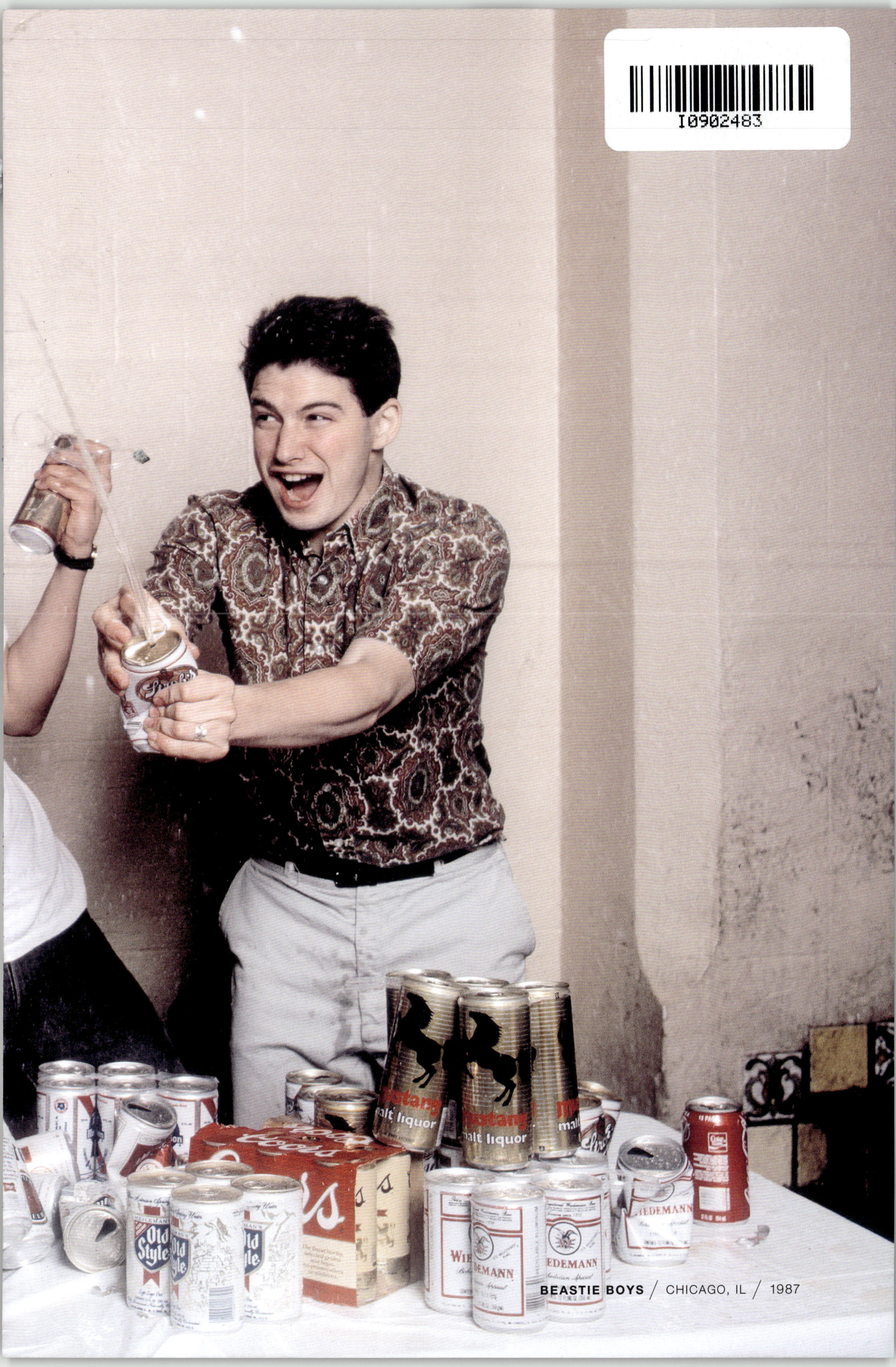

BEASTIE BOYS / CHICAGO, IL / 1987

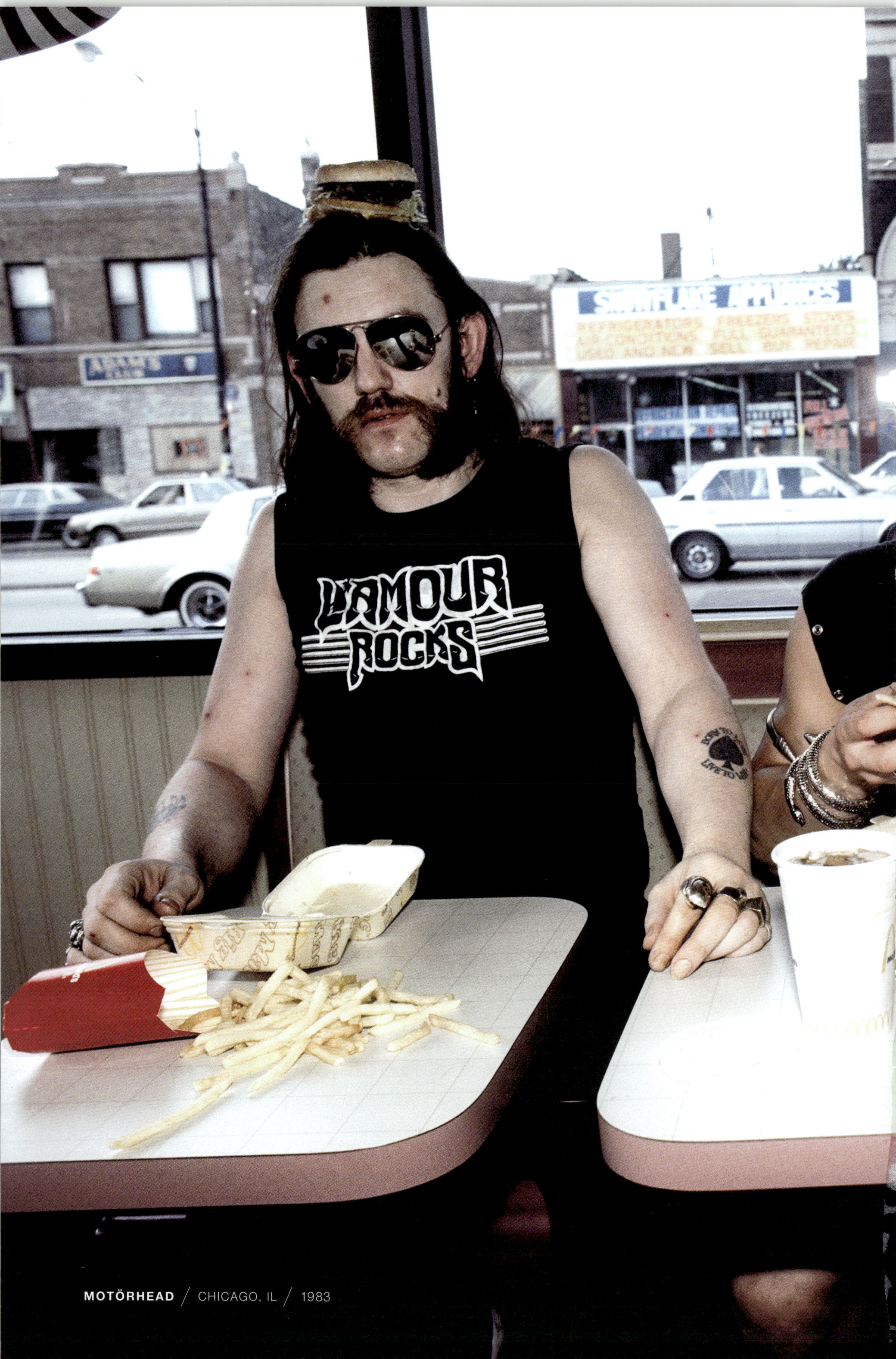

MOTÖRHEAD / CHICAGO, IL / 1983

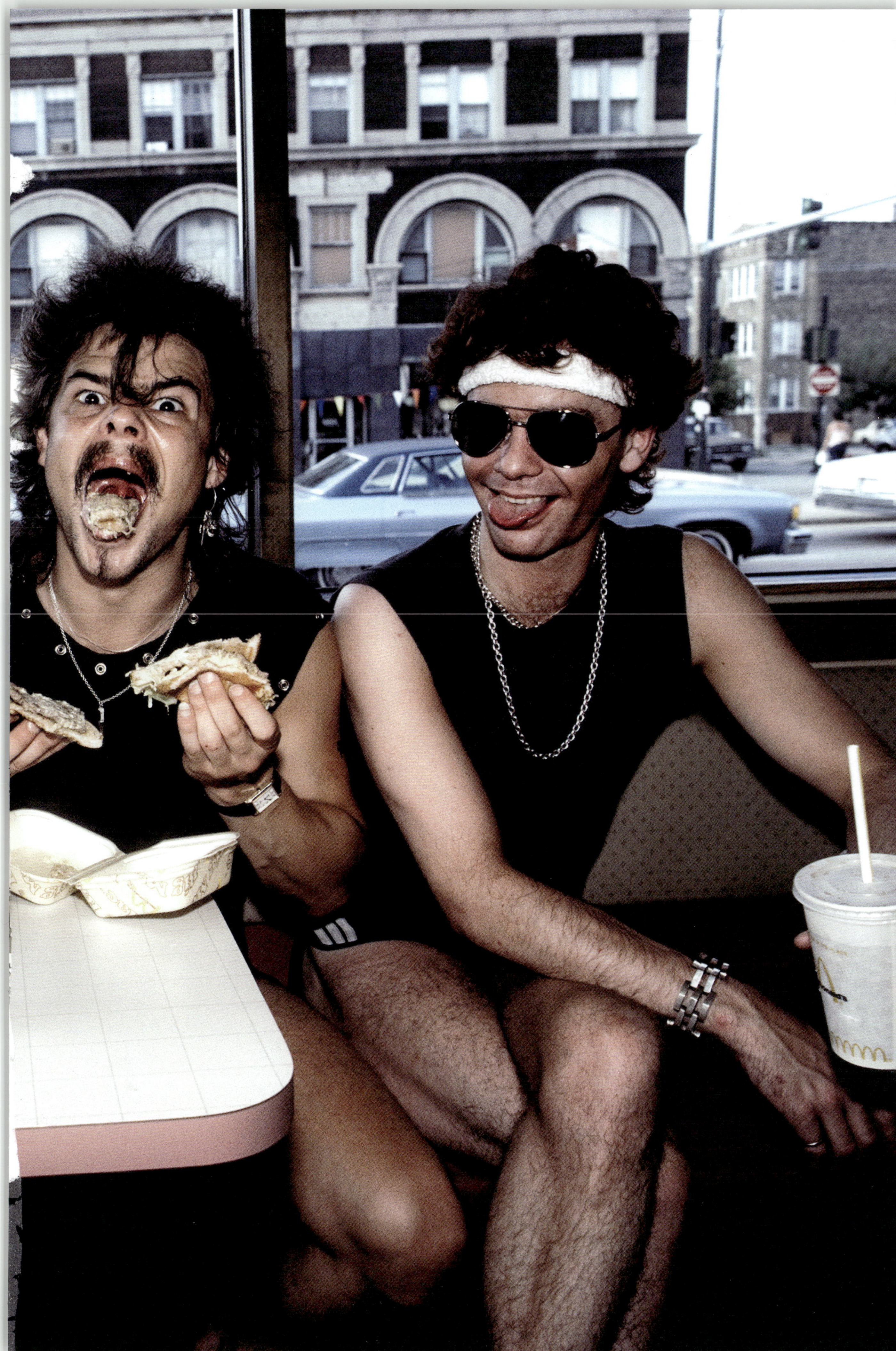

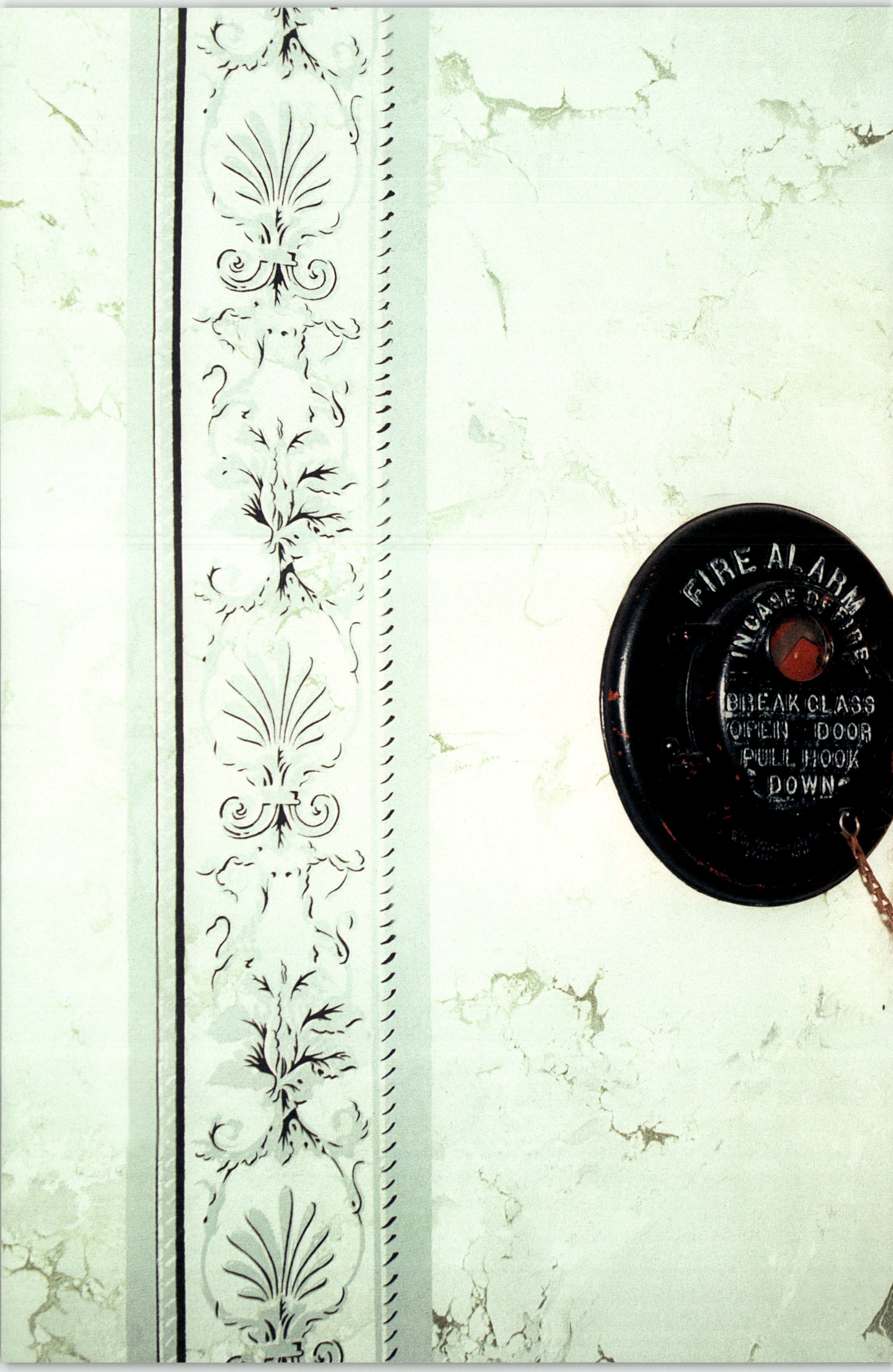
FIRE ALARM
IN CASE OF FIRE
BREAK GLASS
OPEN DOOR
PULL HOOK
DOWN

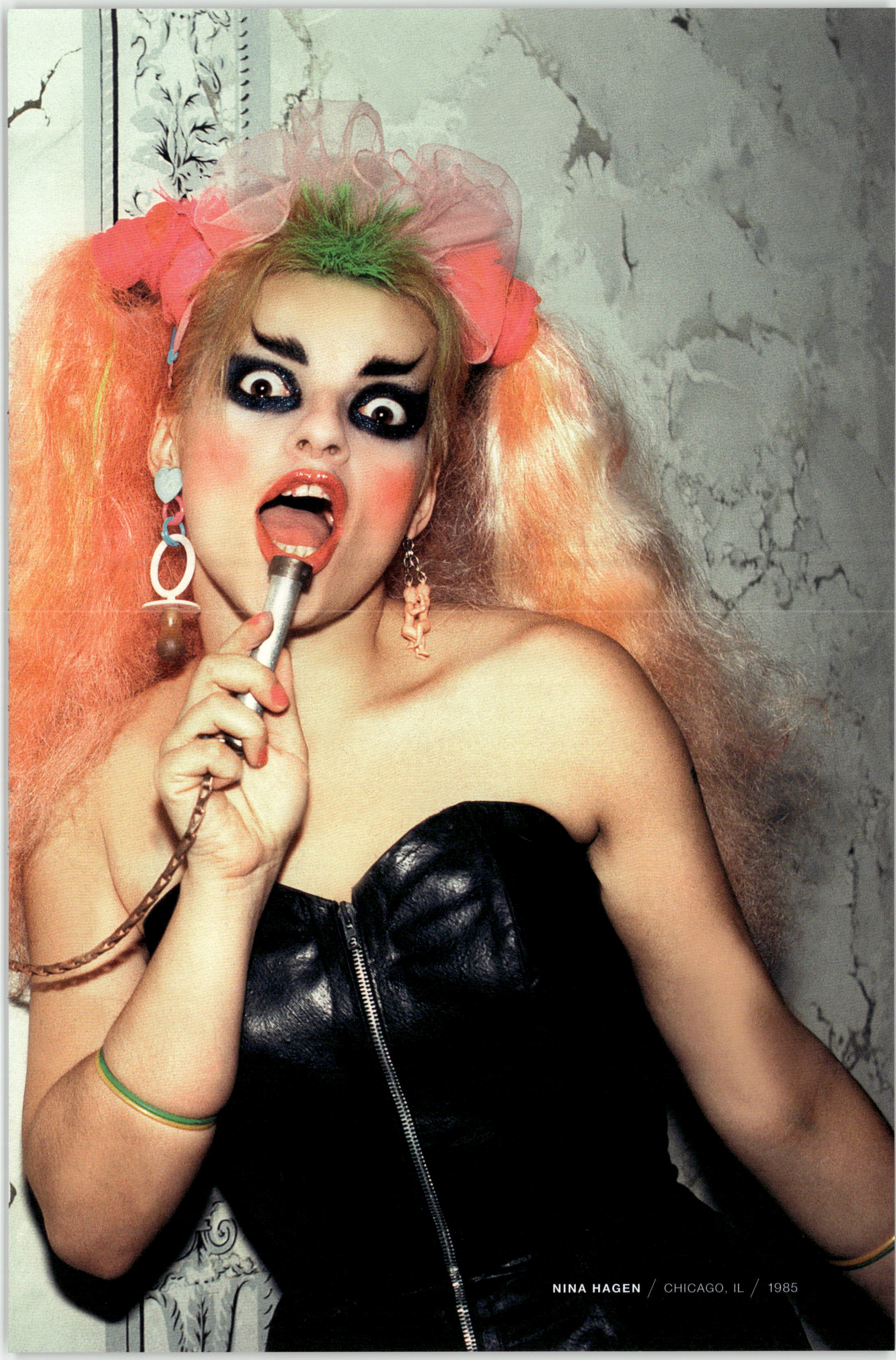

NINA HAGEN / CHICAGO, IL / 1985

Tina Turner & Mick Jagger / Cover
Live Aid was a 1985 benefit to raise money for hunger relief in Africa. Concerts took place simultaneously in Philadelphia and London, while live broadcasts around the world reached almost two billion people. I was one of the photographers invited to the Philadelphia show. Arriving at the stadium about 10 a.m., we were herded onto two platforms in front of the stage and then left to our own devices. For the rest of the day, we had no food or water, and with no intermissions between bands, almost no time for bathroom breaks. Adding to the fun was the audience behind us throwing chunks of sod at our heads all day long! After about 12 hours and around 75 acts, the show started to wrap up with a solo set by Mick Jagger. Tina Turner joined him onstage for two songs, and although I don't remember much of what went on, when I developed the film, I found a shot that became one of my favorites.

Beastie Boys
The Beastie Boys hit it big in 1987 with "(You Gotta) Fight for your Right (To Party)." A major beer company offered them big money to sponsor their first headlining tour, but shortly before they got to Chicago, the sponsorship was canceled–someone from the beer company saw their show and decided that the band did not portray the right image. I got a call to do a photo shoot of the band "auditioning" beers as a ploy to find a new sponsor. We gave a backstage runner $100 and sent him down the block to buy as many six-packs as he could carry. (He came back with a nice selection.) I warned the guys to spray the beer away from my lights while I was shooting–so of course, they sprayed every can directly in my face, on my camera and all over my lighting equipment. The shots turned out to be worth every penny it cost to clean everything.

Motörhead
On the Chicago stop of Motörhead's Another Perfect Tour, their publicist asked me to do a photo shoot with the band. When I picked them up at their (very fancy) hotel, Lemmy settled into the front seat with a bottle of Jack Daniels between his knees, while the other two guys jumped in the back. After seeing the classy hotel they were staying in, I just had to take them to McDonald's to buy them lunch. Hilarity ensued.

Nina Hagen
Heading to the venue to photograph German punk singer Nina Hagen, I crossed my fingers that I could find a crew member to translate. Once Nina understood who I was and what I was doing there, she quickly got dressed and we headed out. I had intended for her to pose against the old marble wall in the venue's lobby, but she had another idea: to play with the fire alarm on the wall. It was definitely the better shot!

NATKIN

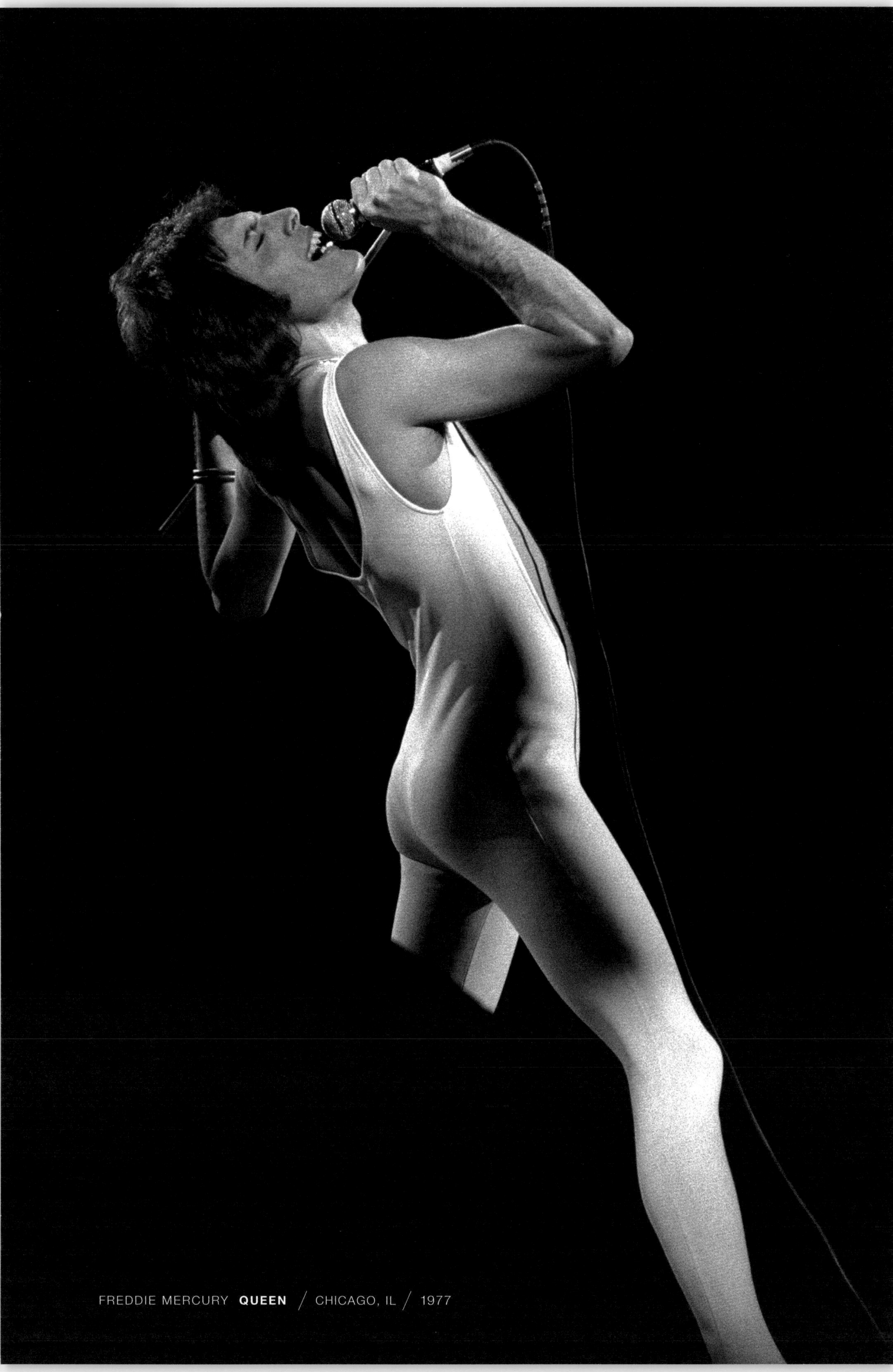

FREDDIE MERCURY **QUEEN** / CHICAGO, IL / 1977

NATKIN
THE MOMENT OF TRUTH

TROPE PUBLISHING Co.

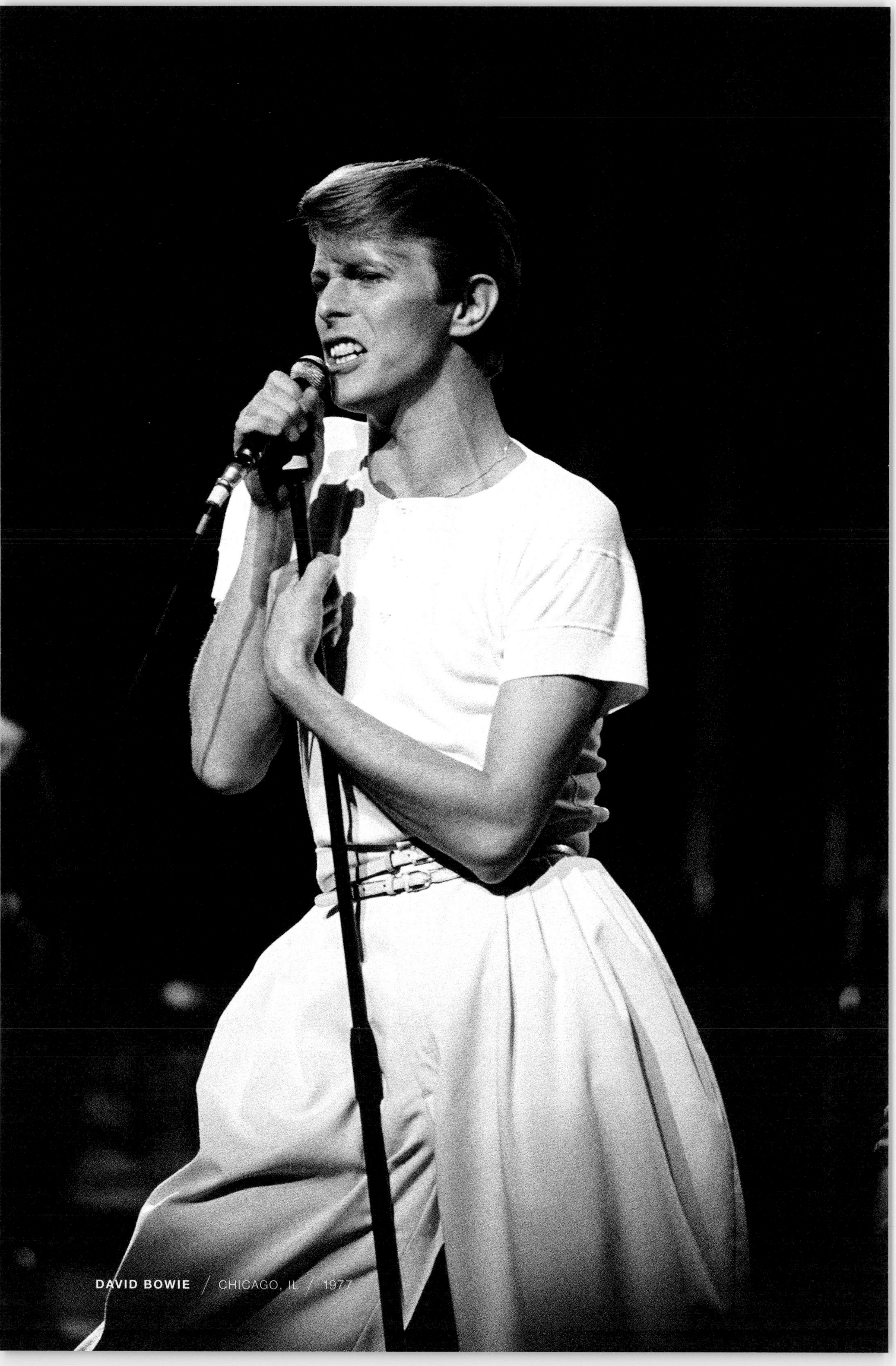

DAVID BOWIE / CHICAGO, IL / 1977

1 METAL
2 FOLK
3 CLASSIC ROCK
4 NEXT WAVE
5 SOUL + R&B
6 JAZZ
7 BLUES
8 COUNTRY
9 GOSPEL
10 RAP + HIP HOP
11 ADULT
12 WORLD

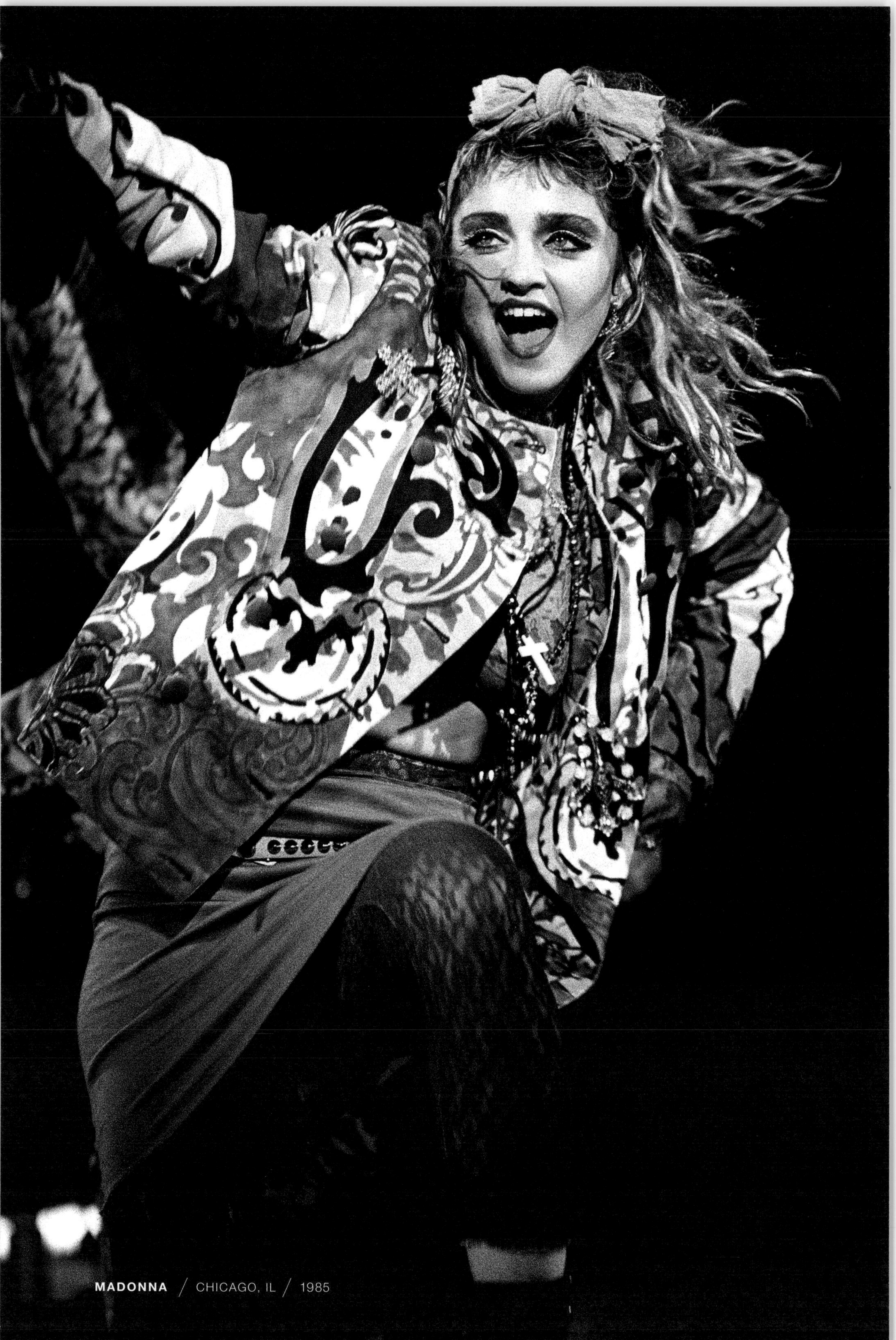

MADONNA / CHICAGO, IL / 1985

PAUL NATKIN OBSERVED

Paul Natkin is a photographer who seizes every moment. He has perfected the skill of catching a musician at an emotional pivot point, but the counterpoint is how Natkin's career is grounded in a distant ethic. His unique access and hustle have made his work known across the world.

Natkin began his career as a popular music photographer in 1976. He has traveled with the Rolling Stones and was the only photographer at Prince's 26th birthday party. Natkin is a diminutive 5'2" but back in the day, he was lugging three Nikon cameras through large concert audiences. Natkin estimates he has shot pictures of 4,200 artists since launching his career.

His style and approach represent an era of photography that no longer exists. Natkin carried a world of imagination in his camera bags. One camera was used for slow speed color, one for high speed color and the third was for black and white. He brought along 20 rolls of film, and if needed, lights and light stands for backstage portraits. (Natkin moved to digital photography in 2000.) The journey has been his promise, a shared rhythm of image-making and music. In his sweet spot of the 1980s and '90s, Natkin was allowed to shoot entire shows–unlike today, where the directive is the first three songs. Photographers are now ushered into the arena by a publicist and escorted back out in a herd after the third song. They do not have concert tickets, so they have to leave the venue.

What you see in the following pages is an extended community in color and black and white. This collection captures a period between 1976 and 2019. His images are the essence of performance; he blends in with the pageantry.

Cheap Trick's Rick Nielsen says, "The interesting thing about Paul is that he was just always there. We never had to officially organize things with him. He was taking great shots of us from the '70s, '80s, '90s to today. And it's always been great material. He's a part of rock history."

Natkin was born among the modest bungalows and delis of Chicago's West Rogers Park neighborhood. His father, the late Robert Natkin, was the official photographer for the Chicago Housing Authority, taking pictures in some of the city's most neglected neighborhoods. This is where Paul learned empathy.

Robert Natkin also was one of the first photographers for the Chicago Bulls, beginning to shoot for the NBA team in 1971. Robert would bring Paul to games at the cavernous Chicago Stadium on the gritty West Side. The first photographs Natkin took, using his father's Nikon, were of future Hall of Famer Kareem Abdul-Jabbar. Paul was 20 years old. He recognized the moment.

"The one thing I learned after the first game I shot is that if you're shooting pictures of a guy while he's dribbling, the ball has to be just coming off his fingertips," Natkin explains over lunch at a West Side restaurant, just a couple of miles from the former Chicago Stadium site. "If the ball is lower it looks like he dropped the ball. You're waiting for that moment. It's the same thing in music. If a guy brings up his guitar, you have to get him at the peak. If he brings it down it looks stupid. And when I started there was no 'you can only shoot three songs.' You could wait for things to happen because you photographed the whole show."

Natkin began shooting musicians in 1976 at the long-gone Ivanhoe Theater on Chicago's North Side. Security allowed him to sneak in the side door. "I shot some great acts there," he says. "Dolly Parton. Kenny Rogers. I remember sitting in the dressing room talking to Kenny Rogers about photography. There was one band that was so terrible I didn't take any pictures of them.

"That was Tom Petty and the Heartbreakers."

Natkin and a couple of Ivanhoe waitresses concluded that Petty sounded too thin and folky, especially during Chicago's punk and Wax Trax! years. "A year later he was at the Riviera Theatre with Elvis Costello (Dec. 2, 1977; tickets were $3)," Natkin continues. "I was there, too. Another key was to get these acts when they started and follow them through their careers. I photographed Bon Jovi when they opened for the Scorpions (May 1984) at the Rosemont Horizon. I walked backstage and said, 'Everybody get in the shower.' The shower wasn't on. But I used the shower tiles as the background for the big hair and spandex. You also had to figure out trends. I figured out real early that hair metal was going to be huge. I started shooting all those bands and they were nice guys to work with."

It is more challenging to shoot in a dark 600-seat club like the Ivanhoe as opposed to a stadium. A large stadium offers more light. "I rarely used a flash," Natkin says. "That's not photography. The band lights the stage with everything they've got and that's what it's supposed to look like. You shoot the flash and all that is blown out. I'd shoot with flash once in a while, but I'd combine it with the stage lights. Once Richard Marx stopped a show at the UIC [University of Illinois at Chicago] Pavilion and kicked me out. And I wasn't even using a flash. The guy behind me was."

Natkin's breakout year was 1984. He shot Prince, Bruce Springsteen and Michael Jackson in one month. His work appeared in *Rolling Stone*, *Newsweek*, *Playboy* and other national magazines. A Warner Brothers publicist called Natkin to invite him to Prince's June 7 birthday party at the First Avenue nightclub in downtown Minneapolis. Prince and his band The Revolution were previewing the music from *Purple Rain*. Natkin was the only photographer invited. He set his camera bag onstage in front of Prince's microphone. Let's see someone try that today.

"I flew home, developed the film and sent a bunch of pictures to *Rolling Stone*," he says. "They called and said Bruce Springsteen's publicist saw my pictures of Prince and wanted to talk to me." Natkin called her. She asked him to return to Minneapolis and shoot the opening three nights of the *Born in the U.S.A.* tour as well as stills of Springsteen's "Dancing in the Dark" video at the St. Paul Civic Center.

Rolling Stone liked his work again. "I guess I proved I was for real," he says. "They asked if I wanted to go to Kansas City and shoot the opening two nights of the Jacksons' *Victory* tour." The world tour launched at Arrowhead Stadium on July 6, 1984. It turned out to be the only tour with all six Jackson brothers. "I hardly had time to get the film processed before I was off again doing something else," Natkin says, "It changed everything. Then, in 1985, I had the cover of *Newsweek* for a Bruce Springsteen story. That's the pinnacle."

Natkin was fortunate to be working at a unique moment in time where he had access to artists. He could take pictures from a pit in front of the stage instead of a soundboard in the middle of the arena, a common practice today. He developed a network of print magazines looking for colorful artwork. "Nobody could do it now," Natkin continues. "The first time I sold pictures to a national magazine, it was Rick Derringer to *Creem*. Full page color! I thought I was rich. I got $35. But I got to be friends with the guys at *Creem* and all of a sudden I had ten pictures in every issue. Then *Circus* [monthly rock magazine] started calling me, *Hit Parader*, [teen fan magazine] *16*. If you sell 40 pictures a month, you could almost make a living." None of those magazines exist today.

Natkin is a fan himself, which is why his pictures create memories and deep associations. He embraces the spectacle of show business. "The energy is huge," he says. He was on board in September 1989 when the Rolling Stones appeared at Foxboro Stadium, south of Boston. "I was on a platform in front of the stage," he recalls. "Someone told me, 'If you need to get up on stage, just go.' The stage was the size of most mid-range venues. Going on stage is the only way you can get pictures of Charlie [Watts, drummer]. I turned around and I'm standing on stage in front of 80,000 people.

"I didn't know anything about touring. The show ended and we got on a private plane. Like, where do you sit? Everybody seemed to have a place to go and I'm just standing there. Bobby Keys (1943–2014, Stones saxophonist) beckons me over and says, 'Hey, sit down with me.' And I sat with him for the whole tour. He'd tell me stories like how the first time he met the Stones he was on tour with [pop singer] Bobby Vee when the Stones were opening for him."

Photography is a nuanced series of open doors. Natkin has used the light to shape his career as a businessman. "You can't scope out a concert," he says. "But there are things you look for. A shot with two or three guys in it is a lot more saleable than one shot each of three guys. I look at what guitar the guy is playing. One of my clients is Gibson. Another is Fender. I make sure you see the name."

He is also extremely organized, having digitized most of his work while also keeping files on his artists in nine large file cabinets. The meticulous upstairs office of his Chicago studio has a bit of a Central Intelligence Agency vibe. "For example, Jaco Pastorius played bass for Weather Report," Natkin says. "He's got his folder, but he's also in the Weather Report folder." Early in his career, Natkin learned how to maintain control over his photographs by almost never signing over a copyright to buyers. He would instead license photos for use by publications and record companies. He has maintained the working-class ethic of his West Rogers Park origins and has mentored many younger photographers and students of Chicago popular culture.

Natkin has photographed five album covers for Chicago-based blues great Buddy Guy as well as the cover of his 2012 autobiography, *When I Left Home: My Story*. Guy says, "It's been a while that I've known Paul, and I've always liked working with him because with most photographers they ask for one photo and they take a thousand. Paul would just do a few clicks and say, 'I've got it.' His camera takes exactly what he sees."

Just like a great guitar solo, photography is about the notes you don't play. Natkin's economical eye allows room for the viewer's hopes and inspirations. He fills spaces in your soul. This was not lost on rock guitarist John Mayer. When Aware Records signed Mayer, they commissioned Natkin to shoot pictures for his 2001 debut album *Room for Squares*. Mayer was appearing at a small club in Chicago, and an Aware representative took Mayer to Natkin's studio before sound check.

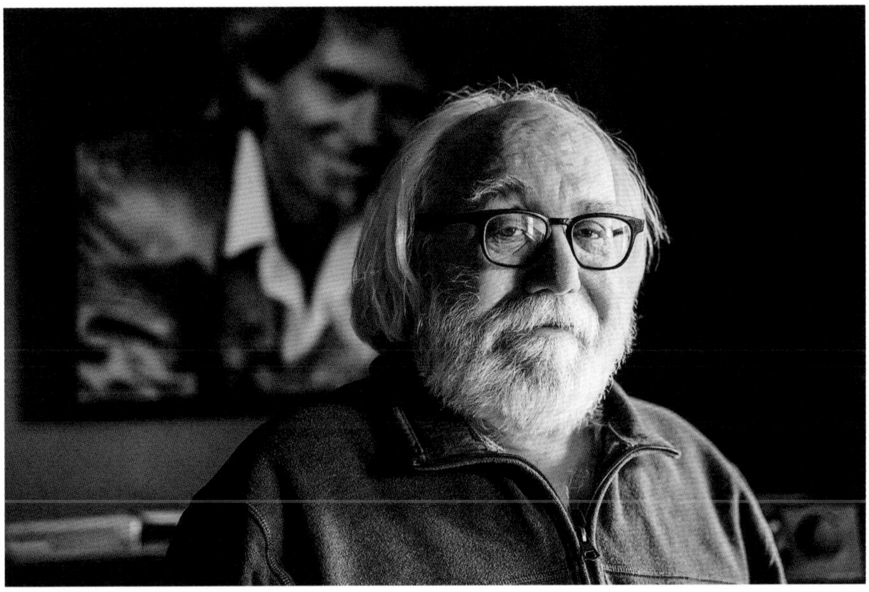

Portrait by Tom Maday

"He started asking me how my business worked, all that," Natkin says. "I said, 'Why don't you go over to the file cabinets and look at artists you like?'" He immediately goes to Stevie Ray Vaughan. He wants to be Stevie Ray Vaughan. About a week later I got a call from a secretary at Columbia Records (Aware's distributor), who said they wanted to buy a picture of Stevie Ray Vaughan to give to John for a Christmas present. So I know there's my Stevie Ray Vaughan picture in his house somewhere."

Like thousands of music fans over the past 40 years, Mayer found Natkin's work to be a conduit for a musical spirit. As he began his career, Natkin learned to rely on his sense of anticipation to set the stage for the most connective photograph. His eye takes the viewer into the heart of the artist at a particular time and place, and their passion can be relived through his image. *The Moment of Truth* is a celebration of all those moments that create the community of music.

Dave Hoekstra
Chicago writer and documentarian
Dave has known Paul for 40 years.

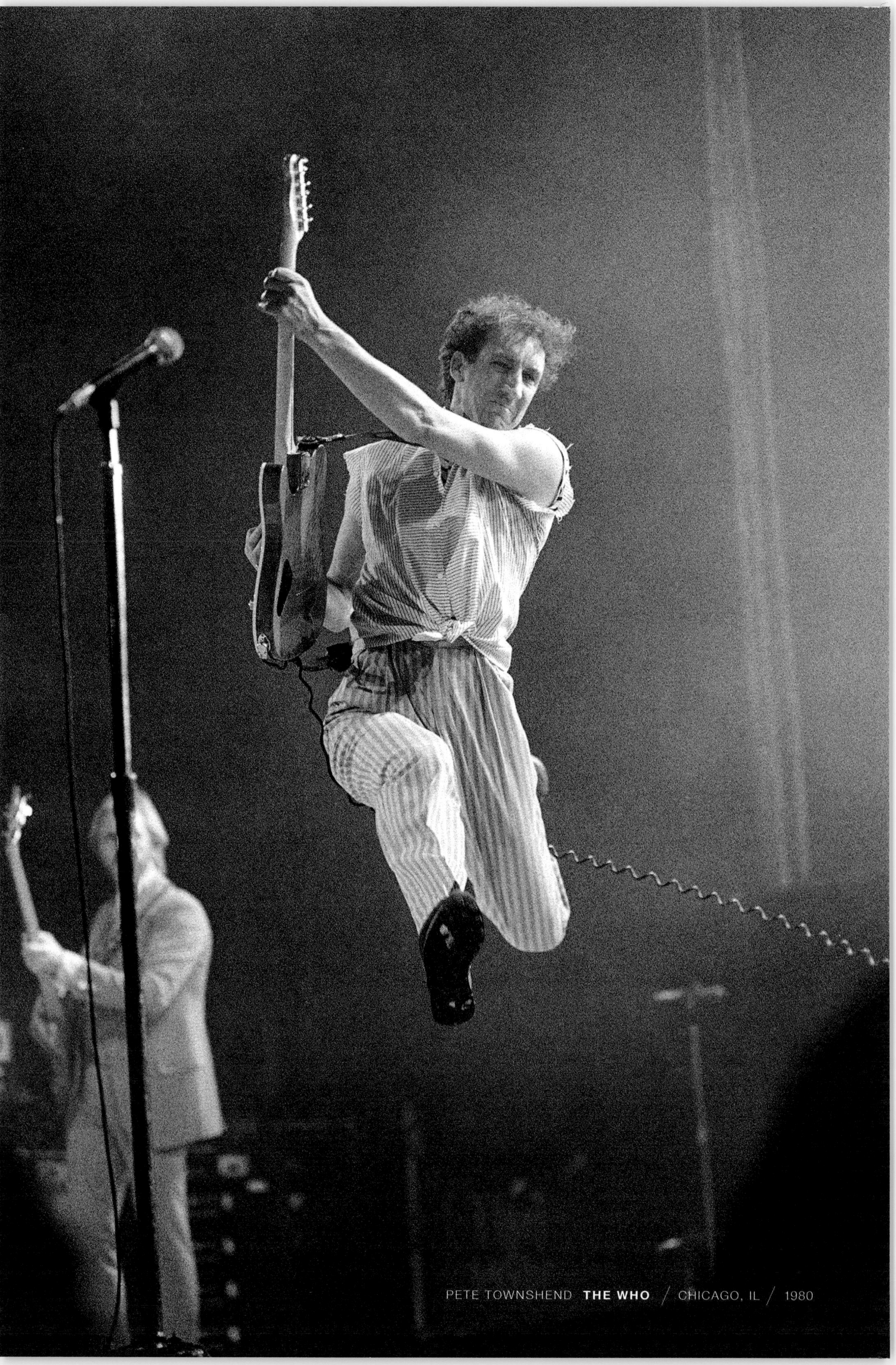
PETE TOWNSHEND THE WHO / CHICAGO, IL / 1980

EVERY PHOTOGRAPHER KNOWS THE MOMENT OF TRUTH

Of all the means of expression, photography is the only one that fixes forever the precise and transitory instant. We photographers deal in things that are continually vanishing, and when they have vanished, there is no contrivance on earth that can make them come back again. We cannot develop a print from memory . . .

***The Decisive Moment* / Henri Cartier-Bresson**

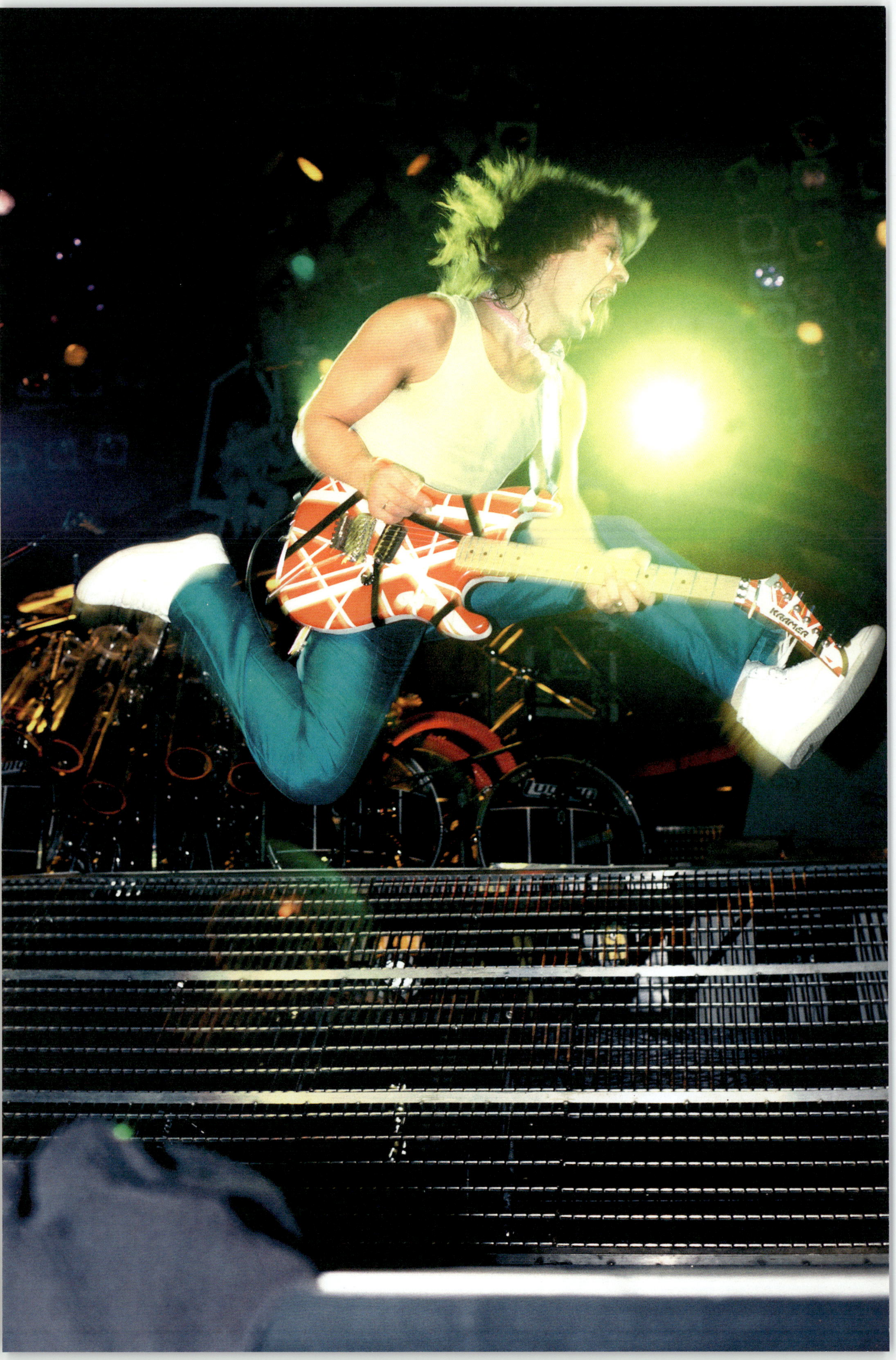
KRAMER

A THEORY

Throughout my career, I have always–above all else–subscribed to a theory that Henri Cartier-Bresson, a founder of modern photojournalism, set forth as the title of his very influential 1952 book *The Decisive Moment.*

By definition, a "decisive moment" is the capture of a unique, fleeting and meaningful moment, ideally one involving movement and action. A precisely timed, unrepeatable, one-chance shot. Every event has a decisive moment; the trick is to find it. It can be captured by shooting thousands of images with a motor drive, and then picking out the "best" one. That is not how I do it. I study the band, watch how they move and anticipate when they are going to do something that can be called a decisive moment. Sometimes it is easy. One of my rules of photography is that if someone climbs up on something (such as a drum riser), he will soon jump off of it. The rest is being prepared to capture that moment.

Sometimes, as was the case with my photograph of Ozzy Osbourne and Randy Rhoads *(page 28)*, a little luck enters into the equation. As I saw Ozzy walking towards Randy, I picked up a camera with a wide-angle lens to be ready to get a photograph of the two of them. When Ozzy picked Randy up, I quickly flipped the camera vertically and captured the most popular image that I have ever taken.

EDDIE VAN HALEN **VAN HALEN** / ROSEMONT, IL / 1986

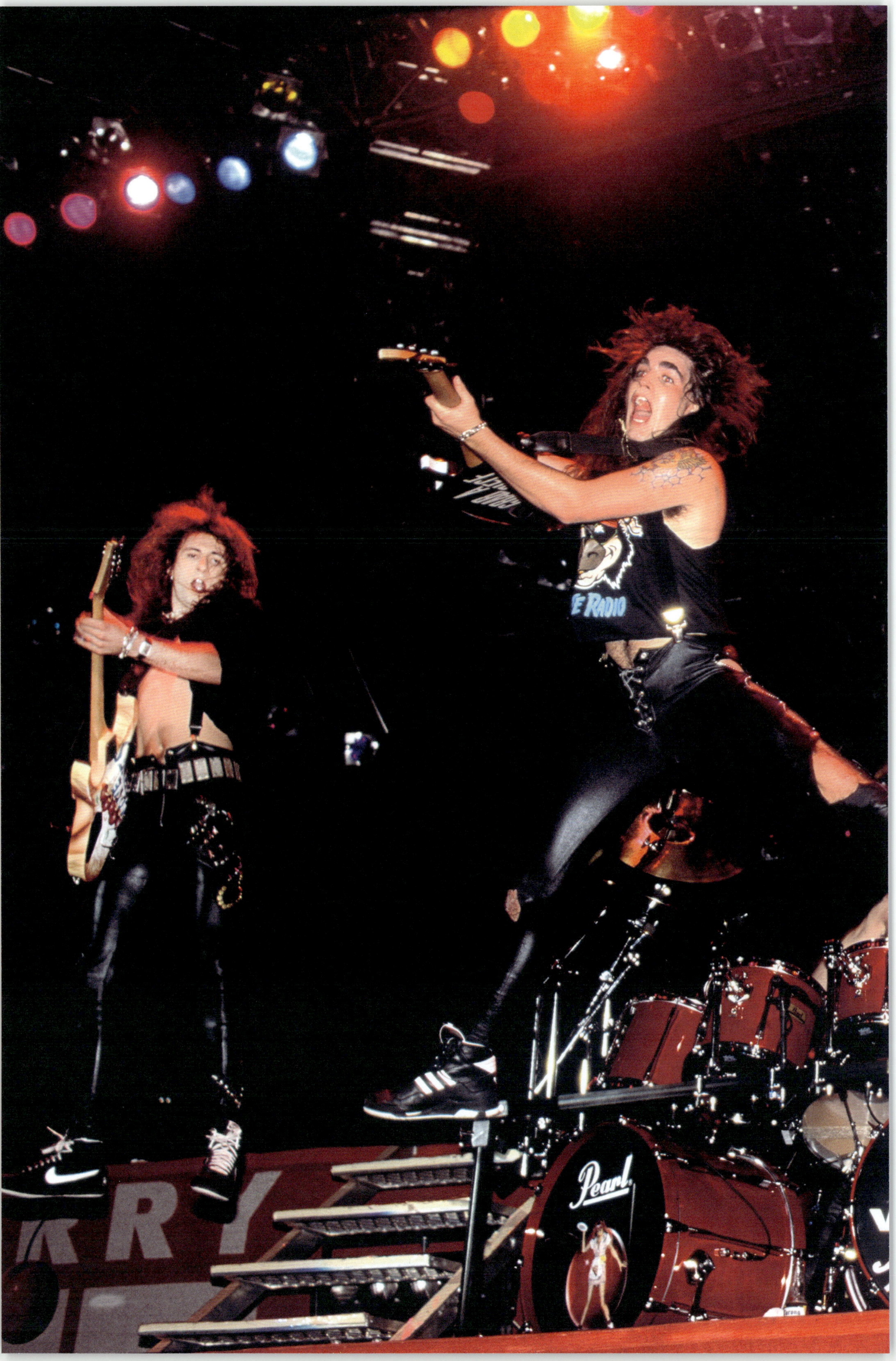
Pearl

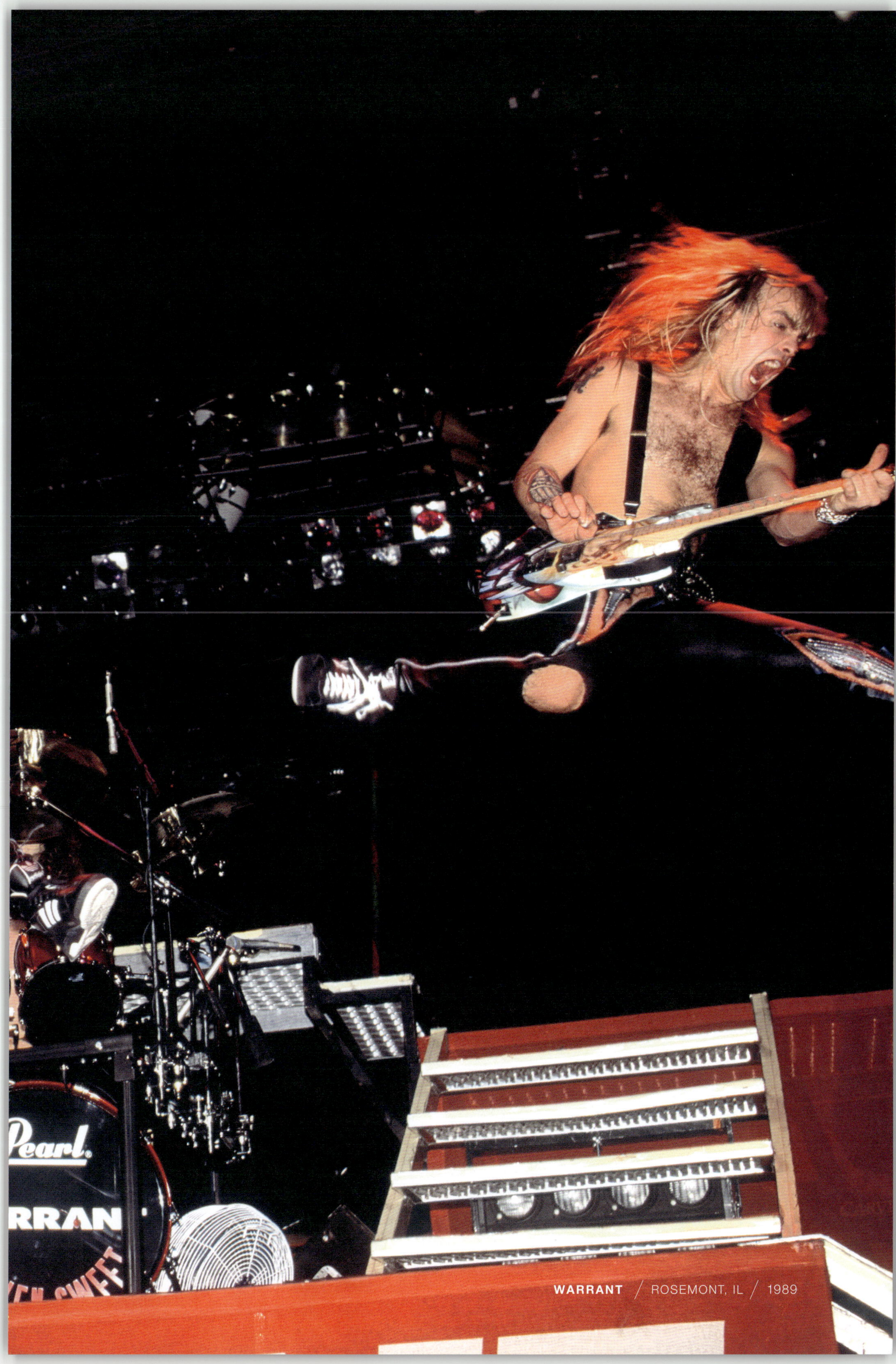

WARRANT / ROSEMONT, IL / 1989

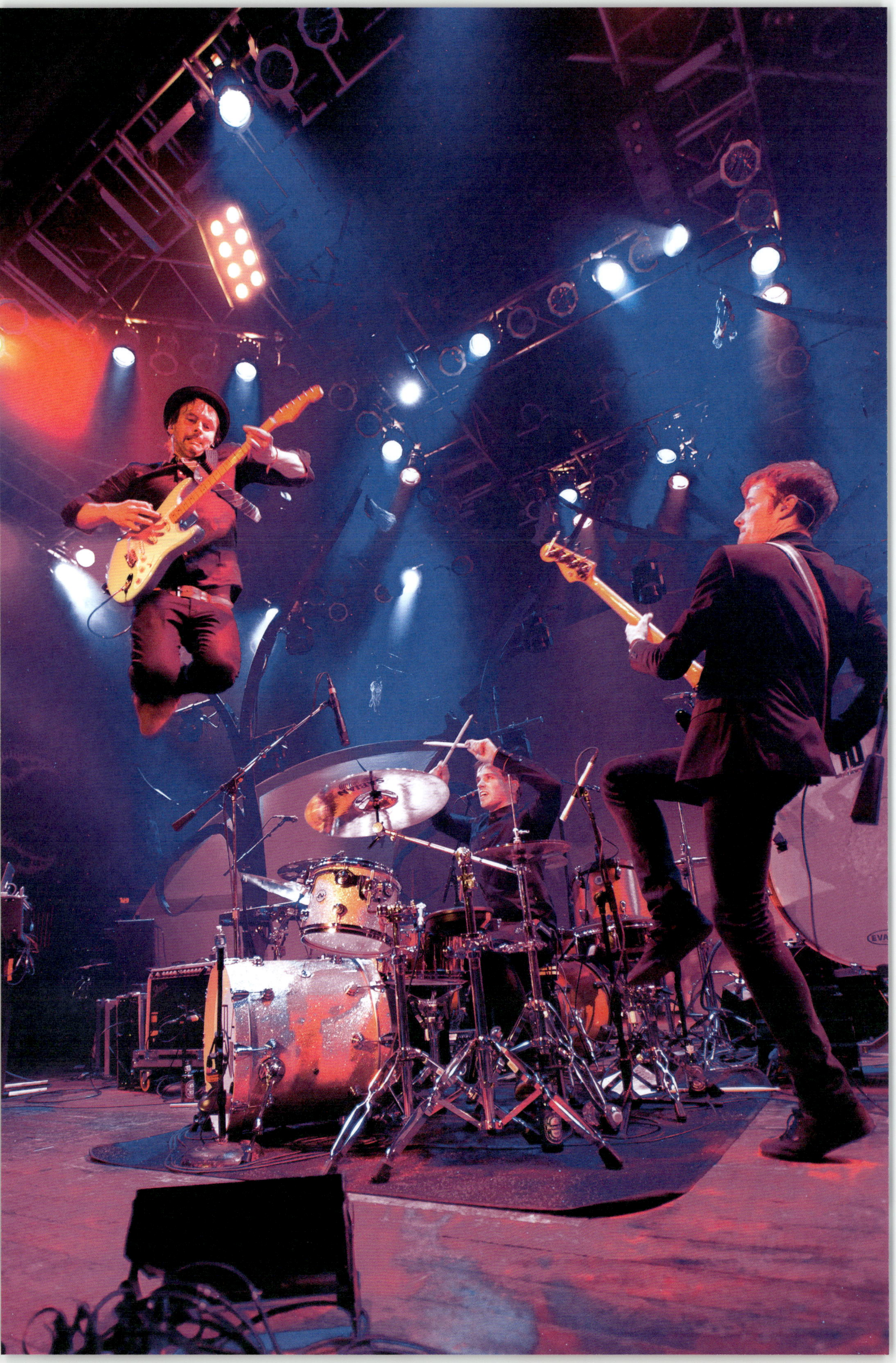

THE LAST PHOTOGRAPH

I always try to get access to photograph the entire show. All the good stuff happens at the end. This was the last picture I took that night. I saw the guitar player climb up on the bass drum, and knew he was going to jump. How else was he going to get down? I waited for the moment, making sure to have a wide enough lens on the camera to capture the floor of the stage and all three guys. Sure enough, he jumped right where I figured he would.

ATLAS GENIUS / CHICAGO, IL / 2013

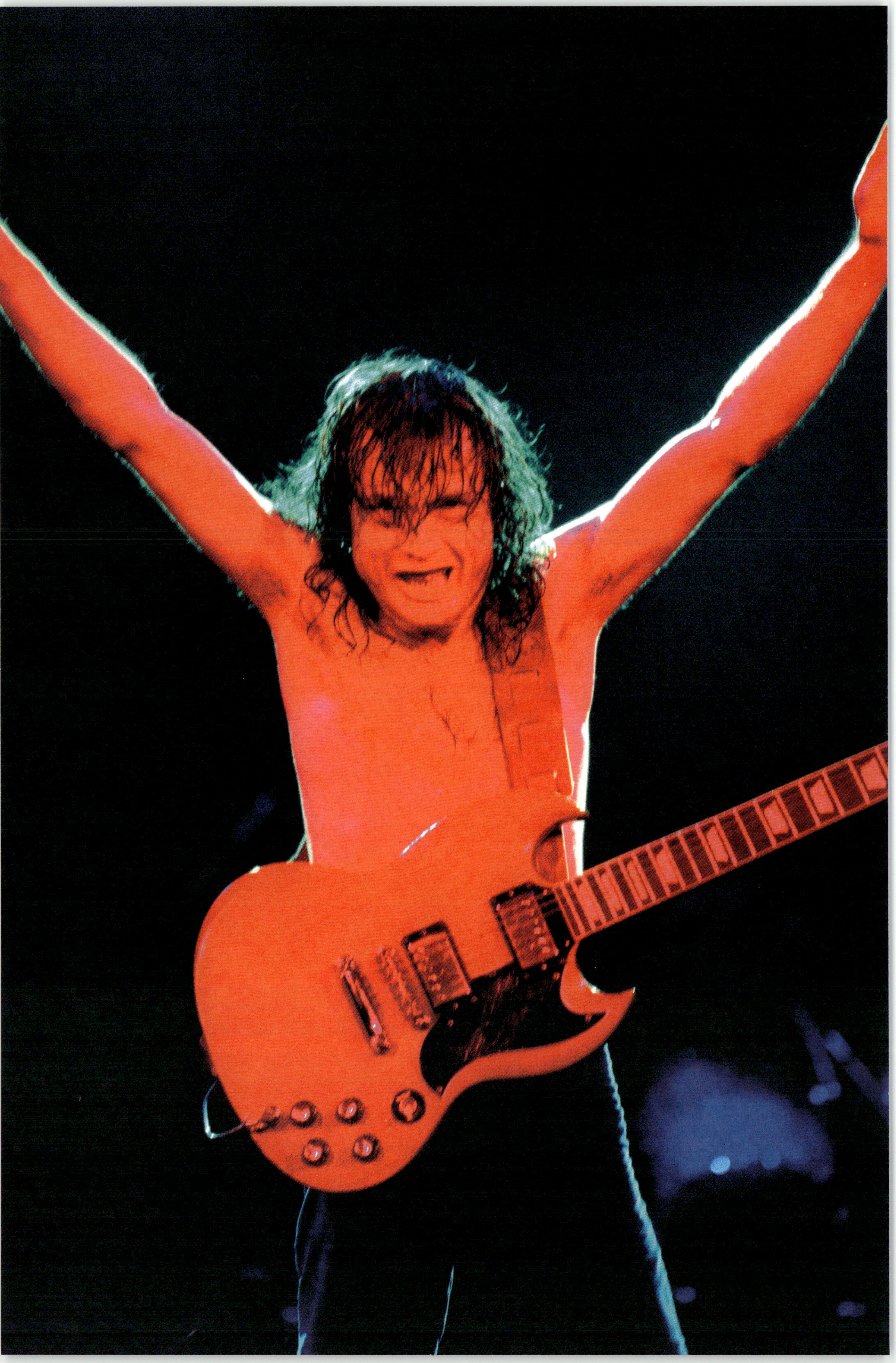

1

METAL
SOUND & SPECTACLE

Metal music is the spectacle of the rock world. Hairspray and spandex combine to make a great subject to photograph. And they certainly don't stand in one place for very long! I spent a long time hanging out with and photographing metal bands in the '80s and '90s, and was welcomed with open arms every time.

ANGUS YOUNG **AC/DC** / CHICAGO, IL / 1979

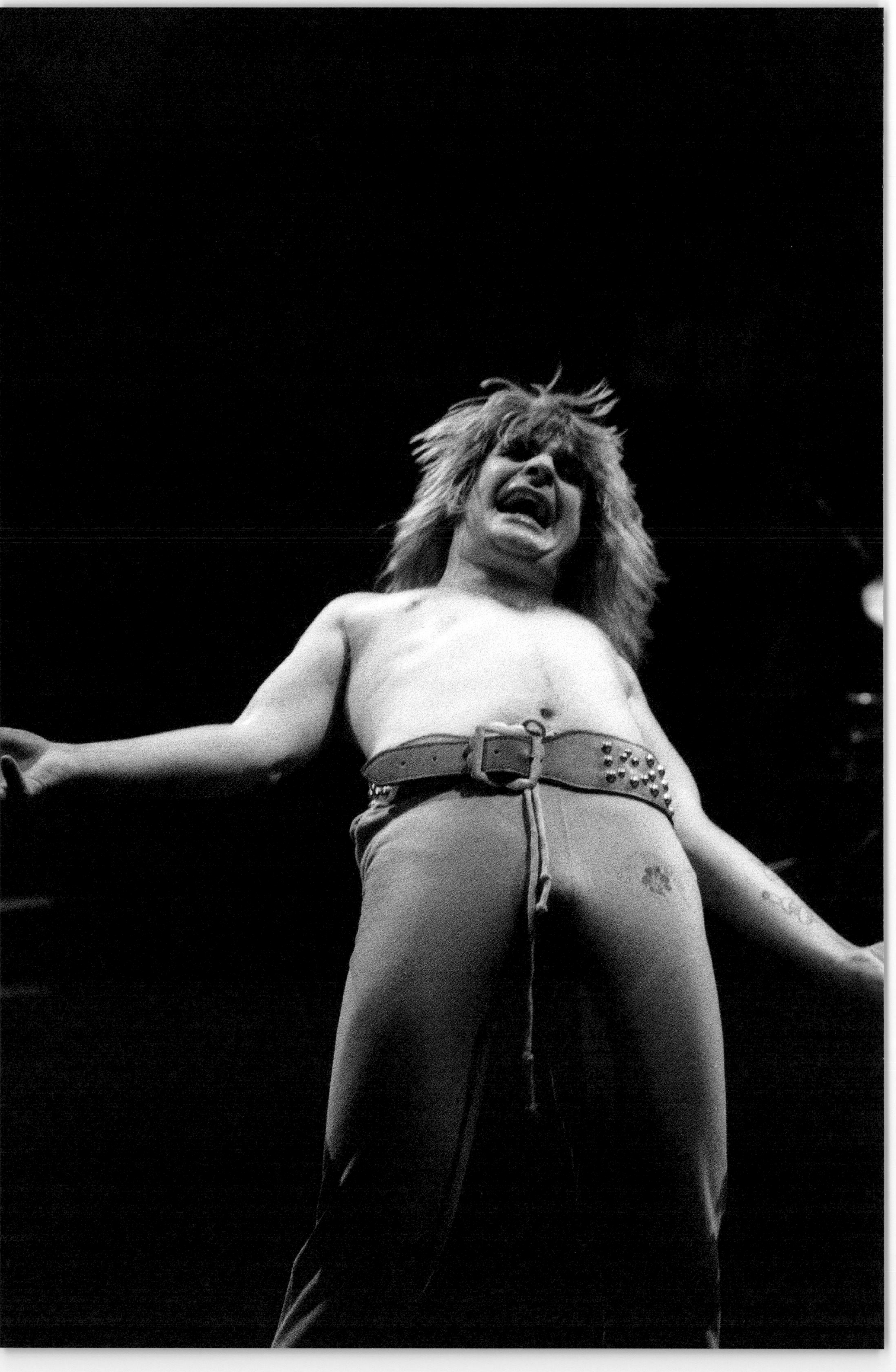

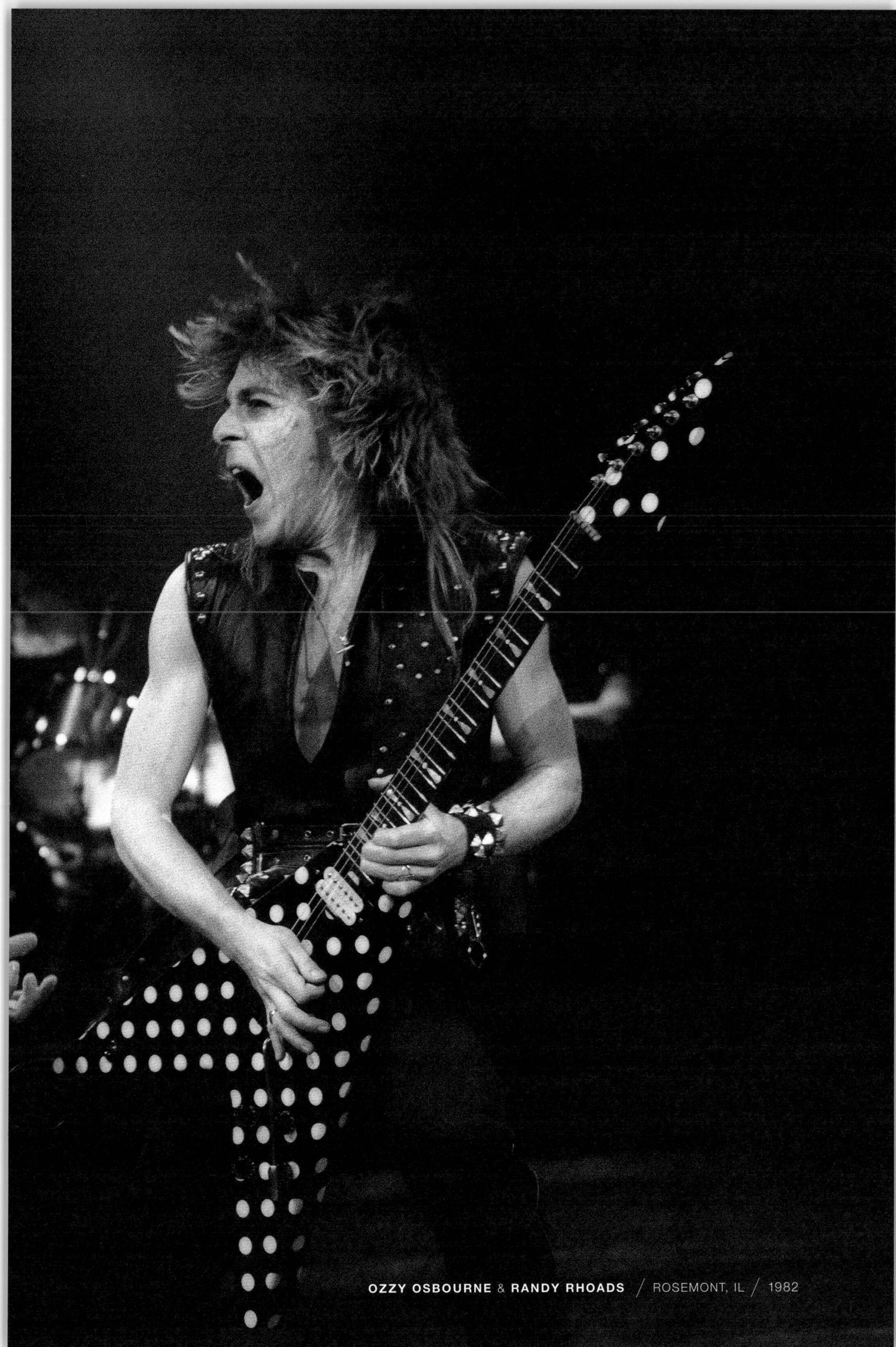

OZZY OSBOURNE & **RANDY RHOADS** / ROSEMONT, IL / 1982

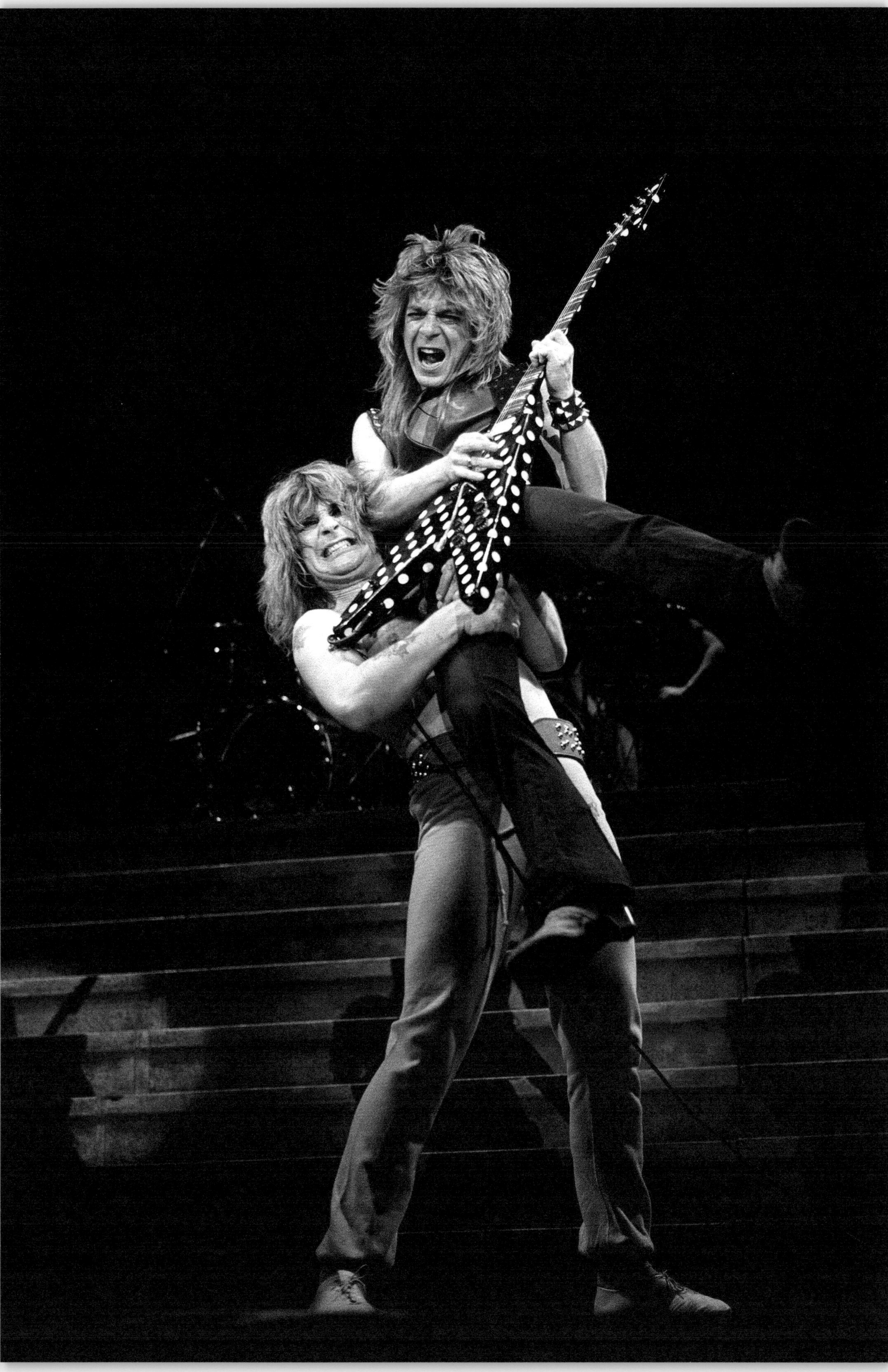

OZZY & RANDY

On Super Bowl Sunday 1982, I went to a sound check to photograph Don Airey, Ozzy's keyboard player, with the hope of getting out of there in time to watch the Super Bowl. Priorities, you know! I was asked to stay and shoot the show–after watching the Super Bowl with the band and crew. During the show I kept noticing this little guy playing guitar and I decided to take some pictures of him. As I did that, Ozzy snuck up behind him and picked him up. I got two photos. Randy Rhoads died in a plane crash shortly after that, and this became the most valuable picture I have ever taken. Book covers, magazine covers, an album cover *(Tribute)*, T-shirts, a doll and–just recently–a limited edition snowboard. All in all, a serendipitous moment.

OZZY OSBOURNE & **RANDY RHOADS** / ROSEMONT, IL / 1982

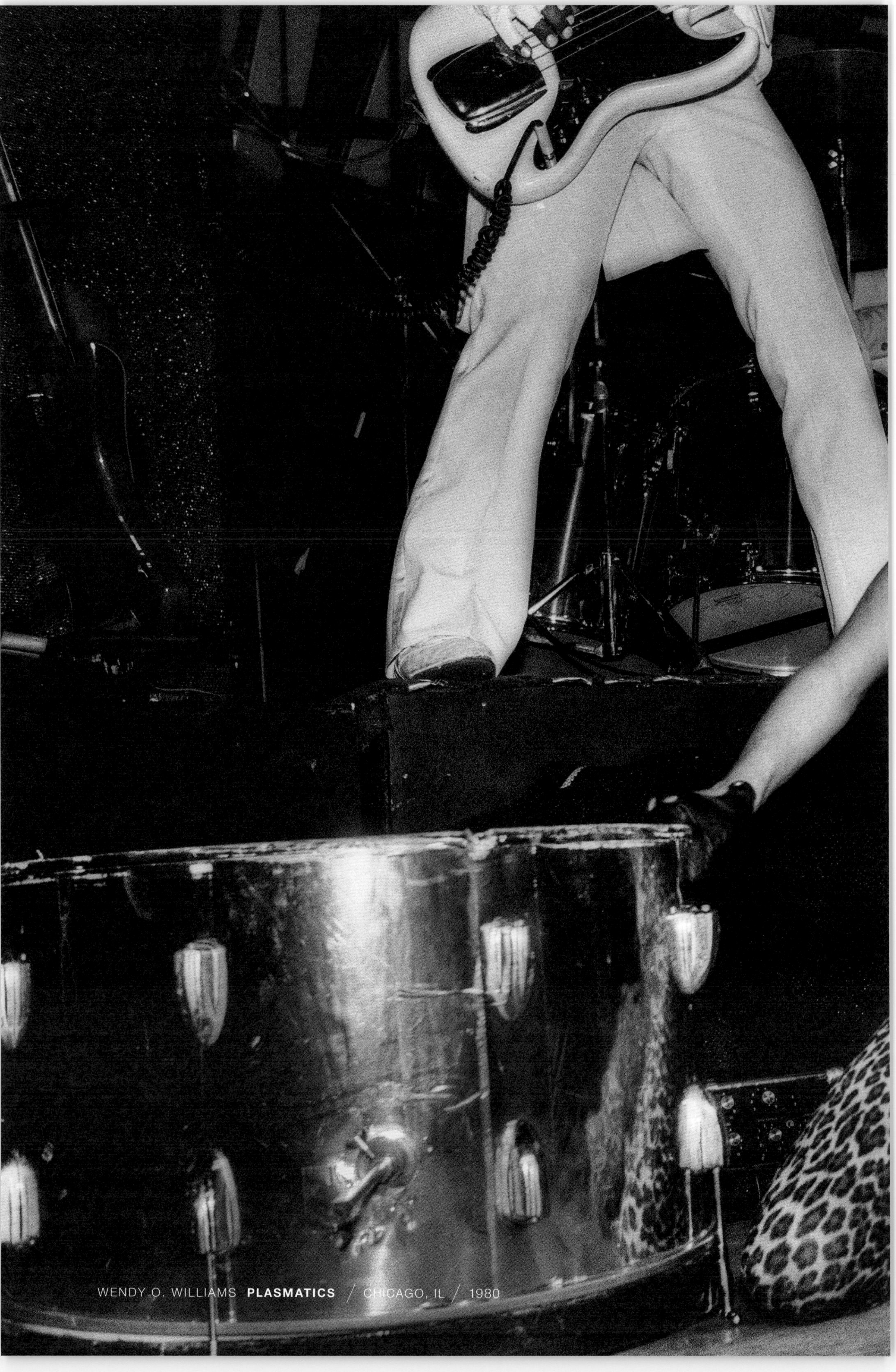

WENDY O. WILLIAMS **PLASMATICS** / CHICAGO, IL / 1980

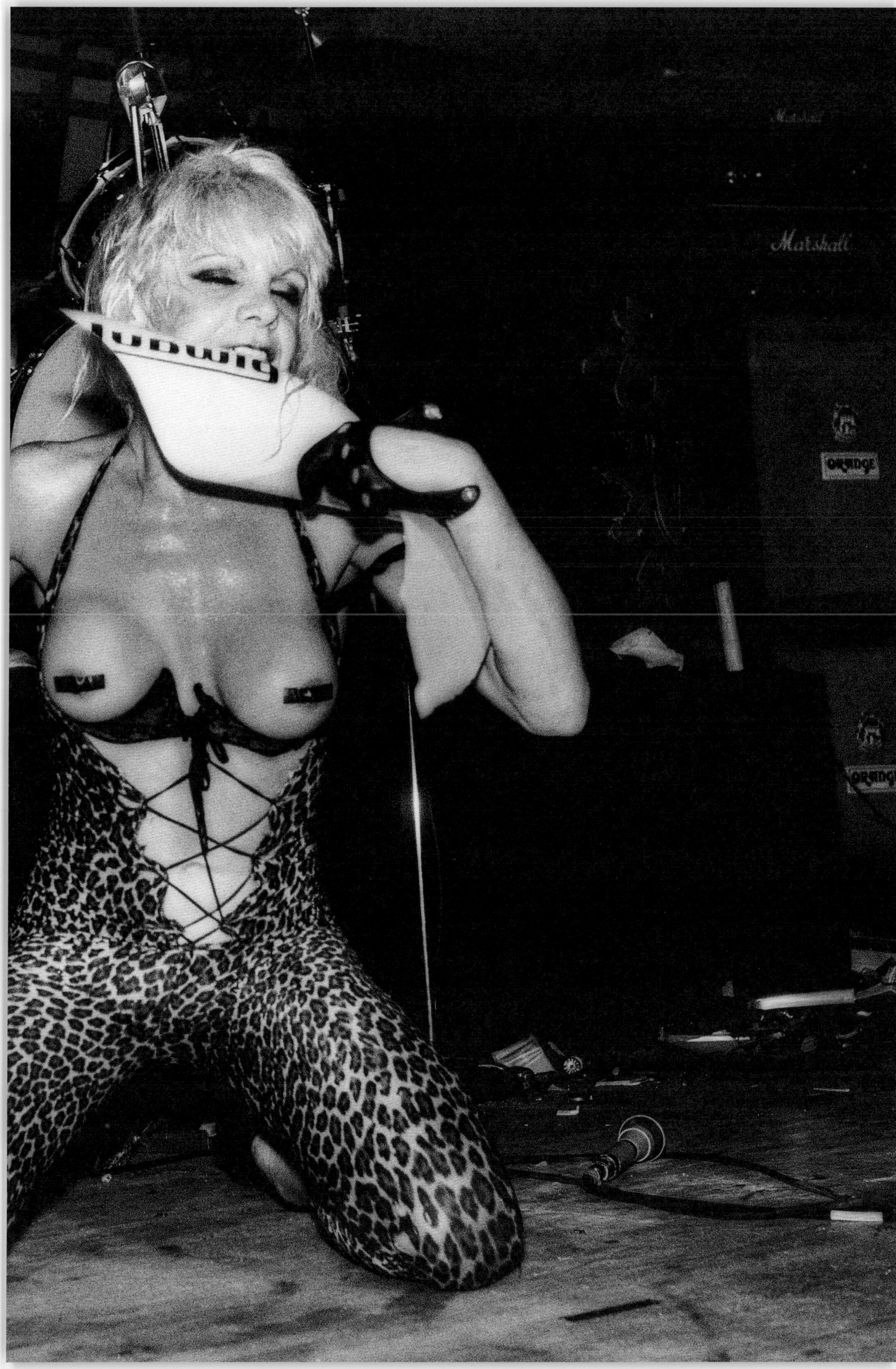
Marshall
Marshall
ORANGE
ORANGE

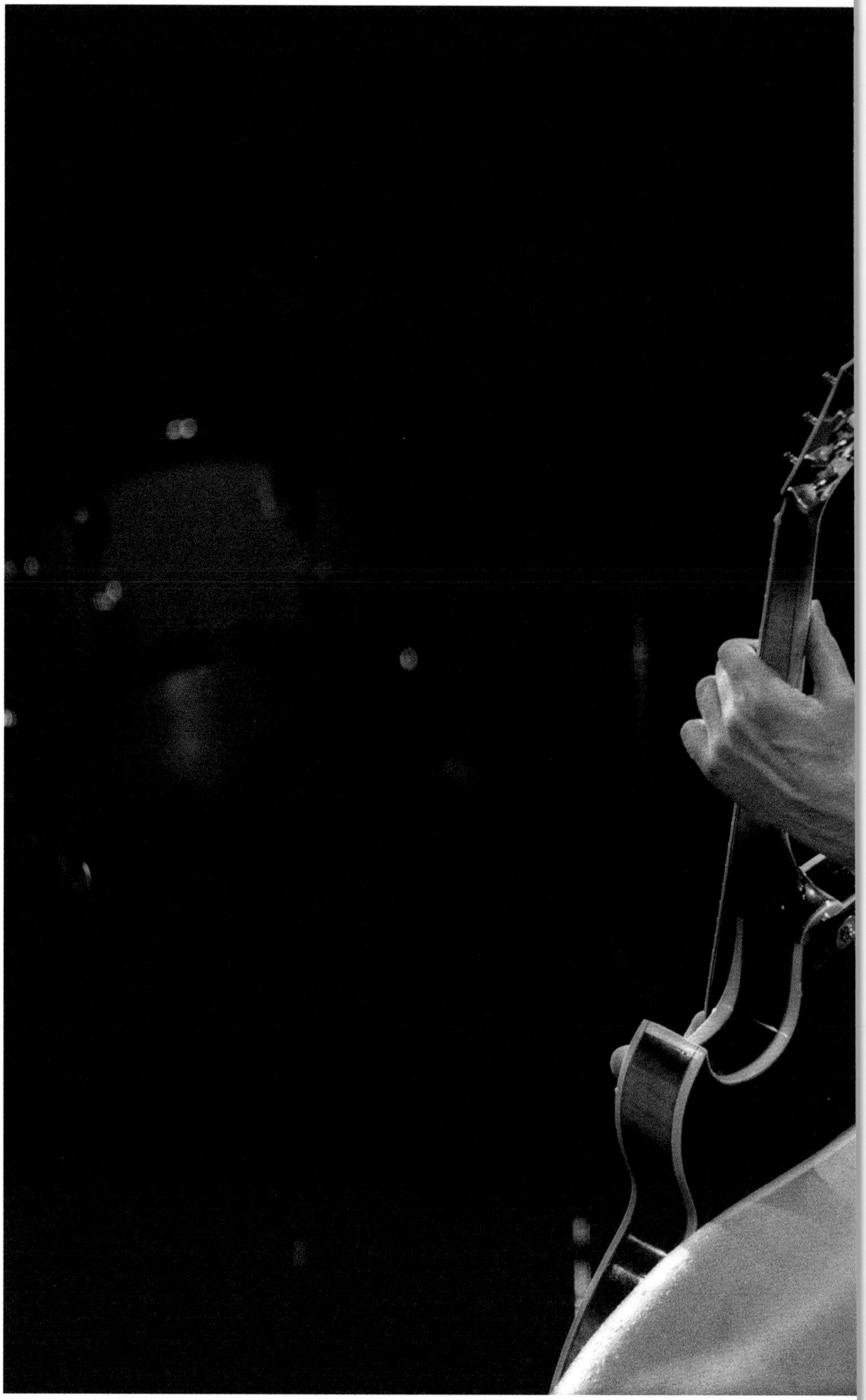

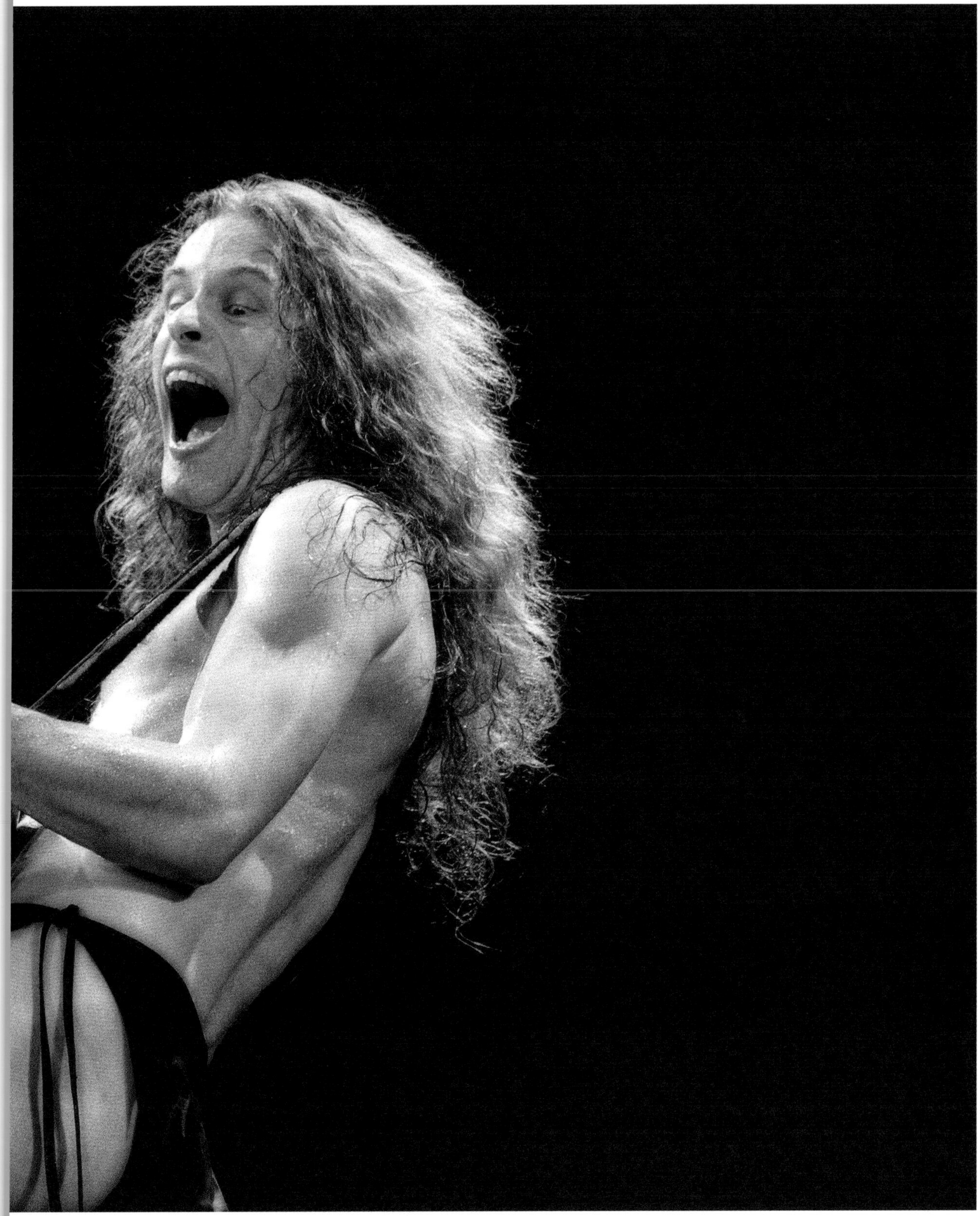

Ted Nugent grew up in the suburbs of Chicago and his parents still lived in the area when he became famous. His mom was asked to write an advice column for a local music magazine, and they used my picture of her and Ted as the column's heading. This led to a great friendship with "Ma" Nugent. She used to invite me out to their house for dinner occasionally–where we would eat something that Ted had shot.

TED NUGENT / ROSEMONT, IL / 1980

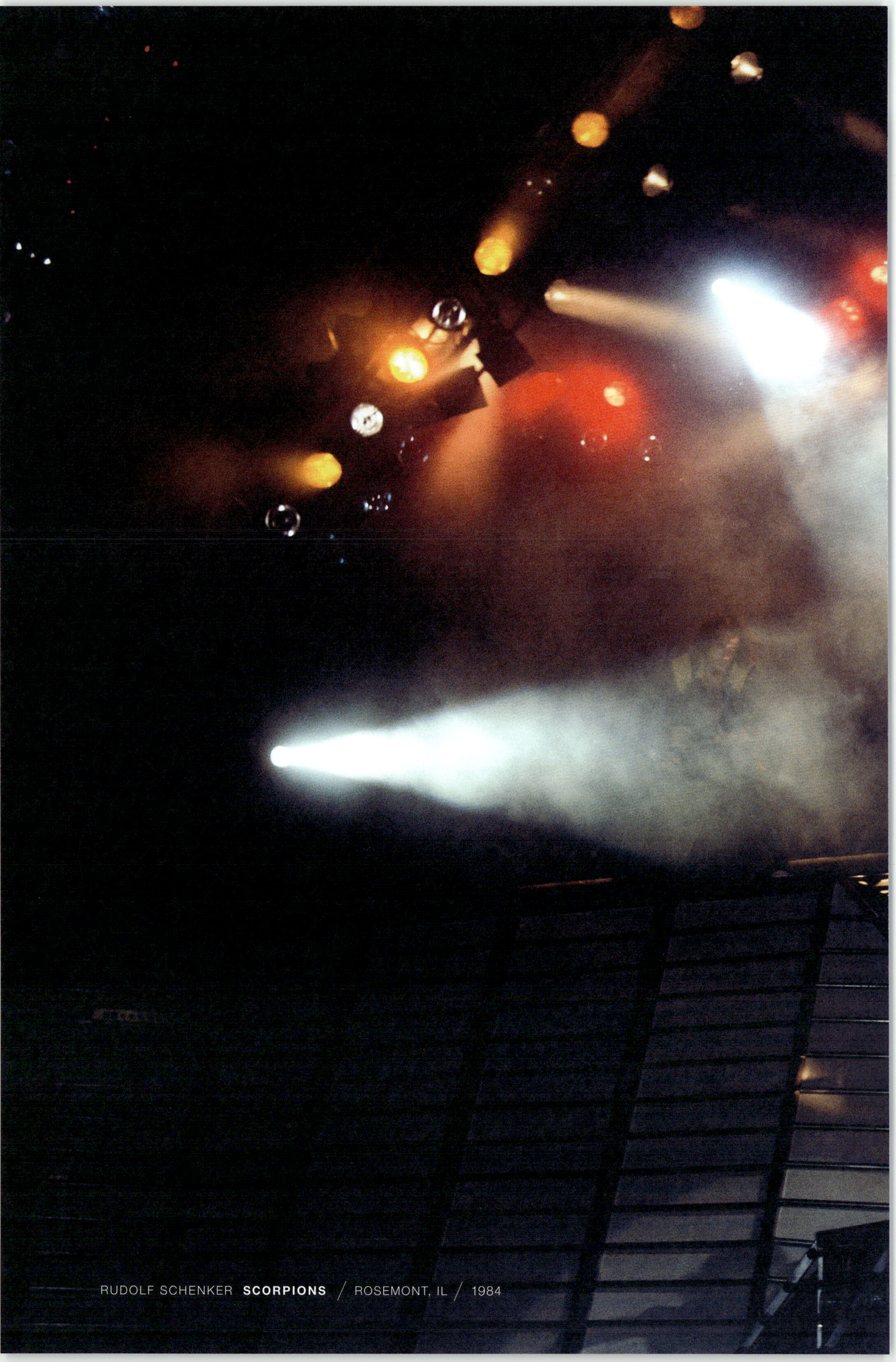

RUDOLF SCHENKER **SCORPIONS** / ROSEMONT, IL / 1984

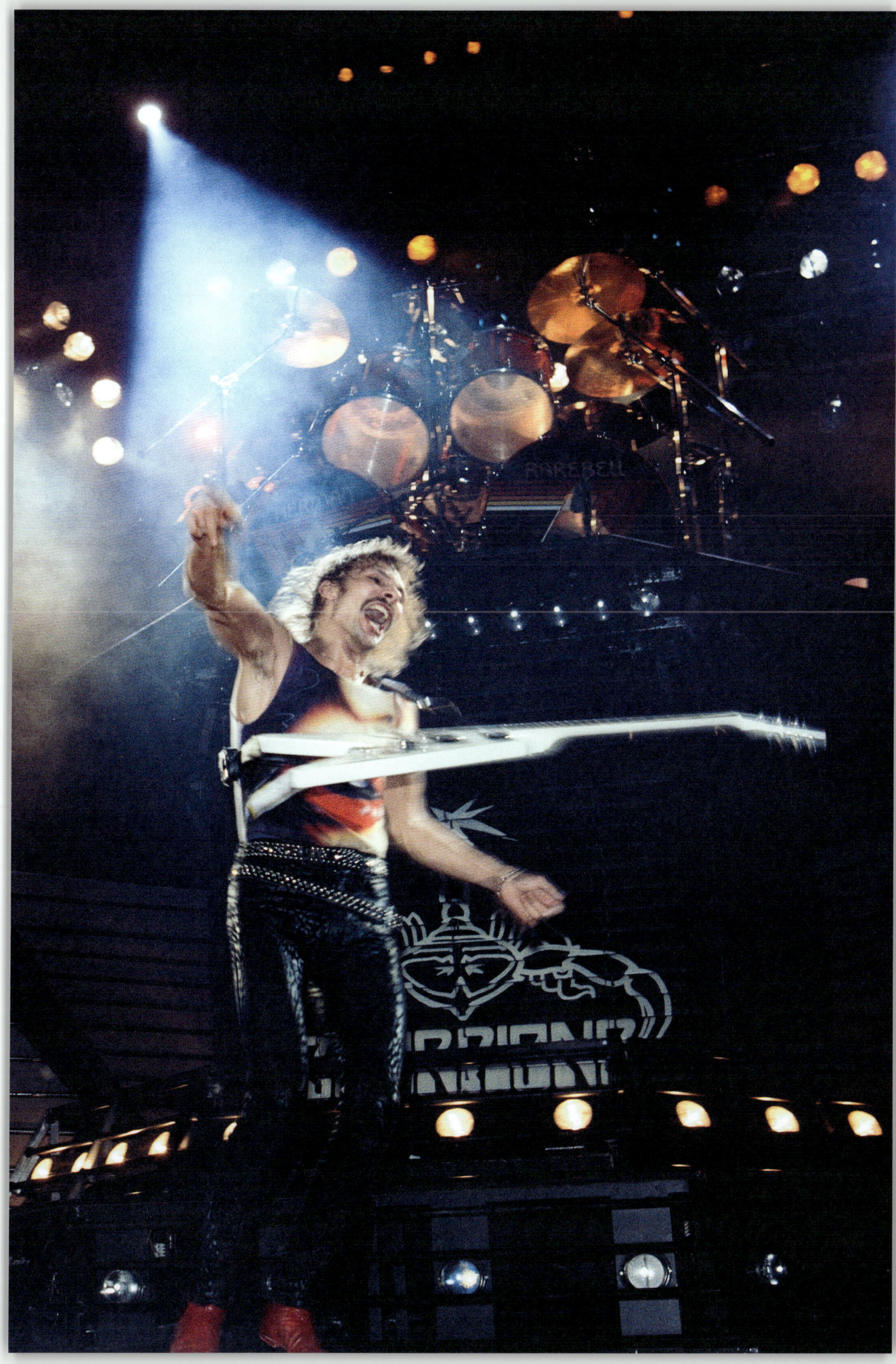

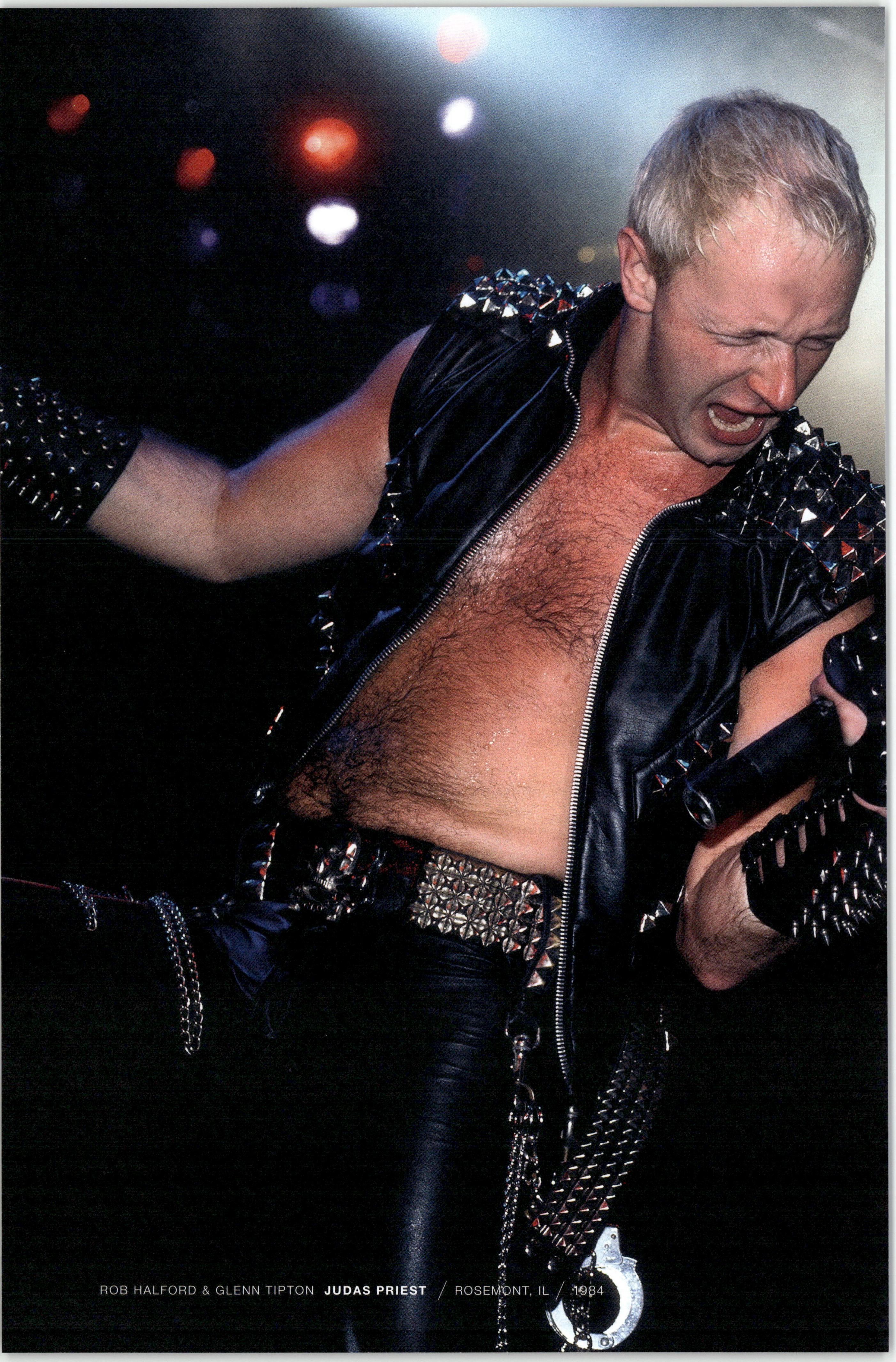

ROB HALFORD & GLENN TIPTON **JUDAS PRIEST** / ROSEMONT, IL / 1984

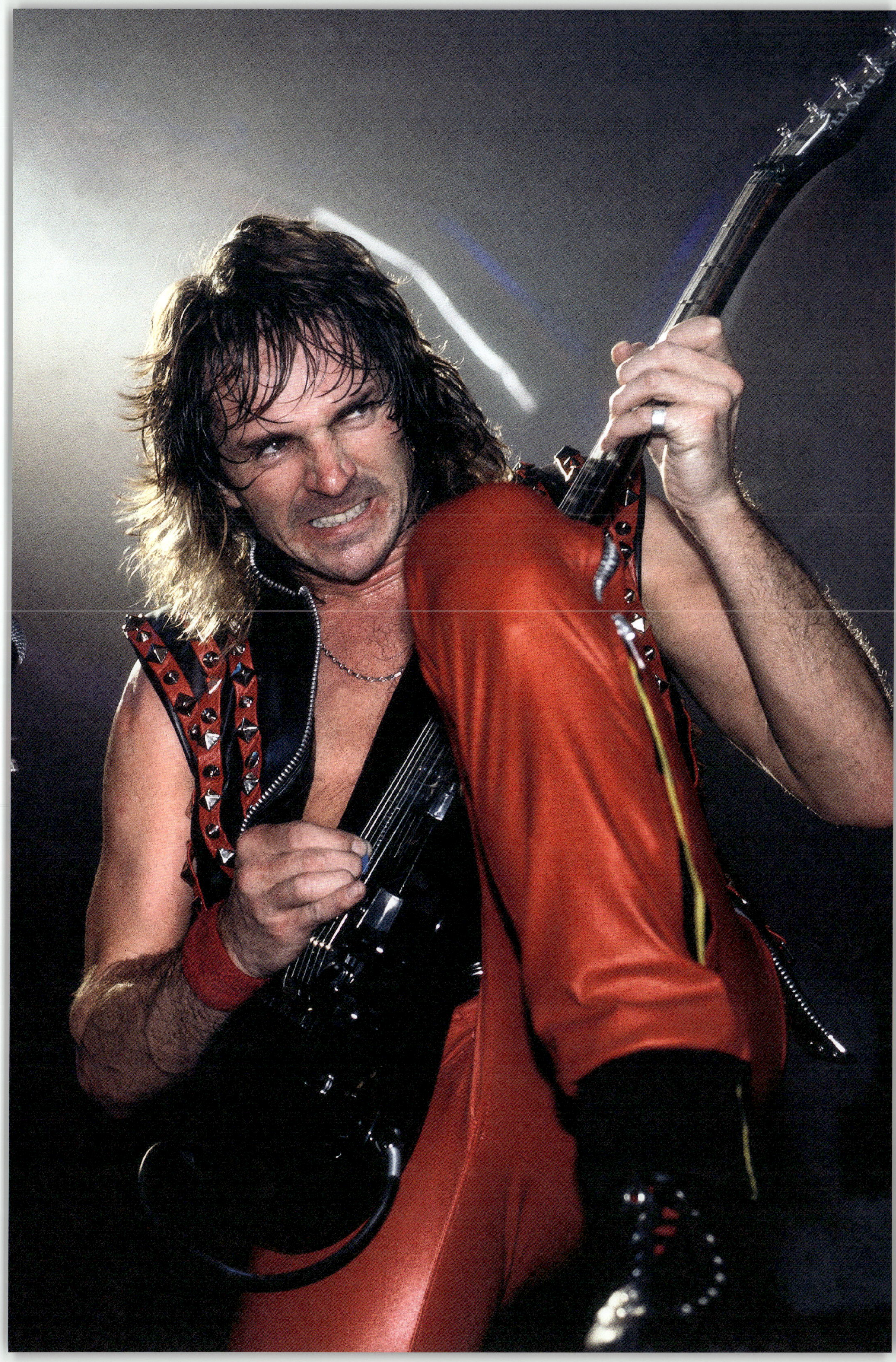

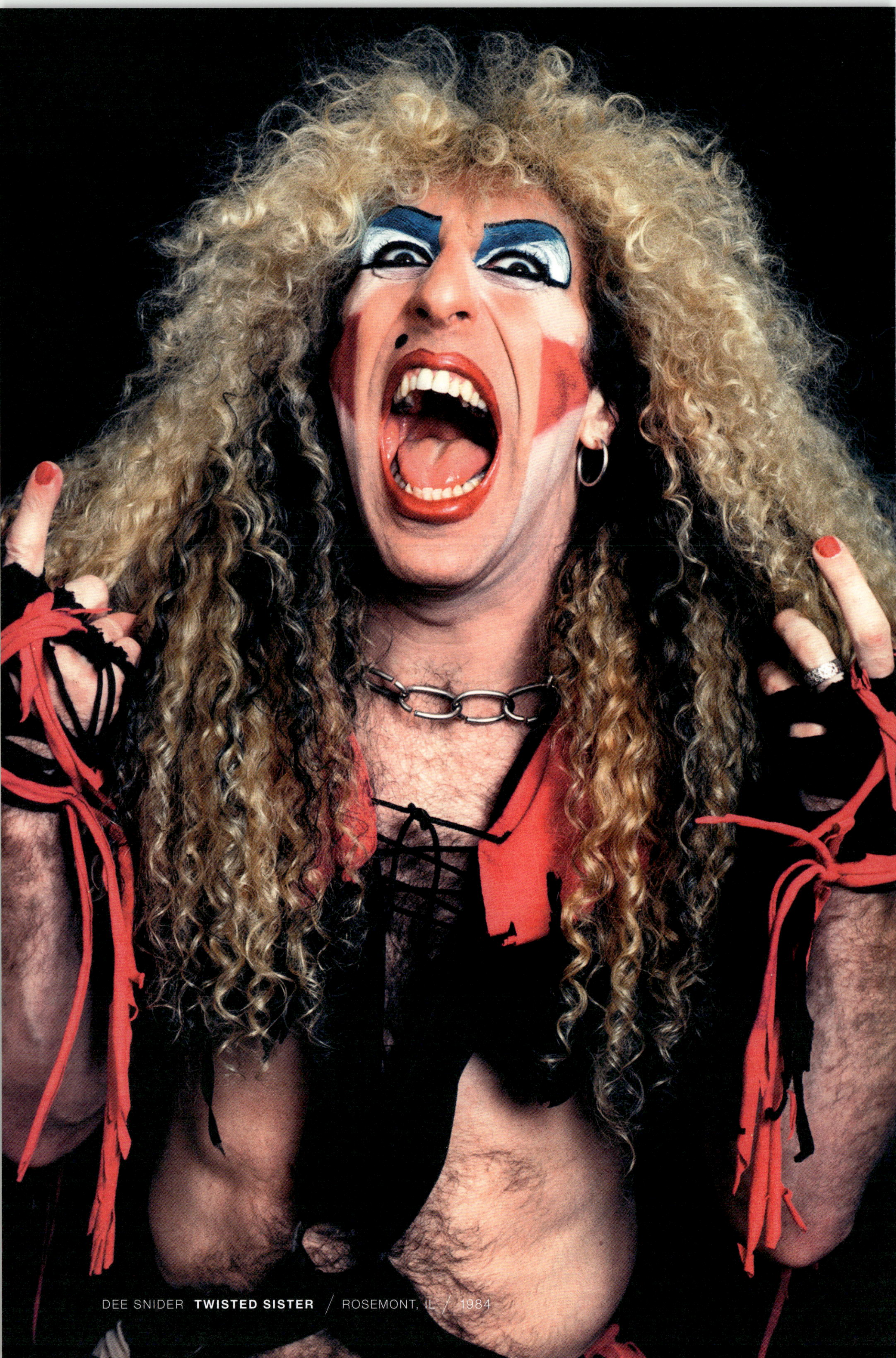

DEE SNIDER **TWISTED SISTER** / ROSEMONT, IL / 1984

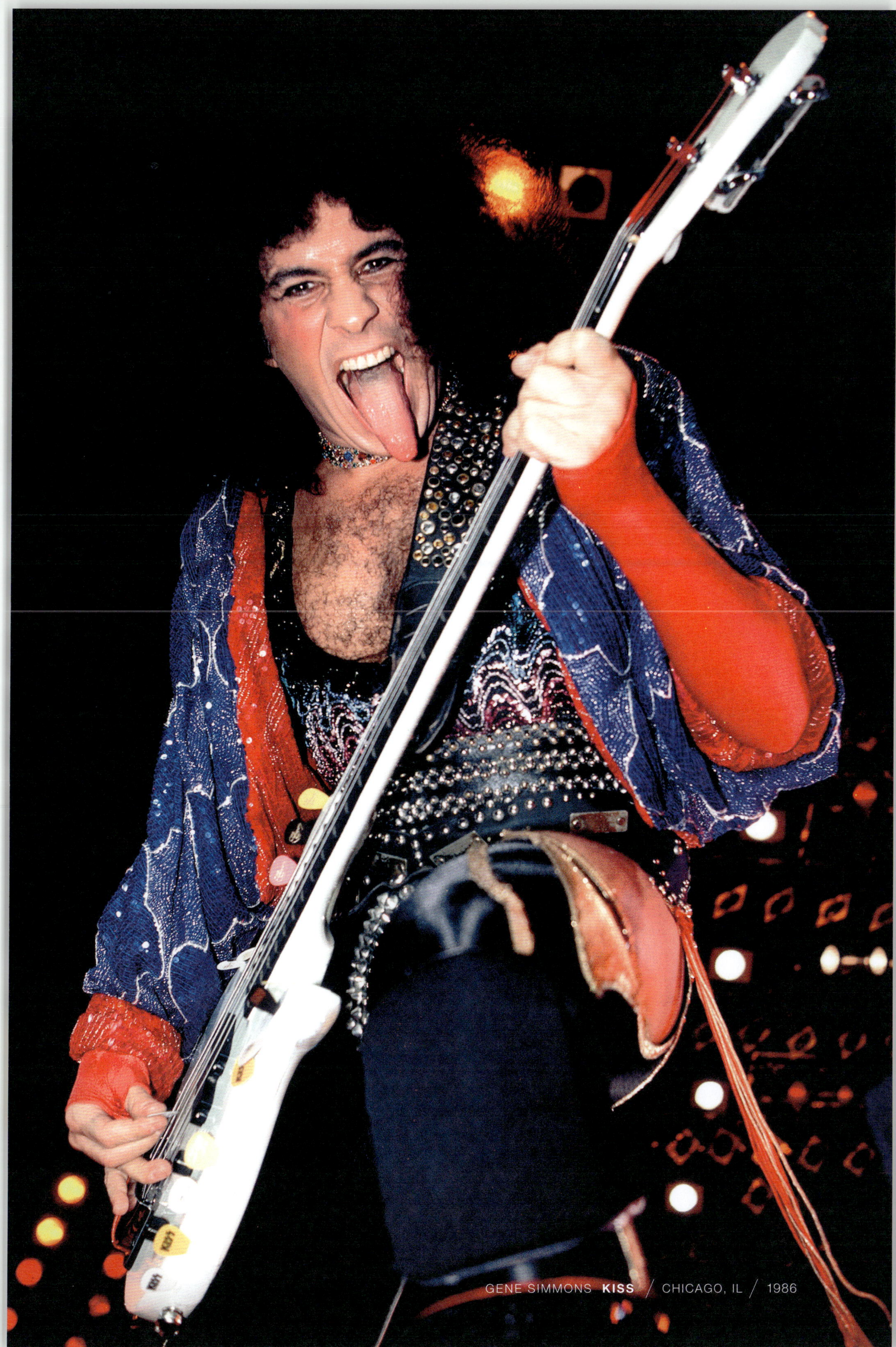

GENE SIMMONS **KISS** / CHICAGO, IL / 1986

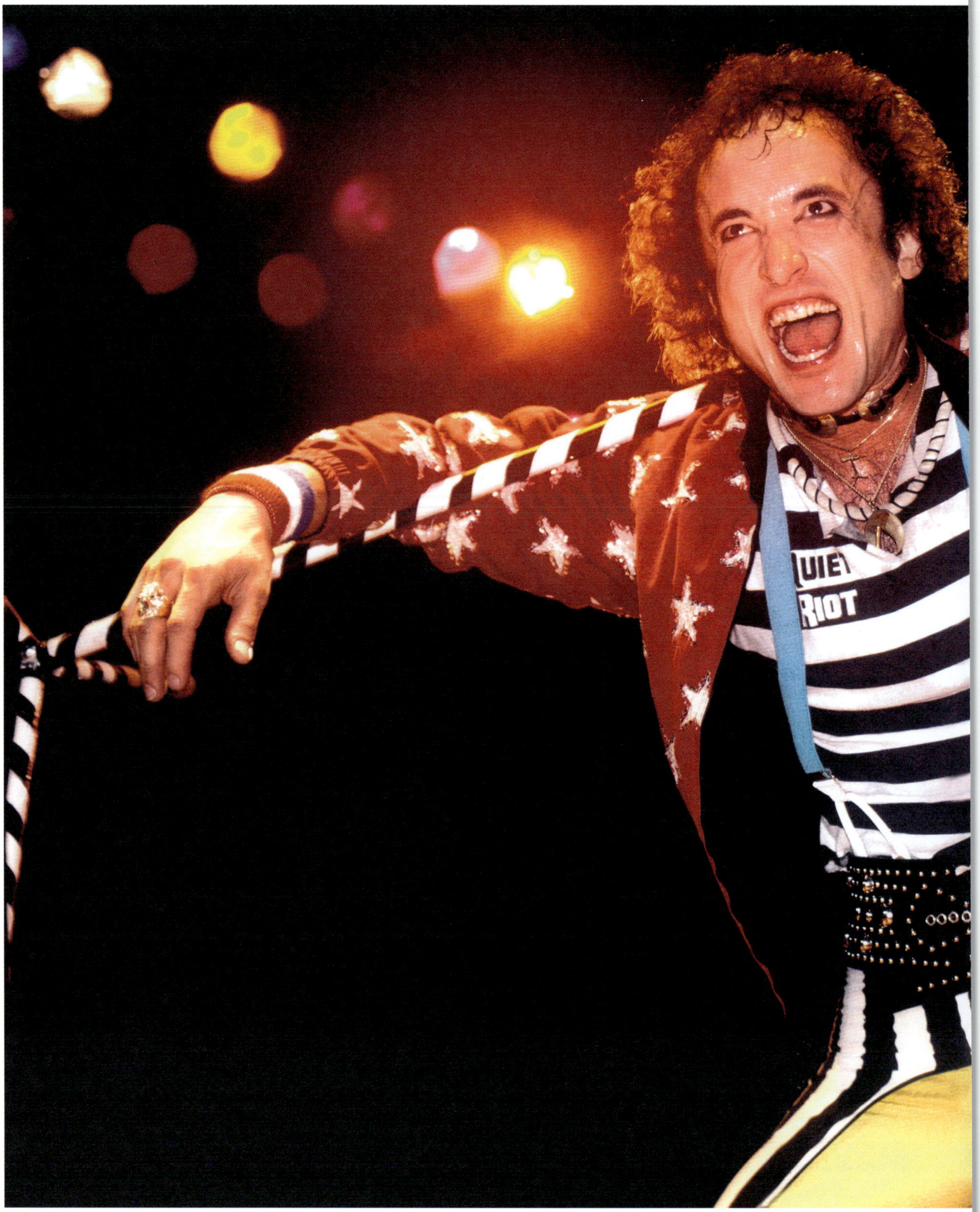

I met Quiet Riot backstage at the US Festival in 1983, before they went on as the first act of the festival's Heavy Metal Day. They were basically unknown outside of Los Angeles, and no other photographers got up early enough to photograph them. So when the band hit it big just a few months later, all the rock magazines came to me for pictures. The first time they came to Chicago, our conversation turned to L.A. vs.

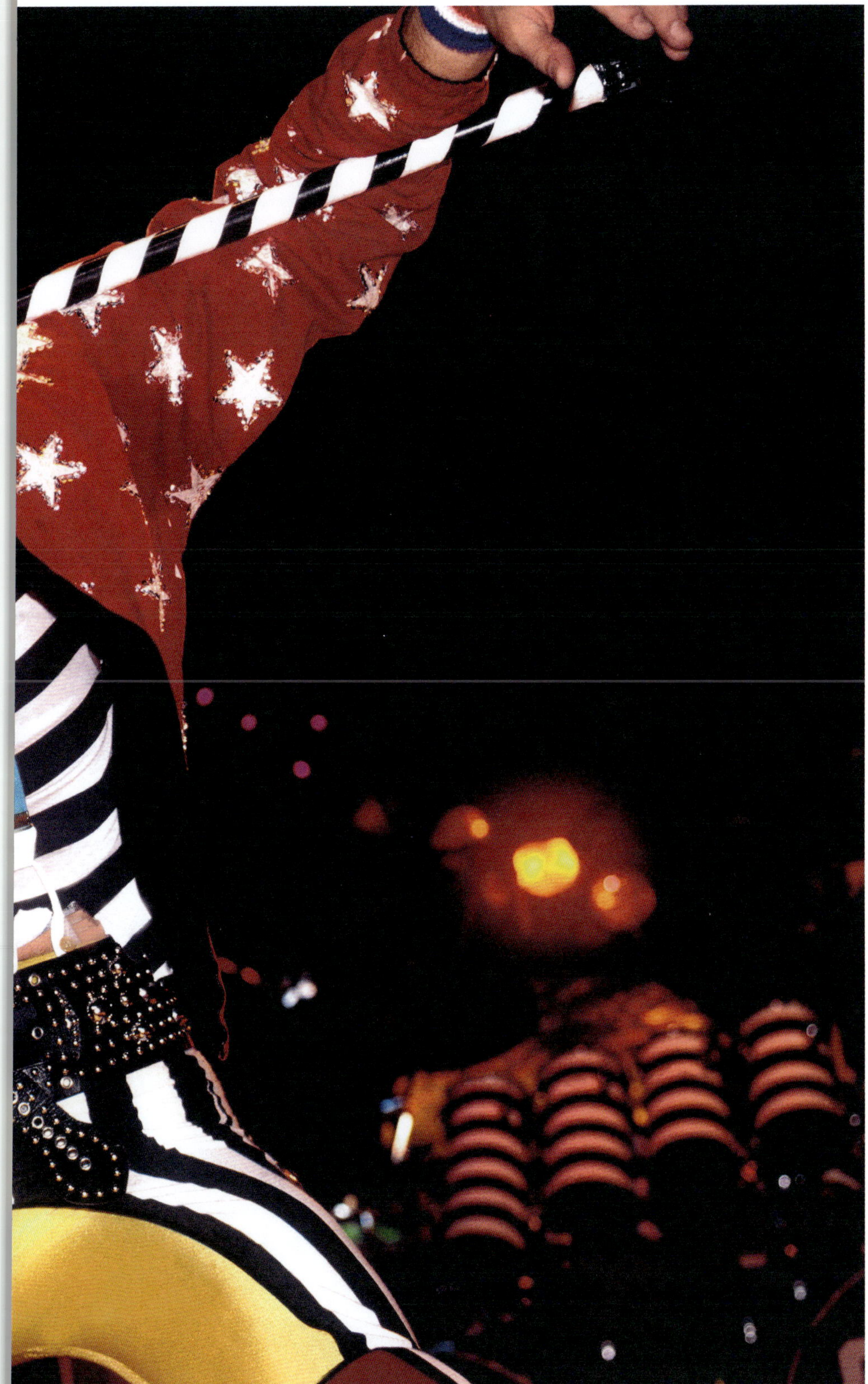

Chicago comparisons: Magic vs. Michael, Lakers vs. Bulls. It eventually escalated to Chicago pizza vs. everybody else's. When they came back to town about three months later, my phone rang the night before the show and on the other end was Kevin DuBrow, their lead singer, saying "Pick me up in half an hour–let's get pizza." That became a tradition for as long as they were touring.

KEVIN DuBROW **QUIET RIOT** / DES MOINES, IA / 1984

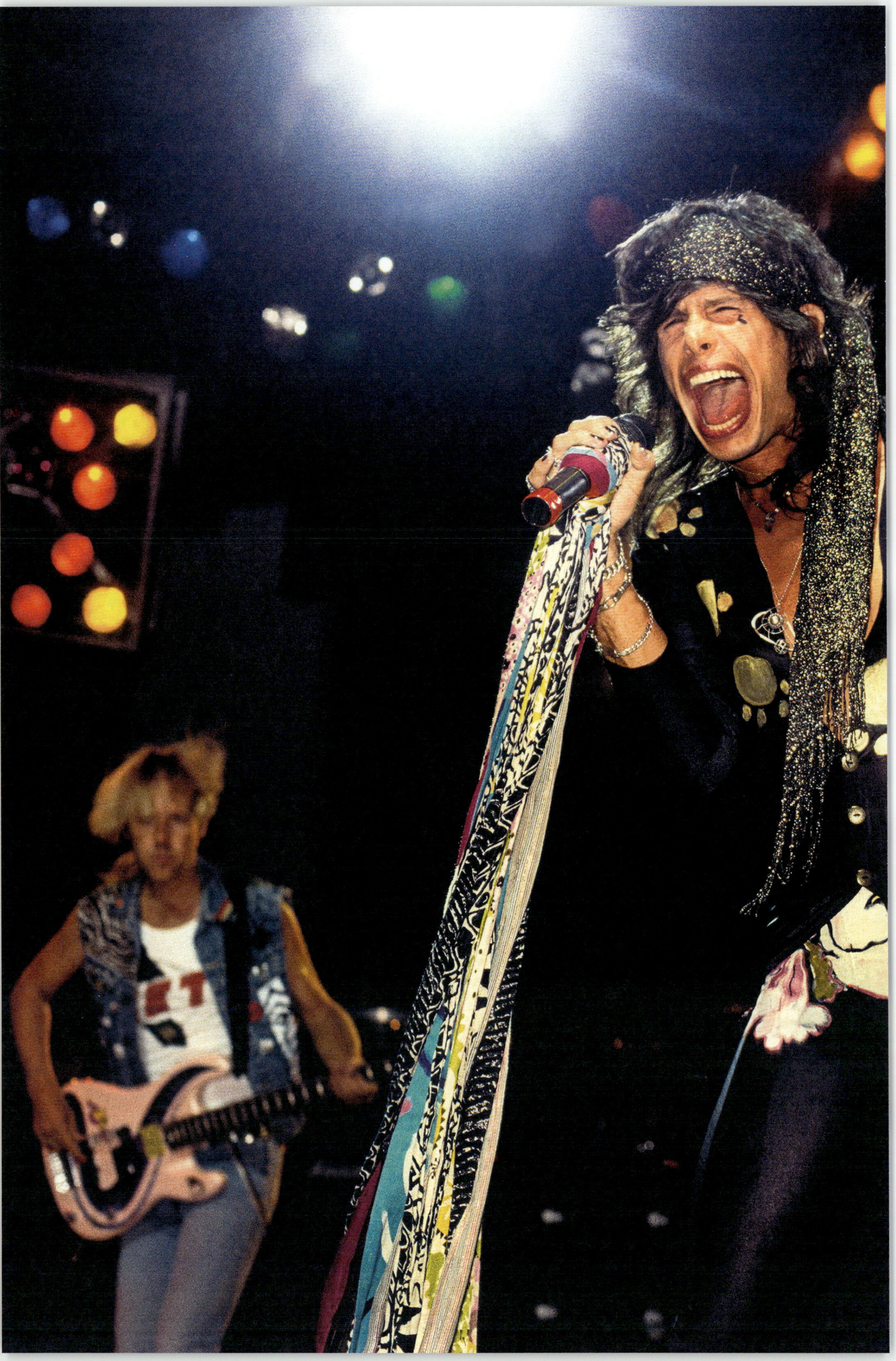

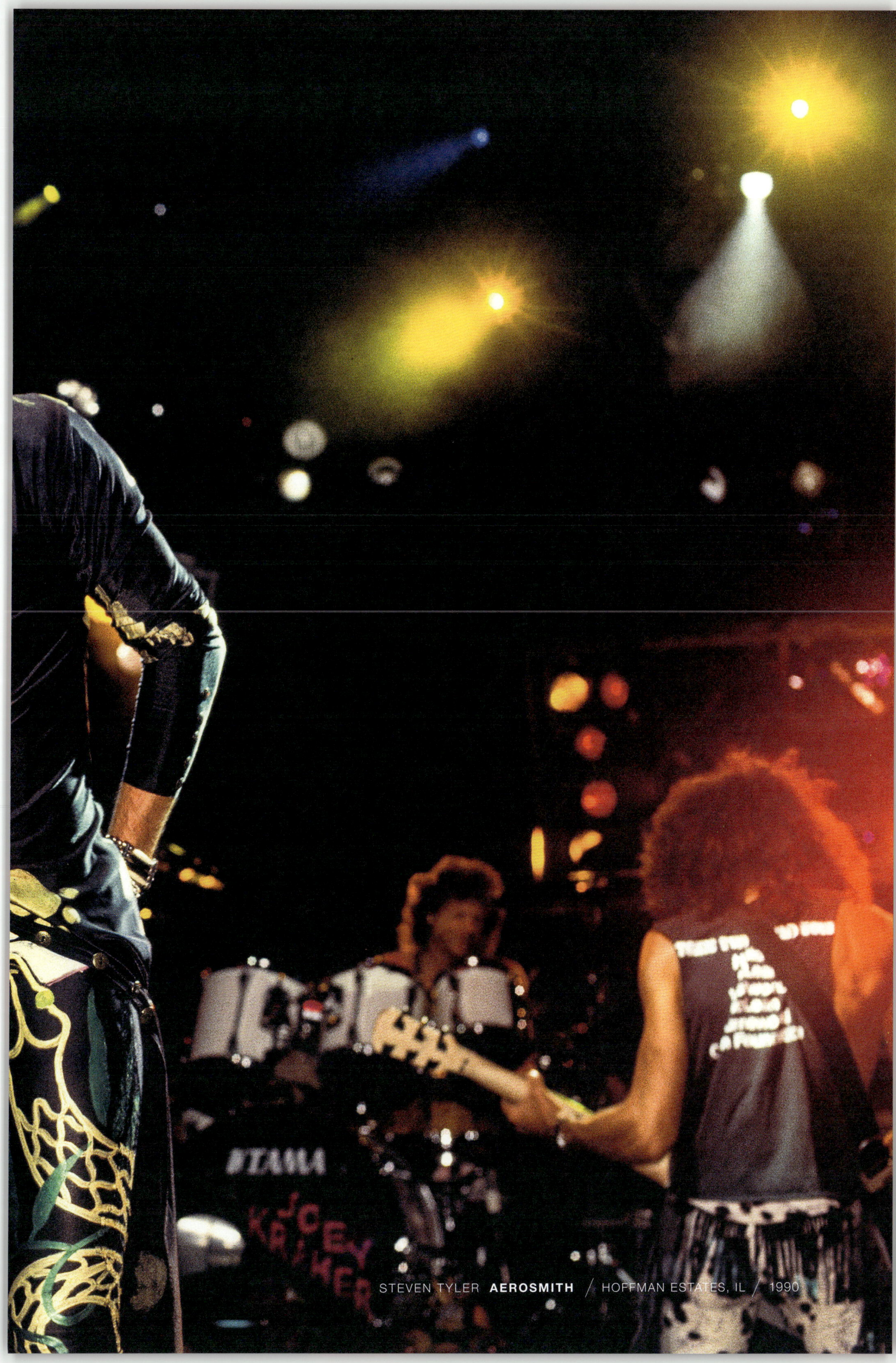

STEVEN TYLER **AEROSMITH** / HOFFMAN ESTATES, IL / 1990

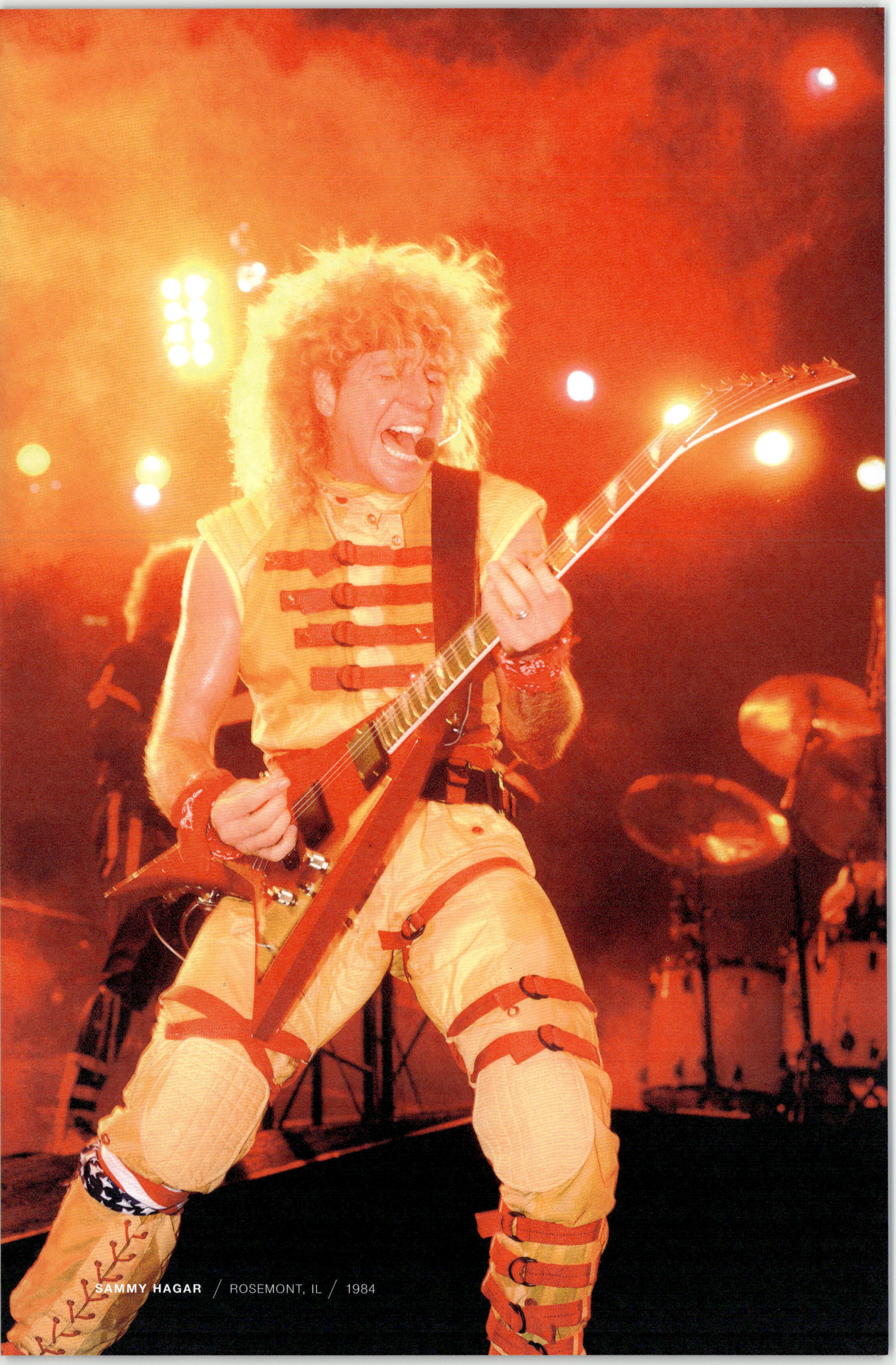

SAMMY HAGAR / ROSEMONT, IL / 1984

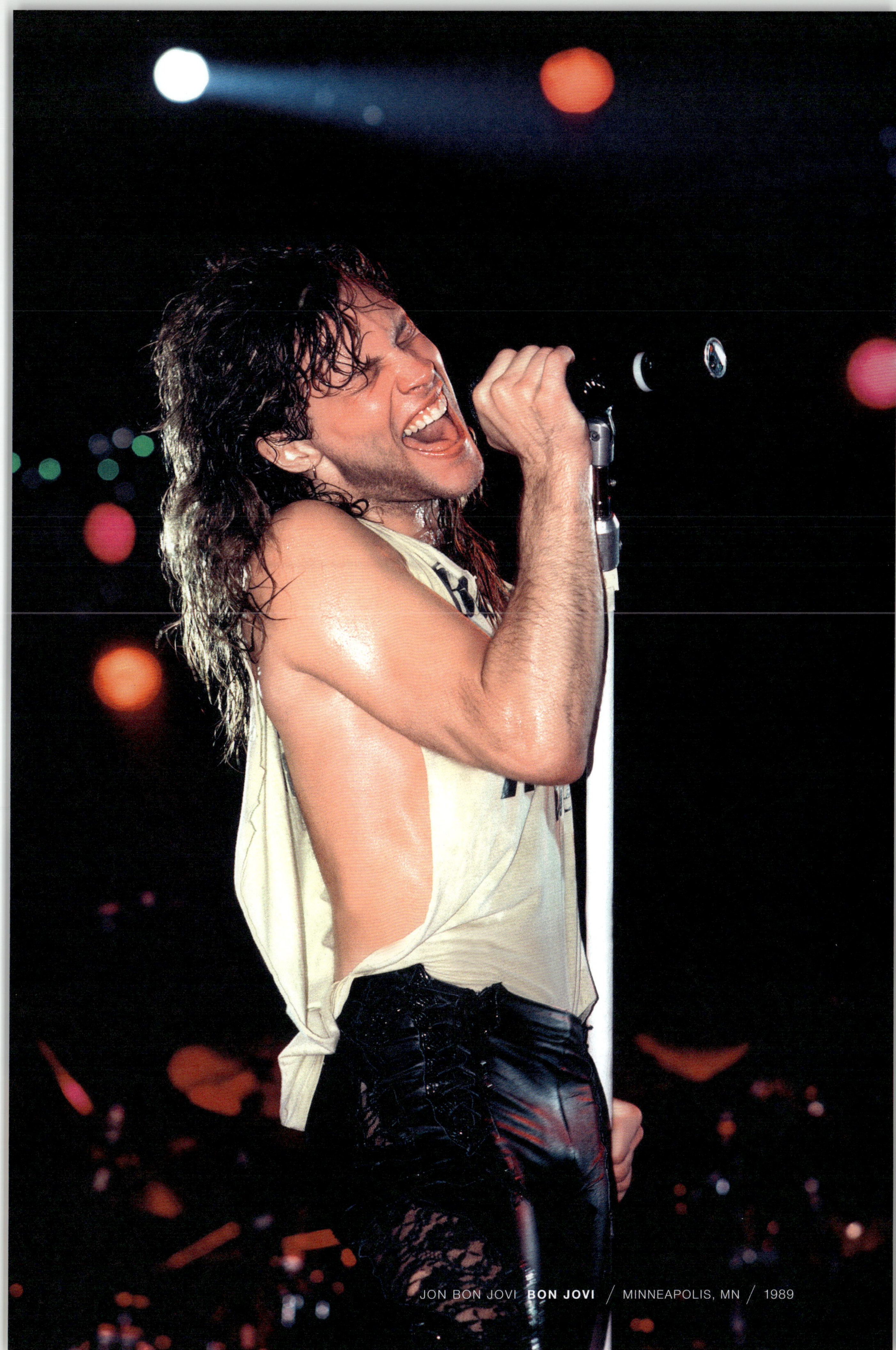

JON BON JOVI **BON JOVI** / MINNEAPOLIS, MN / 1989

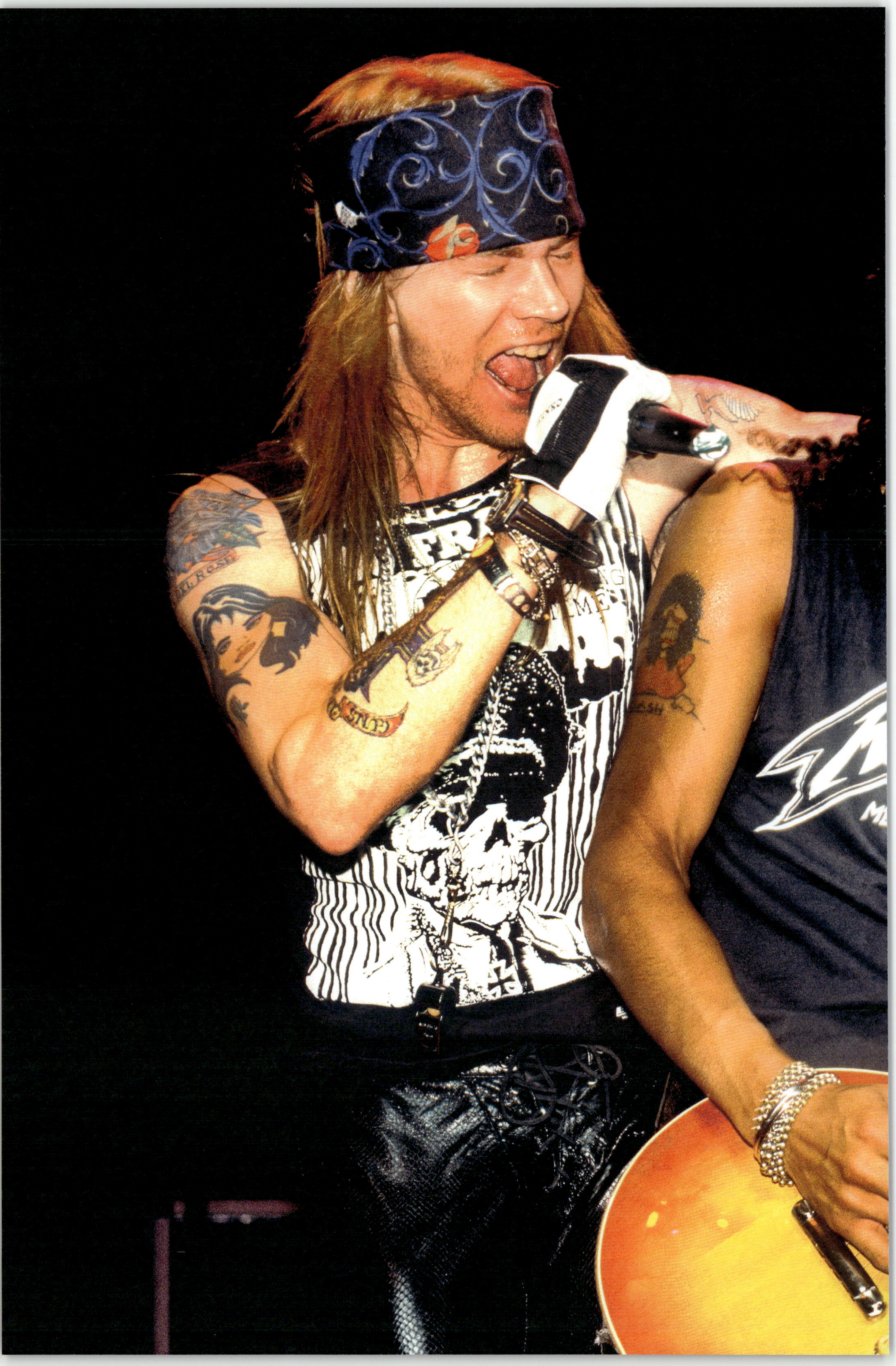

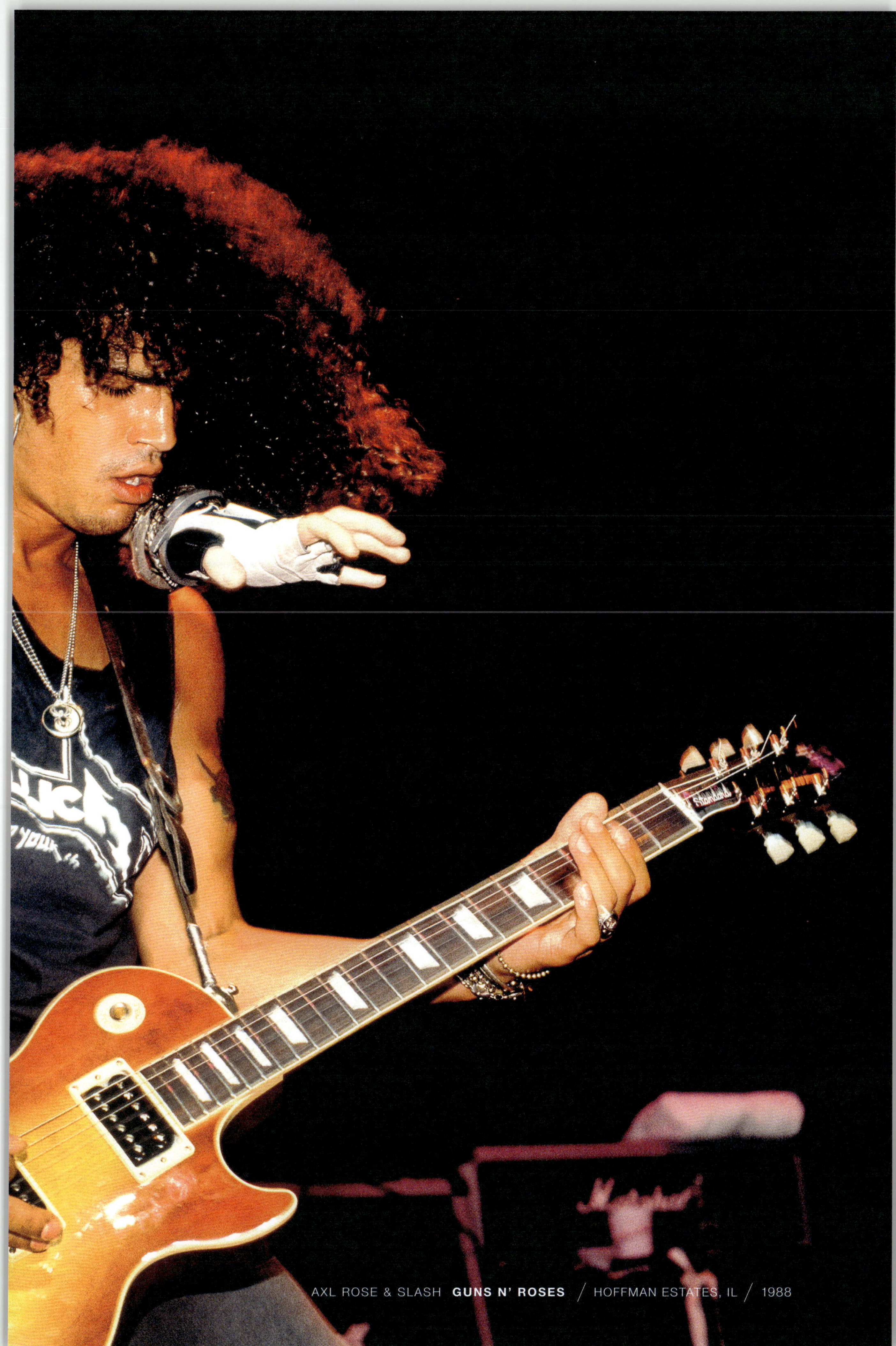

AXL ROSE & SLASH **GUNS N' ROSES** / HOFFMAN ESTATES, IL / 1988

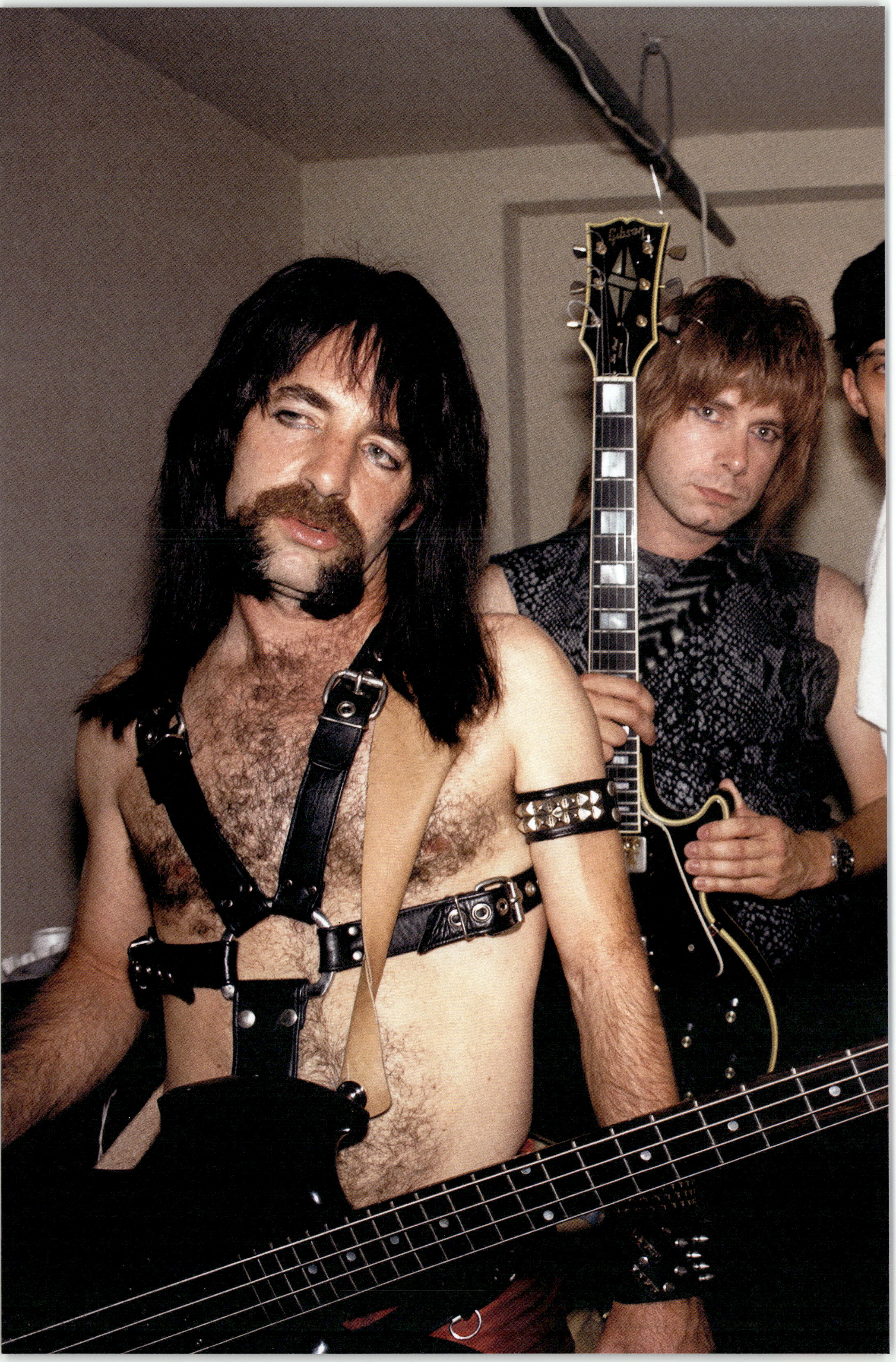
Gibson

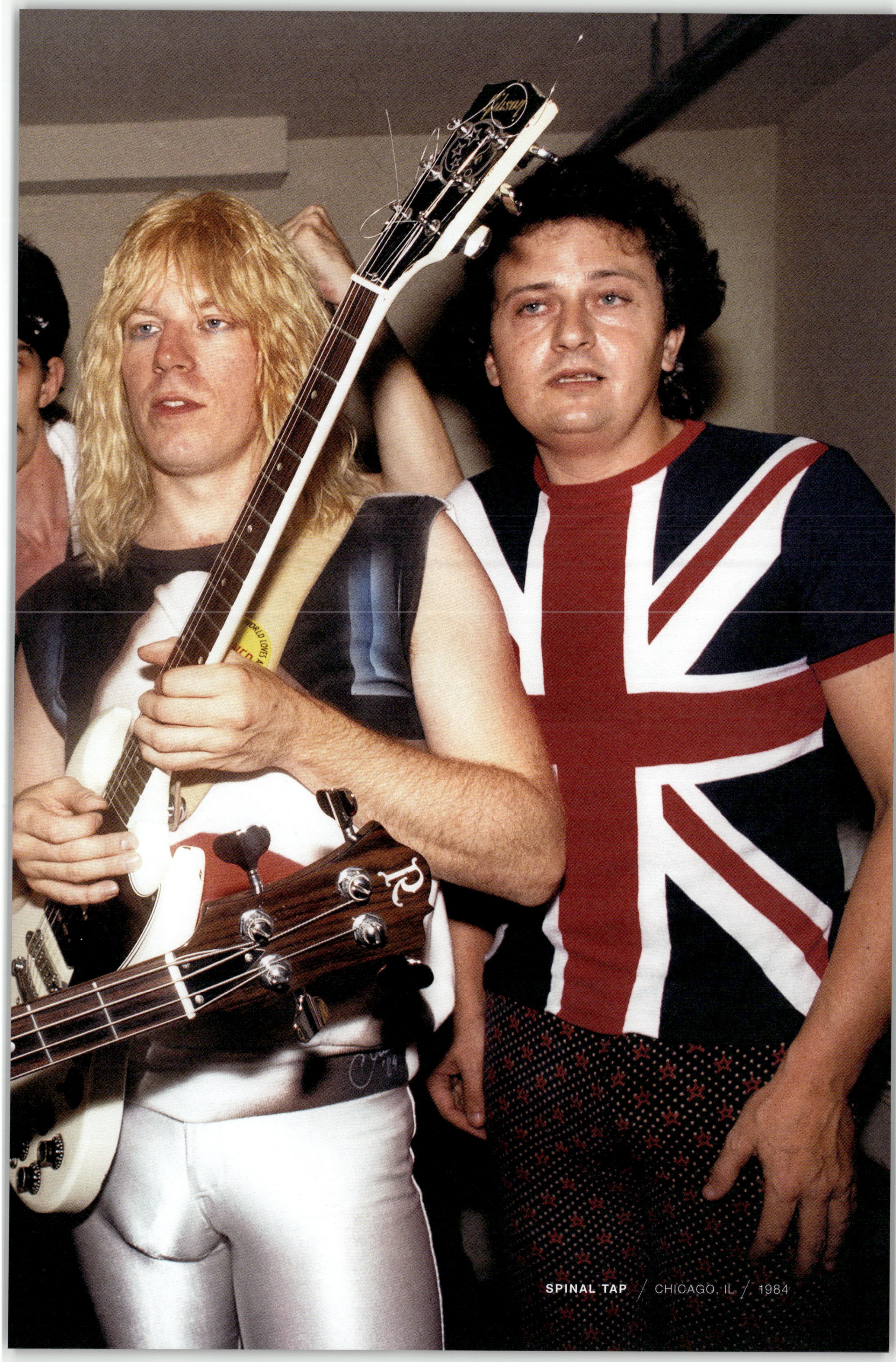

SPINAL TAP / CHICAGO, IL / 1984

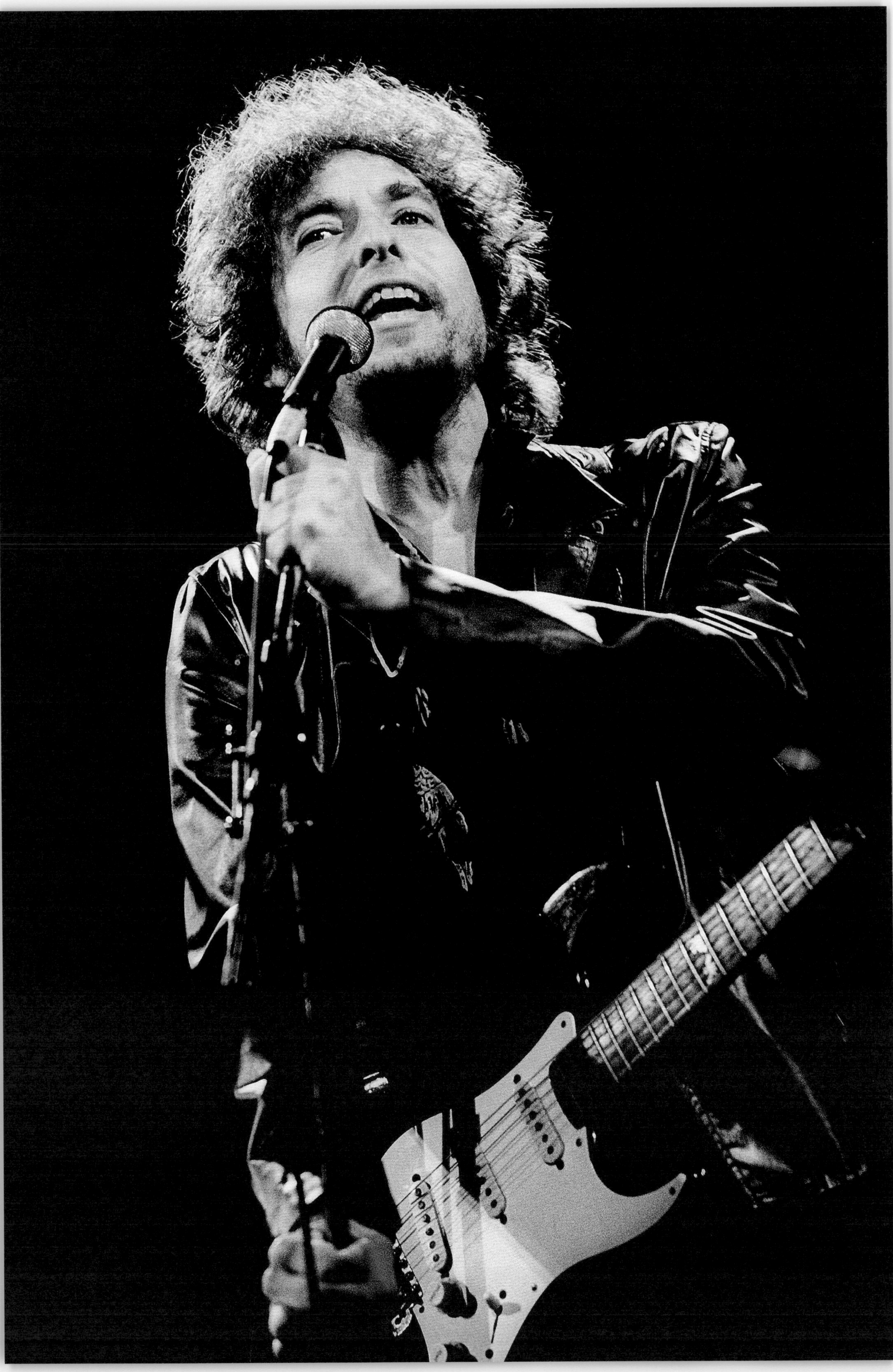

2

FOLK SINGER/SONGWRITERS

Folk music is all about the lyrics. Bob Dylan is the gold standard–he always has something to say, and knows exactly how to say it. The late John Prine is the Chicago-area gold standard. In May of 2010, I was asked to photograph the cover of a concert video John was producing at his old high school. A week earlier, I had photographed three-piece band Muse at a large hockey arena. They had 17 trucks to carry all of their staging, which included three elevators. When I got out to Proviso High School in Maywood, Illinois, I found out that John's contract had stipulated that he and his two bandmates be supplied only with a small card table and three bottles of water. He had the superior show!

BOB DYLAN / HOFFMAN ESTATES, IL / 1981

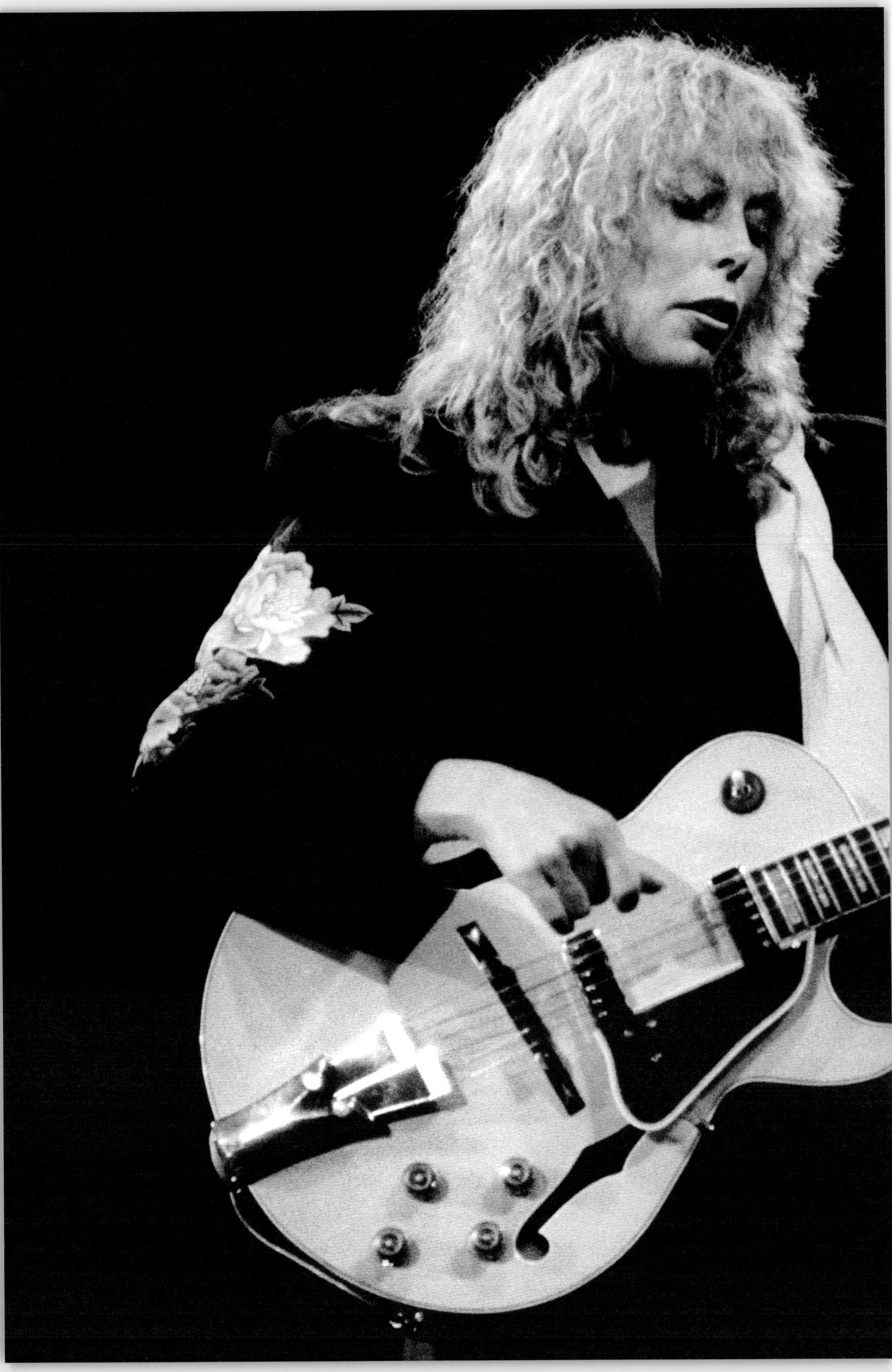

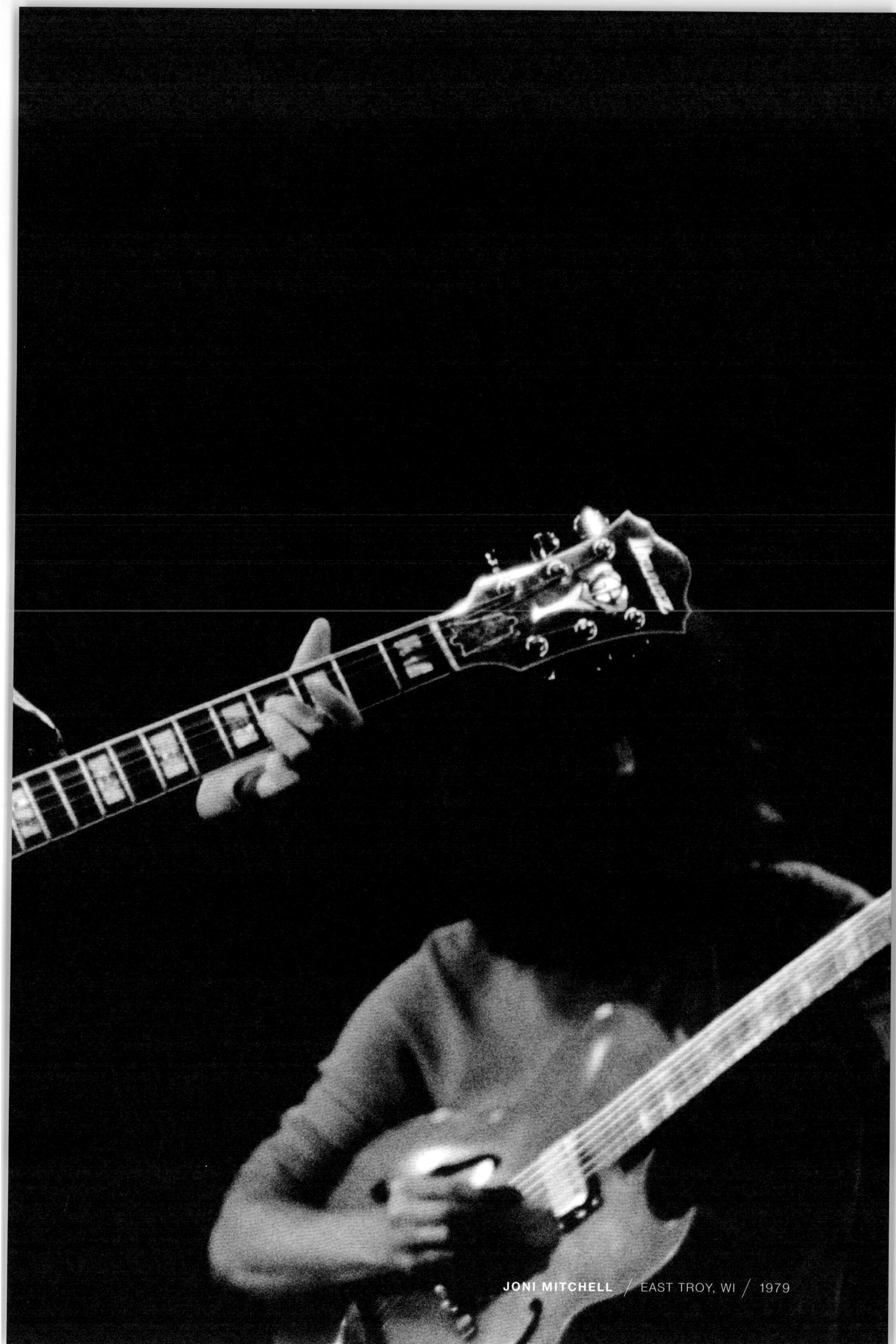

JONI MITCHELL / EAST TROY, WI / 1979

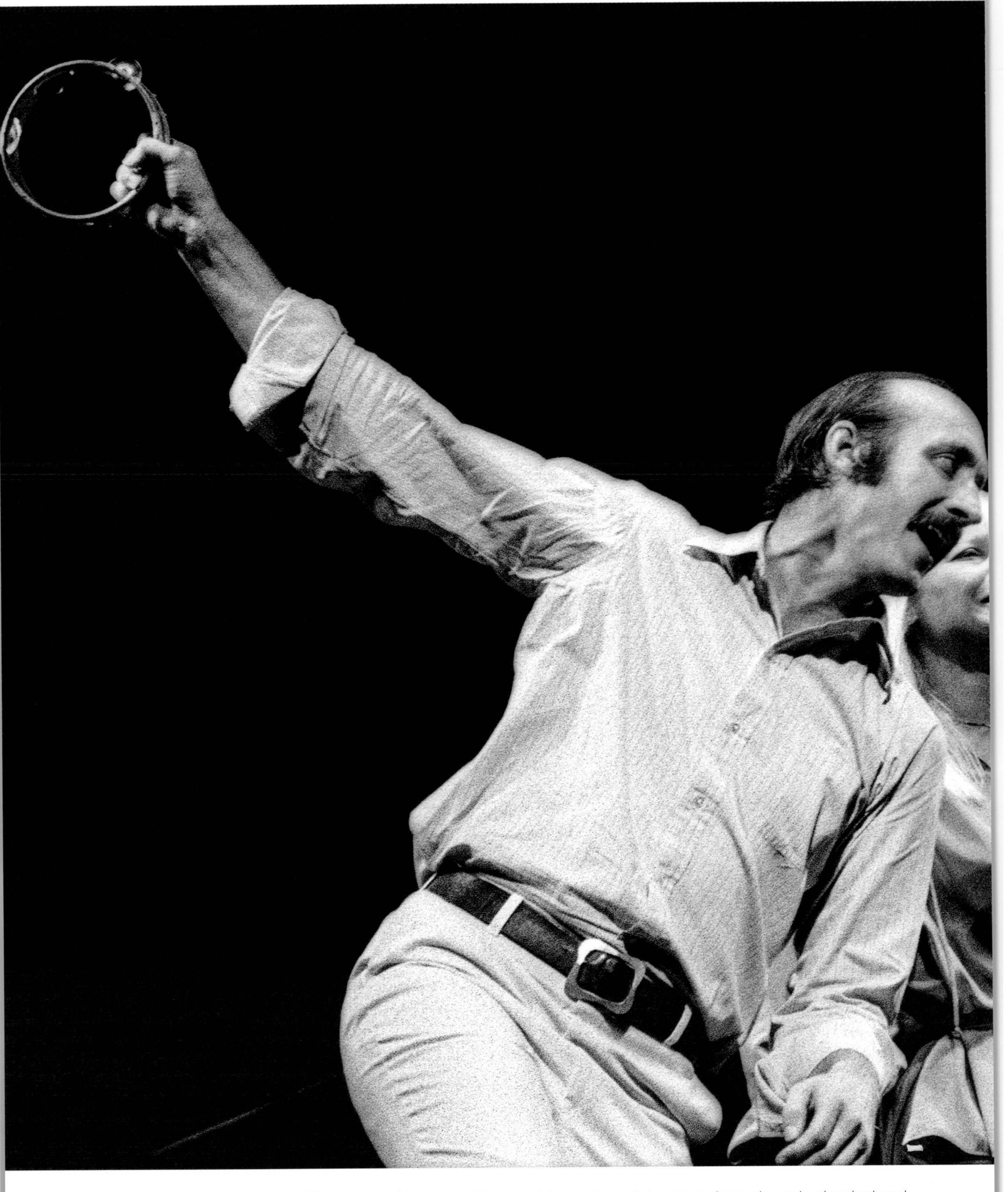

When I was a kid, my mother would not let me listen to rock music, only classical and folk. Peter, Paul and Mary were folk's answer to the Rolling Stones, and when I heard they were coming to town I had to go. I really wanted to get them all in the same shot–fortunately, they were really smart show-biz people and knew that everybody

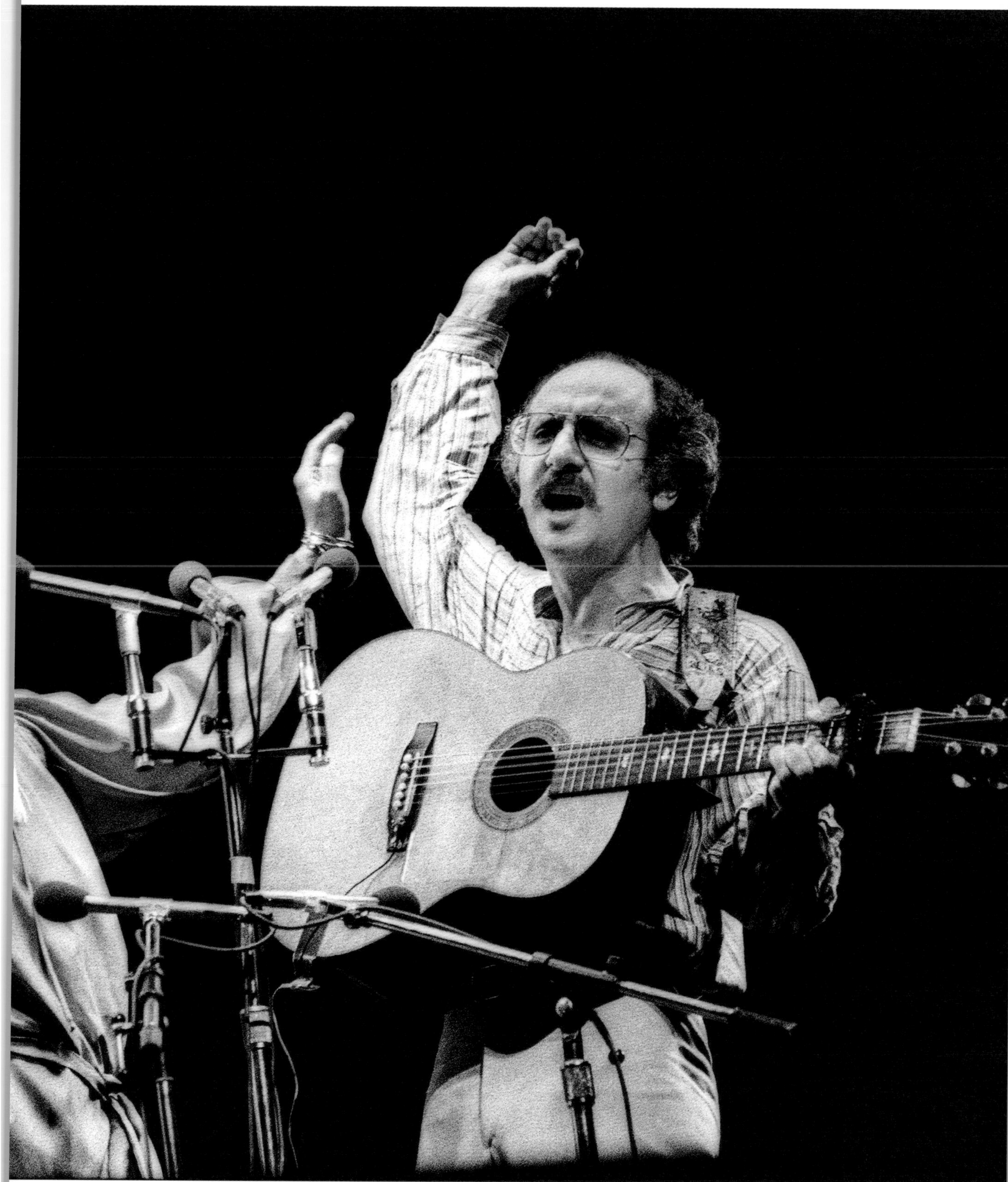

wanted to see them play off each other, so they had a special stand that held three microphones. My only real problem was maneuvering to a spot in the aisle where I could see all three of their faces in the frame. Mission accomplished!

PETER, PAUL AND MARY / CHICAGO, IL / 1978

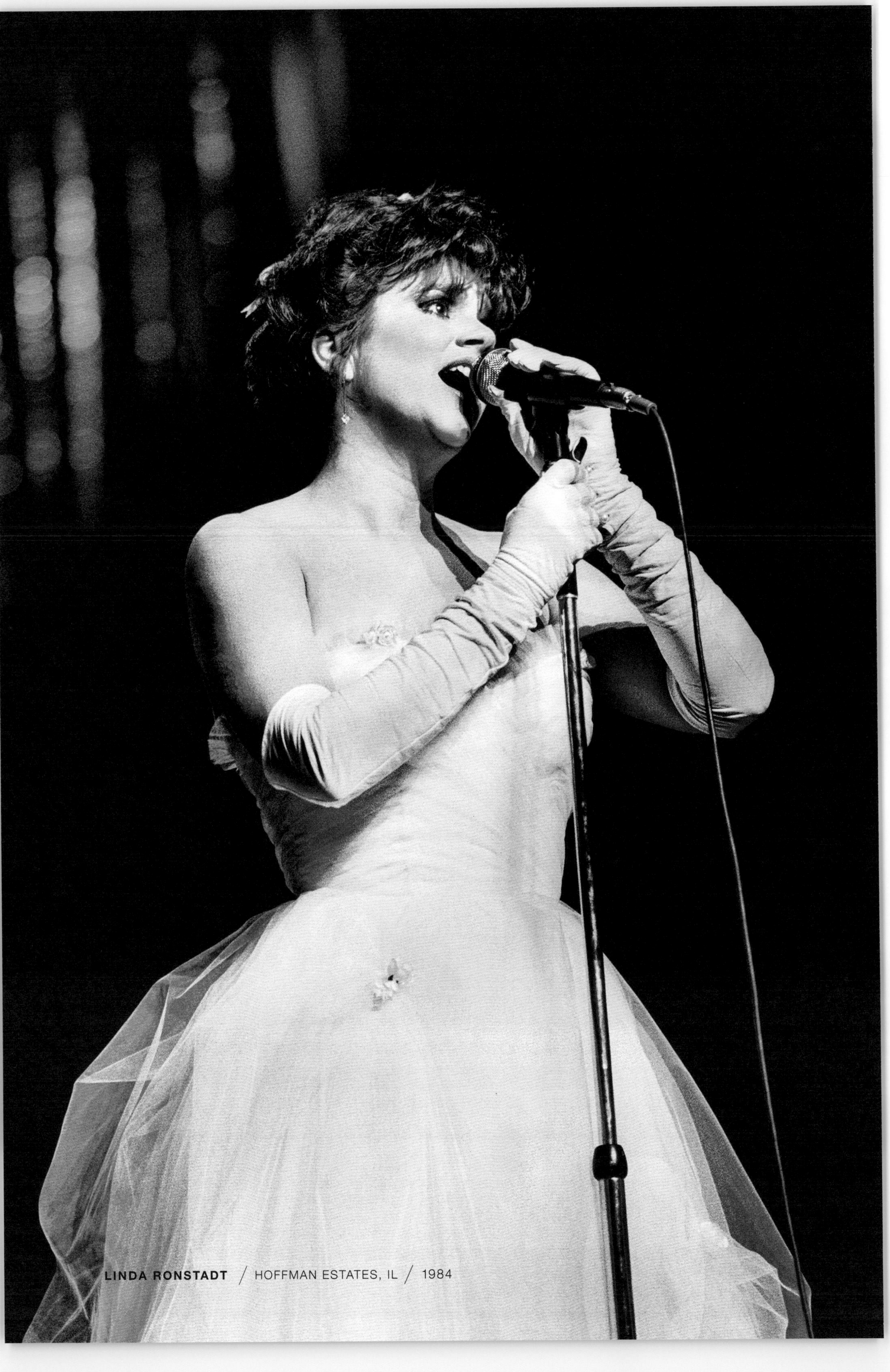

LINDA RONSTADT / HOFFMAN ESTATES, IL / 1984

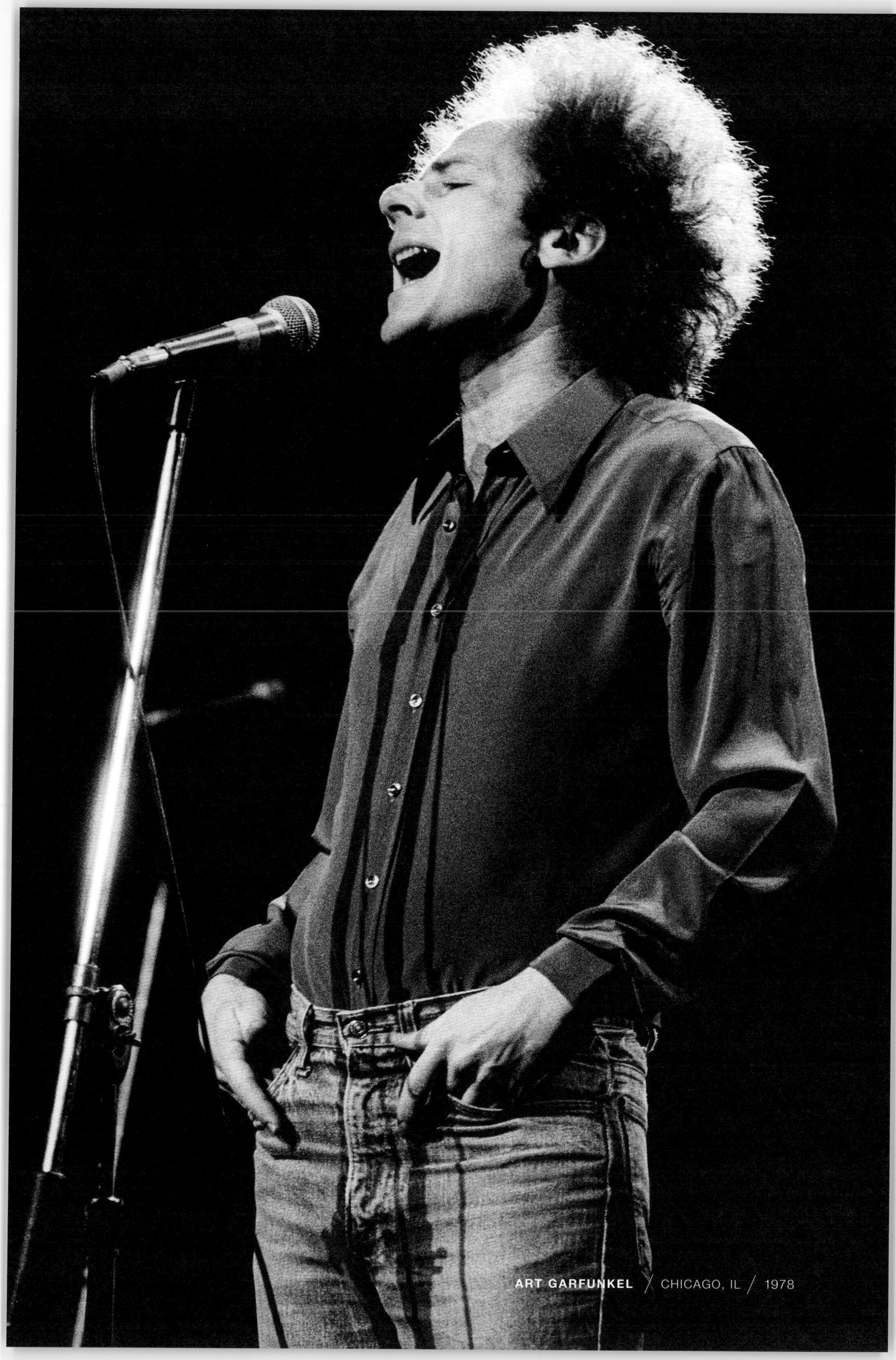

ART GARFUNKEL / CHICAGO, IL / 1978

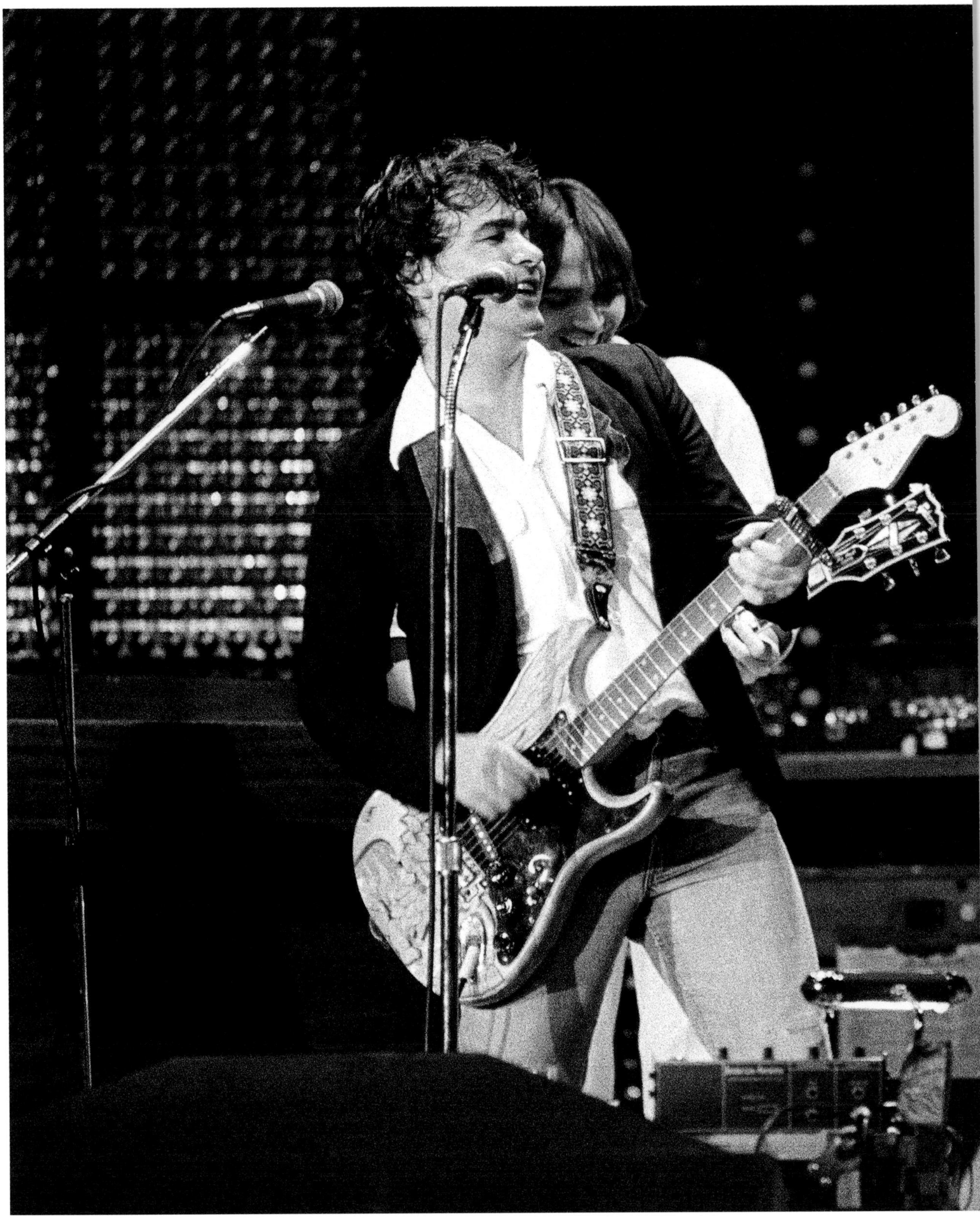

I have always admired how beautifully a great songwriter can convey their thoughts through their lyrics. One of the all-time best was John Prine, who played regularly in folk clubs around Chicago, sometimes with his friend Steve Goodman. Both artists landed record deals around the same time and supported each other as they became world-

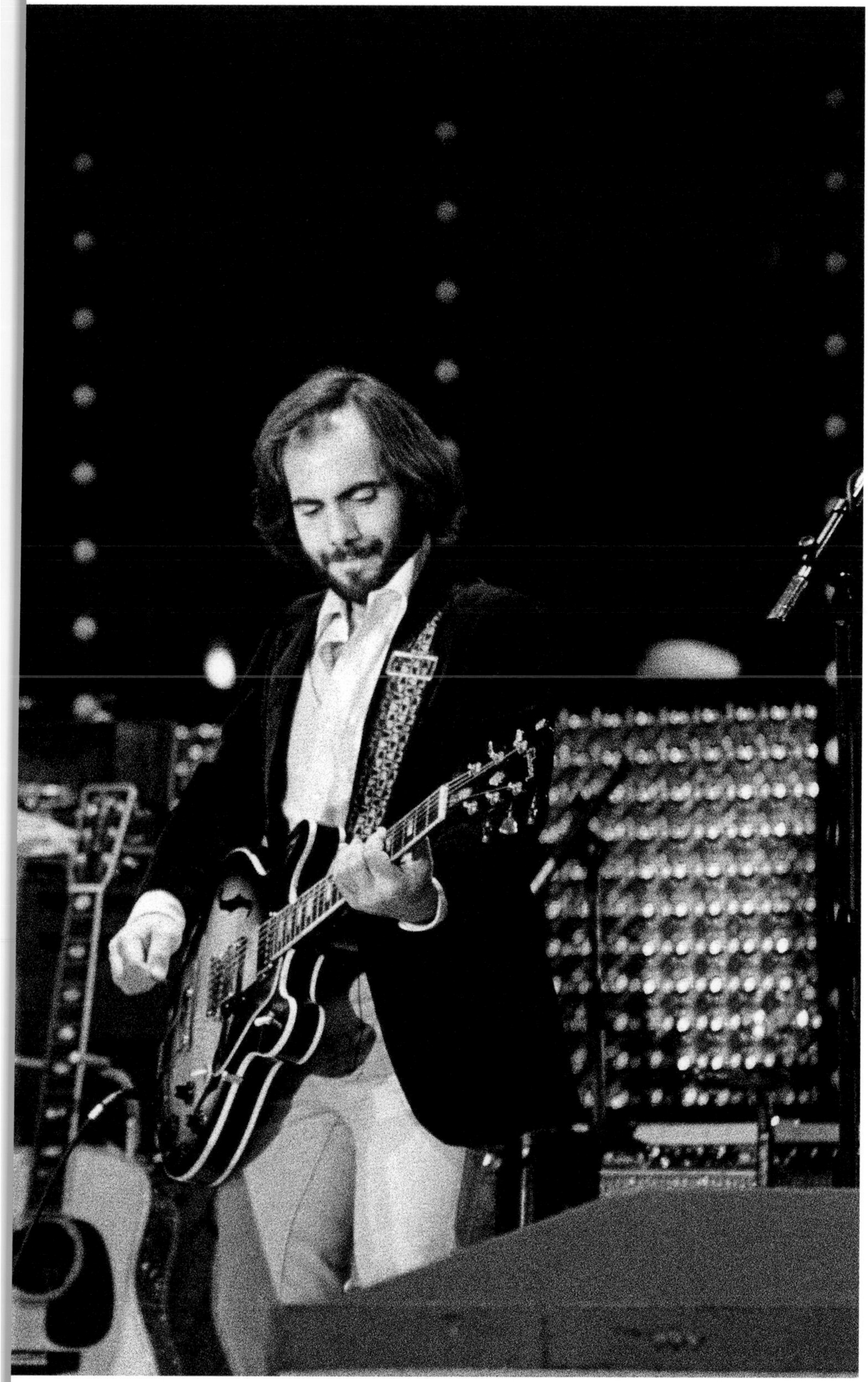

famous. It was always a special night when John was performing and Steve jumped up on stage to play a few songs with him. They loved and covered each other's songs, and reveled in playing them together.

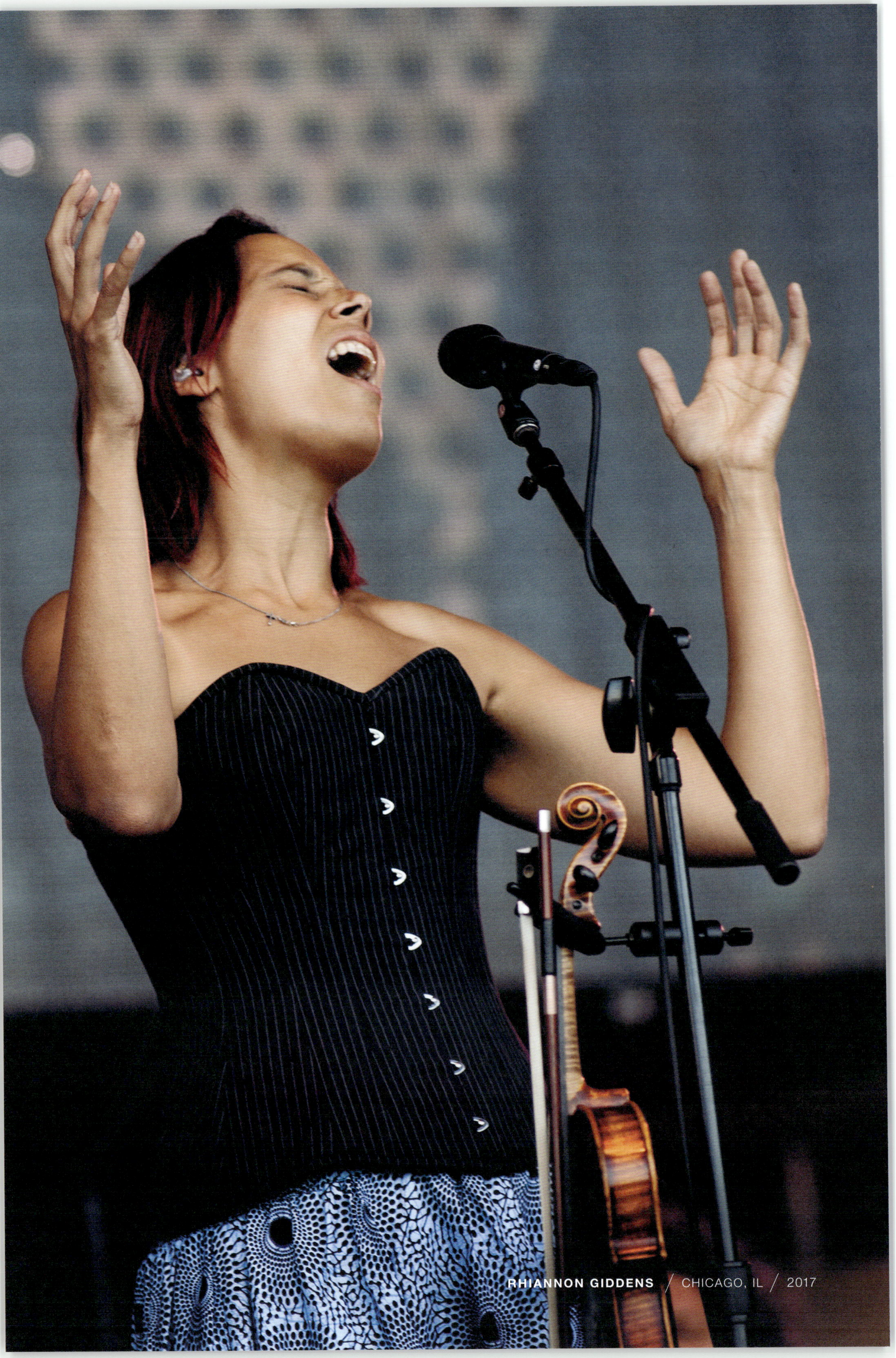

RHIANNON GIDDENS / CHICAGO, IL / 2017

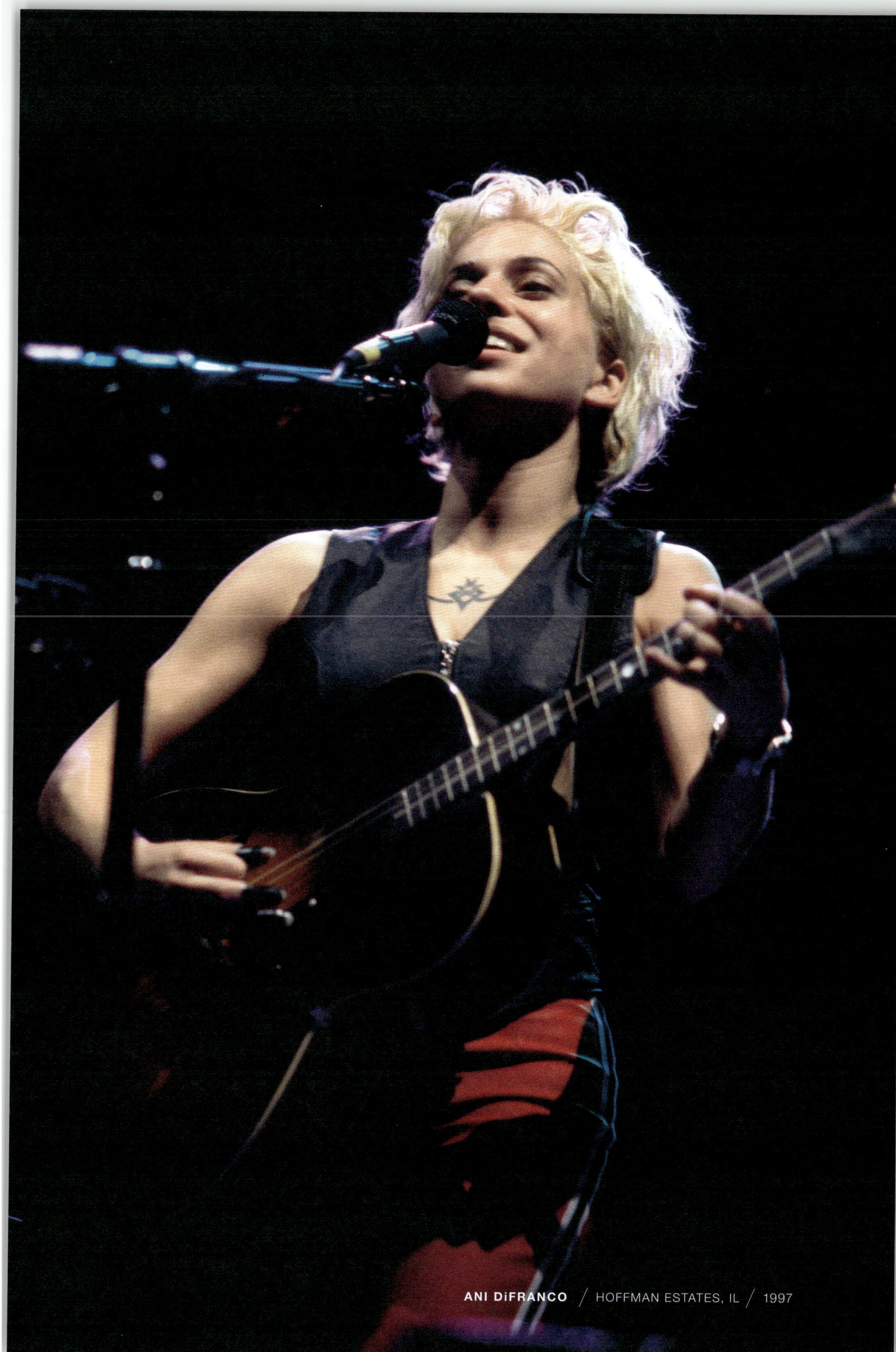

ANI DiFRANCO / HOFFMAN ESTATES, IL / 1997

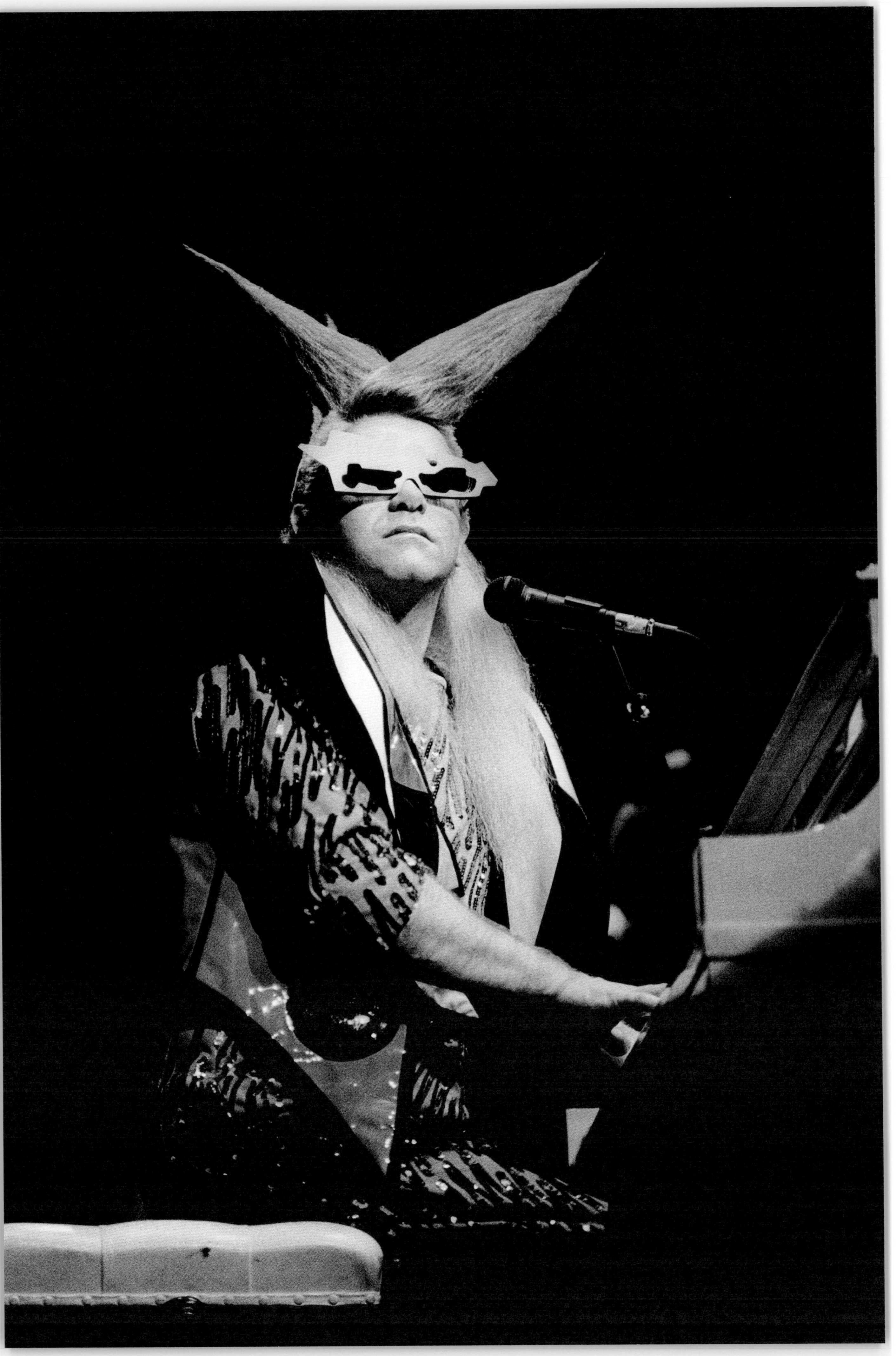

3

ICONIC
CLASSIC ROCK

The backbone of the music and touring business, rock is also the lifeblood of any music photographer. "Discovering" a new talent and seeing them rise to the top is thrilling. For example, introducing myself to R.E.M. in their dressing room on their first tour, then watching them play a 20,000-seat arena only four years later put a smile on my face.

ELTON JOHN / HOFFMAN ESTATES, IL / 1986

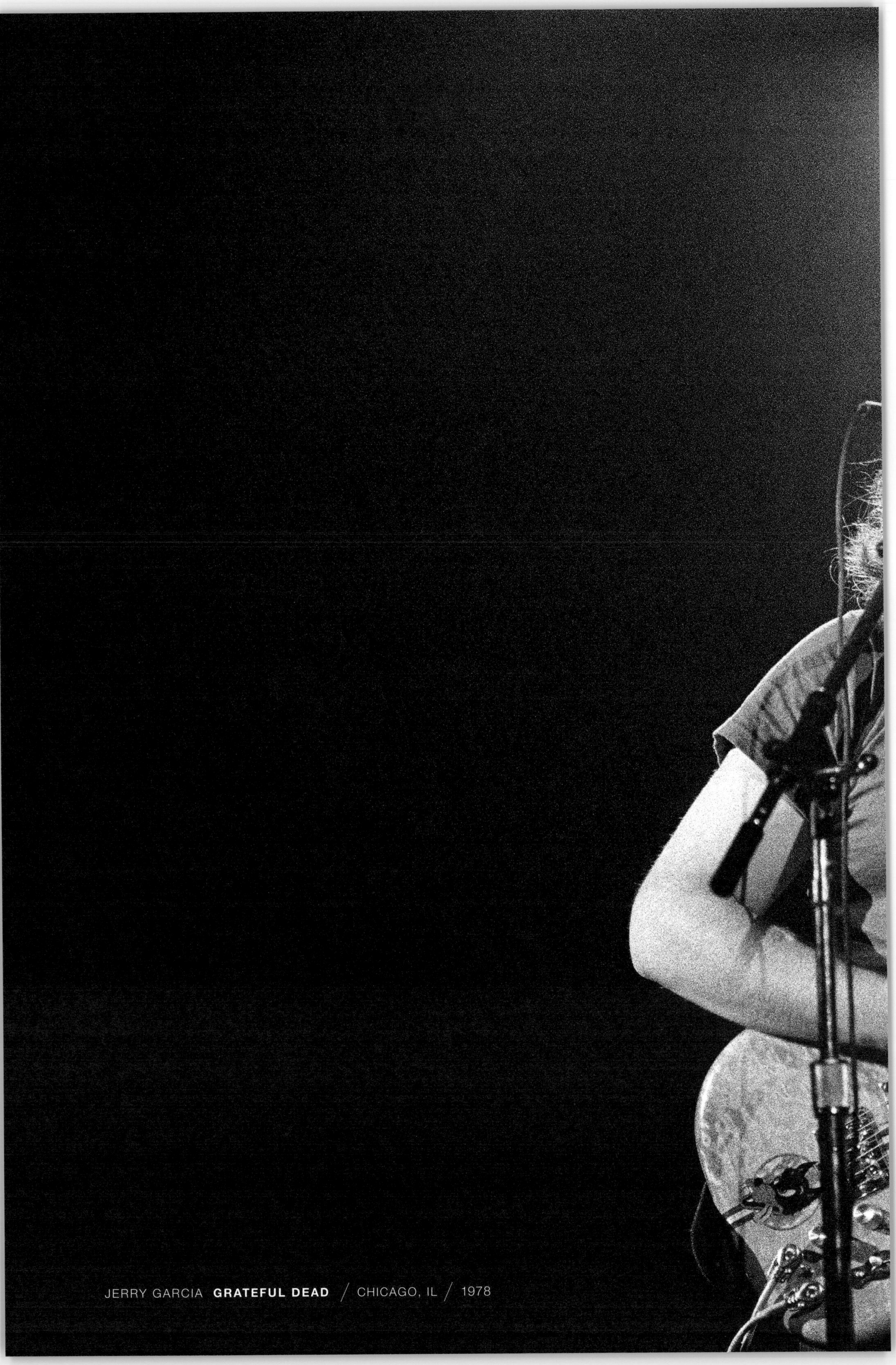

JERRY GARCIA **GRATEFUL DEAD** / CHICAGO, IL / 1978

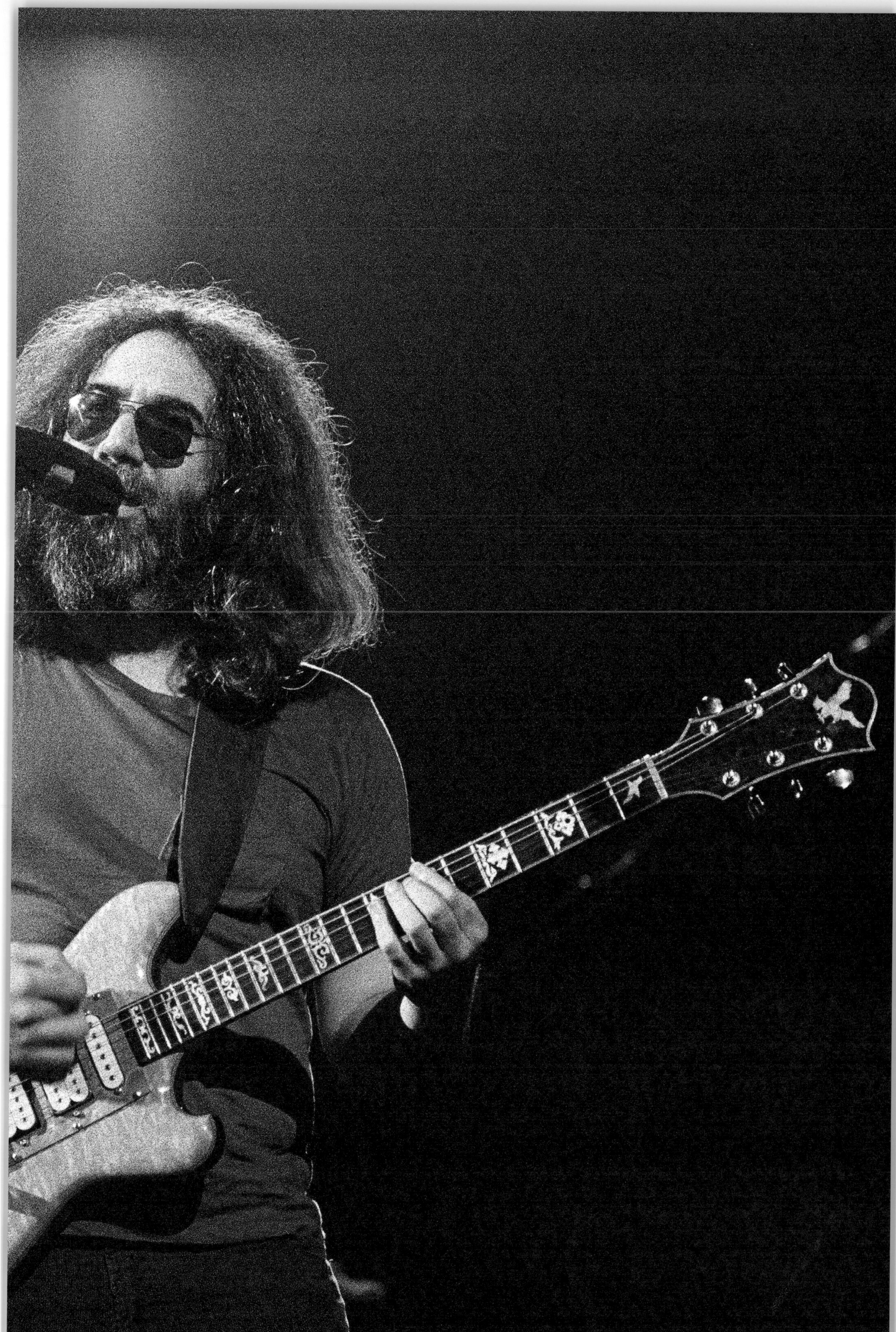

NEIL YOUNG / INDIANAPOLIS, IN / 1990

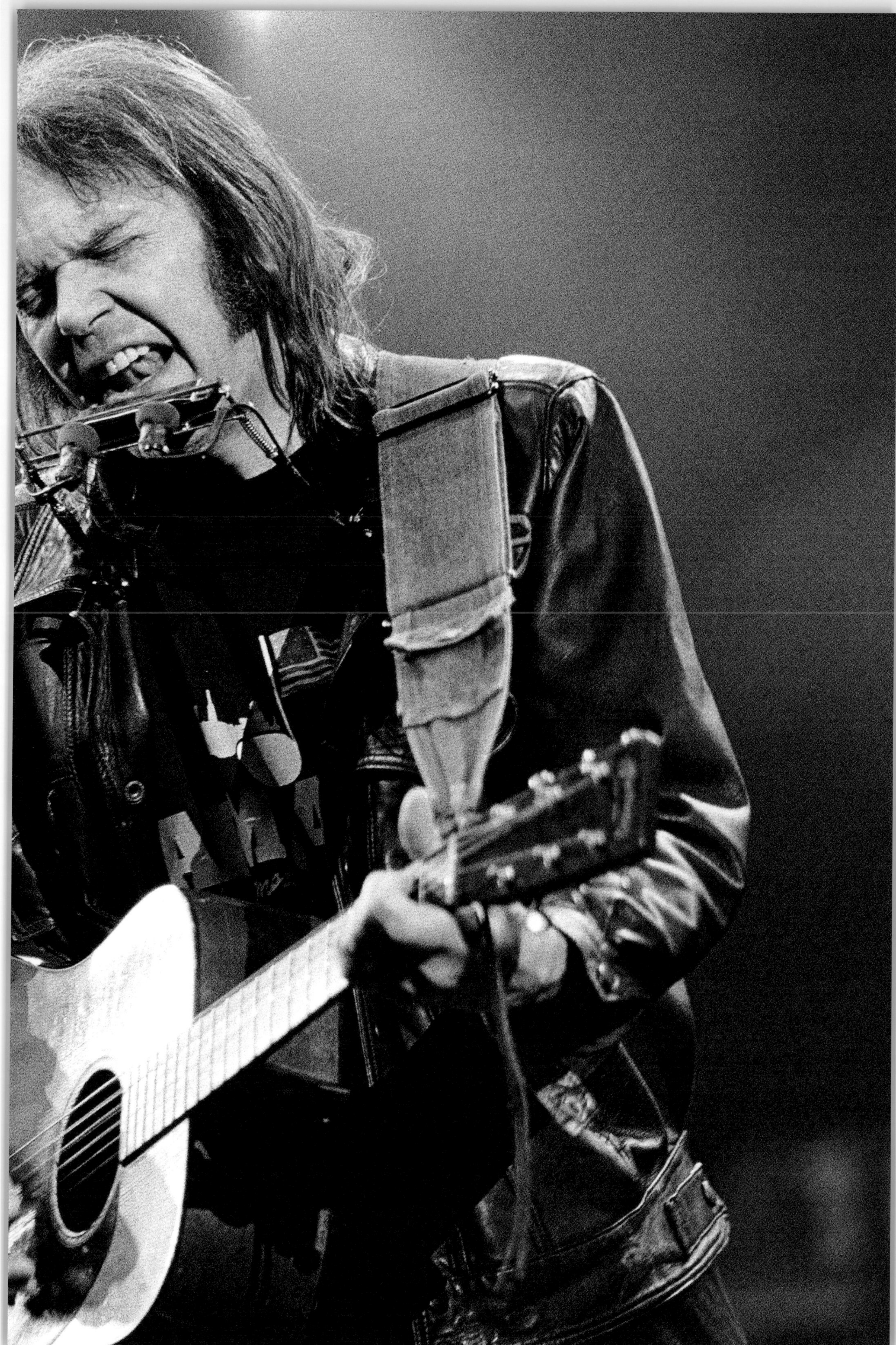

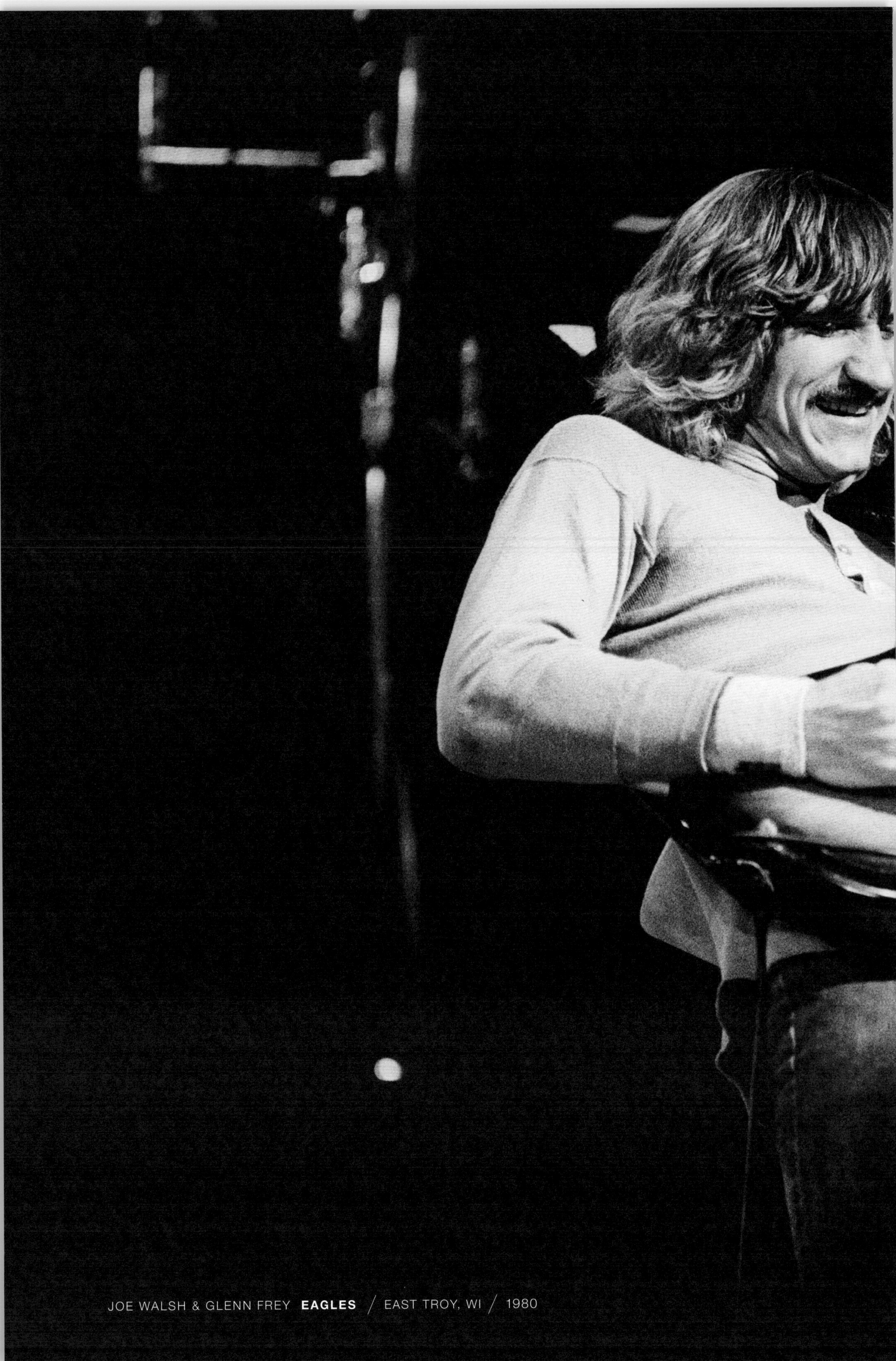

JOE WALSH & GLENN FREY **EAGLES** / EAST TROY, WI / 1980

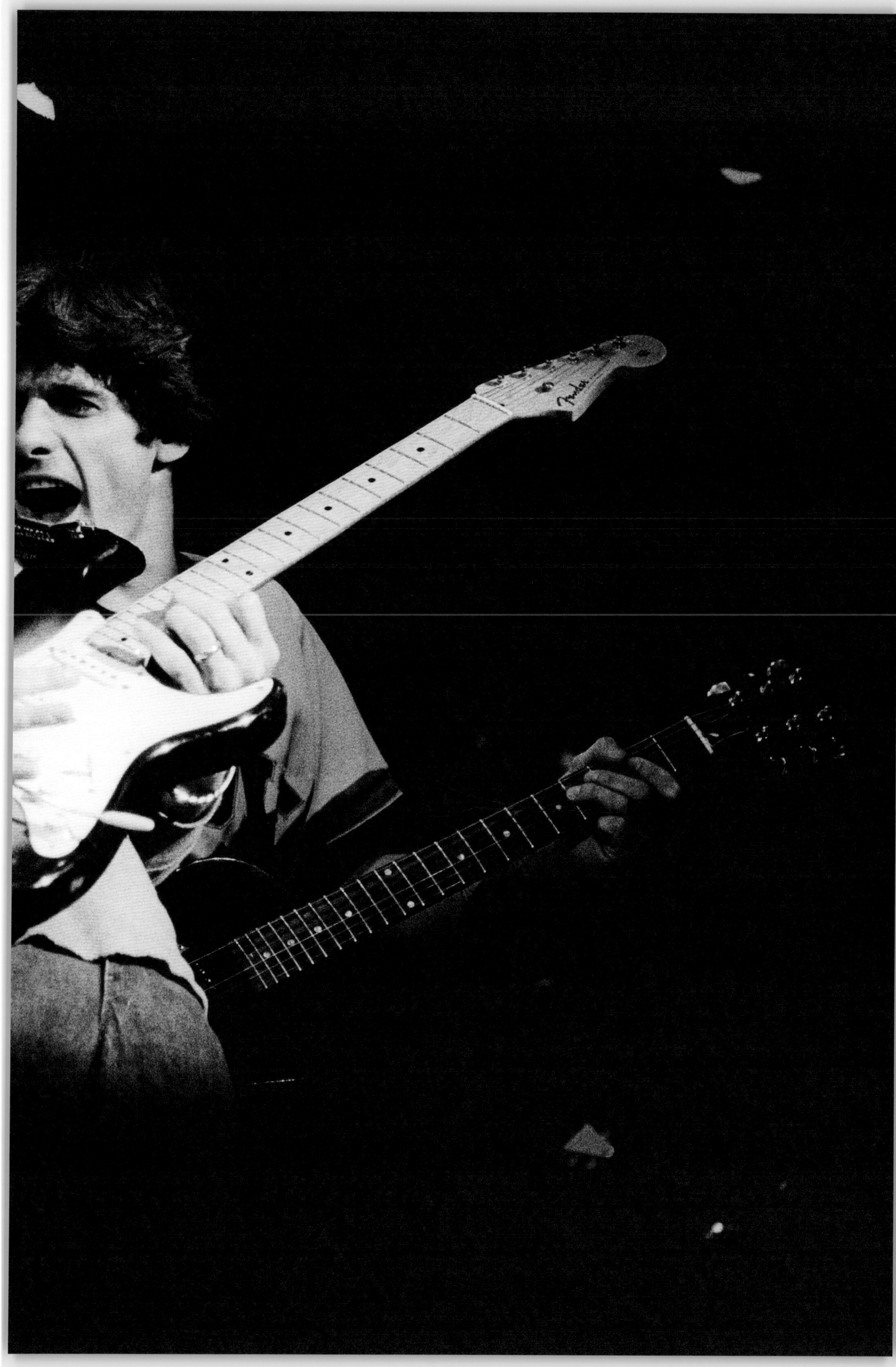

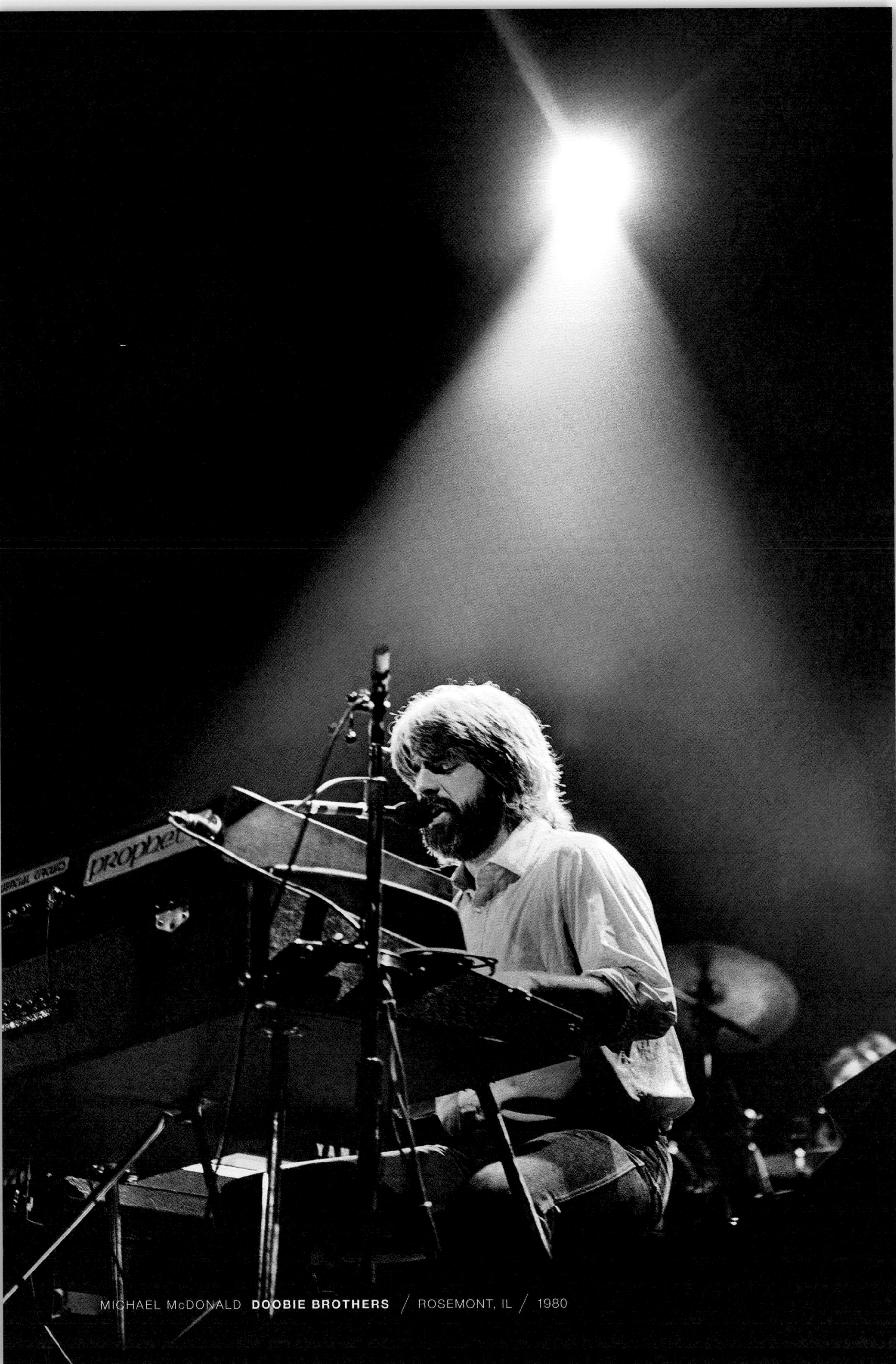

MICHAEL McDONALD **DOOBIE BROTHERS** / ROSEMONT, IL / 1980

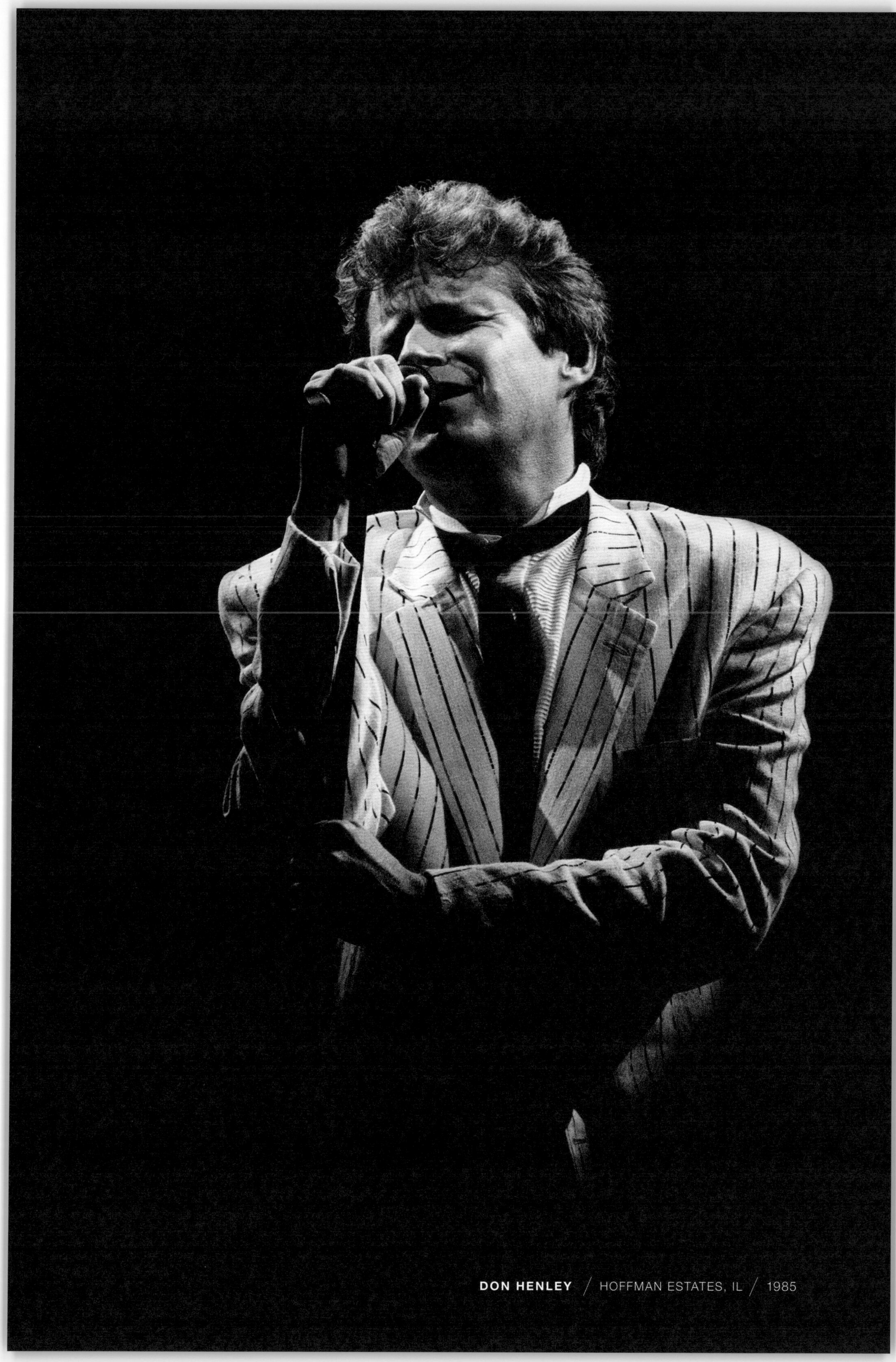

DON HENLEY / HOFFMAN ESTATES, IL / 1985

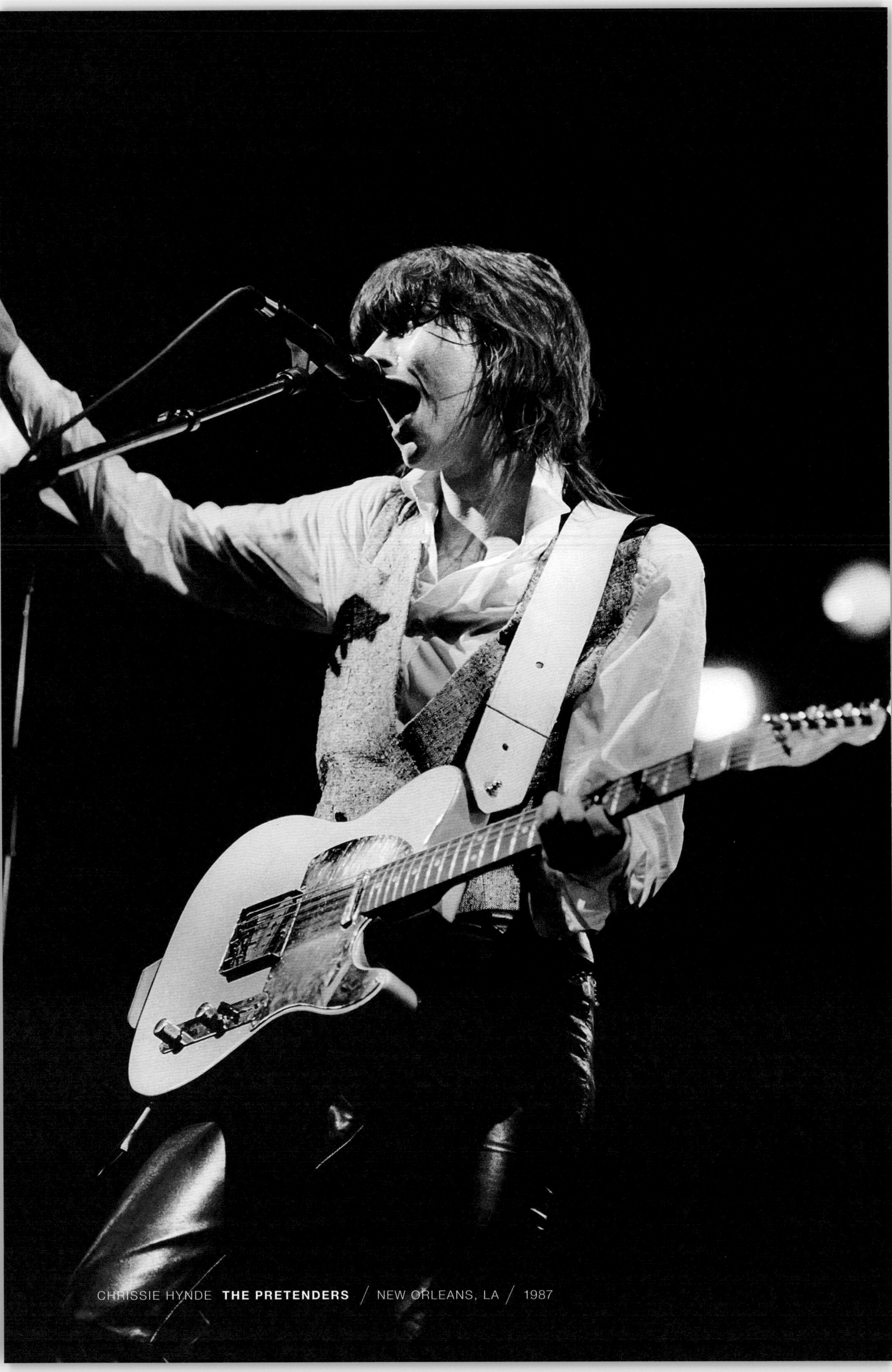

CHRISSIE HYNDE **THE PRETENDERS** / NEW ORLEANS, LA / 1987

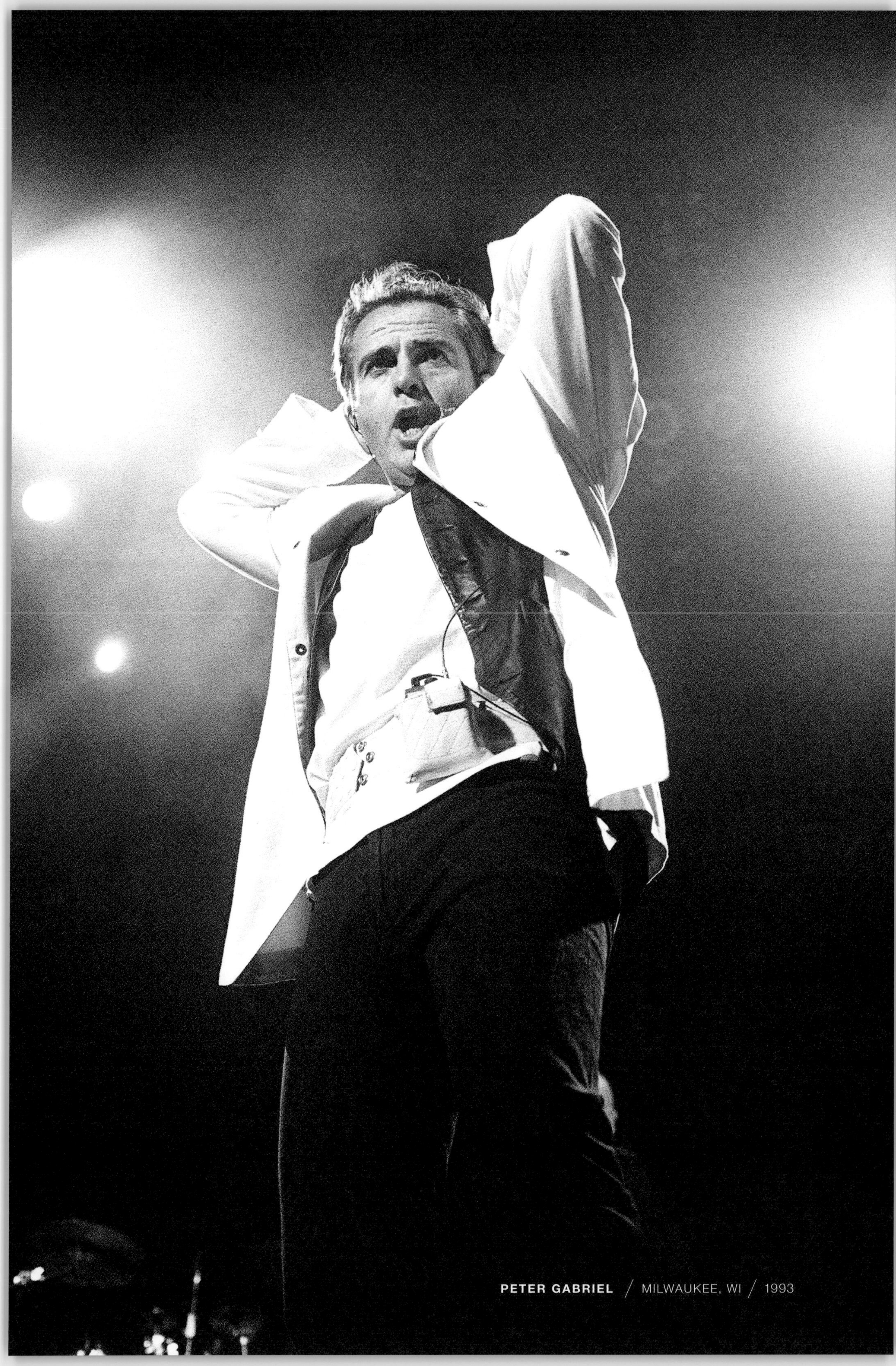

PETER GABRIEL / MILWAUKEE, WI / 1993

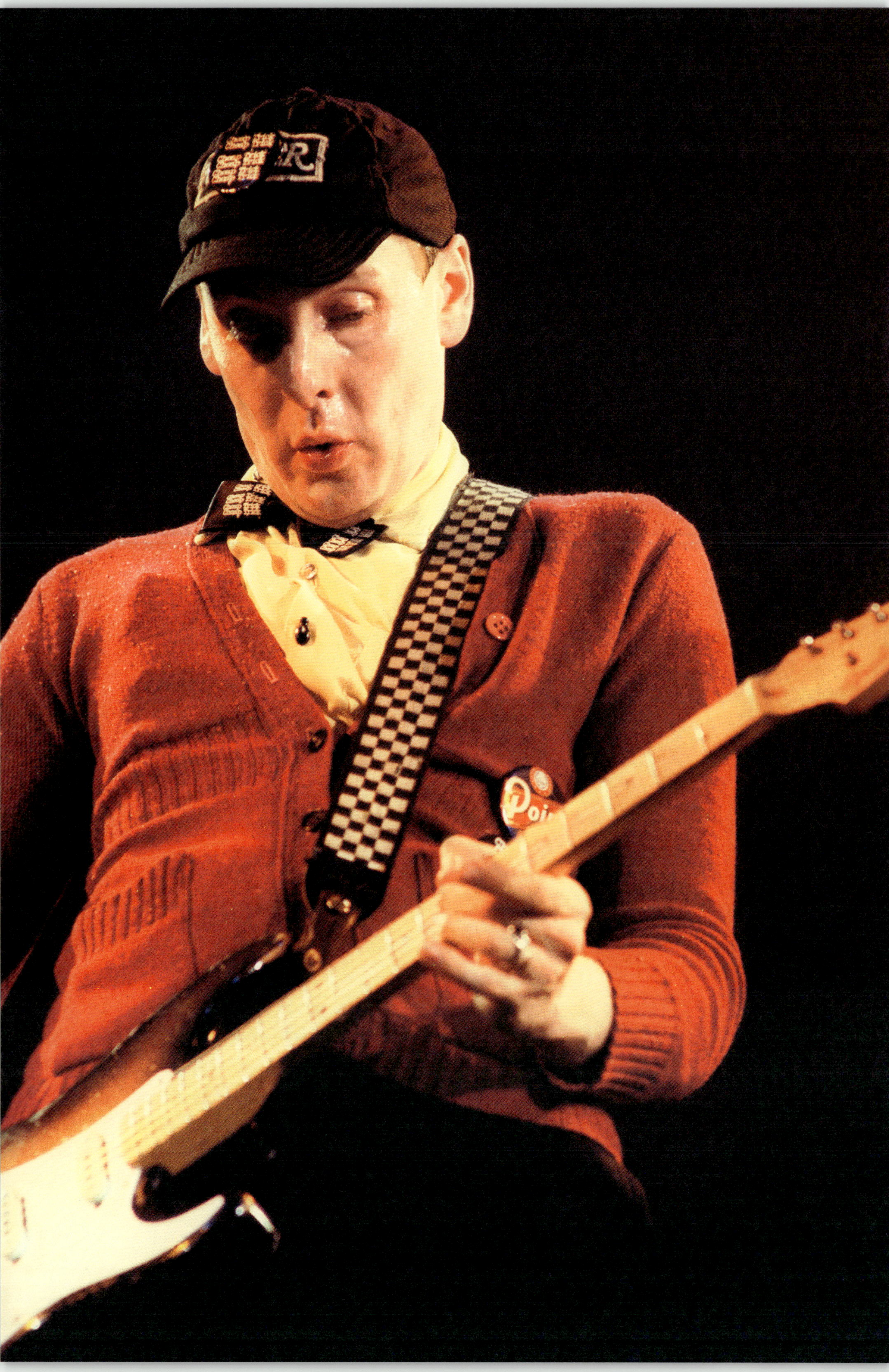

PERFECT STORM

I am often asked who my favorite band is to photograph, and I always answer that it is any band that puts on a show. There's nothing worse than a band that rolls out of bed, throws on T-shirts and jeans and hits the stage just to stand in one spot the entire evening and play with no emotion (British magazines call them "shoegazers"). Yet when I think about my favorite band full of great showmen, I always come back to Cheap Trick. With amazing musicians, great songwriters, a world-class guitarist and one of the best voices in rock 'n' roll history, Cheap Trick is a perfect storm of music and showmanship that is always a joy to be around. The band has also expertly cultivated an image that has withstood the test of time, and they live that look through and through, from their clothes to the shape of Rick Nielsen's guitars. In fact, I have never seen Rick without his baseball hat–even in his kitchen getting something out of the refrigerator. He lives that image 24 hours a day. My photograph of Rick Nielsen jamming with Billy Corgan at Chicago's Metro nightclub shows how Rick's style is revered by many in the business.

RICK NIELSEN **CHEAP TRICK** / CHICAGO, IL / 1977

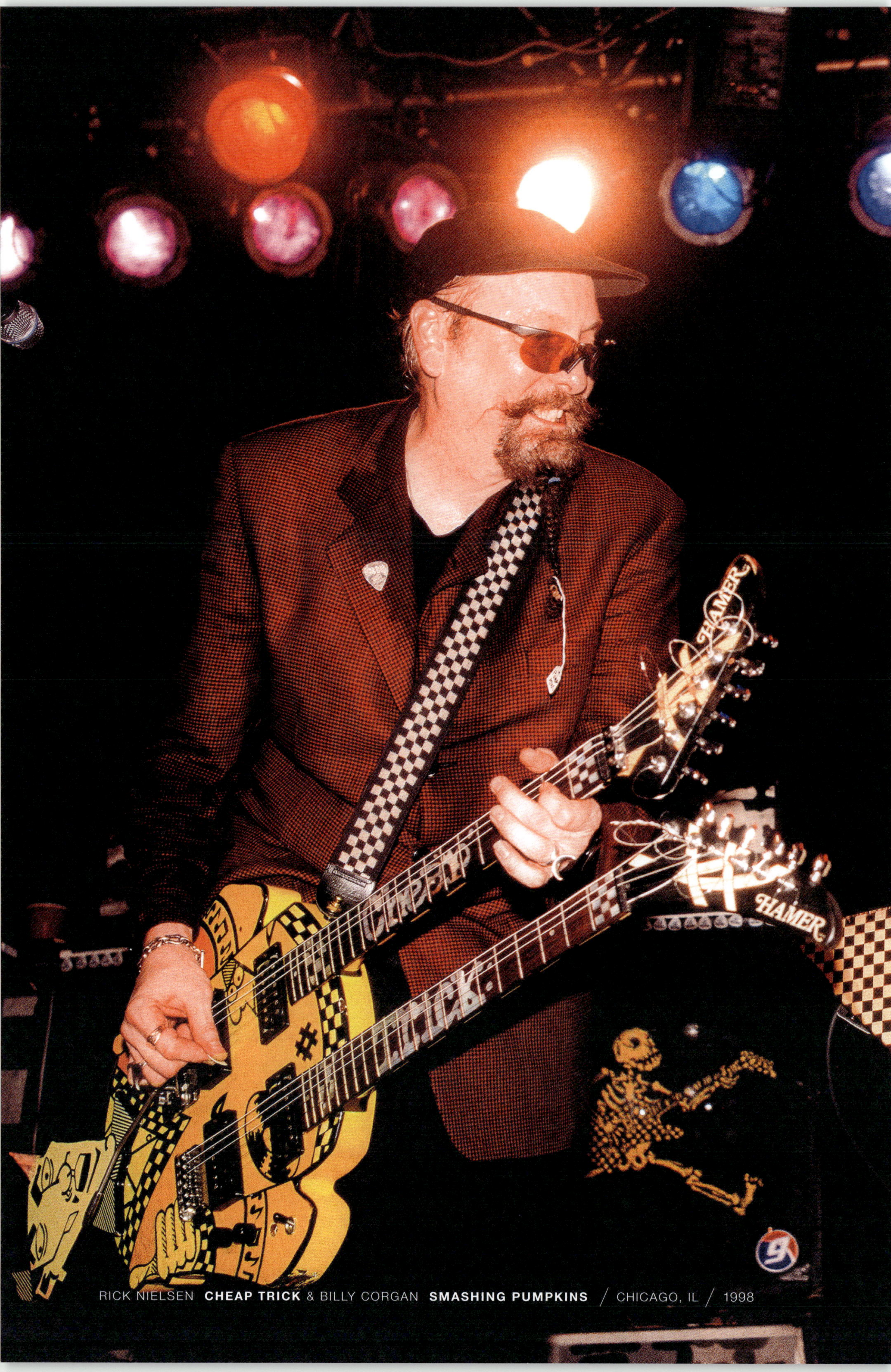

RICK NIELSEN **CHEAP TRICK** & BILLY CORGAN **SMASHING PUMPKINS** / CHICAGO, IL / 1998

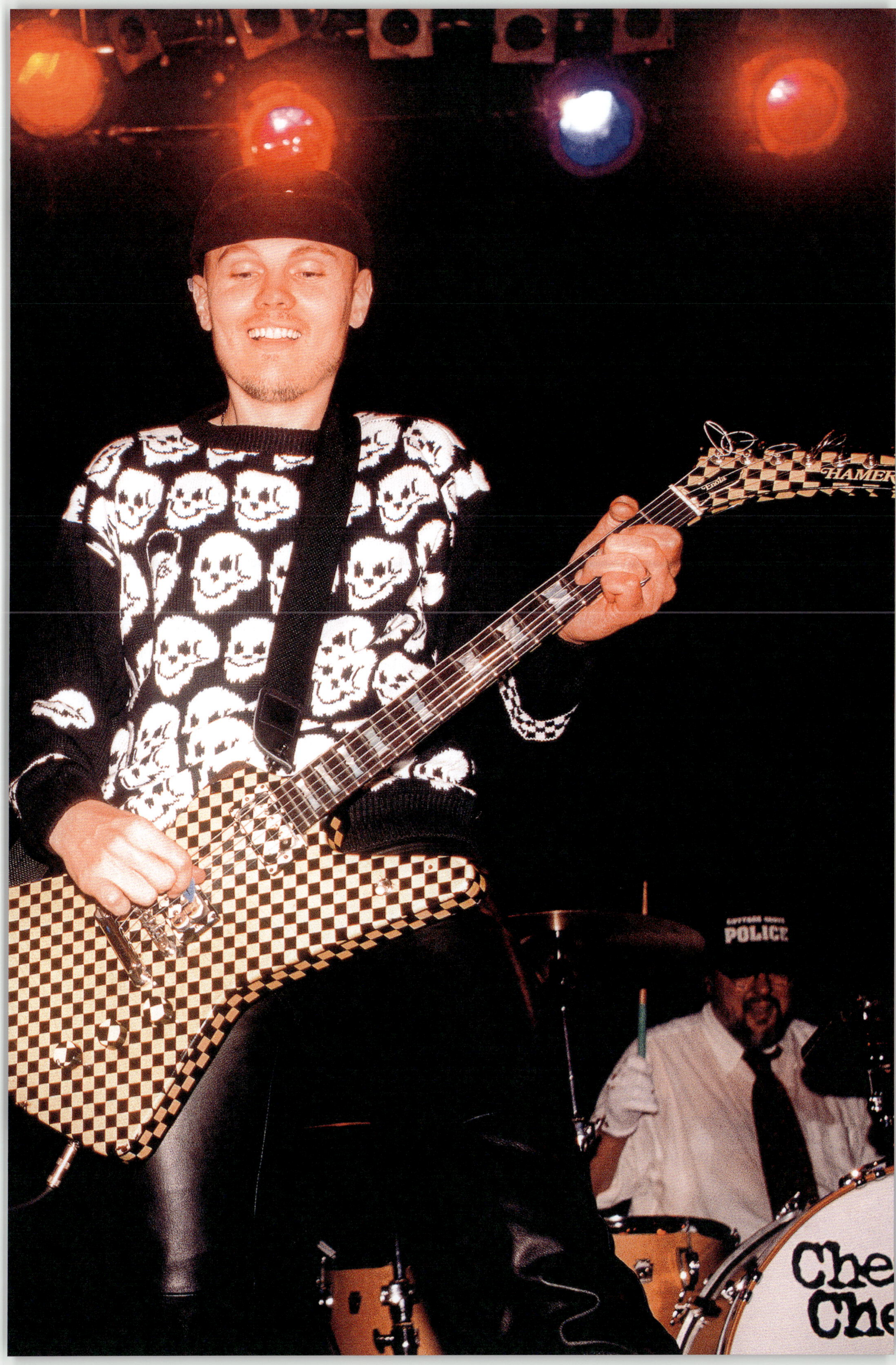
HAMER
POLICE

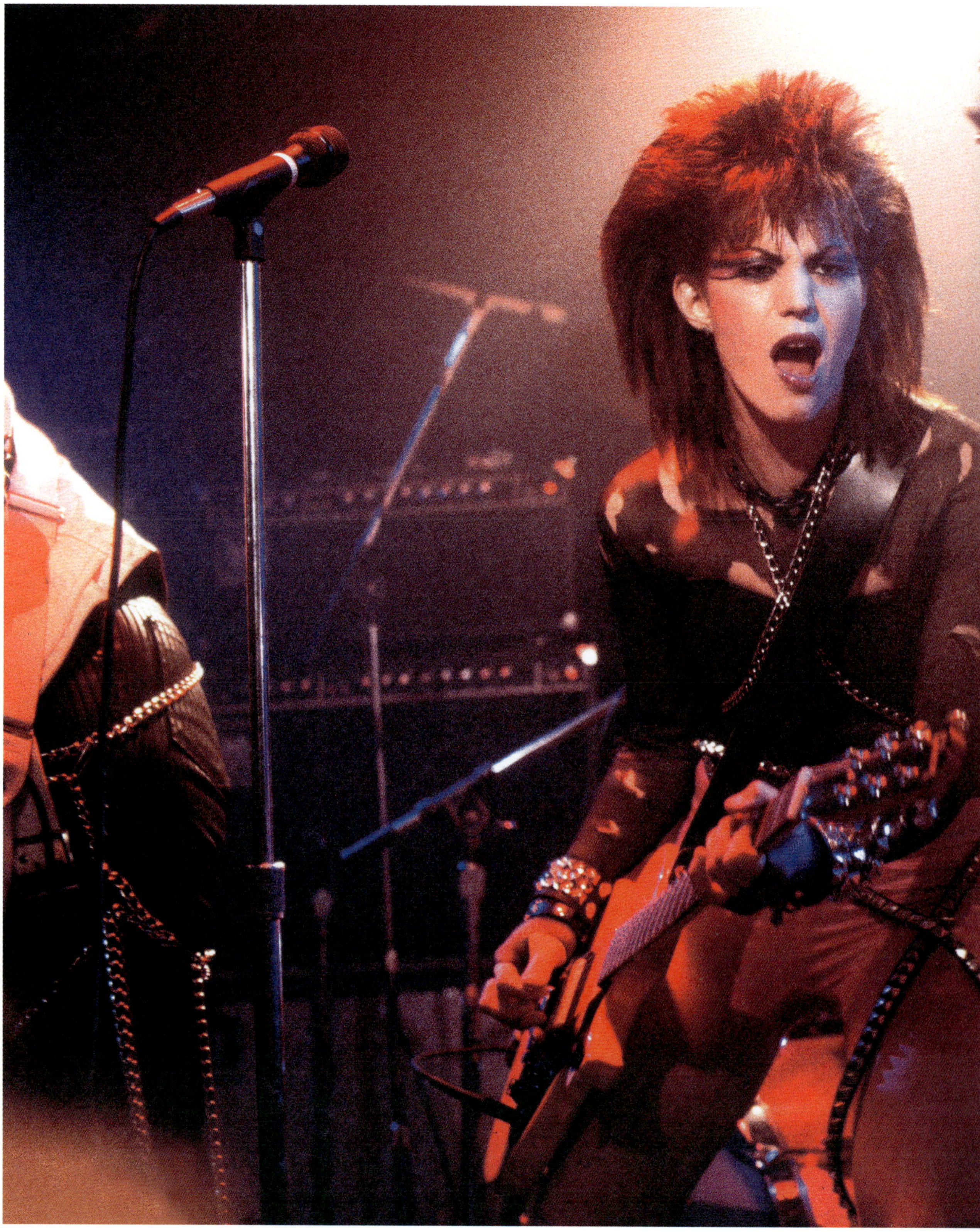

In 1985, a few months after my photograph of Bruce Springsteen was on the cover of *Newsweek*, I was contacted for a meeting with Paul Schrader, the writer of *Taxi Driver* and *Raging Bull* and director of *American Gigolo*. Schrader was directing a film in Chicago called *Light of Day*, named after Springsteen's song "(Just Around the Corner to the) Light of Day," starring Michael J. Fox and Joan Jett as siblings in a Cleveland bar band. Paul asked if I would like to come shoot on the set during the live music scenes.

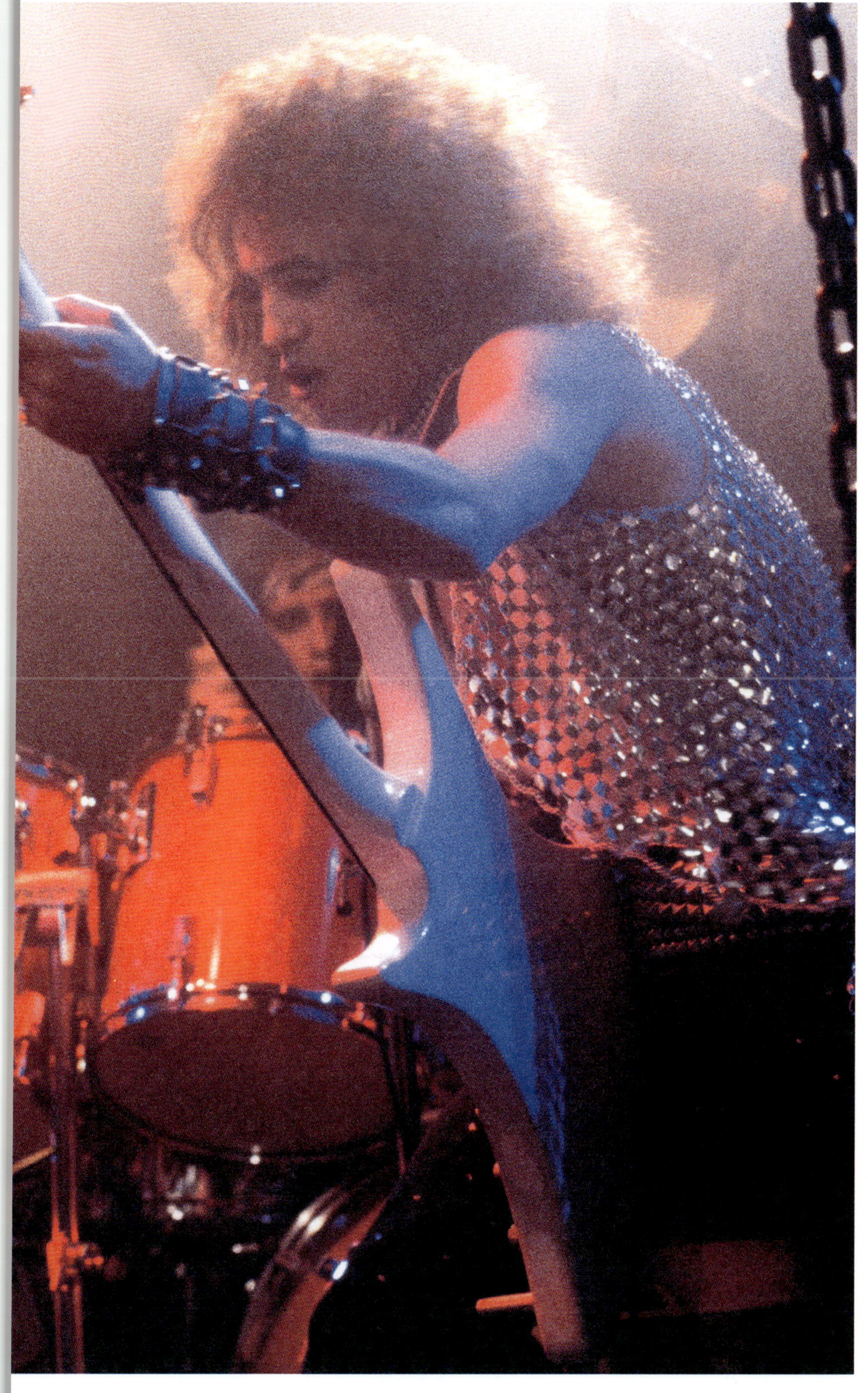

On set, Michael kept asking me between takes whether he looked OK on stage; I later learned that Joan had told him I had been in the business for awhile. I ended up shooting for eight days, including a scene where Joan quits the family band to join a heavy metal band.

JOAN JETT / CHICAGO, IL / 1986

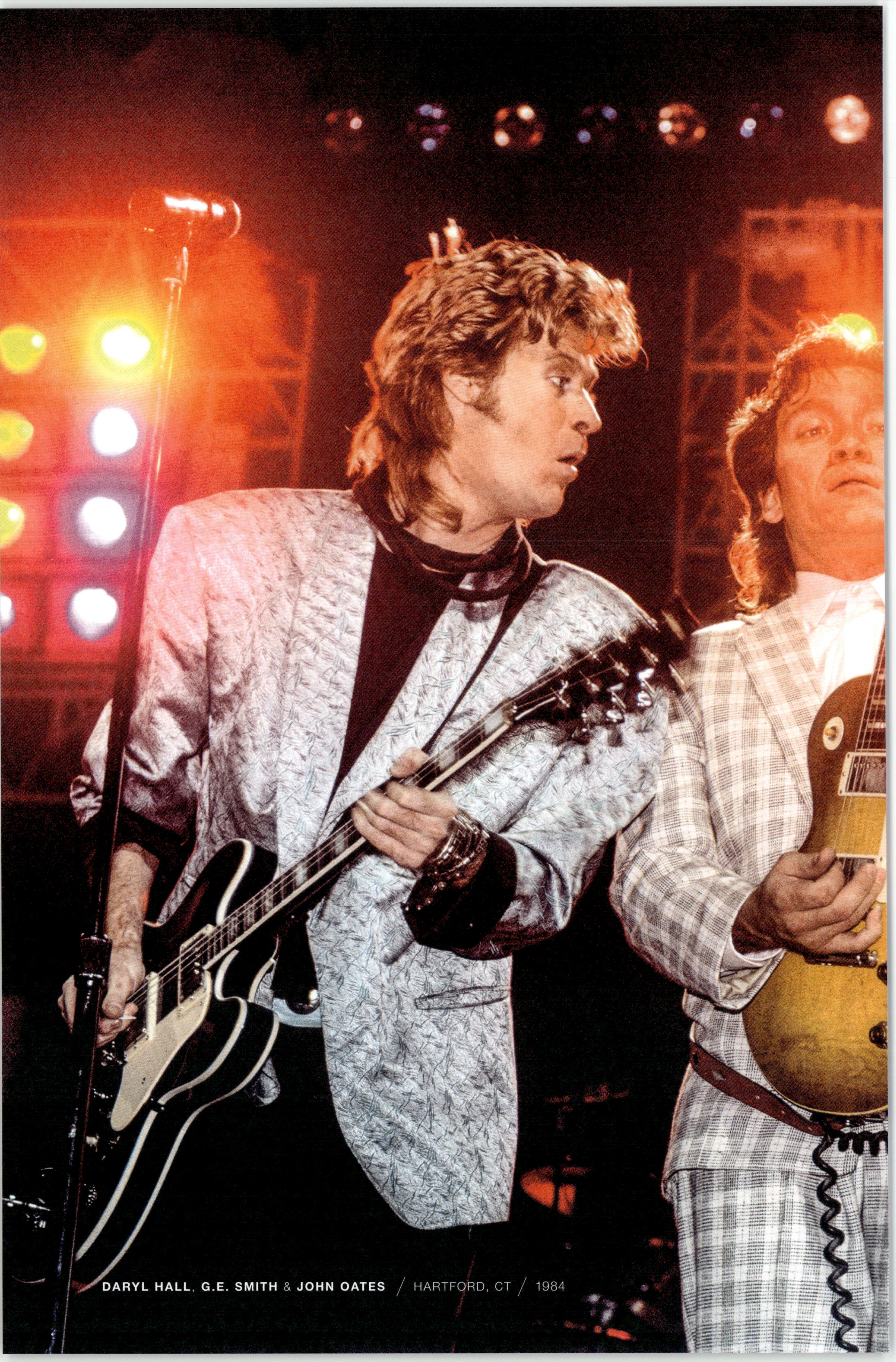

DARYL HALL, G.E. SMITH & JOHN OATES / HARTFORD, CT / 1984

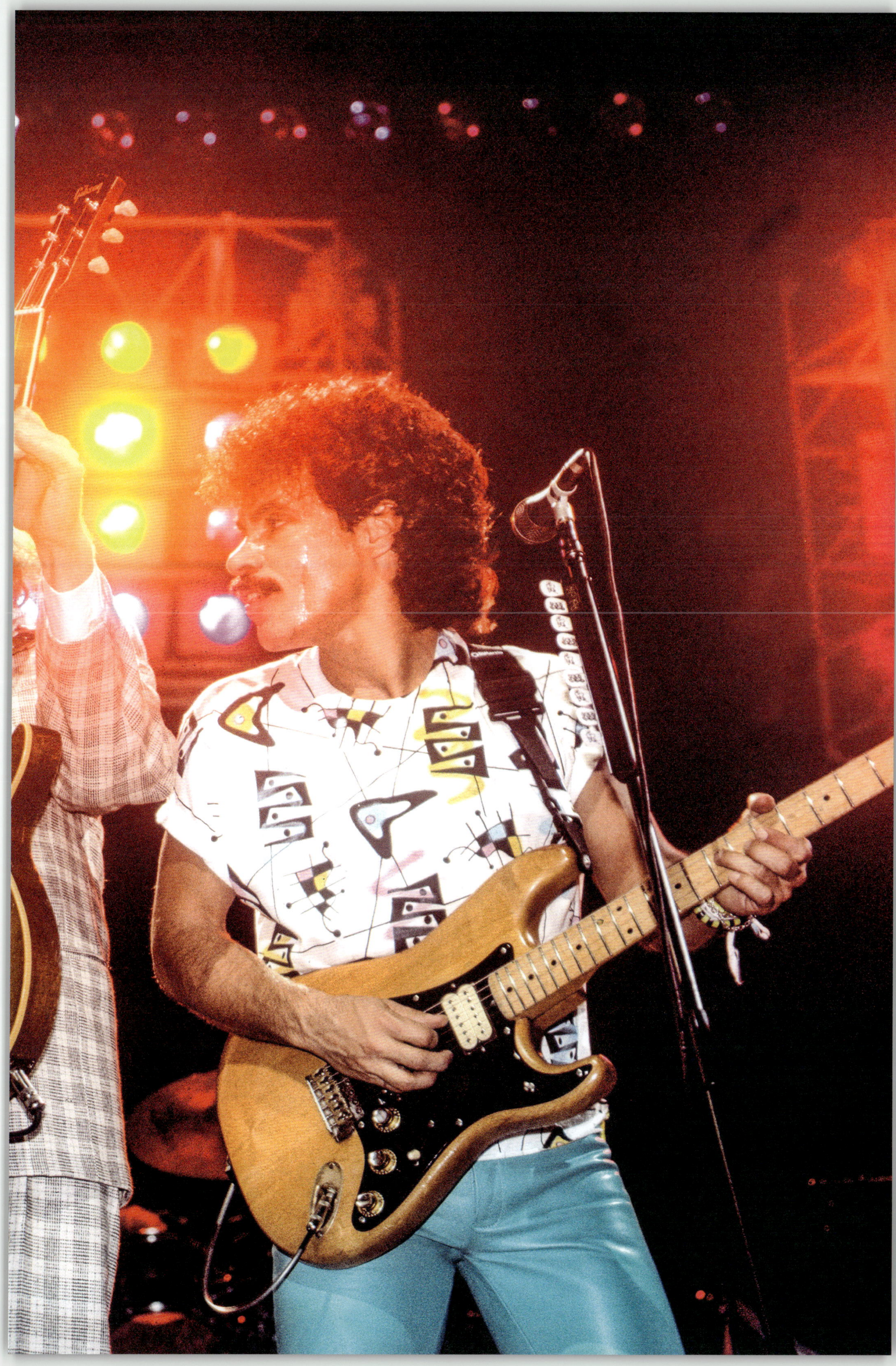

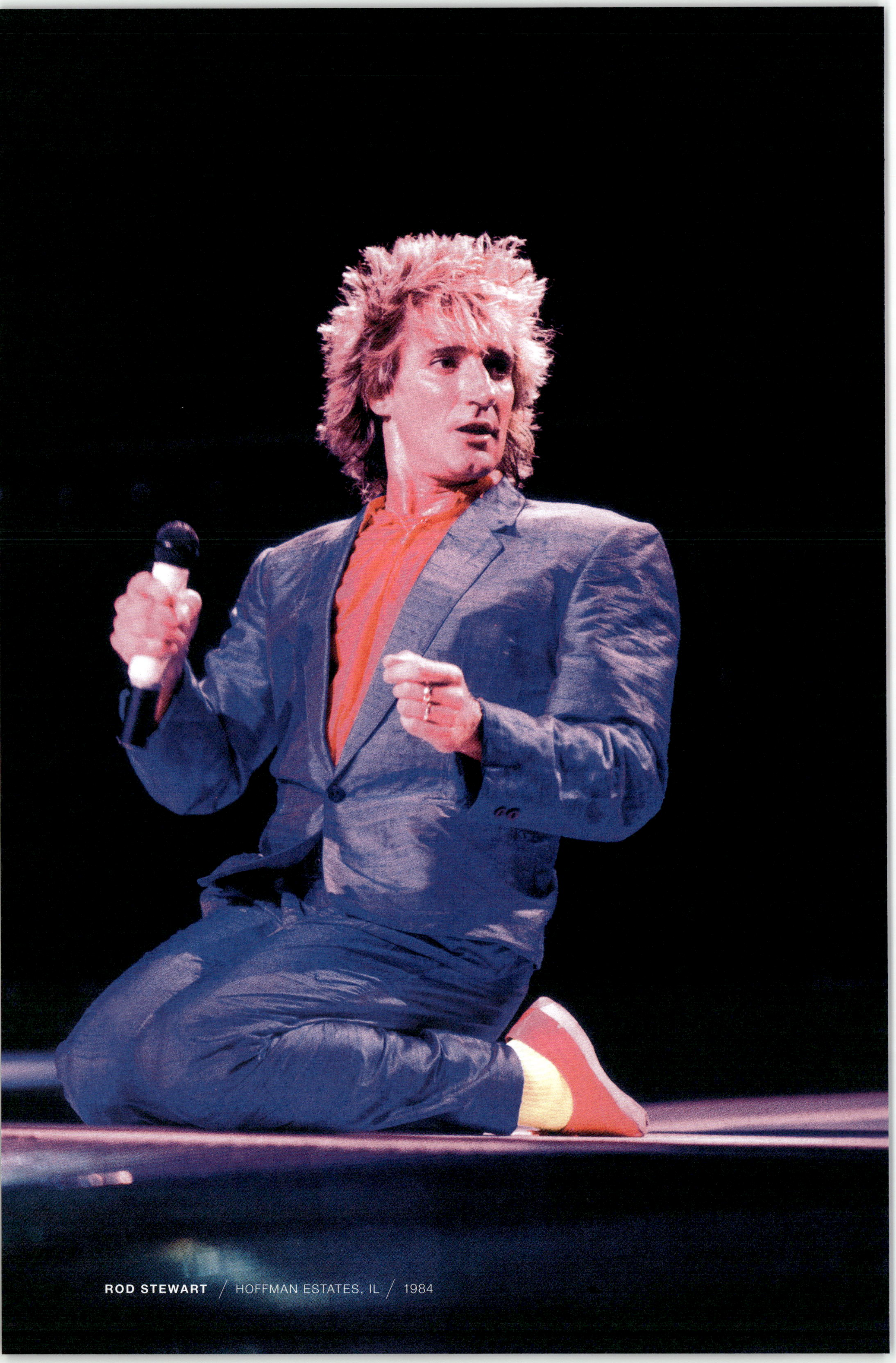

ROD STEWART / HOFFMAN ESTATES, IL / 1984

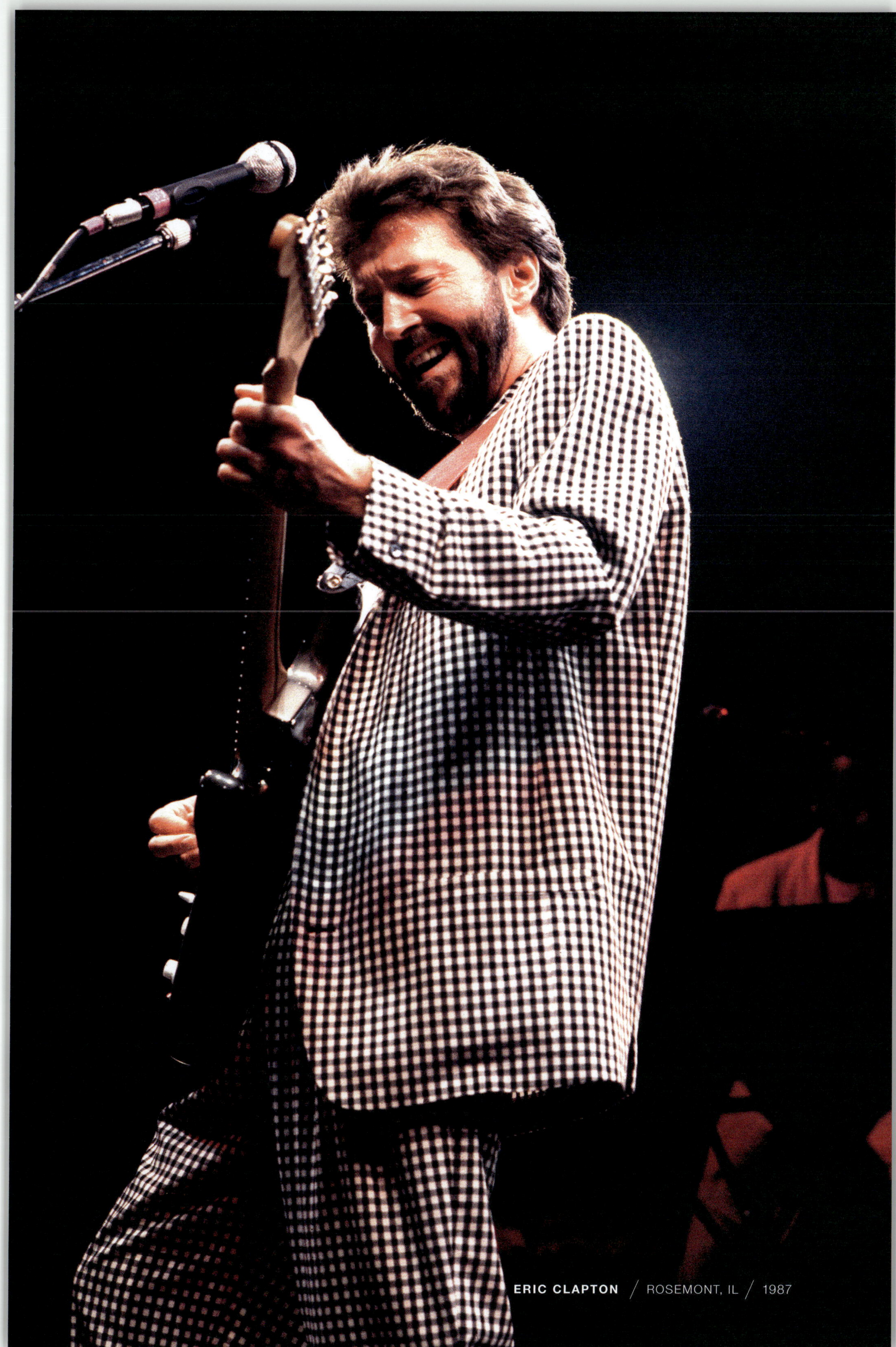

ERIC CLAPTON / ROSEMONT, IL / 1987

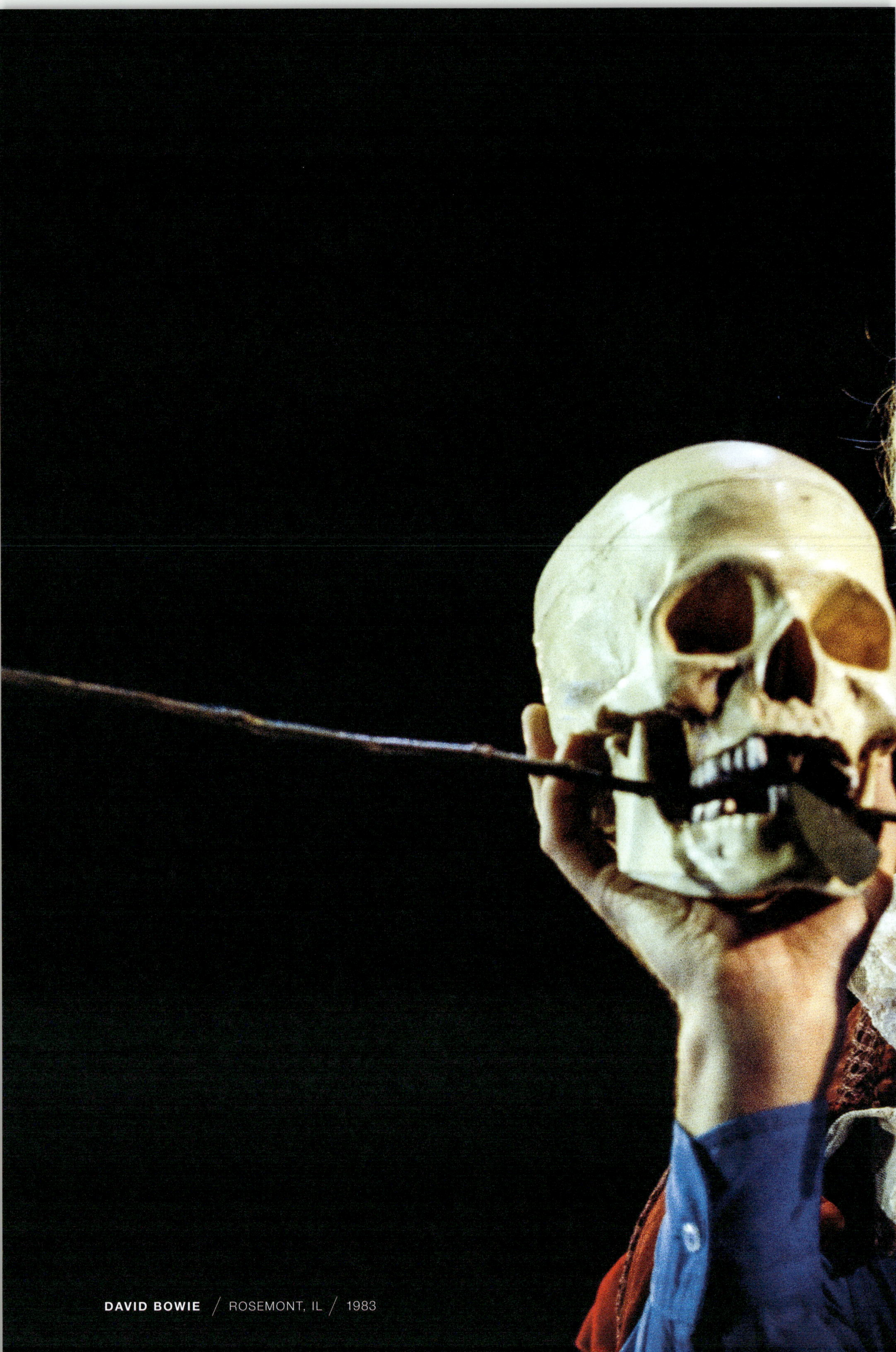

DAVID BOWIE / ROSEMONT, IL / 1983

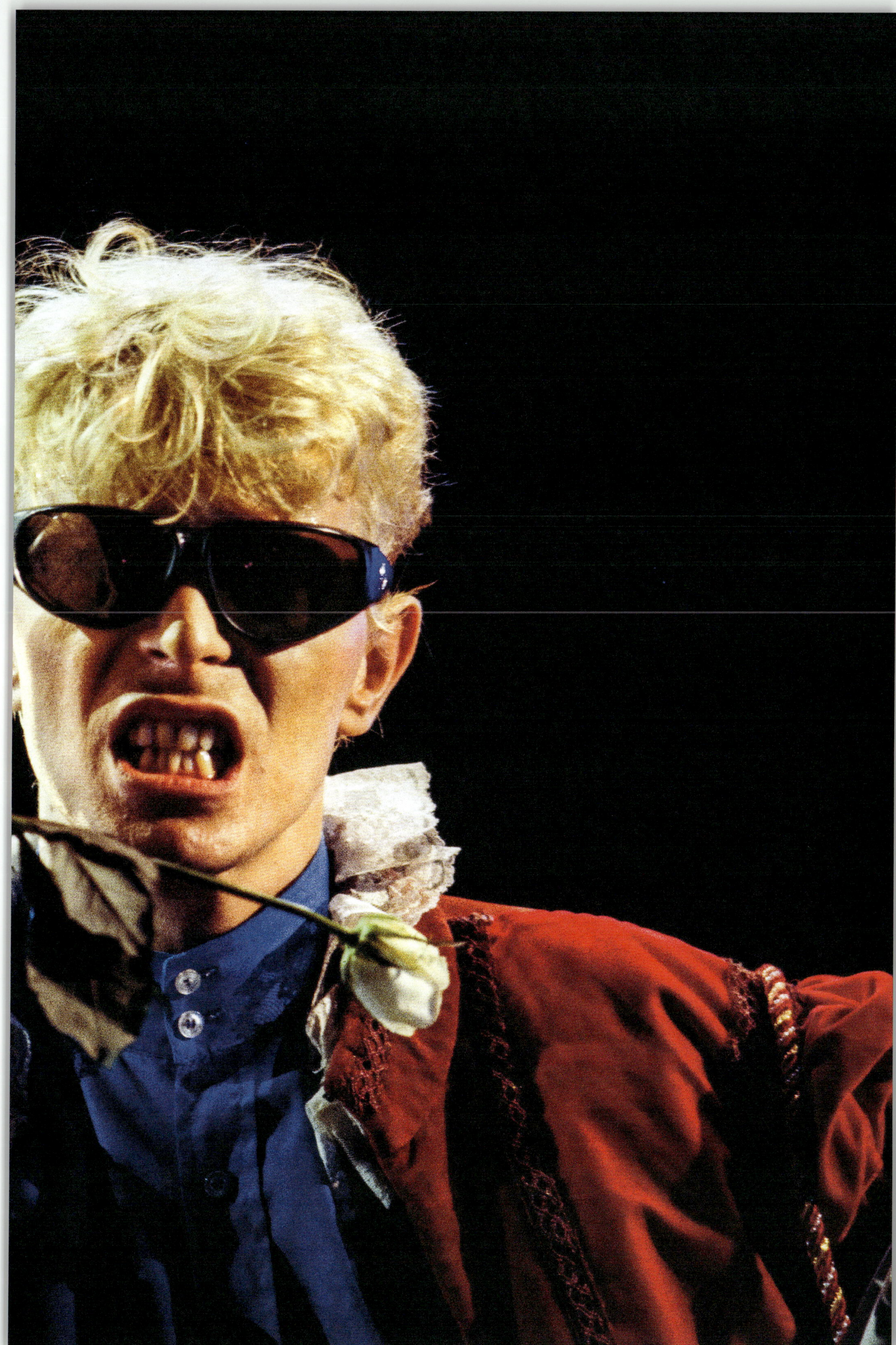

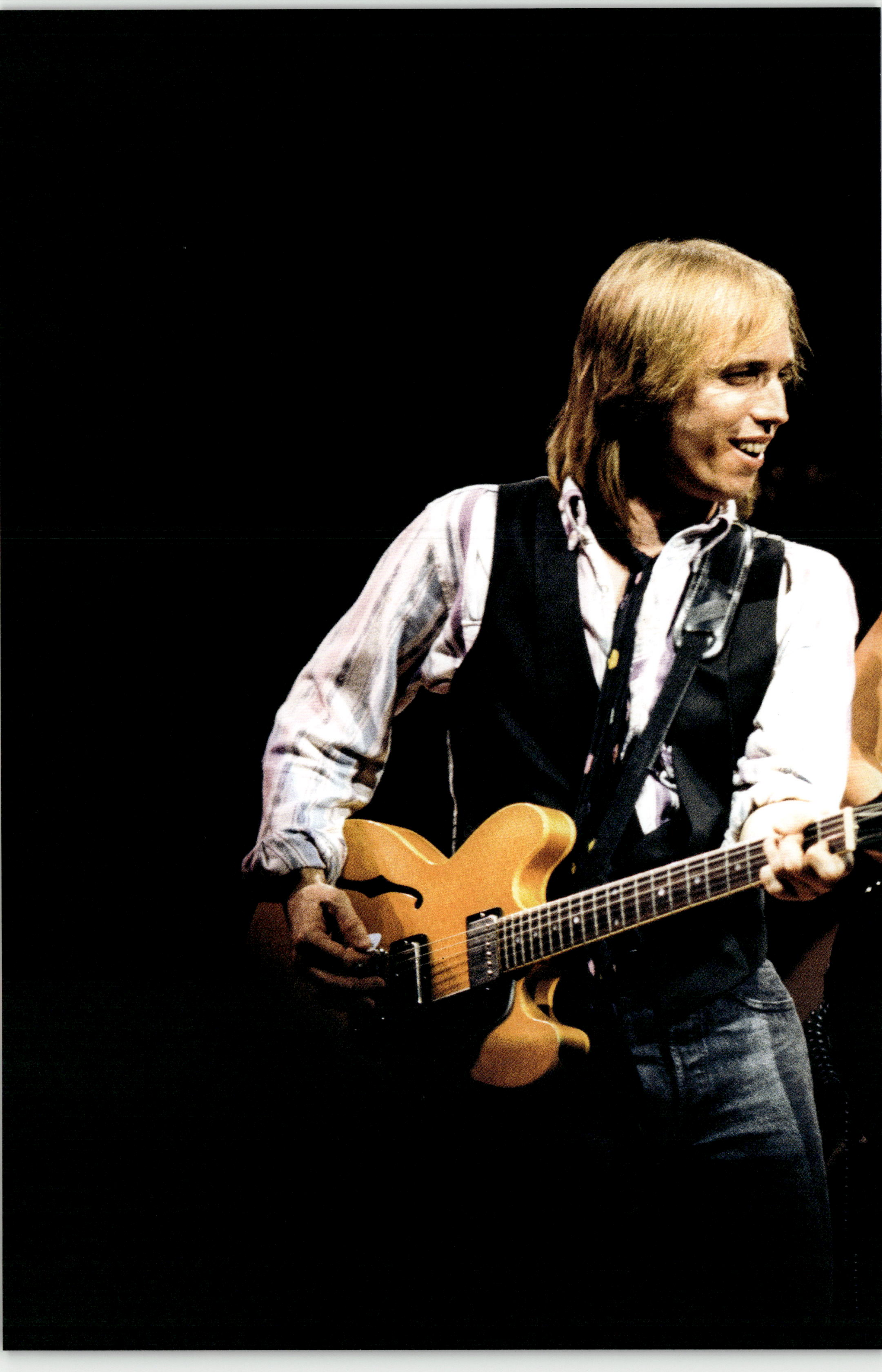

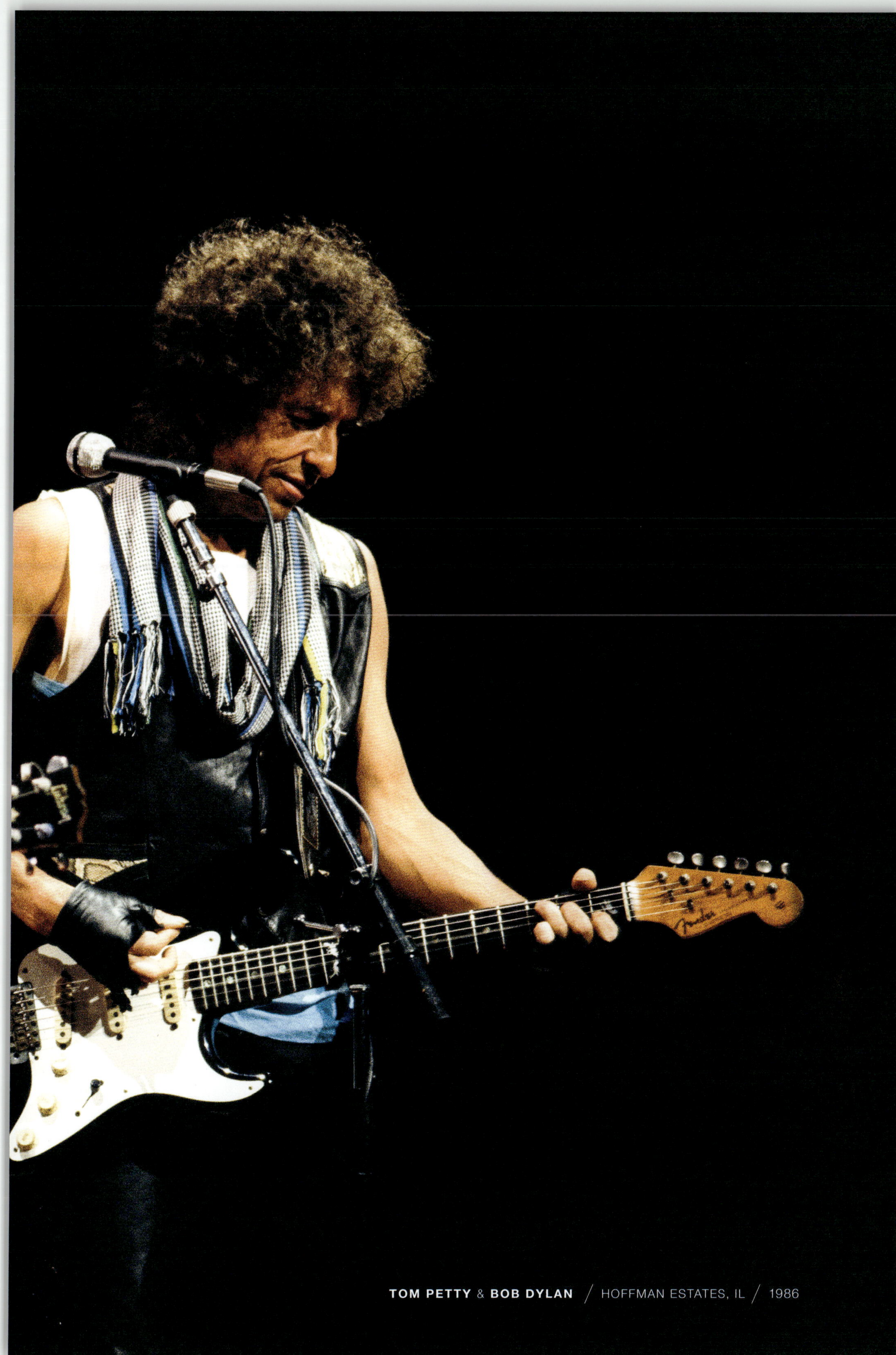

TOM PETTY & **BOB DYLAN** / HOFFMAN ESTATES, IL / 1986

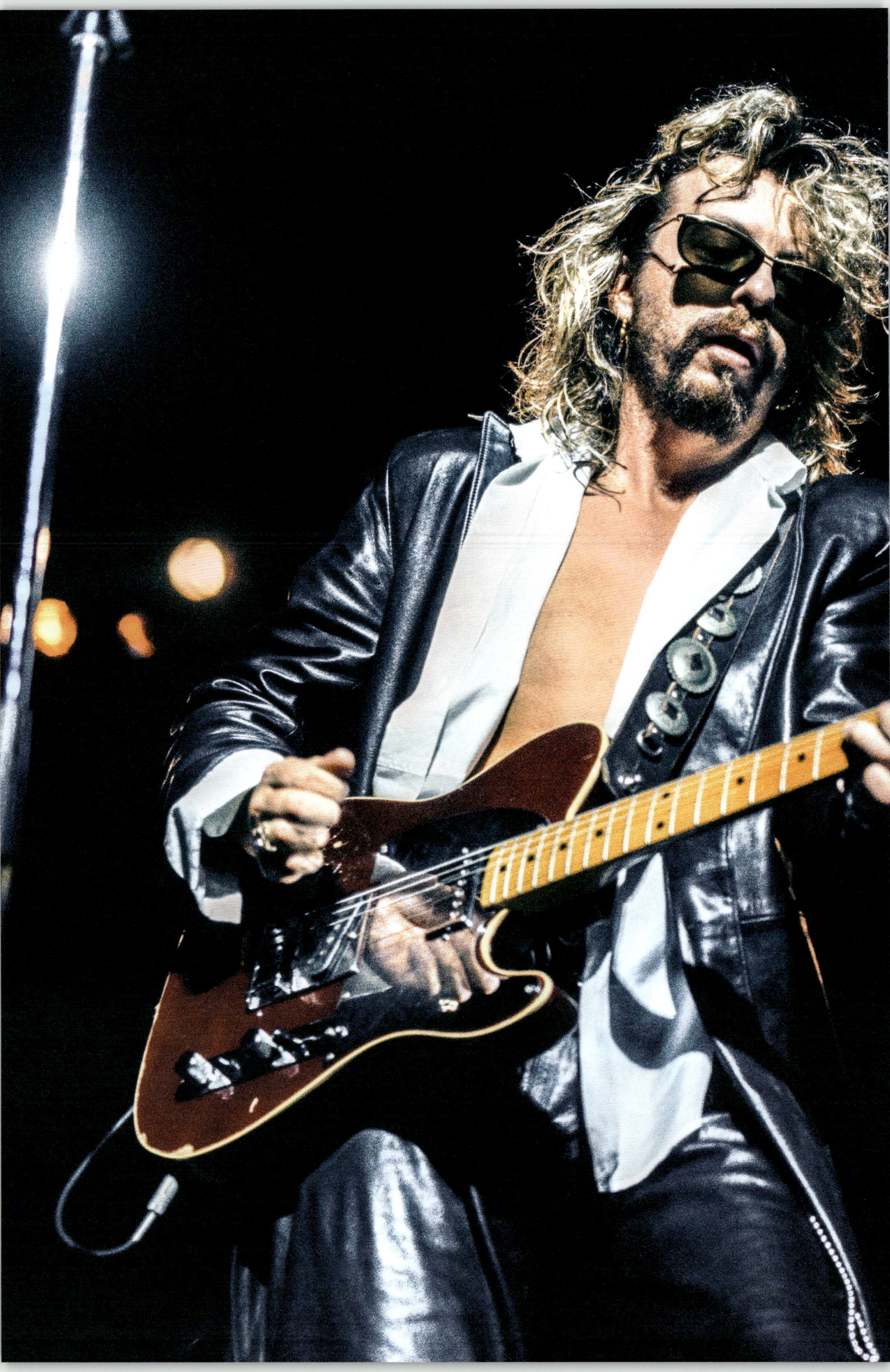

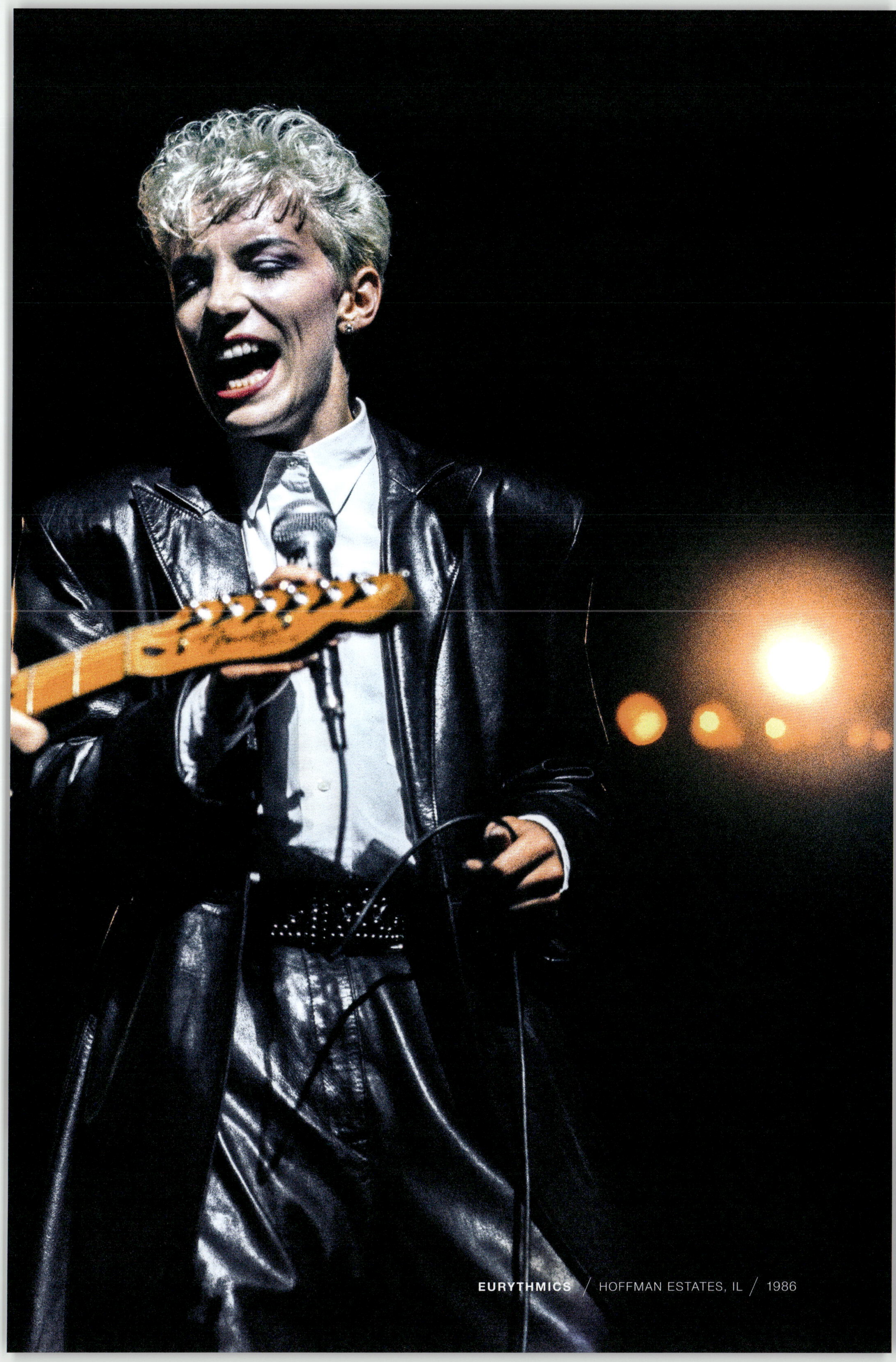

EURYTHMICS / HOFFMAN ESTATES, IL / 1986

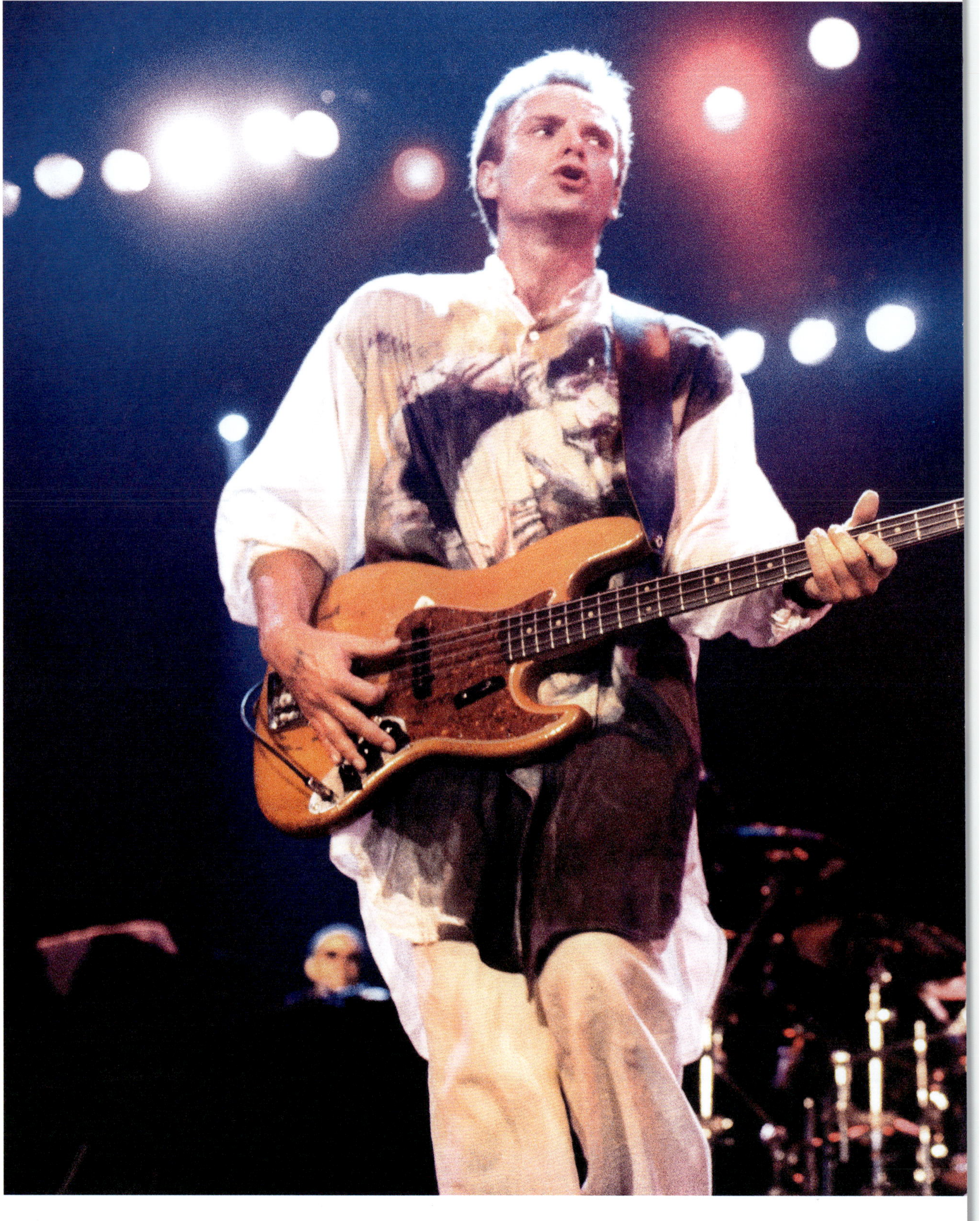

I photographed The Police throughout the band's career, including their first show in the Chicago area, with the staff at the club outnumbering the audience. In 1986, they joined the Amnesty International Tour along with Peter Gabriel, Lou Reed and U2. All the bands were at the top of their game and it made for one of the most exciting days of photography of my career.

THE POLICE / ROSEMONT, IL / 1986

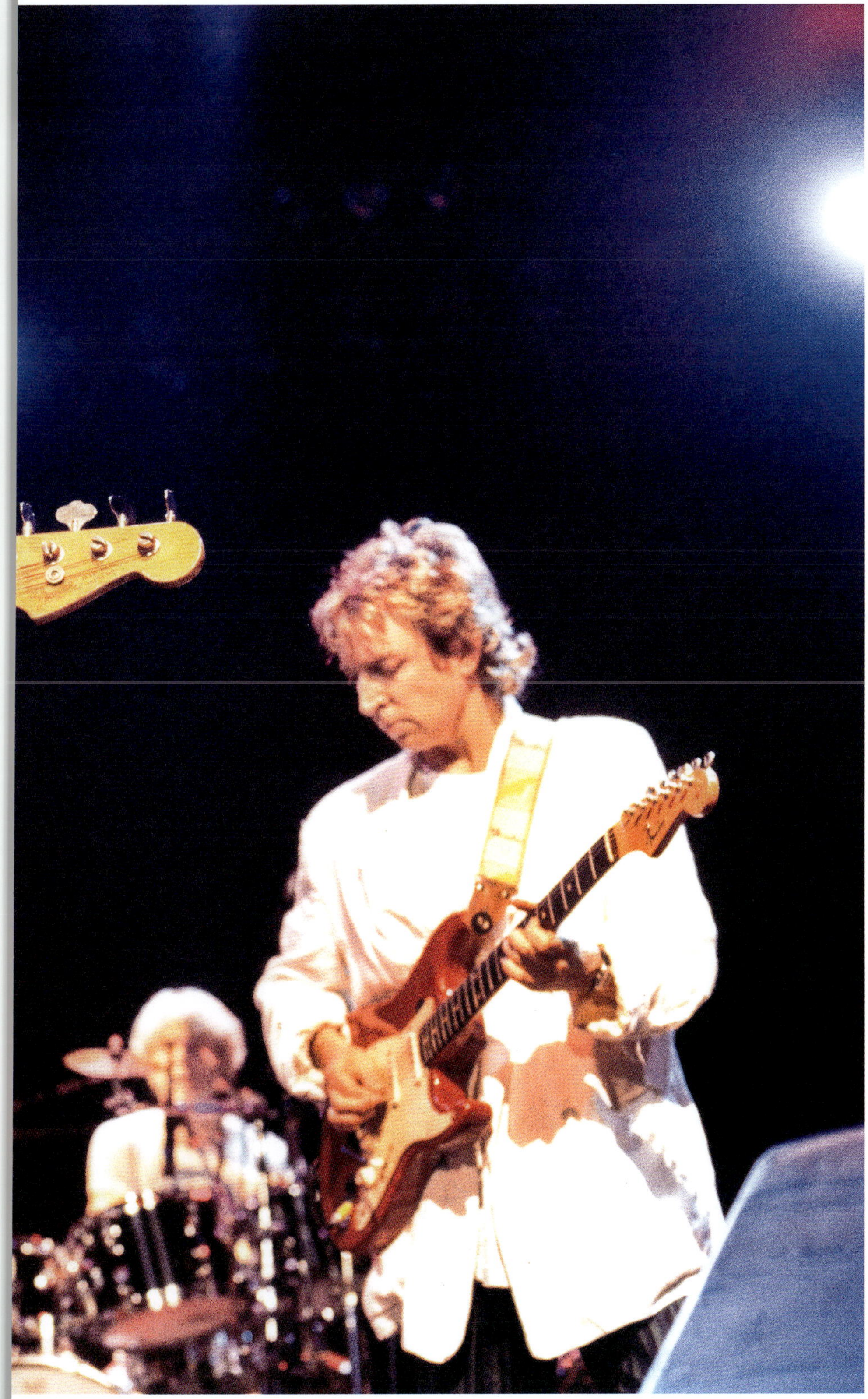

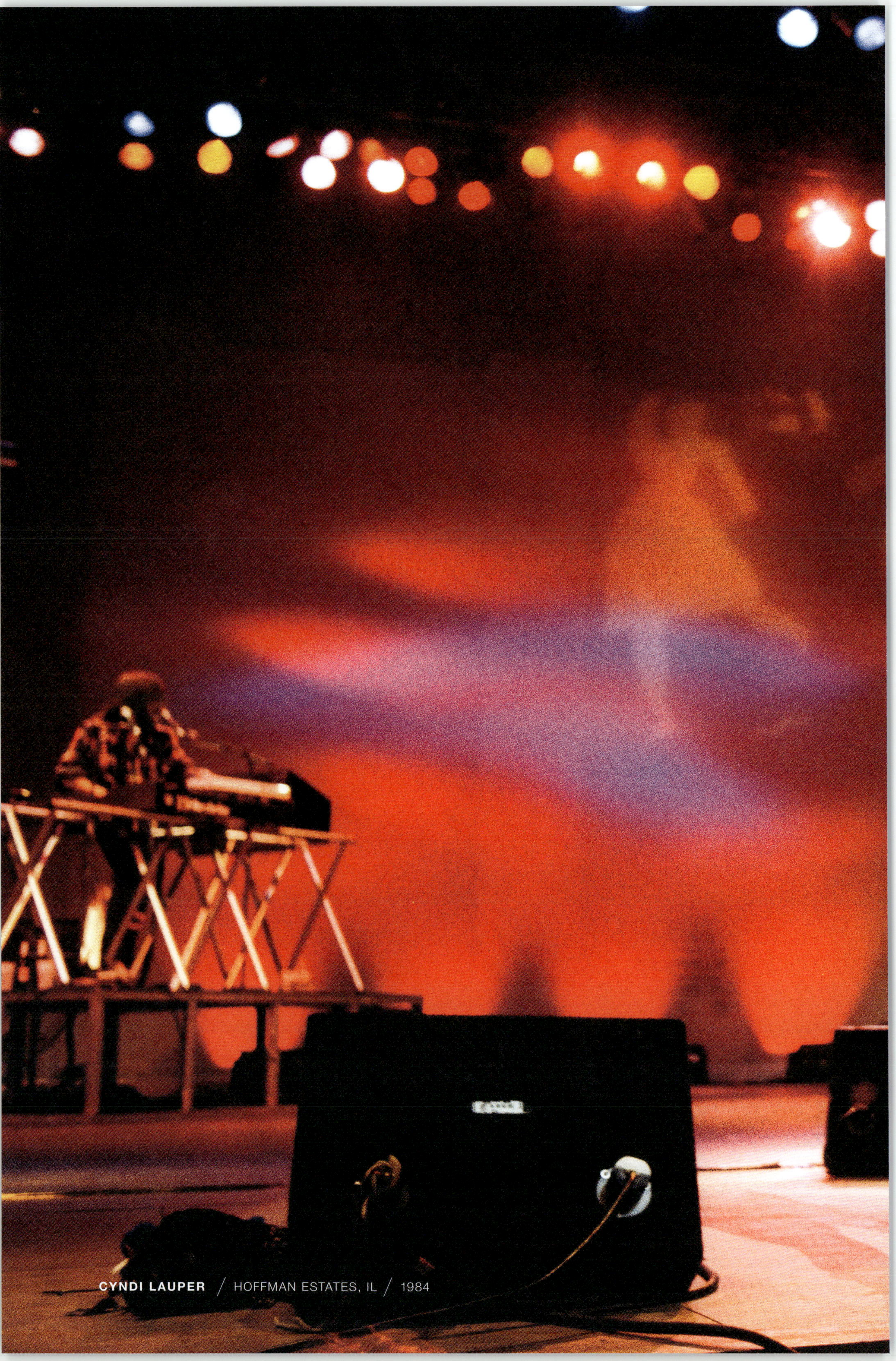

CYNDI LAUPER / HOFFMAN ESTATES, IL / 1984

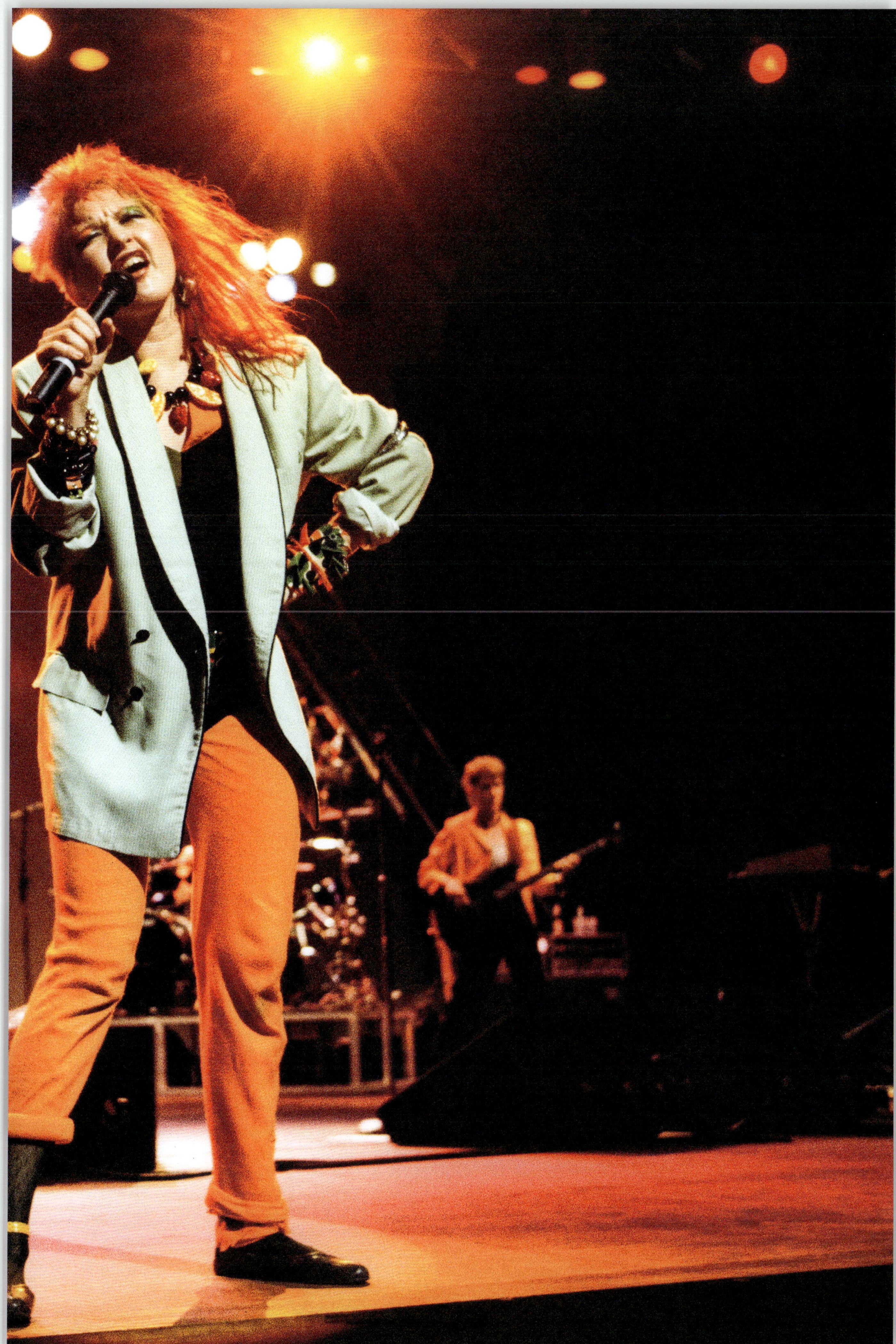

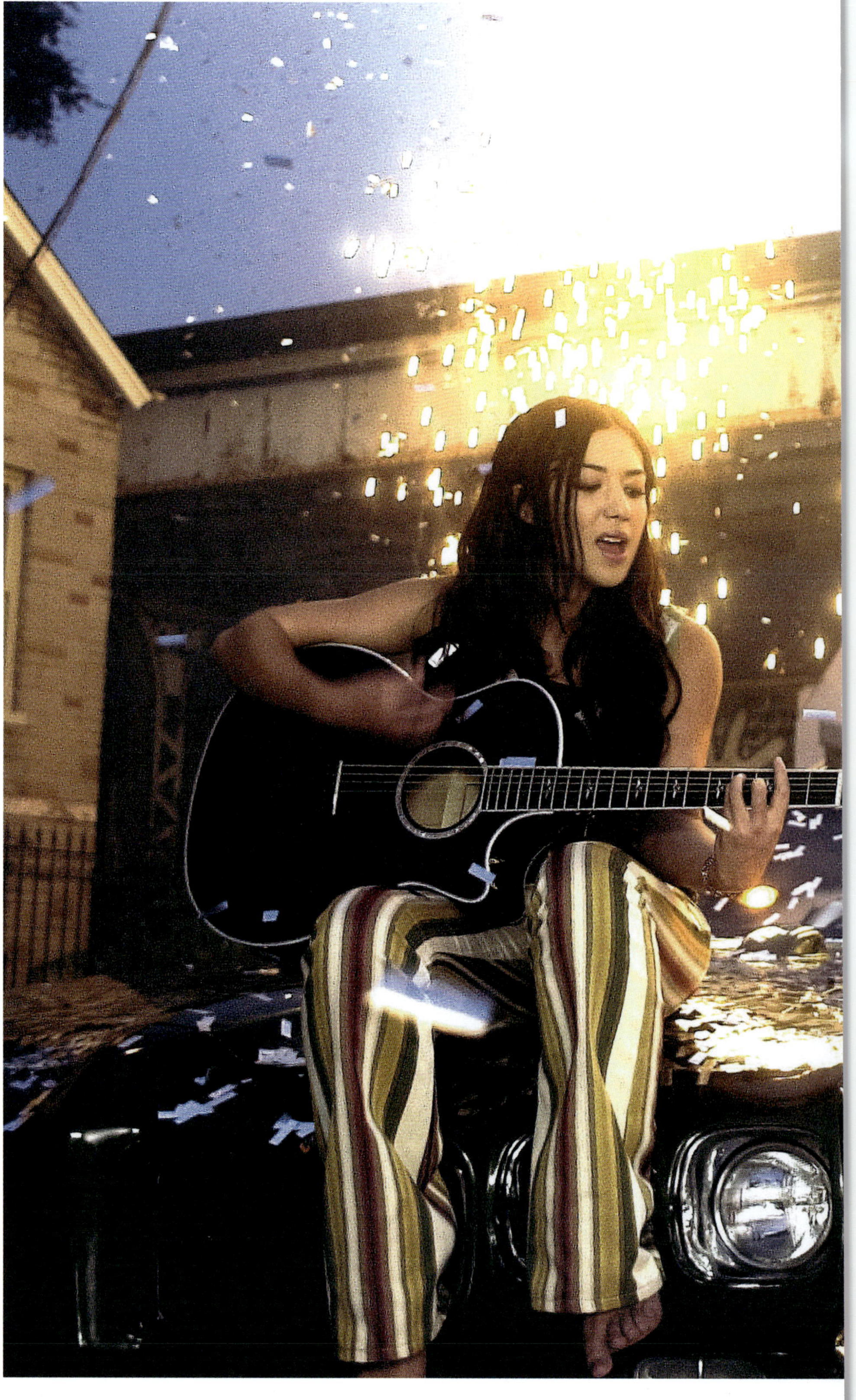

In 2002, Carlos Santana recorded his Grammy-winning song "The Game Of Love" featuring up-and-coming singer Michelle Branch. The video was filmed in the Pilsen neighborhood of Chicago, and the record company asked me to spend a day on the set. It turned out to be a lovely day with two of the nicest people I have ever met in the business. Carlos must

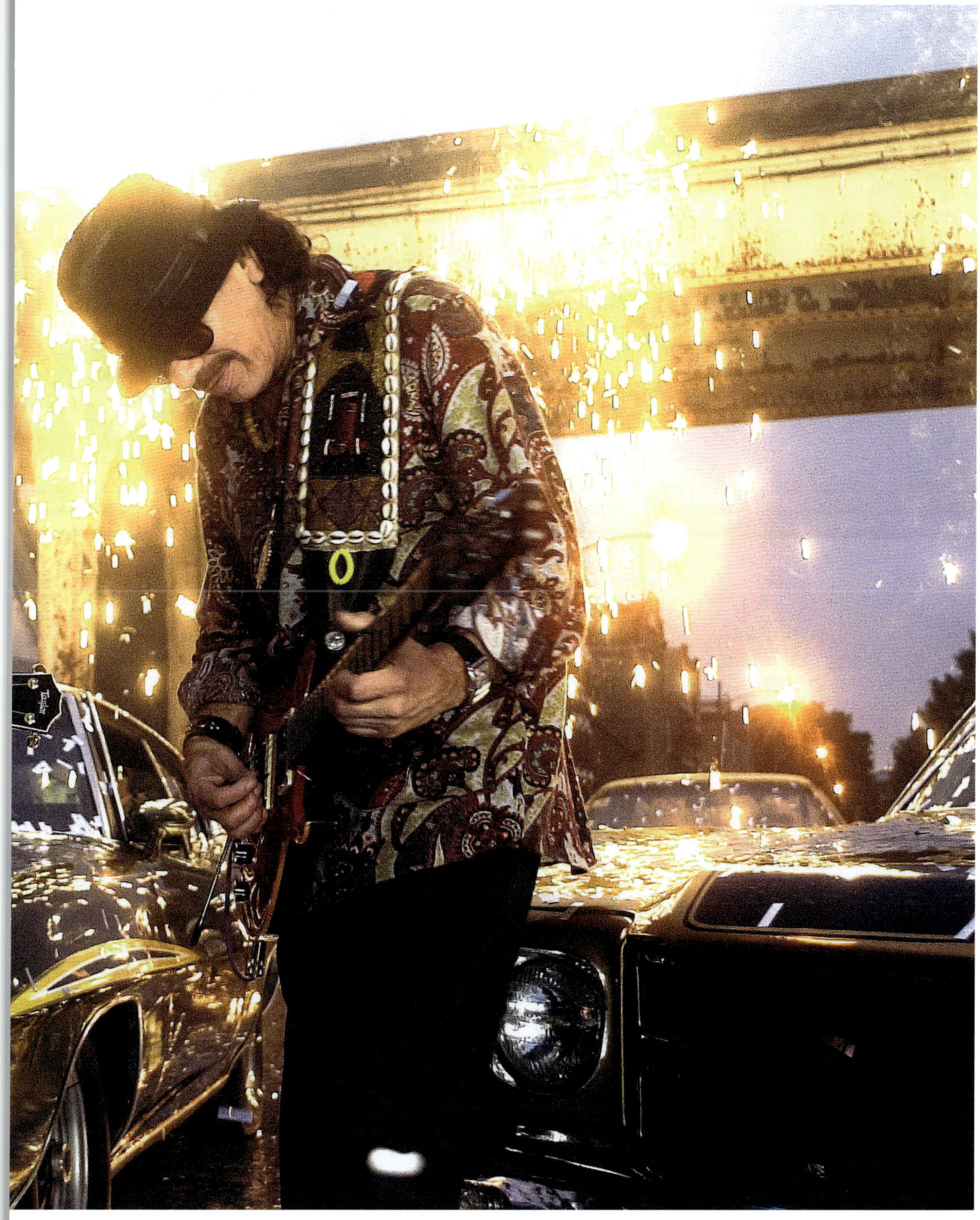

have signed 1000 autographs that day, never turning a fan down. This photograph was taken as a CTA train passed overhead, the sparks generated by special-effects people. I was laying on the ground under another car to stay out of sight of the cameras.

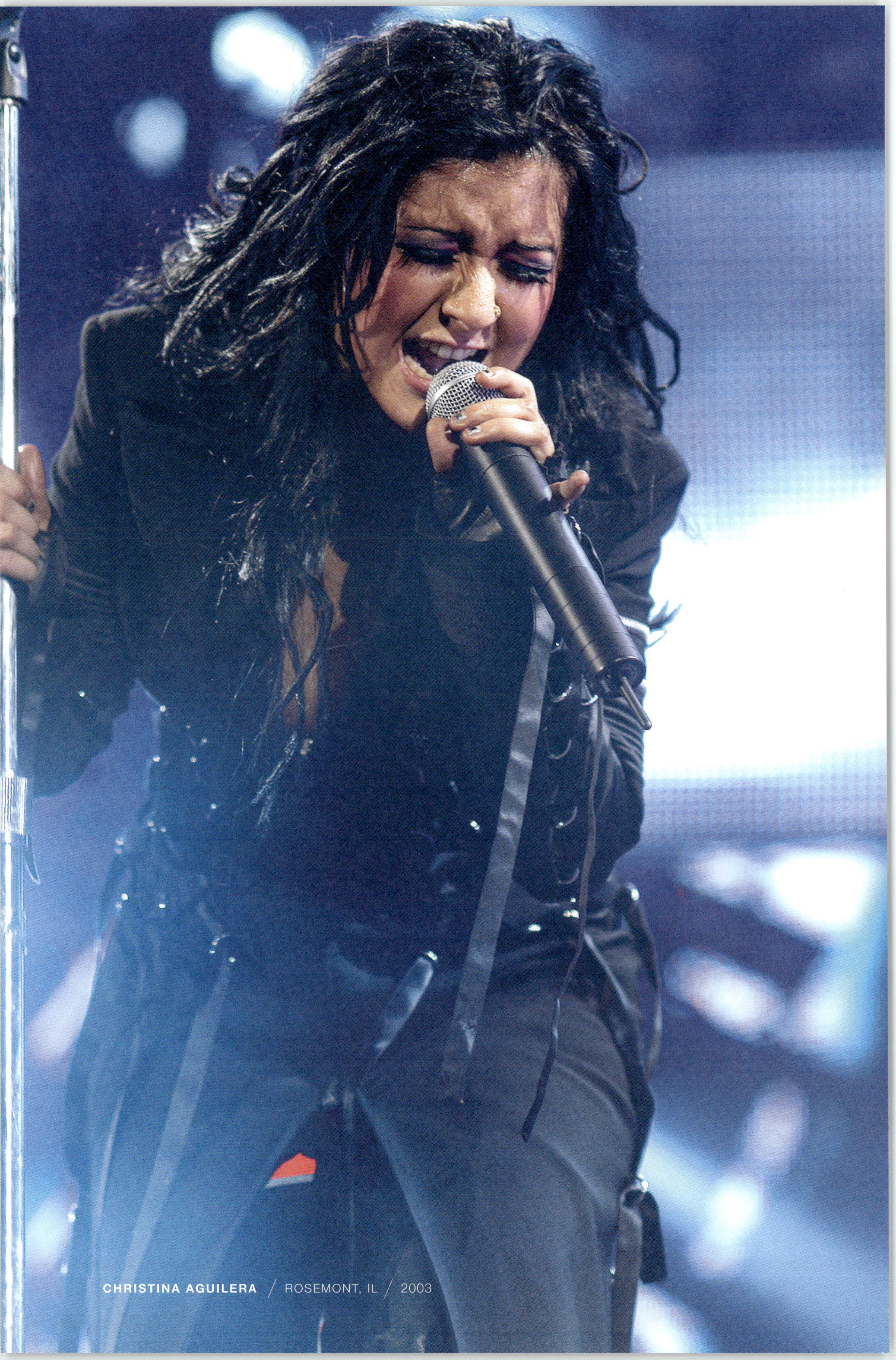

CHRISTINA AGUILERA / ROSEMONT, IL / 2003

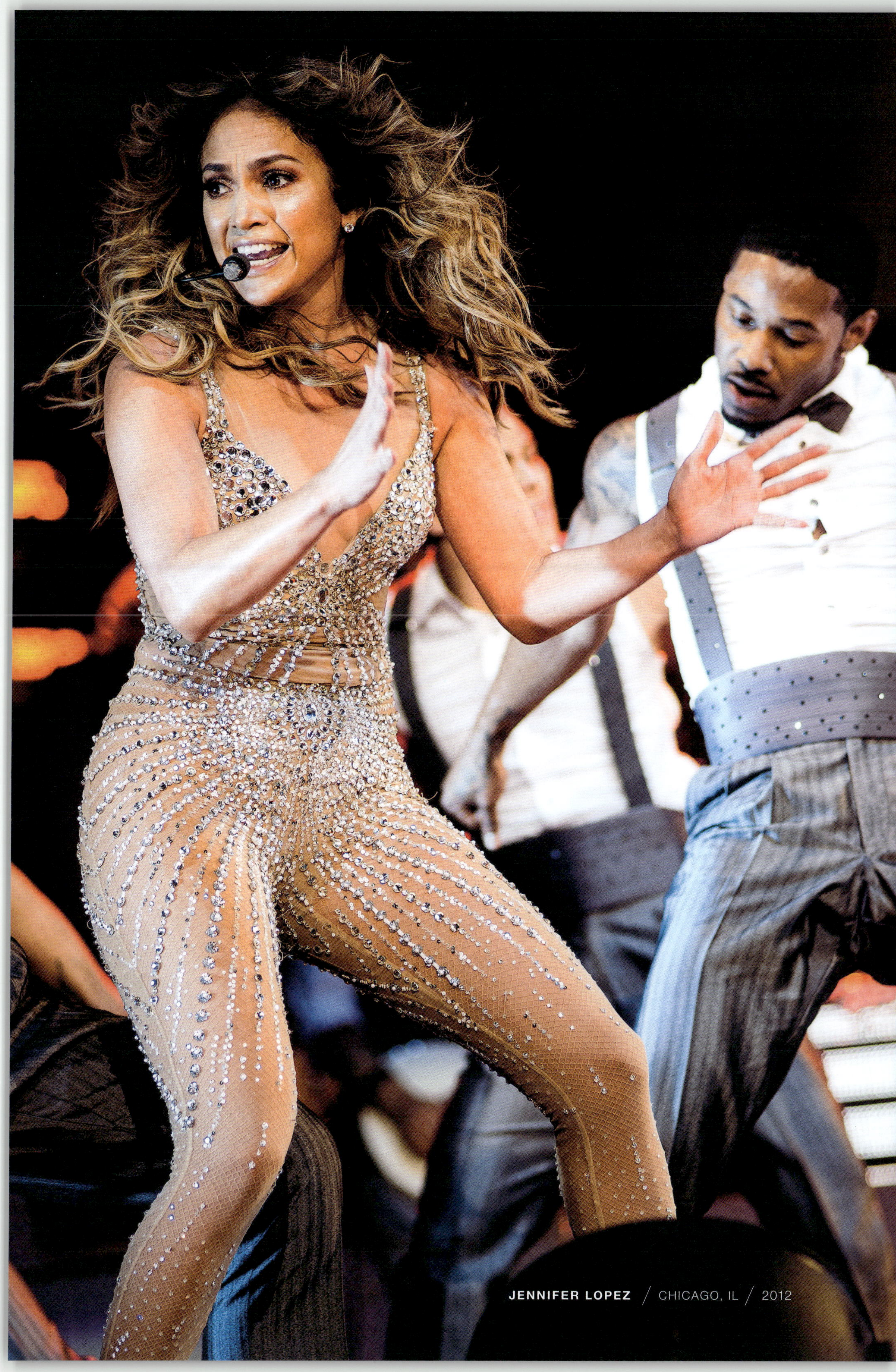

JENNIFER LOPEZ / CHICAGO, IL / 2012

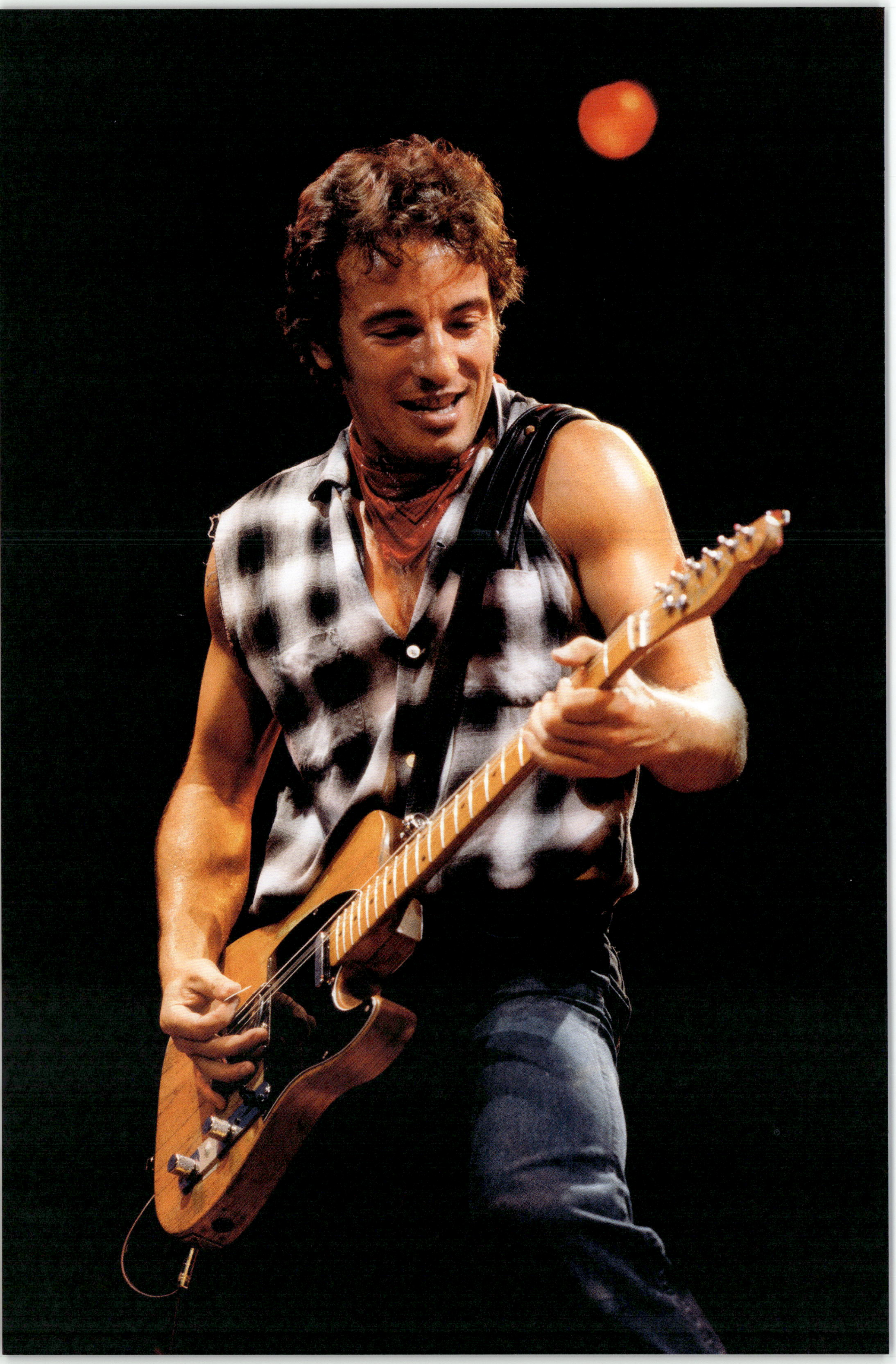

DANCING IN THE DARK

In June of 1984, Bruce Springsteen's publicist invited me to Minneapolis to photograph the first dates of the *Born In the U.S.A.* tour. She asked me to come up a day early as Bruce was shooting his first music video, directed by Hollywood director Brian De Palma, for a song called "Dancing in the Dark." After driving to the St. Paul Civic Center, I was treated to a private five-hour concert that I had free rein to shoot (albeit just one song, played over and over). During the video, Bruce pulls a cute young woman onto the stage and dances with her. Courteney Cox, then unknown, would go on to star in the hit television show *Friends* about a decade later. I stayed for the first three days of the tour; a week after I got home, I asked to shoot two more shows in southern Wisconsin, which netted me the photo that appeared on the cover of *Newsweek* the following week. It was a good week.

BRUCE SPRINGSTEEN / EAST TROY, WI / 1984

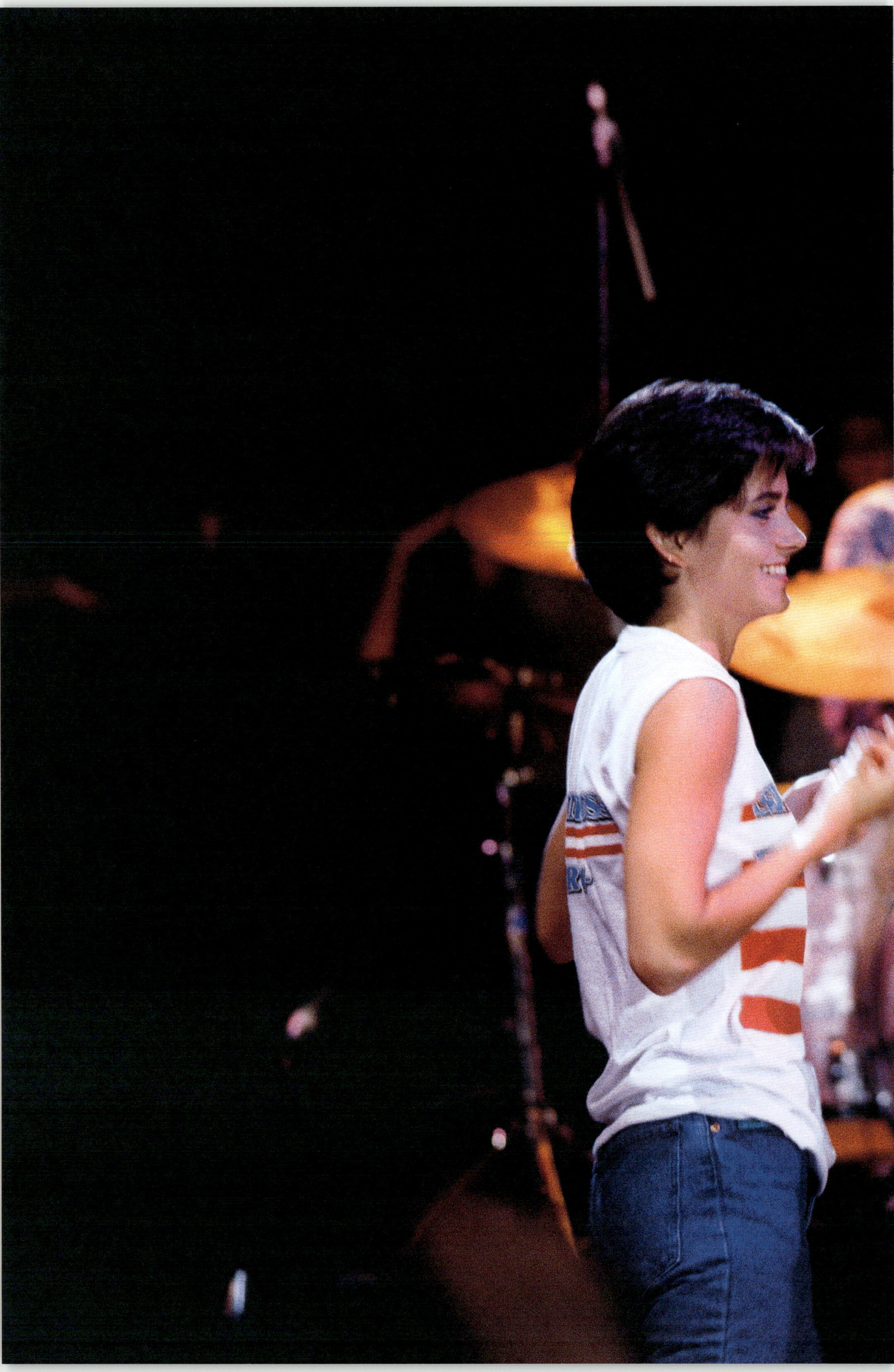

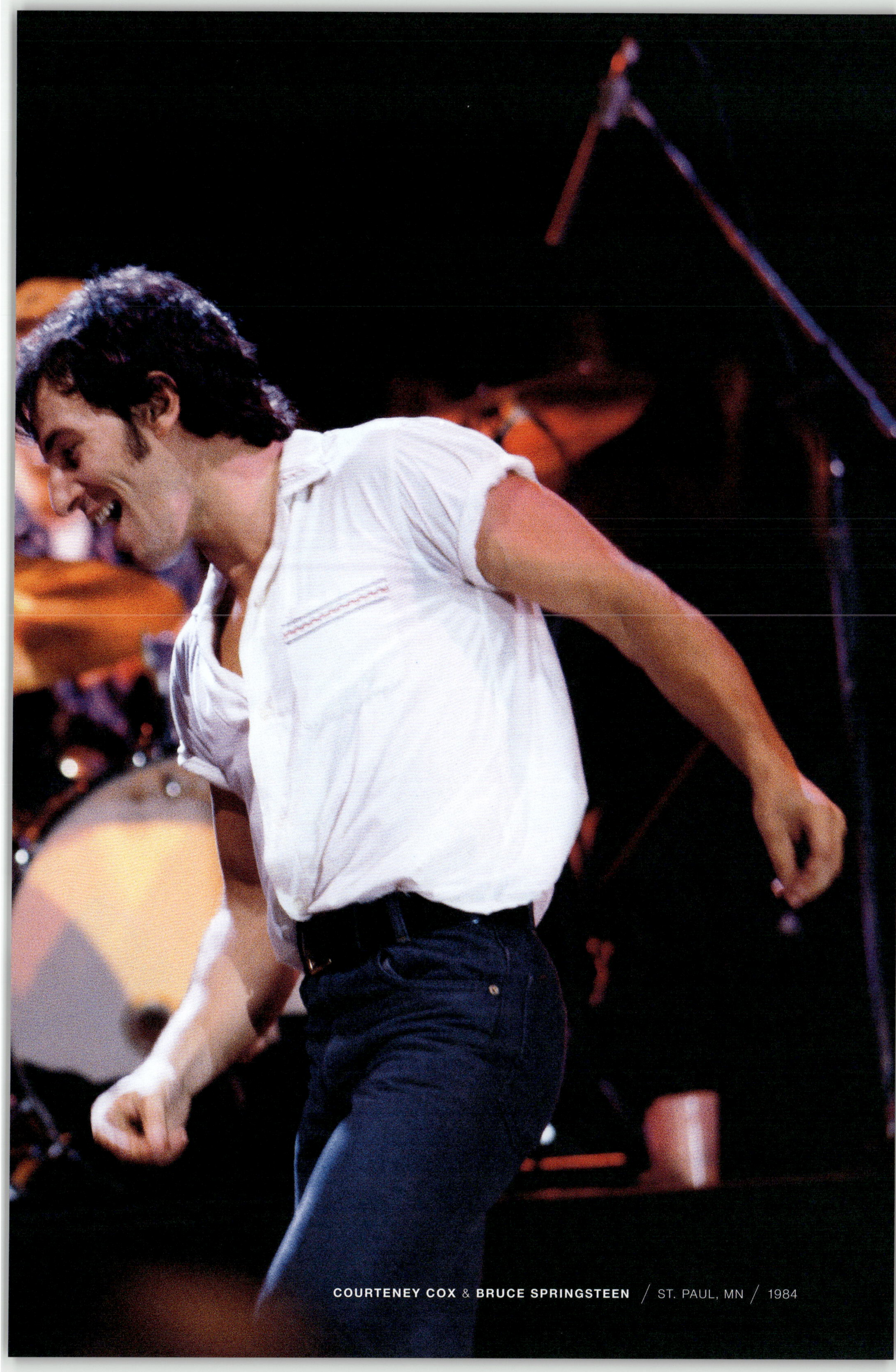

COURTENEY COX & **BRUCE SPRINGSTEEN** / ST. PAUL, MN / 1984

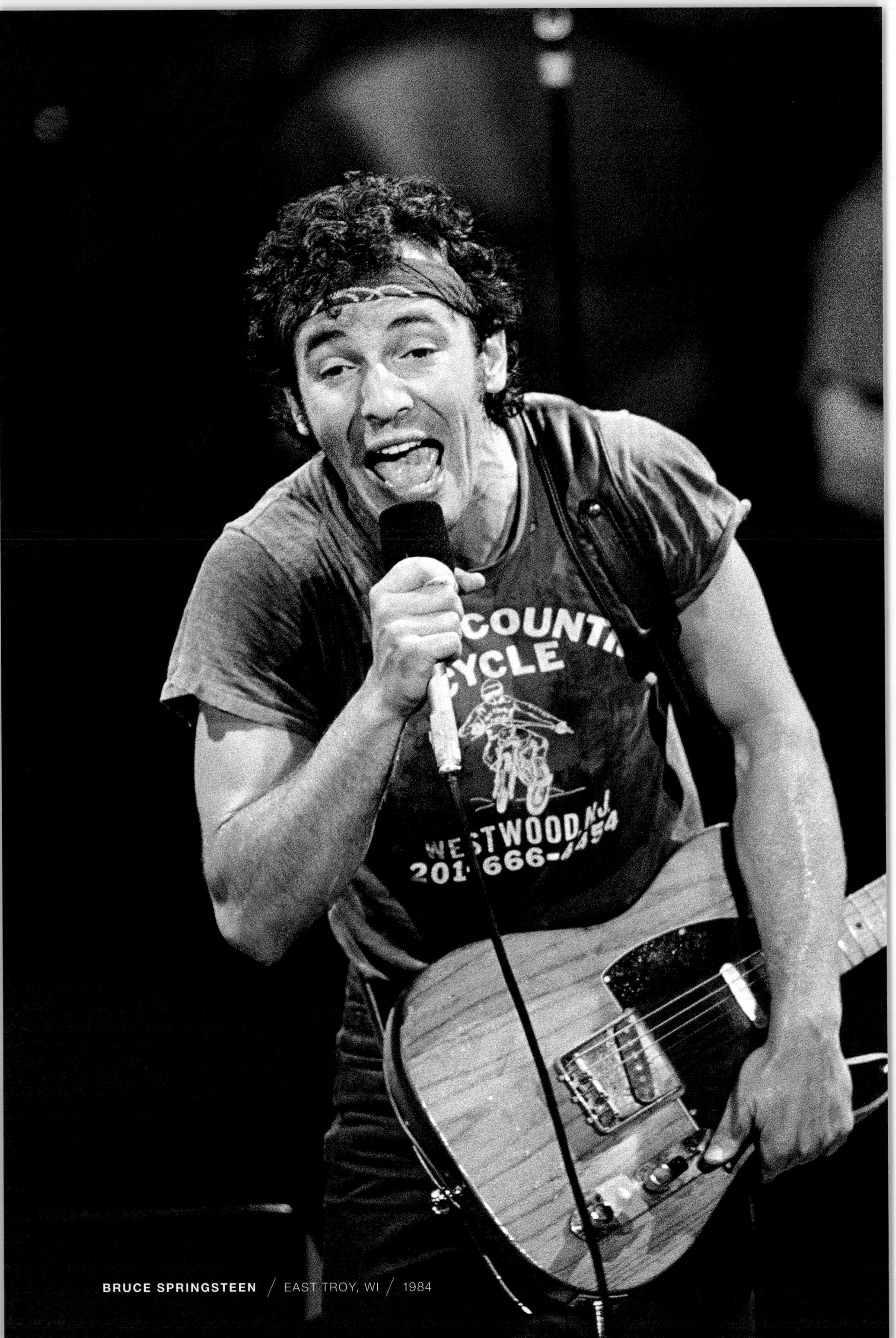

BRUCE SPRINGSTEEN / EAST TROY, WI / 1984

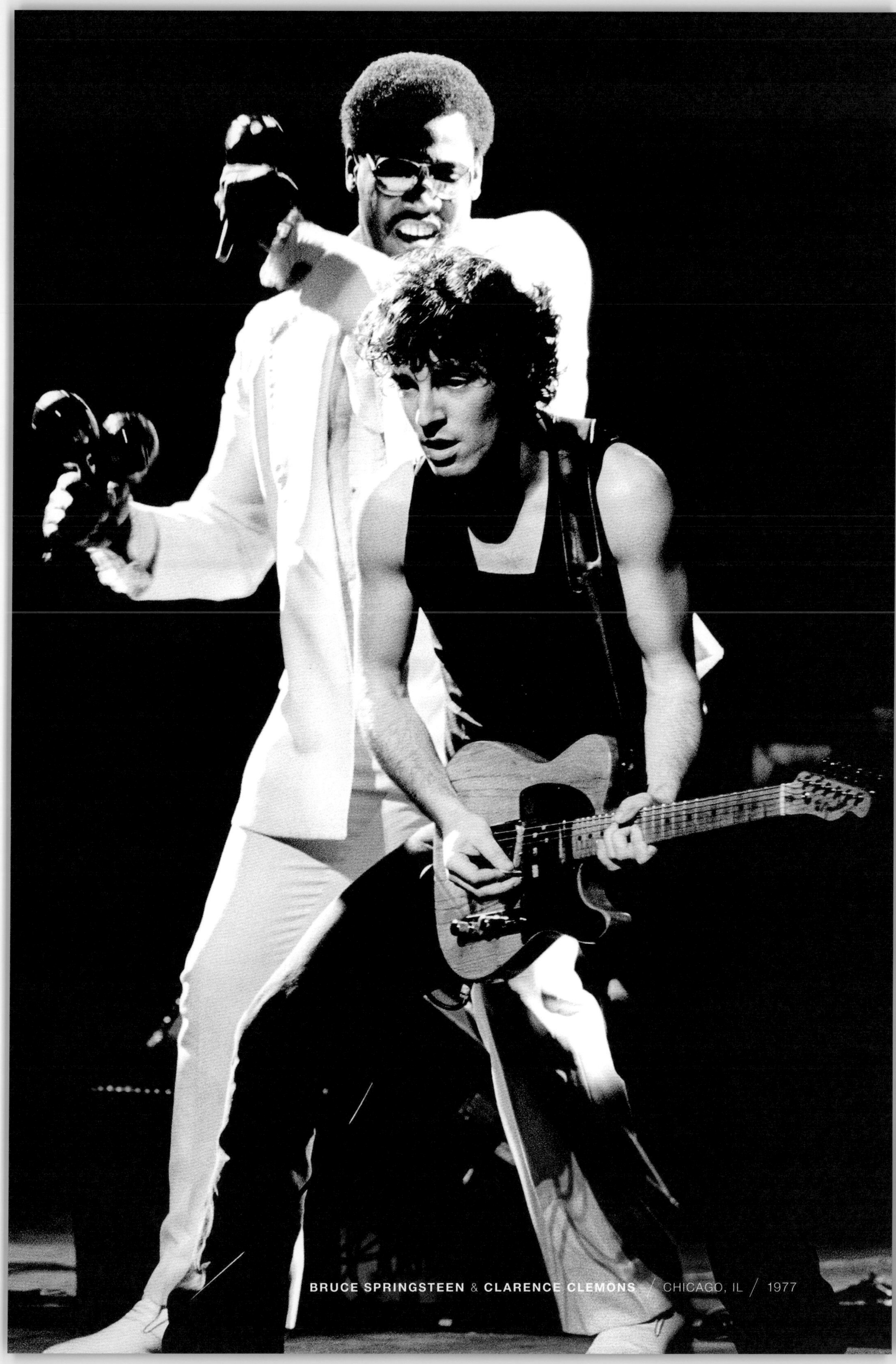

BRUCE SPRINGSTEEN & **CLARENCE CLEMONS** / CHICAGO, IL / 1977

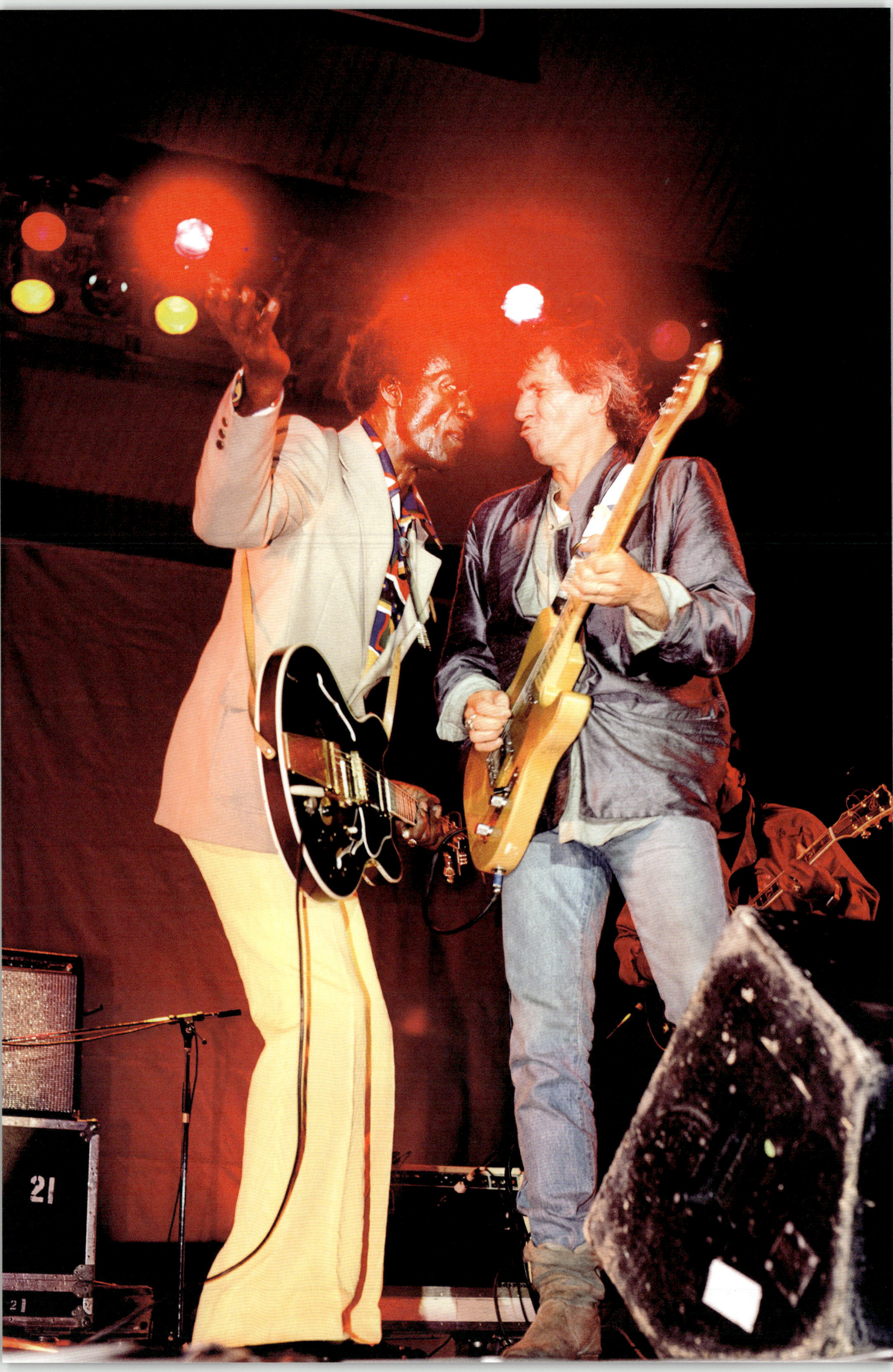
21

ONE SHOT

Years ago, my neighbor Don McLeese was the music critic for the *Chicago Sun-Times*. He called me in July of 1988 and asked if I wanted to go to New York with him to photograph one of my idols, Keith Richards, for a story he was working on. I immediately packed my bags and flew to New York. The next day, we were greeted by Keith at his manager's office. I quickly set up my lights as Don conducted the interview. After he finished, I had five minutes with Keith, and to this day it's still such a blur; I didn't notice Keith was giving me the finger in one of the shots until almost a year later. During the interview, I heard Keith say that he was going on the road with The X-Pensive Winos, the band that appeared on his solo album *Talk is Cheap*. I made a few prints of that session and sent them to his manager with a short note asking if she needed someone to photograph the tour. I got a call a few months later, asking me to come to Atlanta the next day to join the *Talk Is Cheap* tour. That one action led to my job as the tour photographer for the 1989 Rolling Stones *Steel Wheels* tour, Keith's 1993 solo tour and the 1994 Rolling Stones *Voodoo Lounge* tour.

THE FINGER

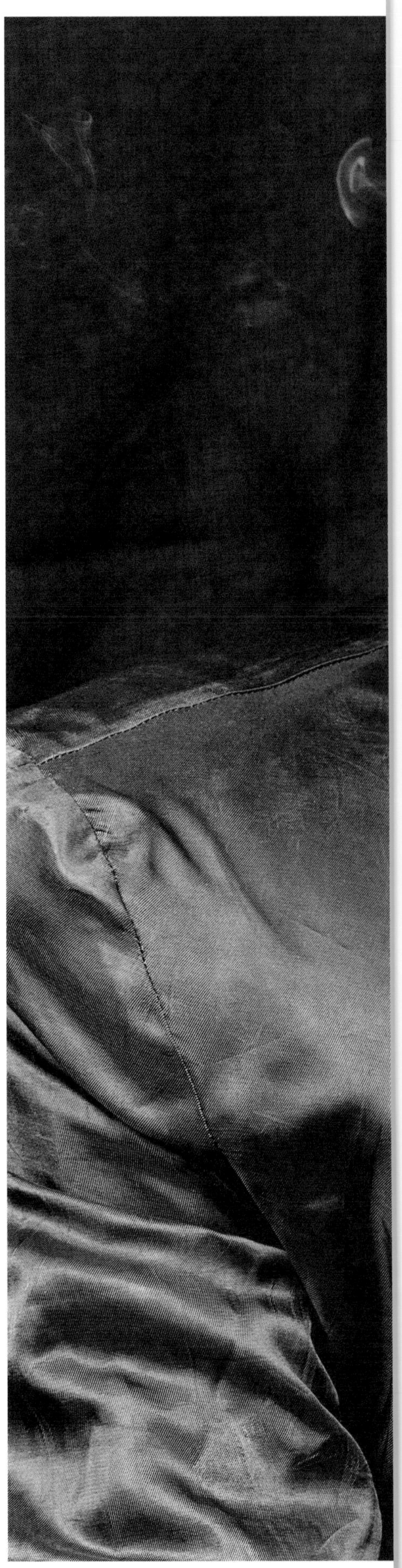

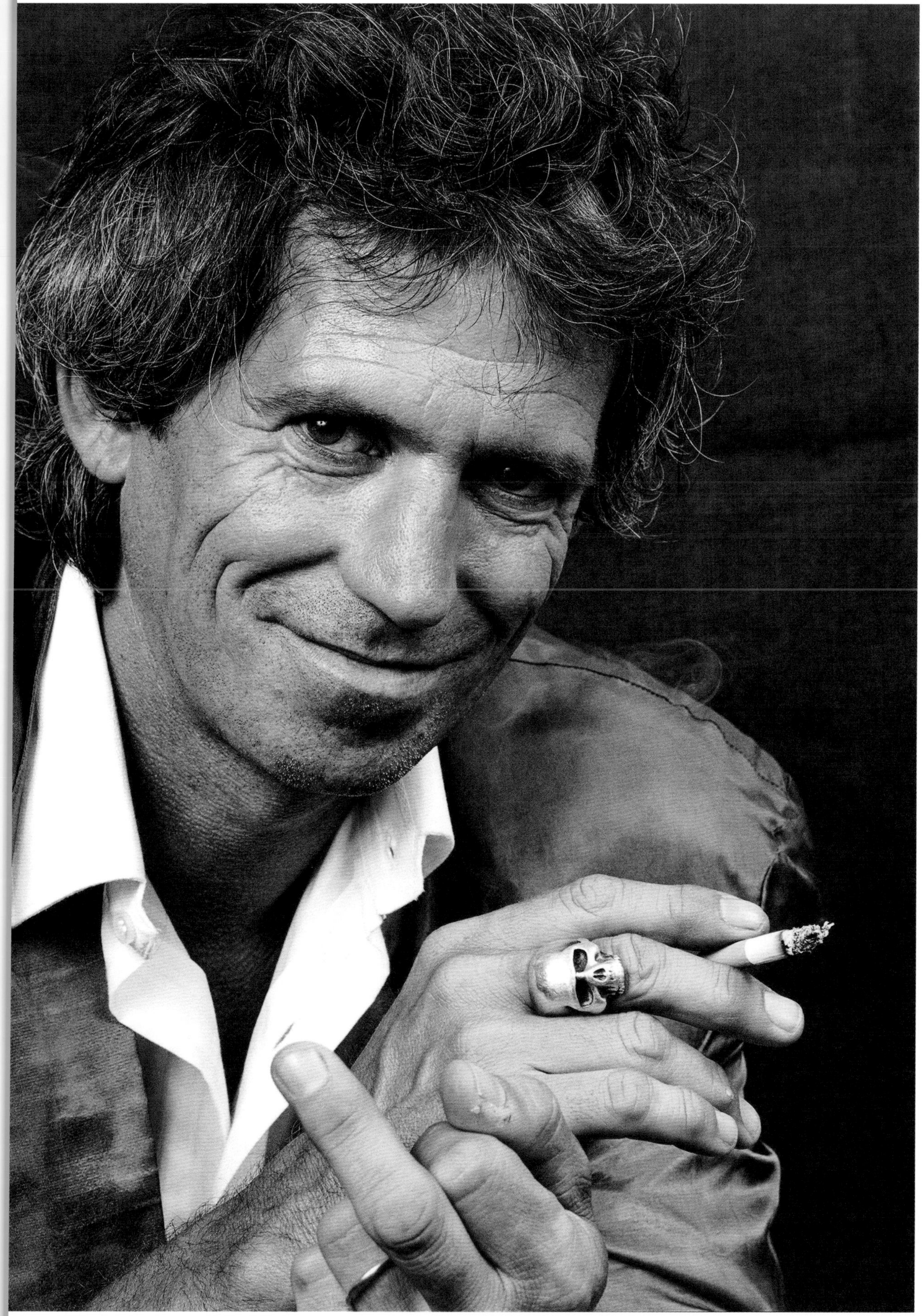

KEITH RICHARDS / NEW YORK, NY / 1988

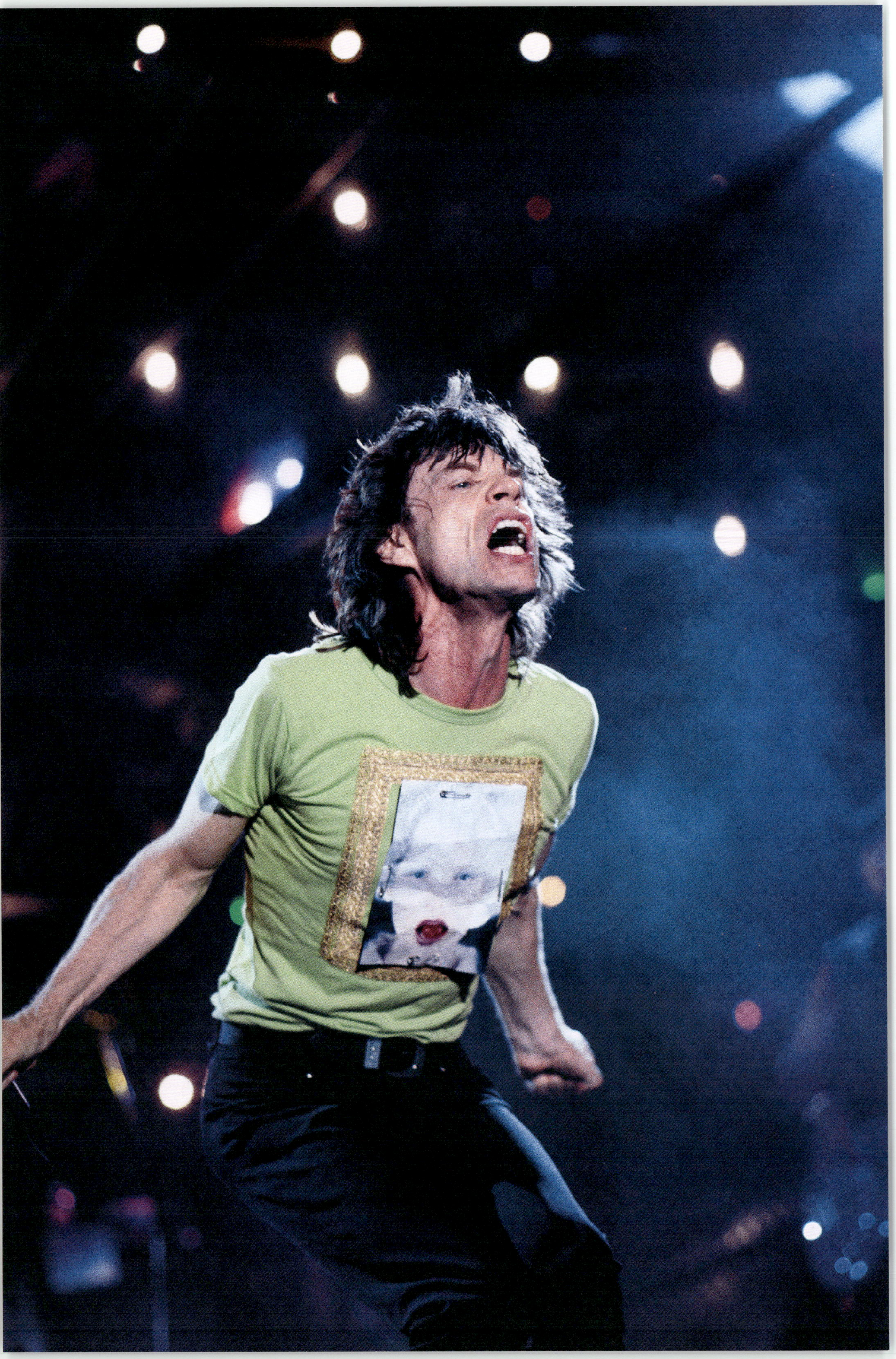

THE ROLLING STONES

A year after working on Keith Richards' 1988 tour, the Stones team called and asked if I would like to do a month on the *Steel Wheels* tour. Of course I said yes! The morning of September 1, 1989, I got on a plane in Chicago and landed in Boston a few hours later. I took a taxi to the hotel, dropped off my luggage with the band's logistics guy, and an hour later was in a van heading to Foxboro, Massachusetts. There I photographed my first Rolling Stones show with total access. I was directed to a small platform hanging from the front of the stage for me and the video crew; I jumped up and started shooting. With 70,000 fans behind me, and the world's greatest rock 'n' roll band in front of me, I felt like I was in the eye of a hurricane for 2 1/2 hours! That feeling continued all month long–and then the management team informed me that I couldn't leave and they wanted me to finish out the tour. One month became three, ending with a pay-per-view event at Trump Casino in Atlantic City. I went home thinking that my career was complete–you can't go up from there!

But in 1993, I was called to do Keith's second solo tour, then did a month on the Stones' *Voodoo Lounge* tour; in 1997, I shot rehearsals and the first days of the *Bridges to Babylon* tour.

MICK JAGGER **THE ROLLING STONES** / MADISON, WI / 1994

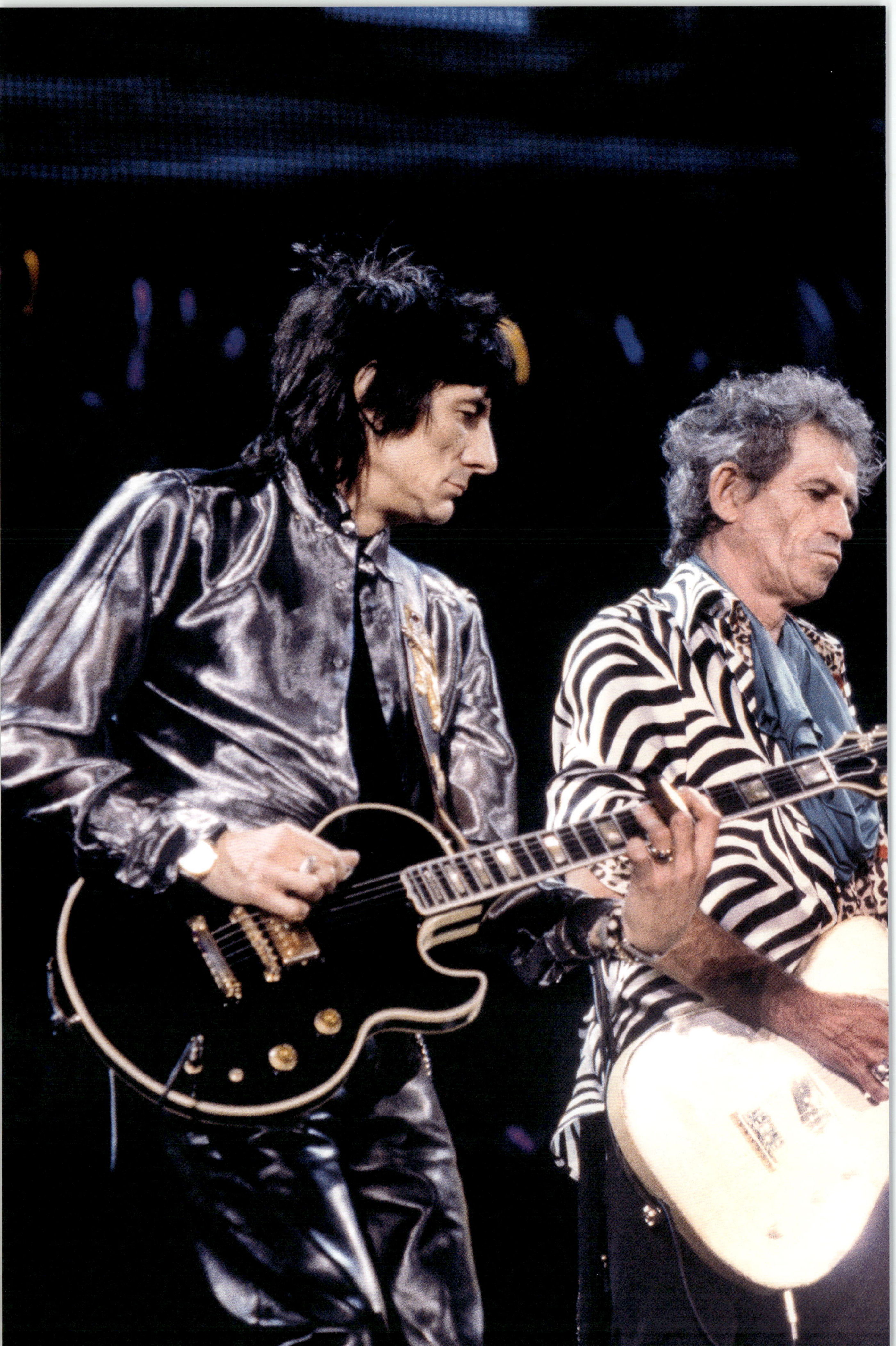

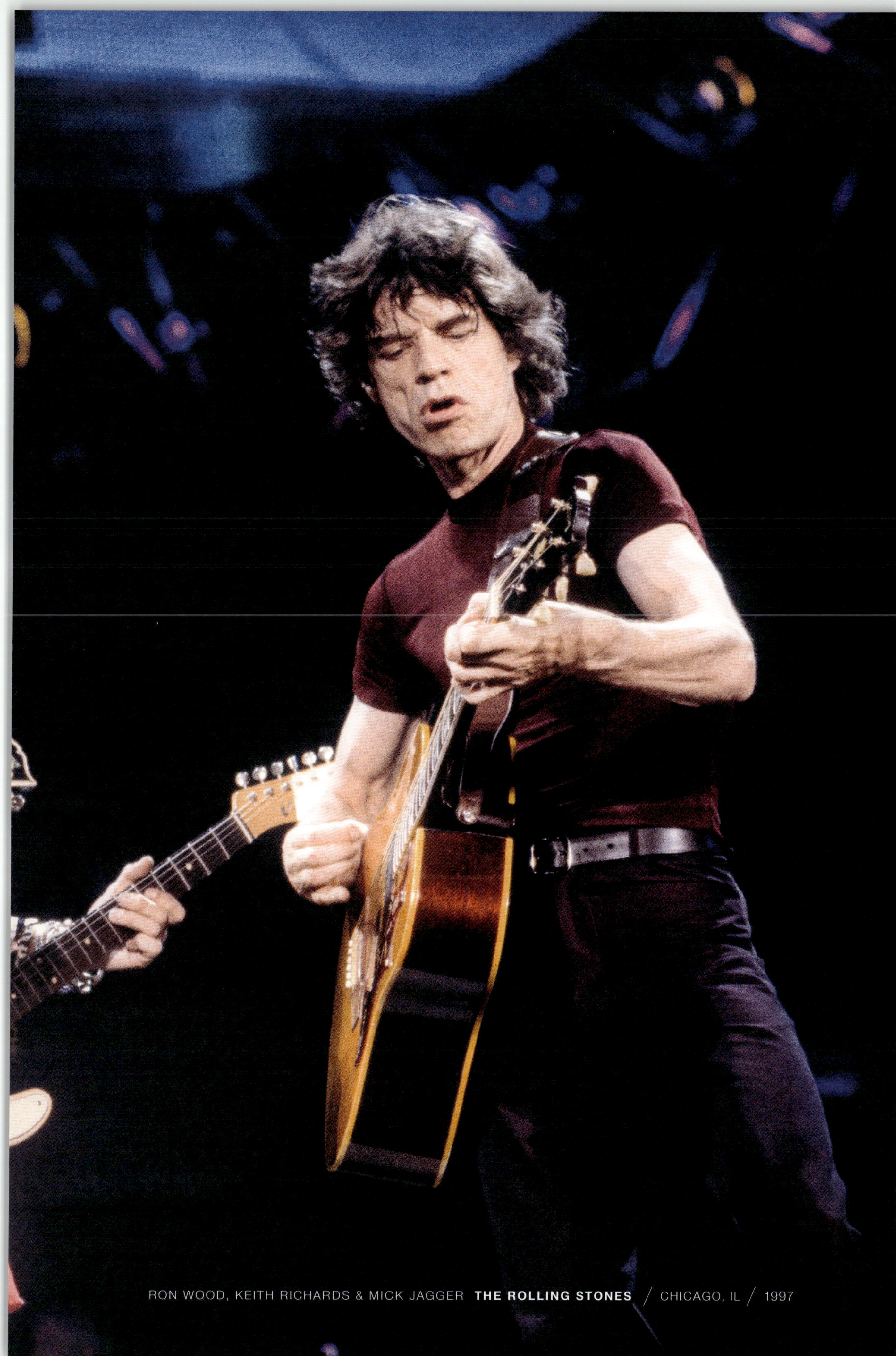

RON WOOD, KEITH RICHARDS & MICK JAGGER **THE ROLLING STONES** / CHICAGO, IL / 1997

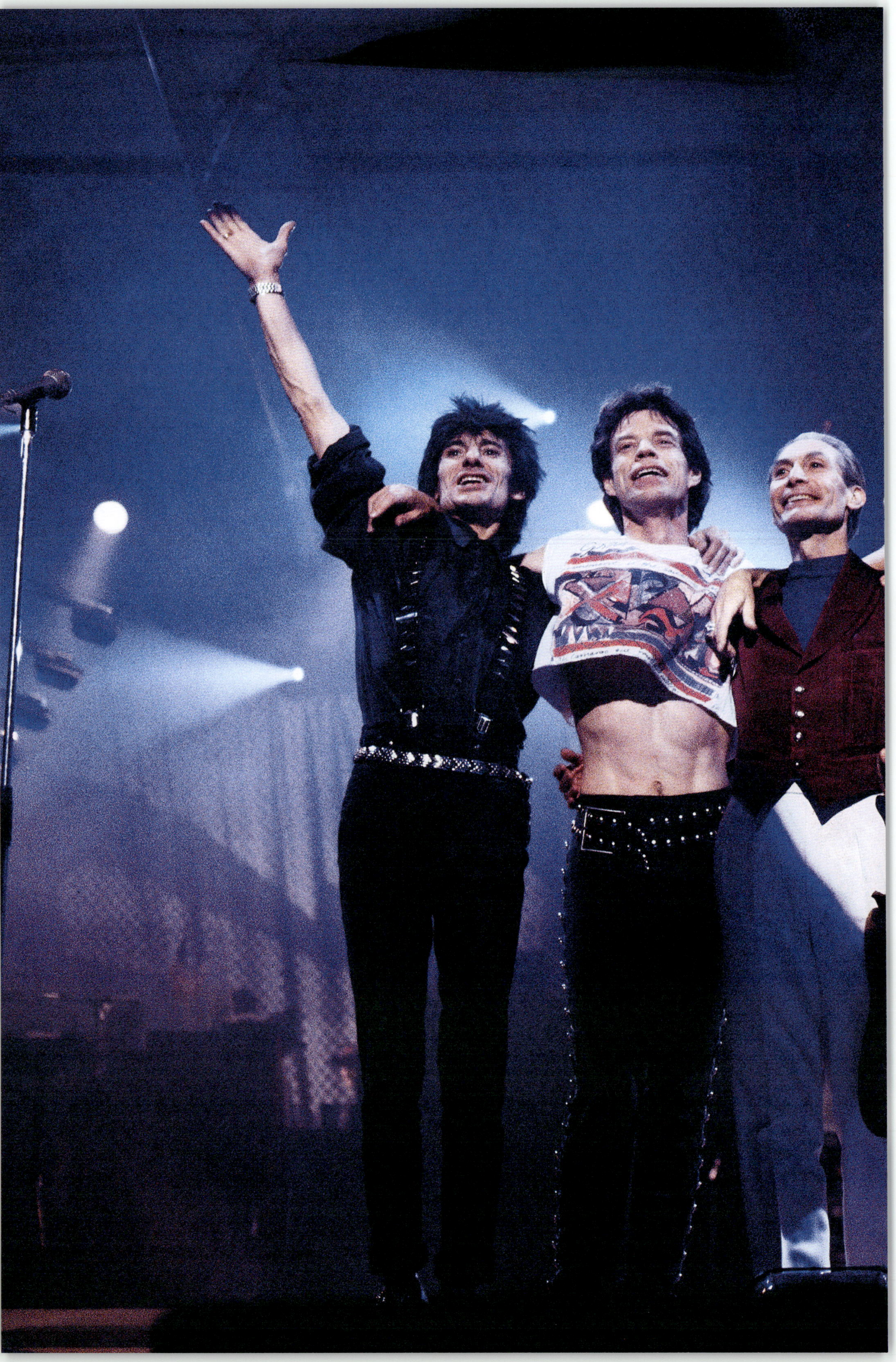

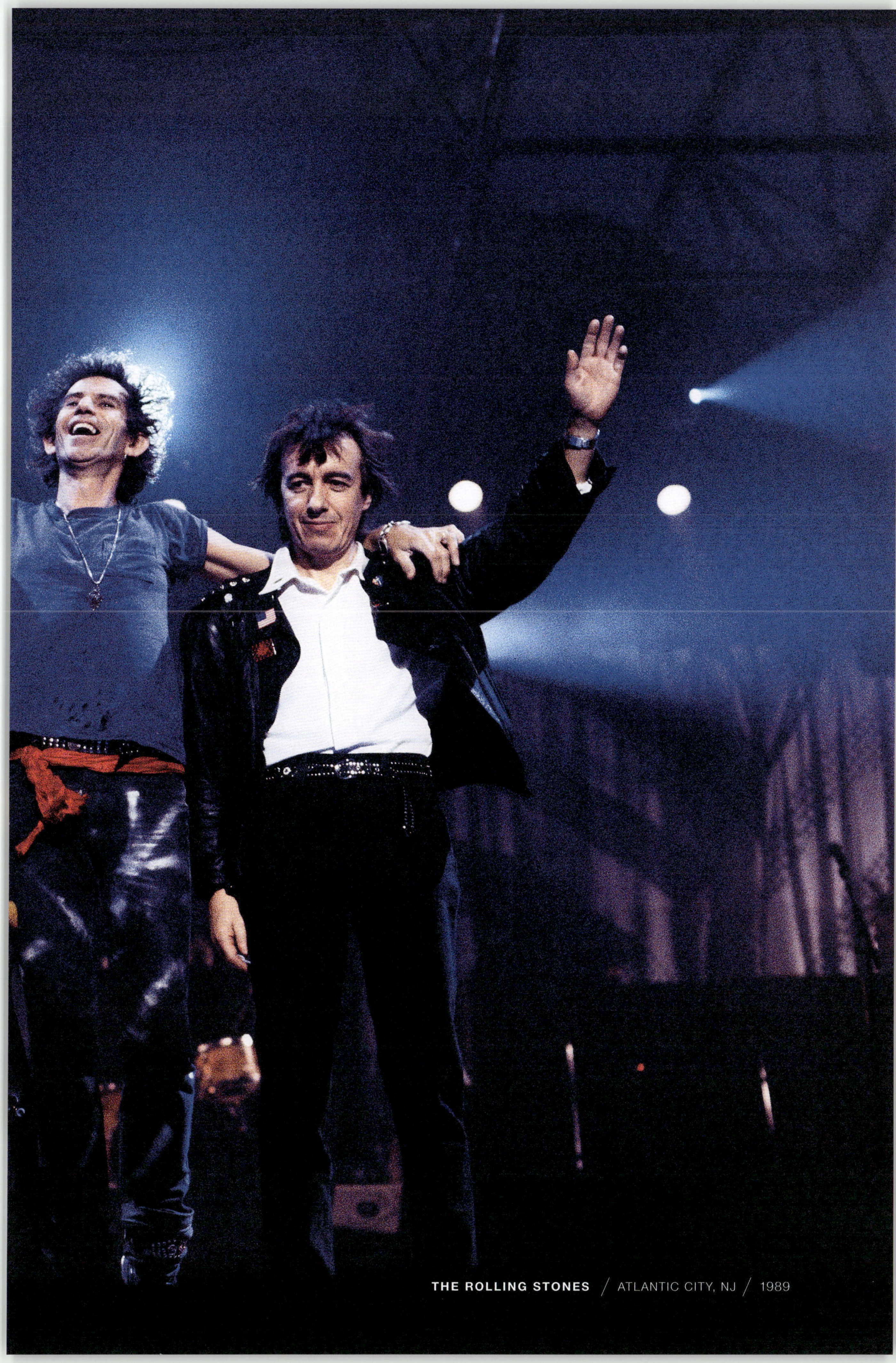

THE ROLLING STONES / ATLANTIC CITY, NJ / 1989

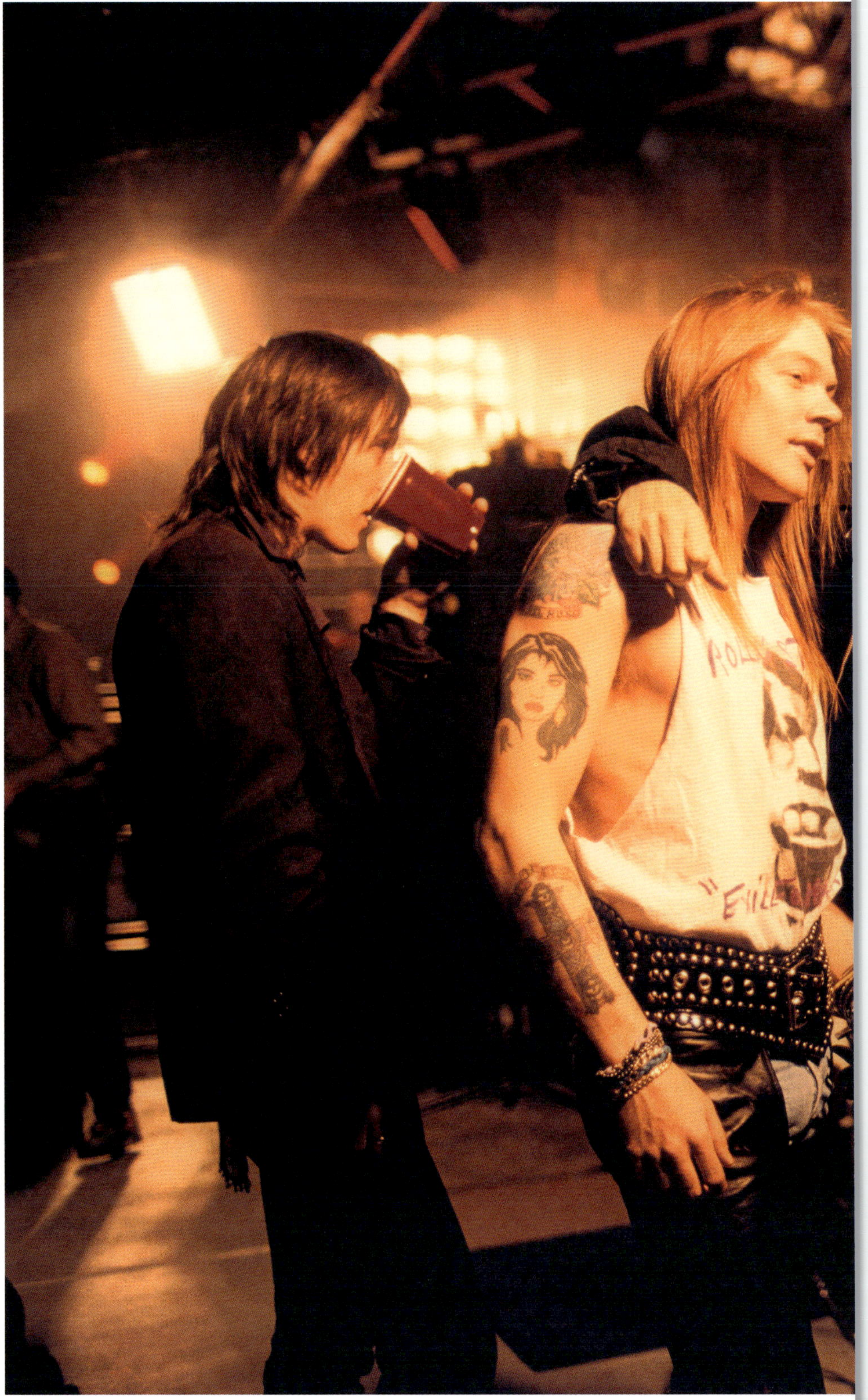

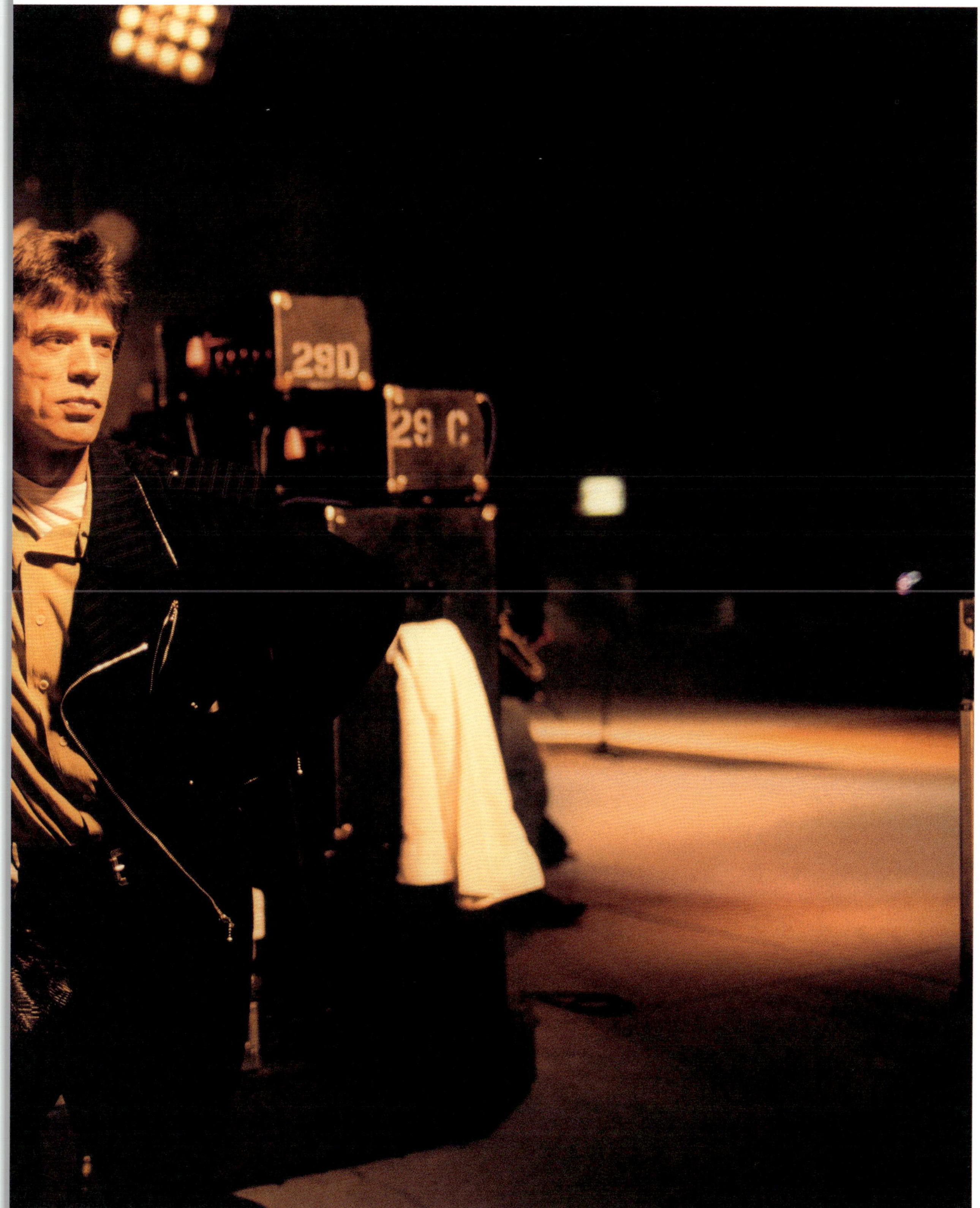

For the Atlantic City pay-per-view concert at the end of the *Steel Wheels* tour, the Stones added guests including Eric Clapton, John Lee Hooker and Axl Rose and Izzy Stradlin from Guns N' Roses. This image was taken before sound check, as Mick and Axl were going through how the song should be split up for their performance together.

AXL ROSE **GUNS N' ROSES** & MICK JAGGER / ATLANTIC CITY, NJ / 1989

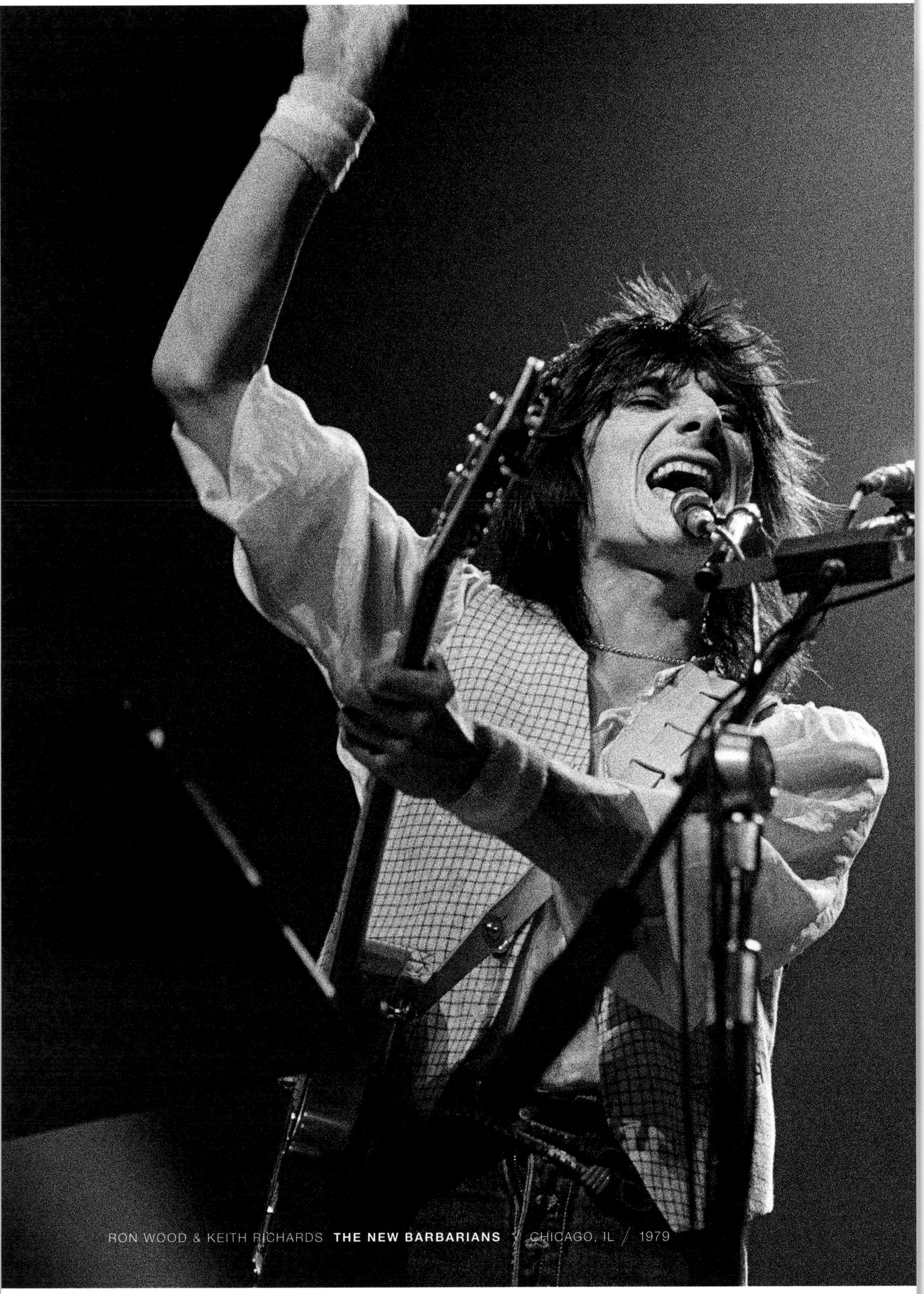

RON WOOD & KEITH RICHARDS **THE NEW BARBARIANS** / CHICAGO, IL / 1979

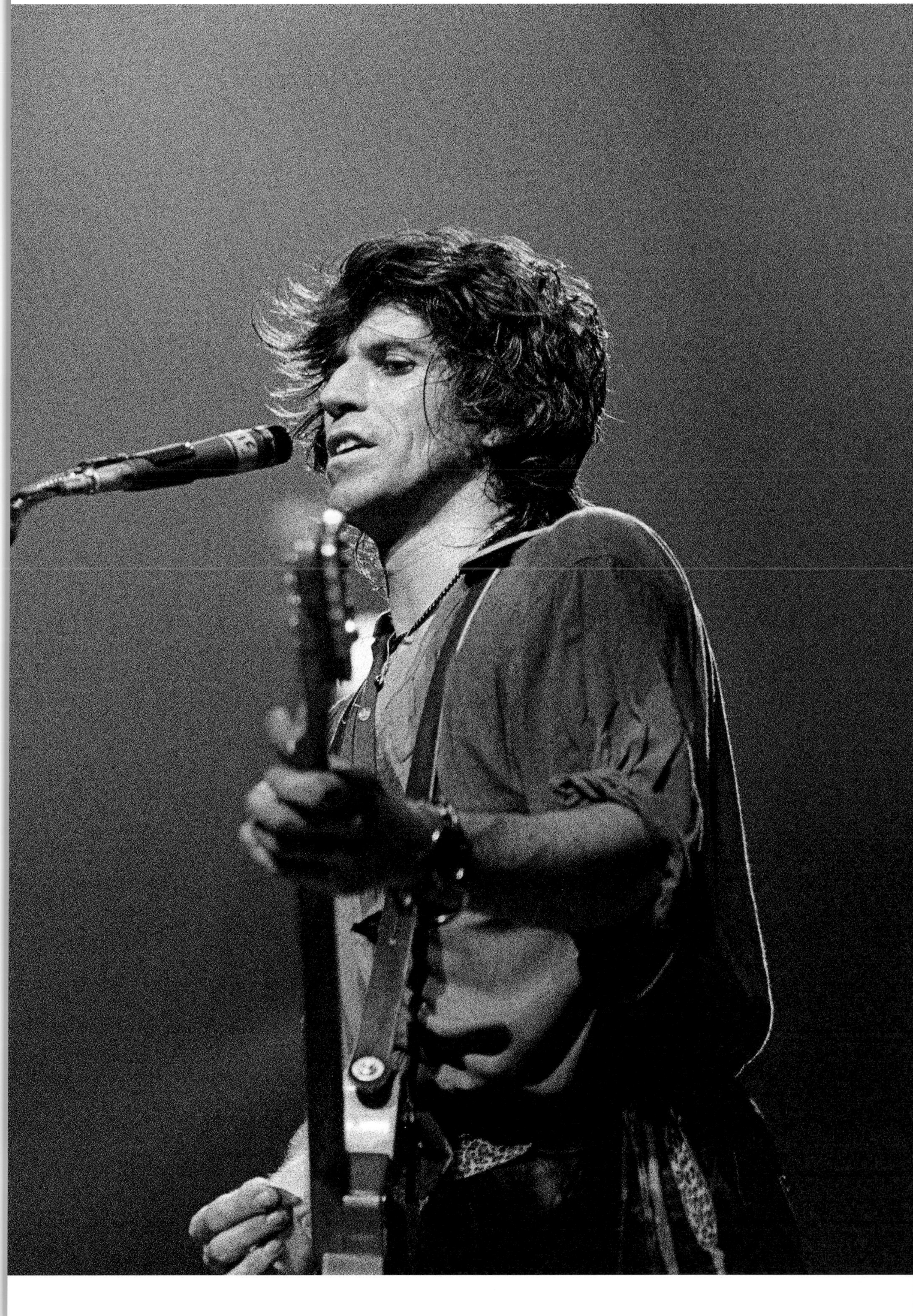

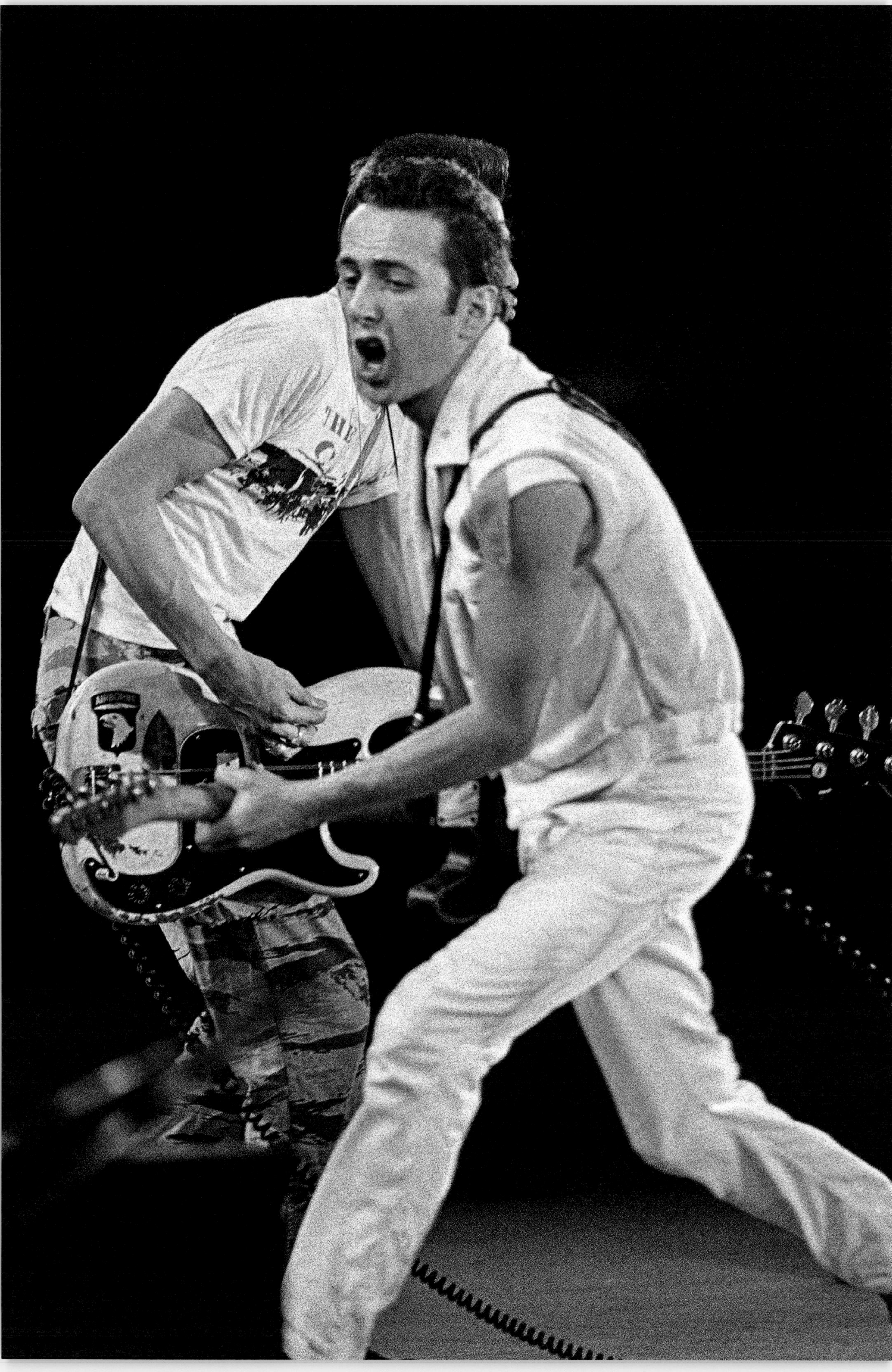

4

NEXT WAVE
PUNK TO GRUNGE

One of the most exciting genres of music to photograph–totally unpredictable and potentially dangerous! Standing between a punk artist and their audience can be risky, at best. I have been spit on (from both sides), had sparks fly from the stage and burn a hole in the coating of a lens, and had beer and ice cubes hit me from behind on many occasions. It is all worth it to get a great photograph.

THE CLASH / ONTARIO, CA / 1983

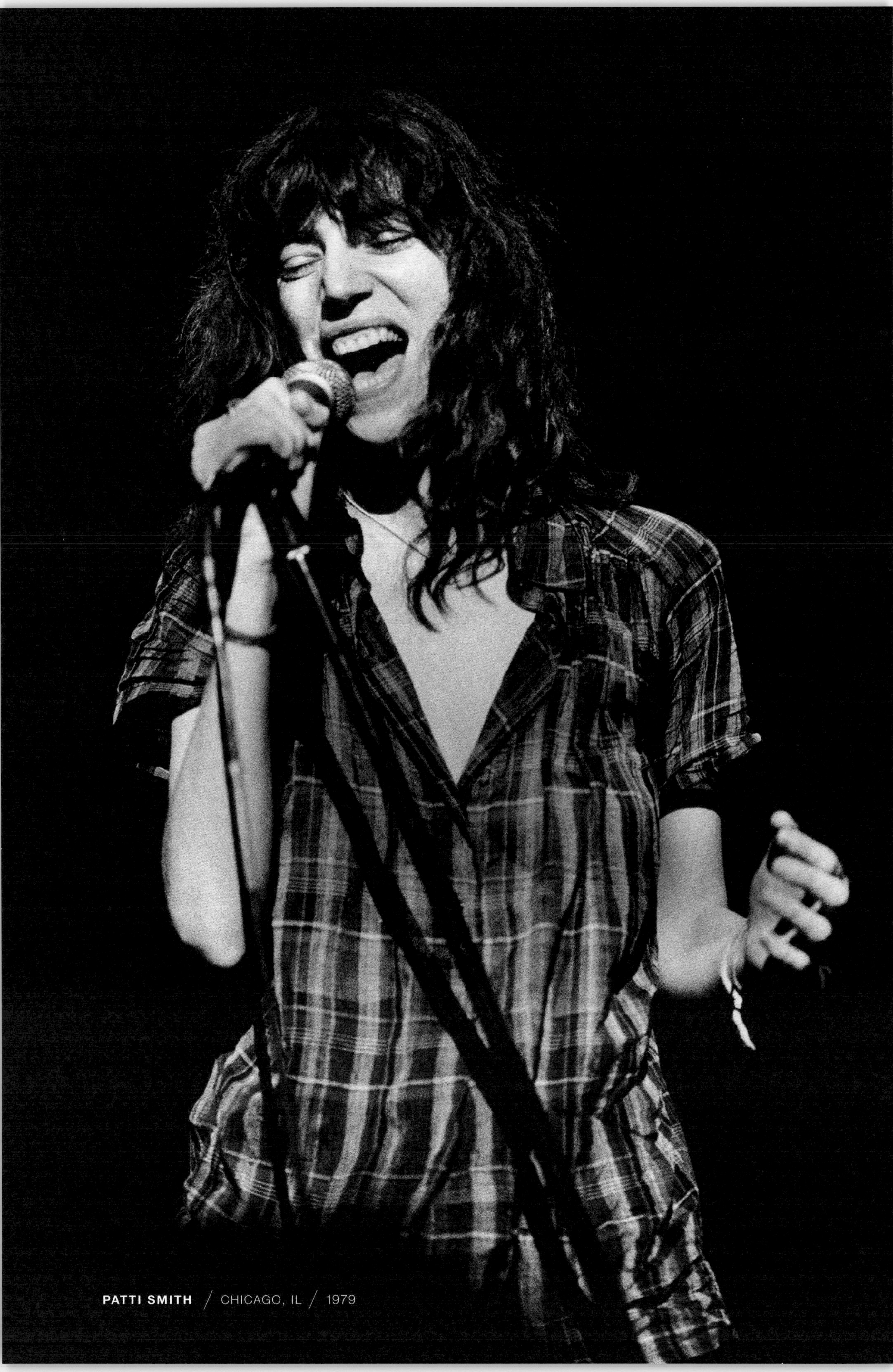

PATTI SMITH / CHICAGO, IL / 1979

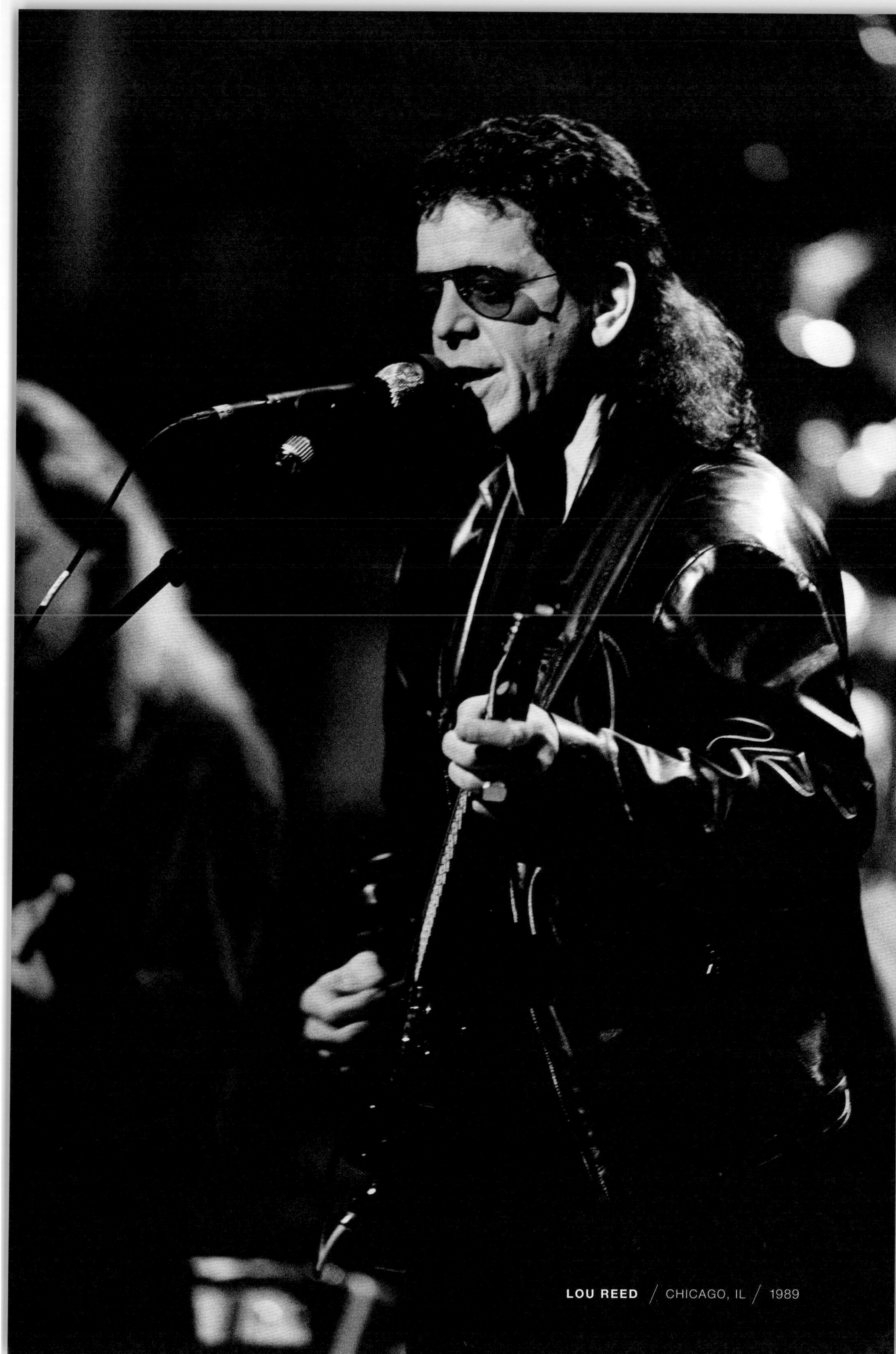

LOU REED / CHICAGO, IL / 1989

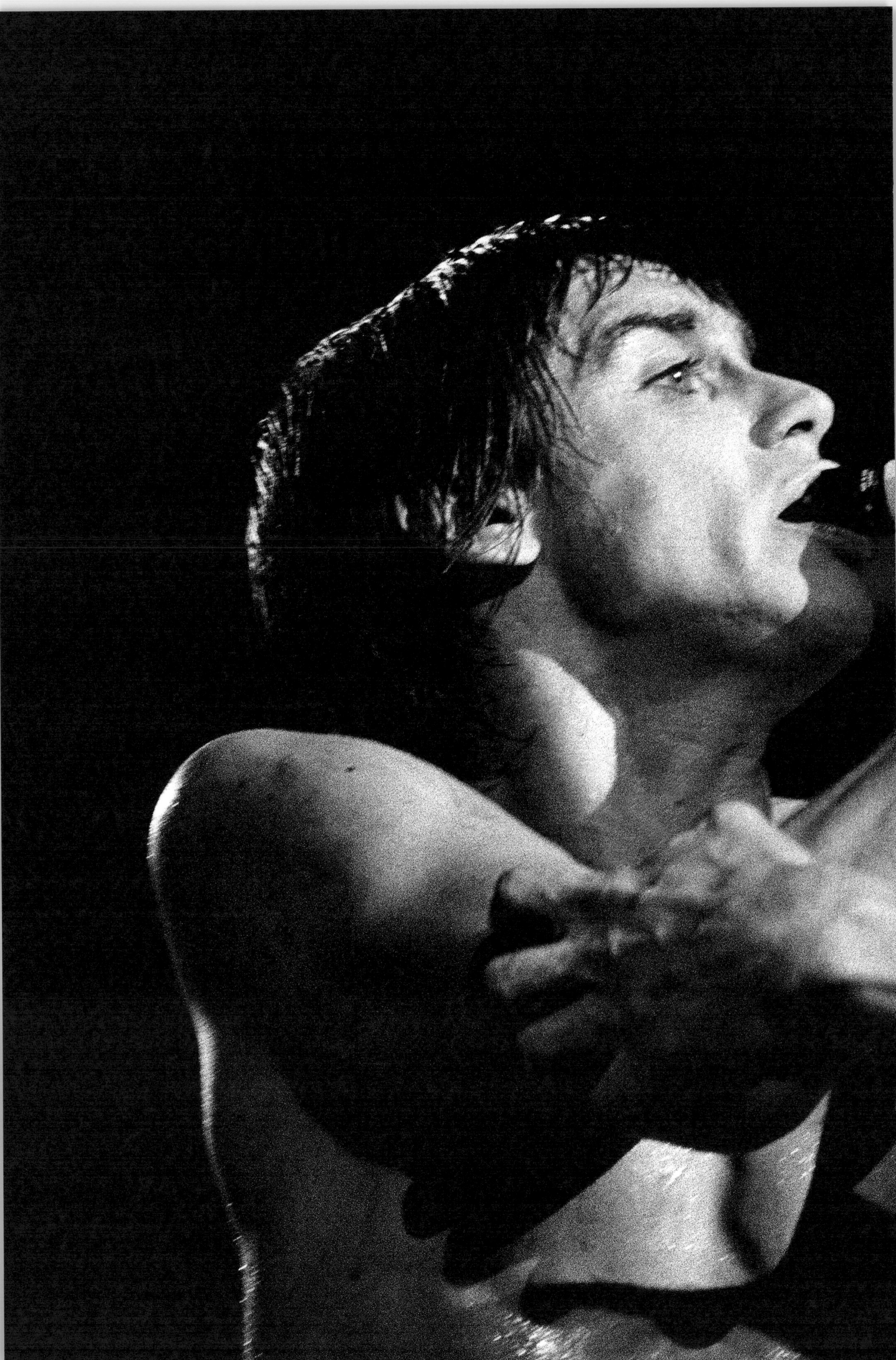

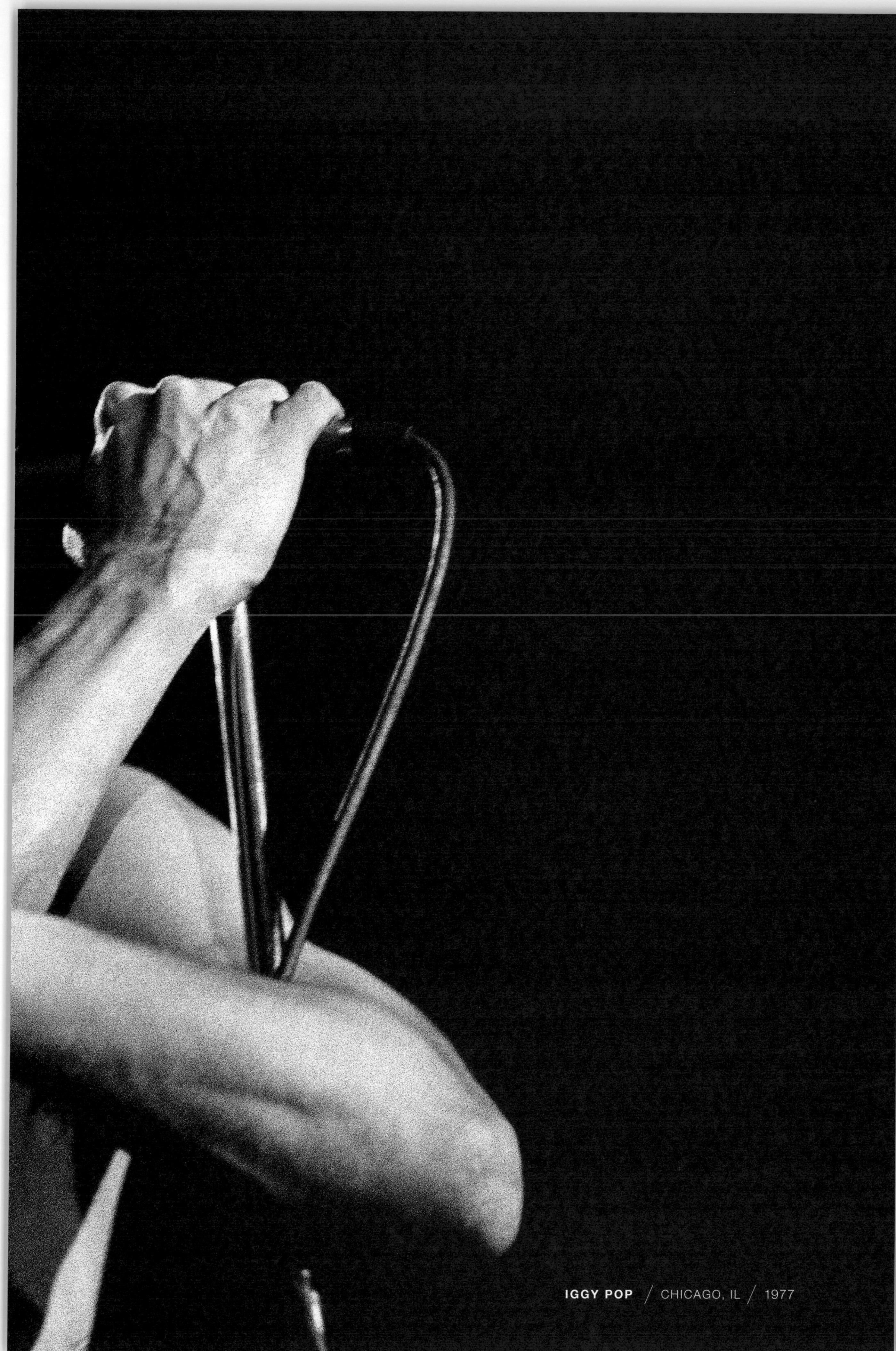

IGGY POP / CHICAGO, IL / 1977

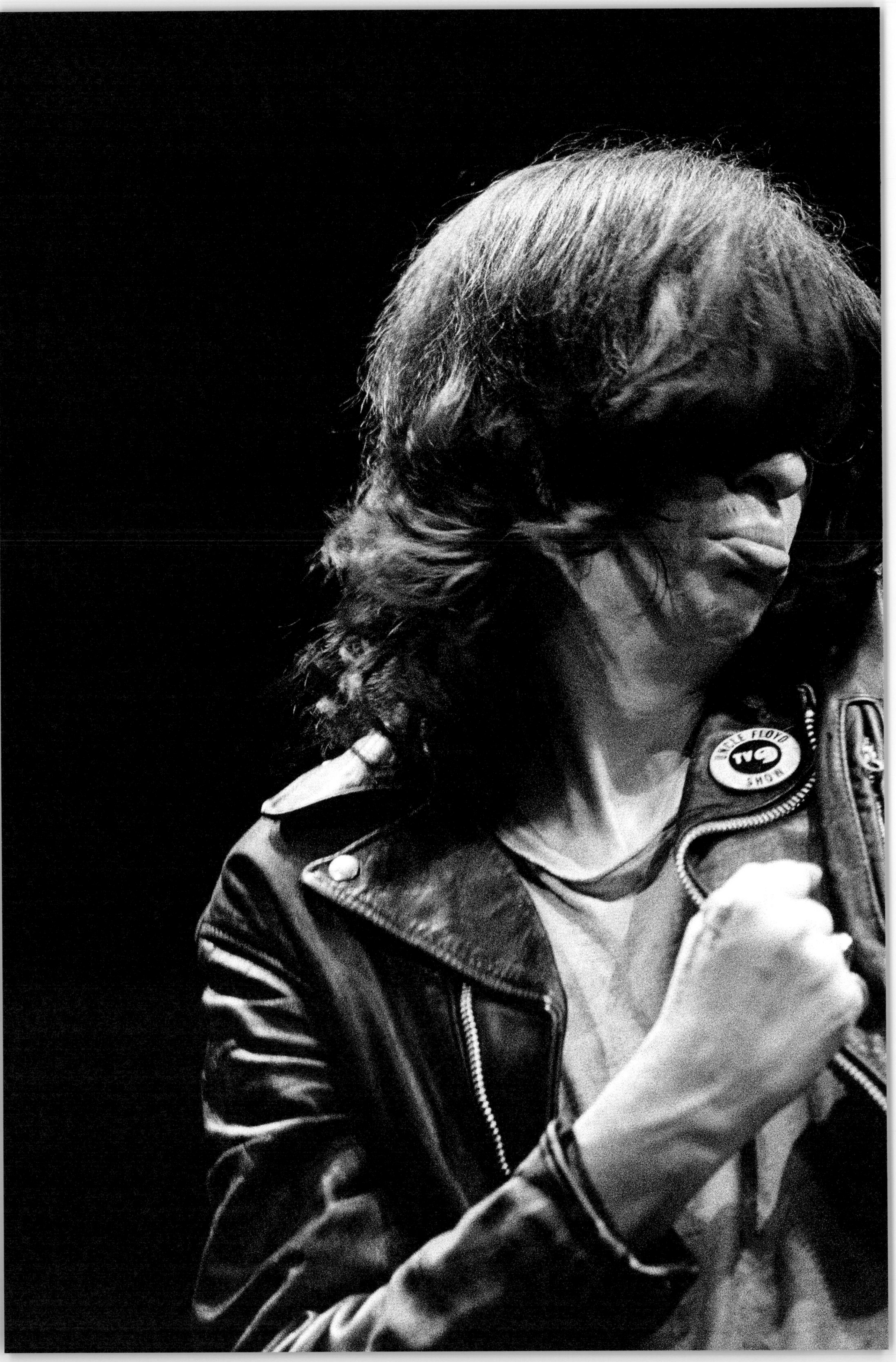
UNCLE FLOYD
SHOW

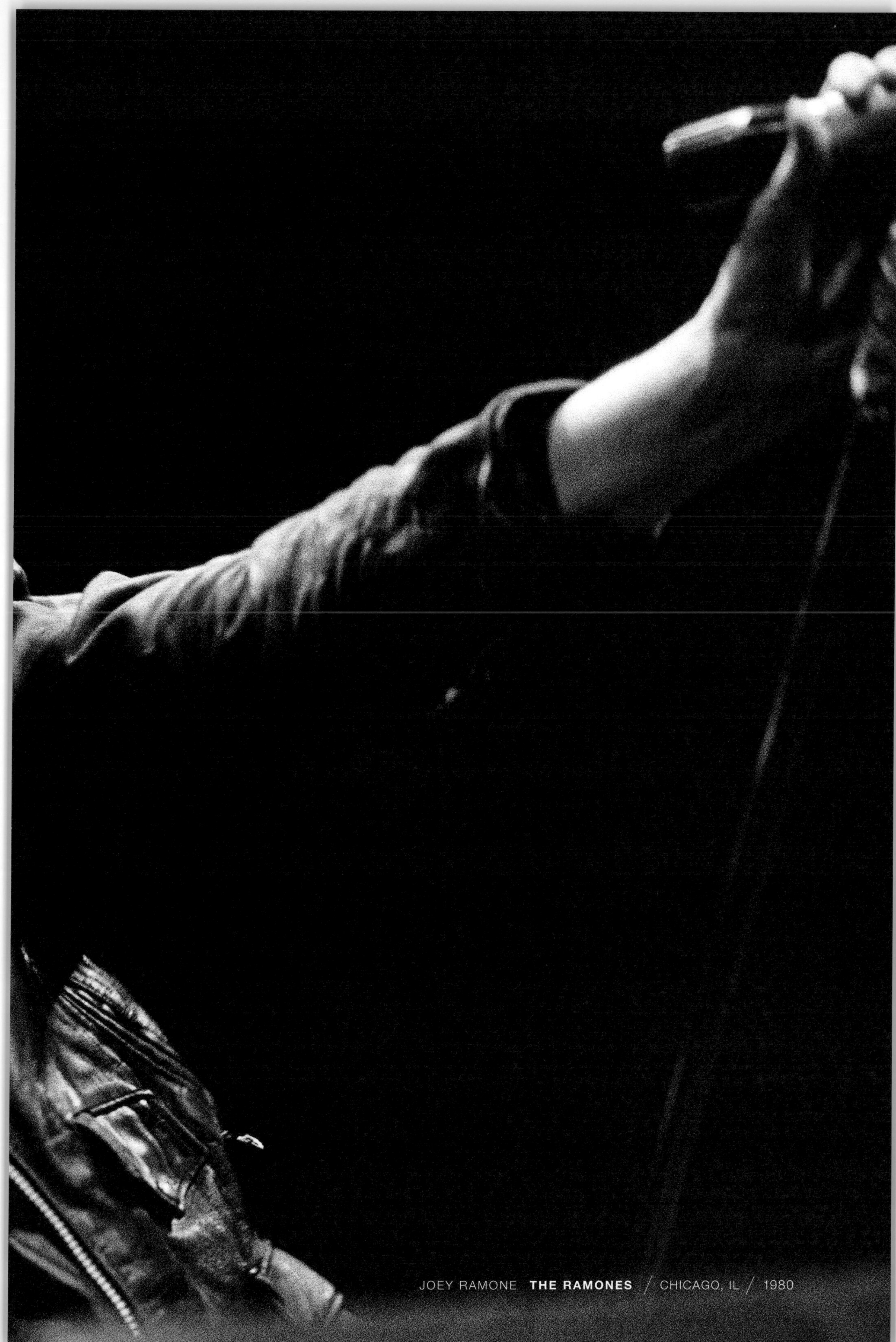

JOEY RAMONE **THE RAMONES** / CHICAGO, IL / 1980

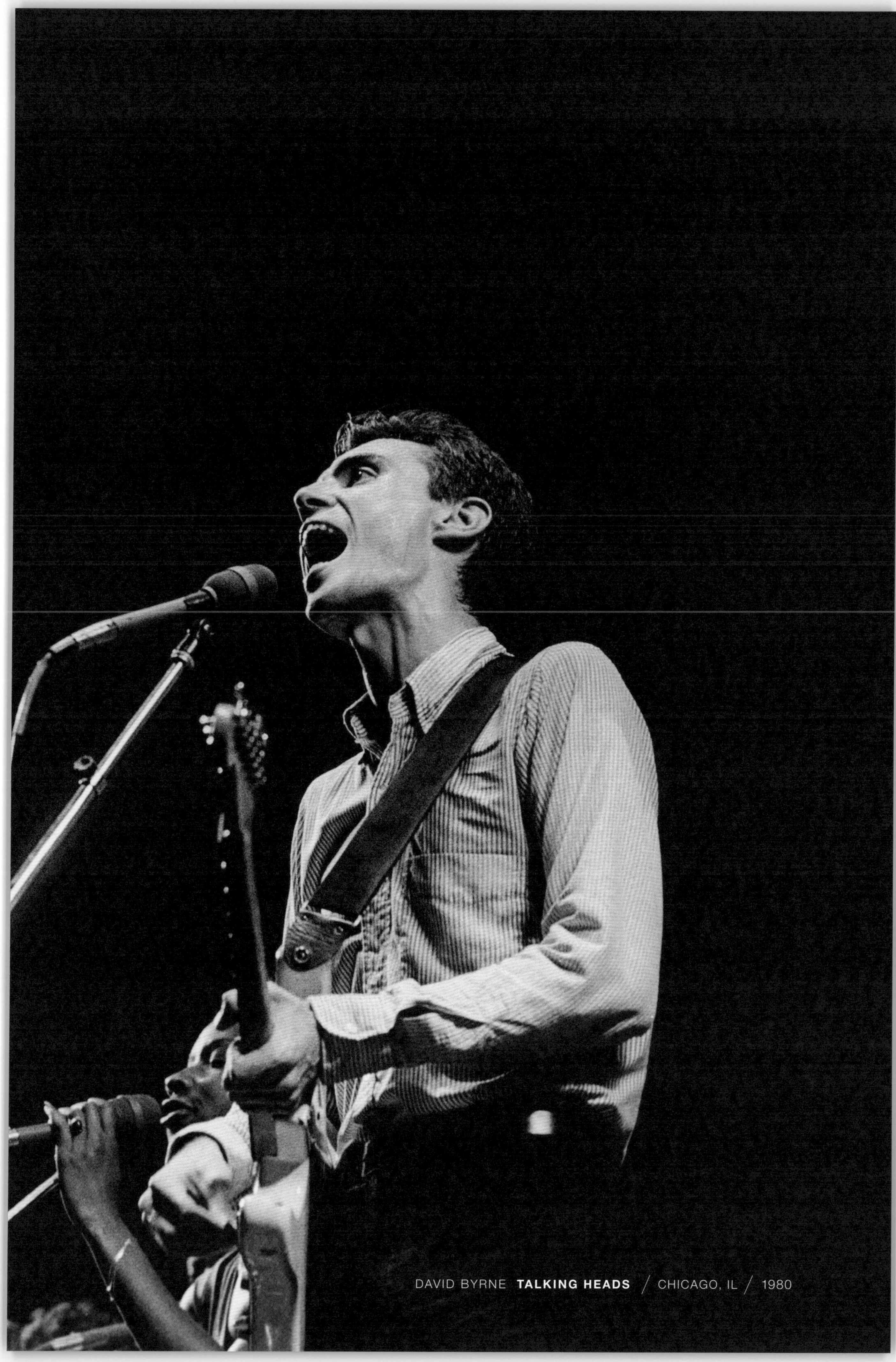

DAVID BYRNE **TALKING HEADS** / CHICAGO, IL / 1980

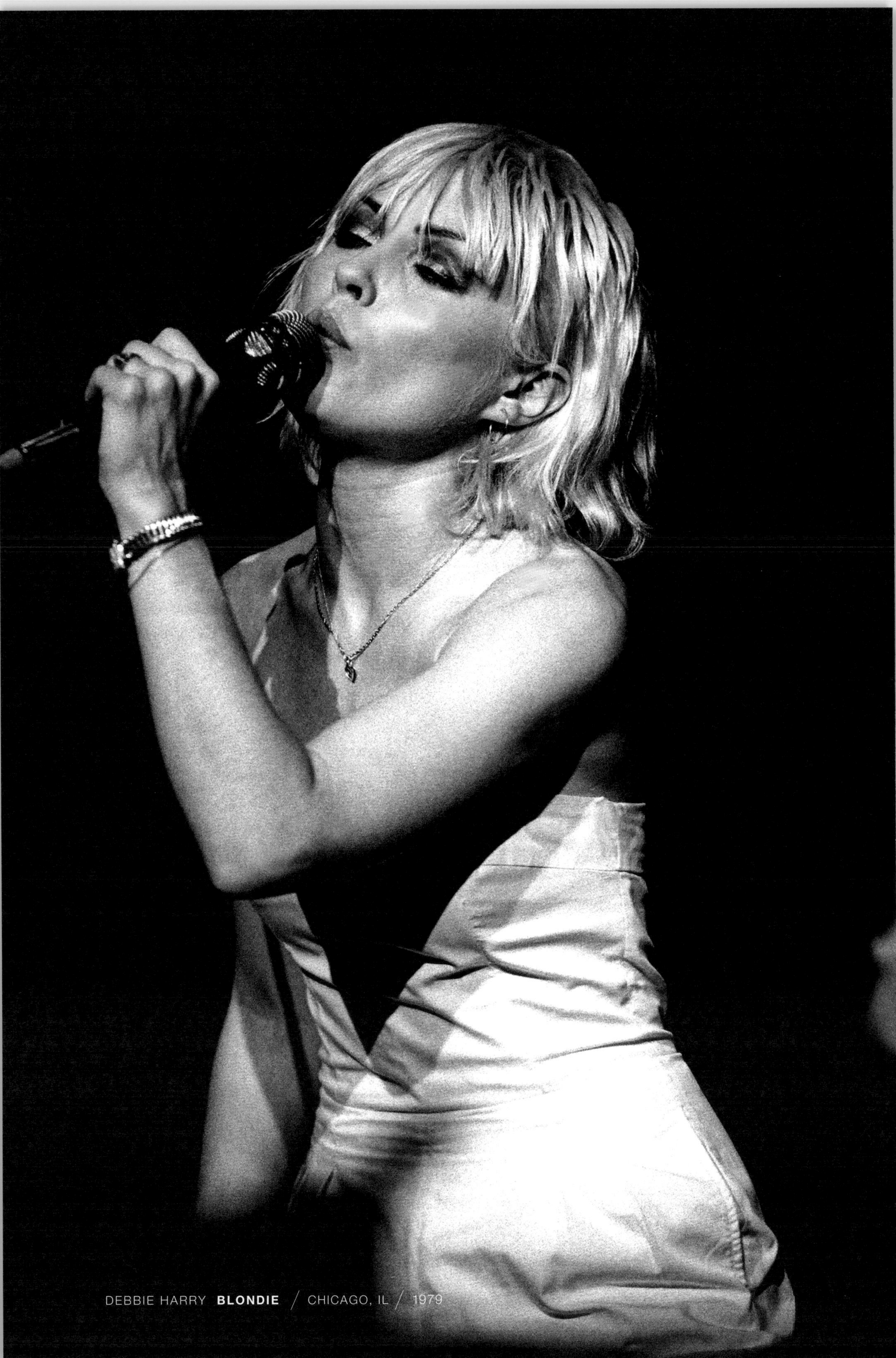

DEBBIE HARRY **BLONDIE** / CHICAGO, IL / 1979

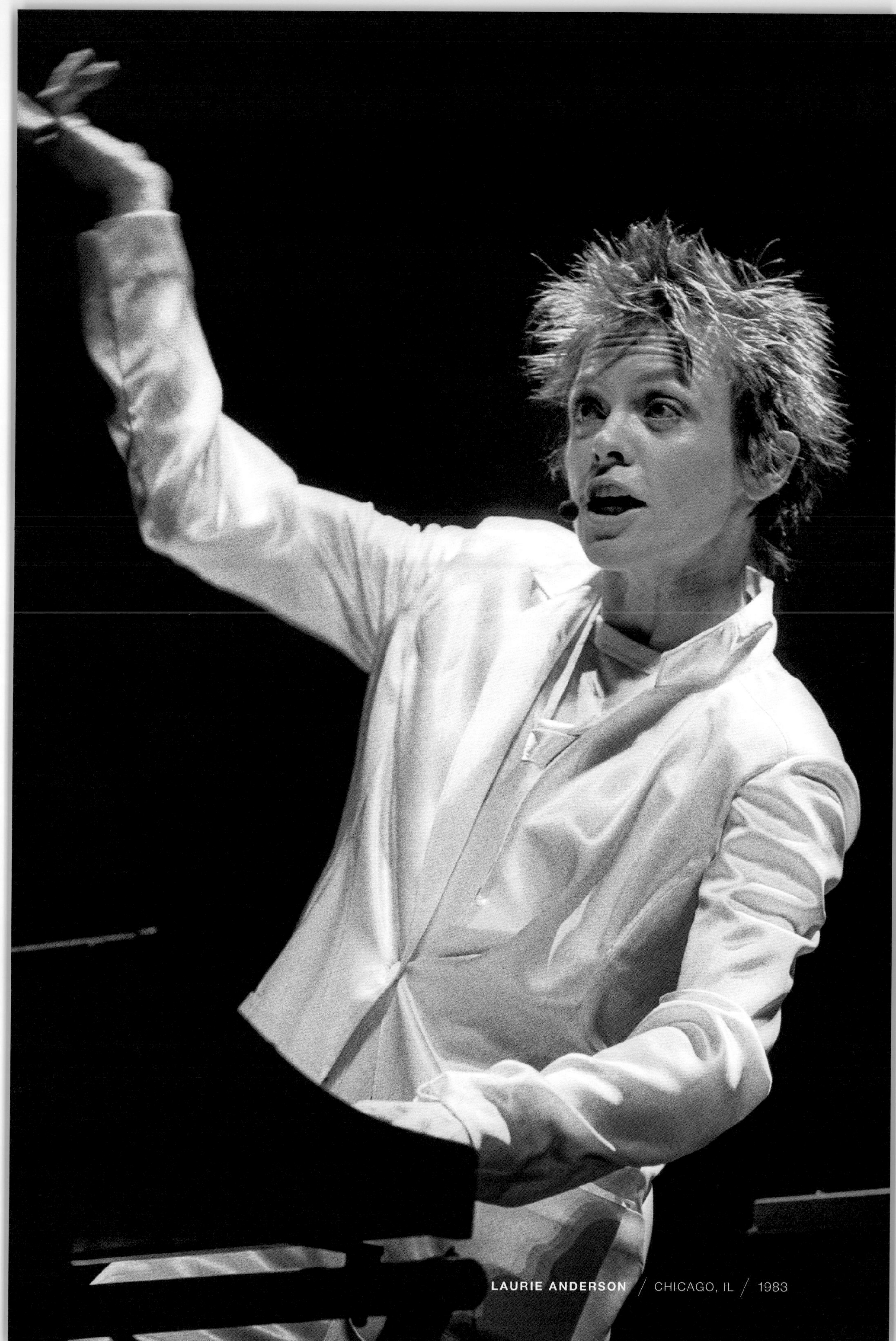

LAURIE ANDERSON / CHICAGO, IL / 1983

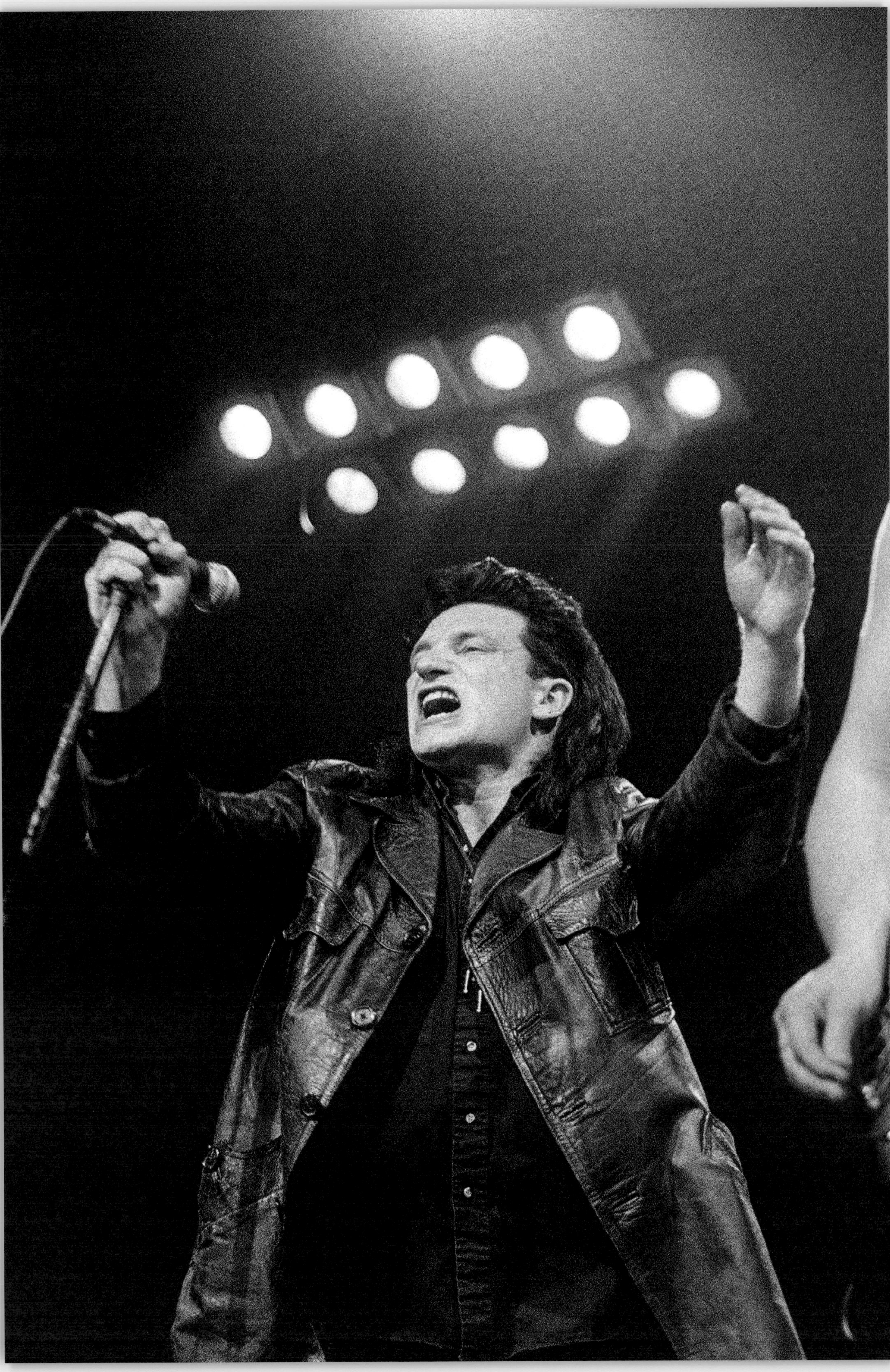

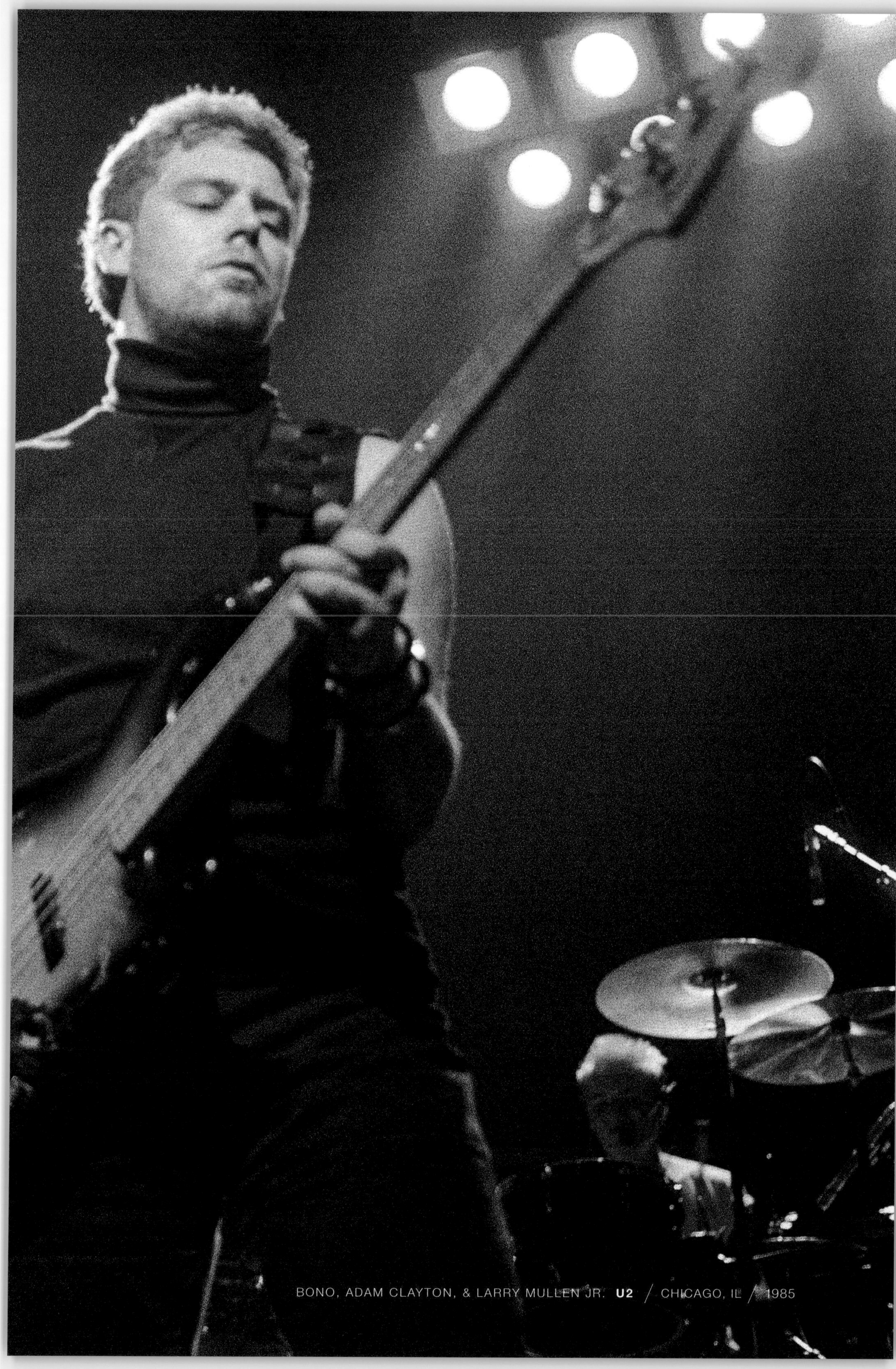

BONO, ADAM CLAYTON, & LARRY MULLEN JR. **U2** / CHICAGO, IL / 1985

EDDIE VEDDER **PEARL JAM** / CHICAGO, IL / 1994

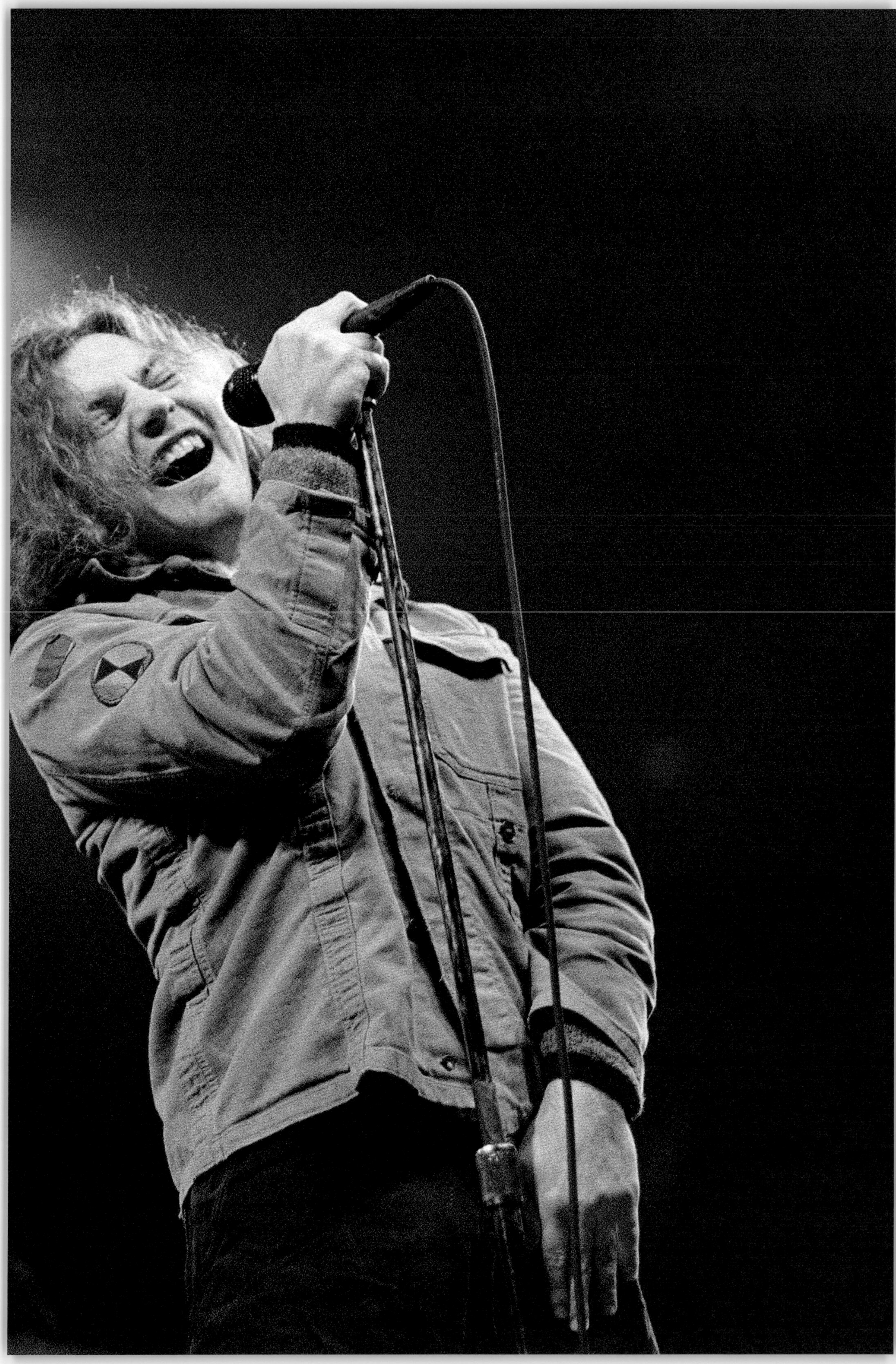

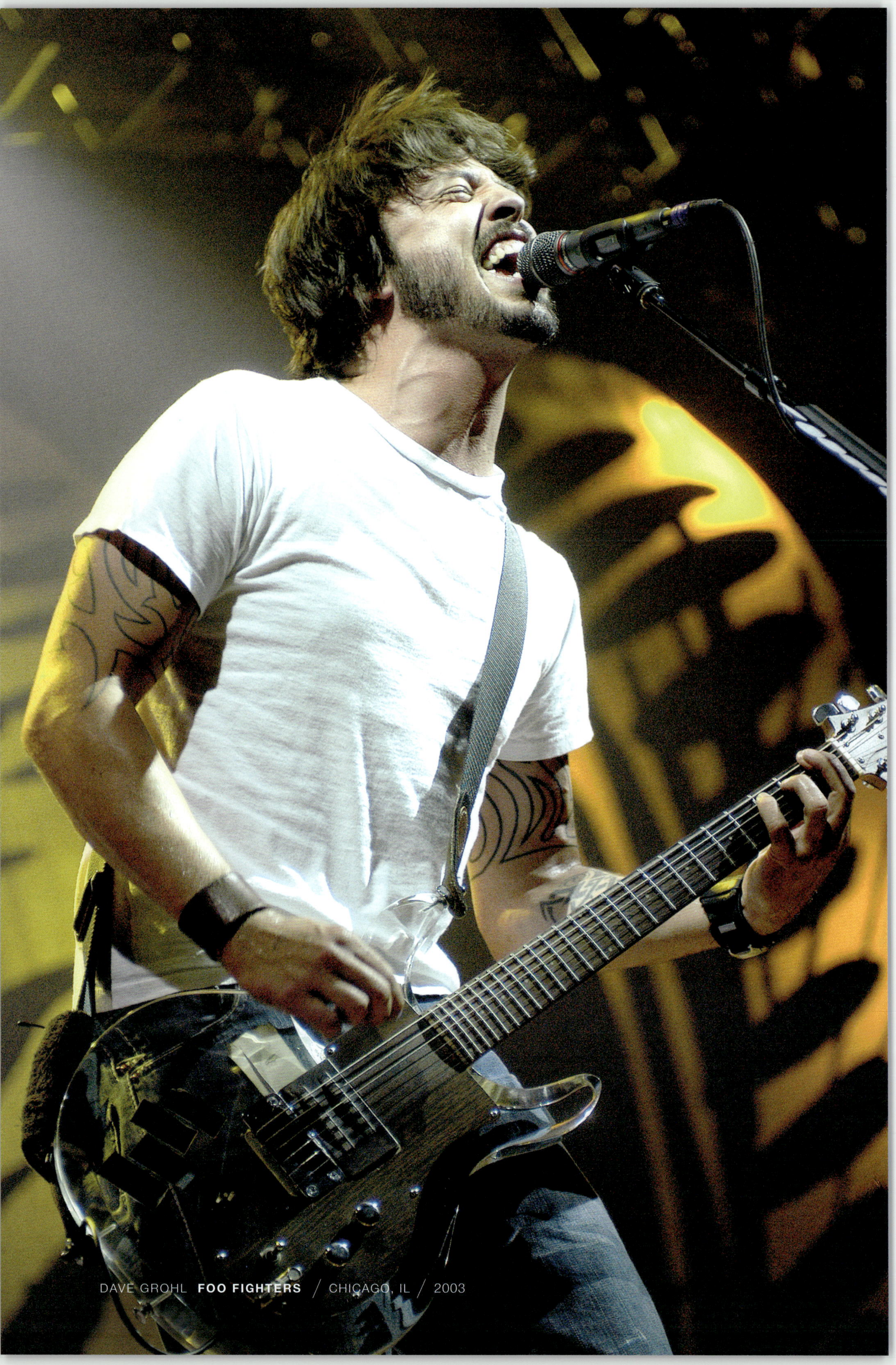

DAVE GROHL **FOO FIGHTERS** / CHICAGO, IL / 2003

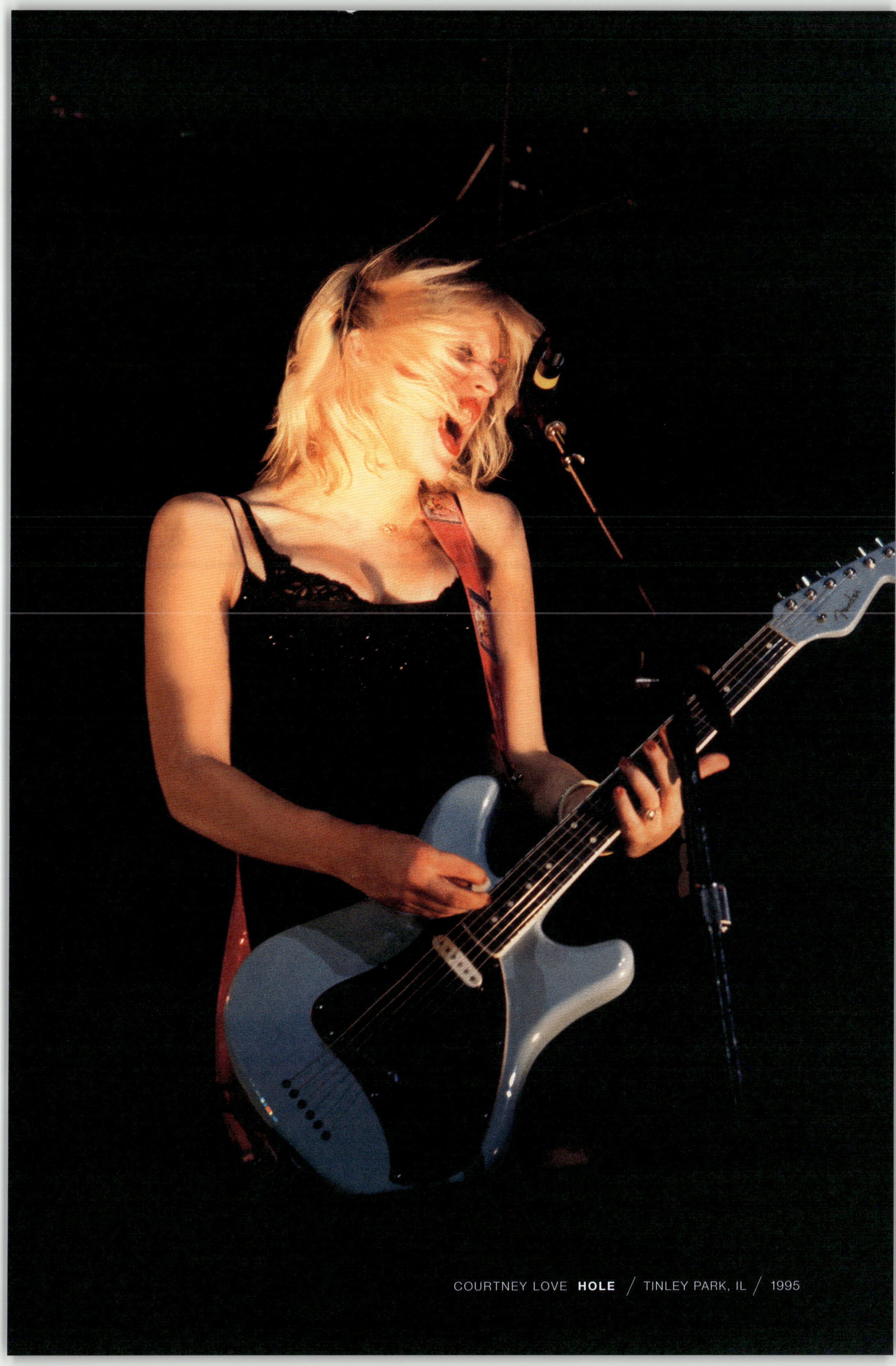

COURTNEY LOVE **HOLE** / TINLEY PARK, IL / 1995

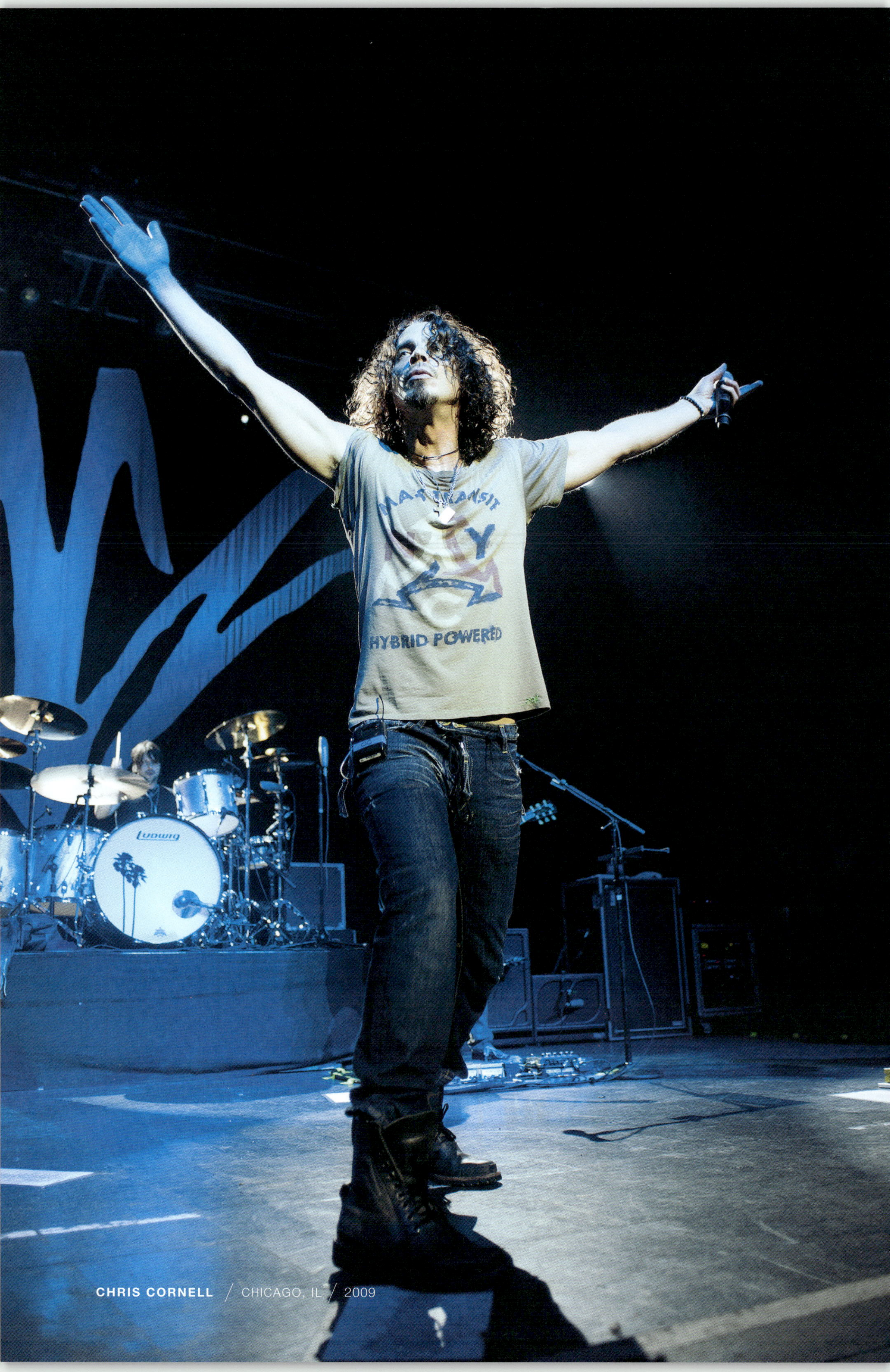

CHRIS CORNELL / CHICAGO, IL / 2009

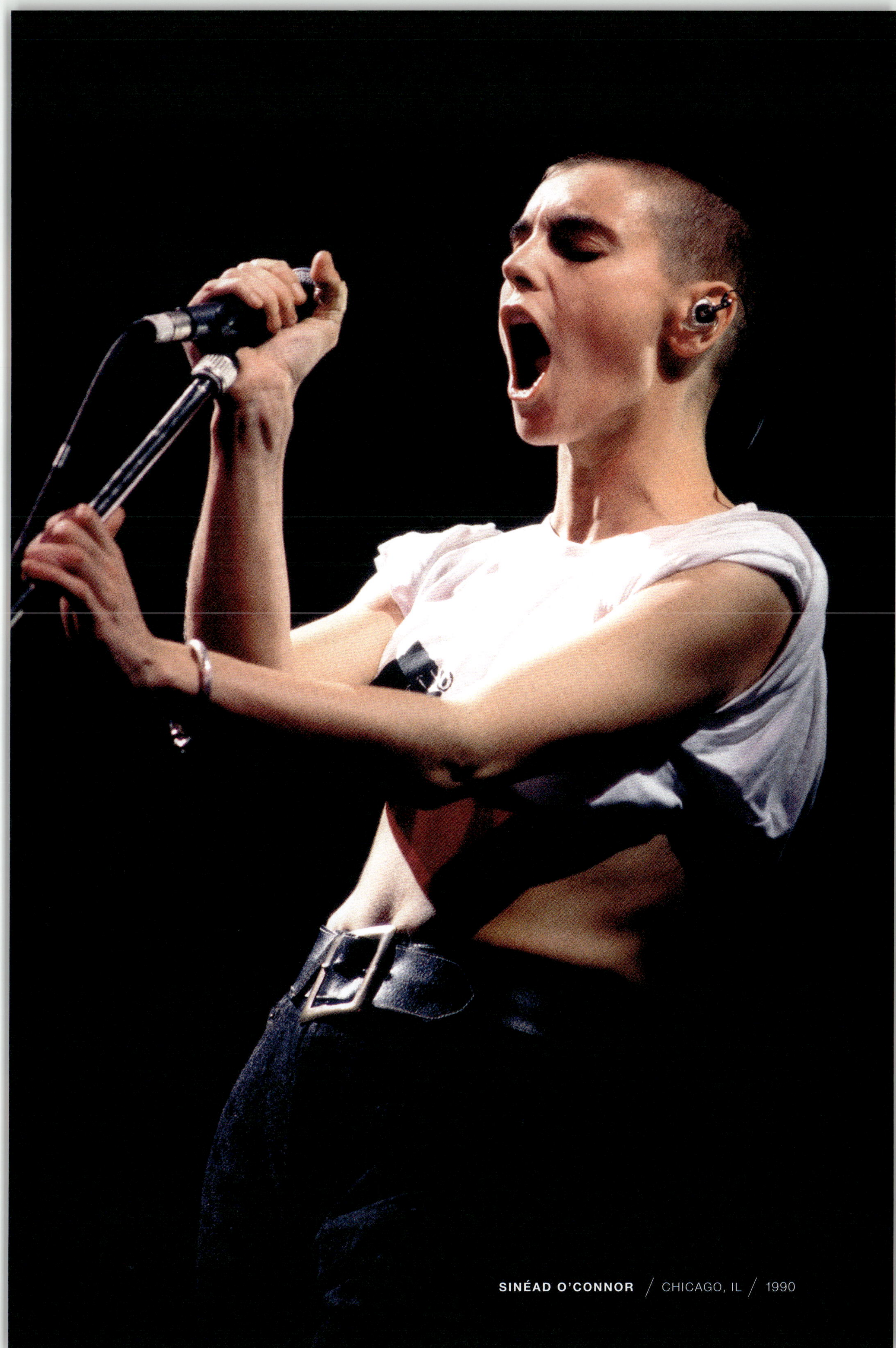

SINÉAD O'CONNOR / CHICAGO, IL / 1990

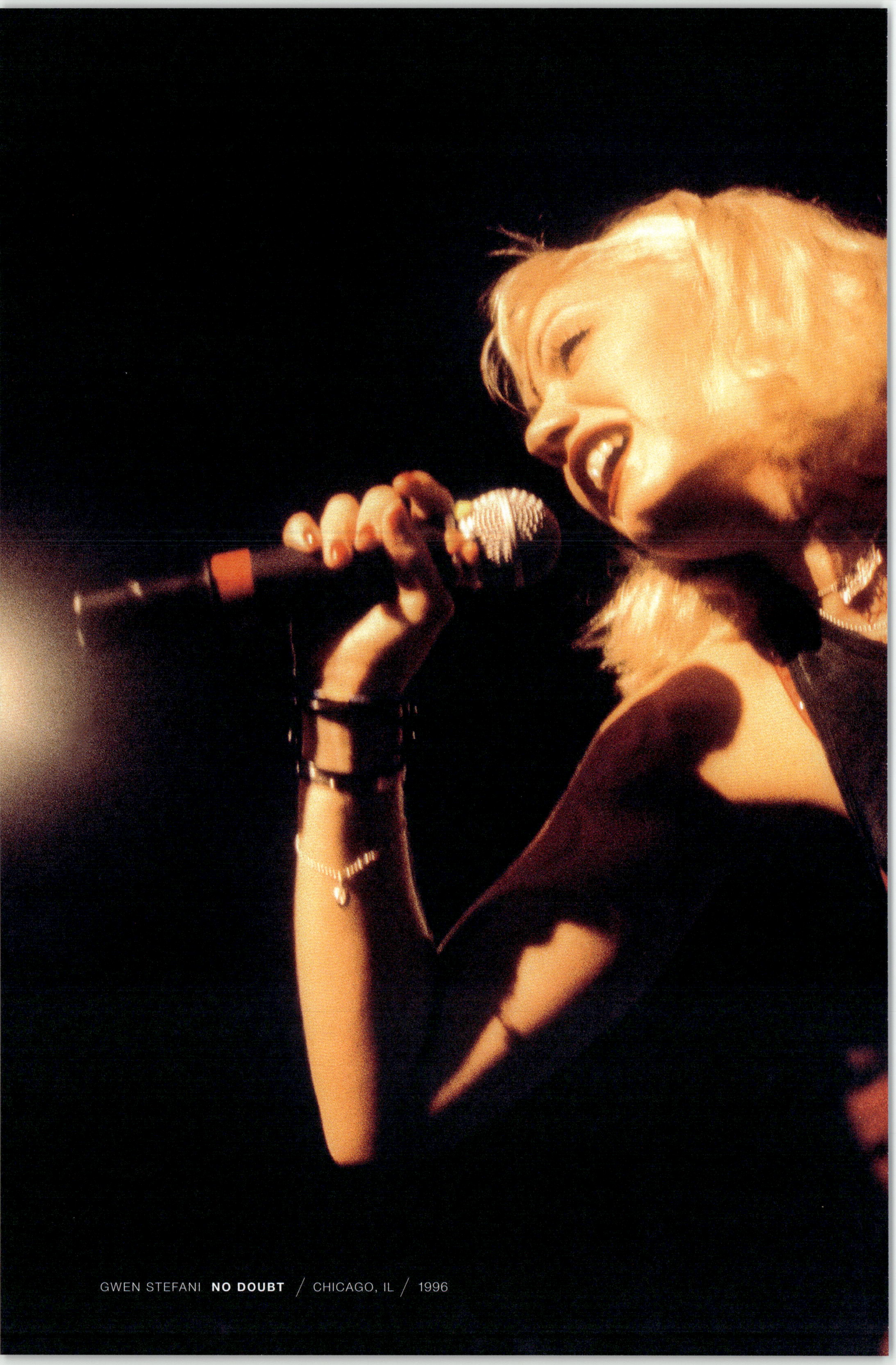

GWEN STEFANI **NO DOUBT** / CHICAGO, IL / 1996

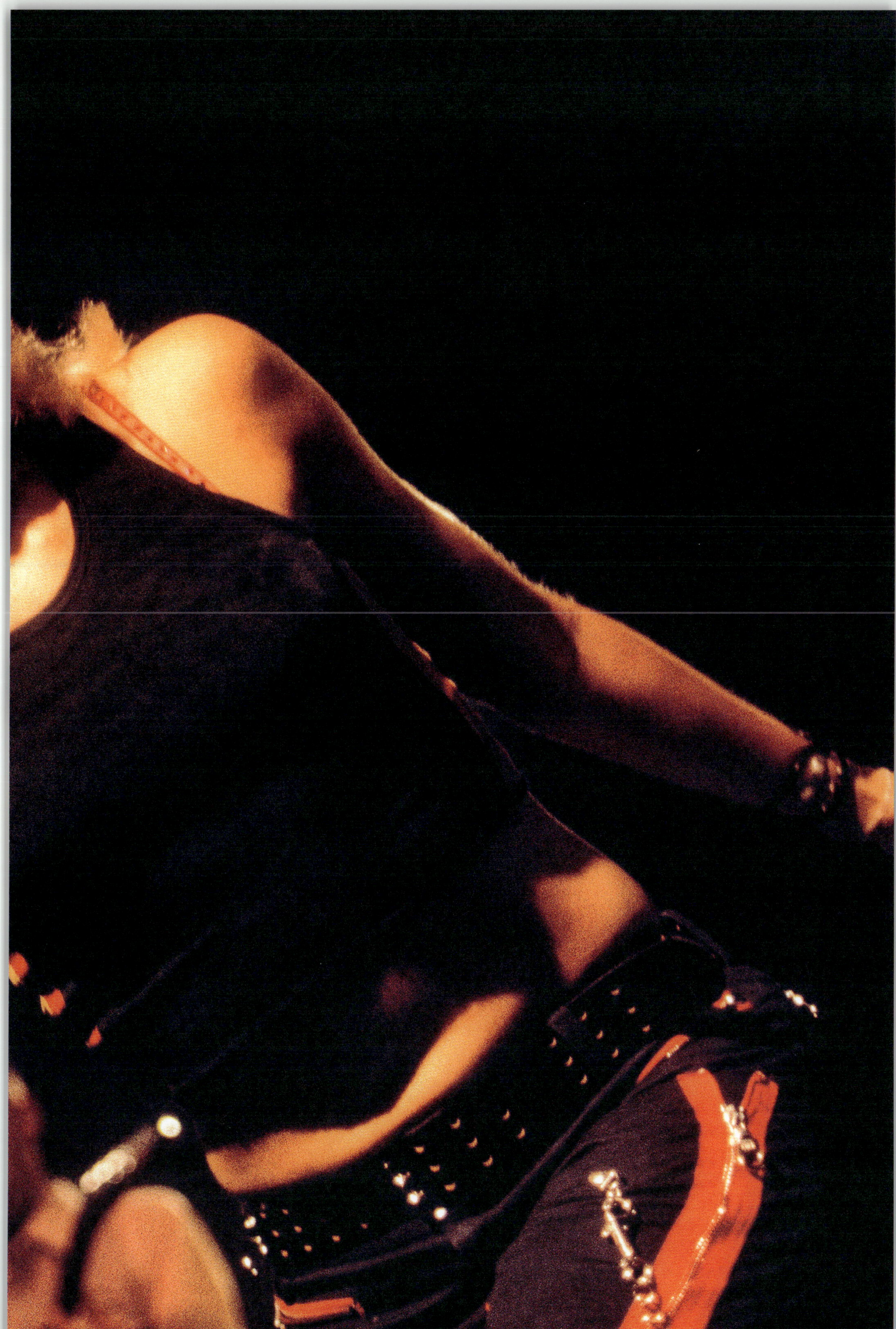

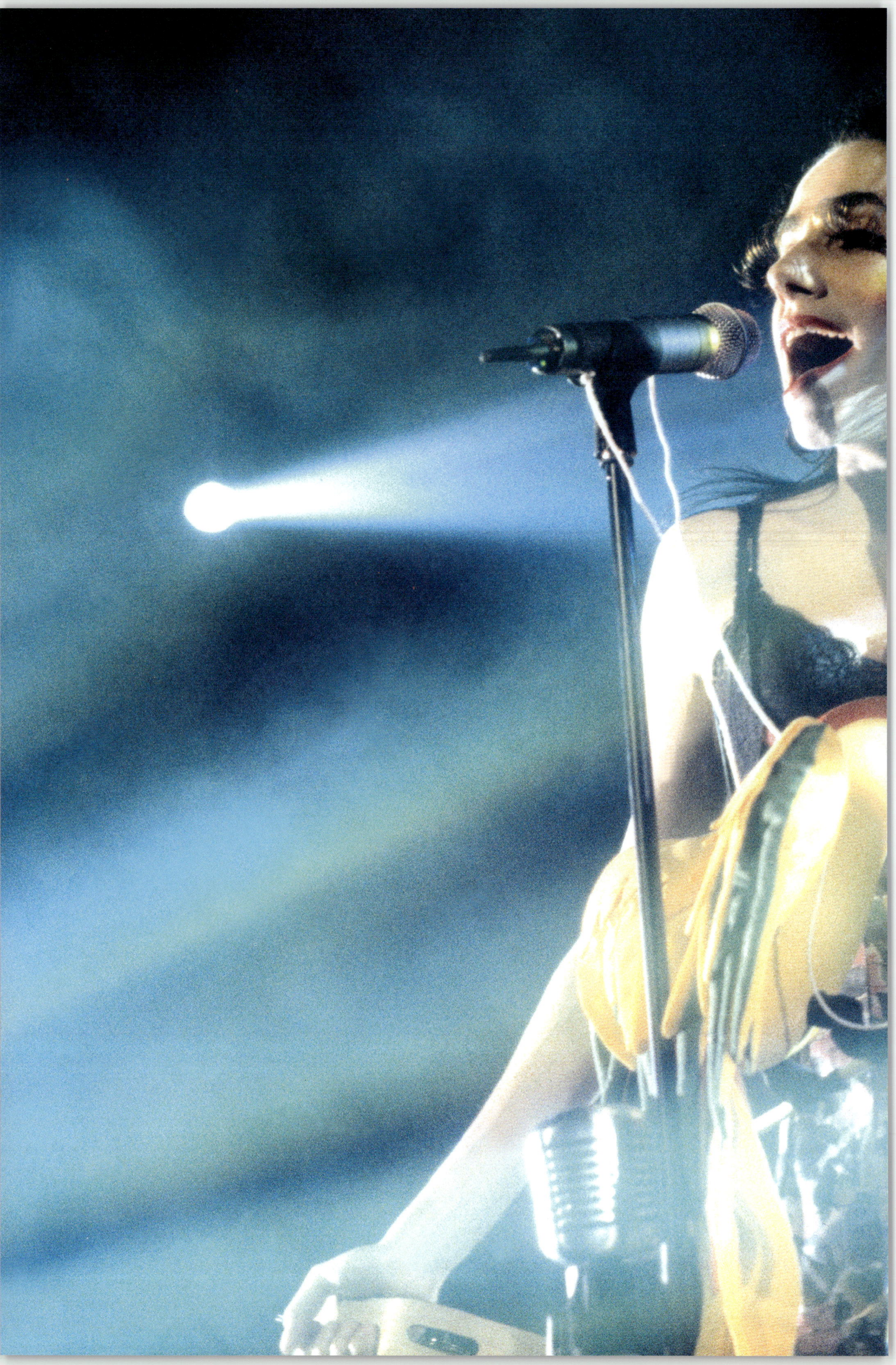

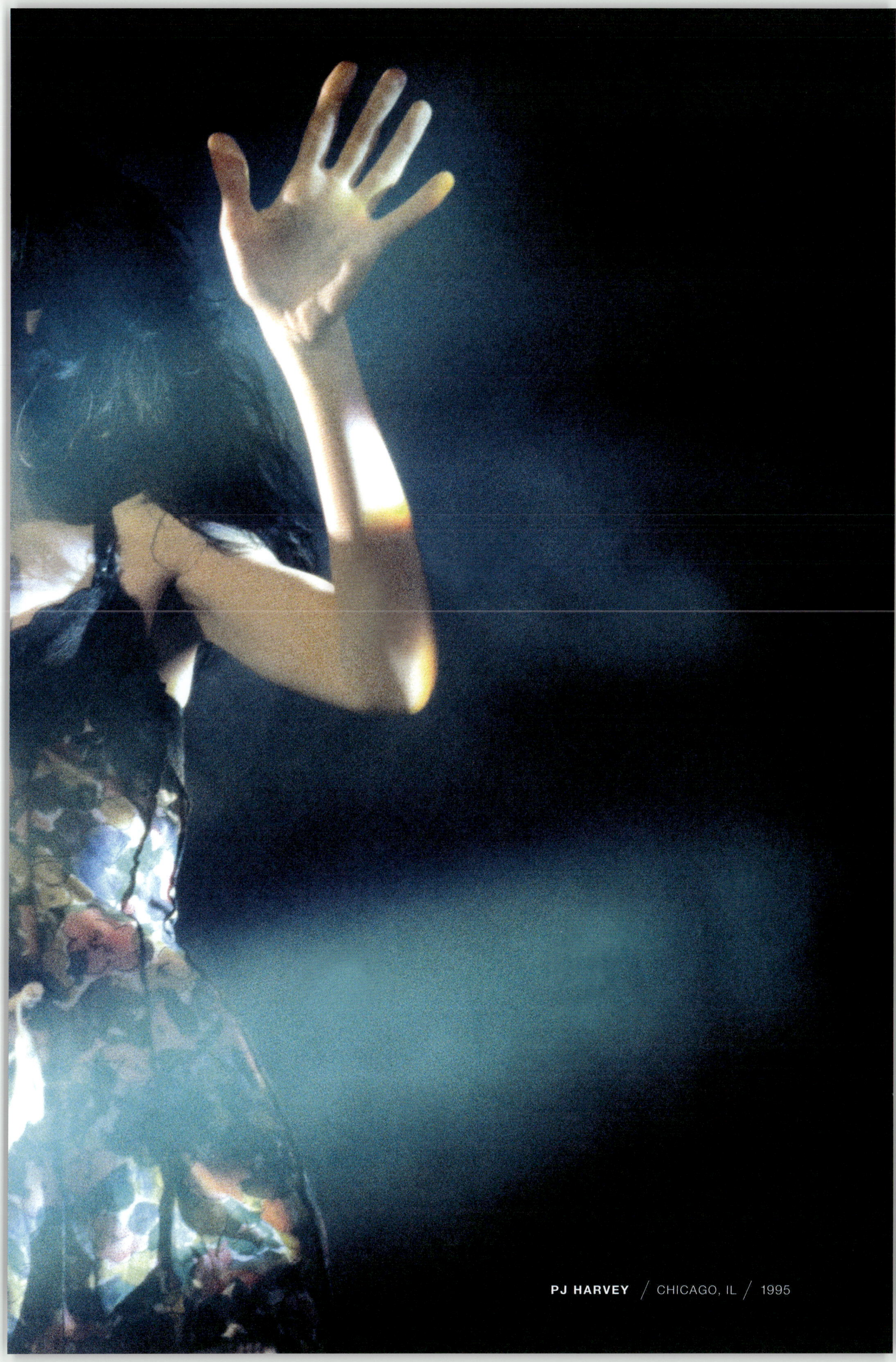

PJ HARVEY / CHICAGO, IL / 1995

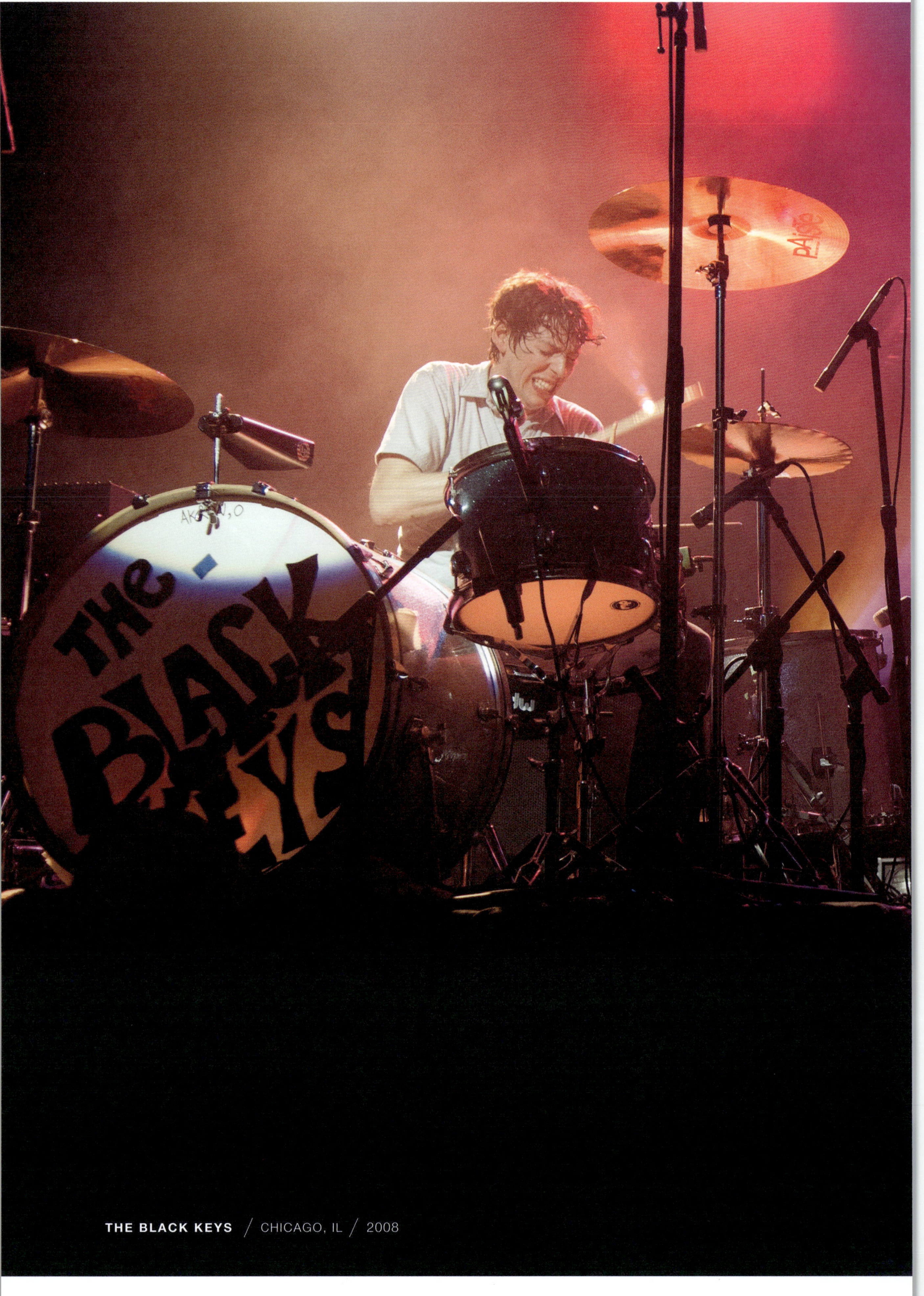

THE BLACK KEYS / CHICAGO, IL / 2008

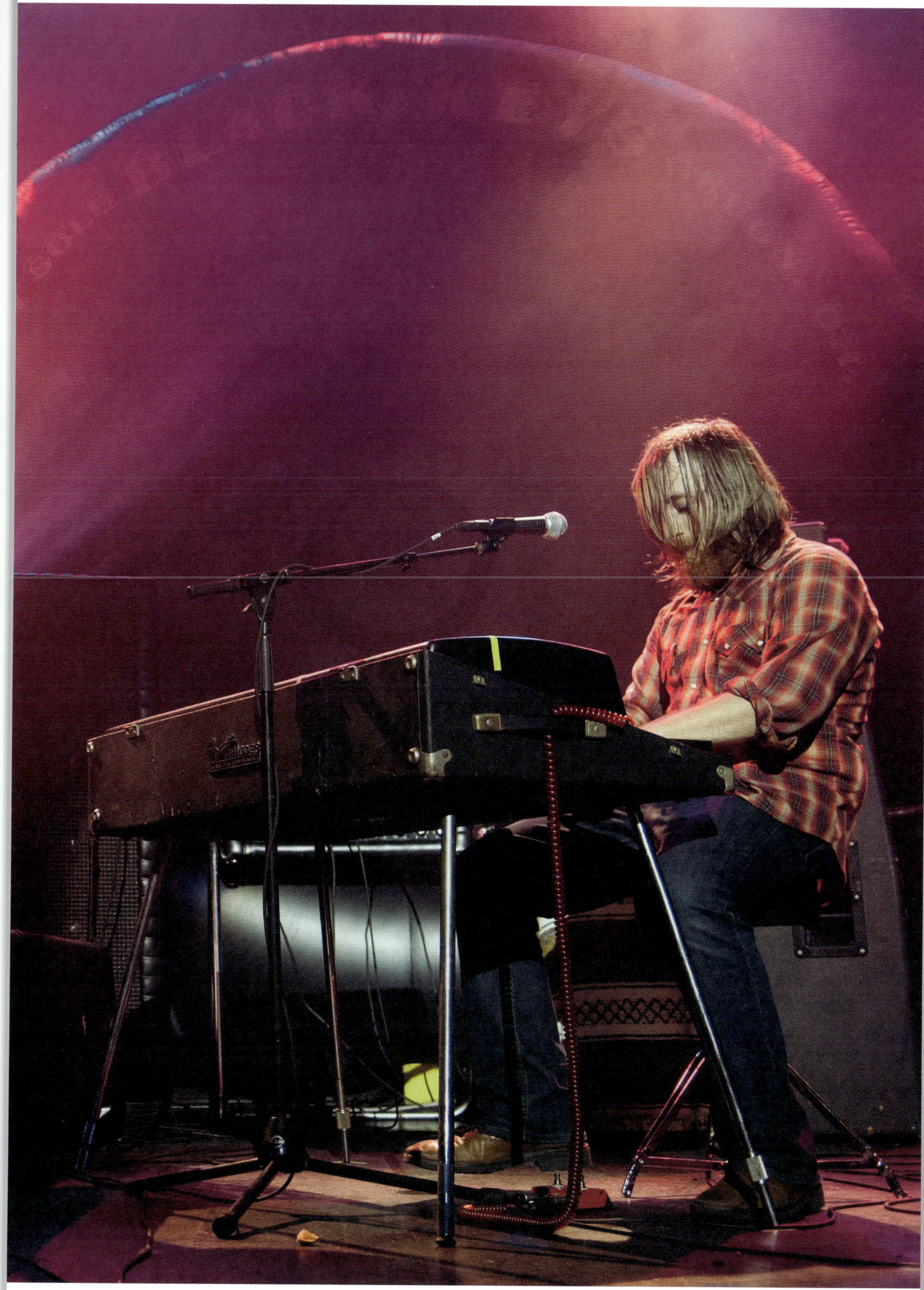

THE ASSISTANT

While traveling with the Rolling Stones in 1989, I was sitting next to keyboard player Chuck Leavell when the subject of new bands came up. He started talking about a new group from Atlanta whose record he had just made an appearance on. They were called The Black Crowes. I filed that information away in the back of my brain until April of the following year, when I read that the band was coming to play a show at Metro. I called their team to set up a photo shoot. A couple of days before the show, I was talking to my friend Keith Van Horne (of the 1985 Chicago Bears Super Bowl championship team) and suggested that he join me to check out this new band. He had just seen their video for "Jealous Again" on MTV and was an enthusiastic yes. I appointed him my "assistant" for the evening. We must have been an interesting sight–me at 5'2" and Keith towering over me at 6'7". We have all remained friends to this day, and not a time goes by when we are together that someone doesn't bring up the time I brought the world's largest assistant to a photo shoot!

Chicago Bear Keith Van Horne:

"We looked like that movie *Twins* with Arnold Schwarzenegger and Danny DeVito. That was the one and only time I was his assistant, but that should be in quotes. I don't think I was very good at it, and he was just being nice by introducing me to the band, who I really liked. I hadn't heard any music like that in a long time, that blues-based rock 'n' roll. It reminded me of Humble Pie and the Stones. We all became good friends and any time they came to town, I was there. That's the great thing about Paul–he is a great connector of people."

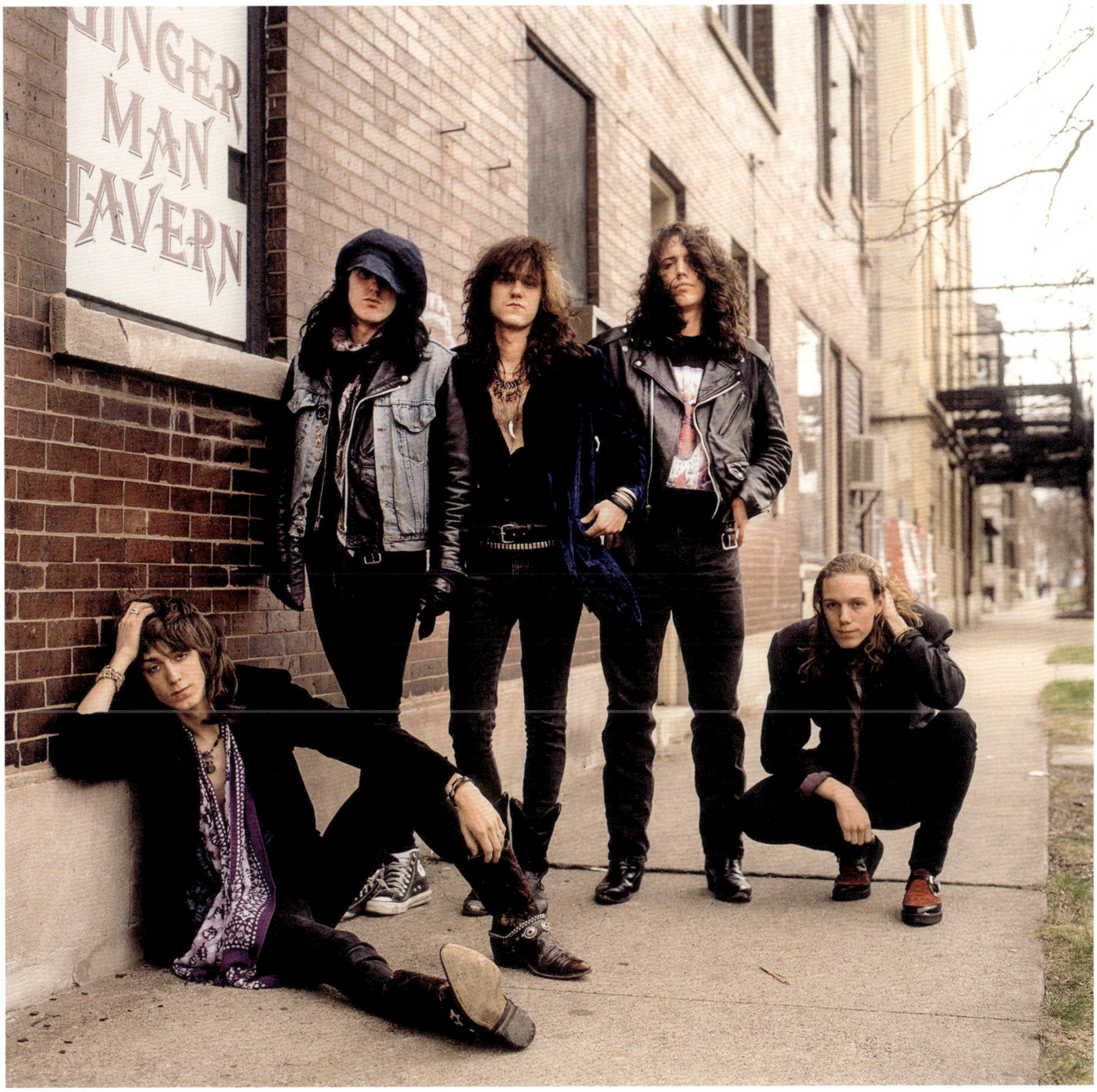

The Black Crowes drummer Steve Gorman:
"It was our first tour and our first time ever in Chicago. I didn't know Paul Natkin's name at the time, but I remember someone said, 'You're doing a shoot with Paul Natkin and he's big time.' There was this sense of, this is a photographer we're supposed to know and care about. And he showed up and brought along Keith Van Horne to that shoot and everyone was struck by that juxtaposition. I remember my first thought was, that's the biggest photo assistant I've ever seen in my life! But both of those guys became a part of our universe right away. And in a short time what I realized was that The Black Crowes became part of Paul's universe. He was far grander and more wide-reaching than anything we had ever done or would do, honestly. The few shows over the next 23 years when Paul wasn't there, his absence was always noted and felt. He was an indelible part of The Black Crowes' Chicago experience from start to finish."

THE BLACK CROWES / CHICAGO, IL / 1990

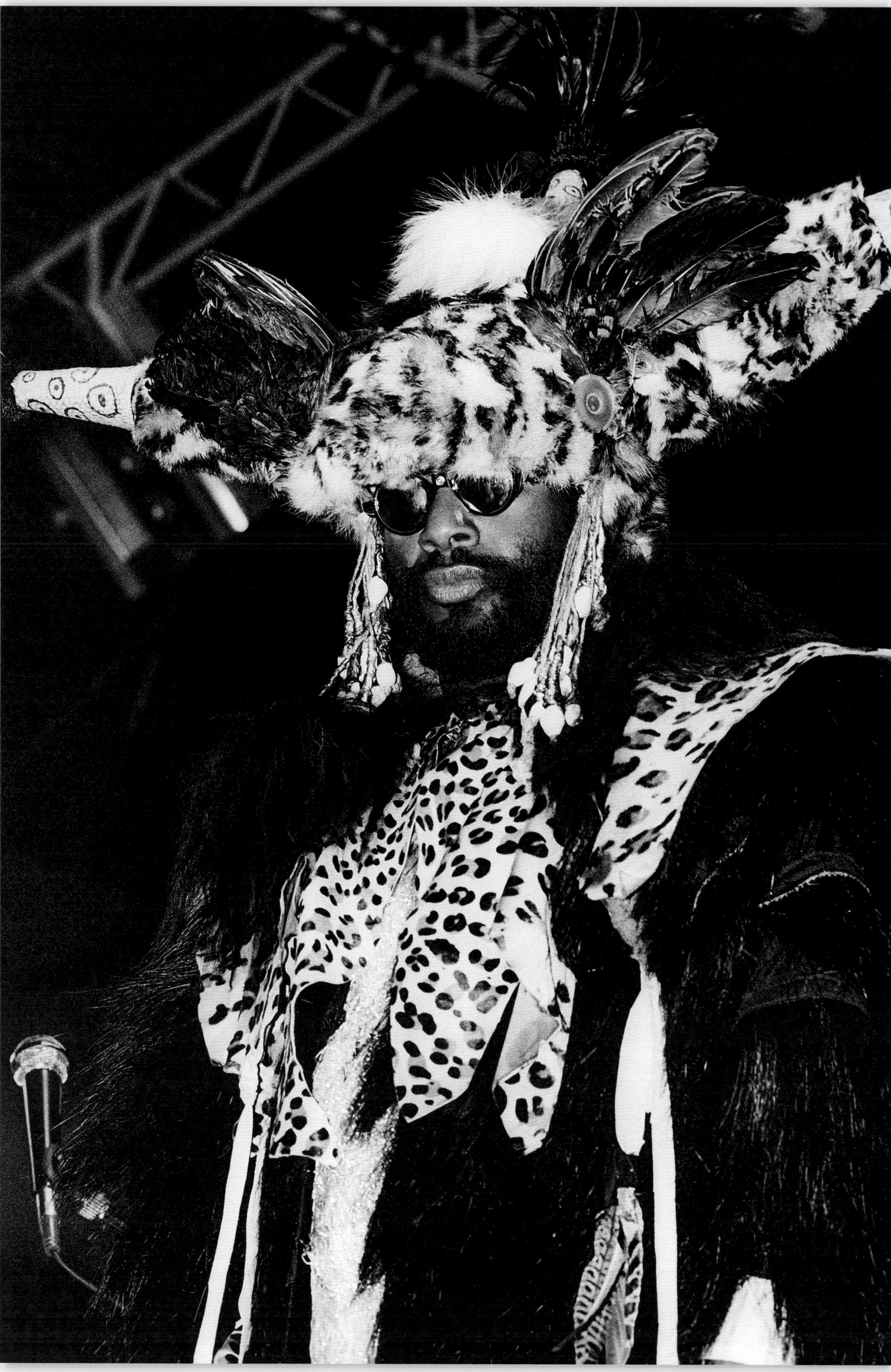

5

SOUL+ R&B
GROOVE, FUNK & POP

To hear a classic song from Aretha's mouth, to hear Whitney Houston's incredible voice or hear the harmonies of The Temptations is what makes it a joy to do what I do.

GEORGE CLINTON **PARLIAMENT FUNKADELIC** / CHICAGO, IL / 1984

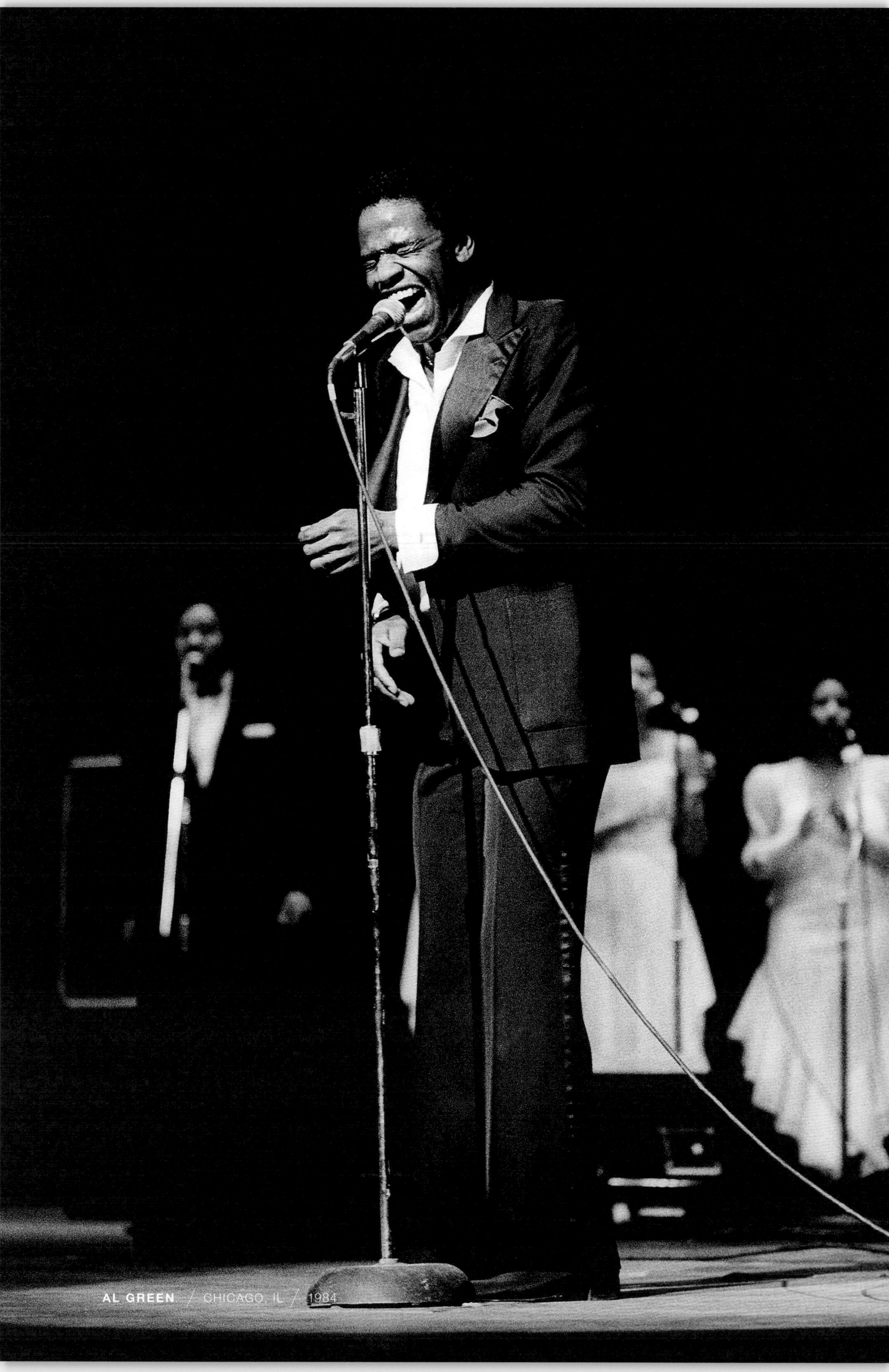

AL GREEN / CHICAGO, IL / 1984

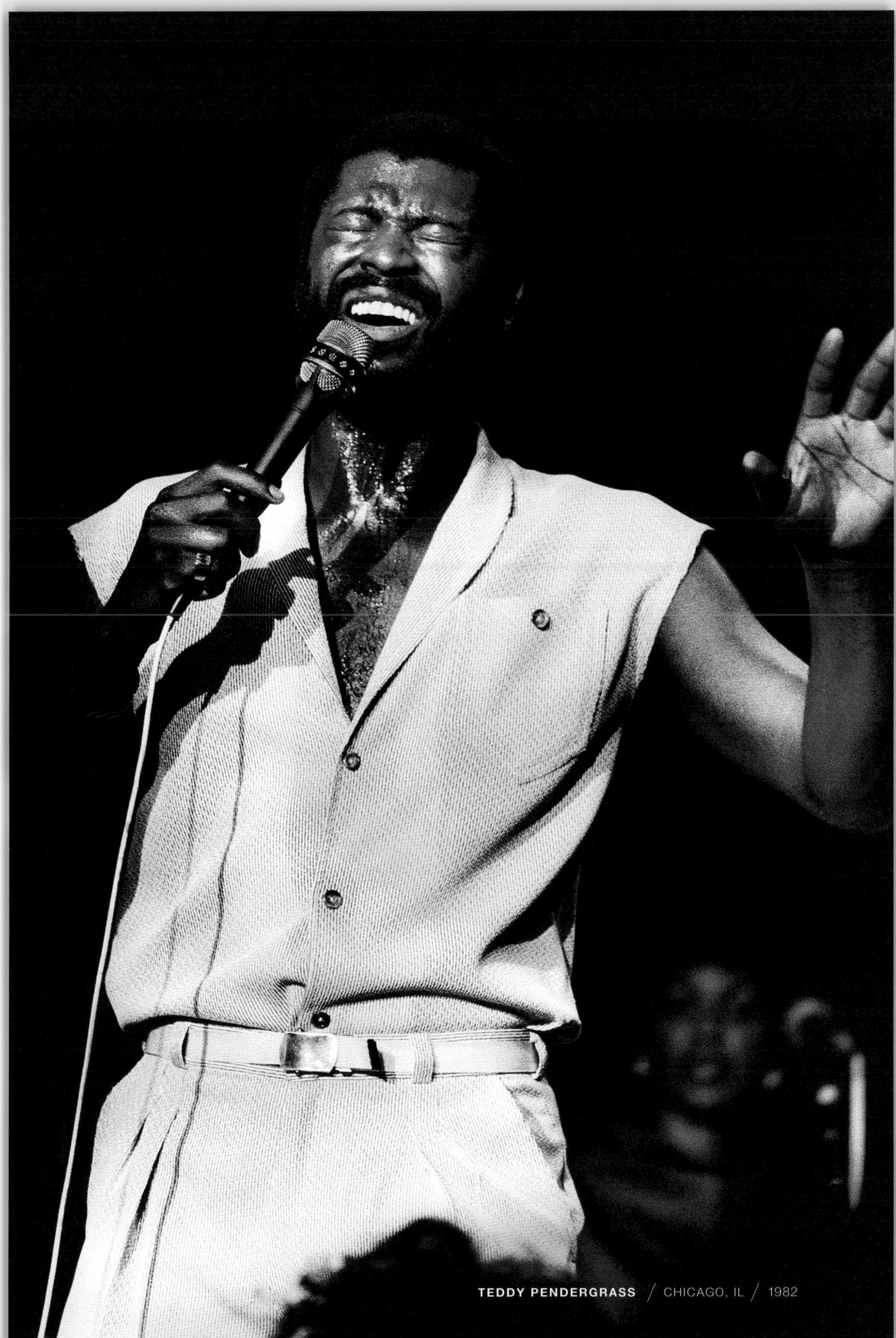

TEDDY PENDERGRASS / CHICAGO, IL / 1982

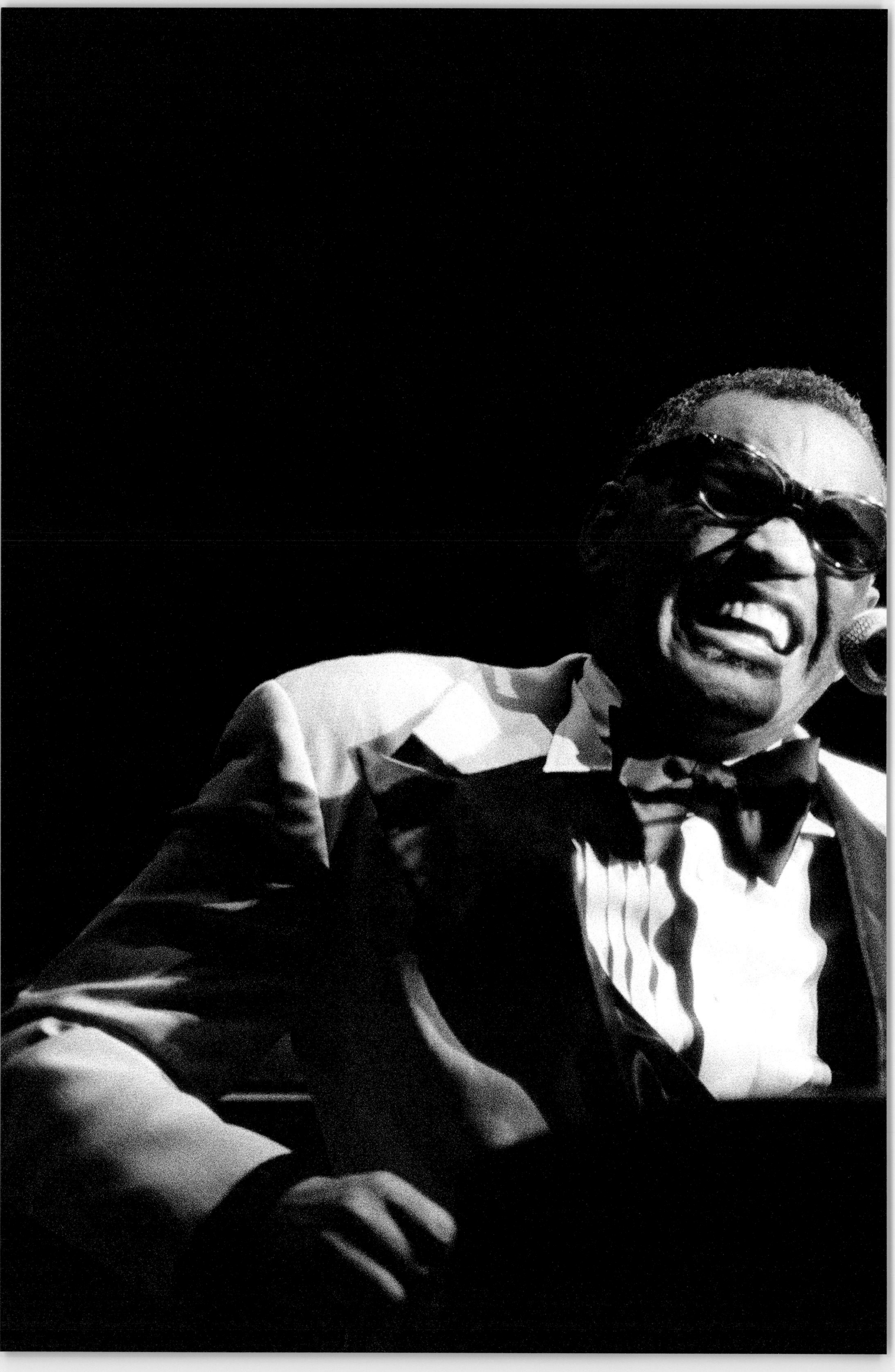

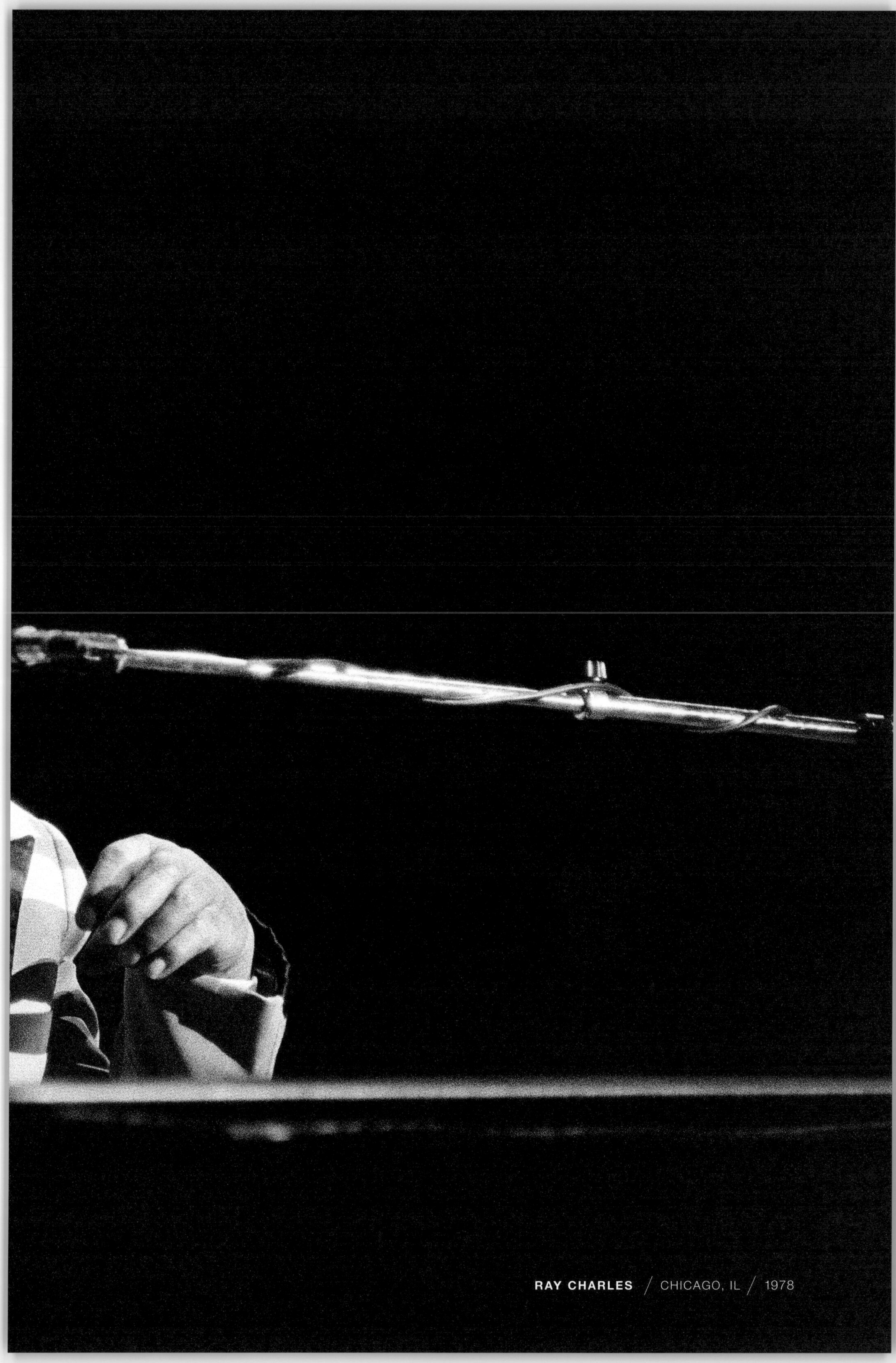

RAY CHARLES / CHICAGO, IL / 1978

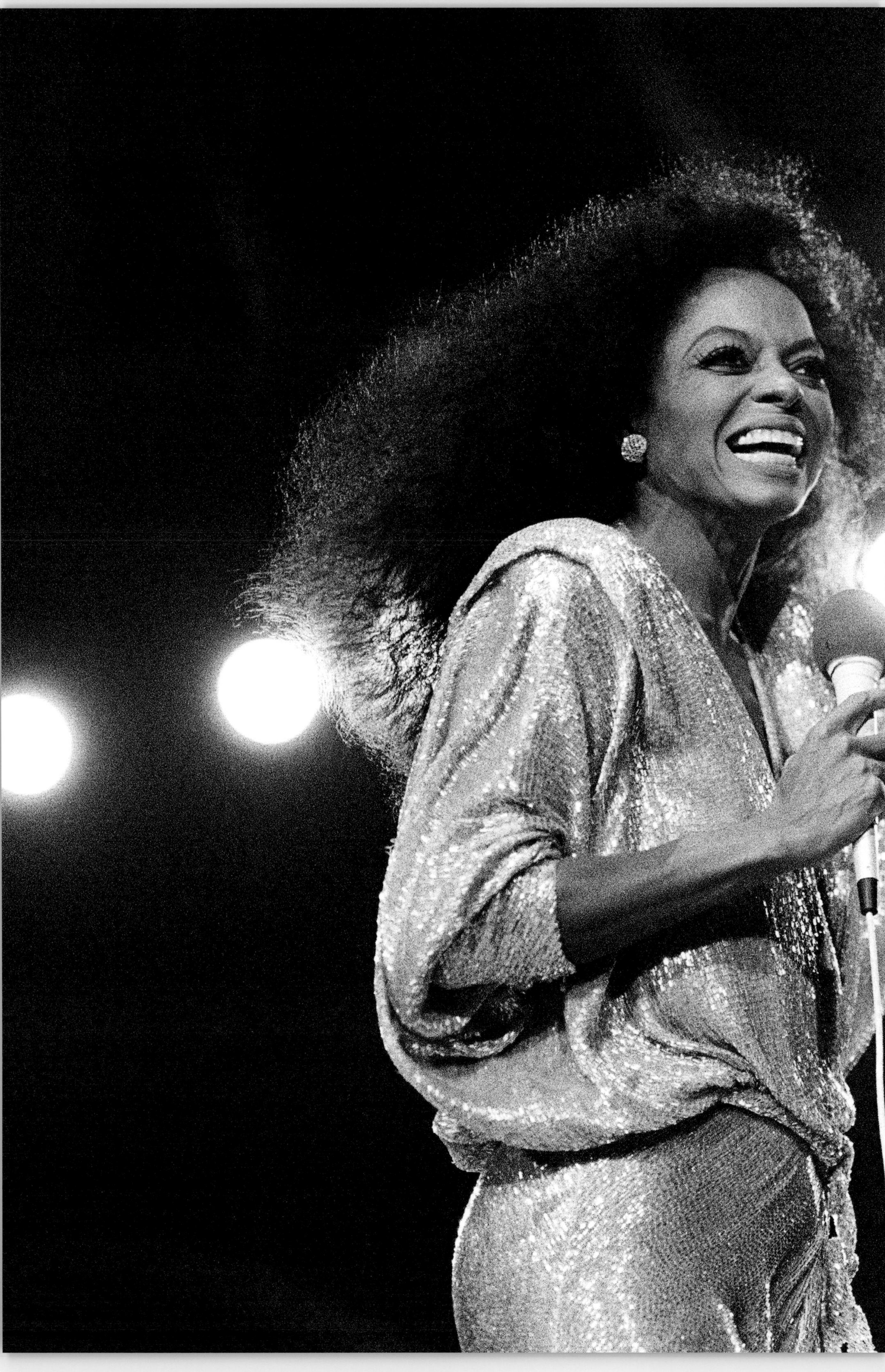

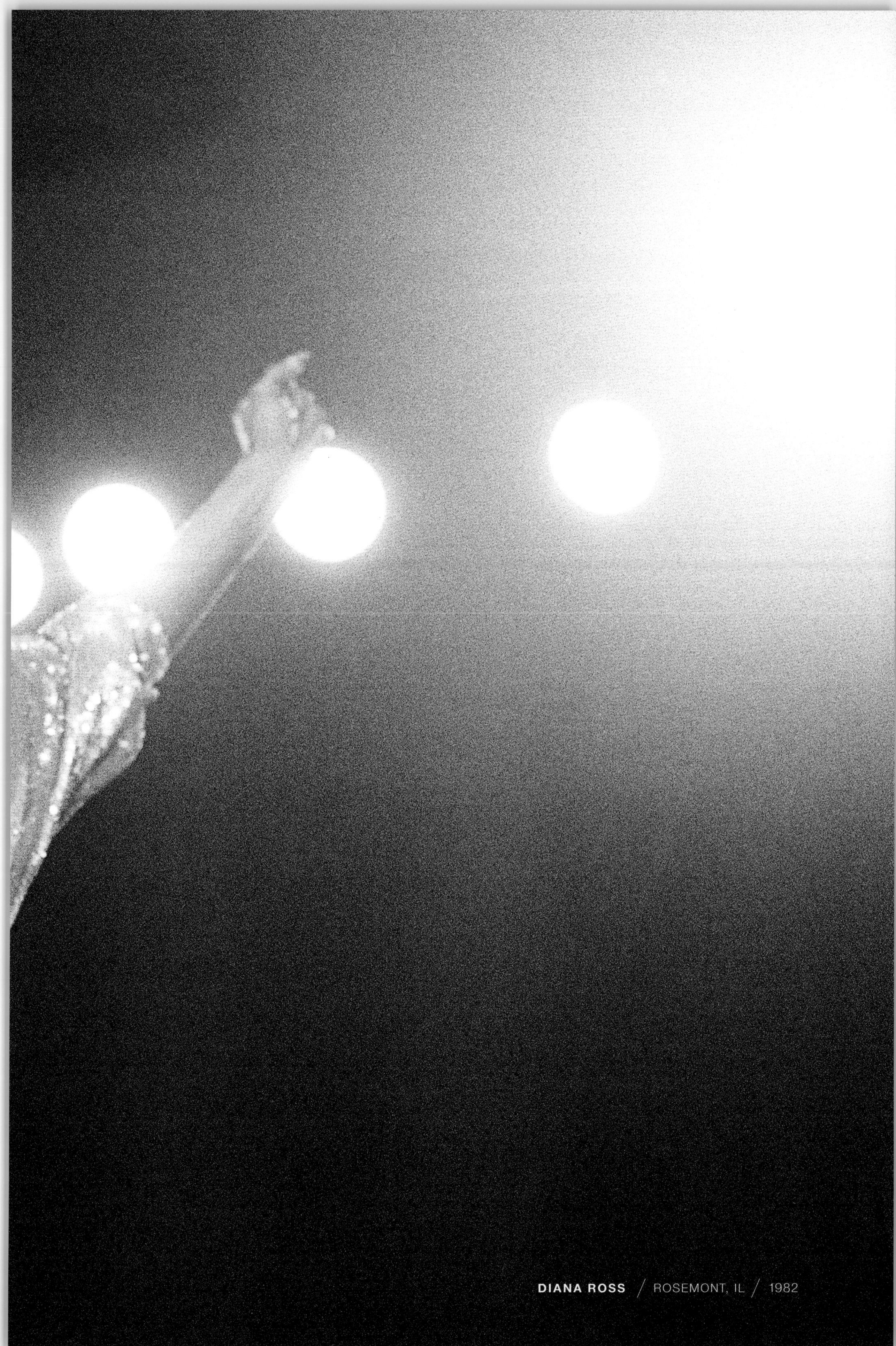

DIANA ROSS / ROSEMONT, IL / 1982

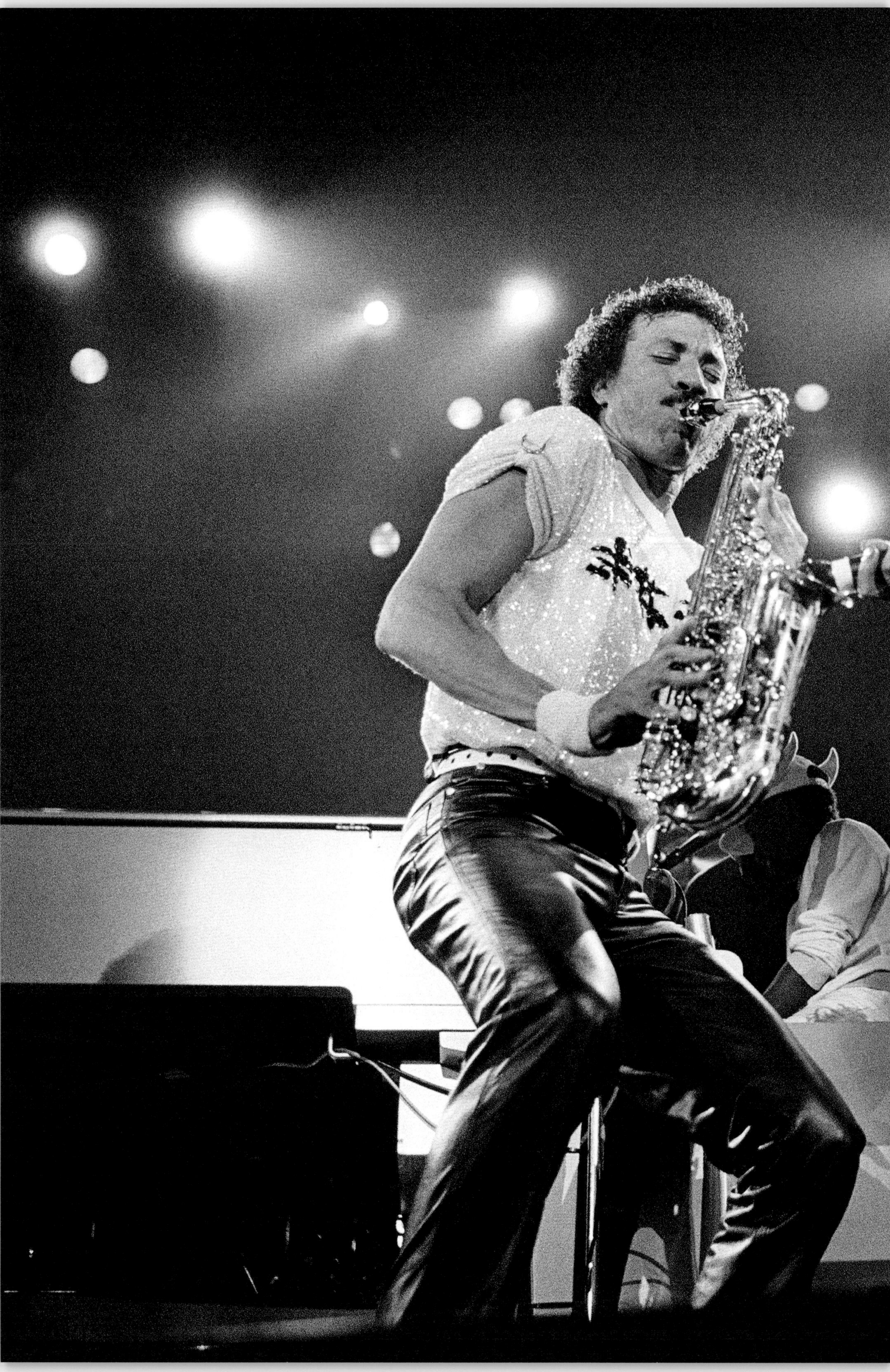

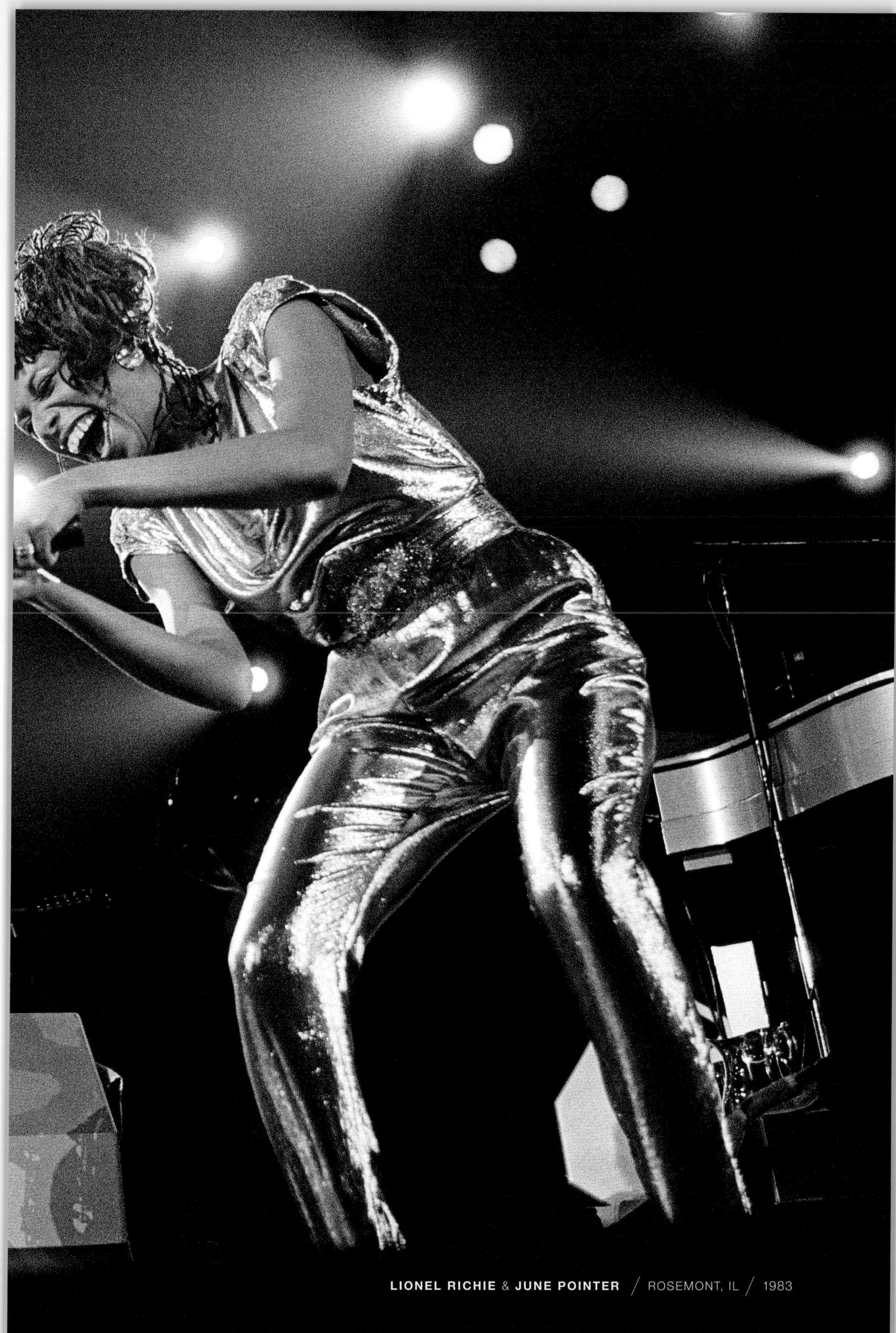

LIONEL RICHIE & **JUNE POINTER** / ROSEMONT, IL / 1983

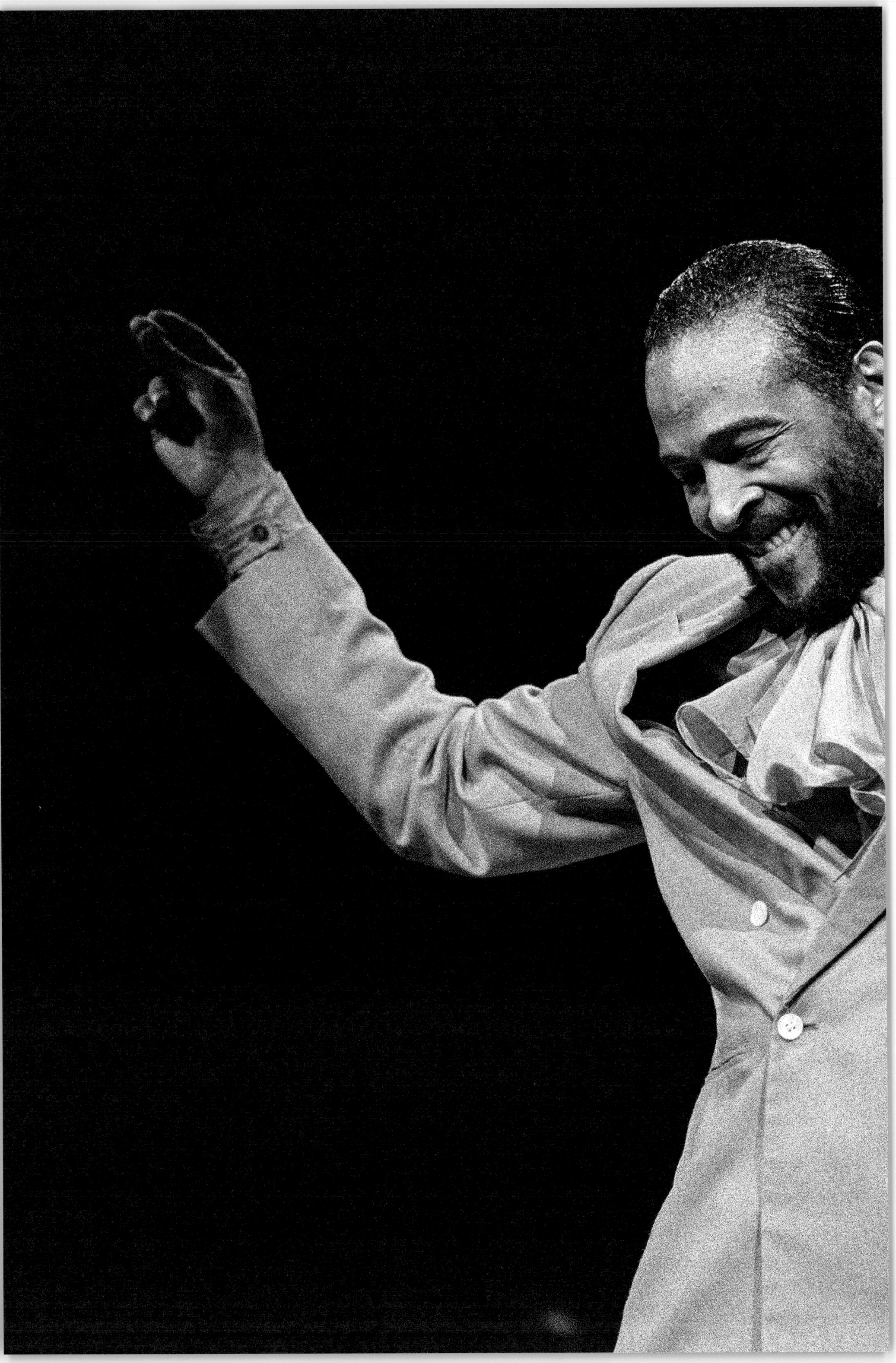

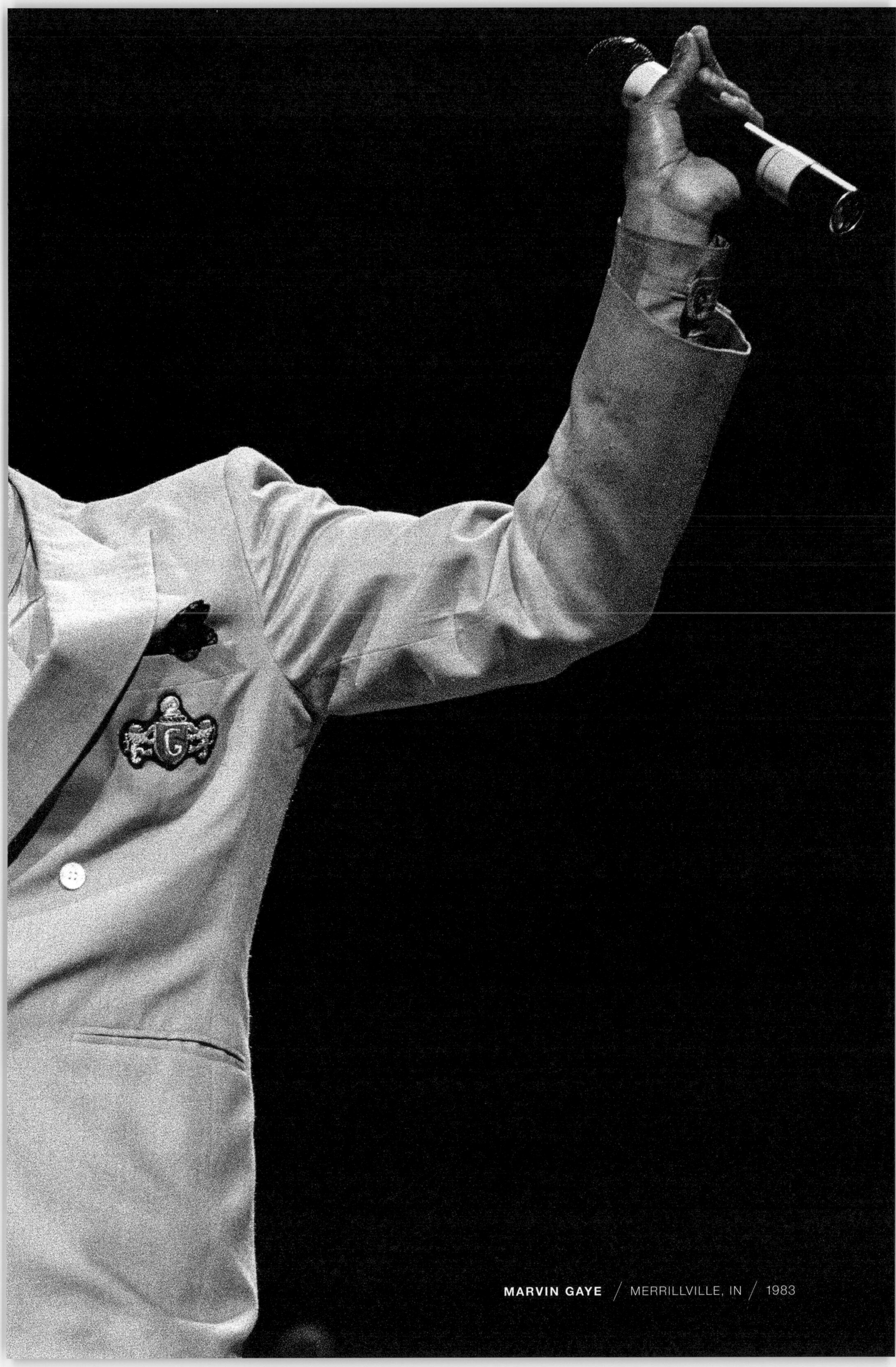

MARVIN GAYE / MERRILLVILLE, IN / 1983

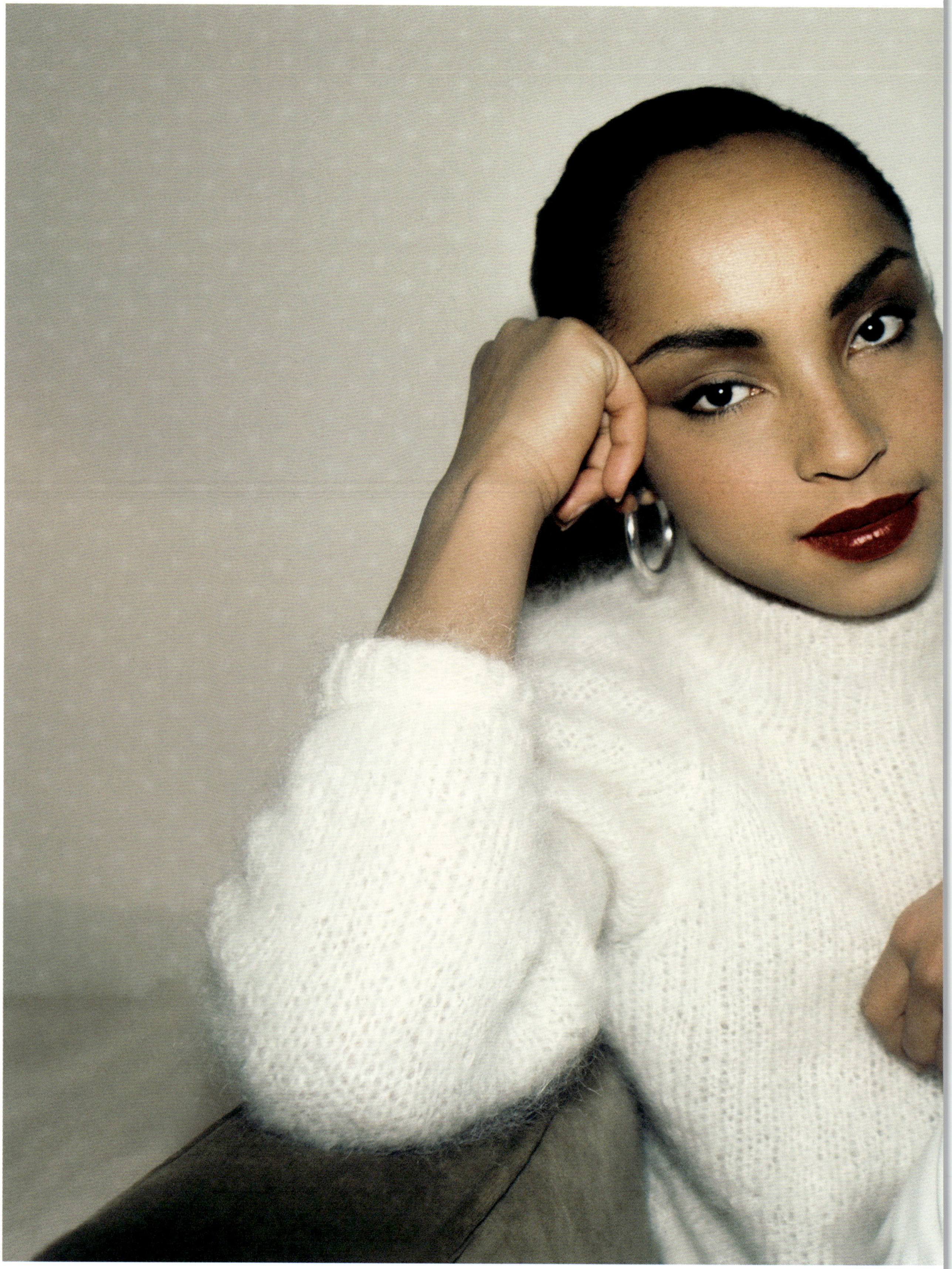

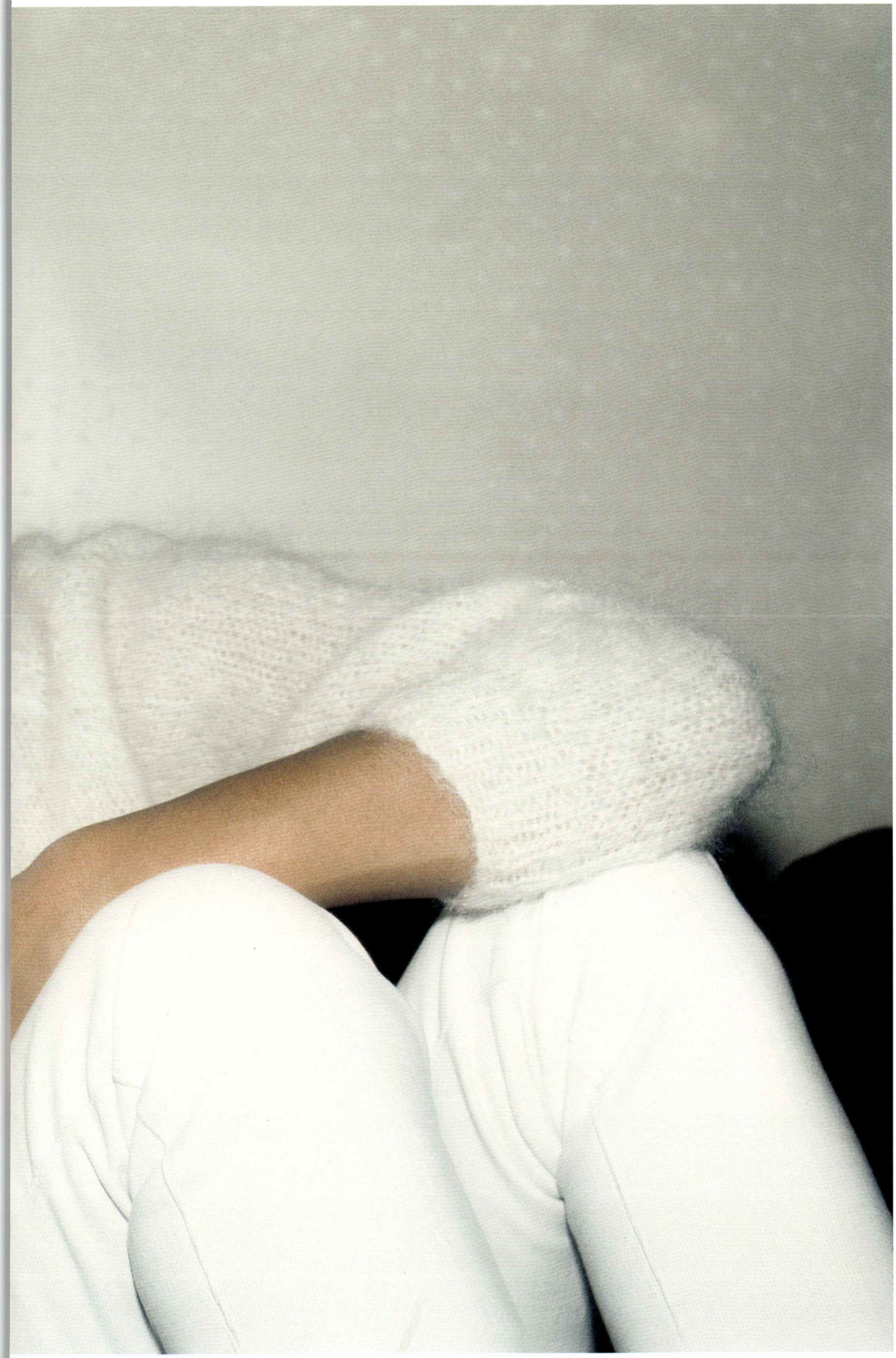

SADE / CHICAGO, IL / 1985

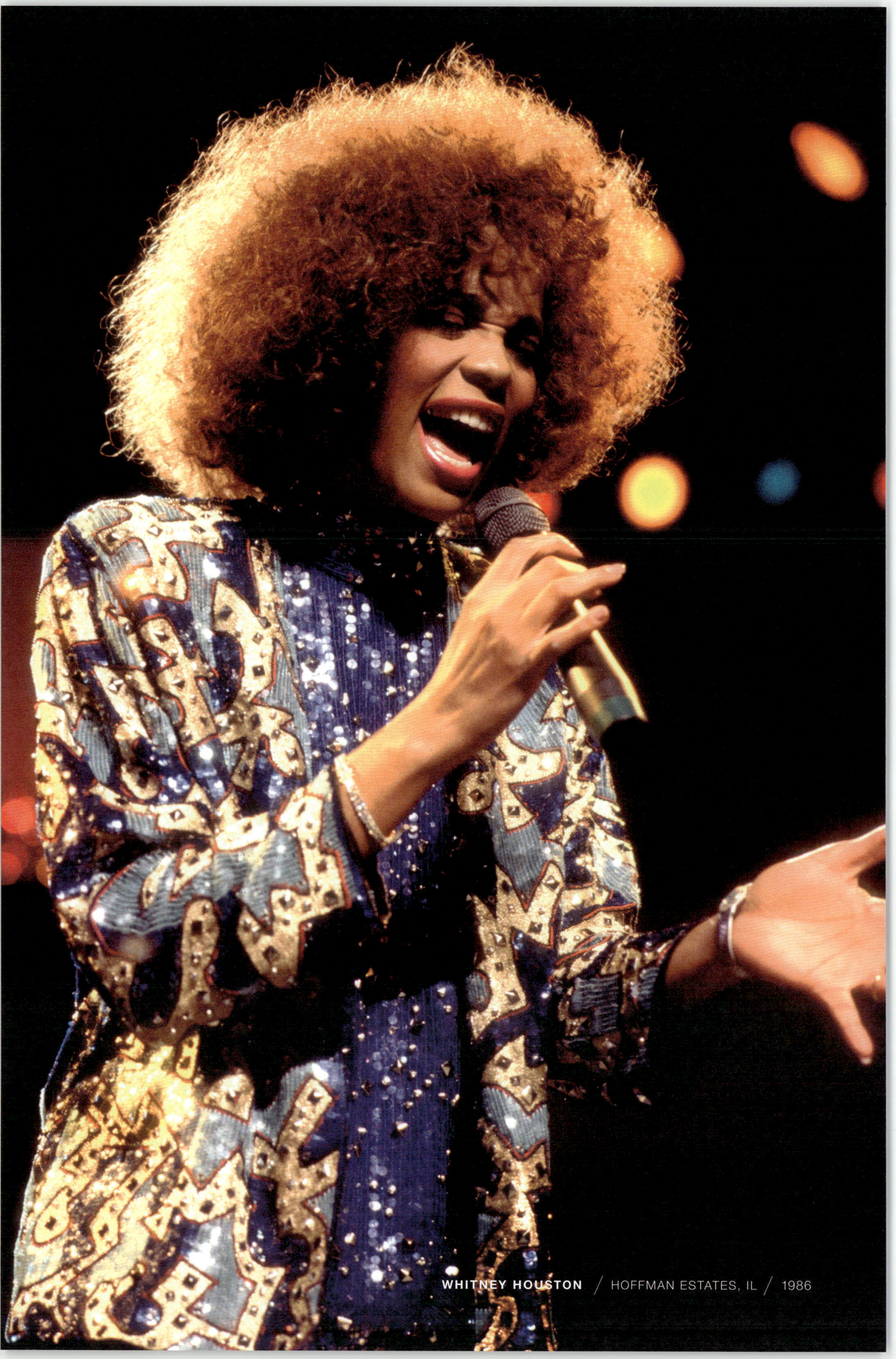

WHITNEY HOUSTON / HOFFMAN ESTATES, IL / 1986

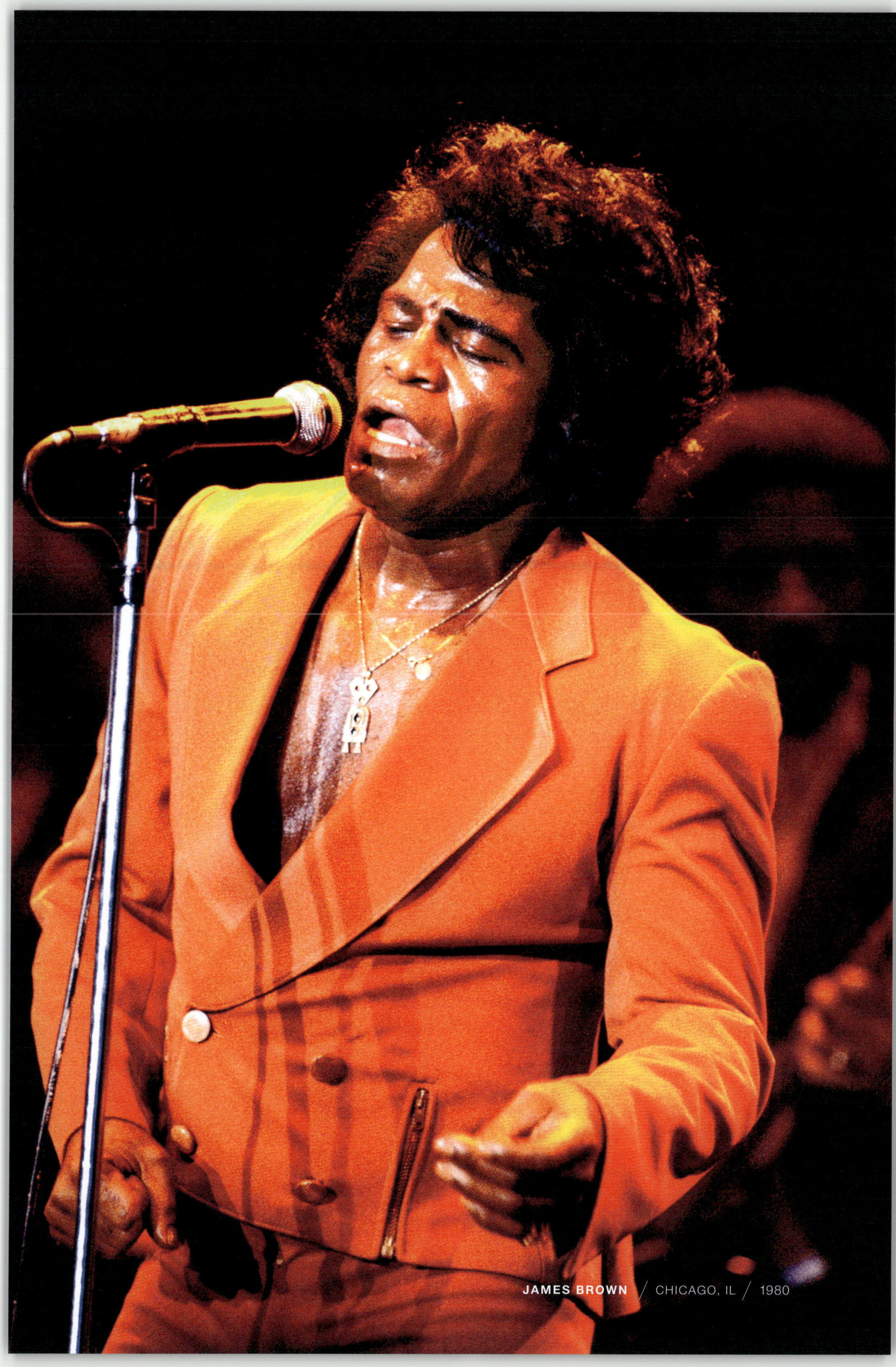

JAMES BROWN / CHICAGO, IL / 1980

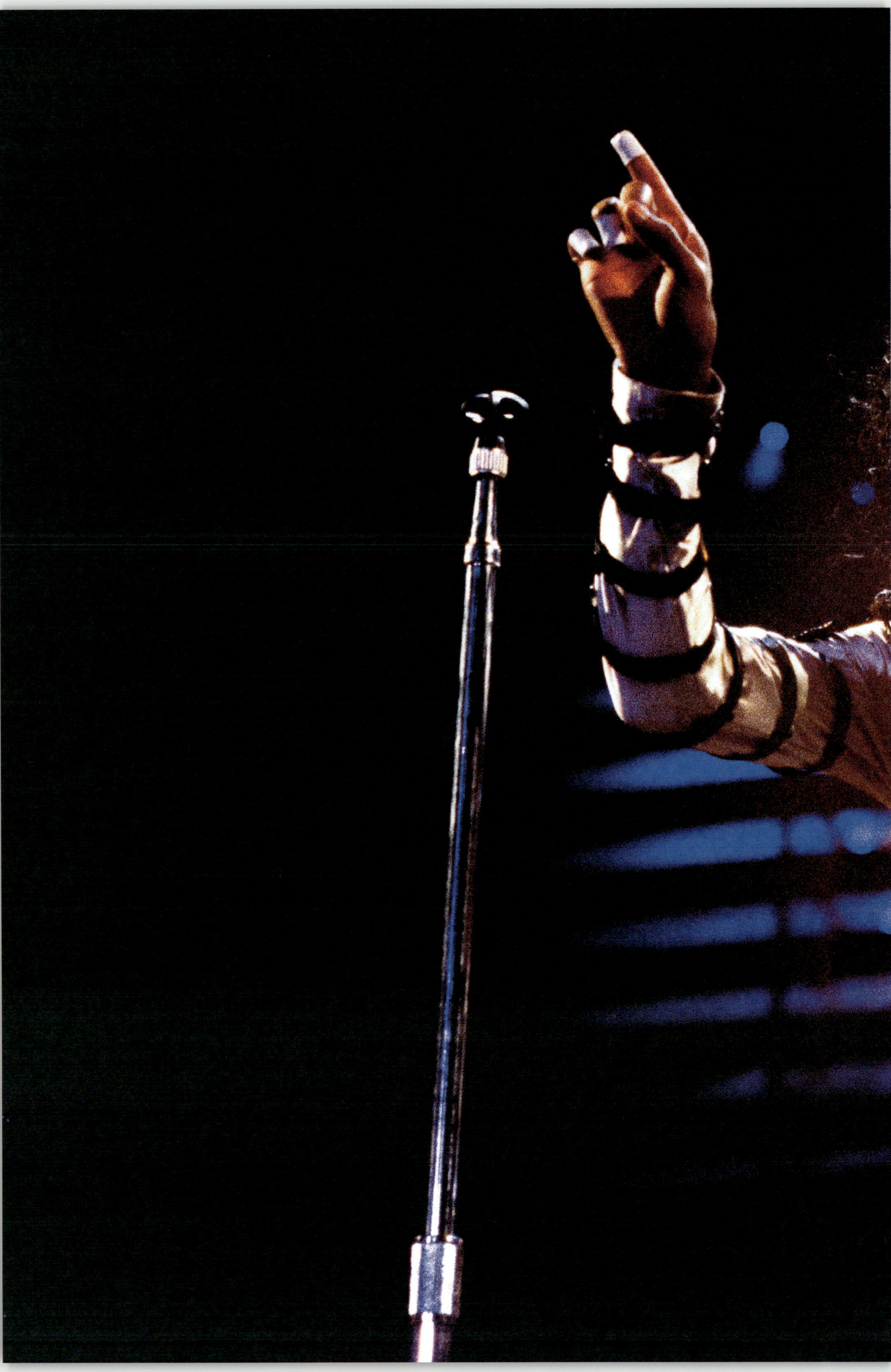

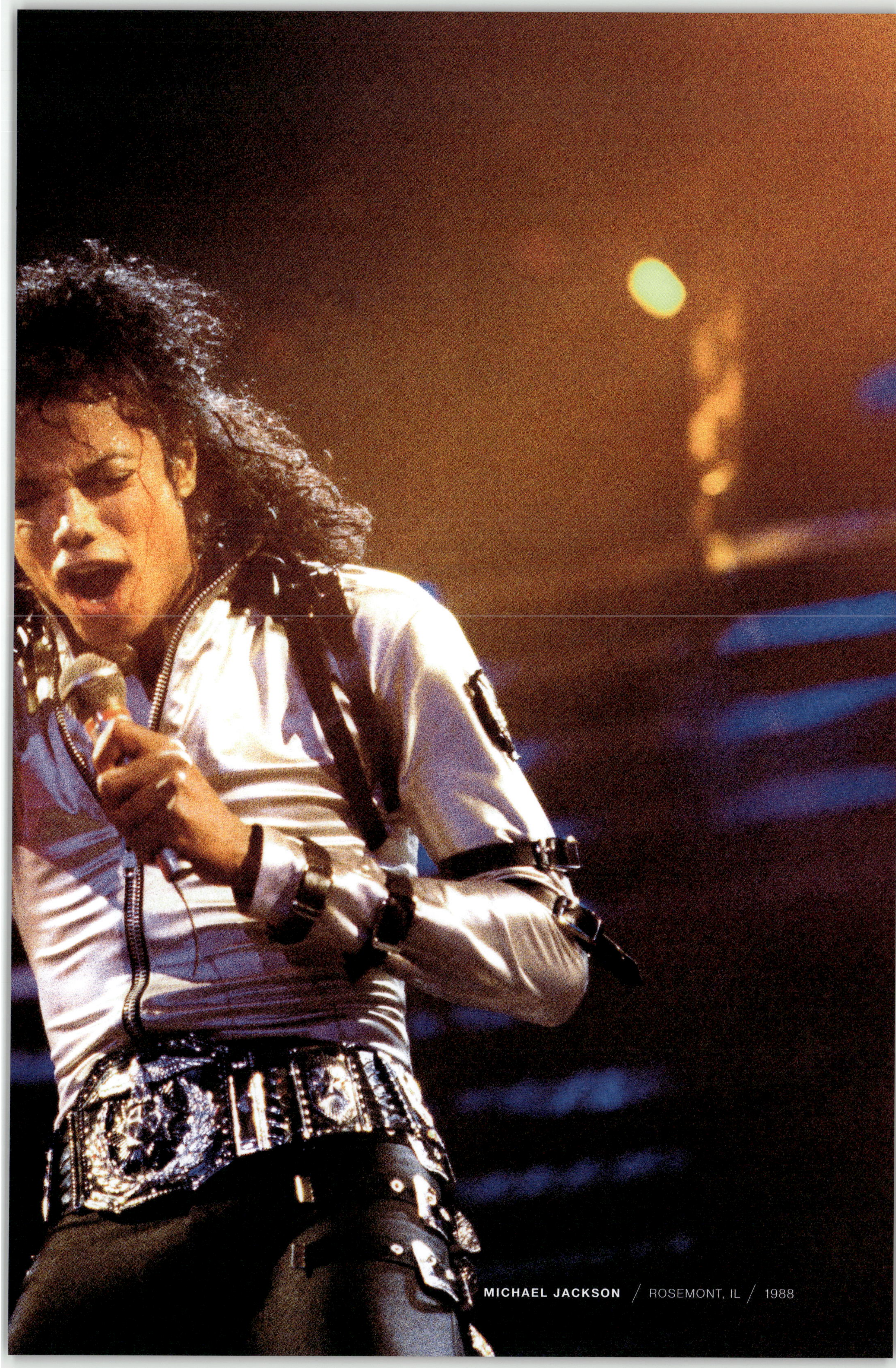

MICHAEL JACKSON / ROSEMONT, IL / 1988

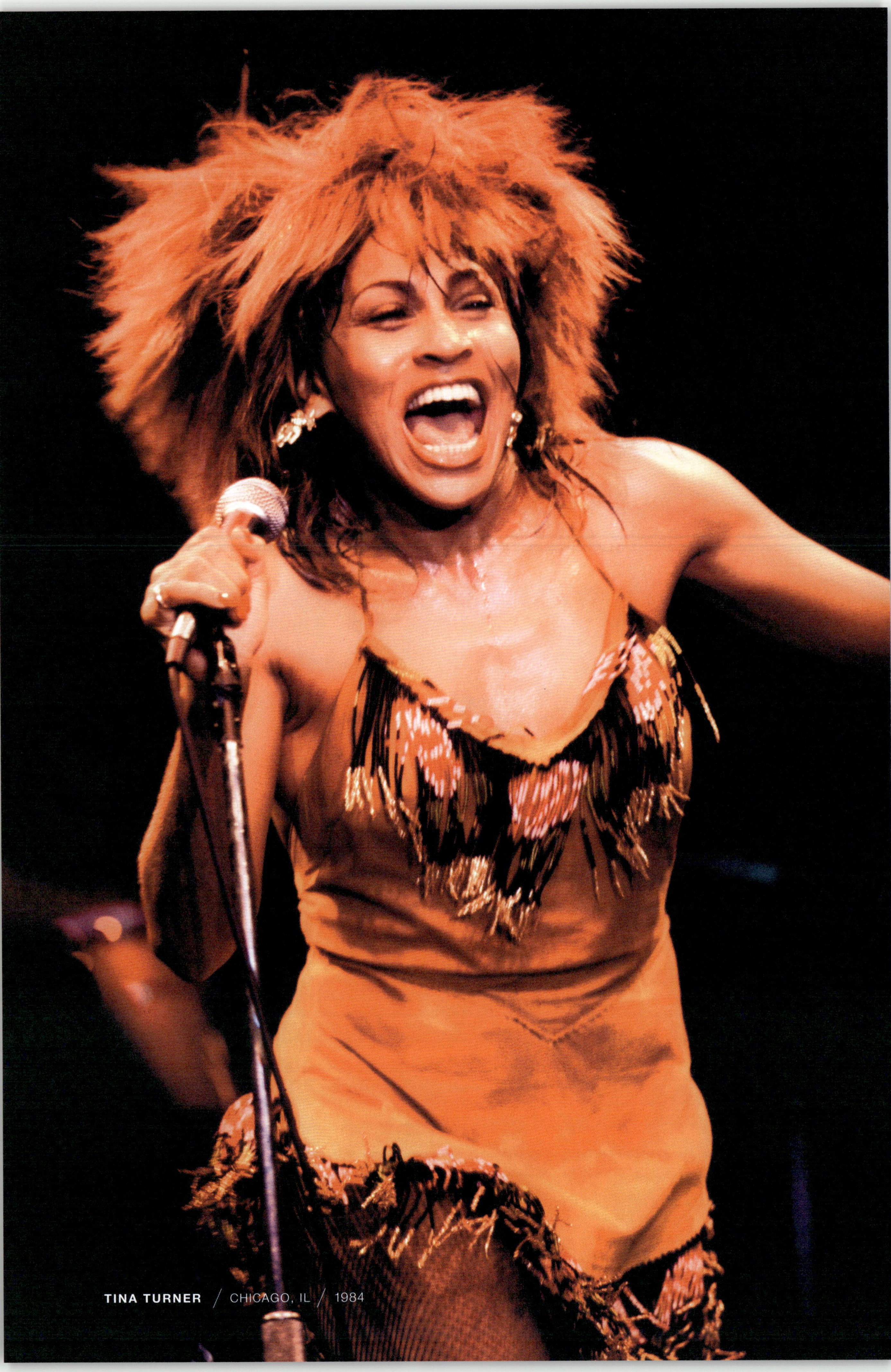

TINA TURNER / CHICAGO, IL / 1984

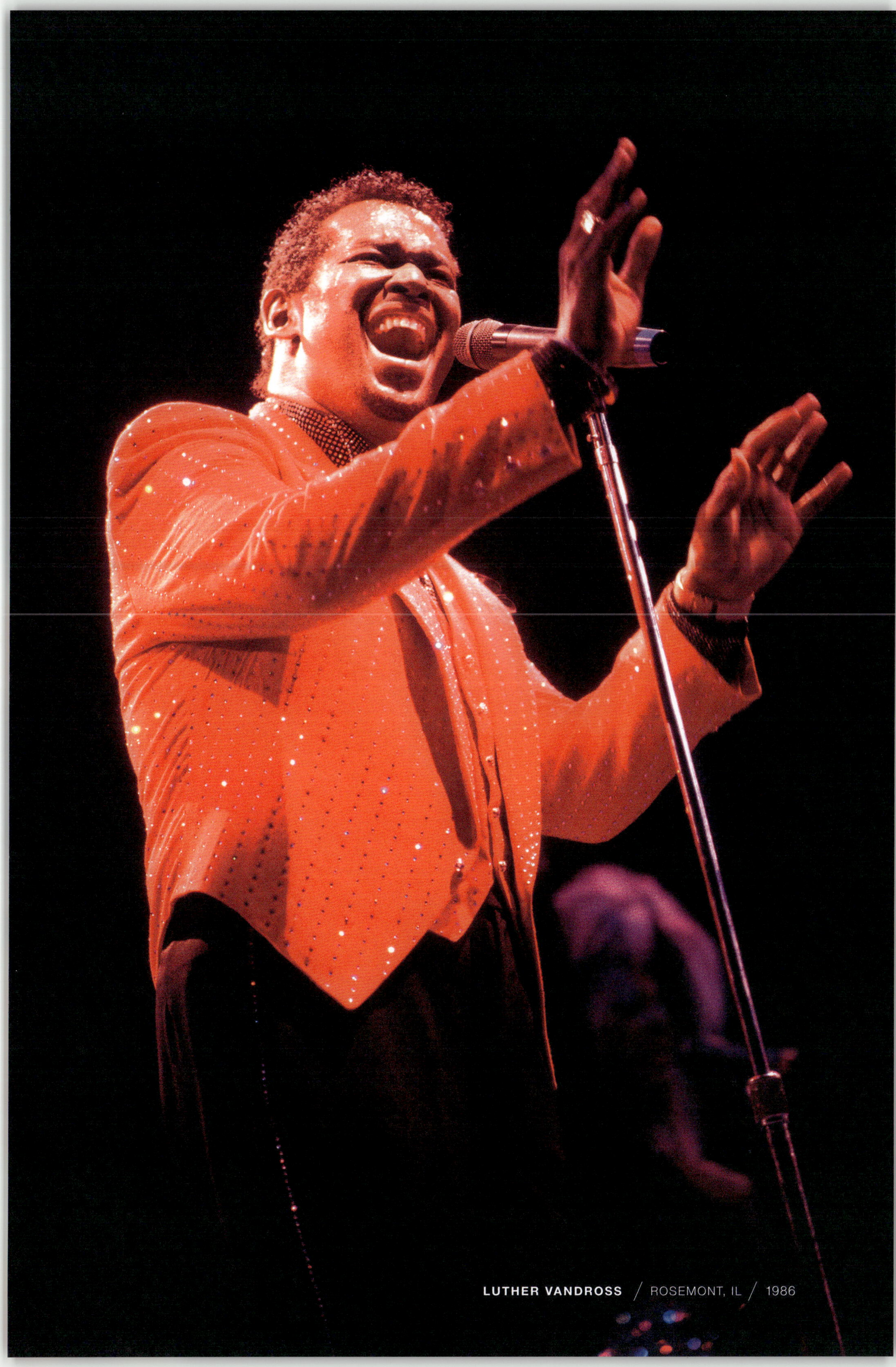

LUTHER VANDROSS / ROSEMONT, IL / 1986

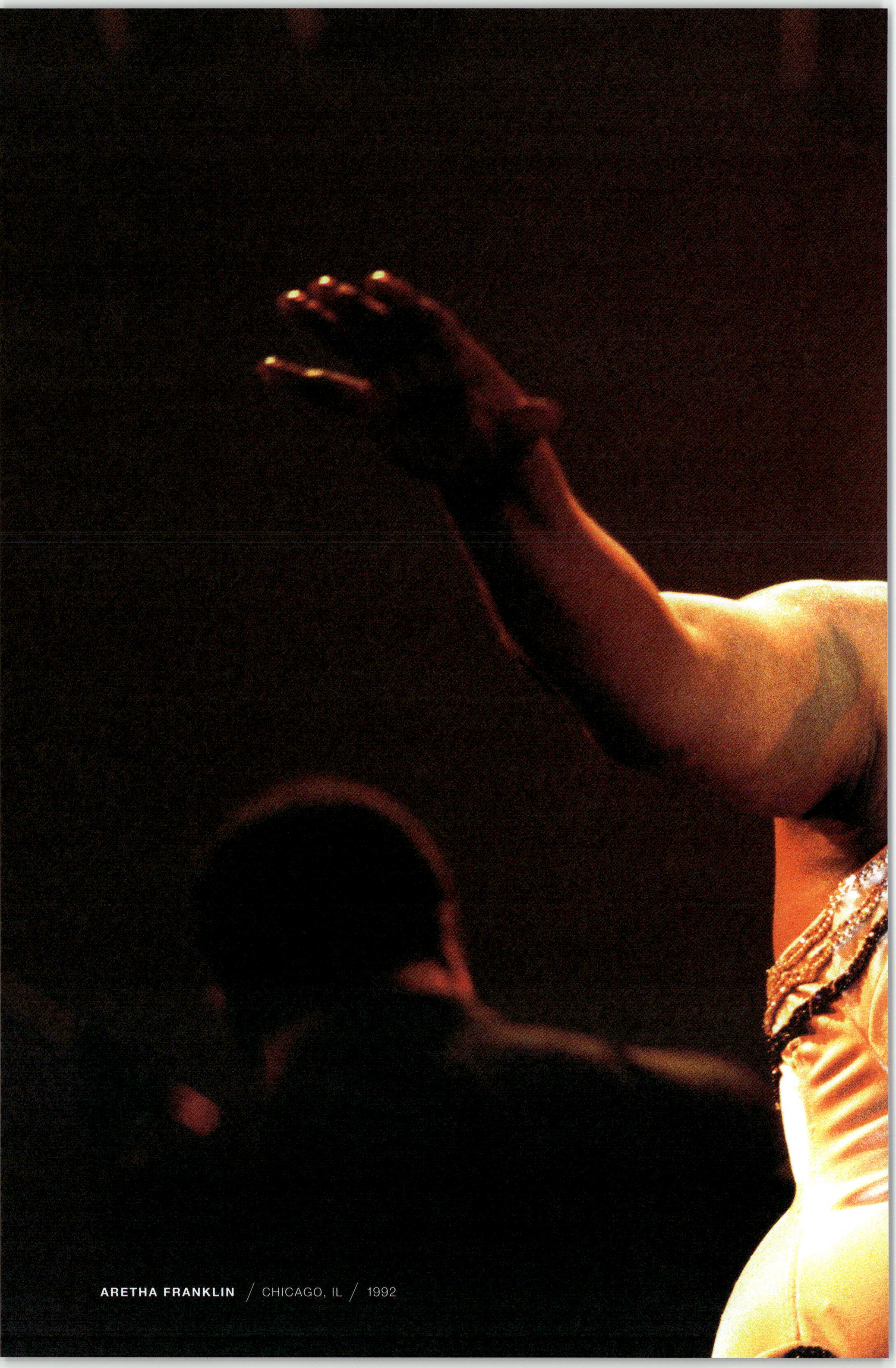

ARETHA FRANKLIN / CHICAGO, IL / 1992

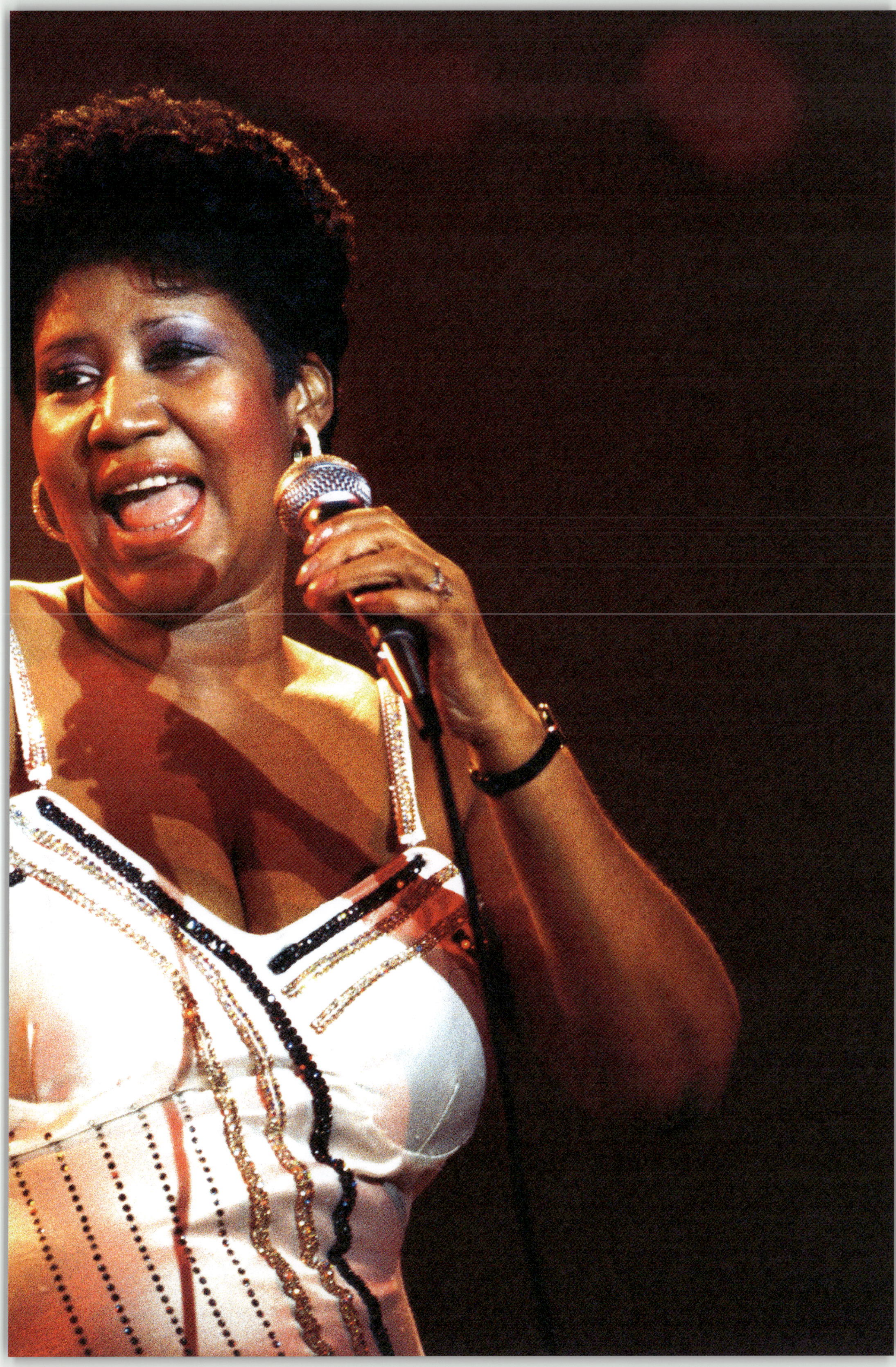

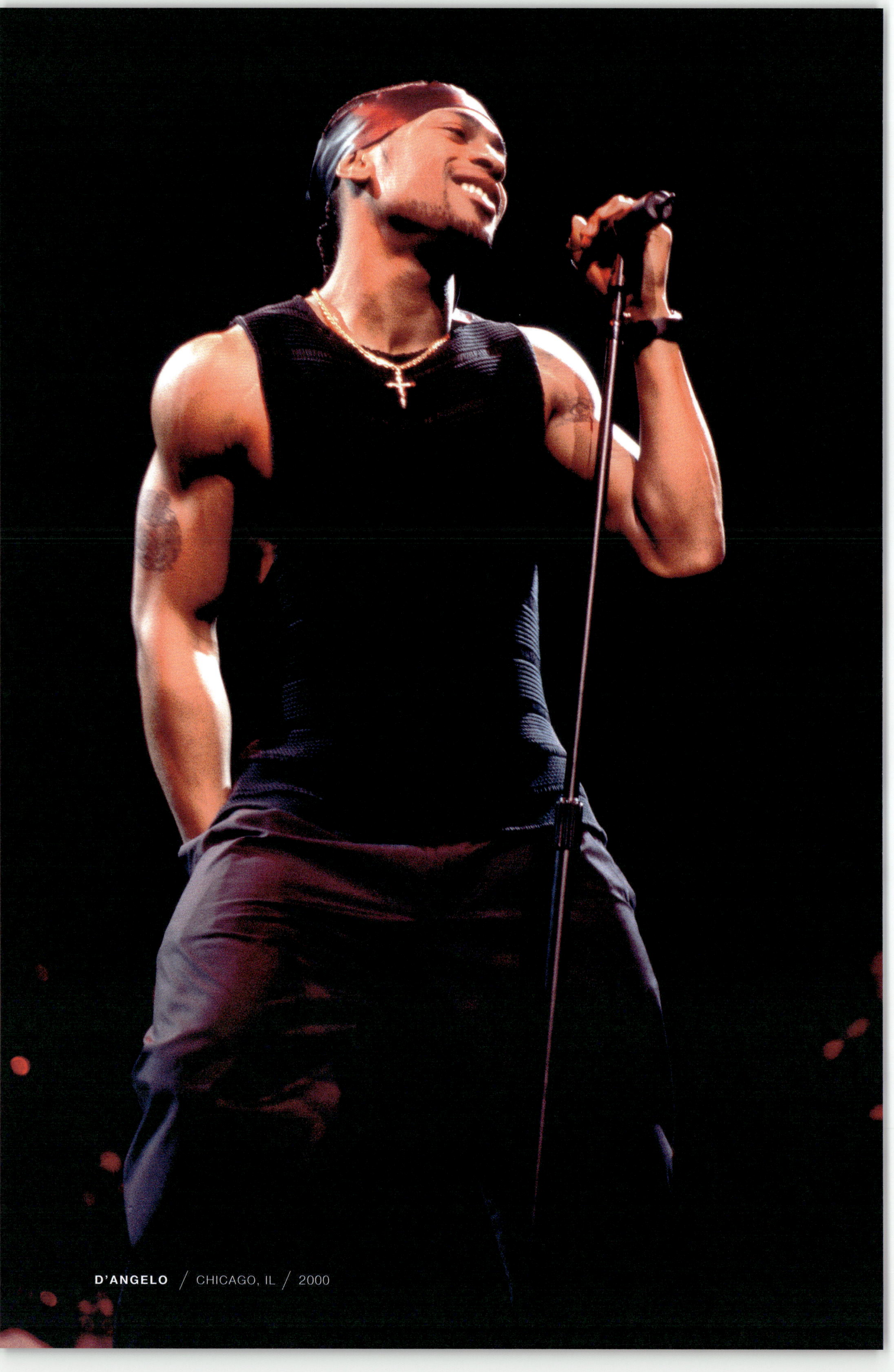

D'ANGELO / CHICAGO, IL / 2000

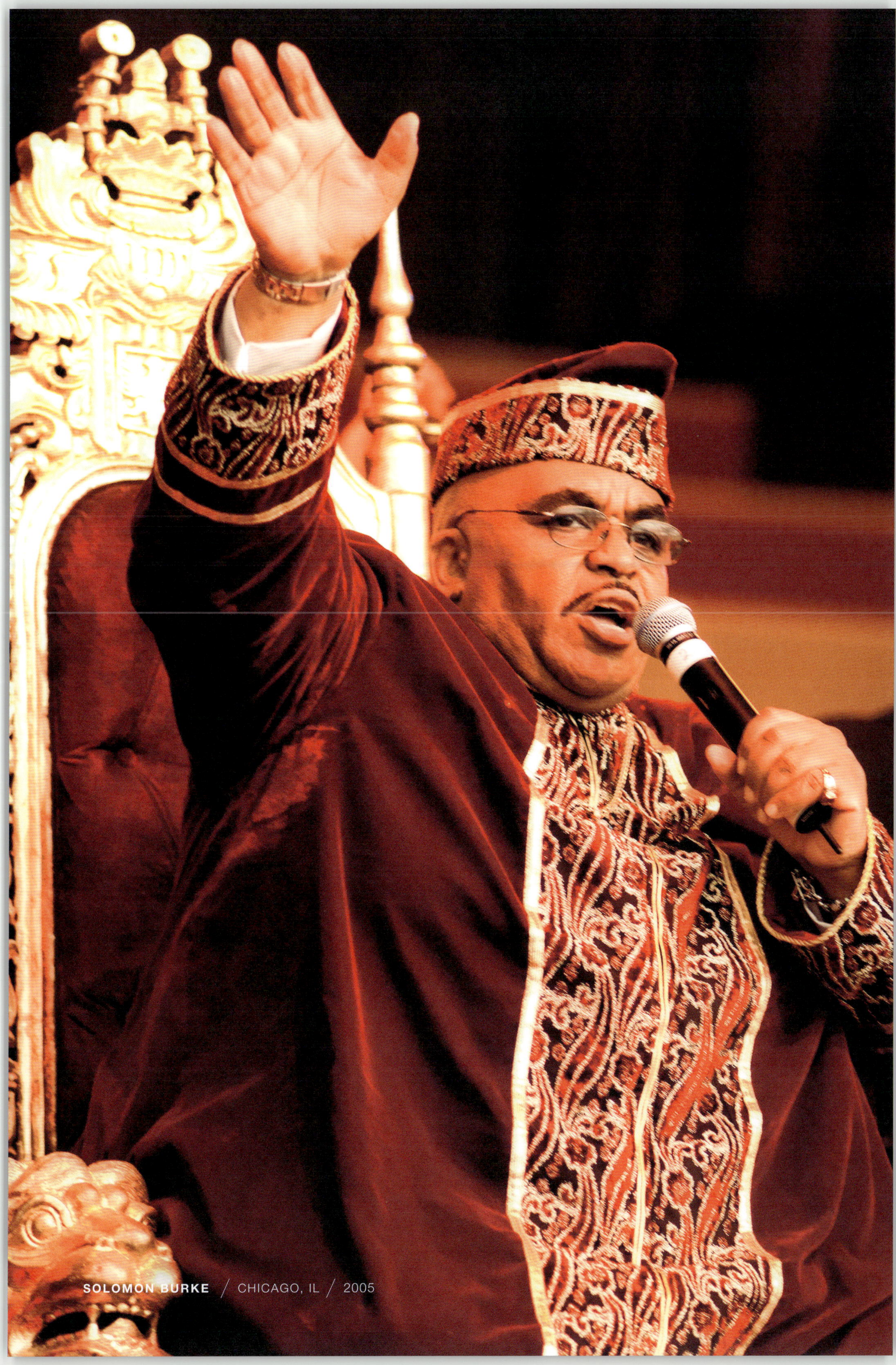

SOLOMON BURKE / CHICAGO, IL / 2005

MAVIS IN THE HOUSE

In early 2004, I was asked by Chicago-based Alligator Records to photograph the legendary Mavis Staples for her album *Have a Little Faith*. Mavis and her sister Yvonne–along with label executives–arrived at my house a week later for the shoot. The record company wanted the front cover to be a picture of her singing, so Mavis sat in my living room for three hours singing to me as I photographed her. As she was getting up to leave, I asked her to do something I have never done before or since–I asked if I could have my picture taken with her. Of course, she said yes, so I quickly taught the Alligator team how to use my camera and got that picture. Having a musical giant like Mavis Staples in my living room/studio remains one of the thrills of my life.

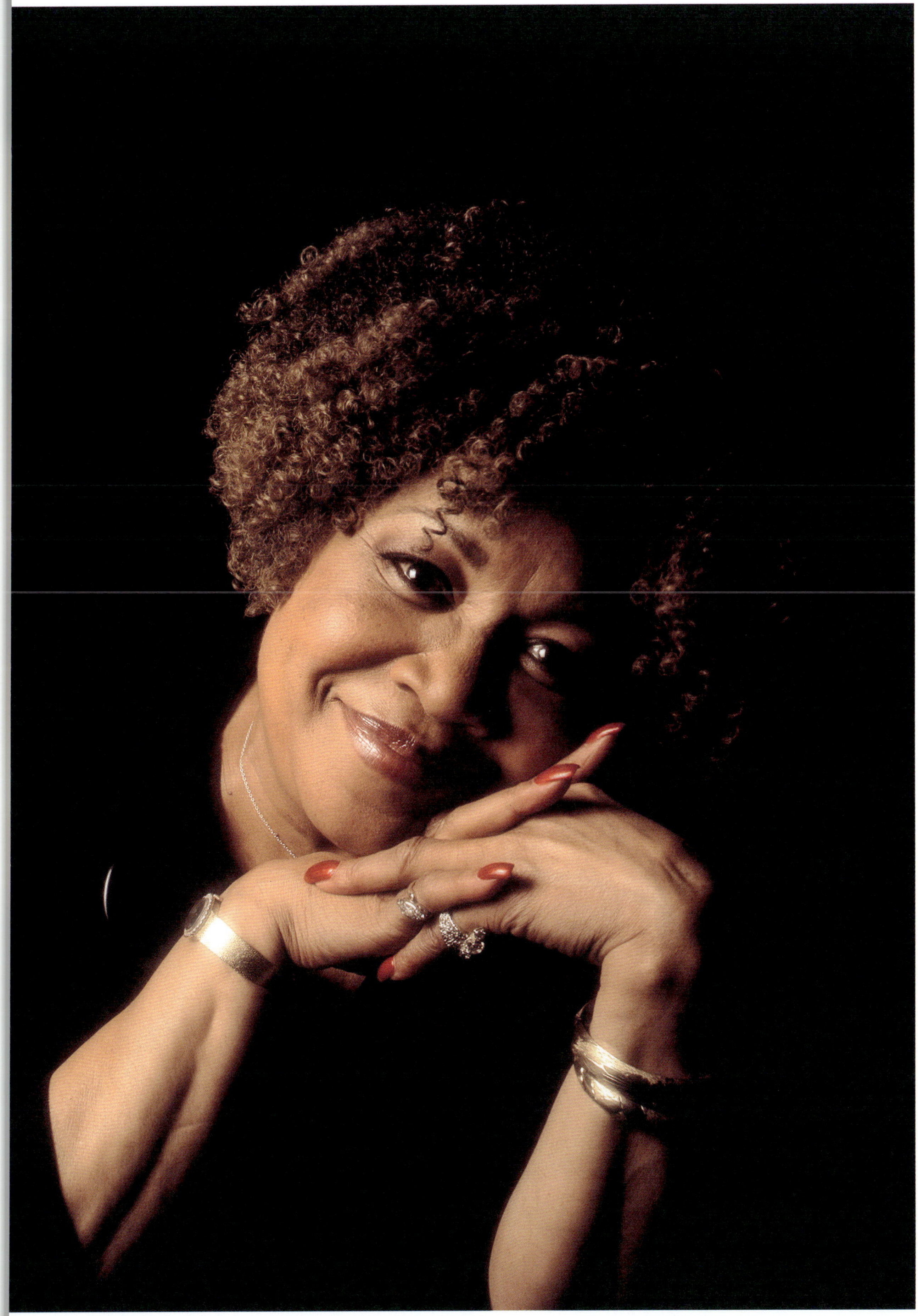

MAVIS STAPLES / CHICAGO, IL / 2004

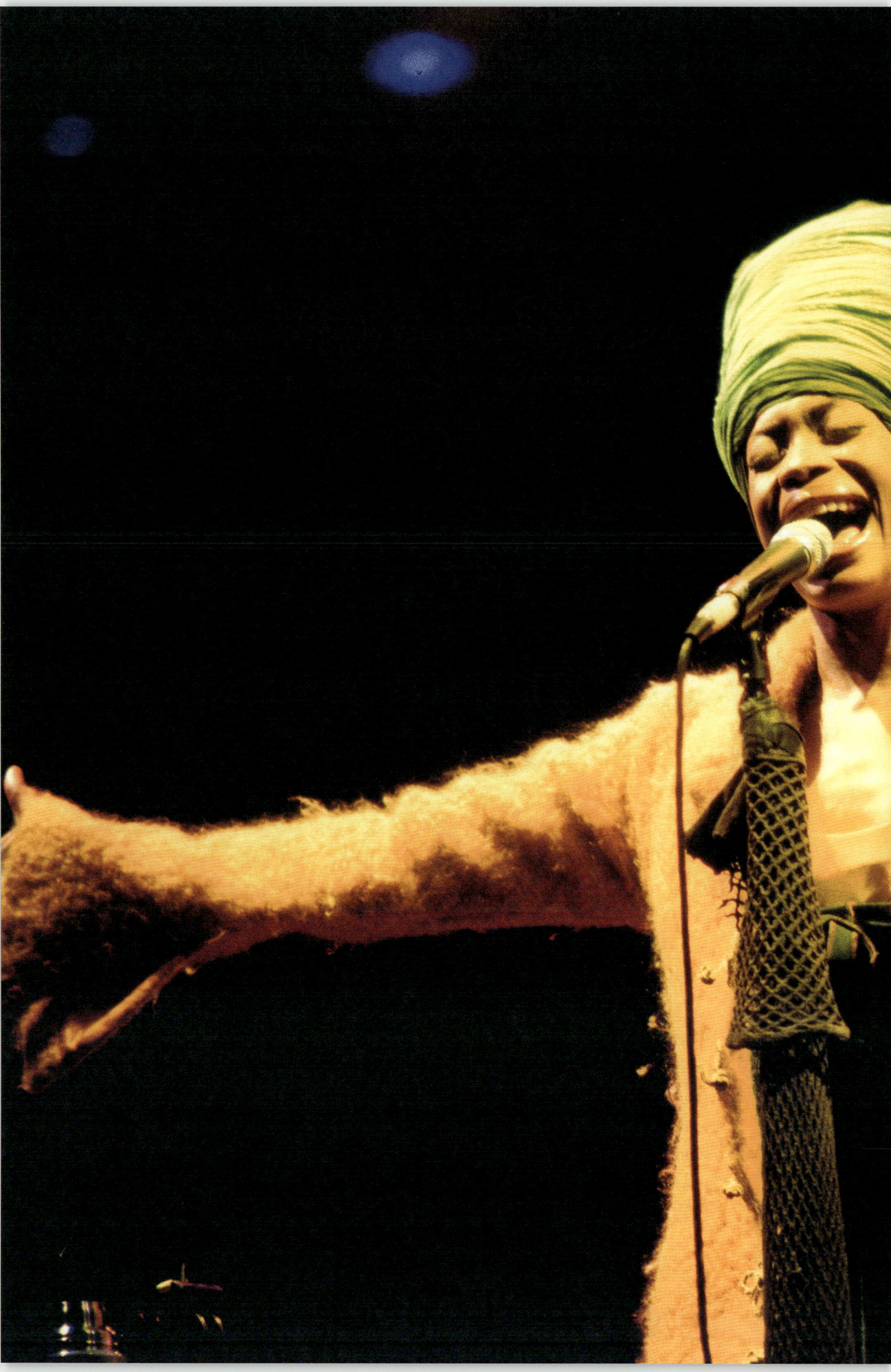

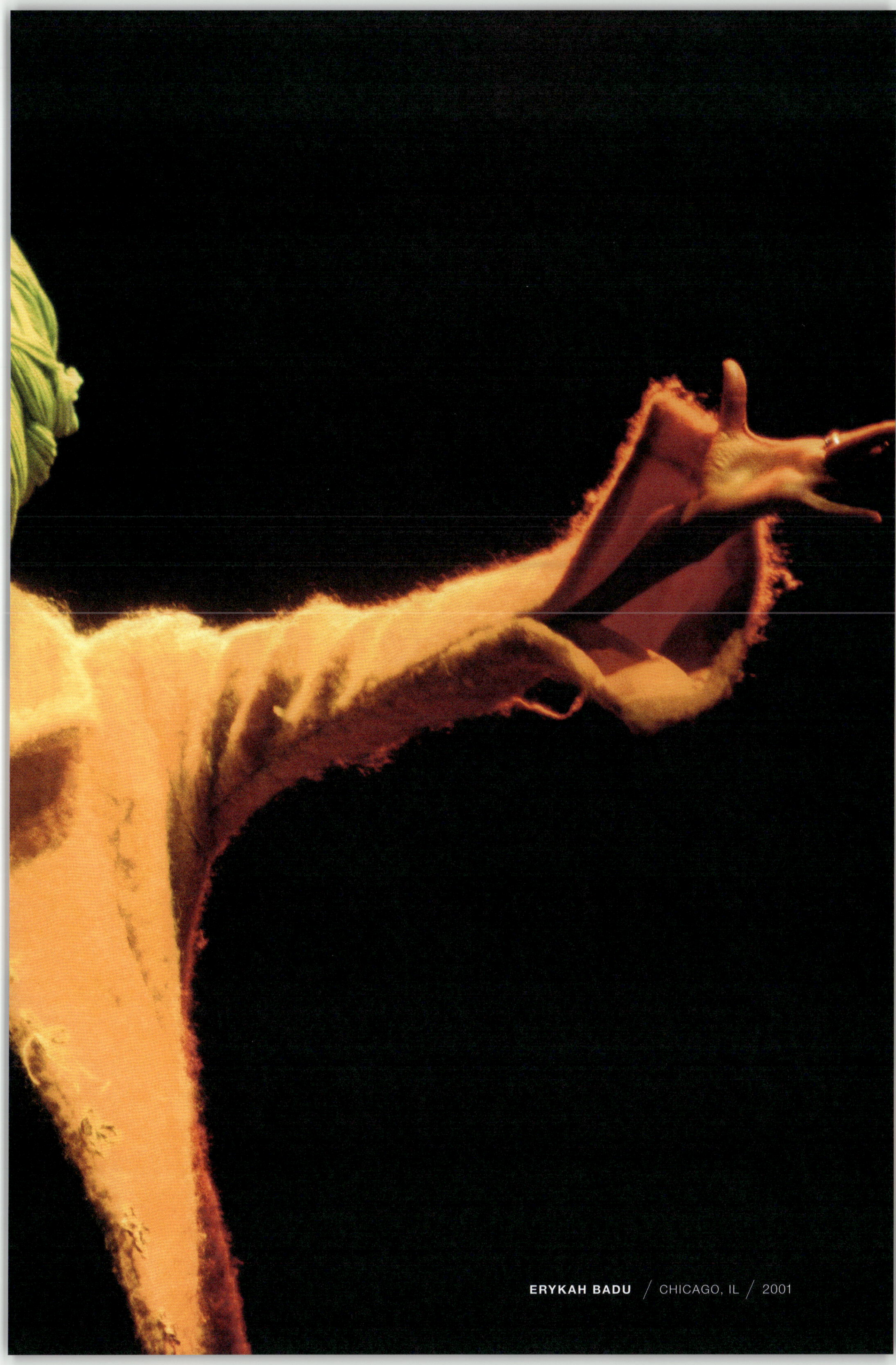

ERYKAH BADU / CHICAGO, IL / 2001

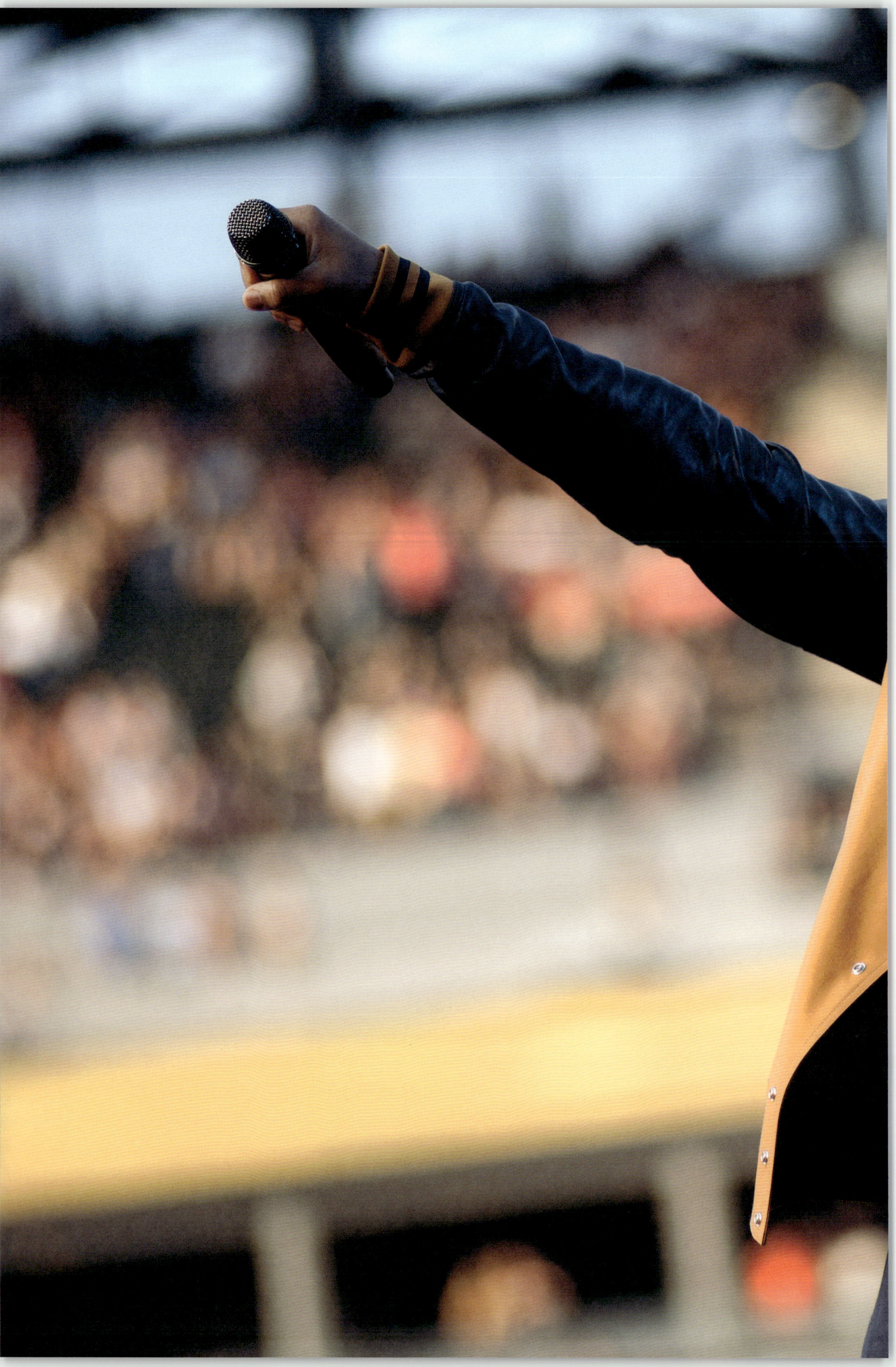

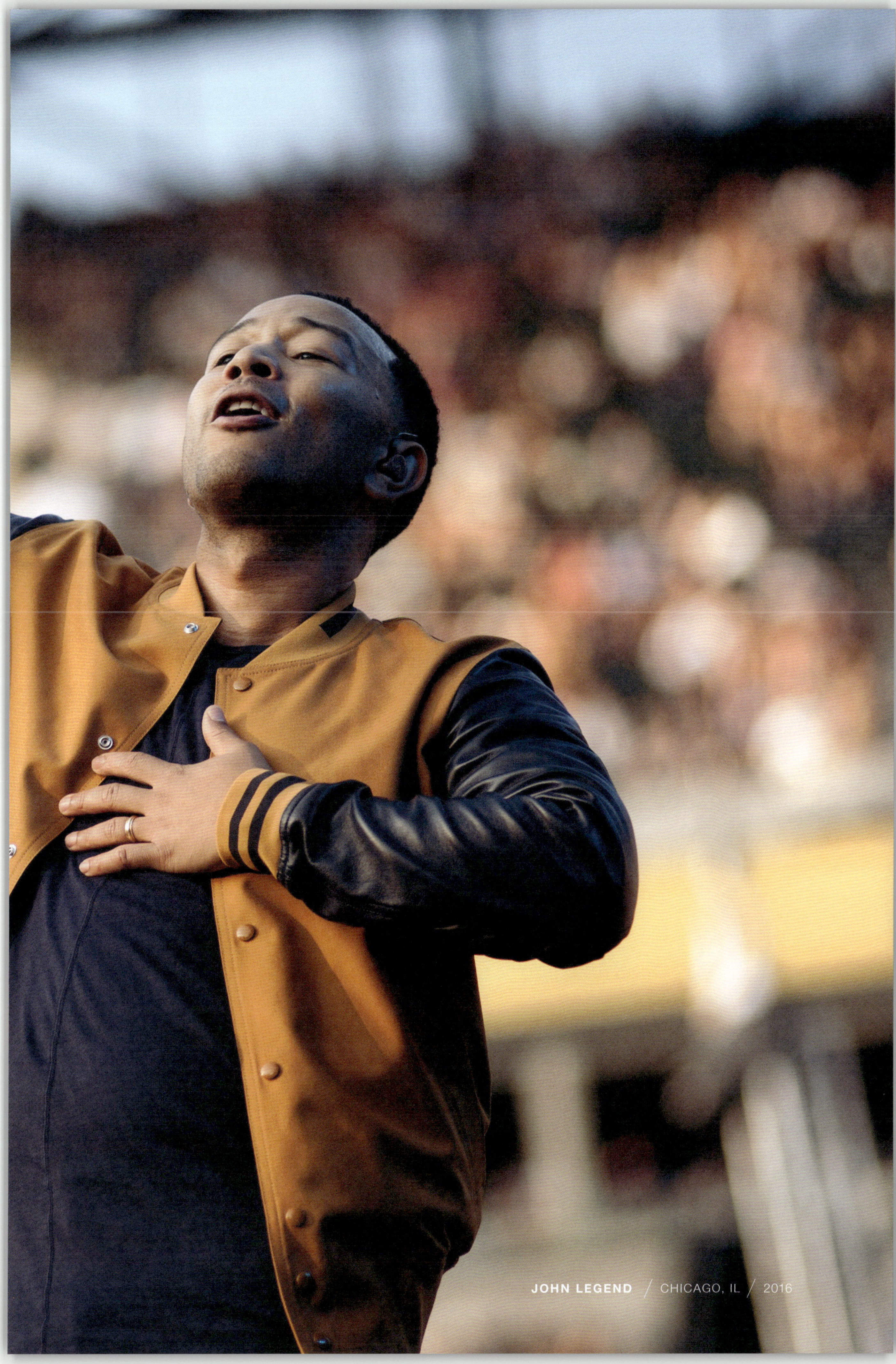

JOHN LEGEND / CHICAGO, IL / 2016

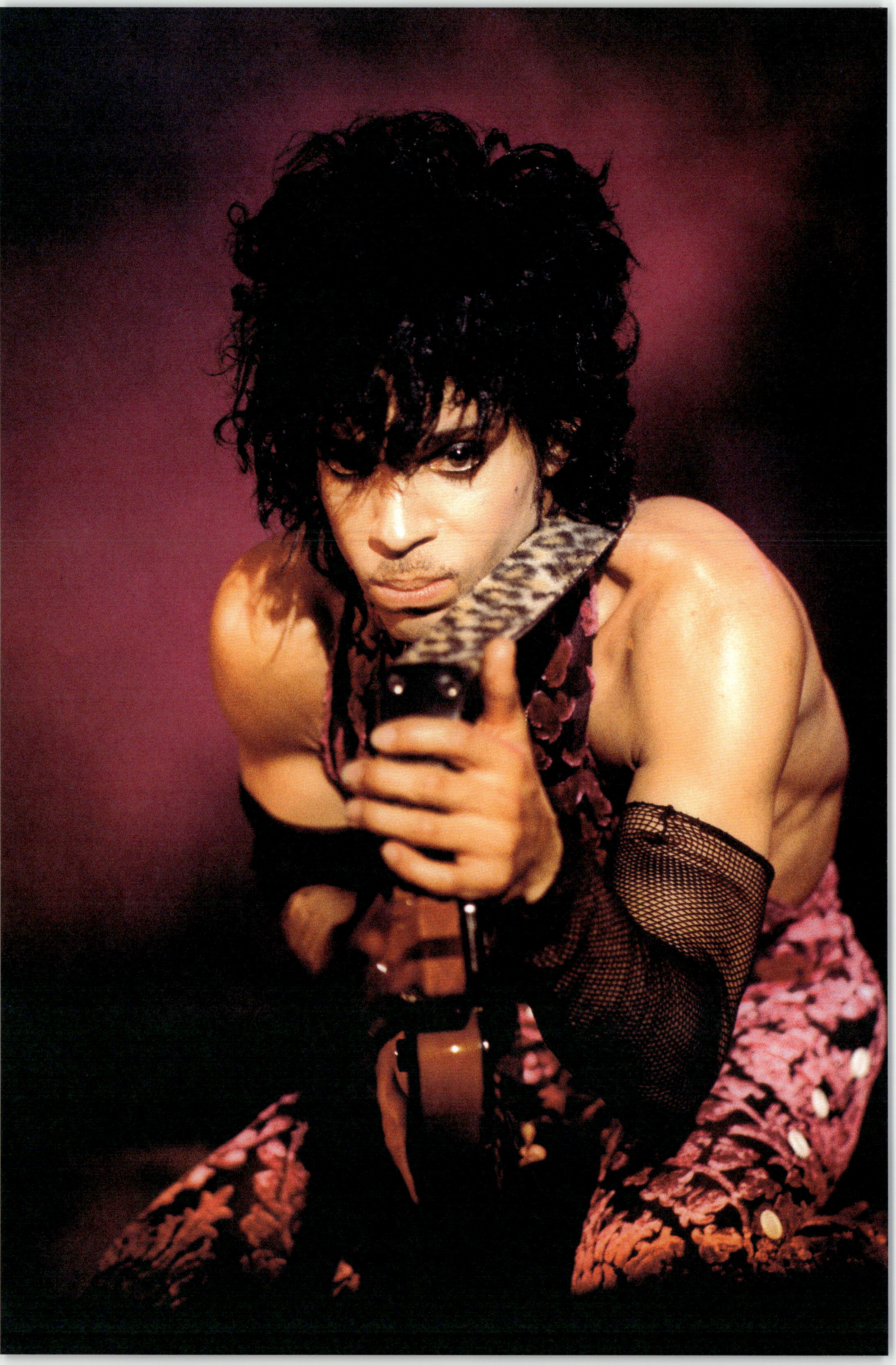

PURPLE RAIN

In June of 1984, a publicist from New York called and asked if I wanted to travel to Minneapolis and photograph Prince's birthday party. He was scheduled to perform with his newest band, The Revolution, and I knew he had a movie and album coming out, a little something called *Purple Rain*. I figured it was probably worth fighting for space amongst all the other photographers that were likely invited to get some new pictures. I purchased a $100 roundtrip plane ticket, grabbed my camera bag, and headed to First Avenue. When I got inside, I found that I was the only photographer allowed into the building that evening. I staked out a position in front of the stage and remained about three feet away from Prince during the 90-minute set, as he posed for me and delivered amazing shot after shot. The next day, I started sending pictures to agencies and publications around the world. As expected, the images were picked up with great success. Prince was hardly seen in public through the rest of that summer until the *Purple Rain* tour started in November. I was, in fact, the only photographer with pictures of him wearing the costumes from the movie. It was the best $100 plane ticket I have ever purchased.

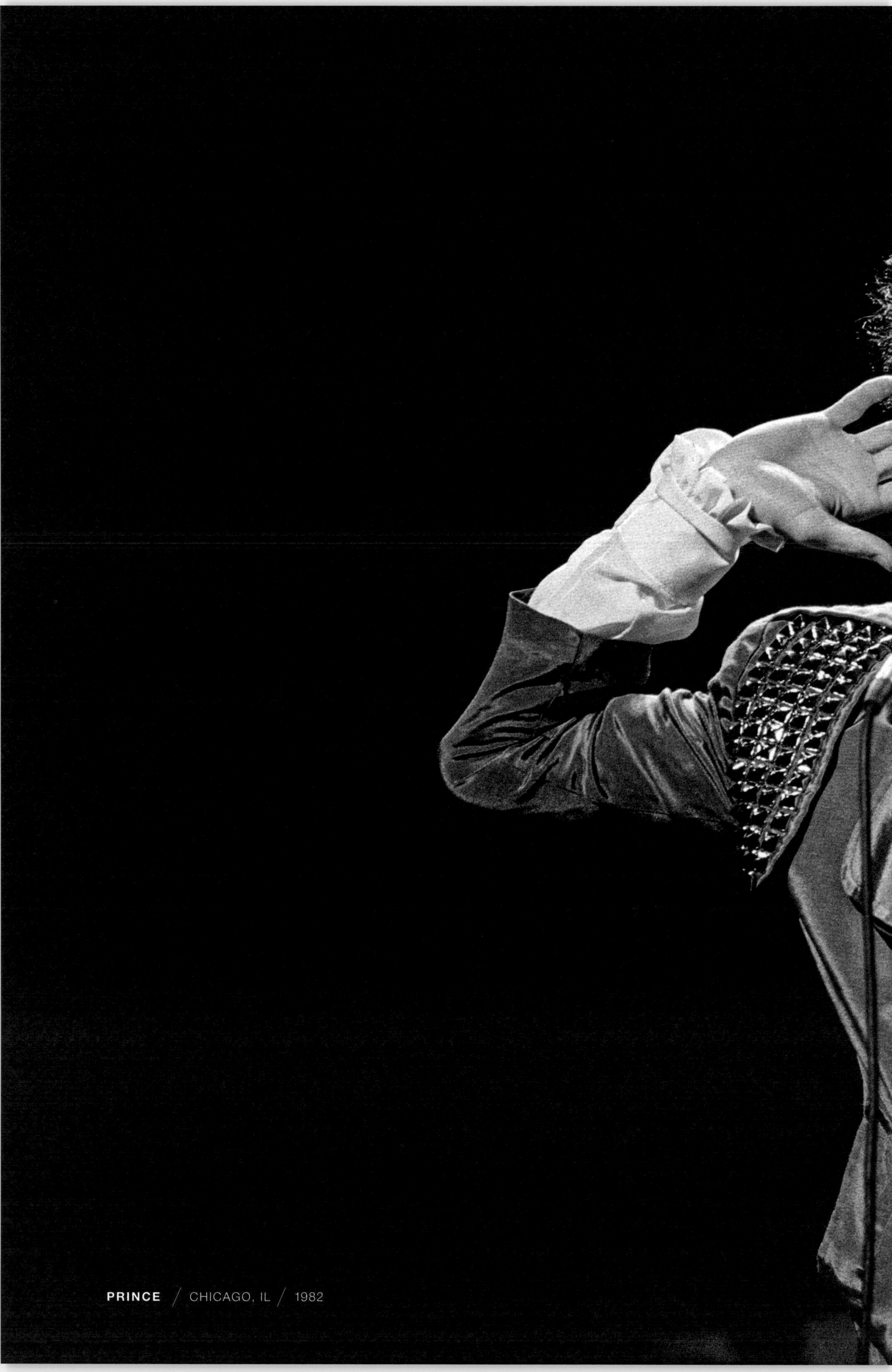

PRINCE / CHICAGO, IL / 1982

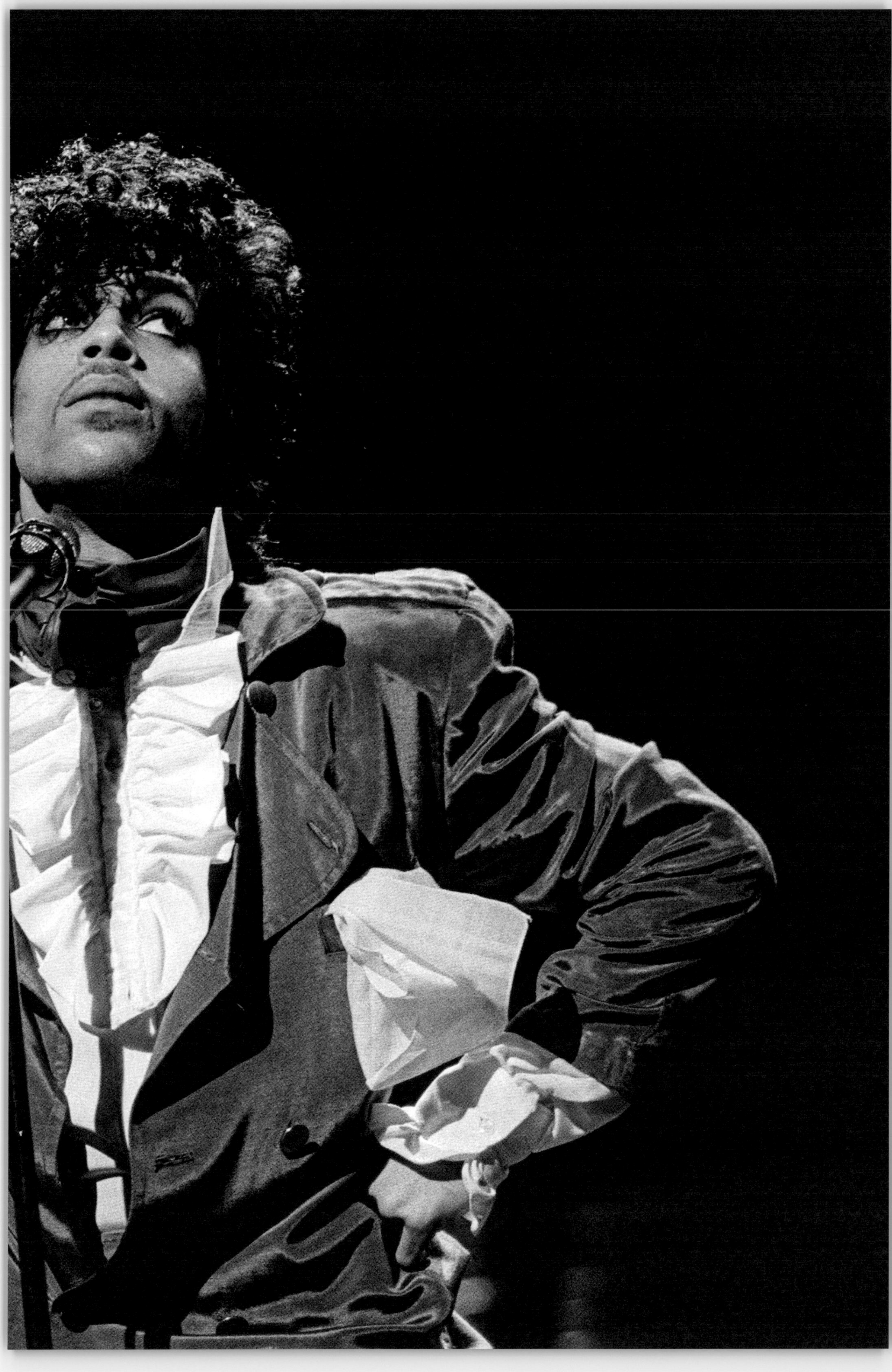

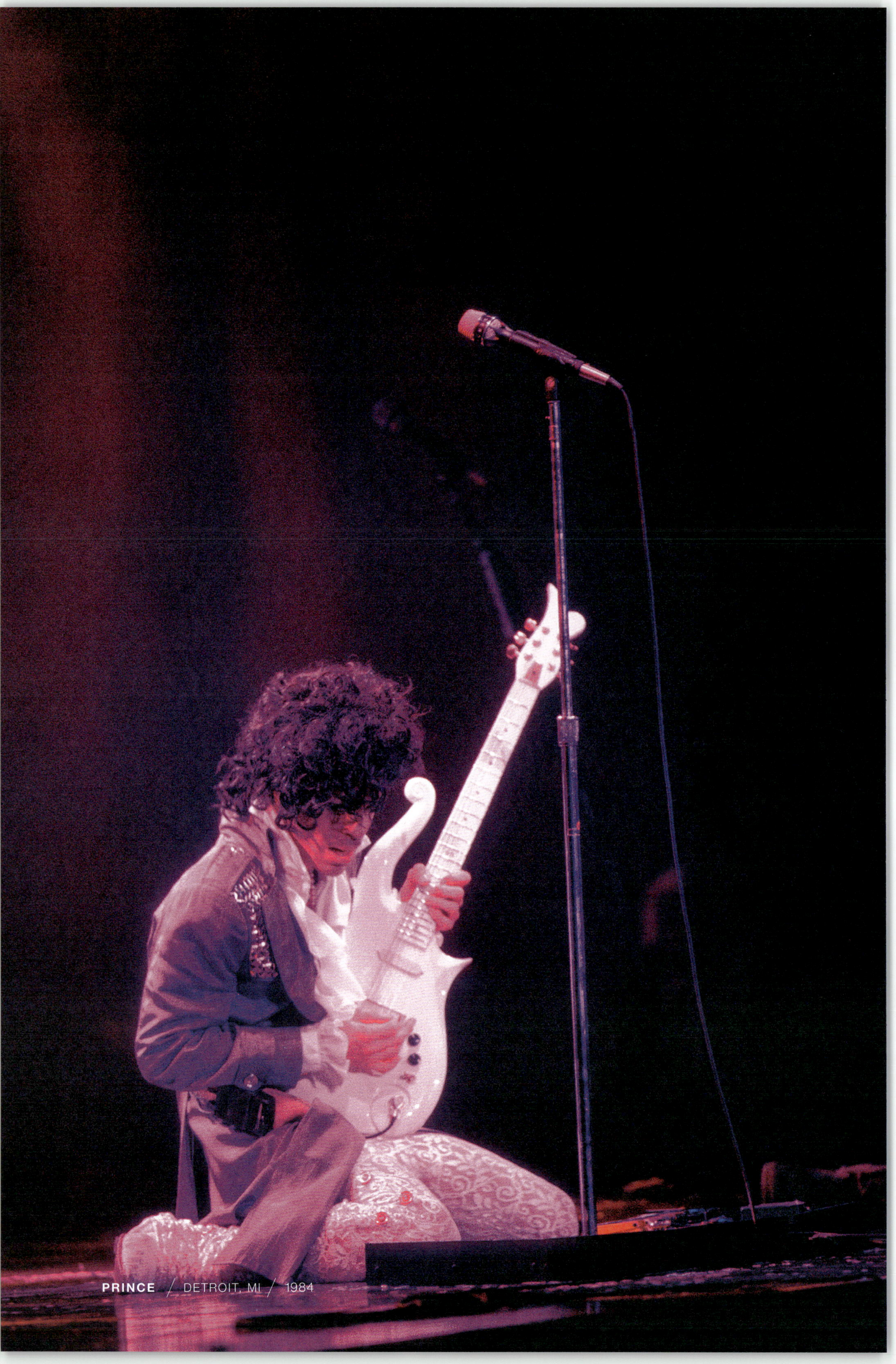

PRINCE / DETROIT, MI / 1984

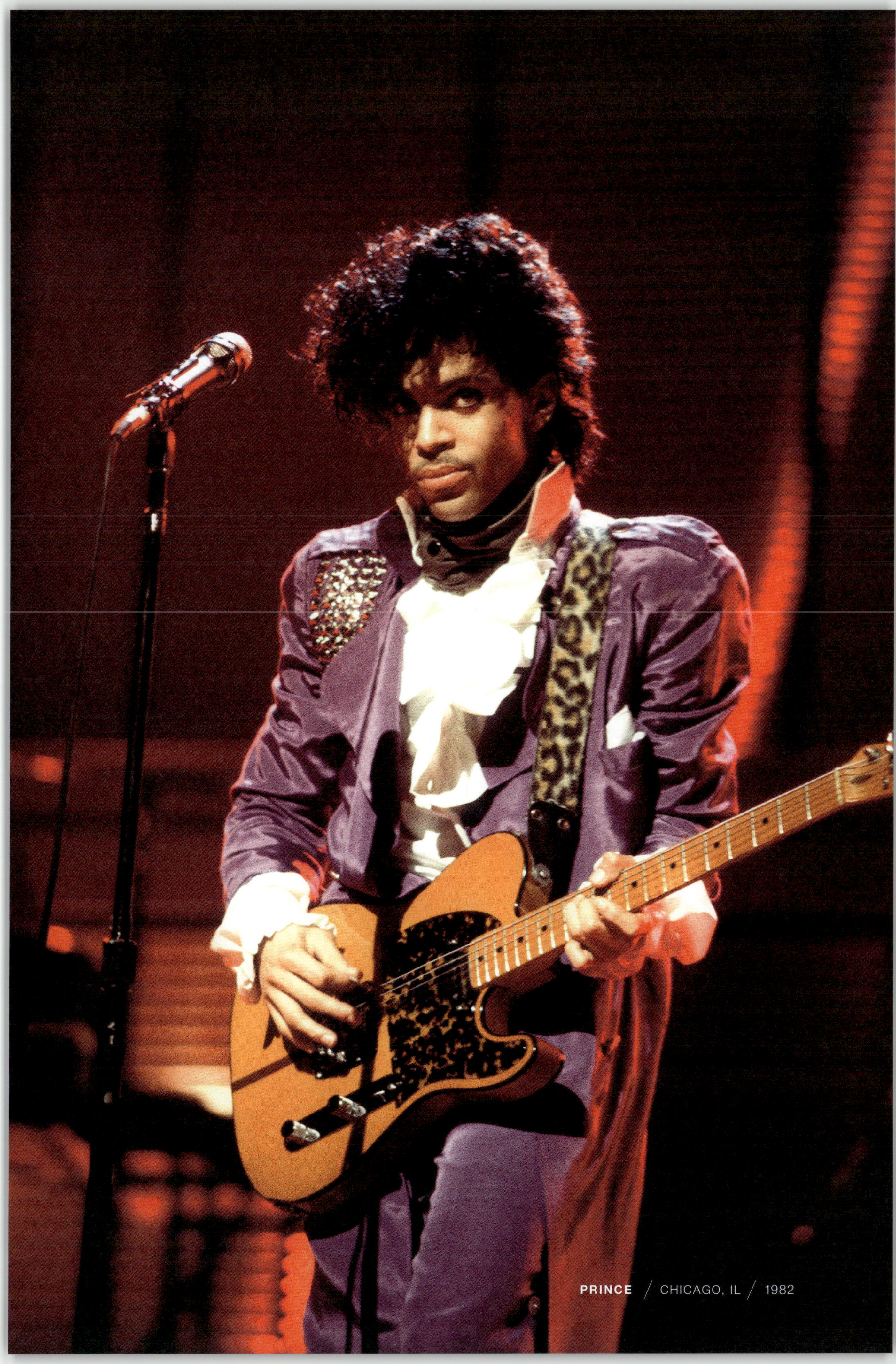

PRINCE / CHICAGO, IL / 1982

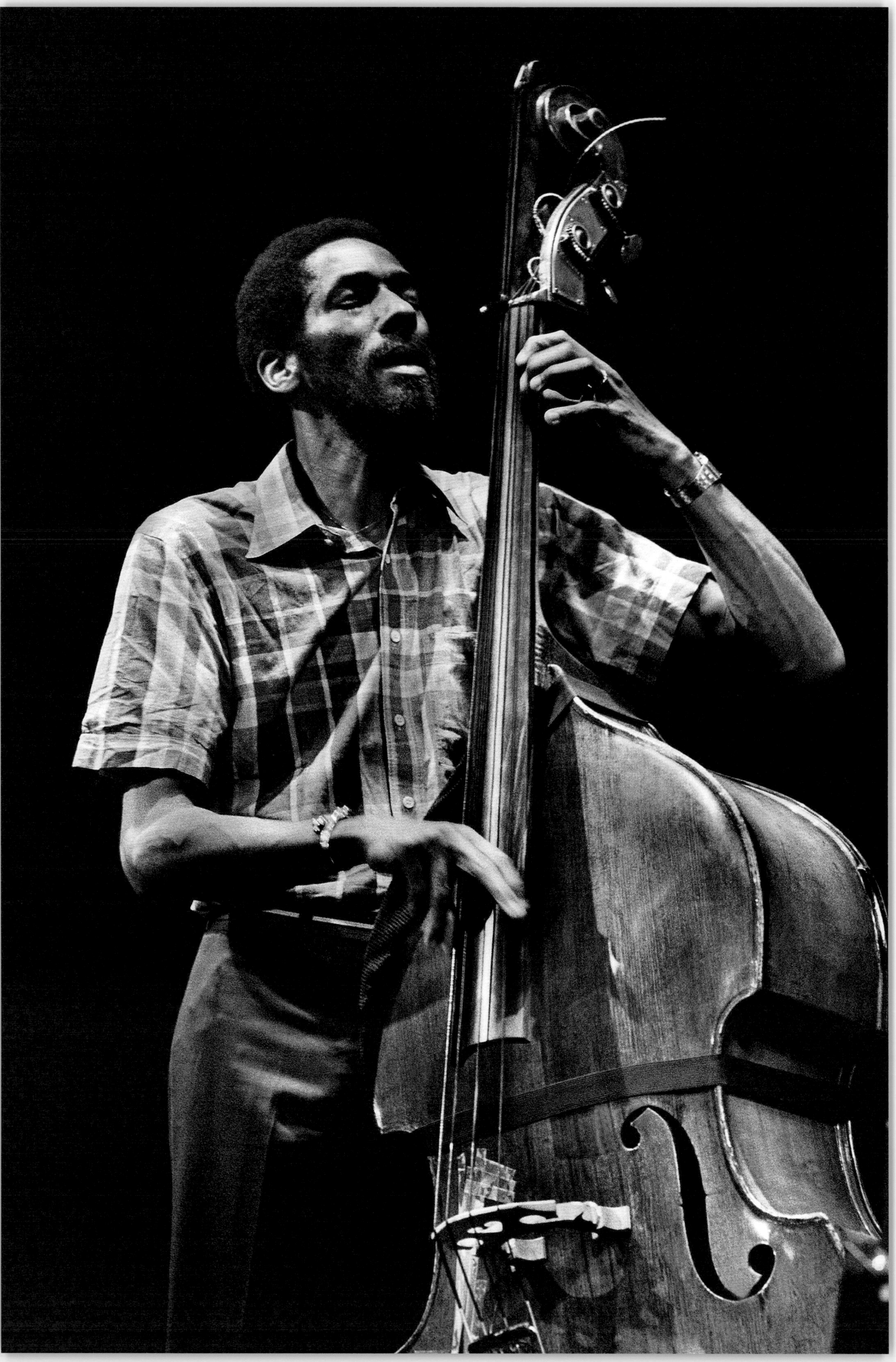

6

JAZZ
HEROES & LEGENDS

I have been able to photograph many legends of jazz over the years, and they always make for great pictures (and a great show). Seeing Miles Davis or Wynton Marsalis control an audience with their horns, or hearing a gifted vocalist like Ella Fitzgerald blend in with their band is always cause for a great night. I have also photographed many younger, up-and-coming players, making me believe that jazz is in good hands for years to come.

RON CARTER / CHICAGO, IL / 1981

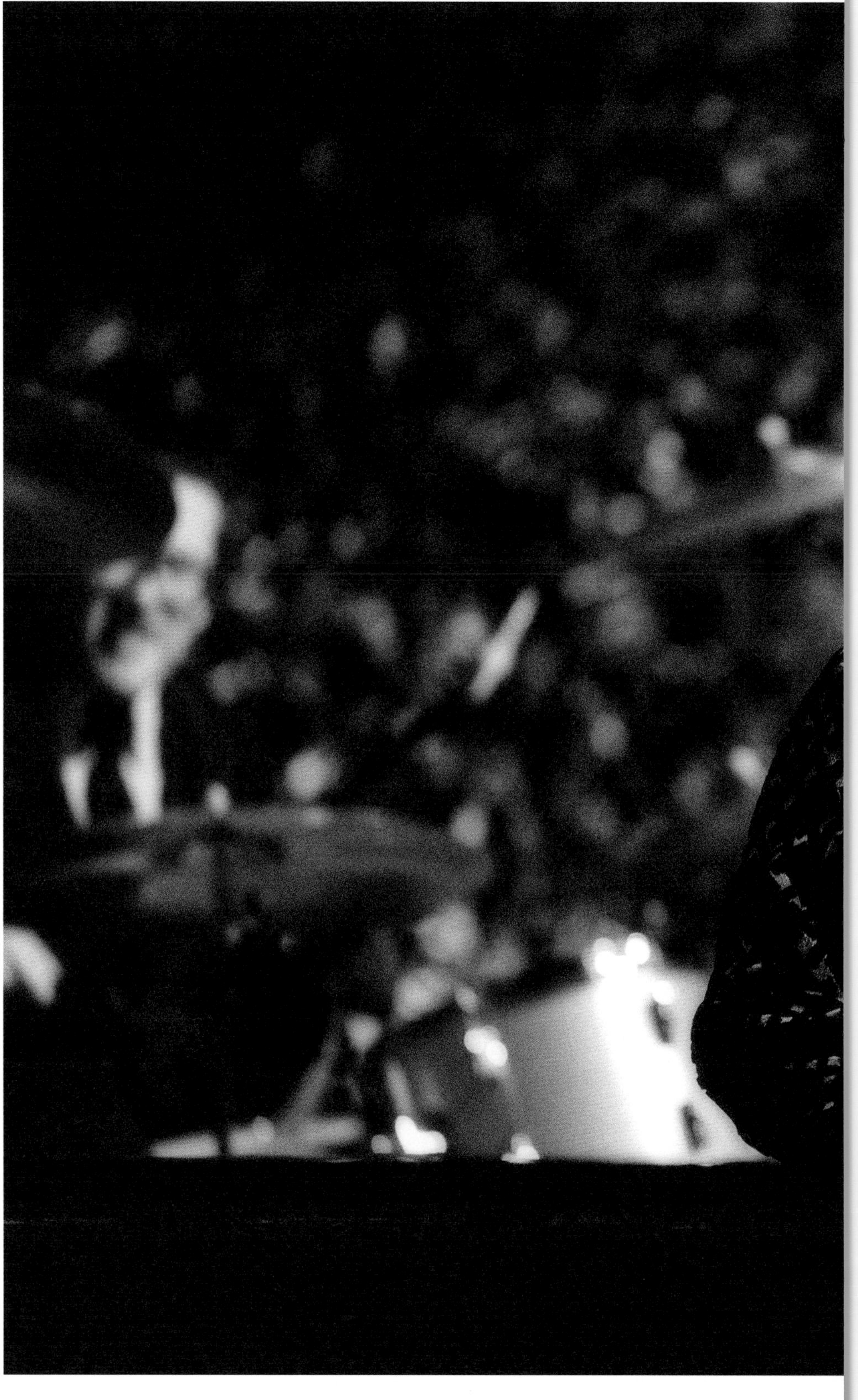

For many years, I worked on a television series called *Soundstage* that was shot at Chicago's PBS station. It featured a diverse selection of subjects, from Johnny Paycheck to Muddy Waters. In November of 1979, I was asked to photograph a jazz show featuring Count Basie and Ella Fitzgerald. The first day was a rehearsal, and I was allowed to

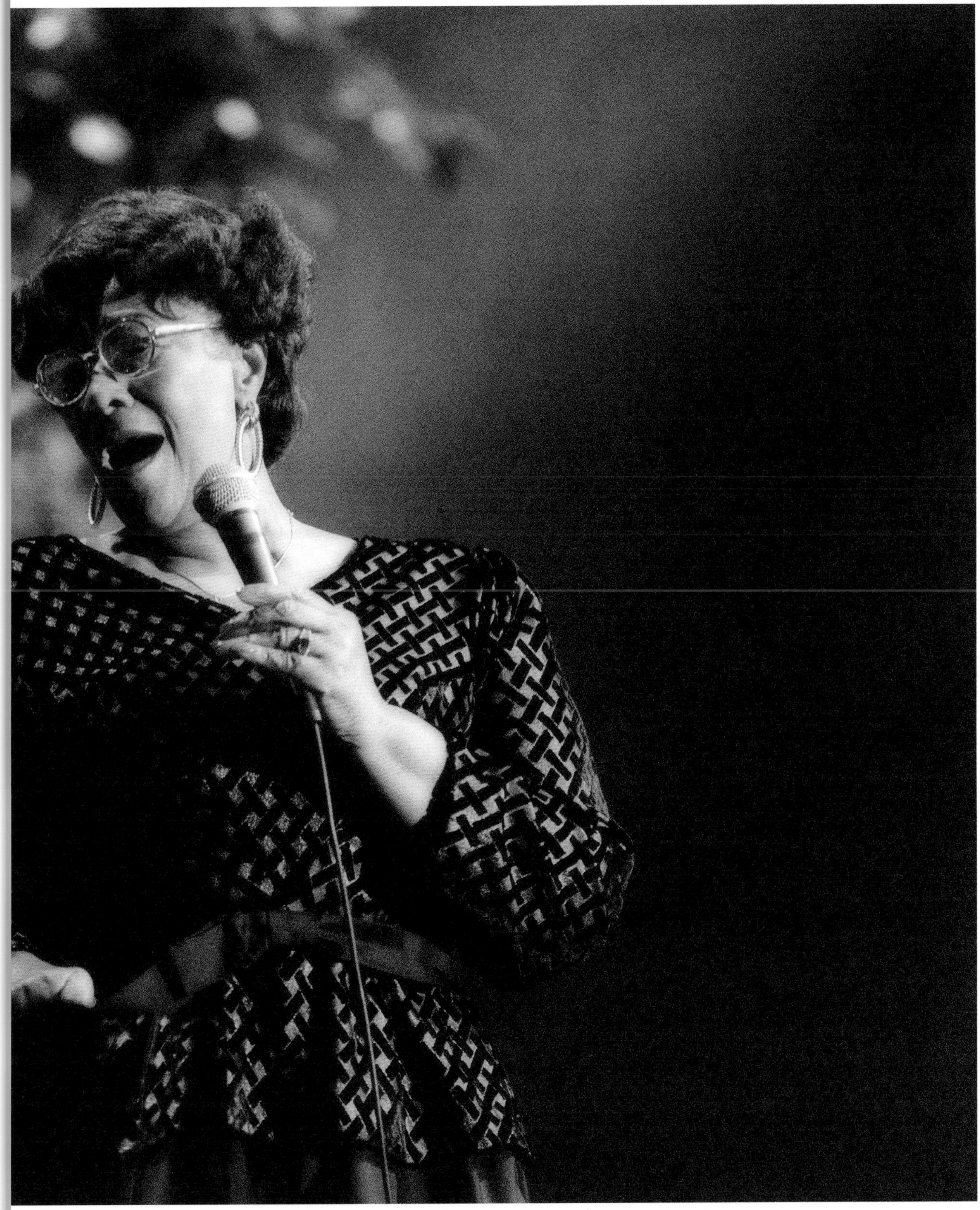

wander anywhere I needed to be, including onstage at the end of the piano. The second day was the taping, where I captured the interaction between the two jazz giants for several hours!

ELLA FITZGERALD / CHICAGO, IL / 1979

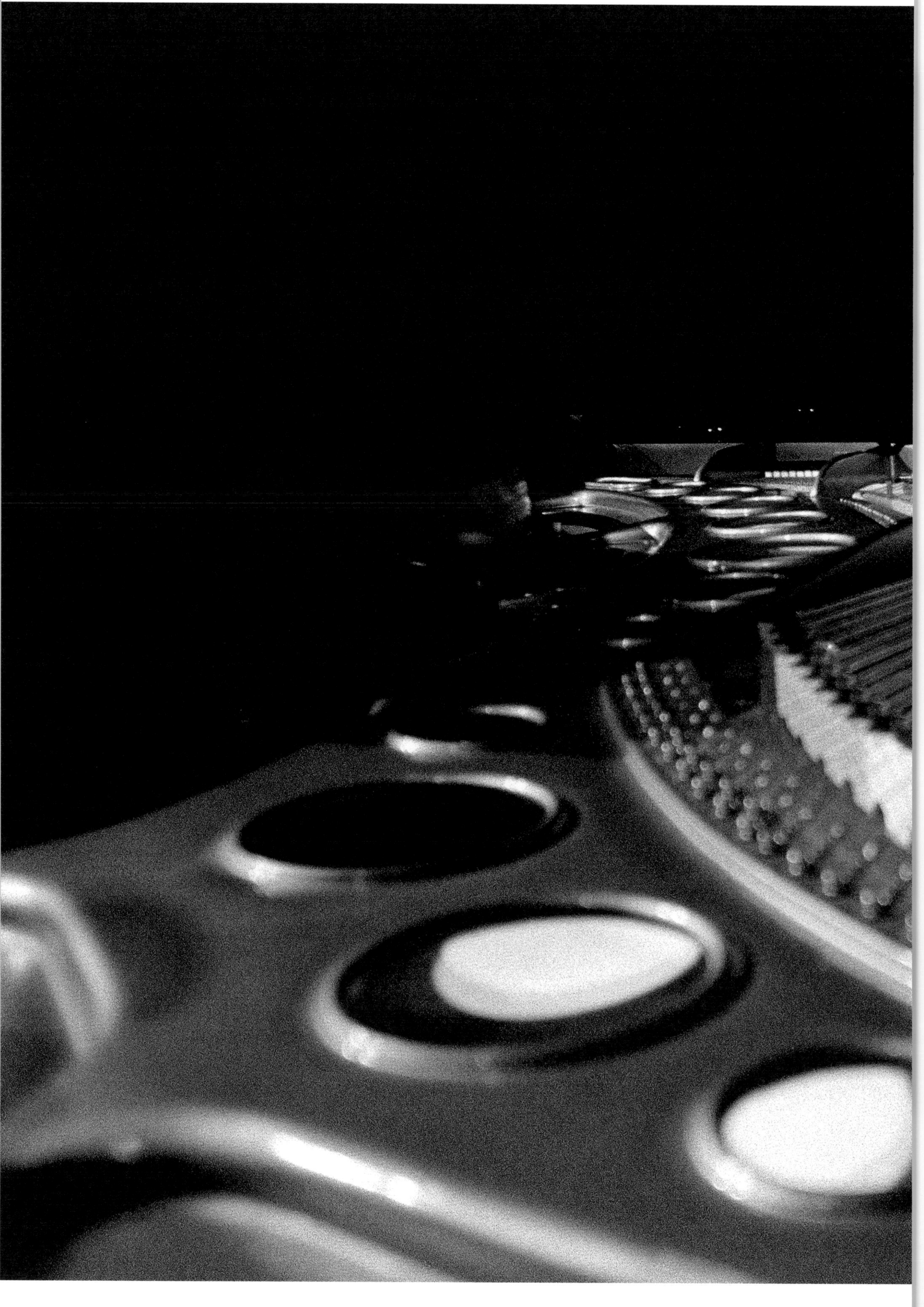

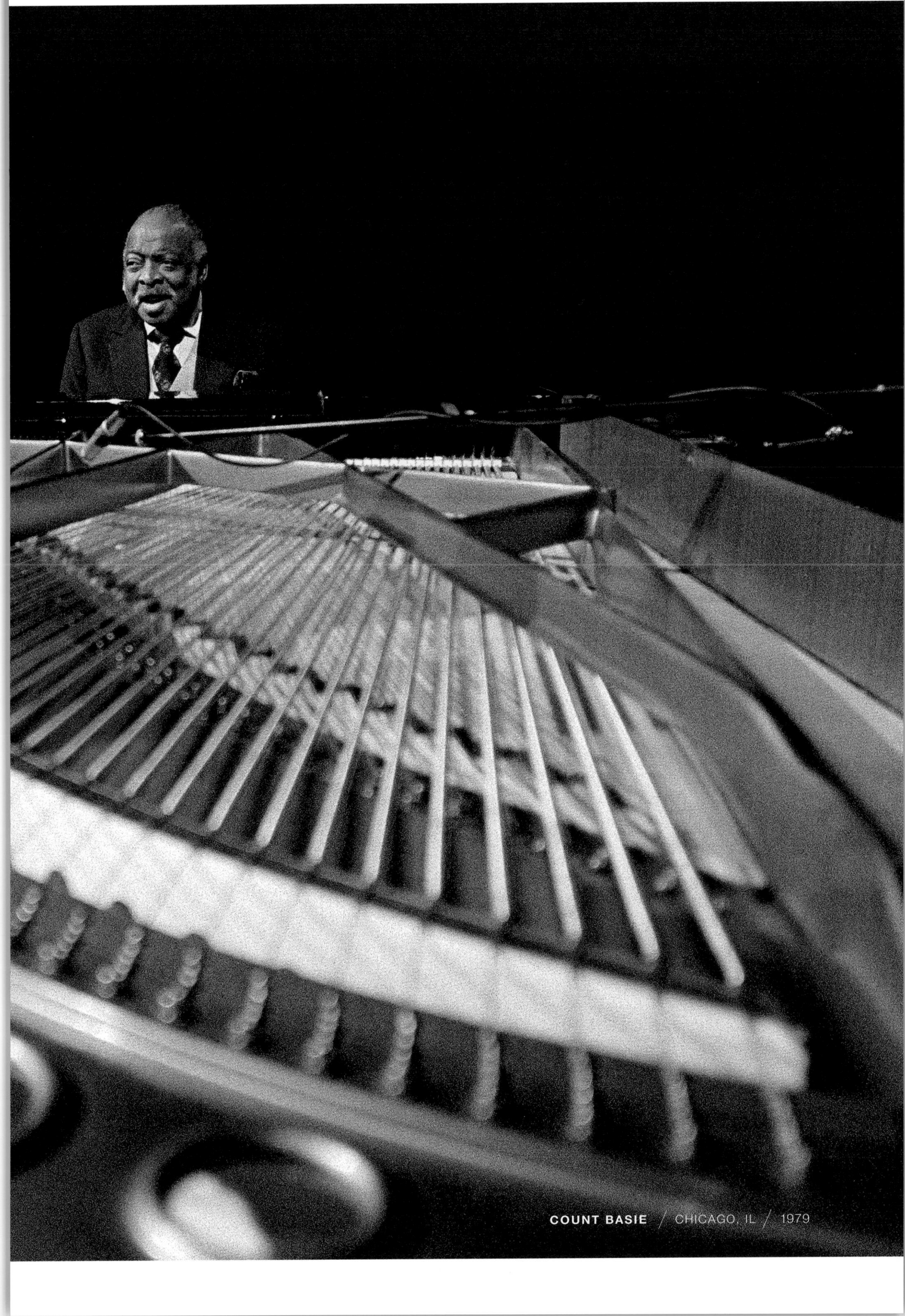

COUNT BASIE / CHICAGO, IL / 1979

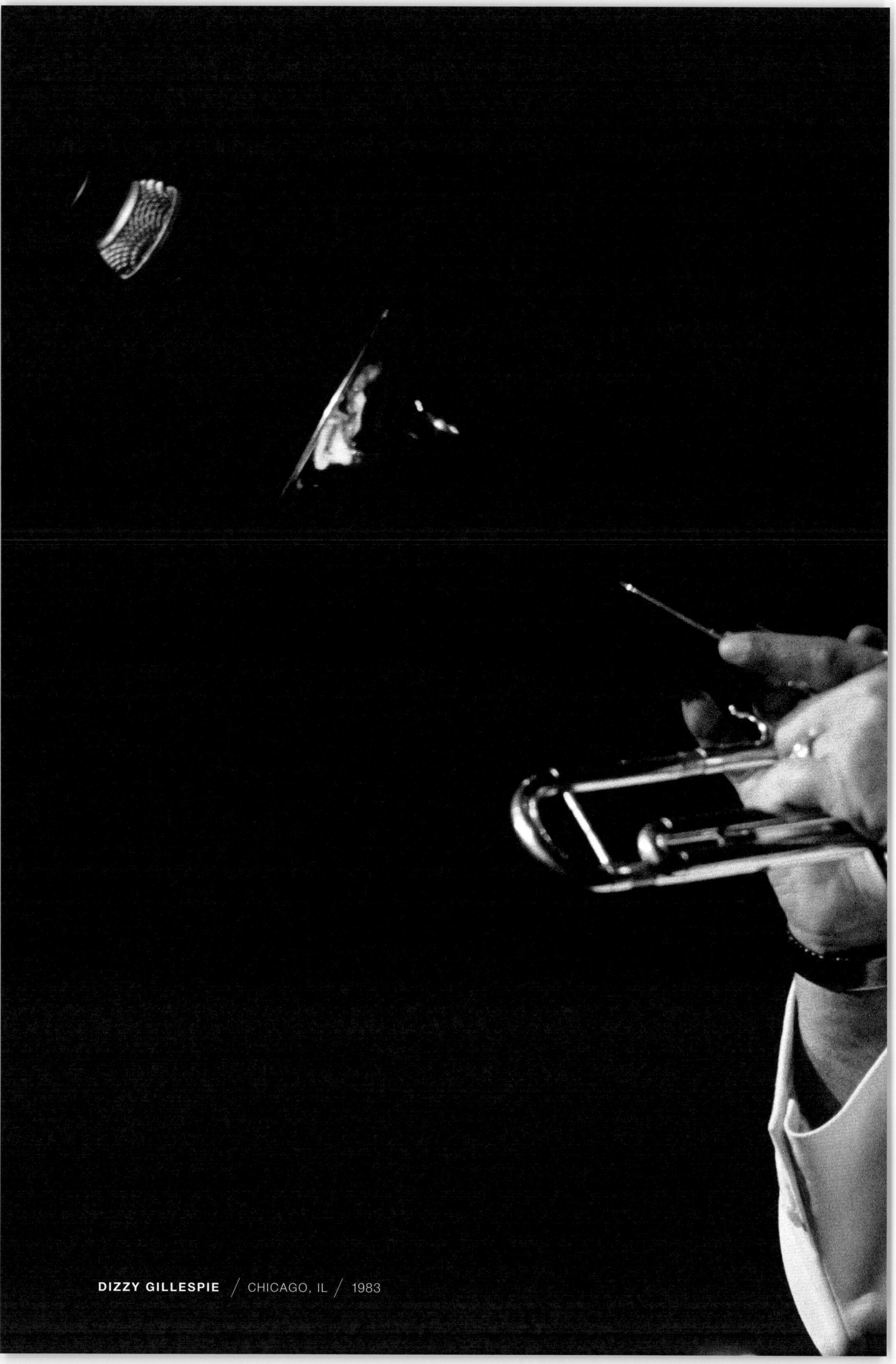

DIZZY GILLESPIE / CHICAGO, IL / 1983

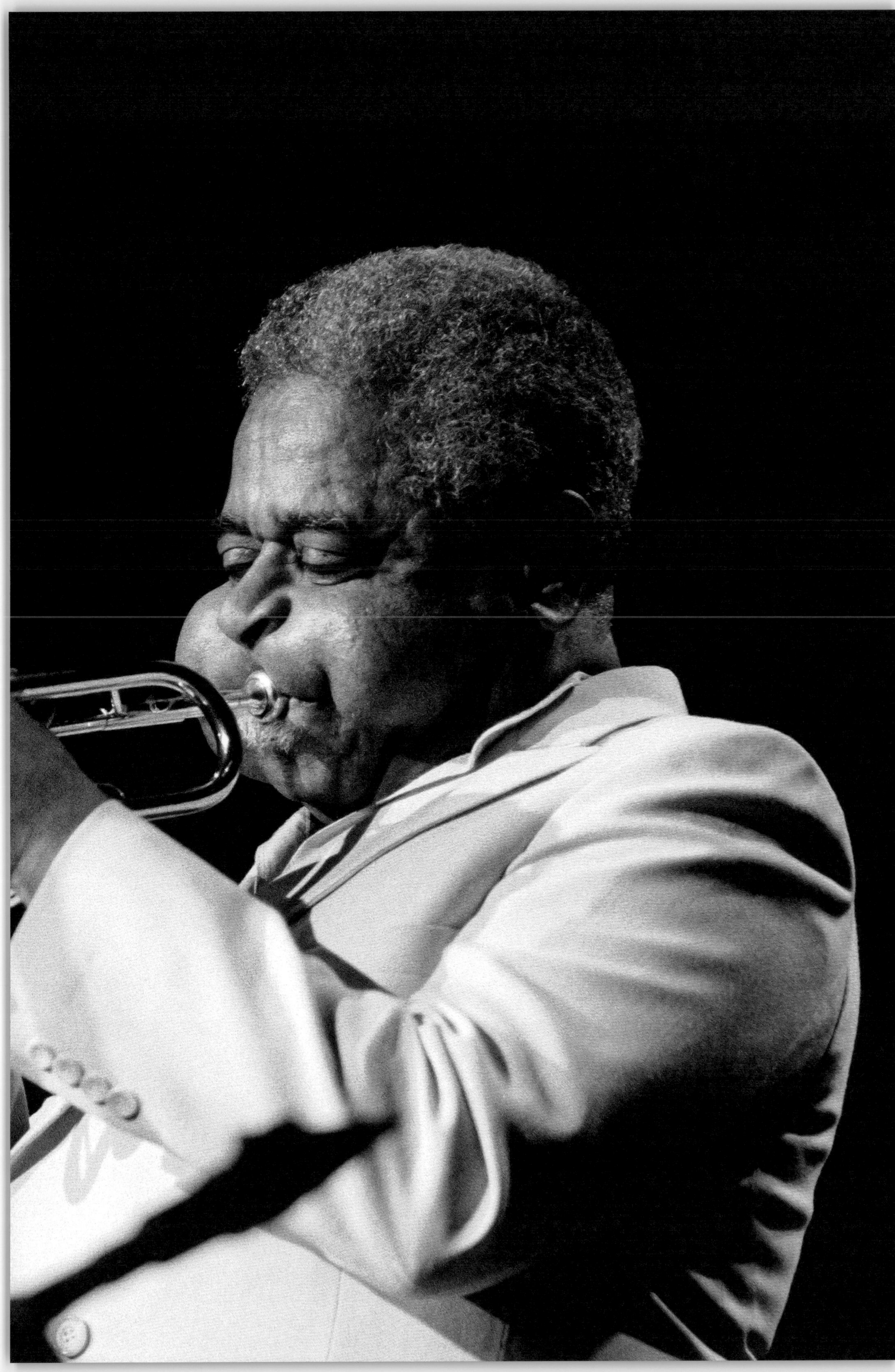

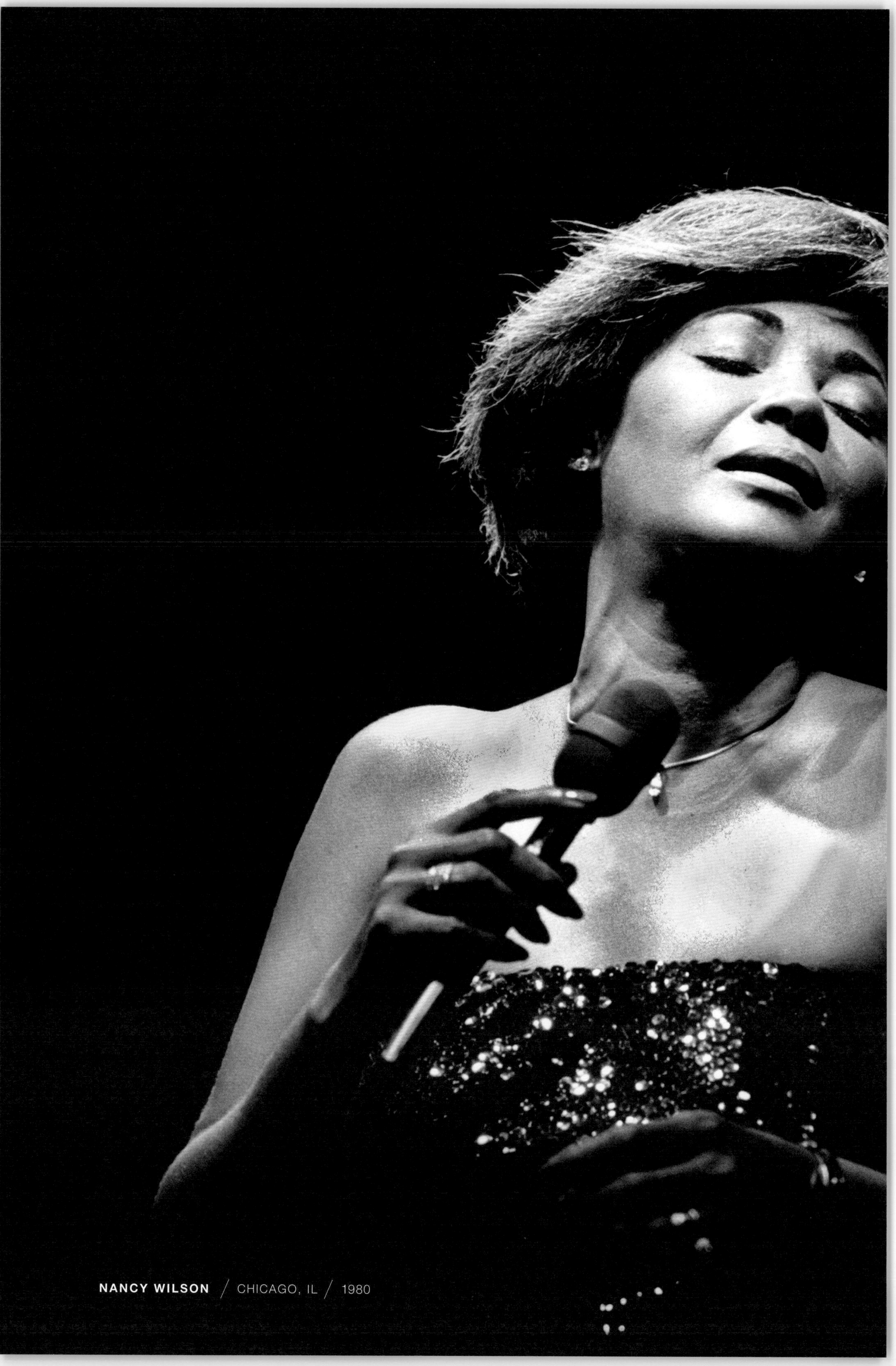

NANCY WILSON / CHICAGO, IL / 1980

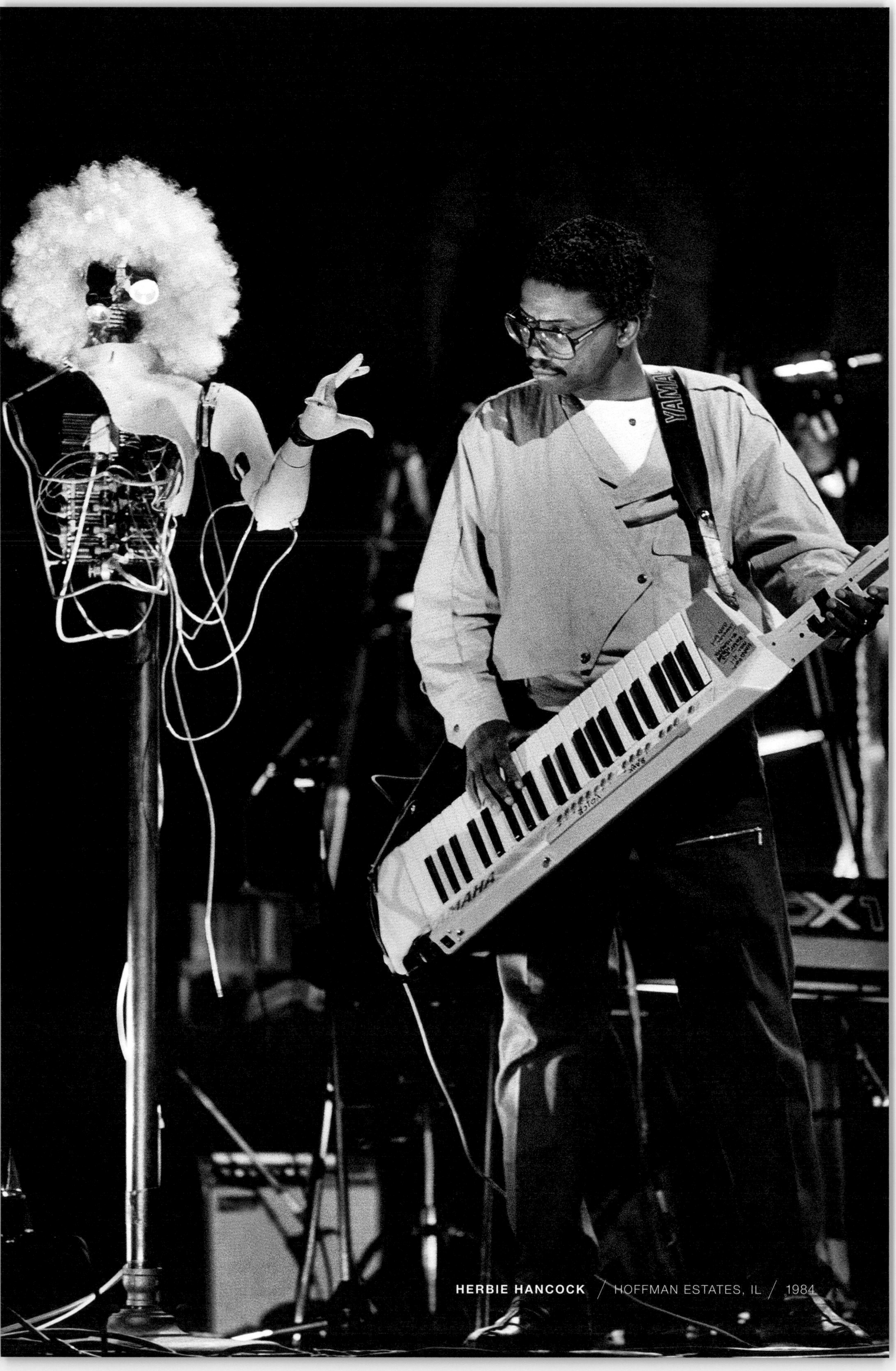

HERBIE HANCOCK / HOFFMAN ESTATES, IL / 1984

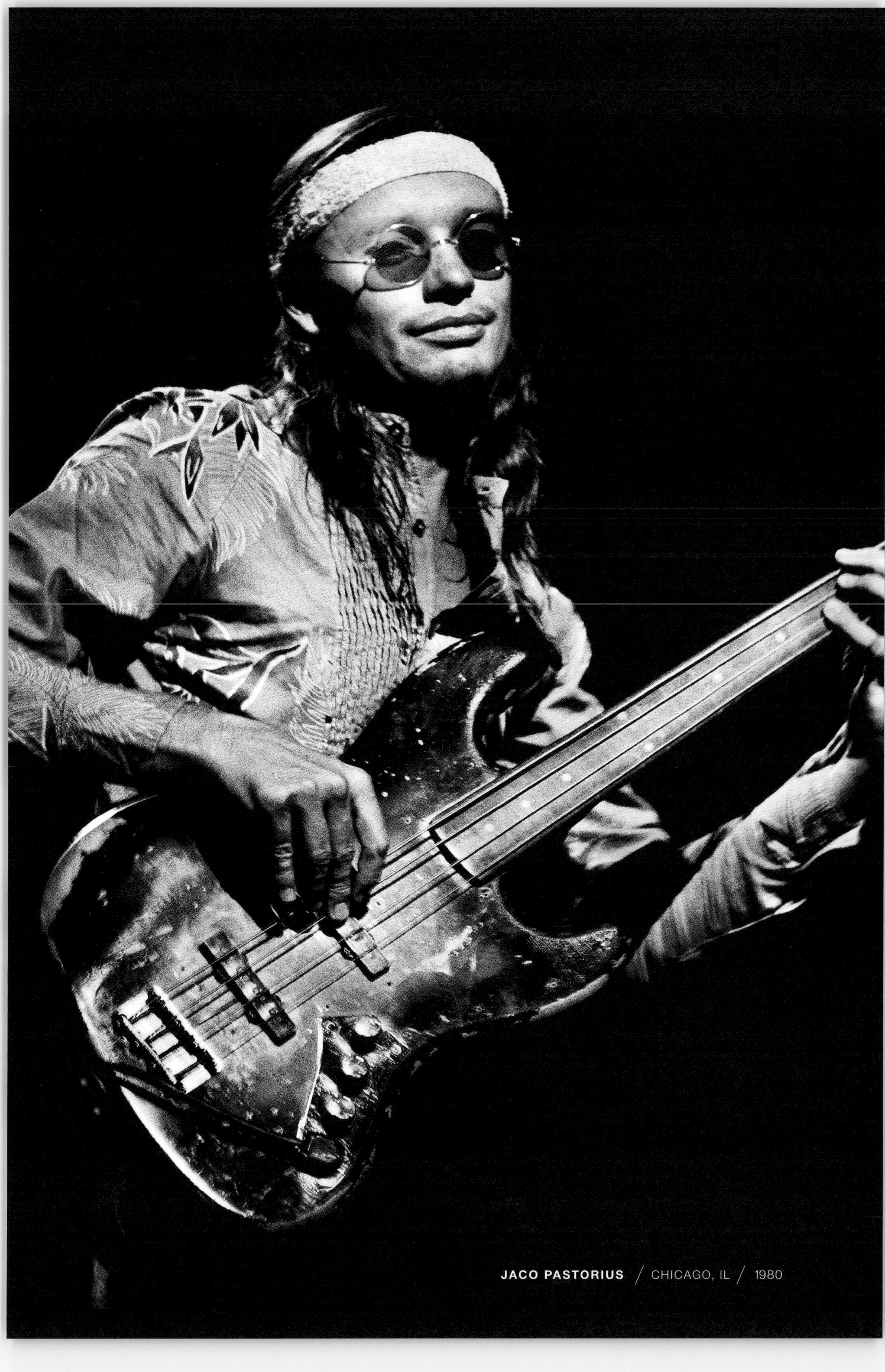

JACO PASTORIUS / CHICAGO, IL / 1980

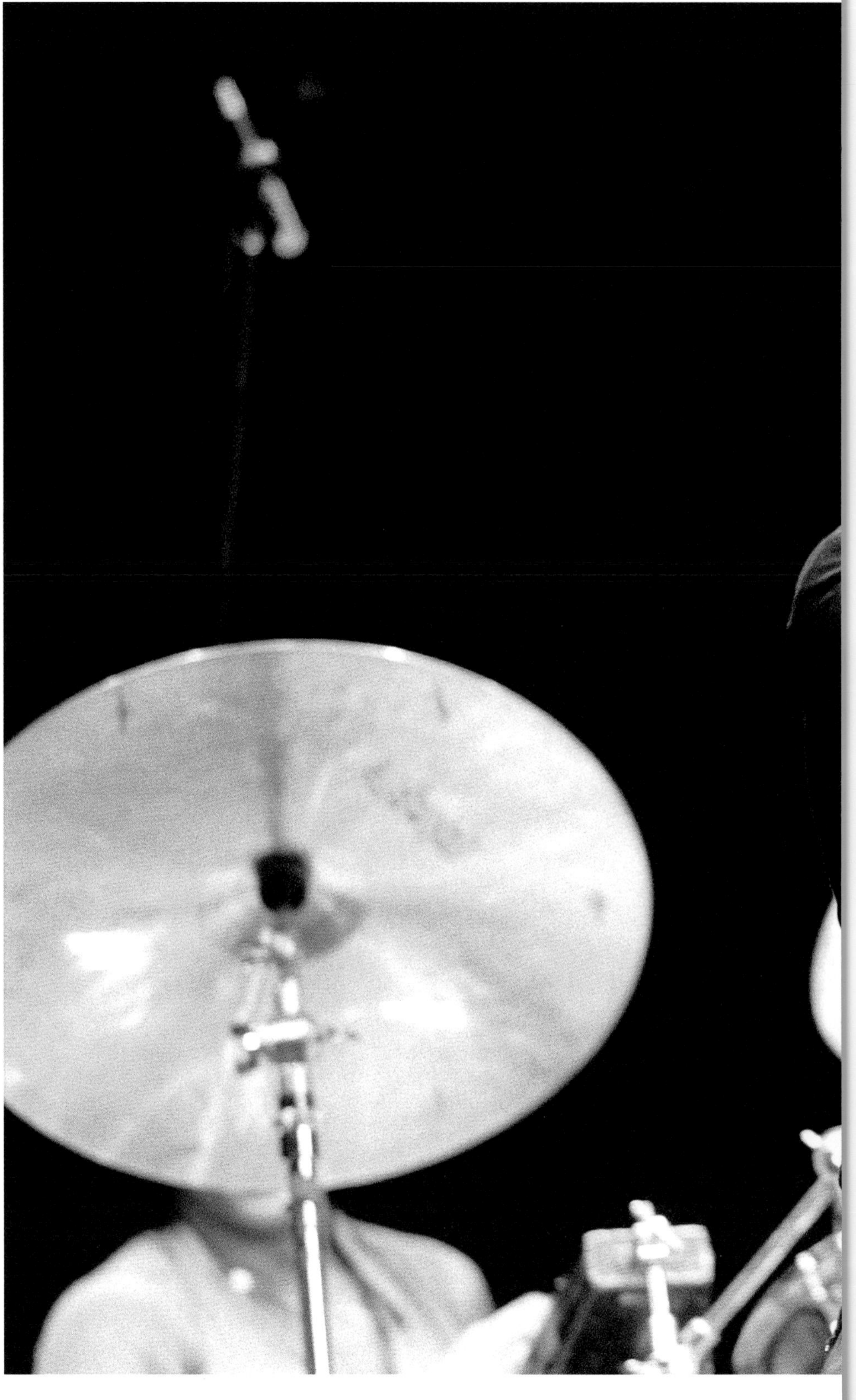

I was on assignment for the *Chicago Reader* in 1983 to photograph the incomparable Miles Davis at the Park West nightclub. Before the show started, I settled myself near the front of the stage, kneeling in an uncomfortable position on the hardwood floor in order to capture the perfect shot. Much to my chagrin, Miles played with his back to the audience for song after song after song. I tried to wait him out and remained where

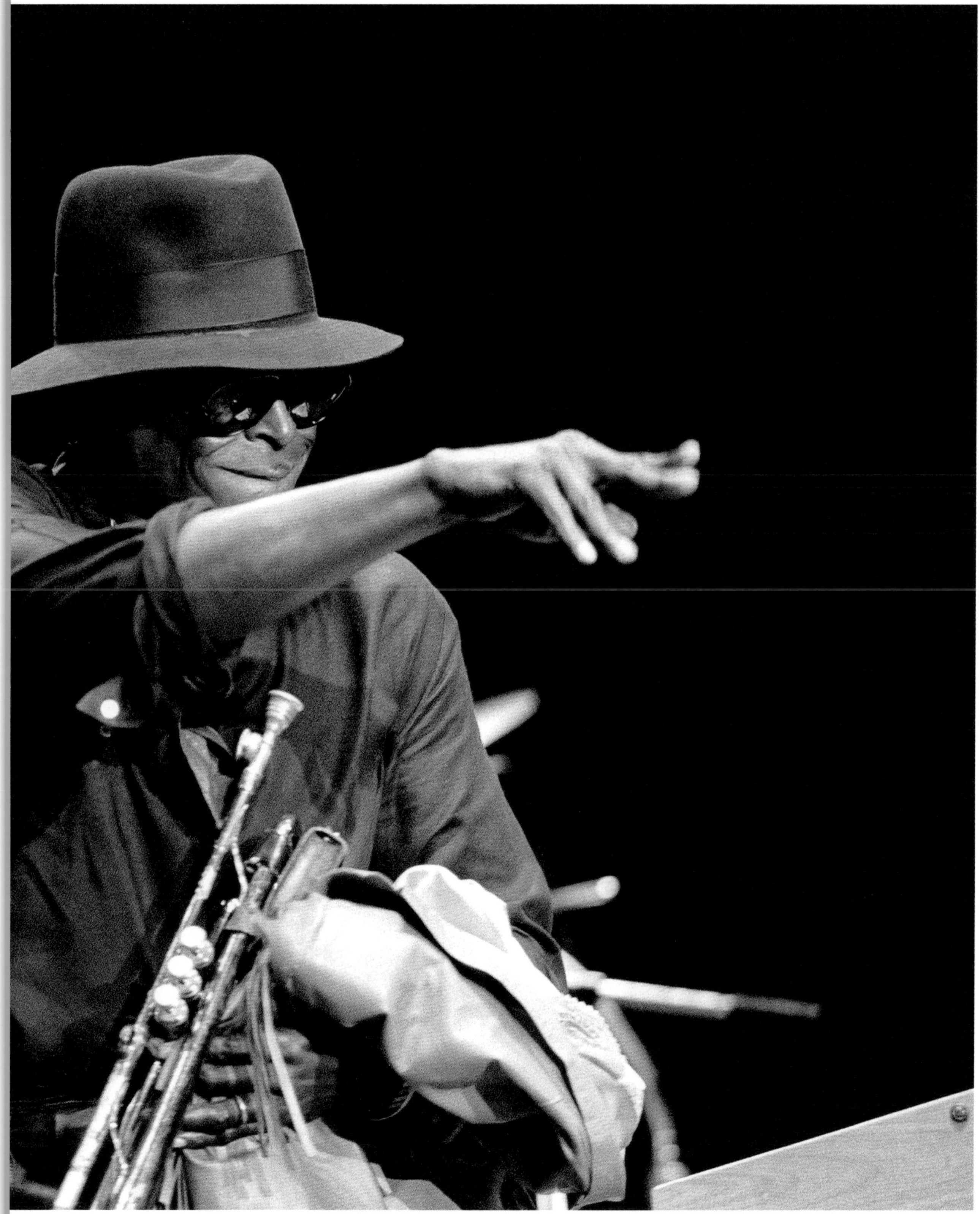

I was, camera ready for the moment he turned around. But as the show continued, he stayed put. Still I waited, trying to stay out of the way as the waitstaff served drinks to the crowd. Two hours later, just as the show was ending, Miles picked up his jacket, turned to the audience, waved and walked off the stage. In that brief moment, I took one picture. And to this day, it is one of my favorites.

MILES DAVIS / CHICAGO, IL / 1983

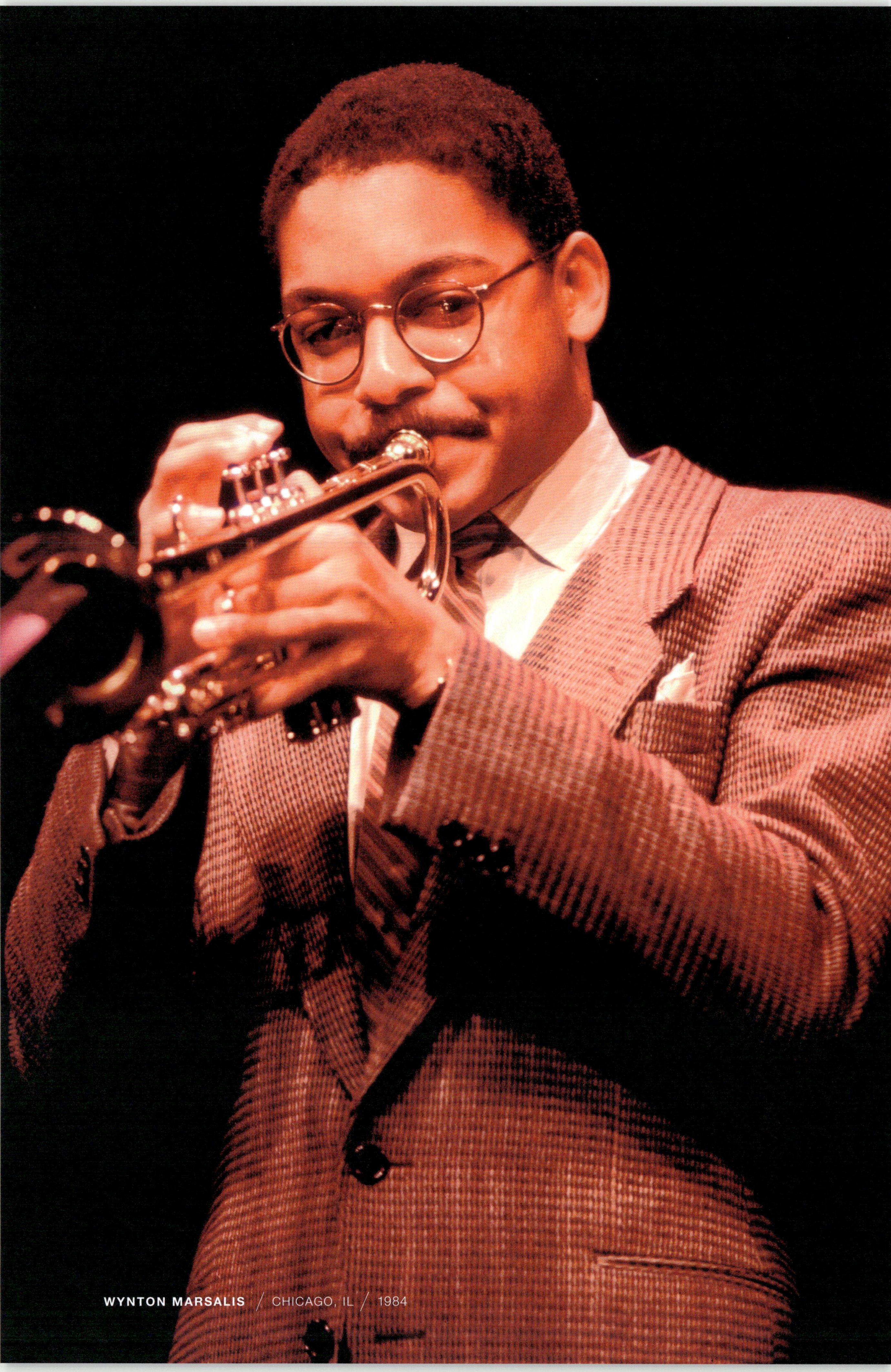

WYNTON MARSALIS / CHICAGO, IL / 1984

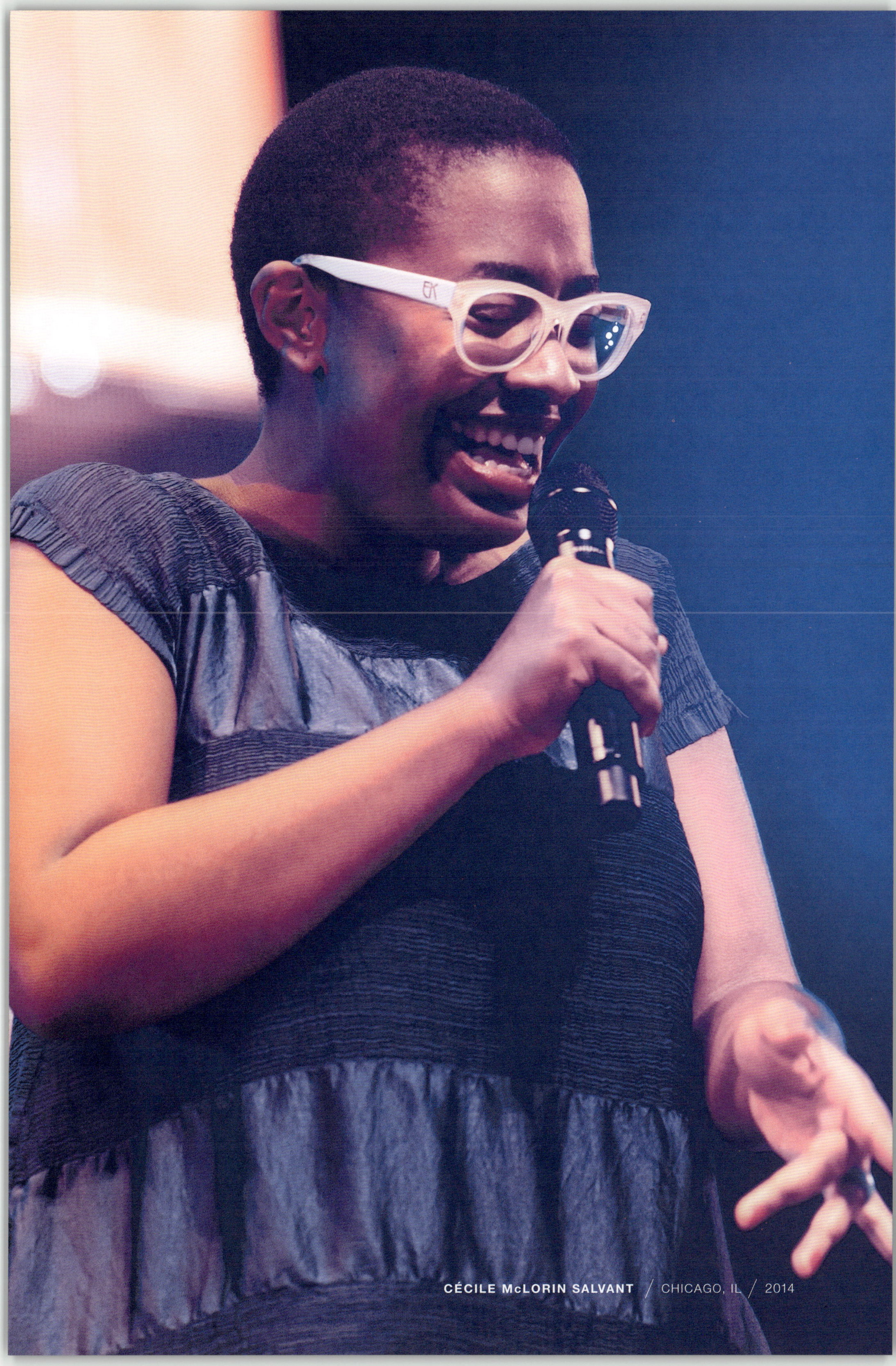

CÉCILE McLORIN SALVANT / CHICAGO, IL / 2014

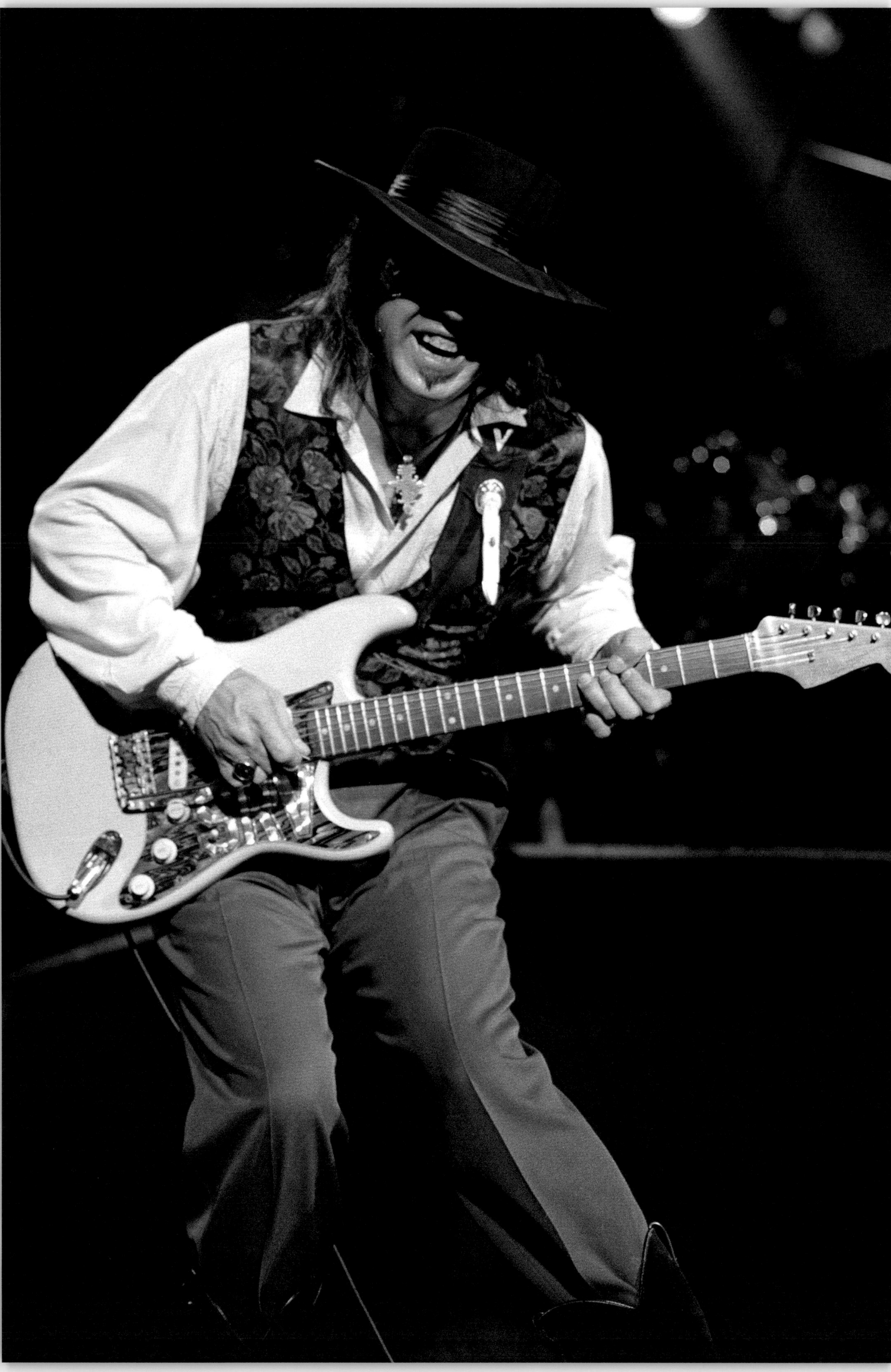

7

BLUES
NOTES & CHORDS

When I first started going out to hear live music, it was almost always blues or folk. The first time I heard Buddy Guy, I knew that I had found a reality that I could listen to for the rest of my life. Then I discovered Muddy Waters and Willie Dixon and I knew that life was good!

STEVIE RAY VAUGHAN / EAST TROY, WI / 1990

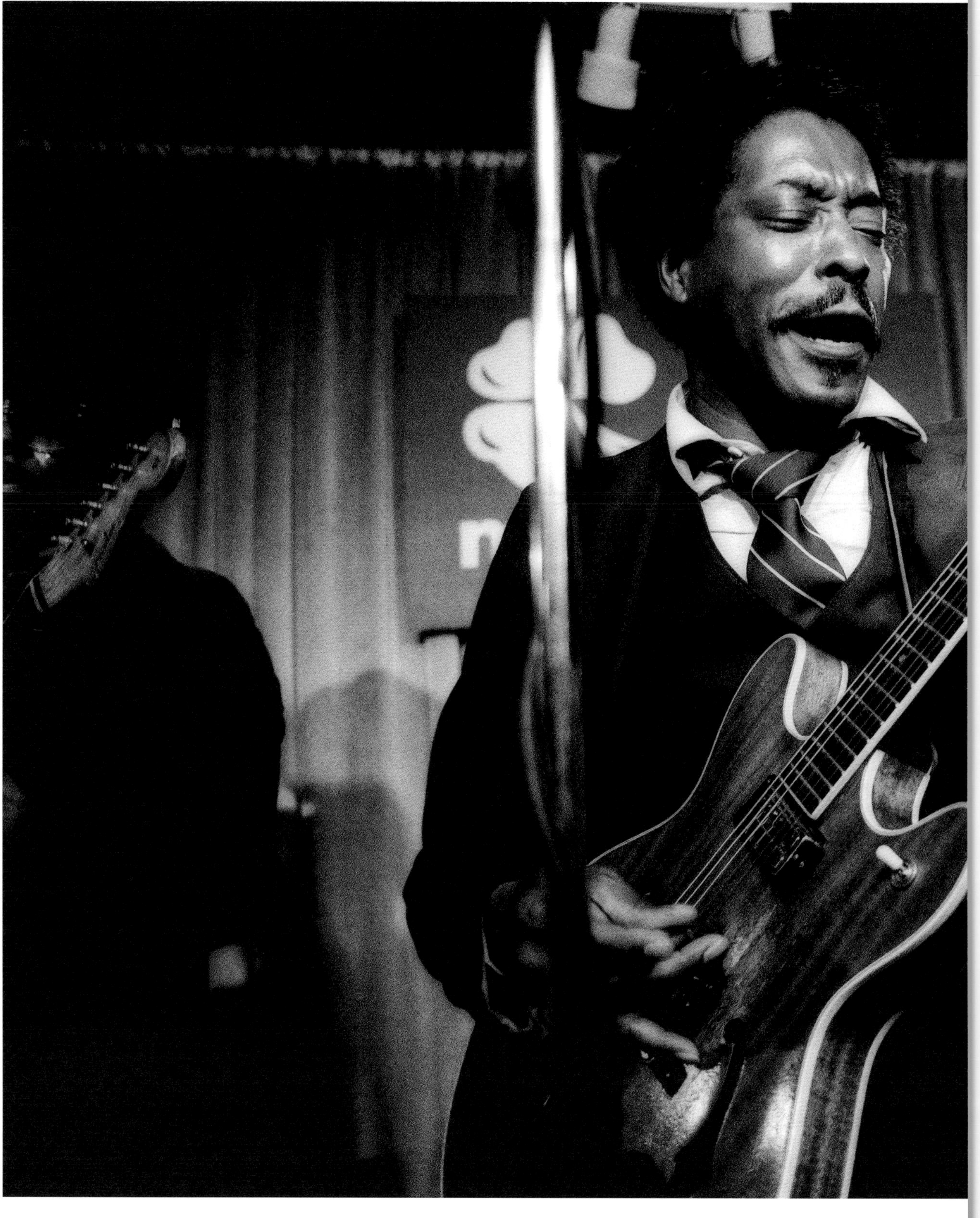

I met Buddy Guy in 1980 when I was working for Journey, photographing whatever they were doing in Chicago for the week they were based in town. The band was filming a documentary where each member of the band was granted a wish off their "bucket list." Guitarist Neal Schon's wish was to play on stage with blues greats Buddy Guy and Junior Wells. The documentary crew rented a blues club called Biddy Mulligan's, hired Buddy and Junior to play, and then filmed the entire event. During filming, there was a lot of downtime, so I had the opportunity to sit down with Buddy. We had a great

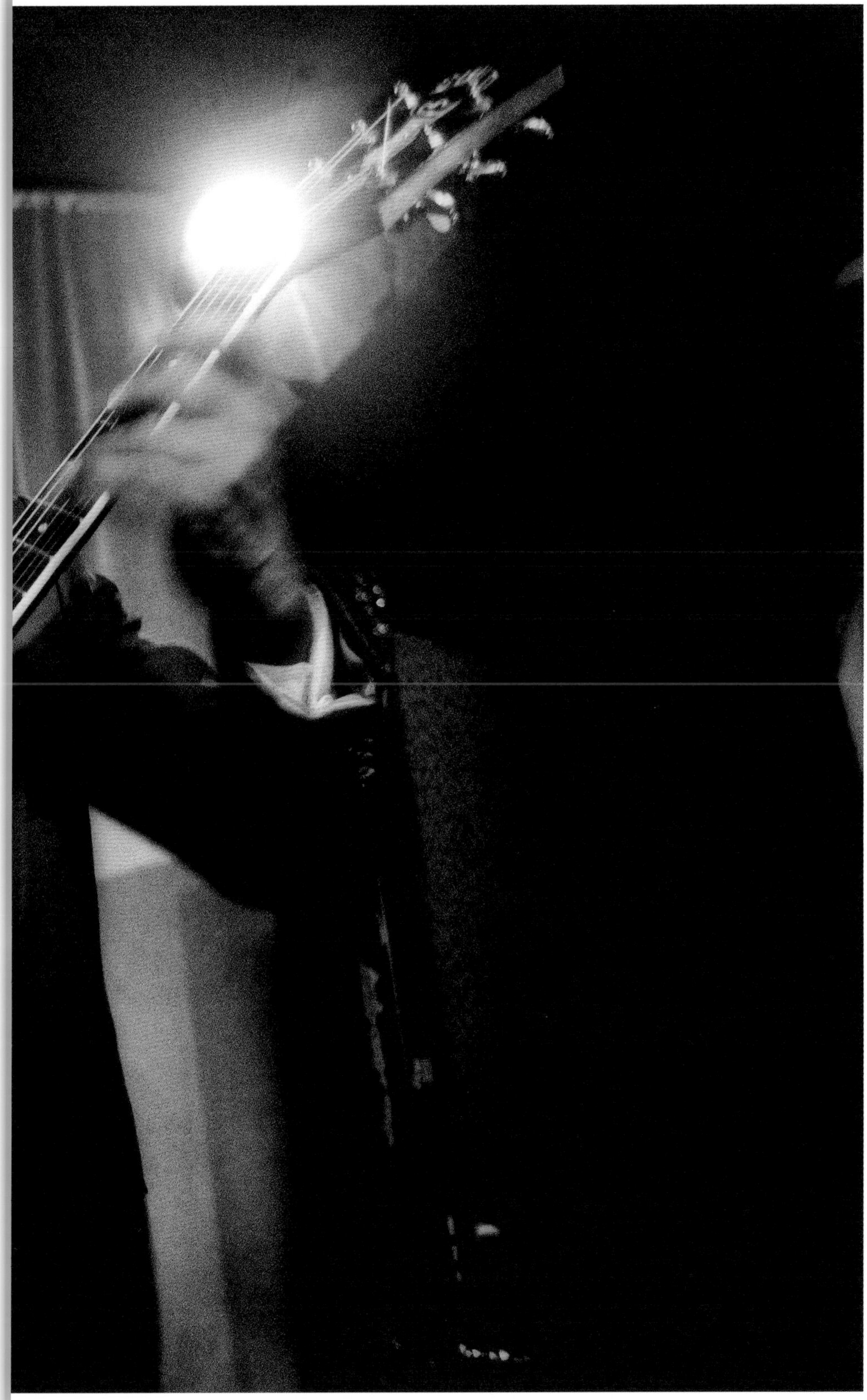

conversation about the world in general and other random subjects that turned into a 40-year friendship that continues to this day. One thing I love about being around Buddy is that it's like having a front-row seat to musical history. I have photographed him through the years in amazing situations: playing with the Rolling Stones, David Bowie, John Mayer, and even the president of the Czech Republic, among many others.

BUDDY GUY / CHICAGO, IL / 1980

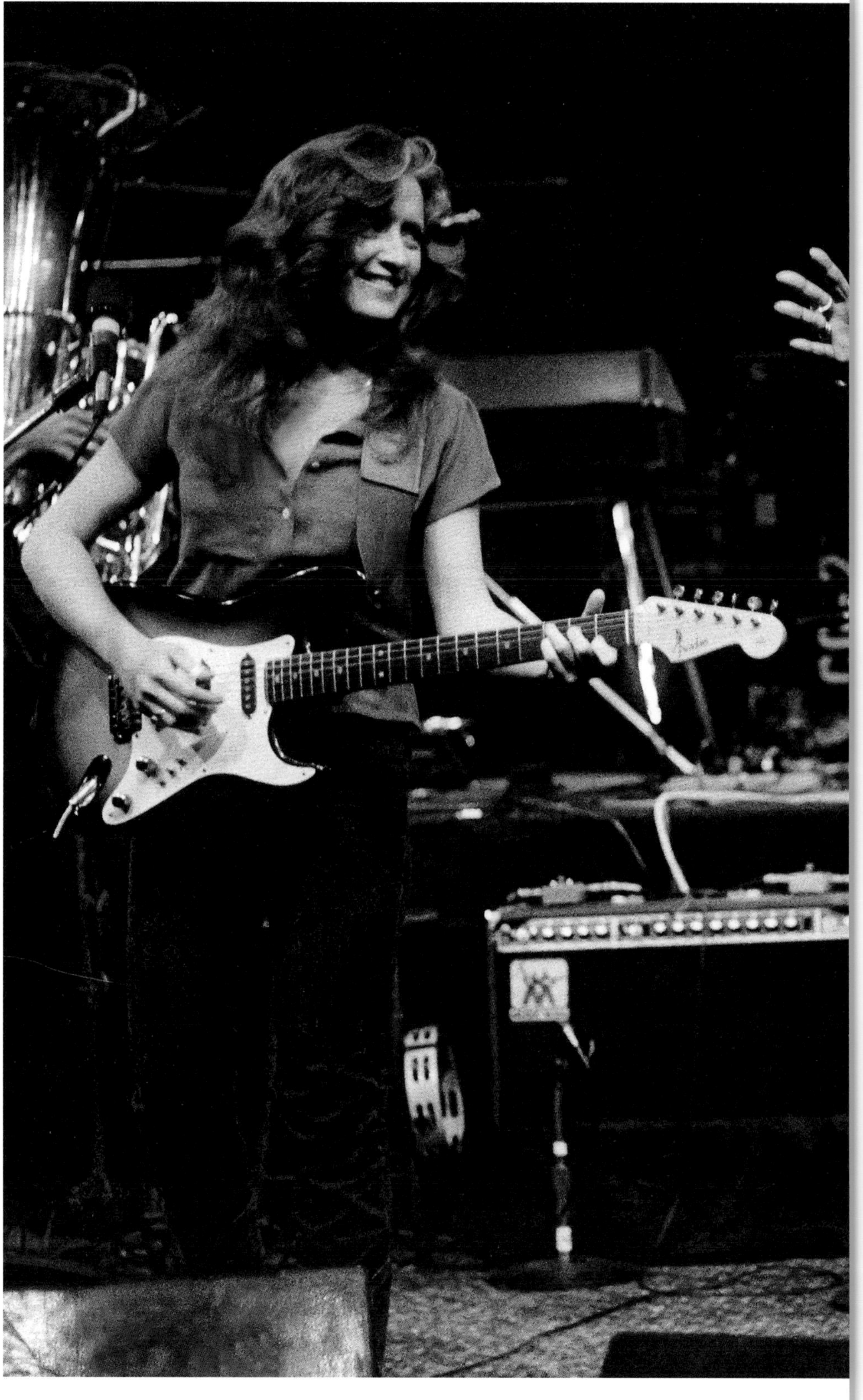

One day in 1980 I was scheduled to photograph a Bonnie Raitt concert in the suburbs of Chicago. When I arrived, I found out that the opening act was Sippie Wallace, a legendary Southern blues singer and Bonnie's all-time hero. I hoped that Bonnie would invite Sippie back onstage during her set, and I stayed at the ready for the entire show.

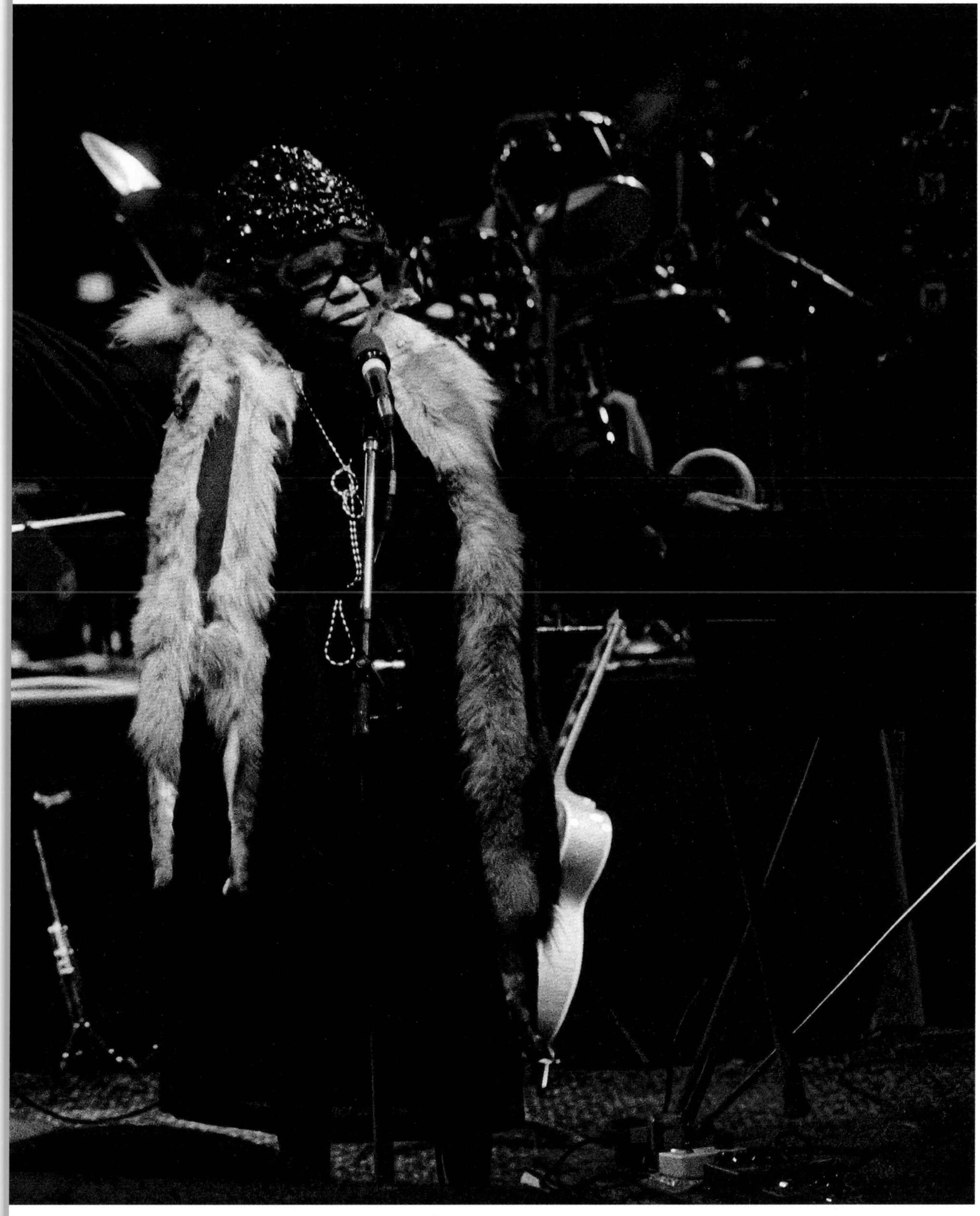

The invitation did eventually come, and the women performed several songs together. It wasn't until I developed the film the next day that I noticed Sippie was wearing a fox fur stole around her neck, complete with head and feet–quite the fashion statement.

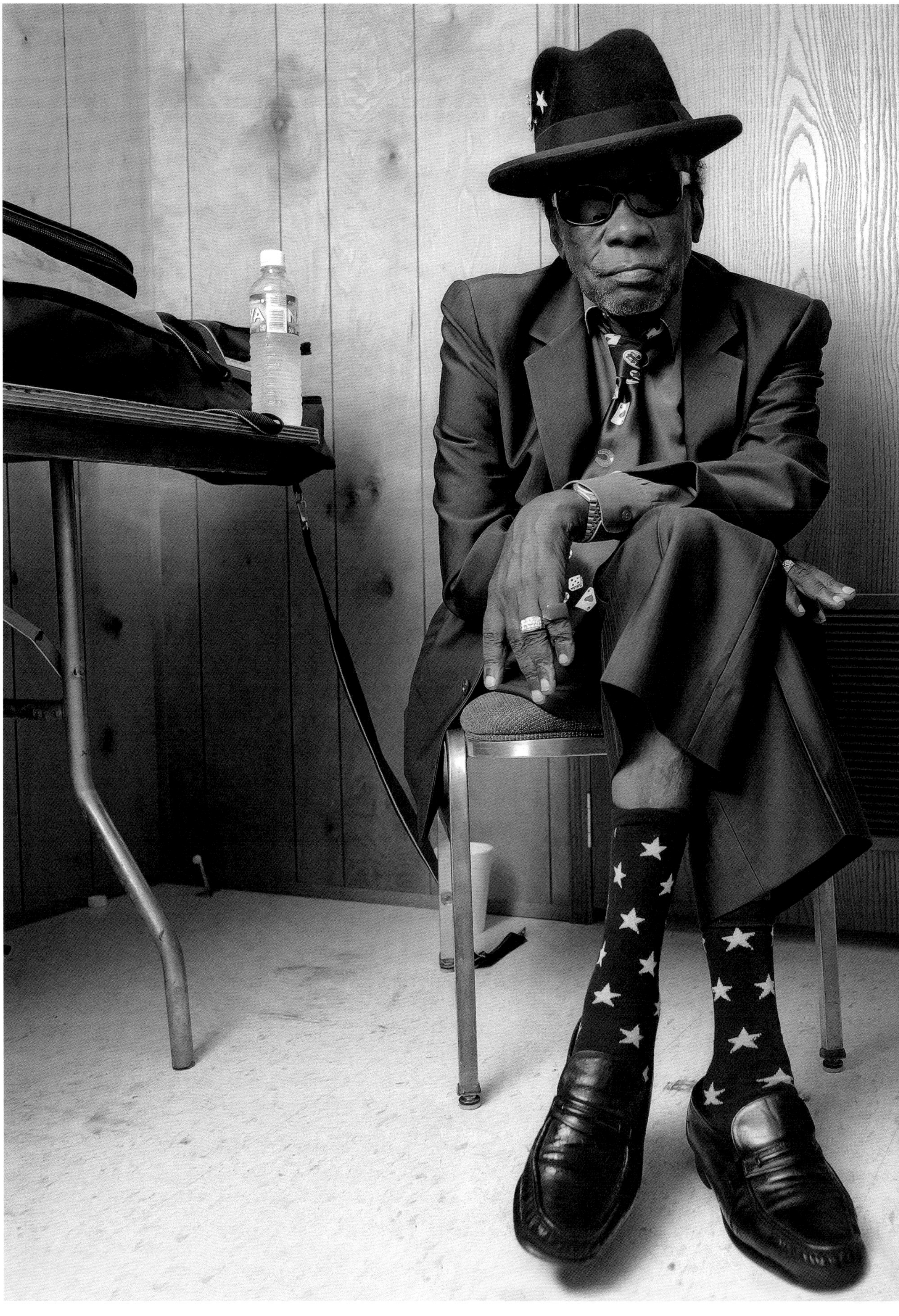

JOHN LEE HOOKER / ARLINGTON HEIGHTS, IL / 1998

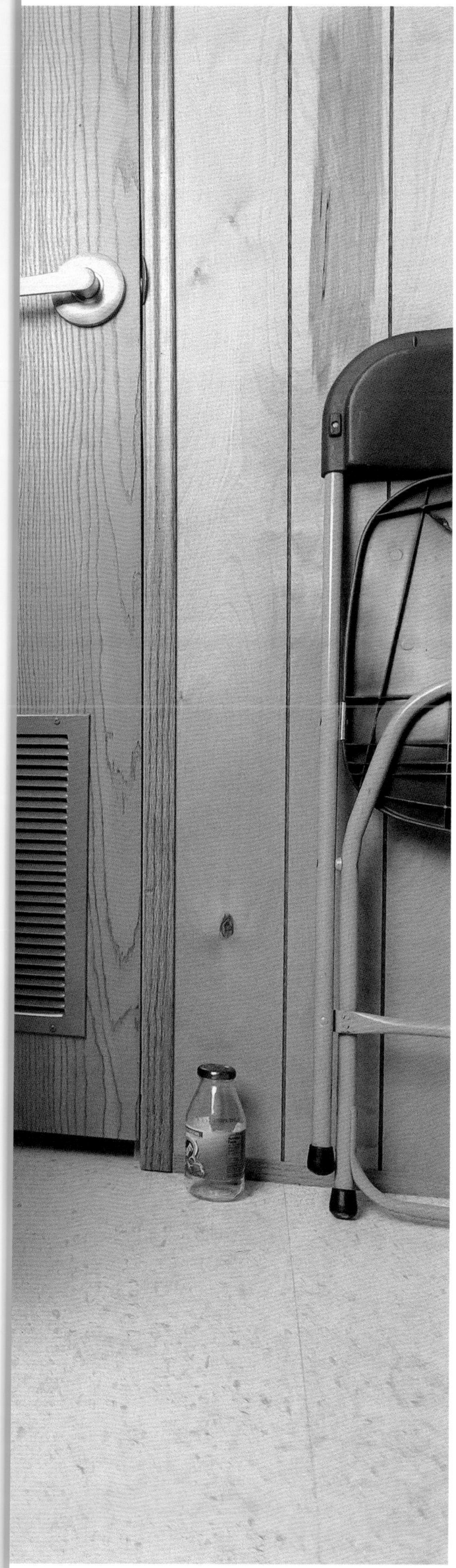

In June of 1998, I was asked to do a portrait of John Lee Hooker. He was playing at a festival in the infield of a racetrack. When I reached his trailer, I discovered that the room was too small for me to stand far enough back to fit his full body in the frame. My only choice was to take the camera off the tripod and crawl under a table on my stomach to rest the camera on the floor–allowing me a great angle to capture him (and his socks) for history.

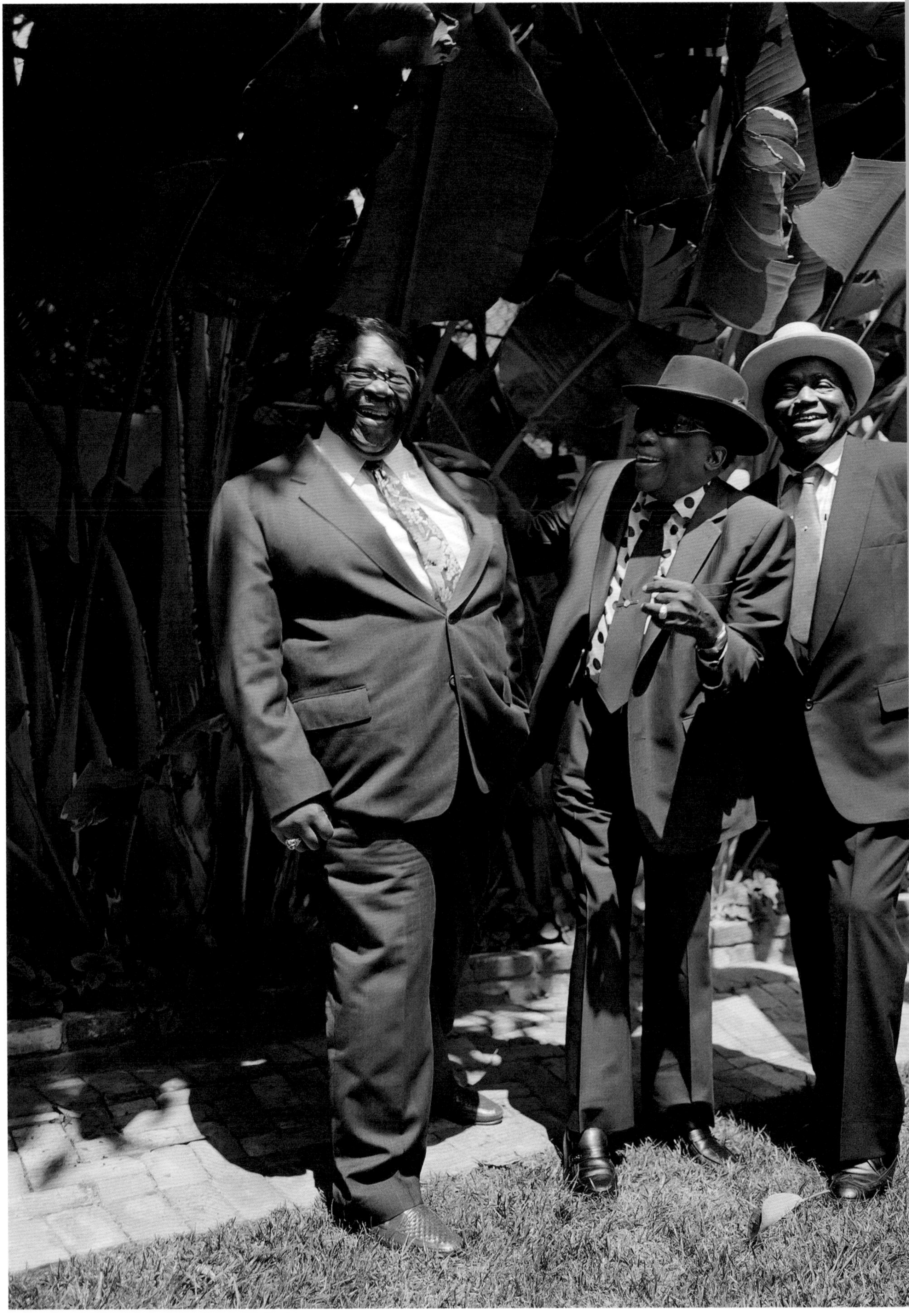

B.B. KING, **JOHN LEE HOOKER** & **WILLIE DIXON** / LOS ANGELES, CA / 1991

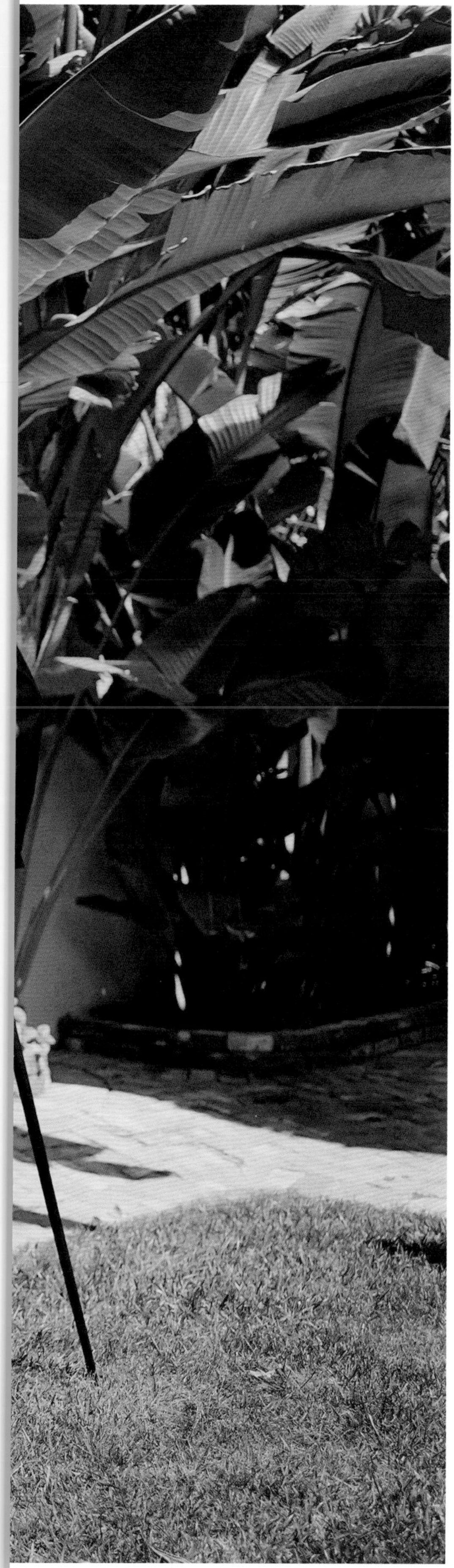

In April 1991, a press conference was held for a blues tour that was going to take place over the summer. I was hired to shoot the official portrait of the headliners, and I had one hour with the three blues giants. After shooting each artist individually around a piano, we went outside where this unscripted moment took place. I asked them to just ignore me and talk to each other. Their subject was women on the road; nice to see that in their 80s, that was still a viable topic!

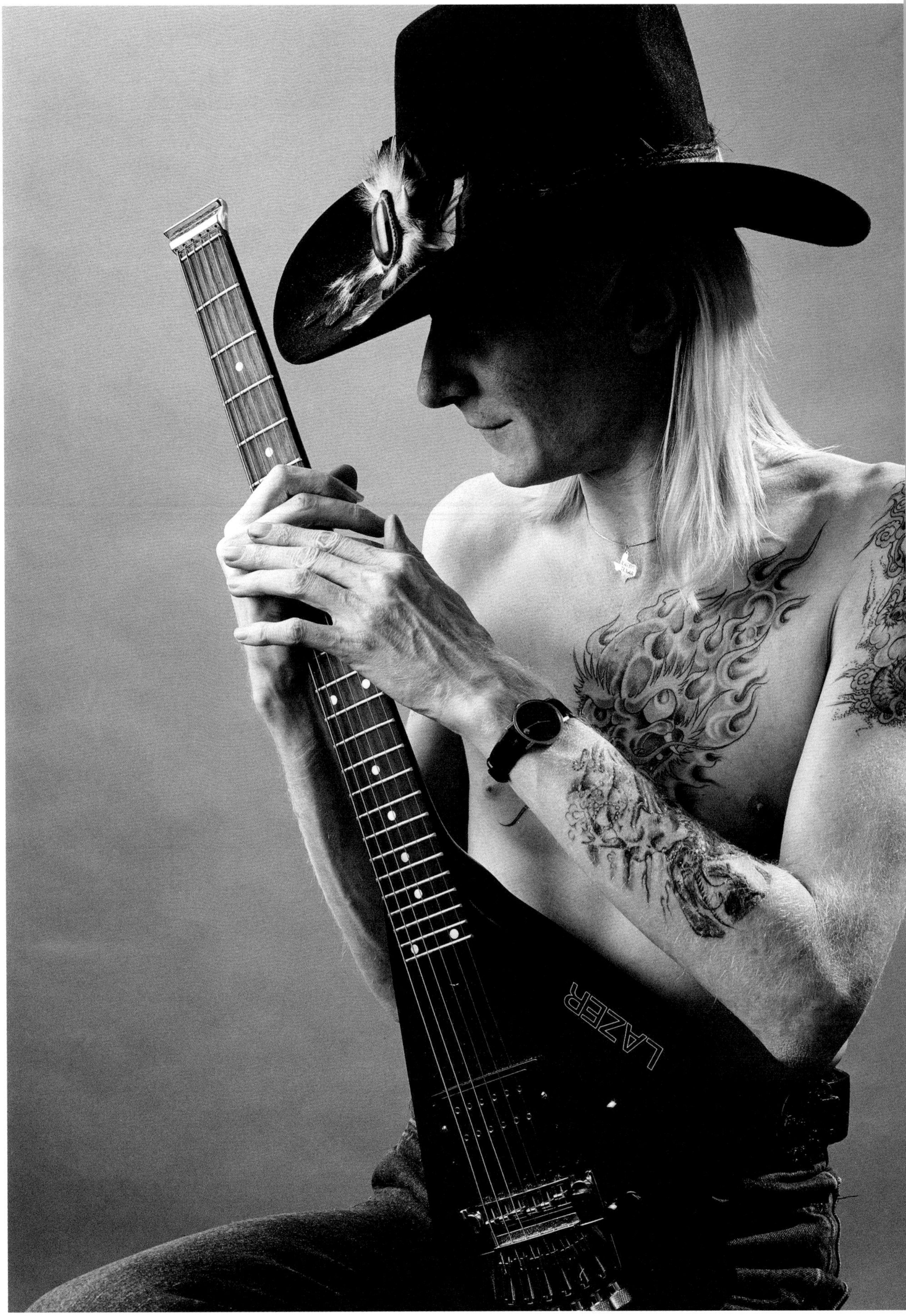

JOHNNY WINTER / CHICAGO, IL / 1984

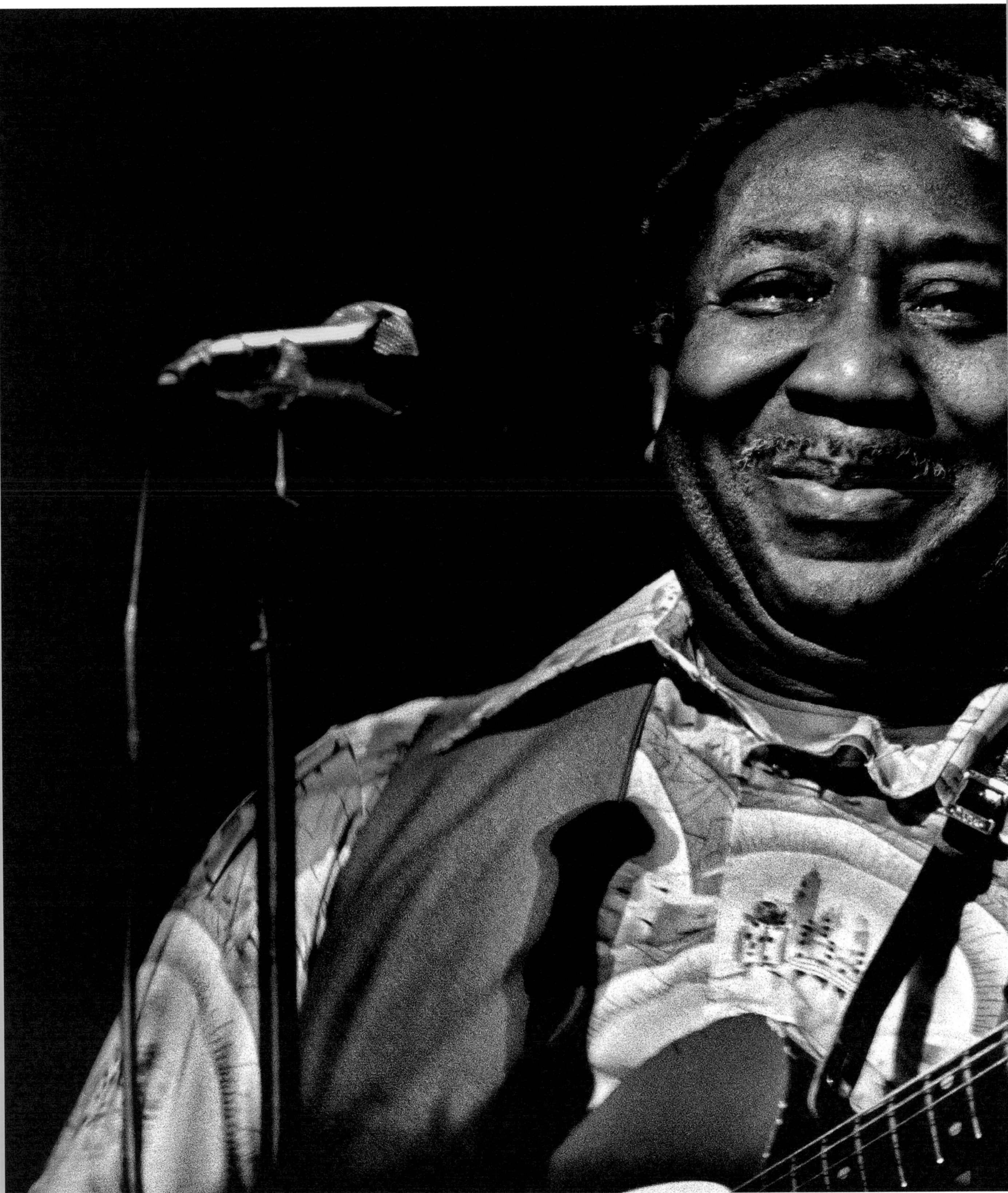

Early in my career, I set out to meet and photograph as many Chicago-based blues artists as possible. The name at the top of my list was Muddy Waters, and I would go see him play wherever and whenever I could. One day I was introduced to Scott Cameron, his manager, who took a liking to my work and started to call and invite me to Muddy's shows. This was before I could just call someone up and request

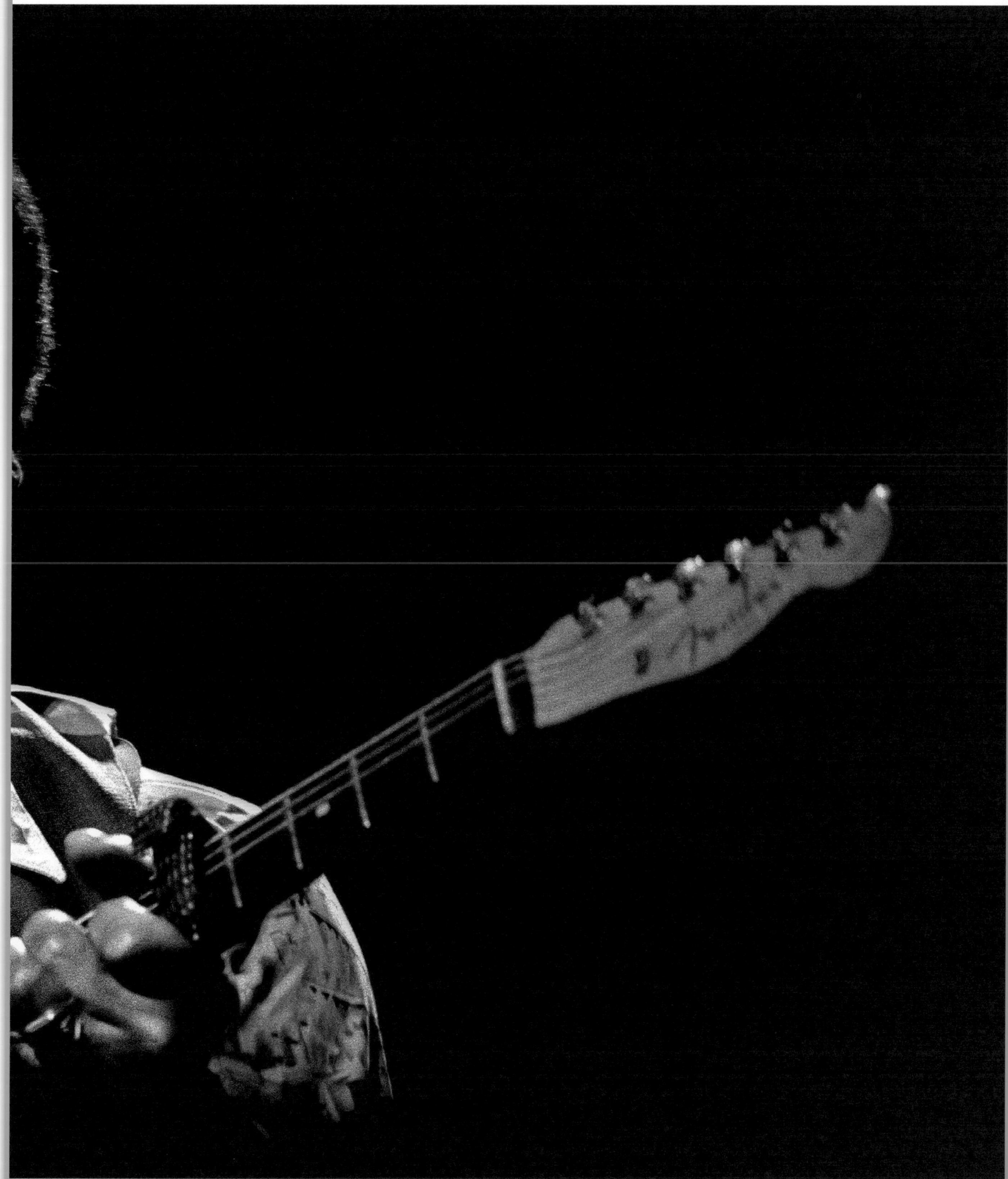

a photo pass, so it was a great feeling. This photograph was taken at the Auditorium Theater in Chicago, and was the first photograph I ever licensed to a major publication, in this case the *Chicago Reader*. It kicked off a stretch of assignments for the *Reader* that lasted about 10 years.

MUDDY WATERS / CHICAGO, IL / 1977

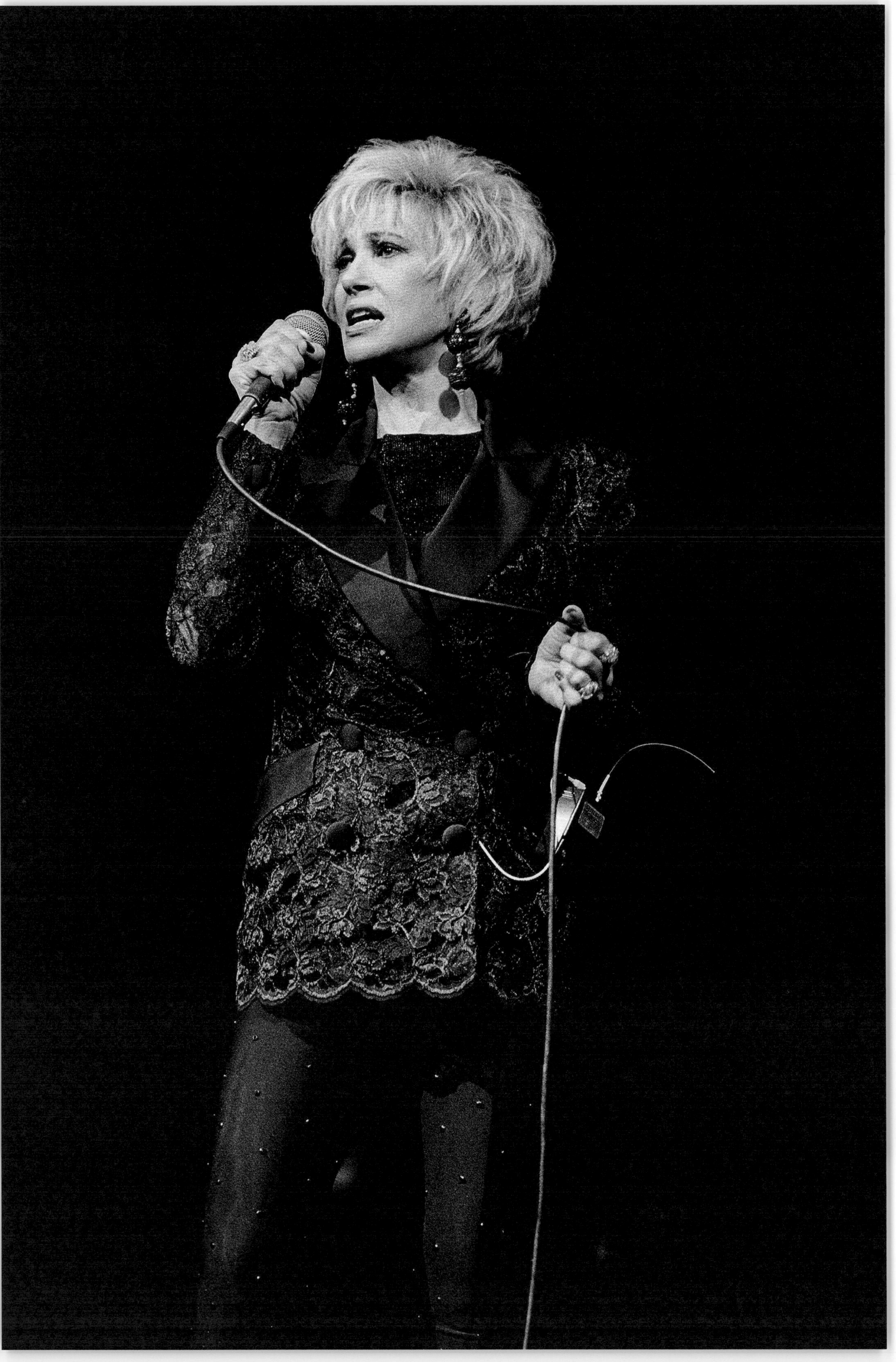

8

COUNTRY
BALLADS & HARMONIES

Legendary songwriter Harlan Howard once described country music as "three chords and the truth." You can hear that every time Willie Nelson, Merle Haggard, Dolly Parton or anyone from that era sings or plays a note. They are what country music is about. They are real and their songs convey that feeling. They are a joy to photograph.

TAMMY WYNETTE / MERRILLVILLE, IN / 1993

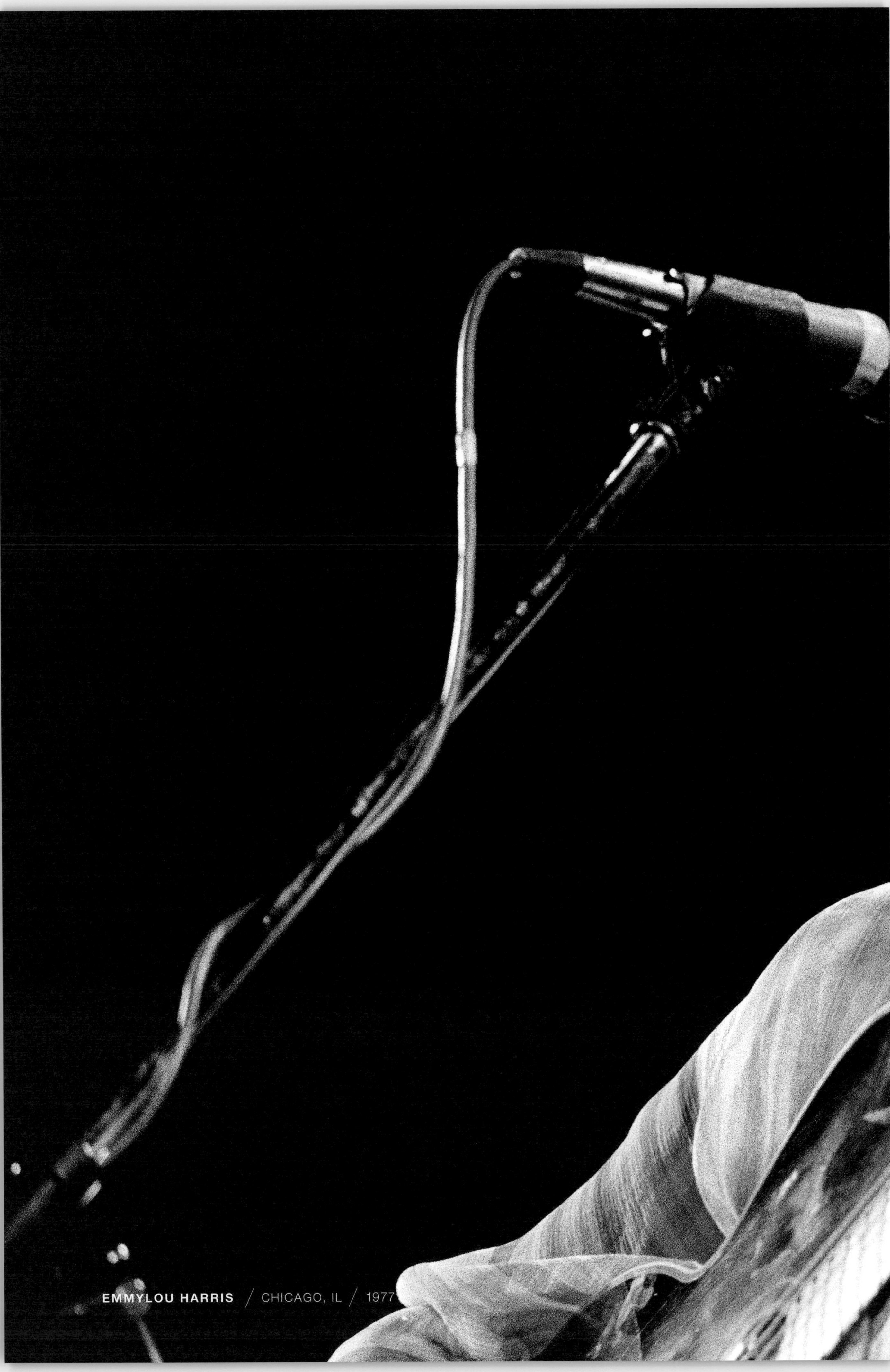

EMMYLOU HARRIS / CHICAGO, IL / 1977

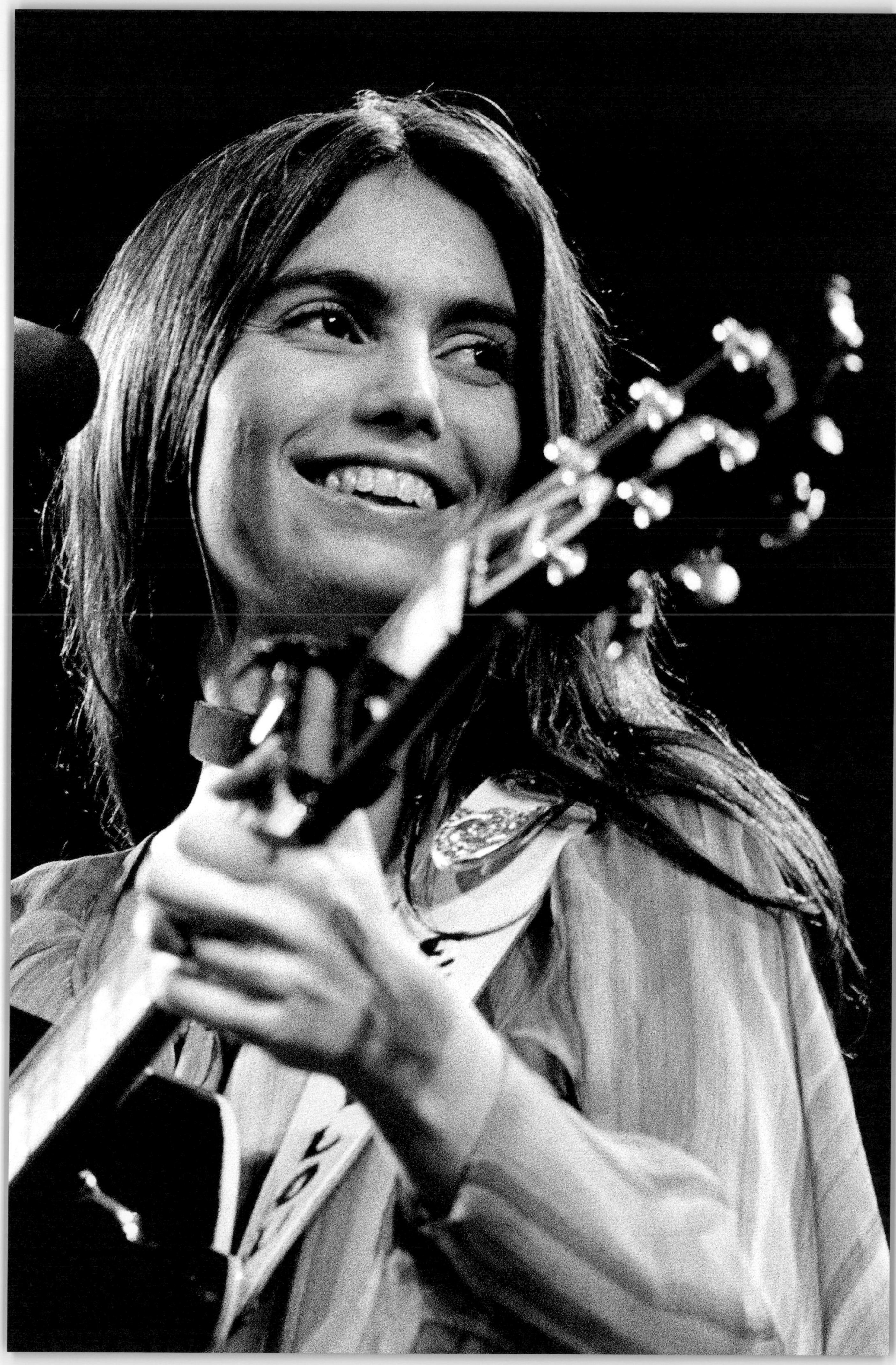

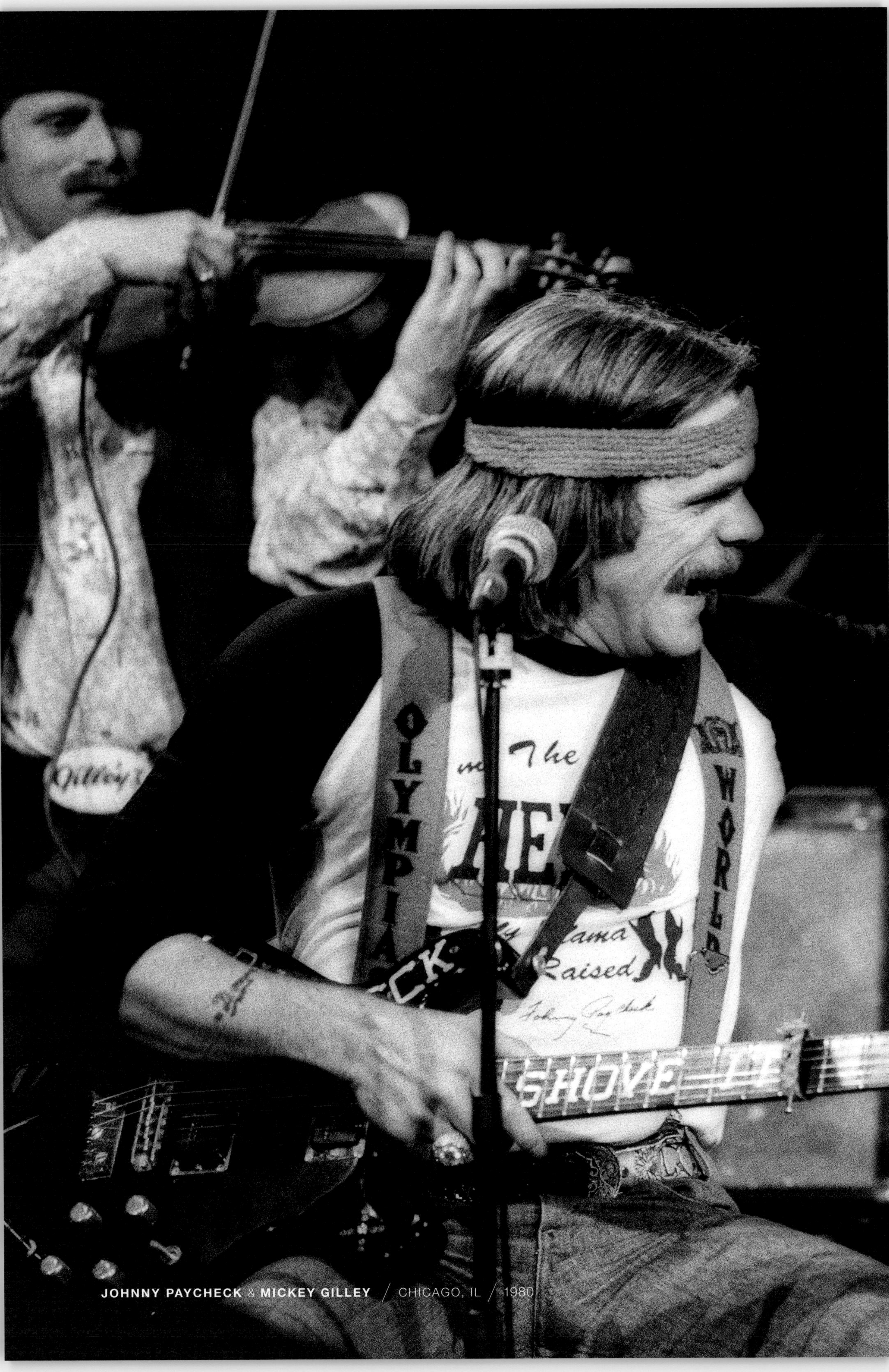

JOHNNY PAYCHECK & **MICKEY GILLEY** / CHICAGO, IL / 1980

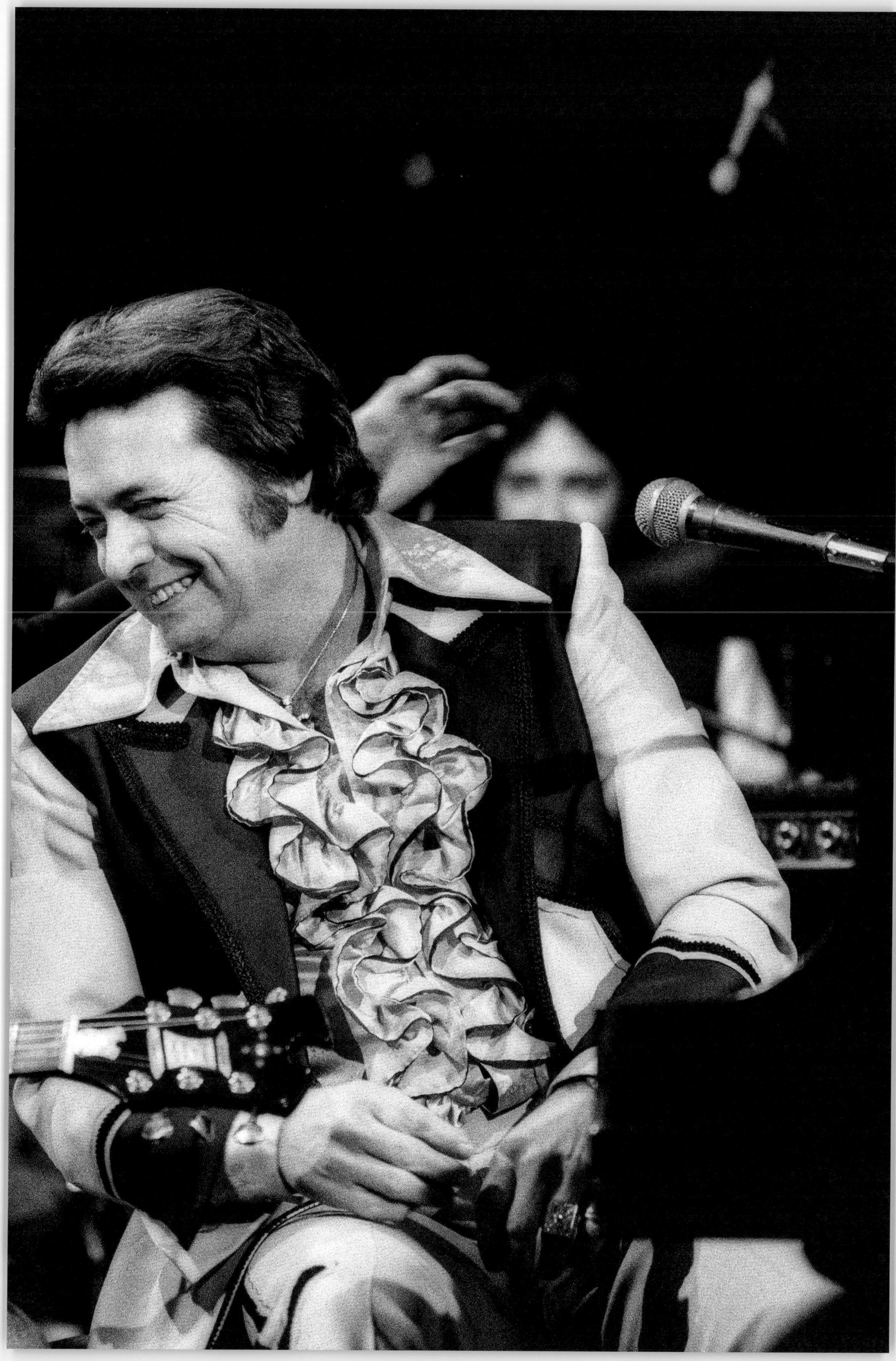

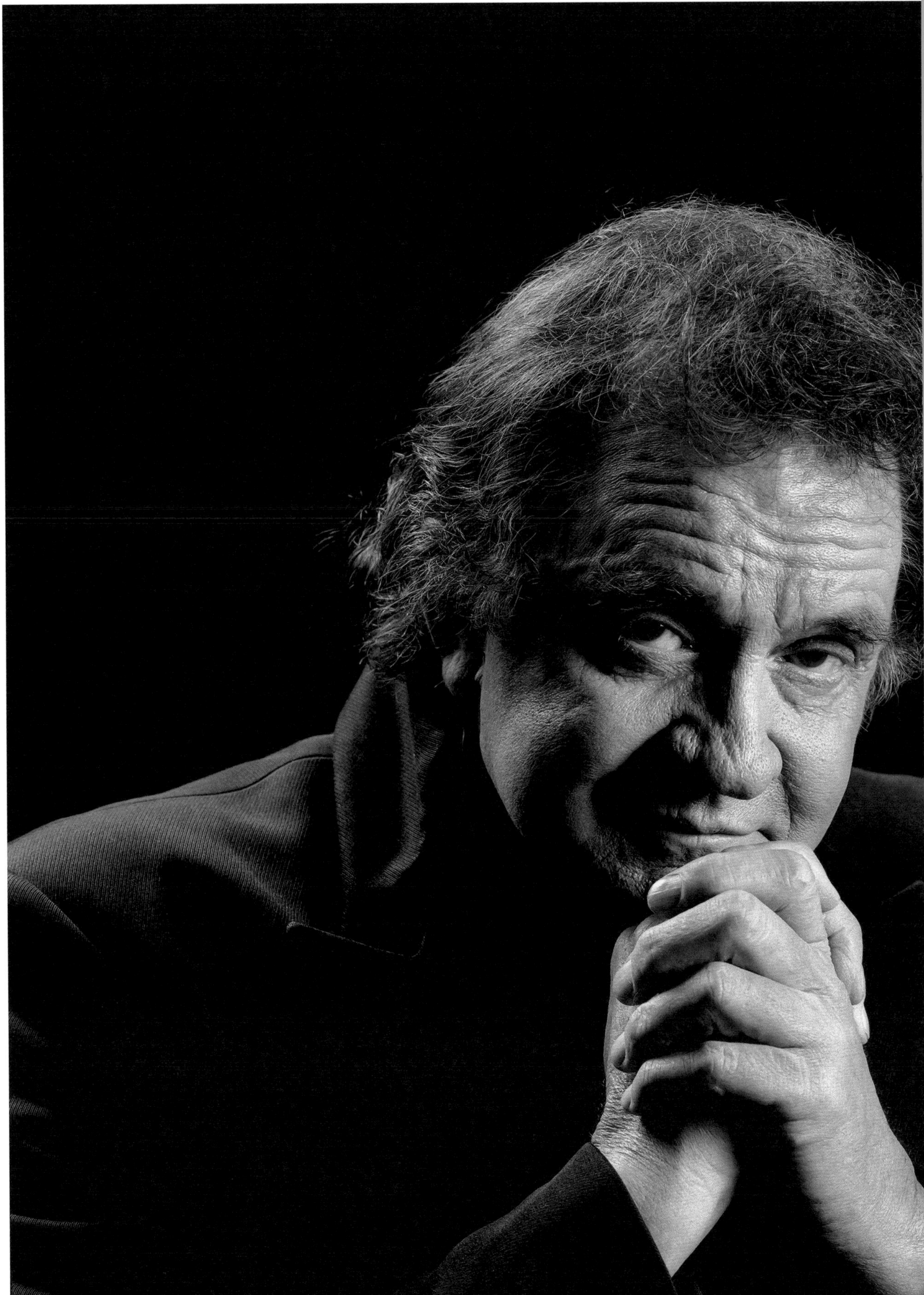

JOHNNY CASH / MERRILLVILLE, IN / 1994

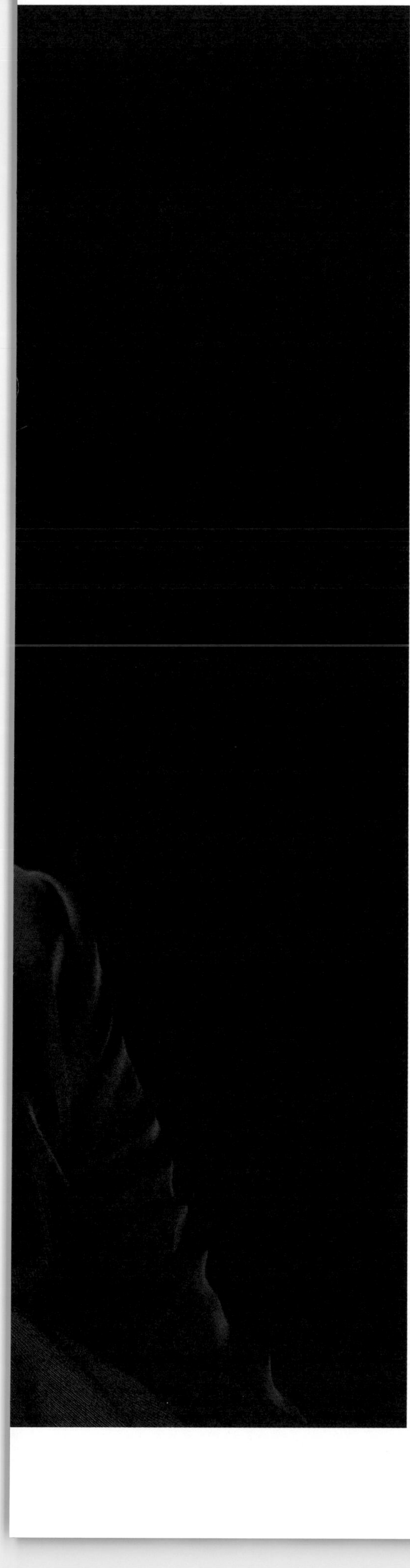

In May of 1994, a country music magazine asked me to do a cover shoot with Johnny Cash. Off to northern Indiana I went to meet the "Man in Black." I could not have found a nicer person. Meeting Johnny was one of the highlights of my life, and he lived up to all of my expectations.

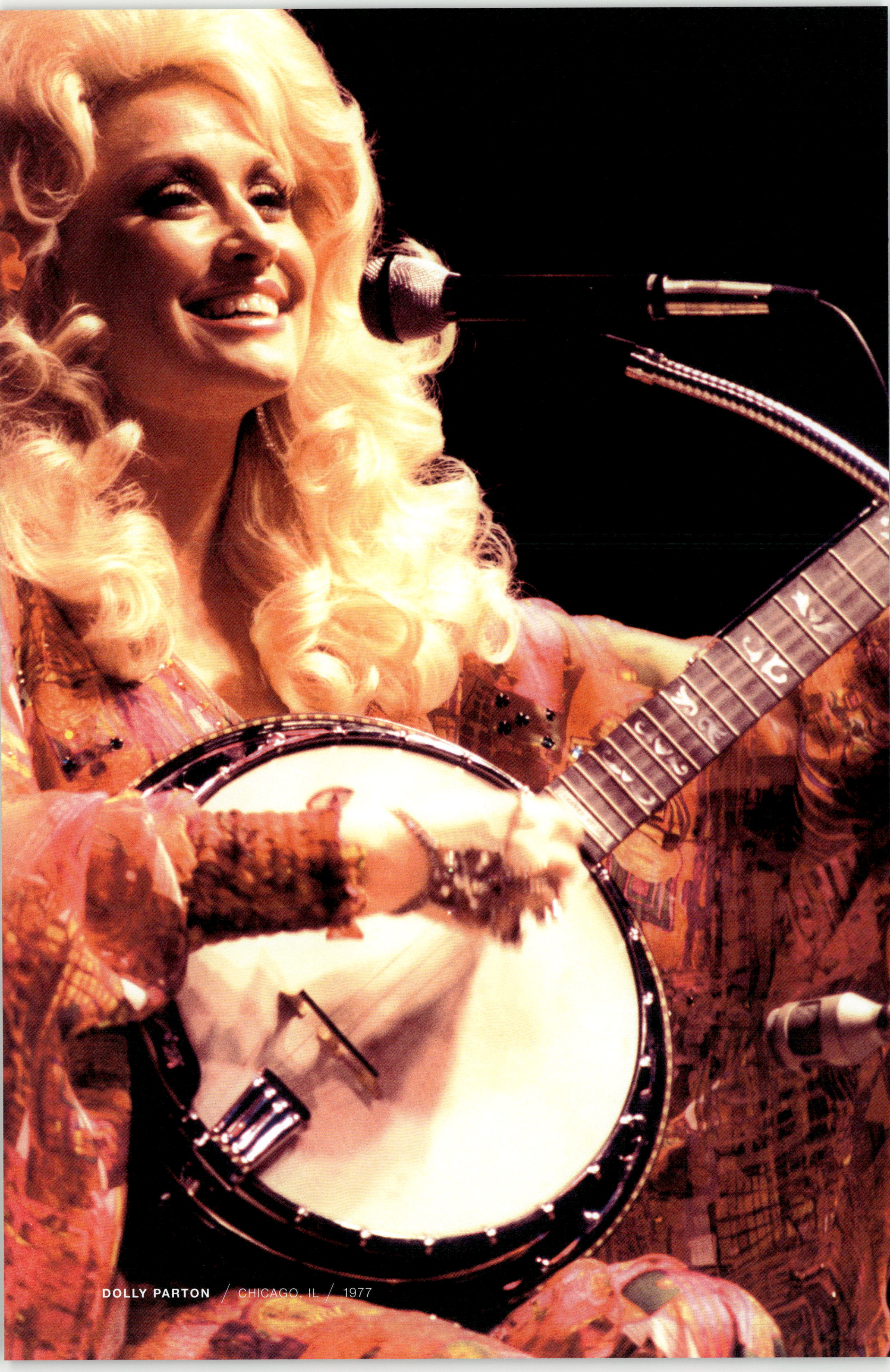

DOLLY PARTON / CHICAGO, IL / 1977

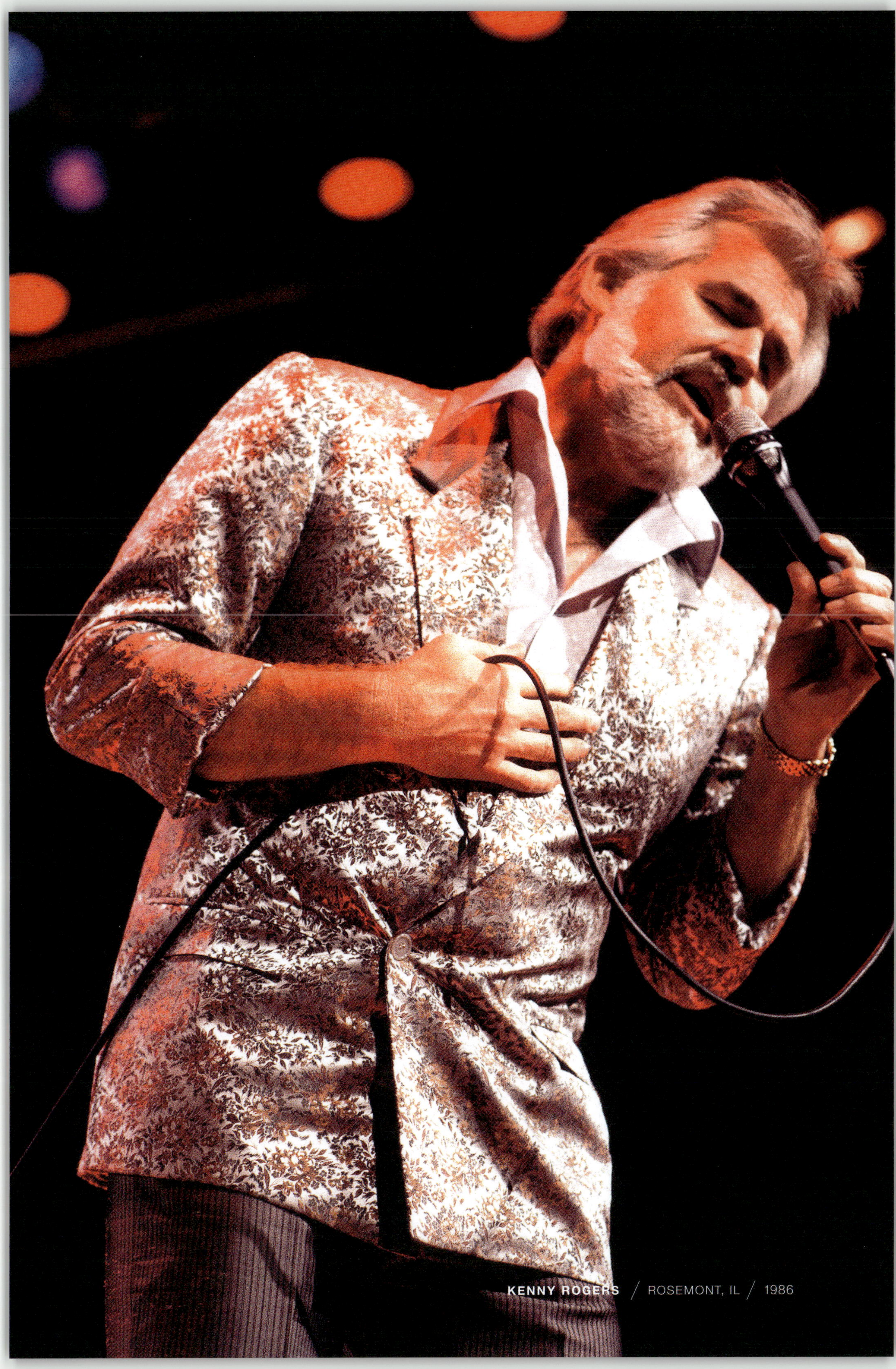

KENNY ROGERS / ROSEMONT, IL / 1986

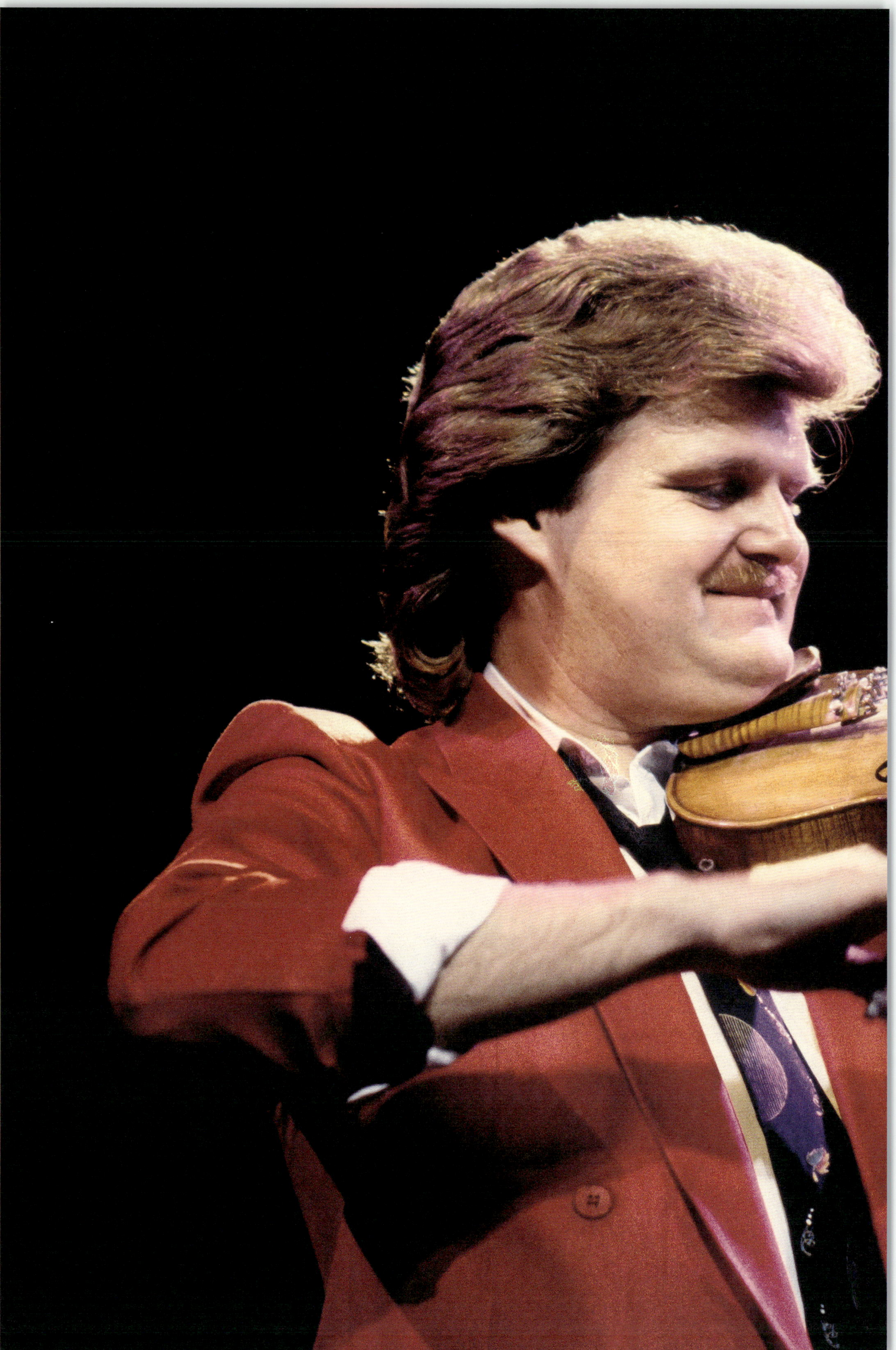

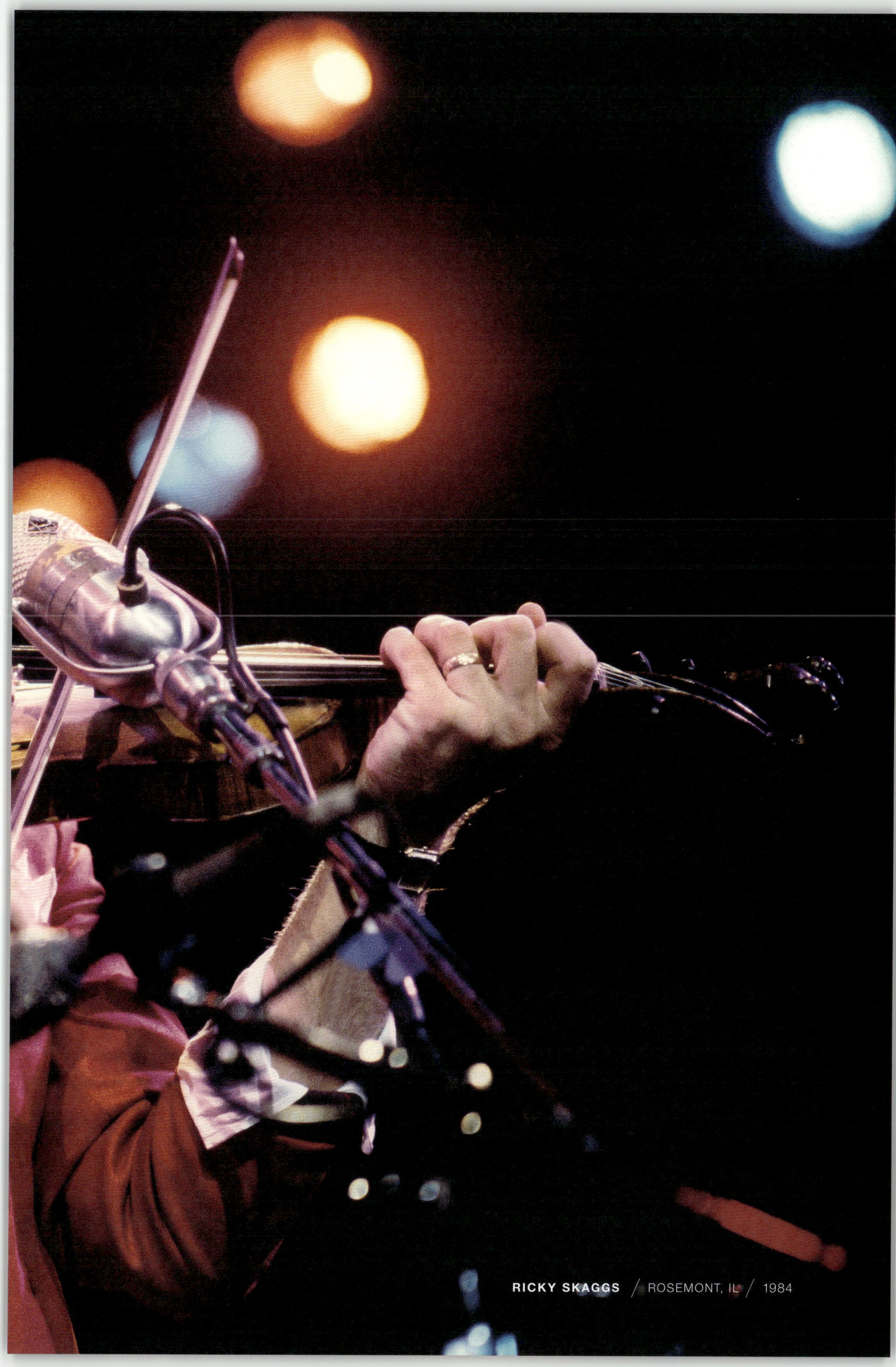

RICKY SKAGGS / ROSEMONT, IL / 1984

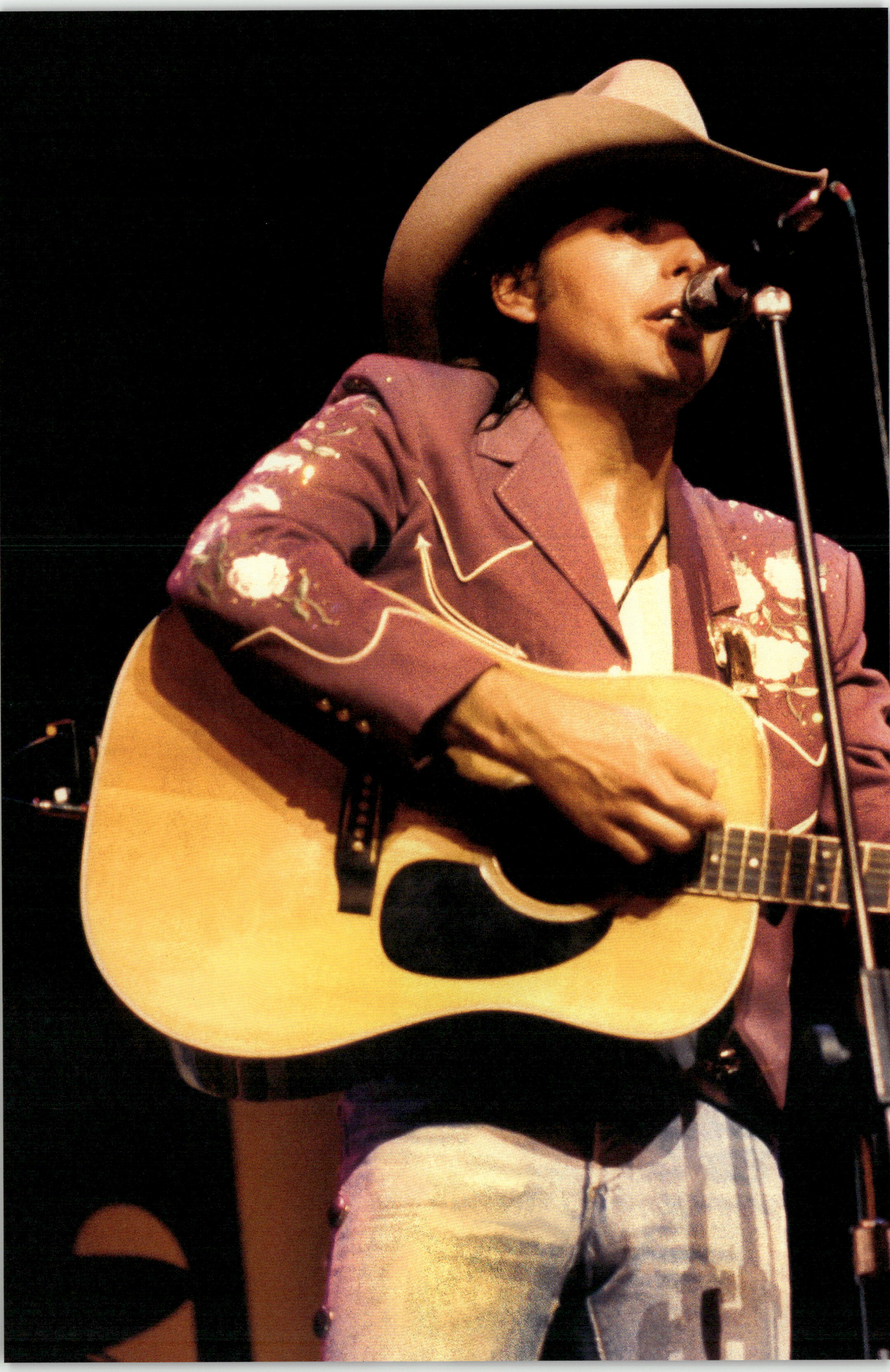

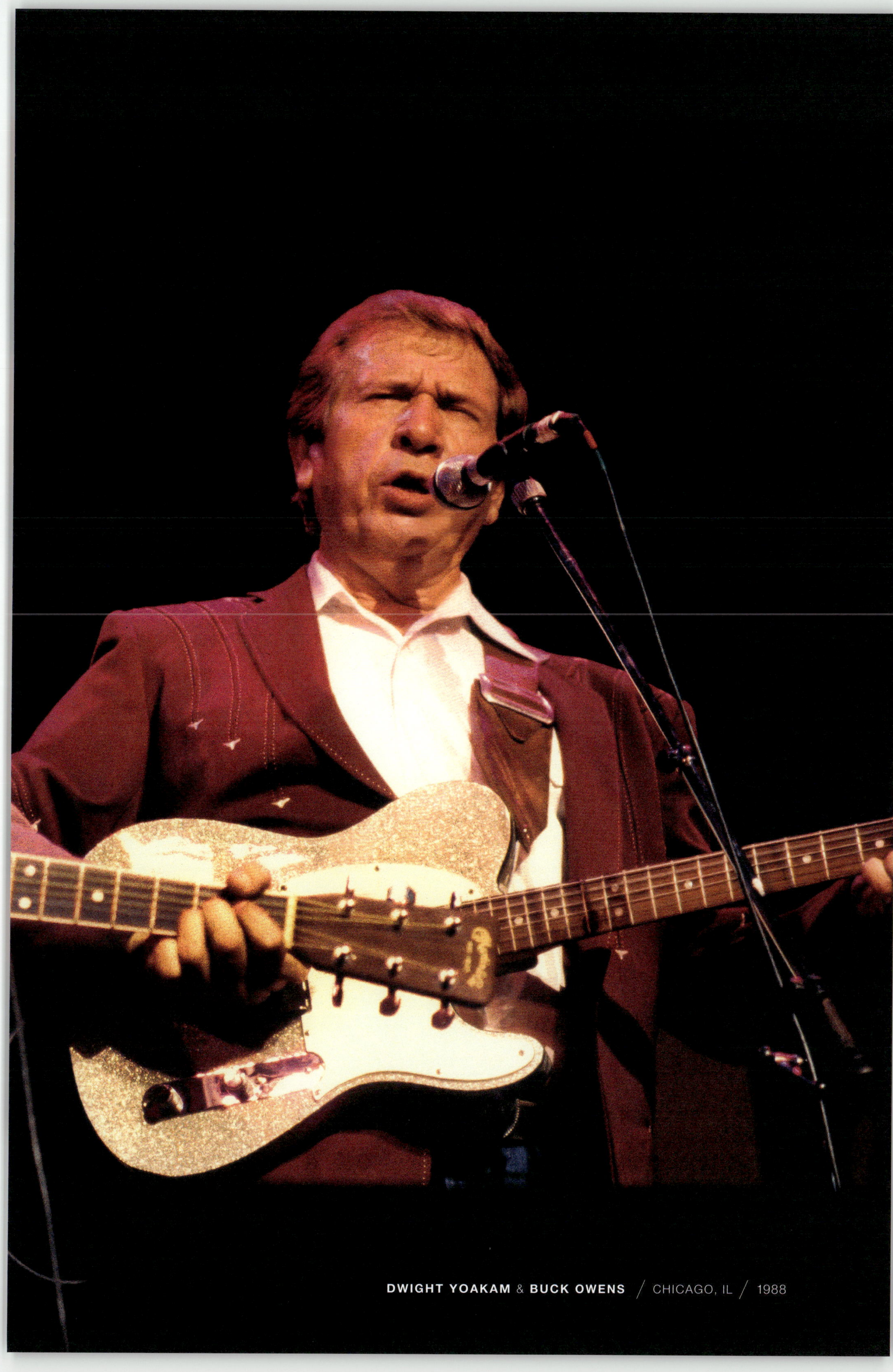

DWIGHT YOAKAM & **BUCK OWENS** / CHICAGO, IL / 1988

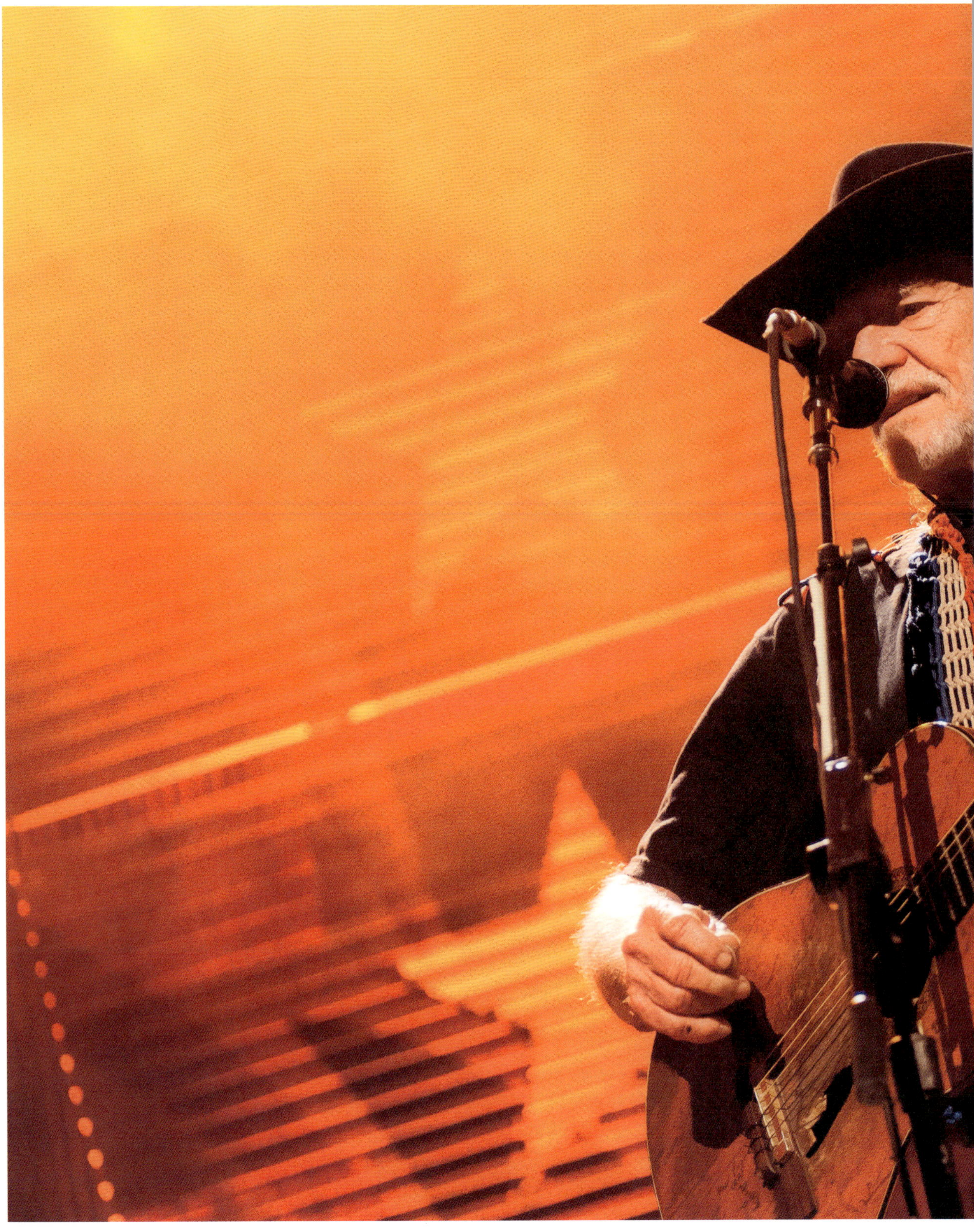

Legend has it that Bob Dylan, who played the London Live Aid show with Keith Richards and Ron Wood in 1984, called his friend Willie Nelson and asked why there wasn't something similar for the American farmer. Willie ran with the idea, called his friends Neil Young and John Mellencamp, and Farm Aid was born. The first Farm Aid concert took place in September 1985 in Champaign, Illinois, with 75 bands in one day! It was a long day, but I

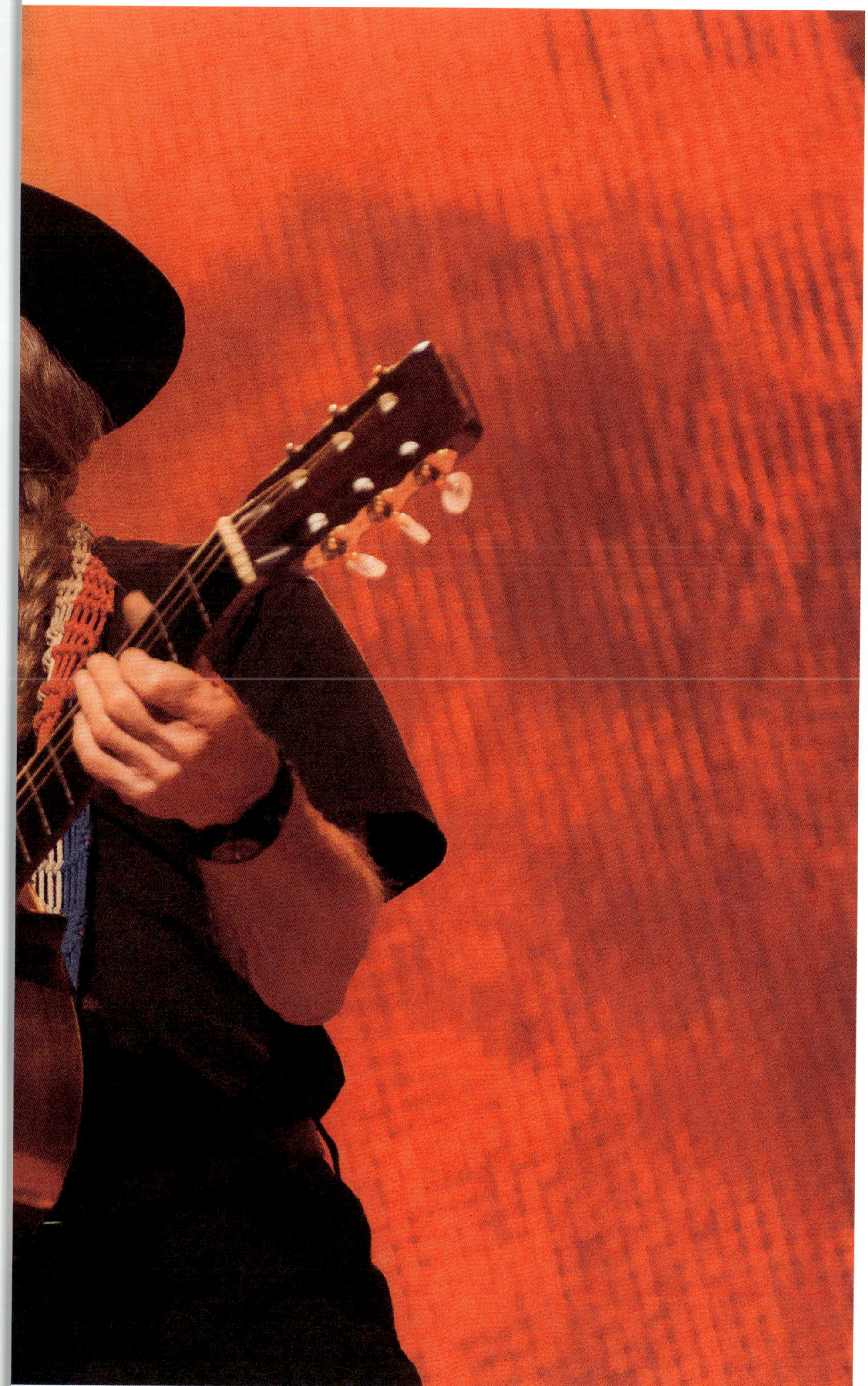

had incredible access. I lost touch with the concept for a few years, but I was assigned by *Rolling Stone* to photograph the April 1990 press conference for Farm Aid 4 in Indianapolis. At that event, I met the staff and volunteered my services, which I then continued to do for about 25 years. Great music every year, and the program taught me how to eat healthy food and support local family farms.

WILLIE NELSON / MILWAUKEE, WI / 2010

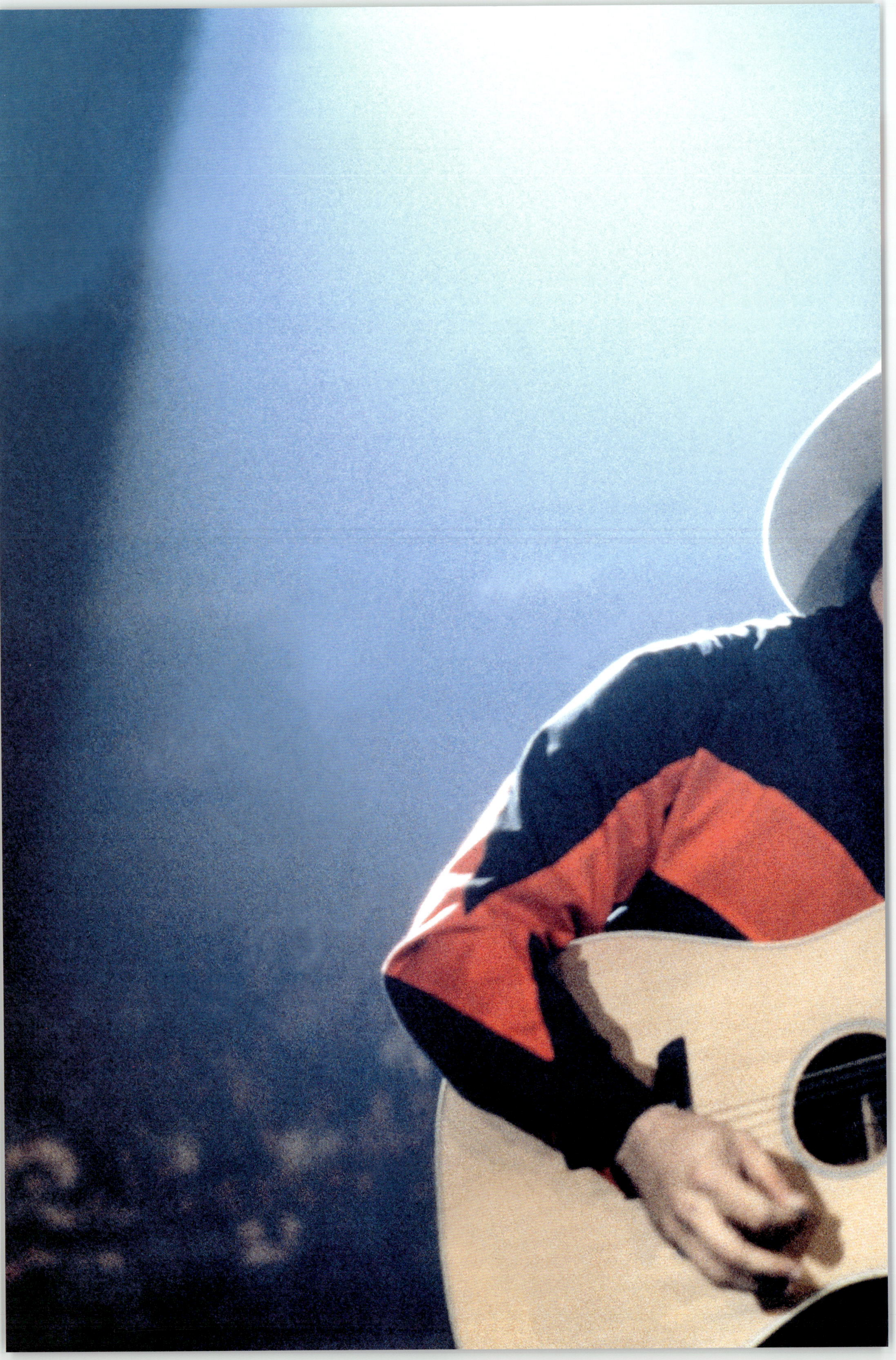

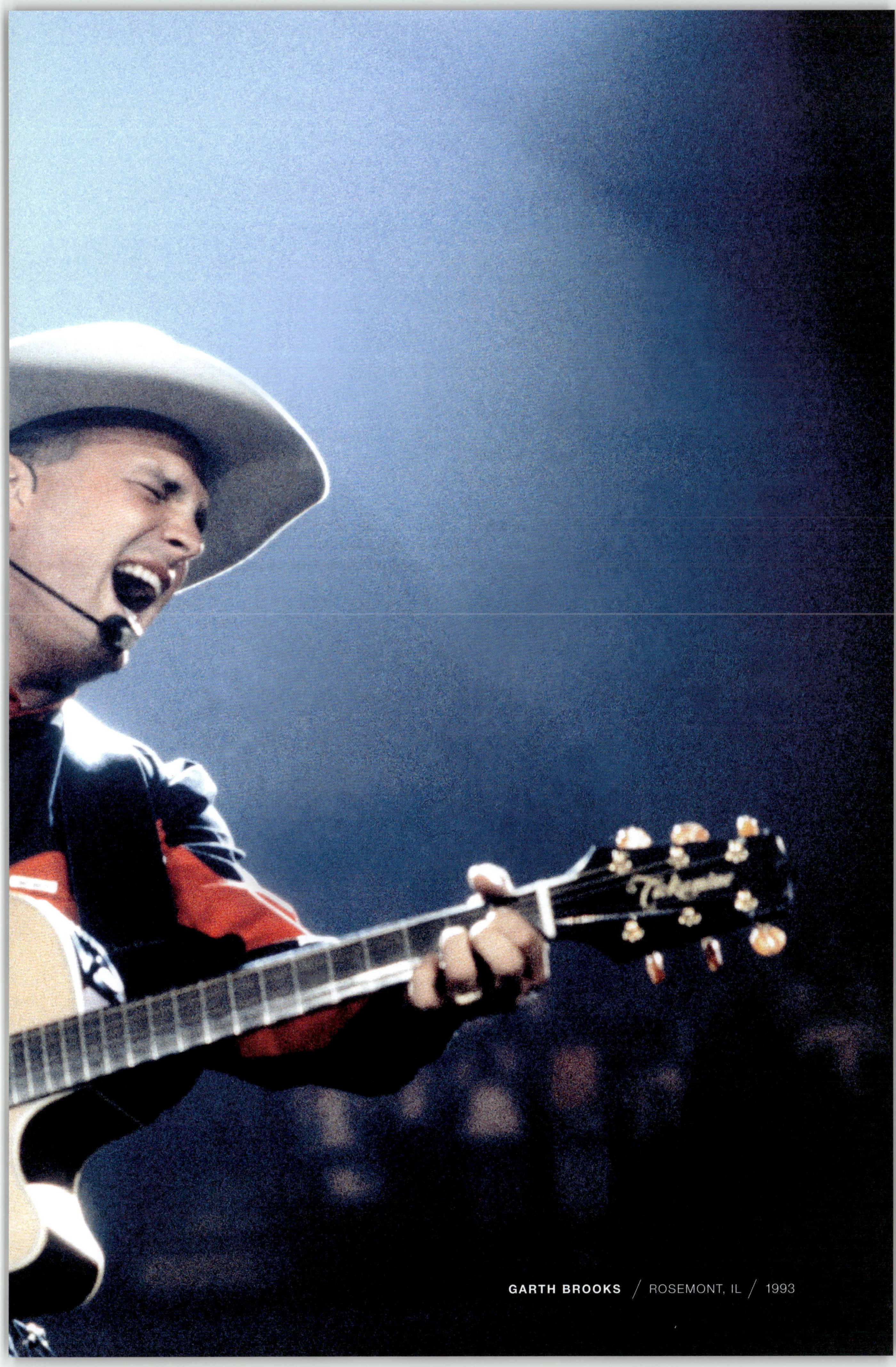

GARTH BROOKS / ROSEMONT, IL / 1993

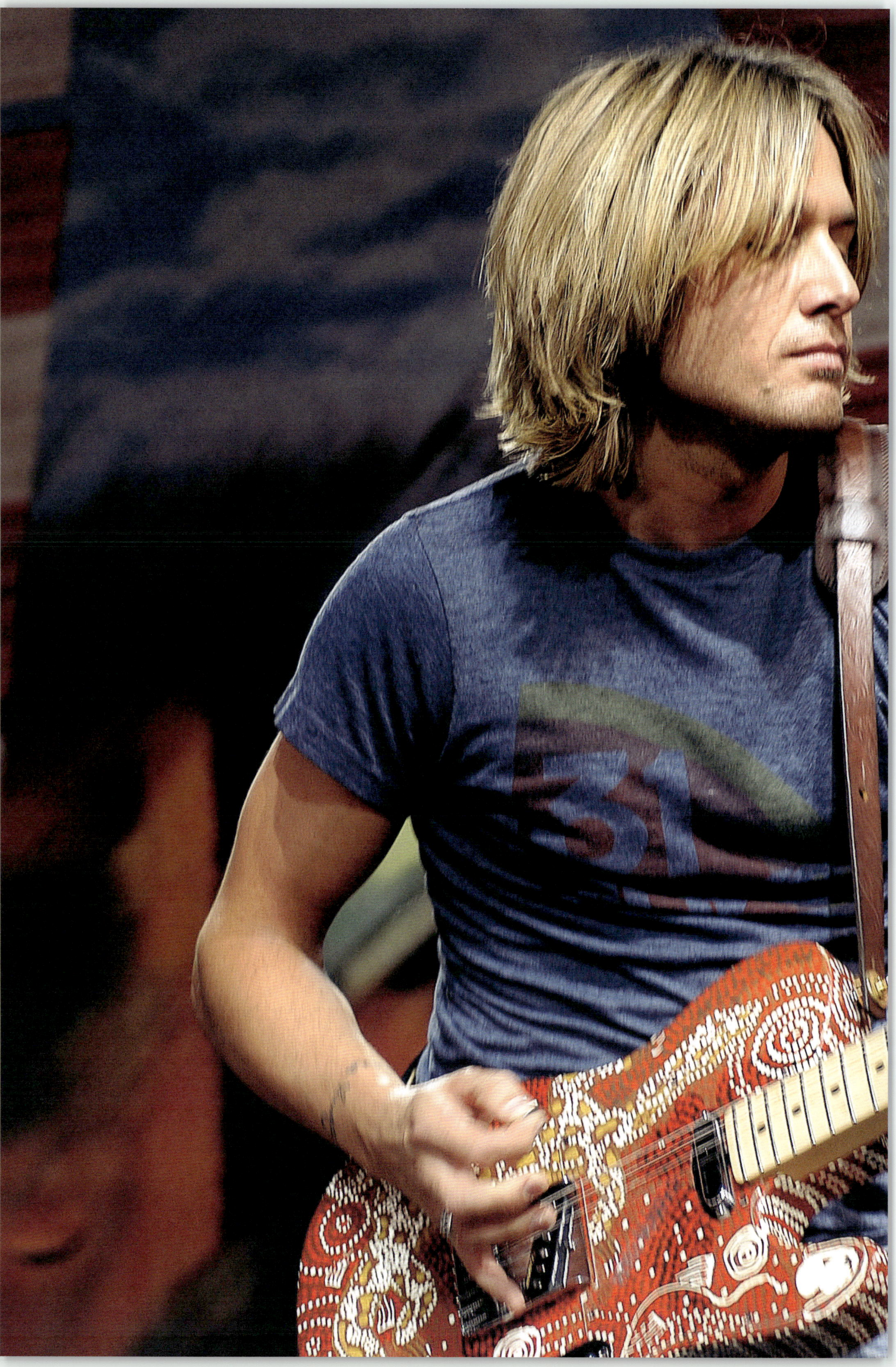

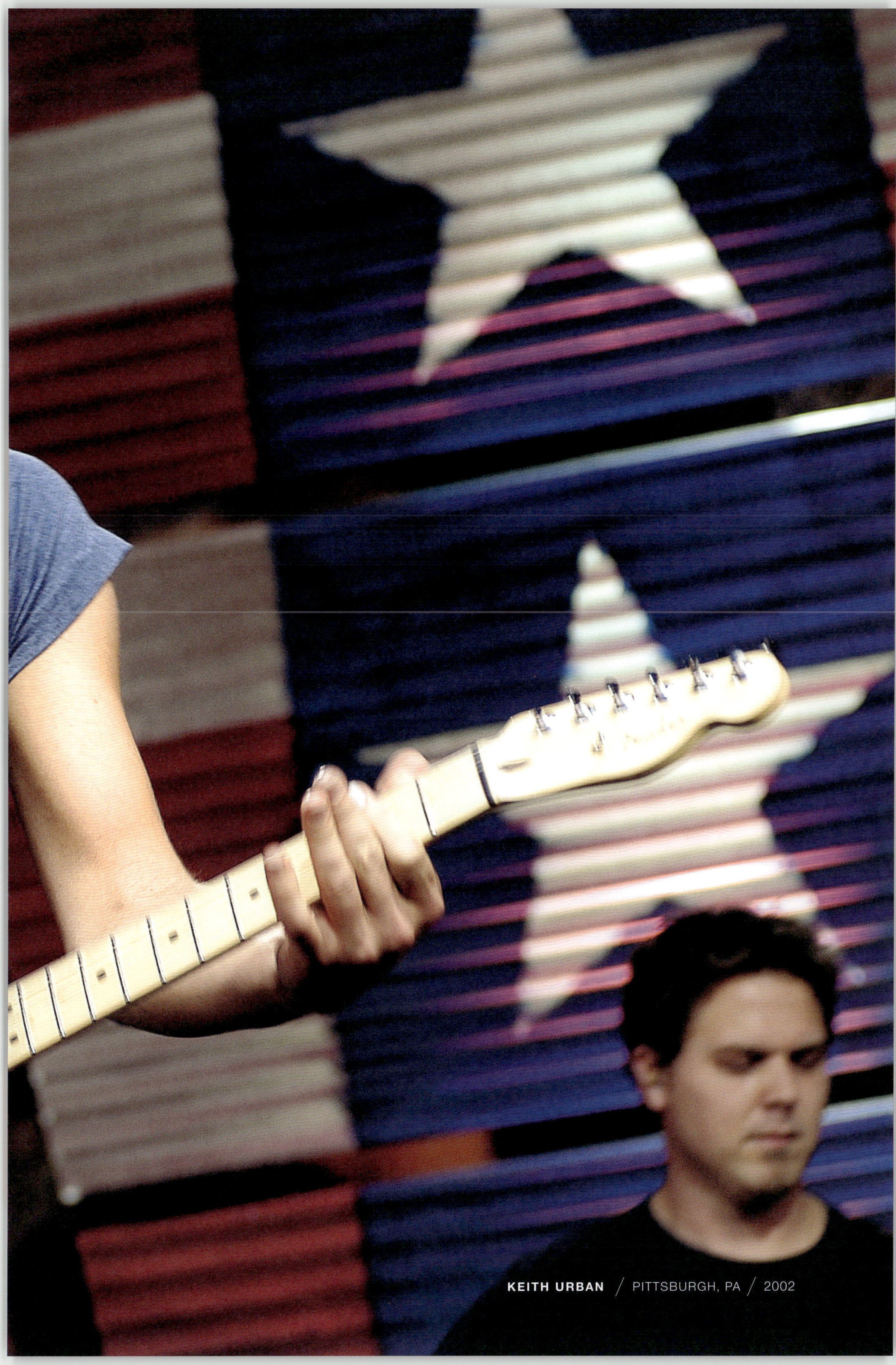

KEITH URBAN / PITTSBURGH, PA / 2002

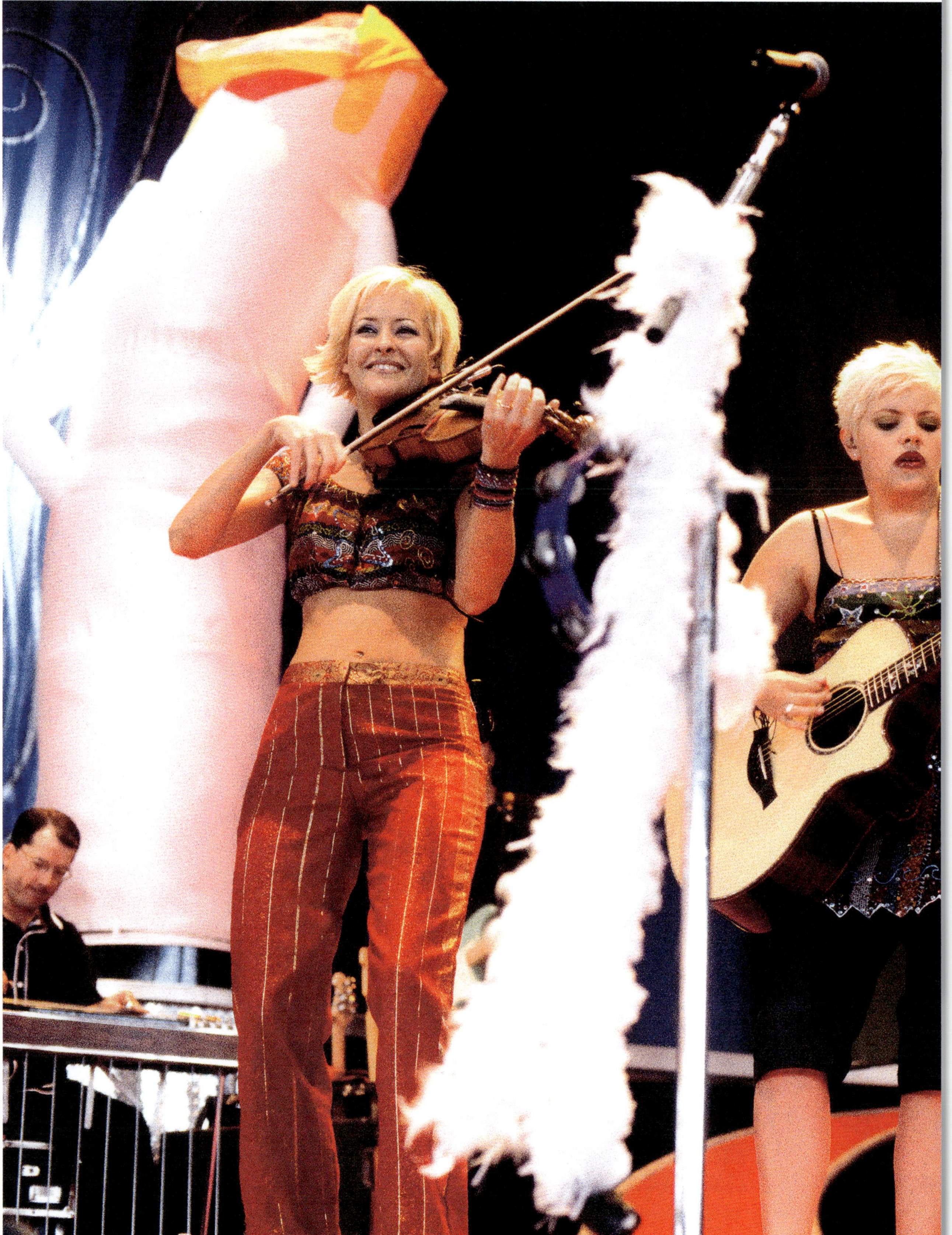

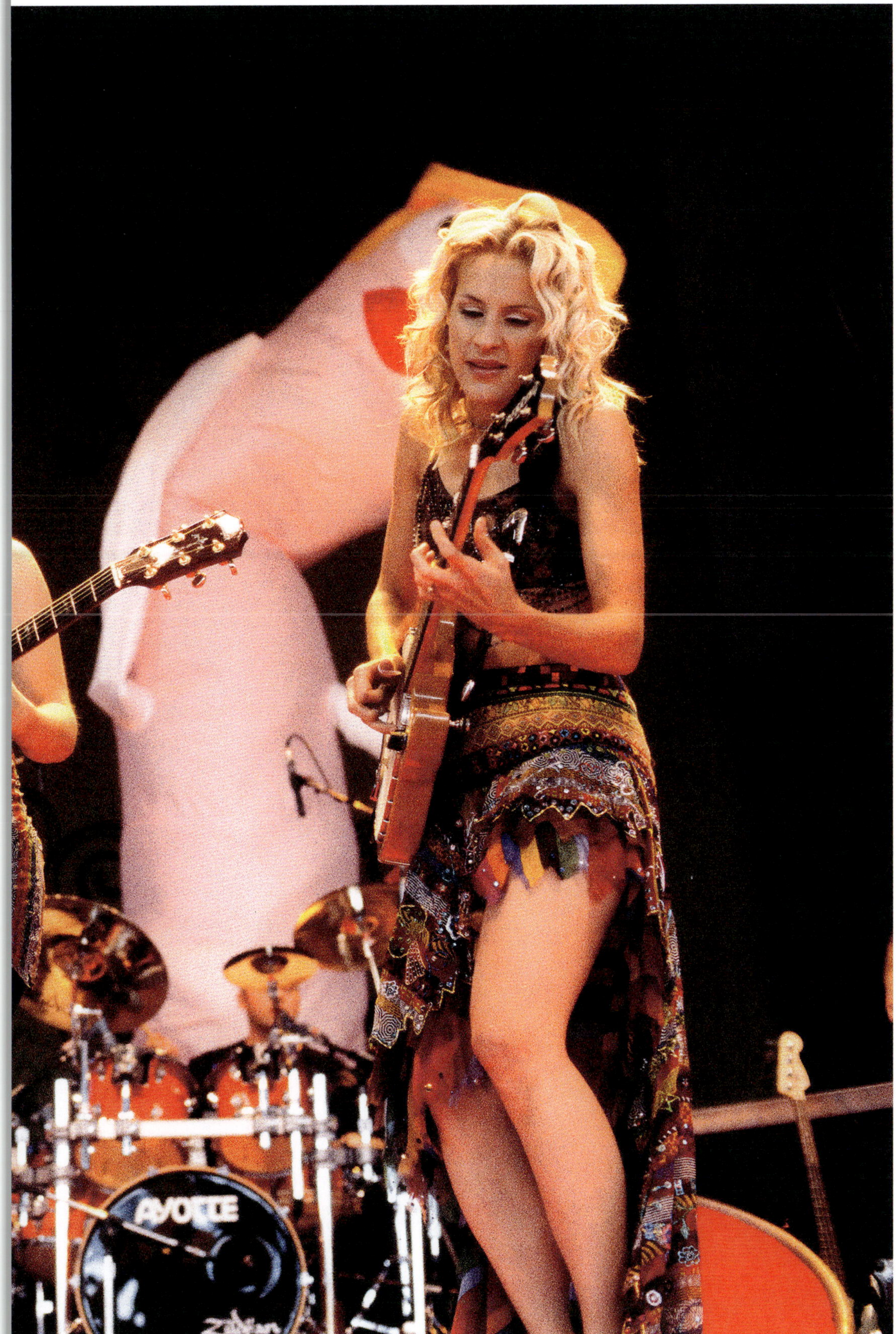

DIXIE CHICKS / CHICAGO, IL / 1999

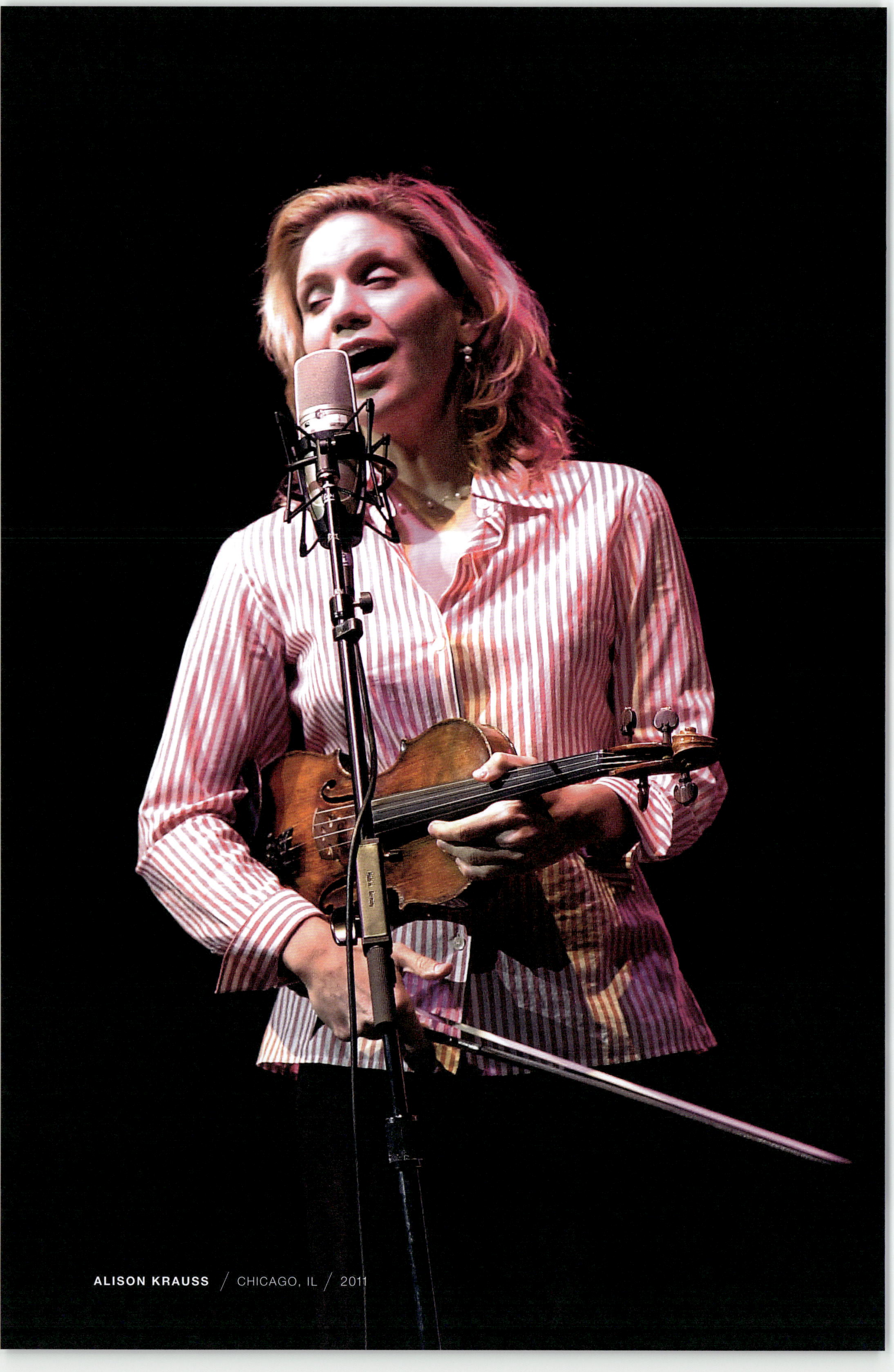

ALISON KRAUSS / CHICAGO, IL / 2011

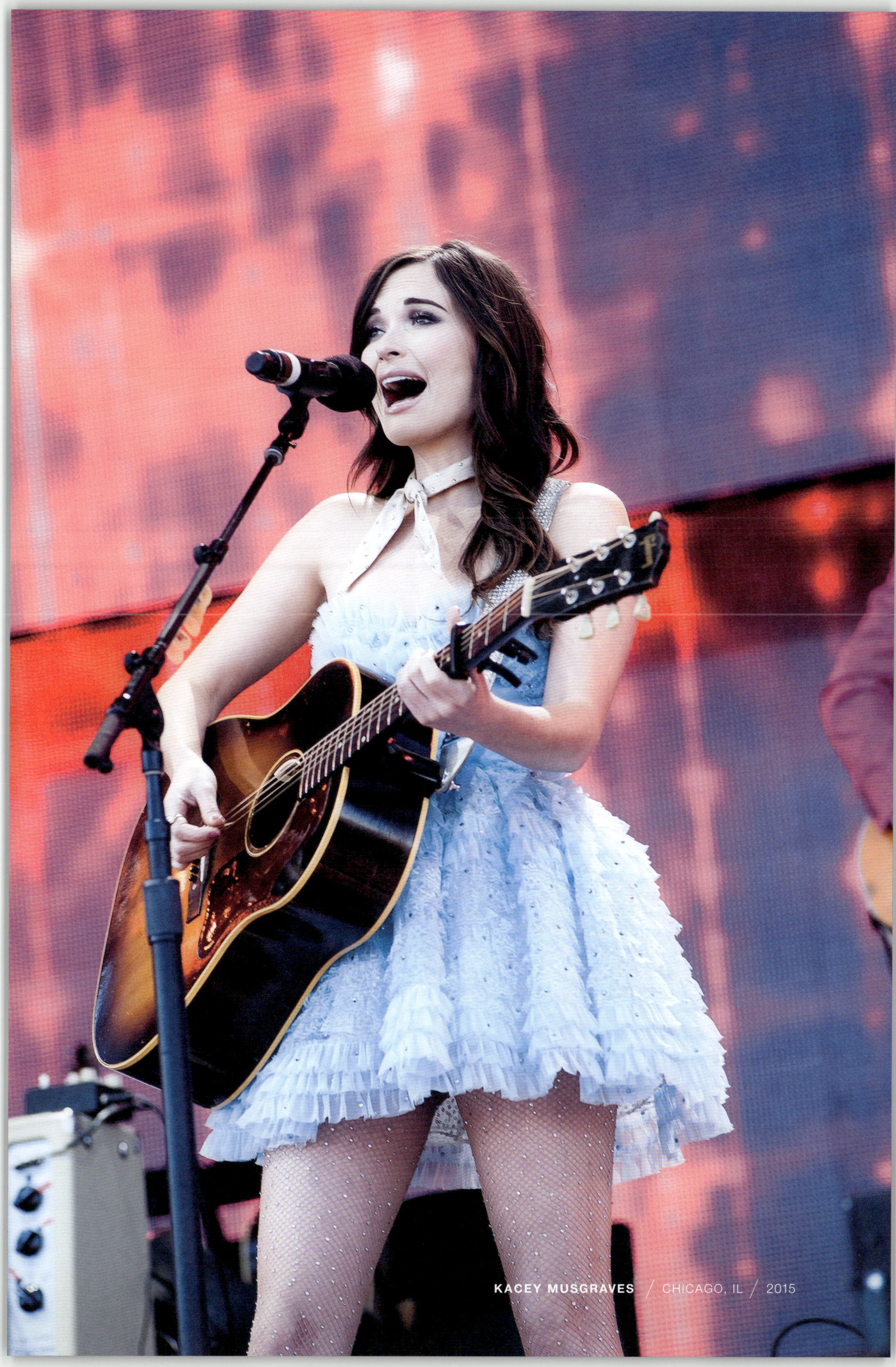

KACEY MUSGRAVES / CHICAGO, IL / 2015

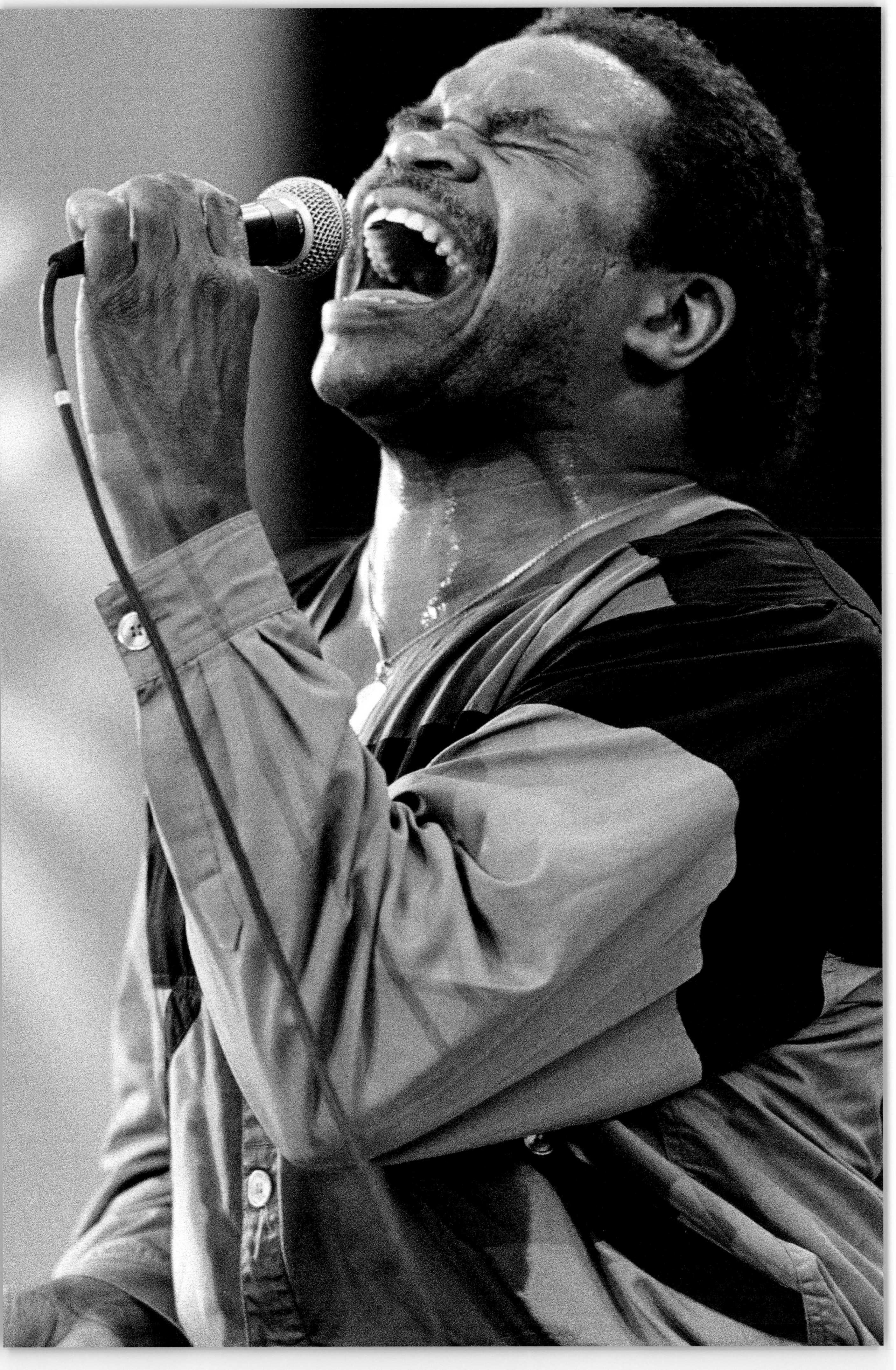

9

GOSPEL

PRAISE & WORSHIP

Although I am not a religious person, I greatly appreciate the music that comes out of the church. To hear a talented choir sing is the definition of great music. To hear Albertina Walker sing sends chills up and down my spine.

OTIS CLAY / CHICAGO, IL / 1990

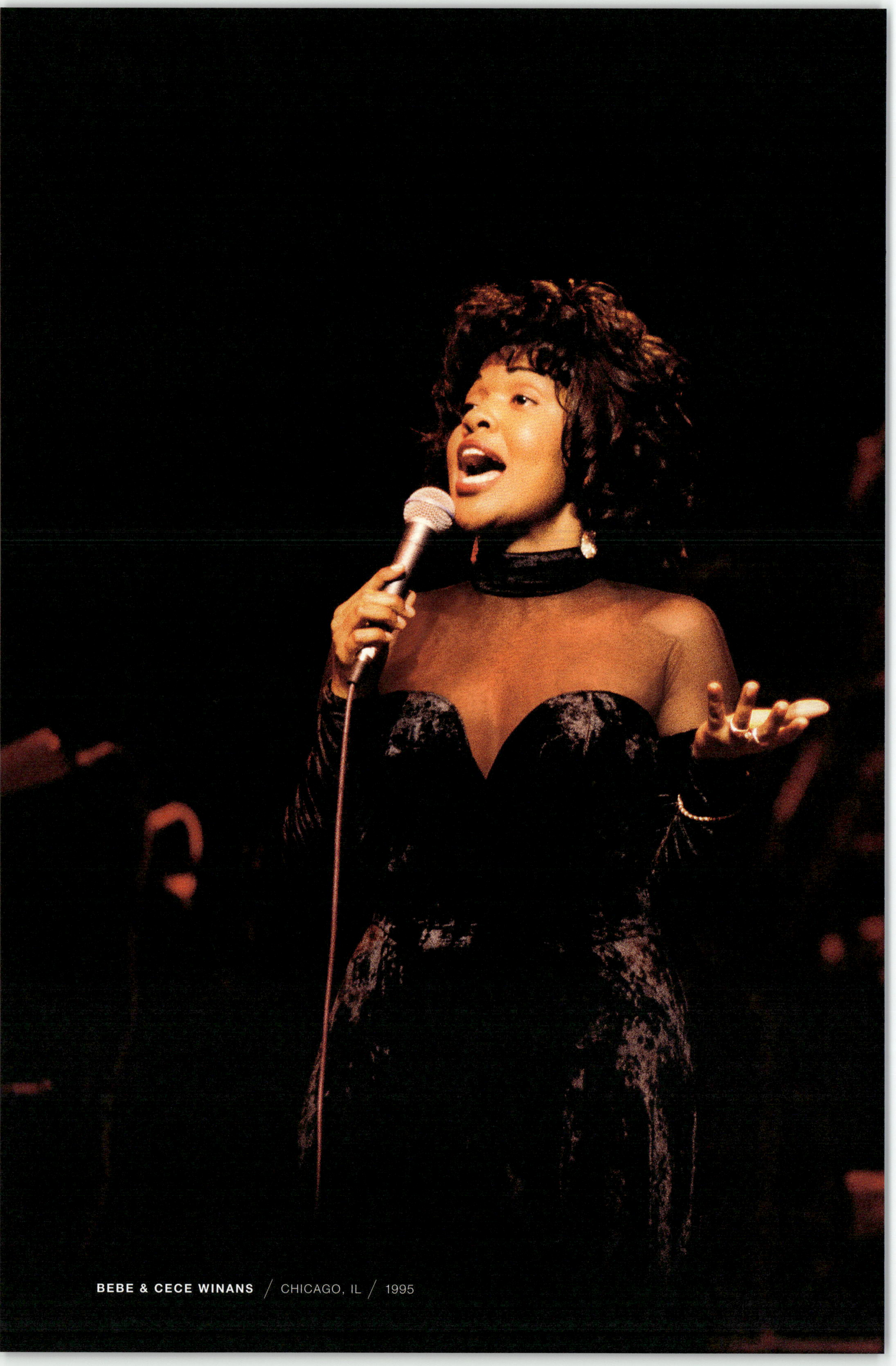

BEBE & CECE WINANS / CHICAGO, IL / 1995

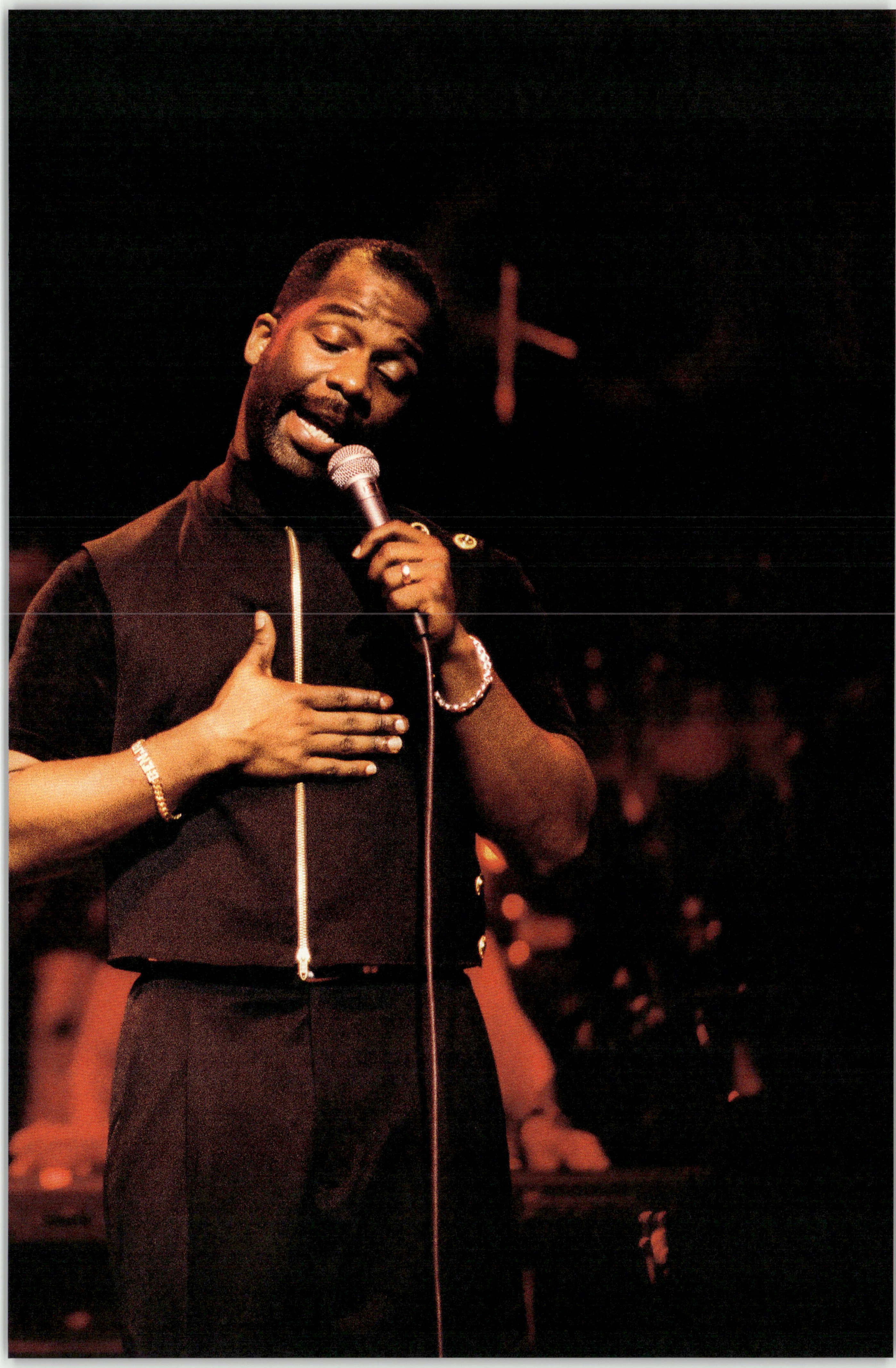

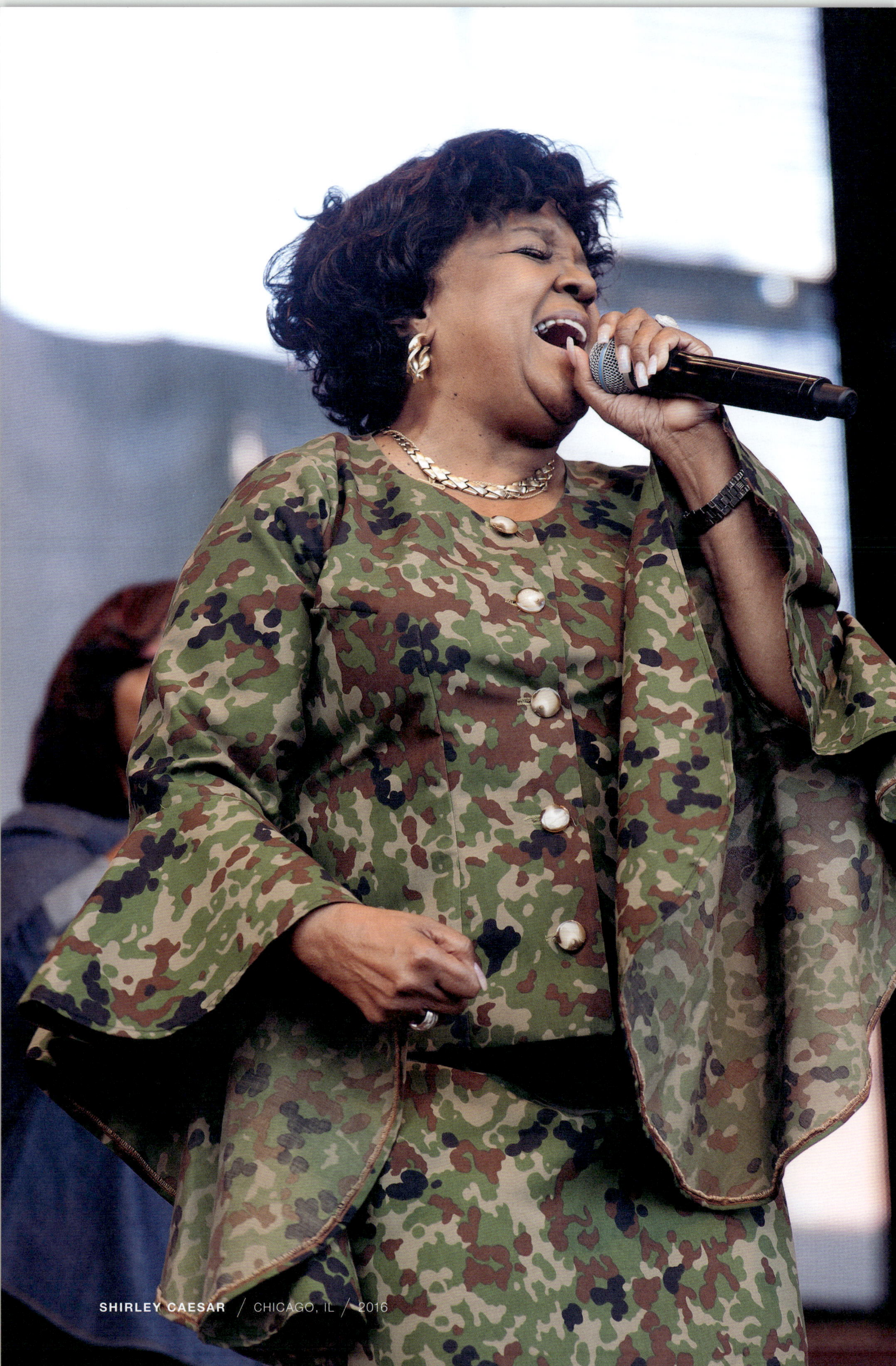

SHIRLEY CAESAR / CHICAGO, IL / 2016

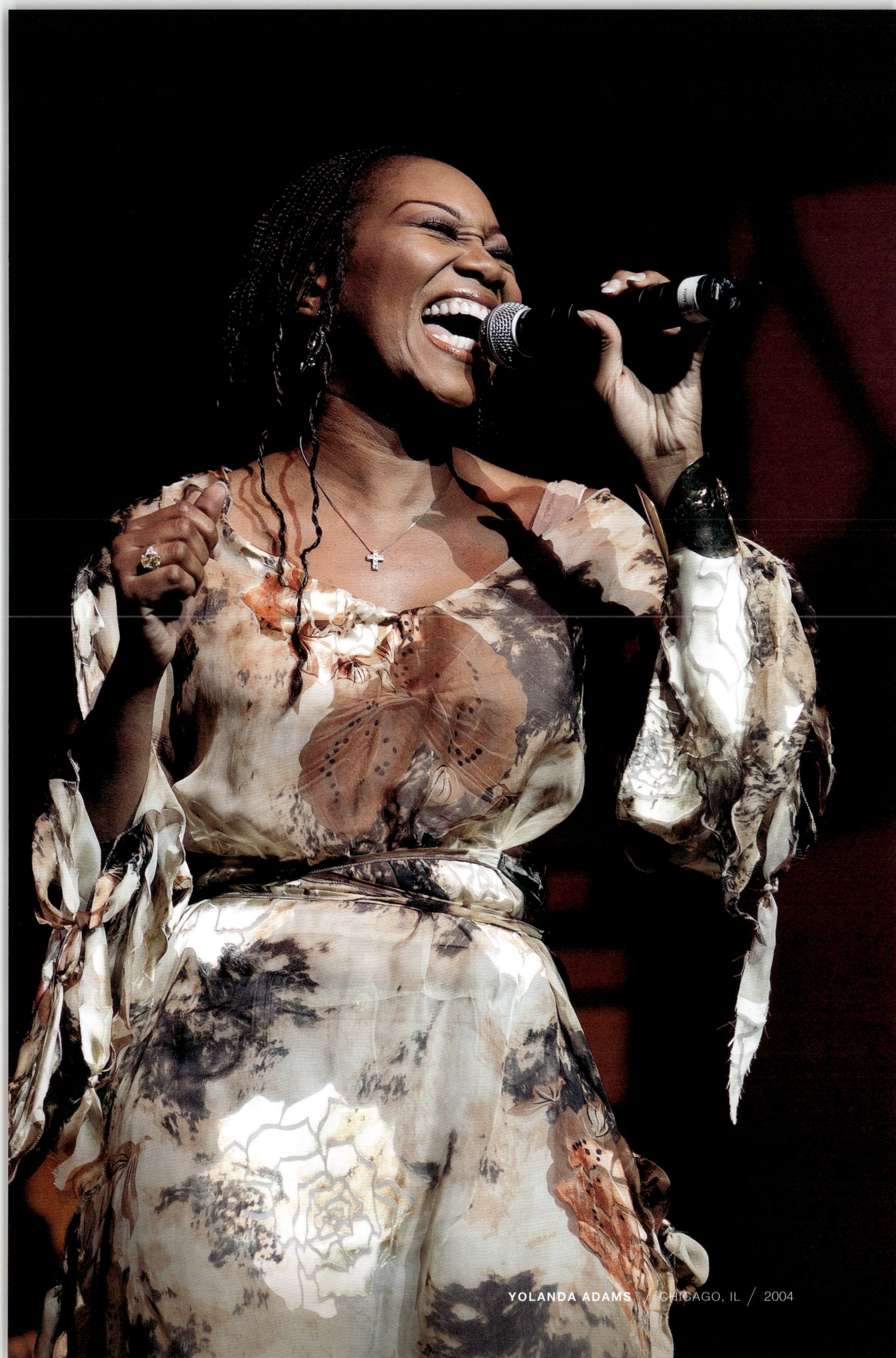

YOLANDA ADAMS / CHICAGO, IL / 2004

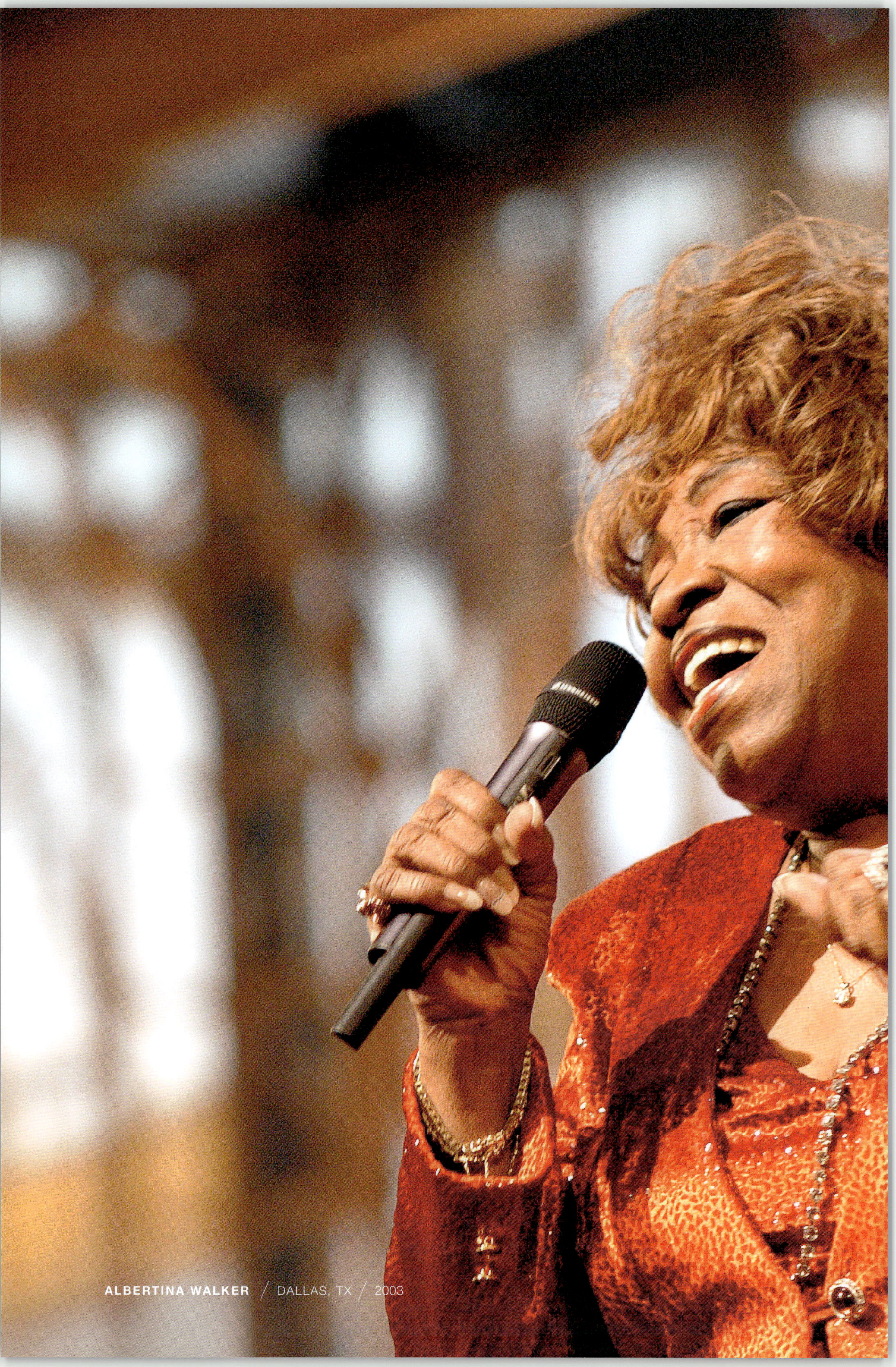

ALBERTINA WALKER / DALLAS, TX / 2003

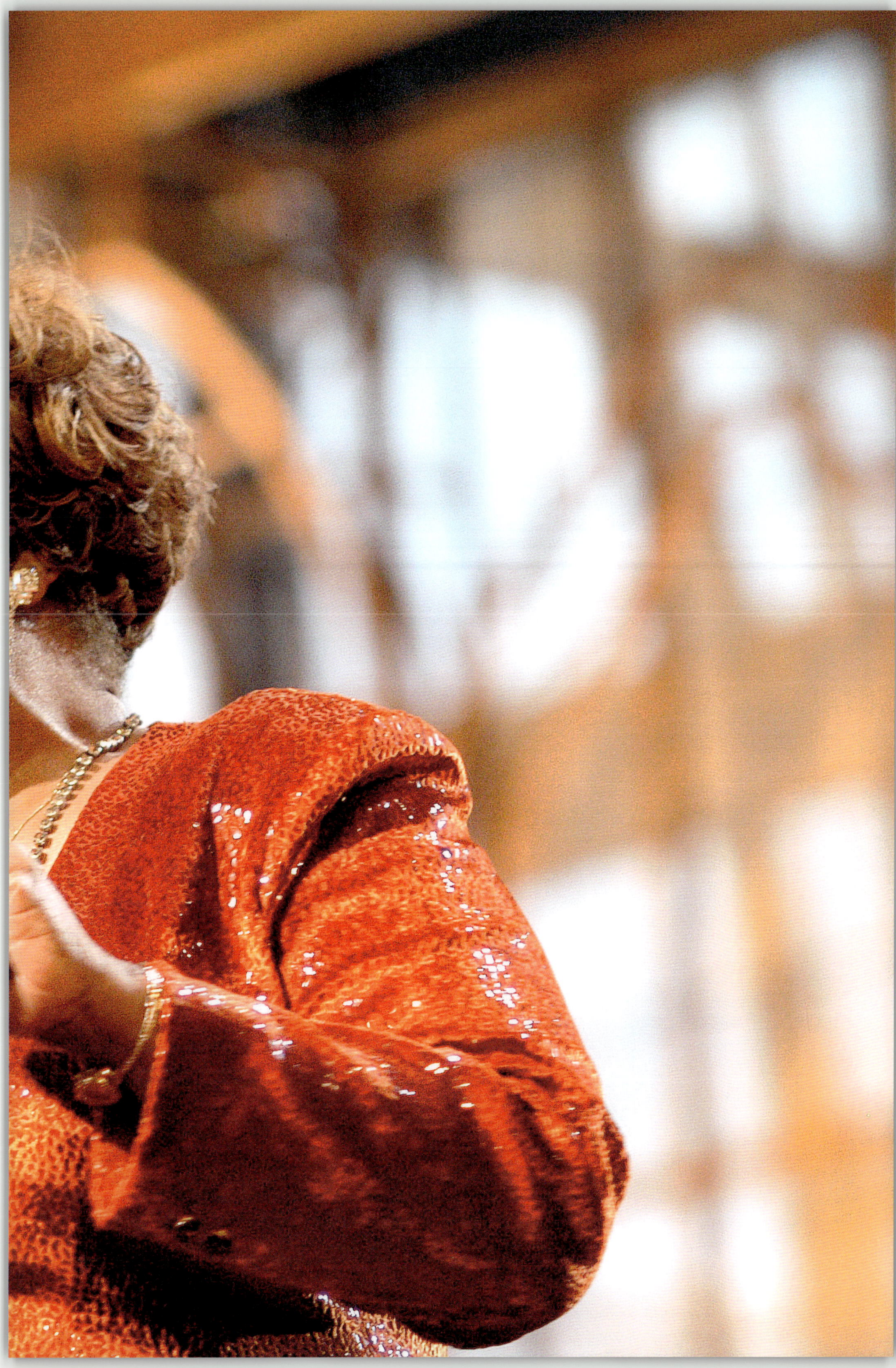

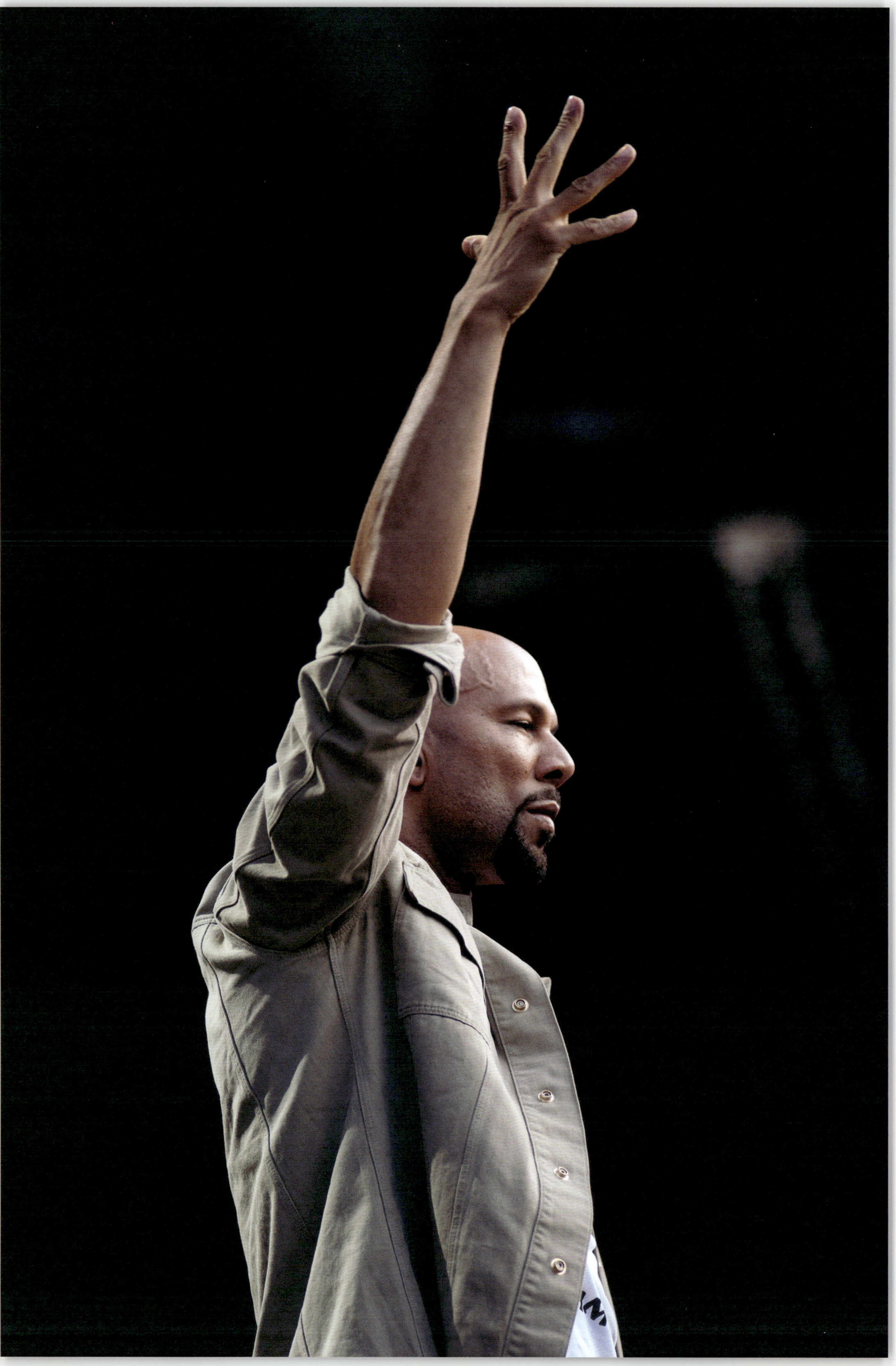

10

RAP + HIP HOP
URBAN CULTURE

Hip hop is the folk music of the Black community. It speaks truth about the world today. Performances are intense, and great to photograph. The performers are very interesting people to photograph offstage as well as on.

COMMON / CHICAGO, IL / 2016

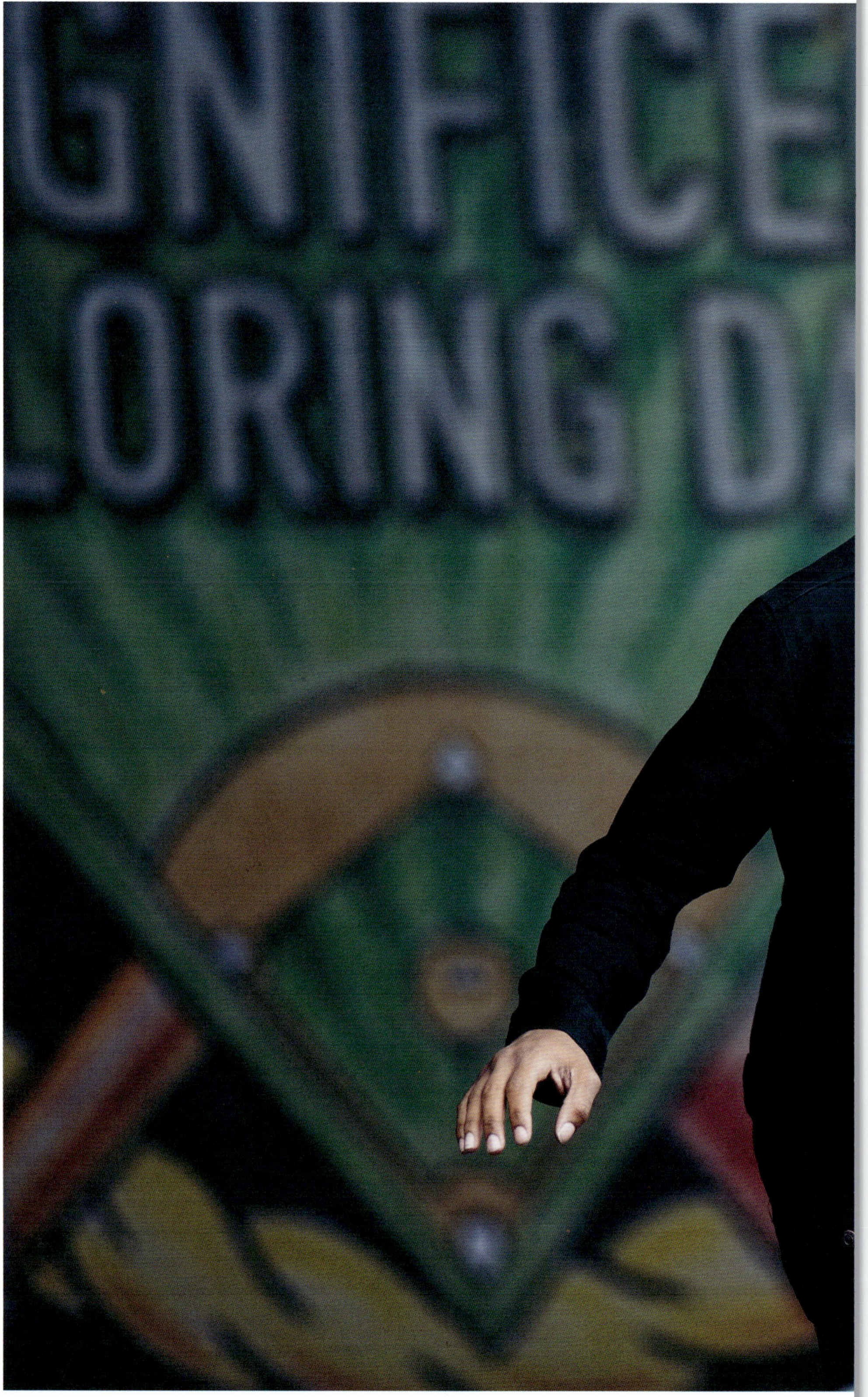

On September 24, 2016, Chance the Rapper produced the Magnificent Coloring Day festival, a one-day extravaganza where it seemed that he invited every rapper in America to come play–and they all showed up! The show started at noon and continued until 11 p.m. with performances by Chance, Kanye West, Common, John Legend, Alicia Keys,

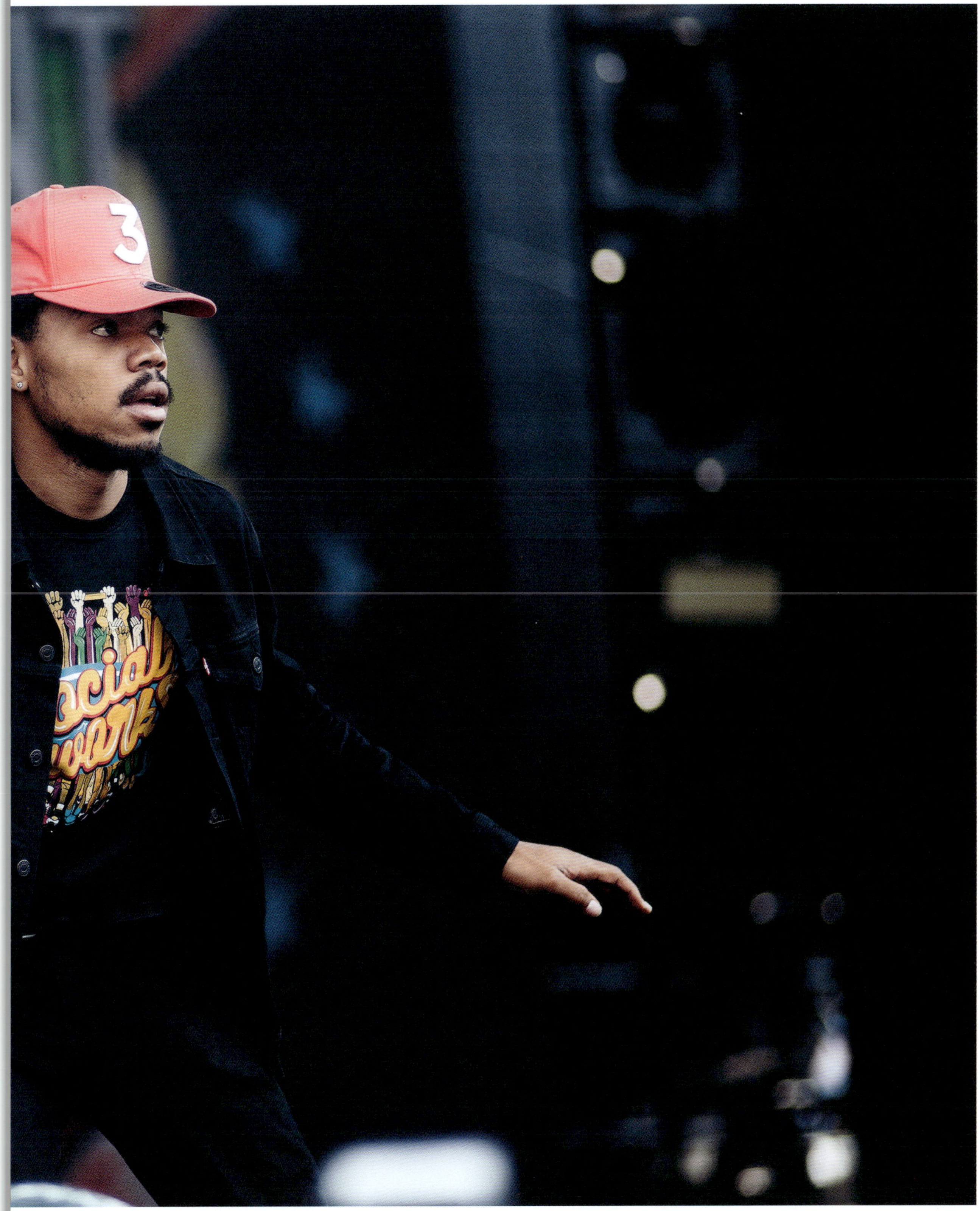

Lil Wayne, 2 Chainz and many more. I couldn't stop photographing throughout the day. The highlight was John Legend and Common collaborating on their Academy Award-winning hit "Glory" from the movie of the same name, with 60,000 people in the audience singing along to every word.

CHANCE THE RAPPER / CHICAGO, IL / 2016

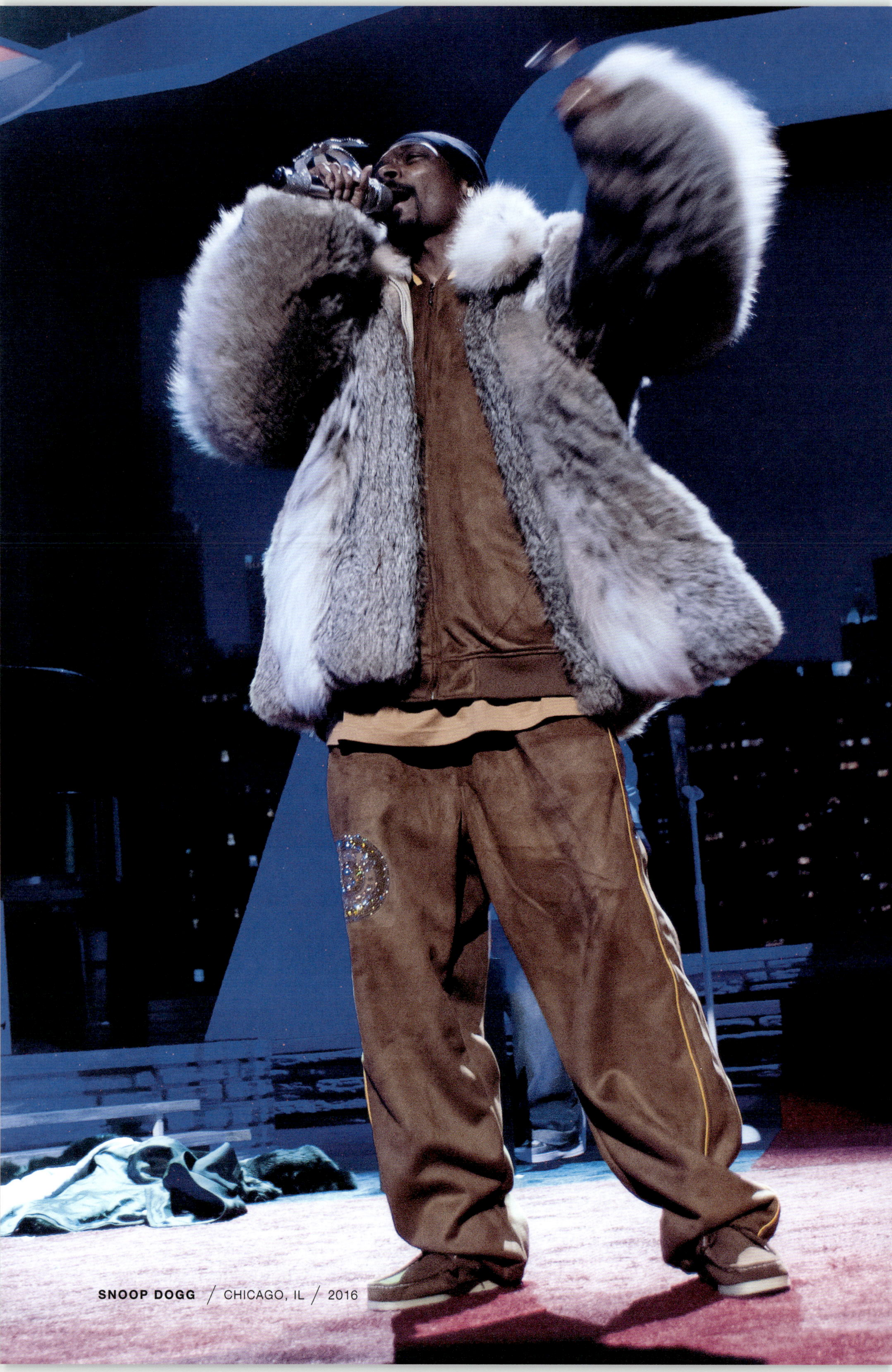

SNOOP DOGG / CHICAGO, IL / 2016

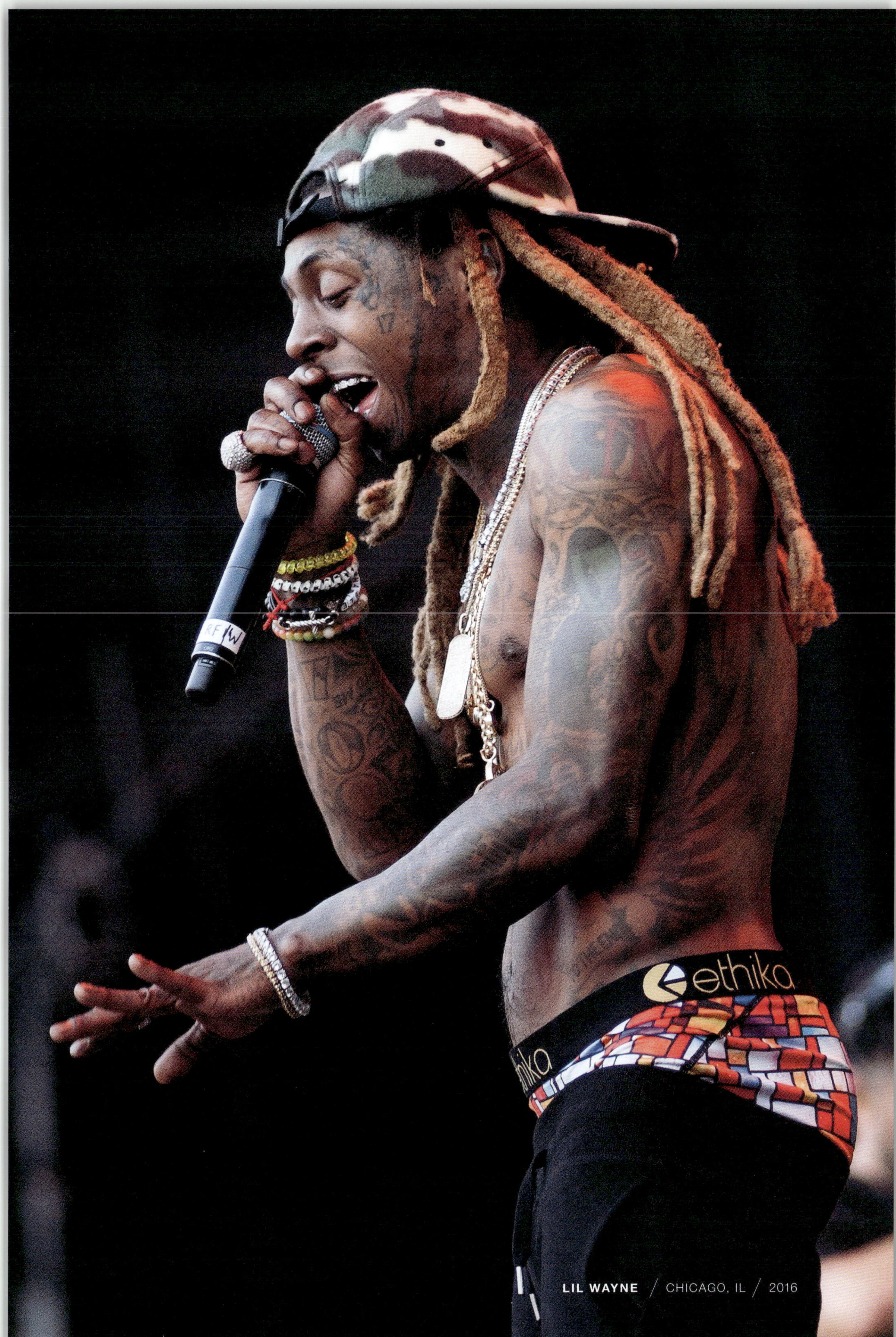

LIL WAYNE / CHICAGO, IL / 2016

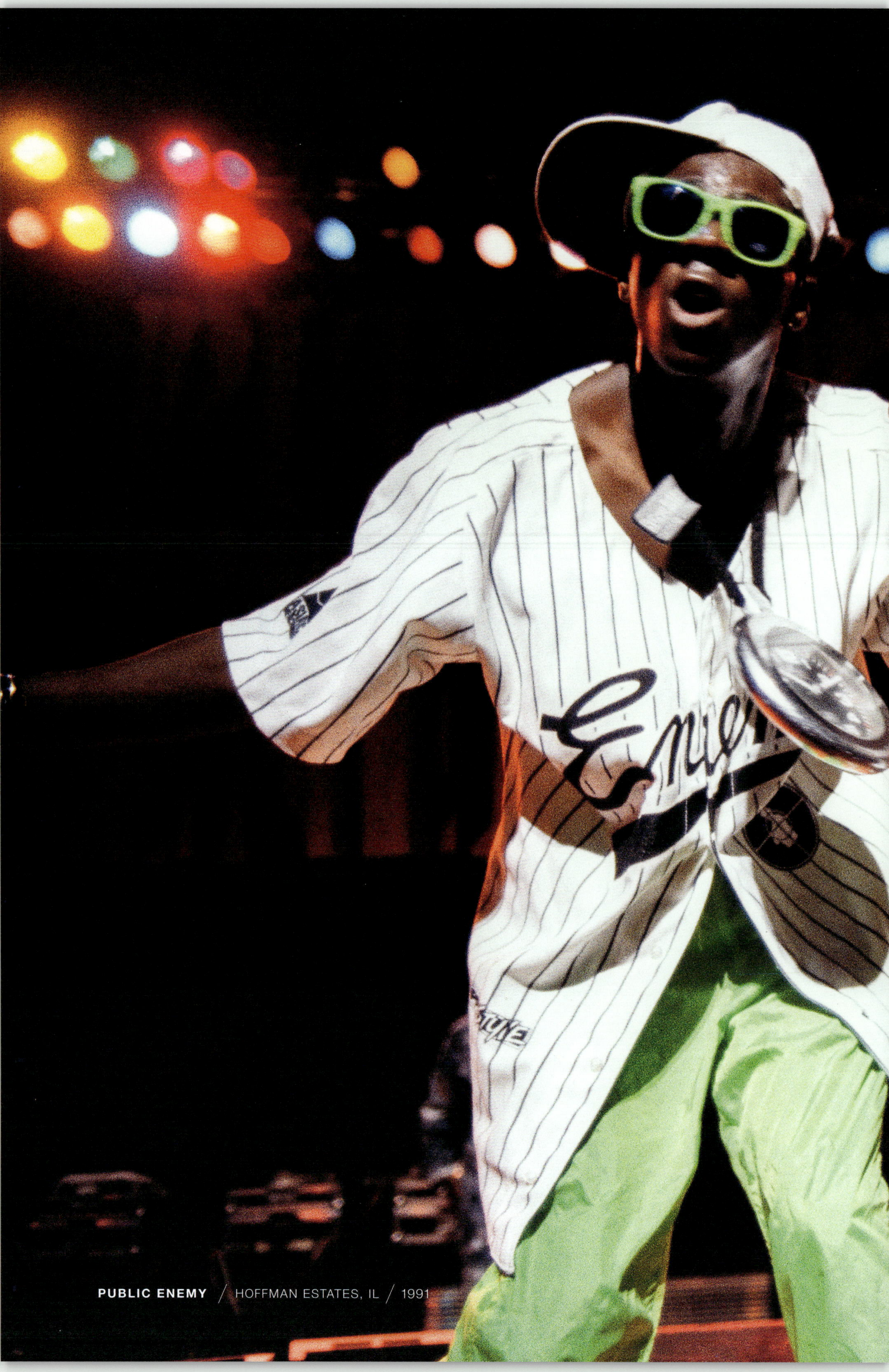

PUBLIC ENEMY / HOFFMAN ESTATES, IL / 1991

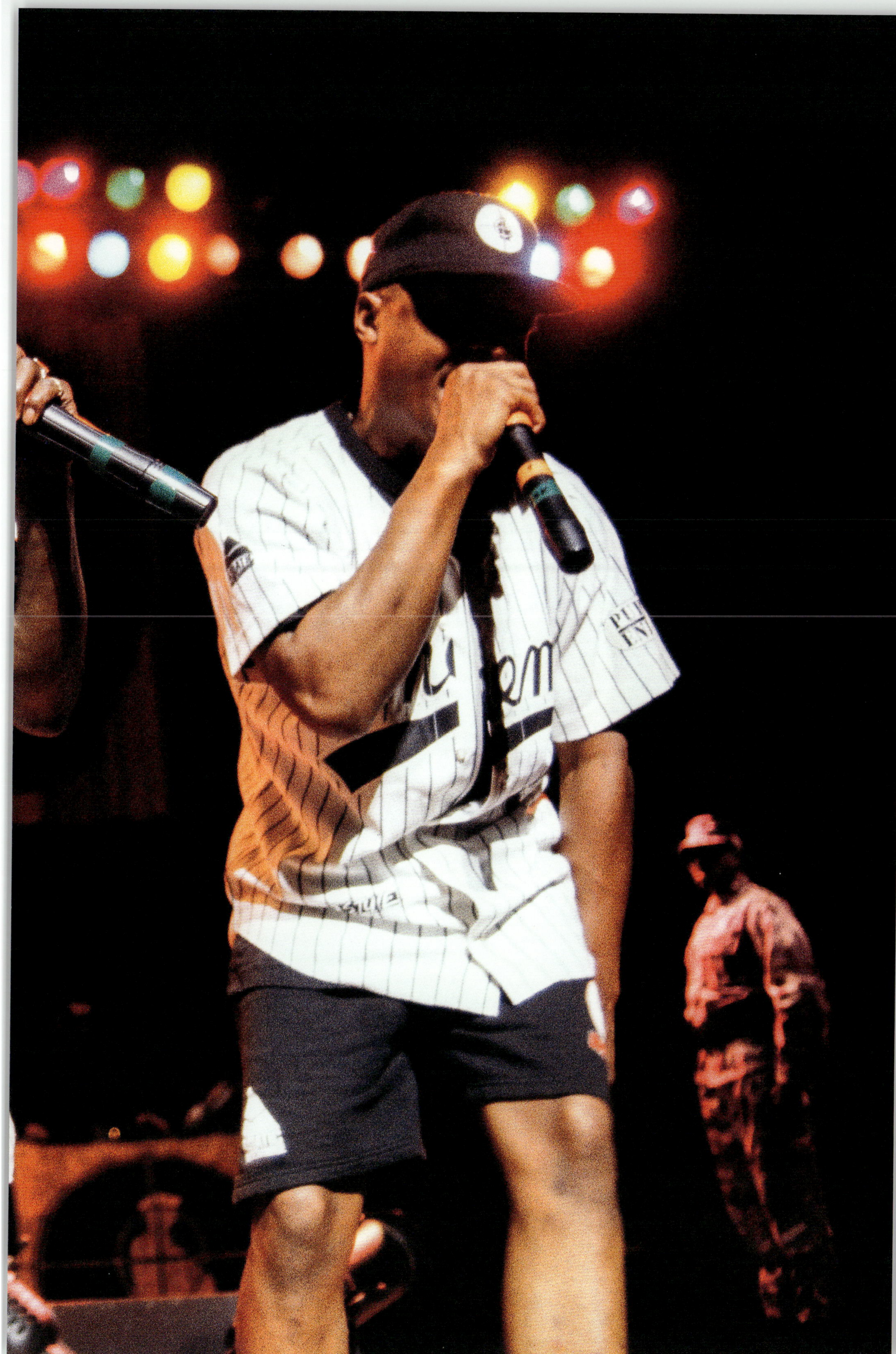

I was asked to photograph rapper Ice Cube for a magazine story on government censorship in music. I purchased three rolls of tape–one red, one white and one blue–and off to Los Angeles I went. When I got to his house he was just sitting down to watch *Raising Arizona*. I set up my stuff, cut three pieces of tape to make one red, white and blue piece, grabbed an ice cream bar out of the refrigerator, and sat down with him to watch the movie. When it was over, I handed him the piece of tape and asked him to put it over his mouth. He looked at me like I was crazy, then started laughing and said, "Great idea." The entire shoot took five minutes.

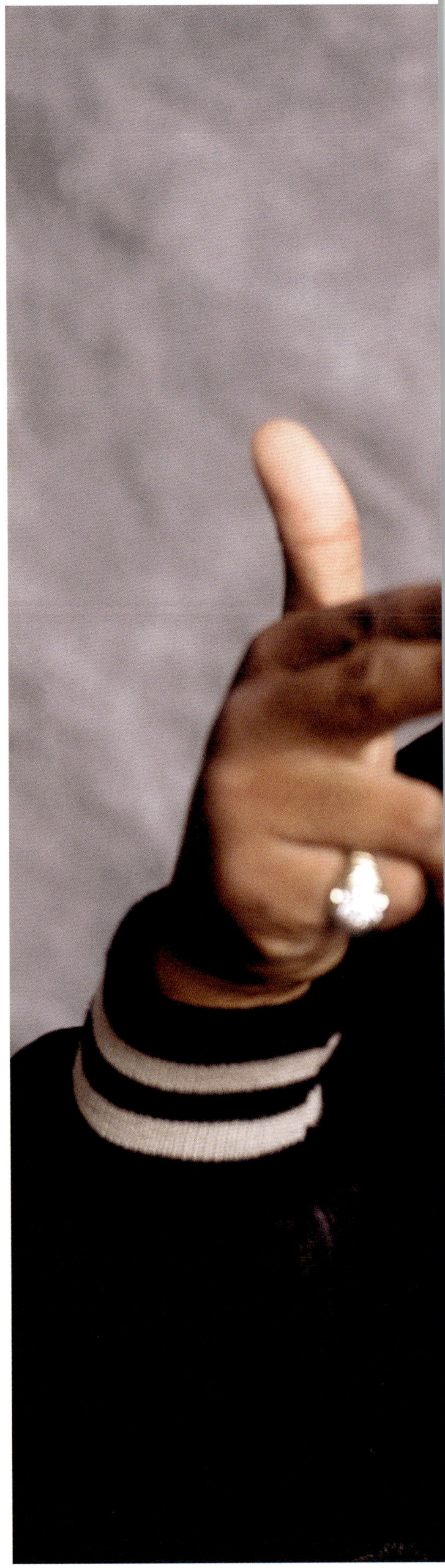

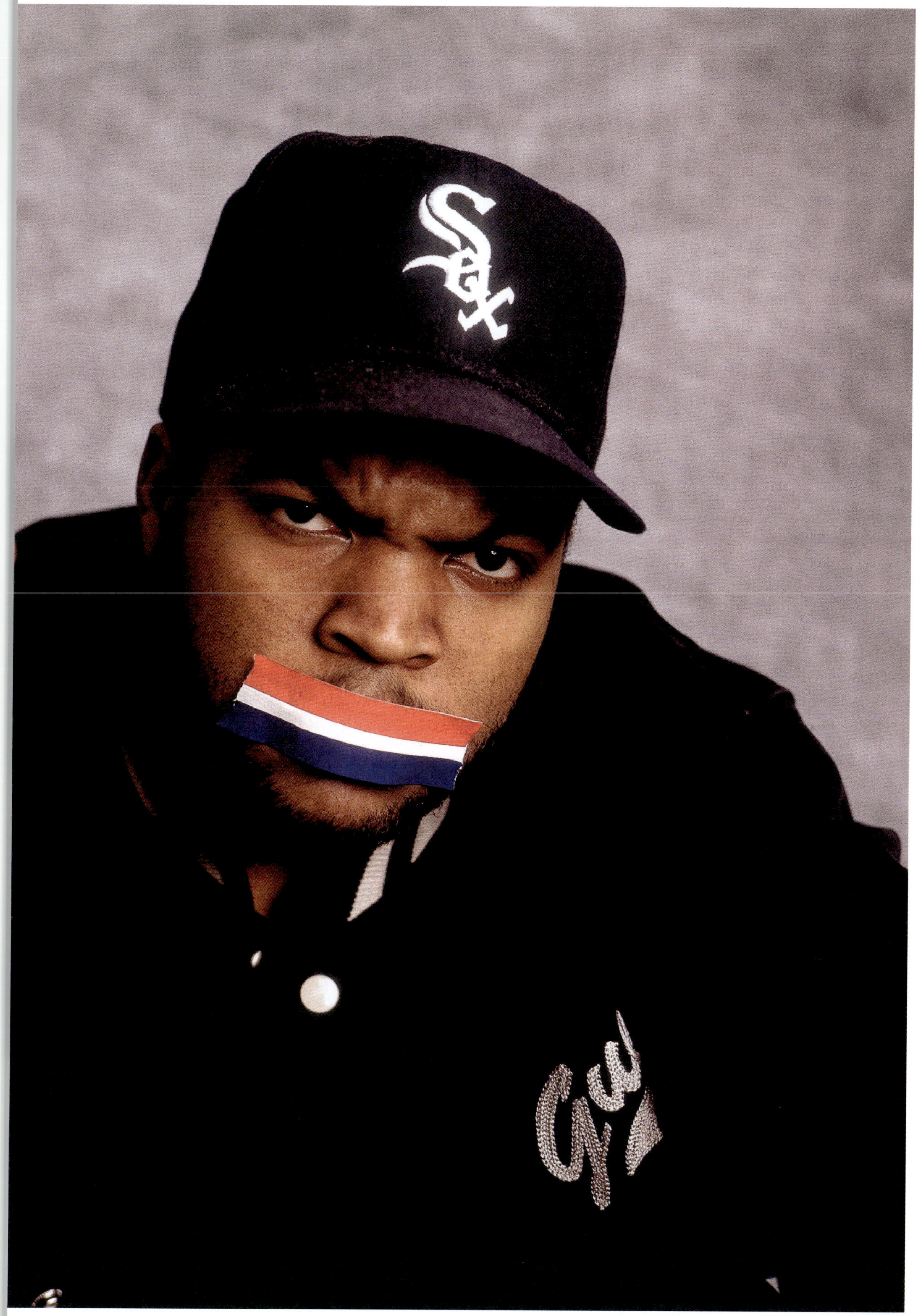

ICE CUBE / LOS ANGELES, CA / 1991

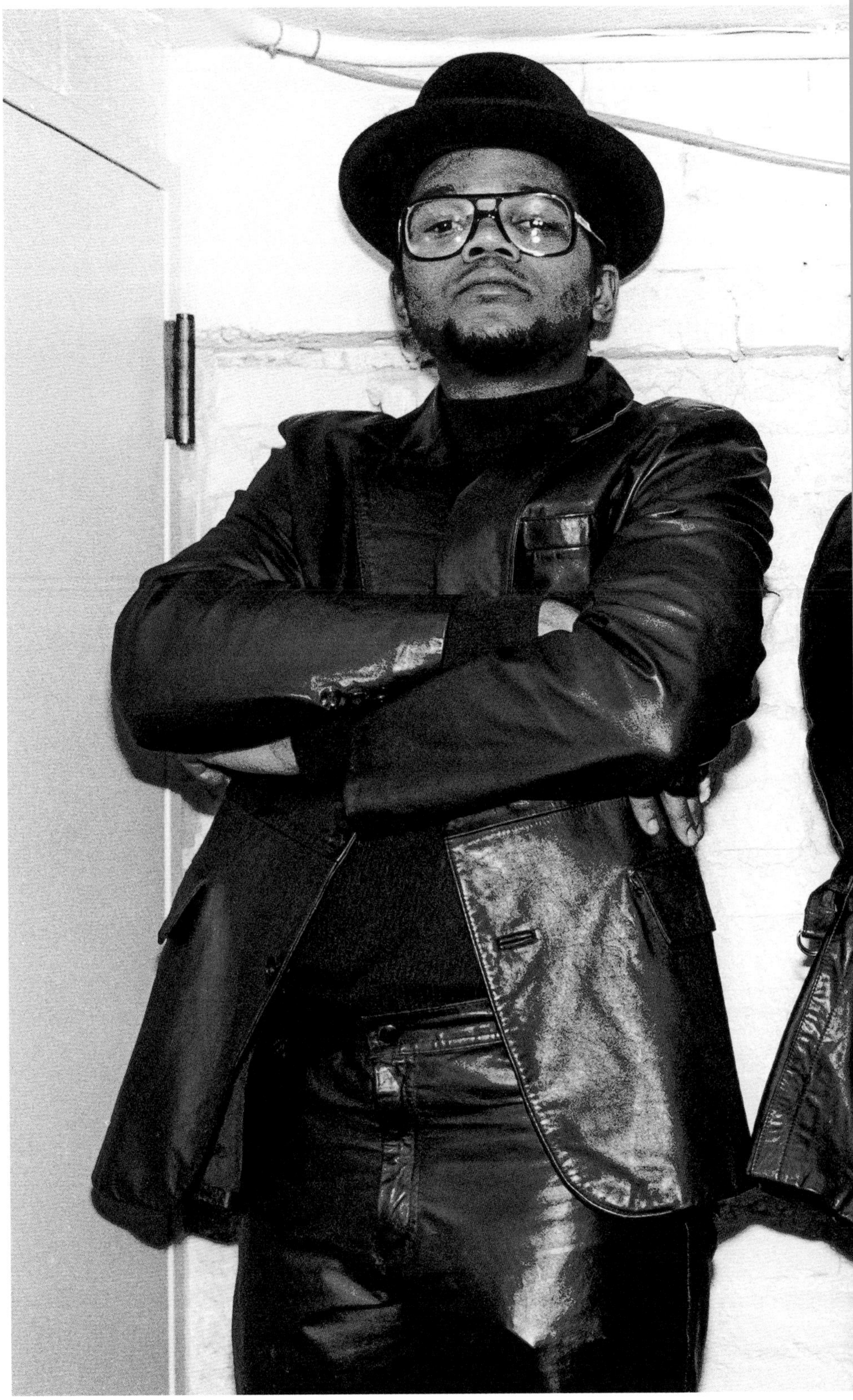

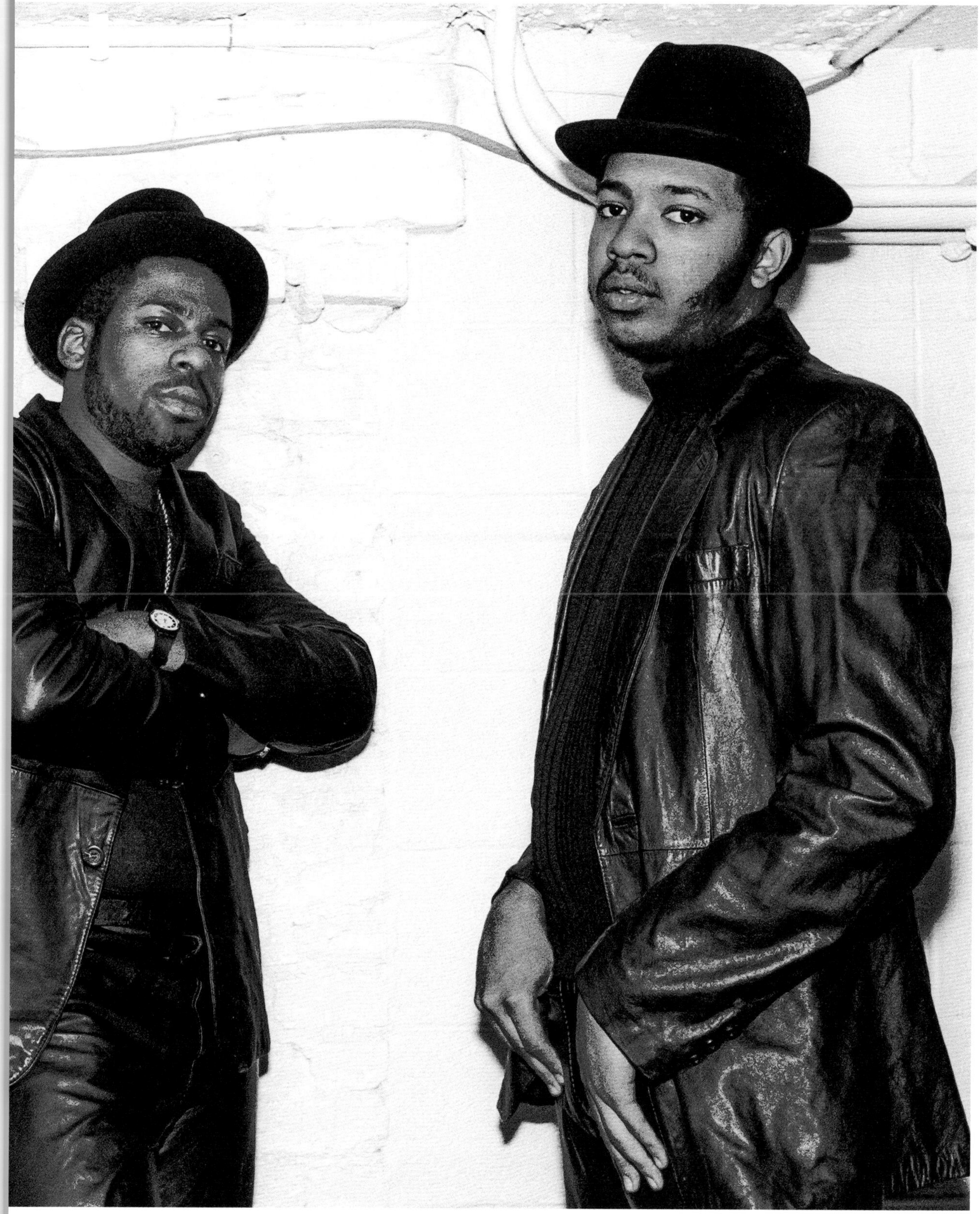

While photographing a music festival at the University of Chicago, I went backstage between acts and saw these three striking guys dressed in black leather standing against the wall. I approached them and asked if they were in a band. They said yes, so I asked if I could take a few pictures of them. A few years later everyone knew who they were.

RUN-DMC / CHICAGO, IL / 1984

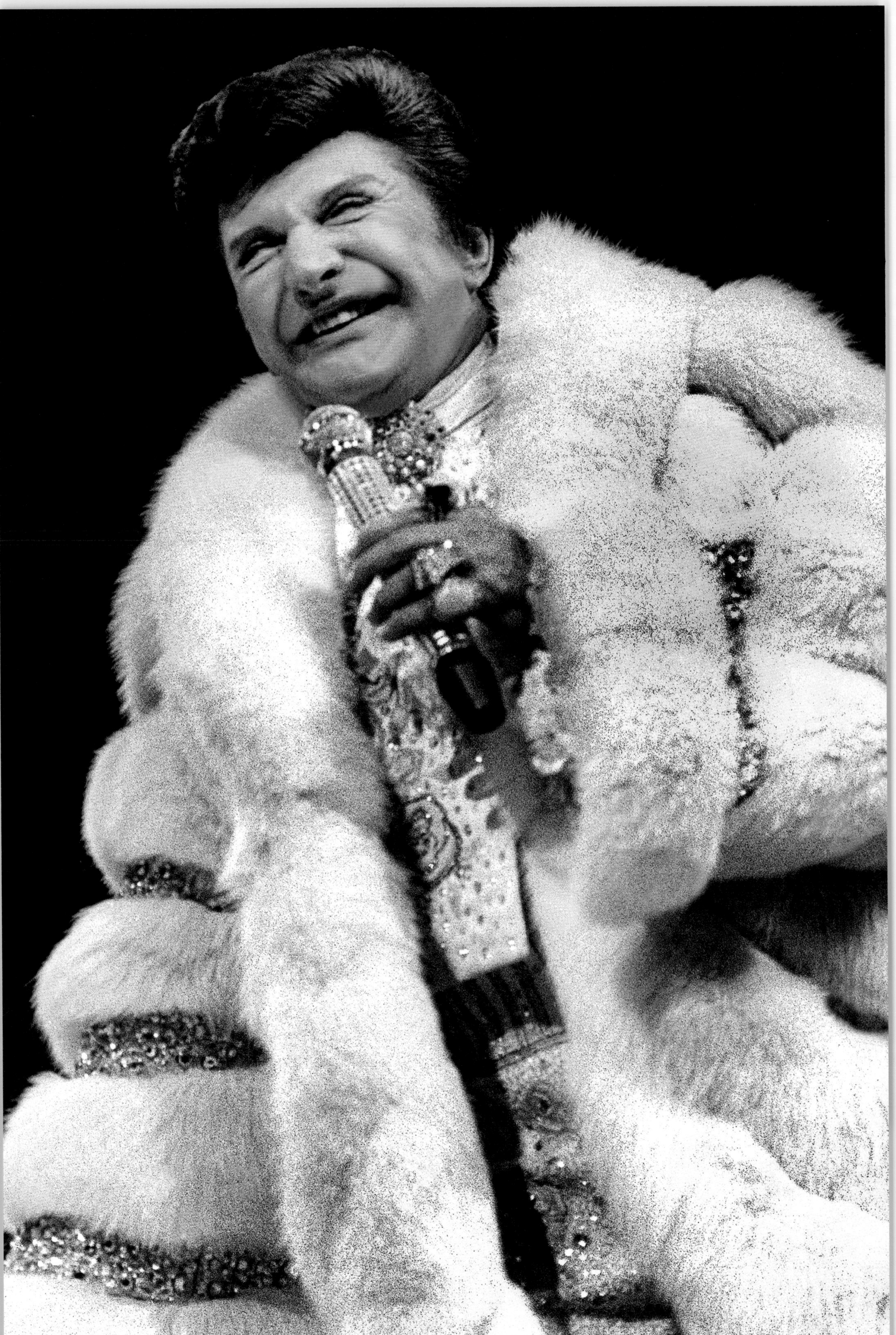

11

ADULT
POP STANDARDS

This is music that has been around forever, like Frank Sinatra, and is still as great as when it first came out. To be in the presence of Frank (or Dean or Sammy) is a privilege not to be forgotten.

LIBERACE / MERRILLVILLE, IN / 1982

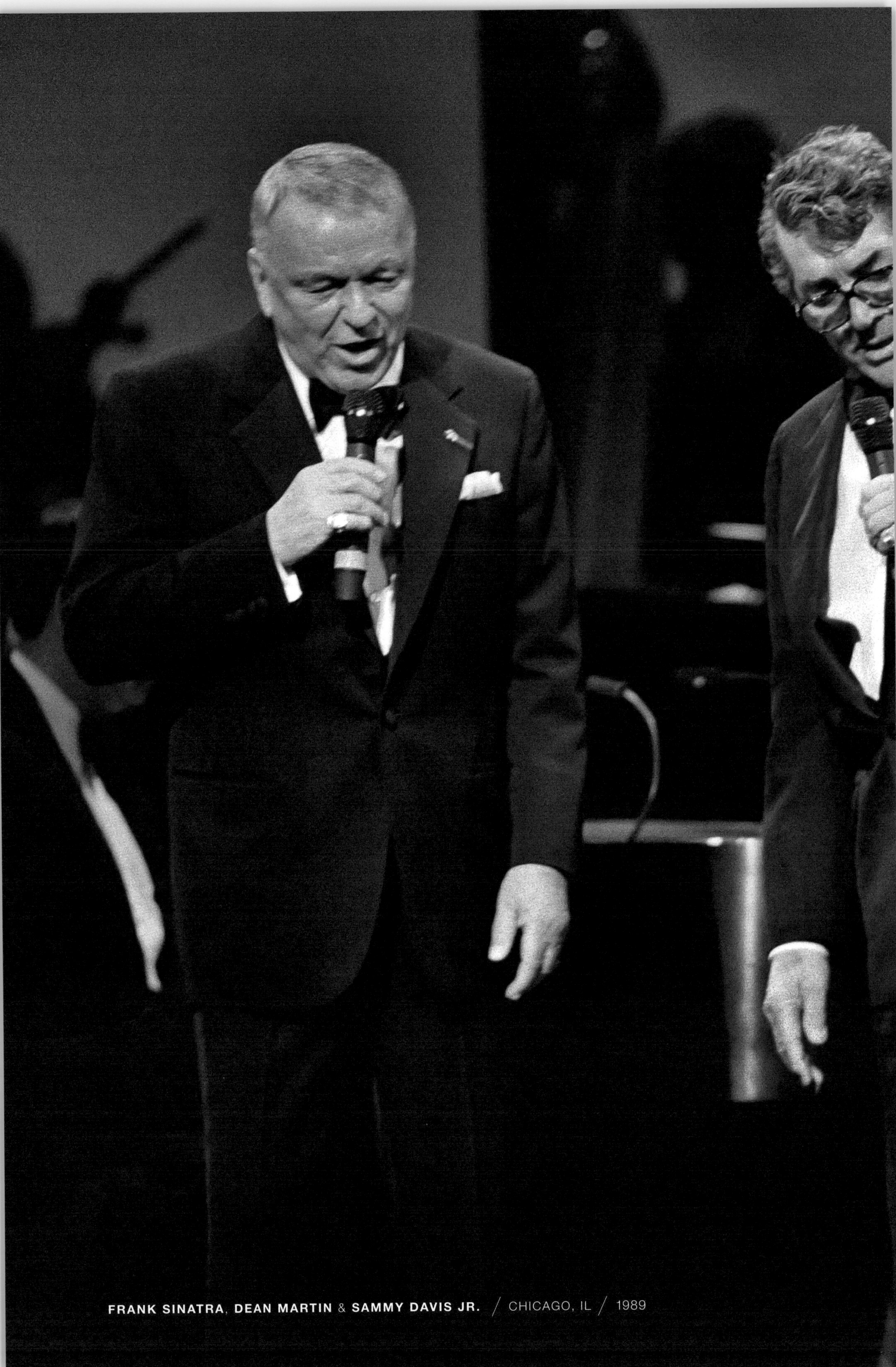

FRANK SINATRA, DEAN MARTIN & SAMMY DAVIS JR. / CHICAGO, IL / 1989

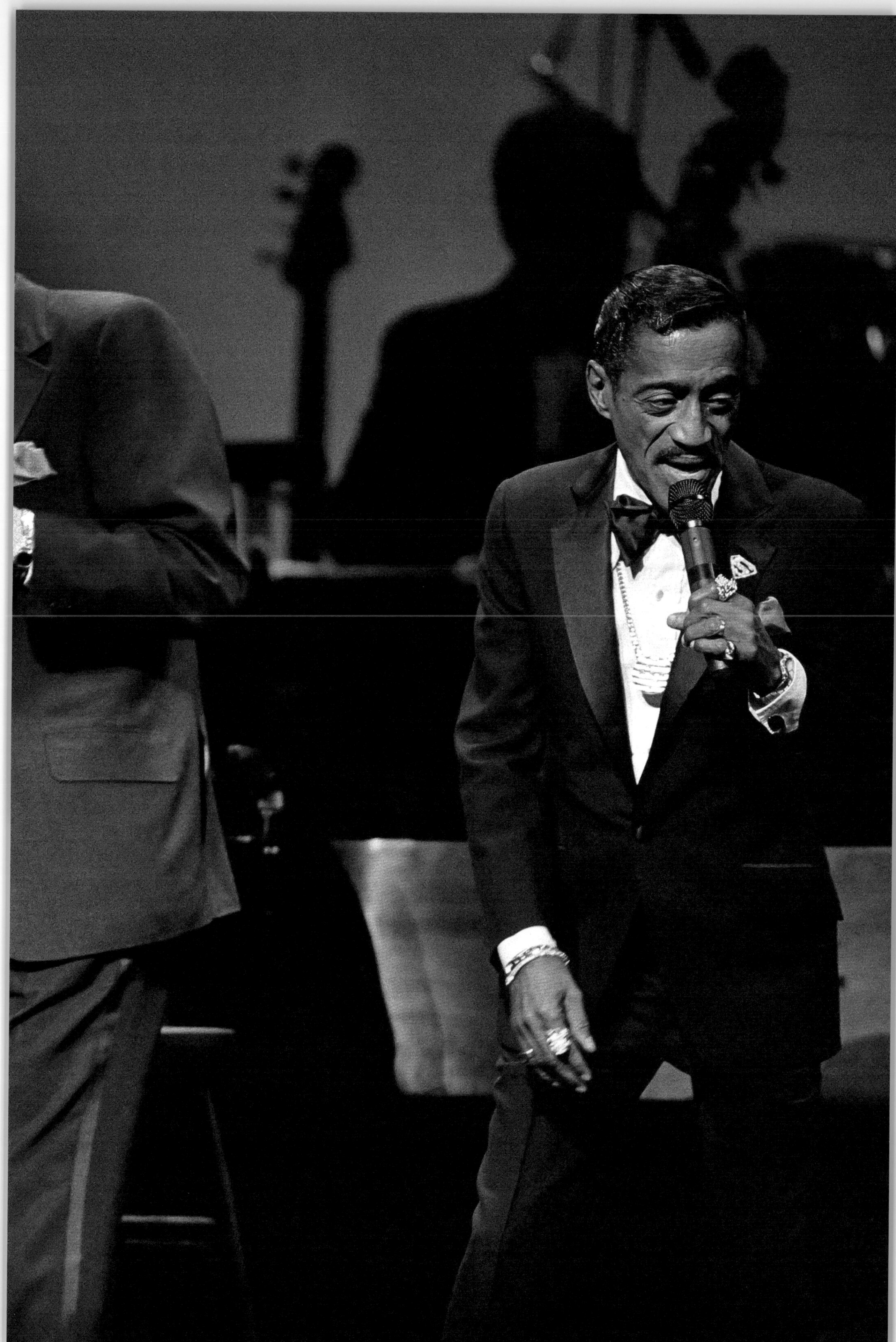

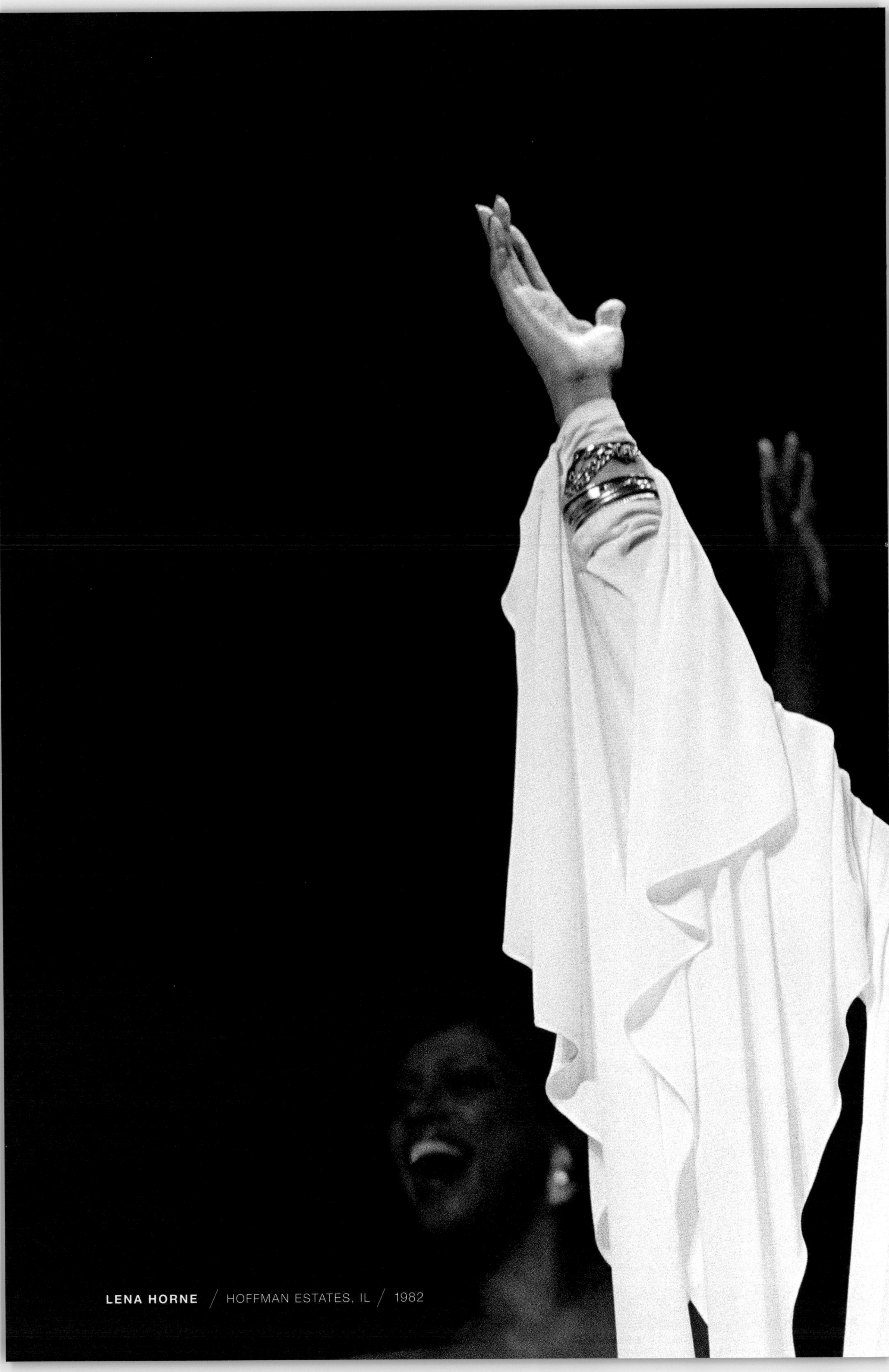

LENA HORNE / HOFFMAN ESTATES, IL / 1982

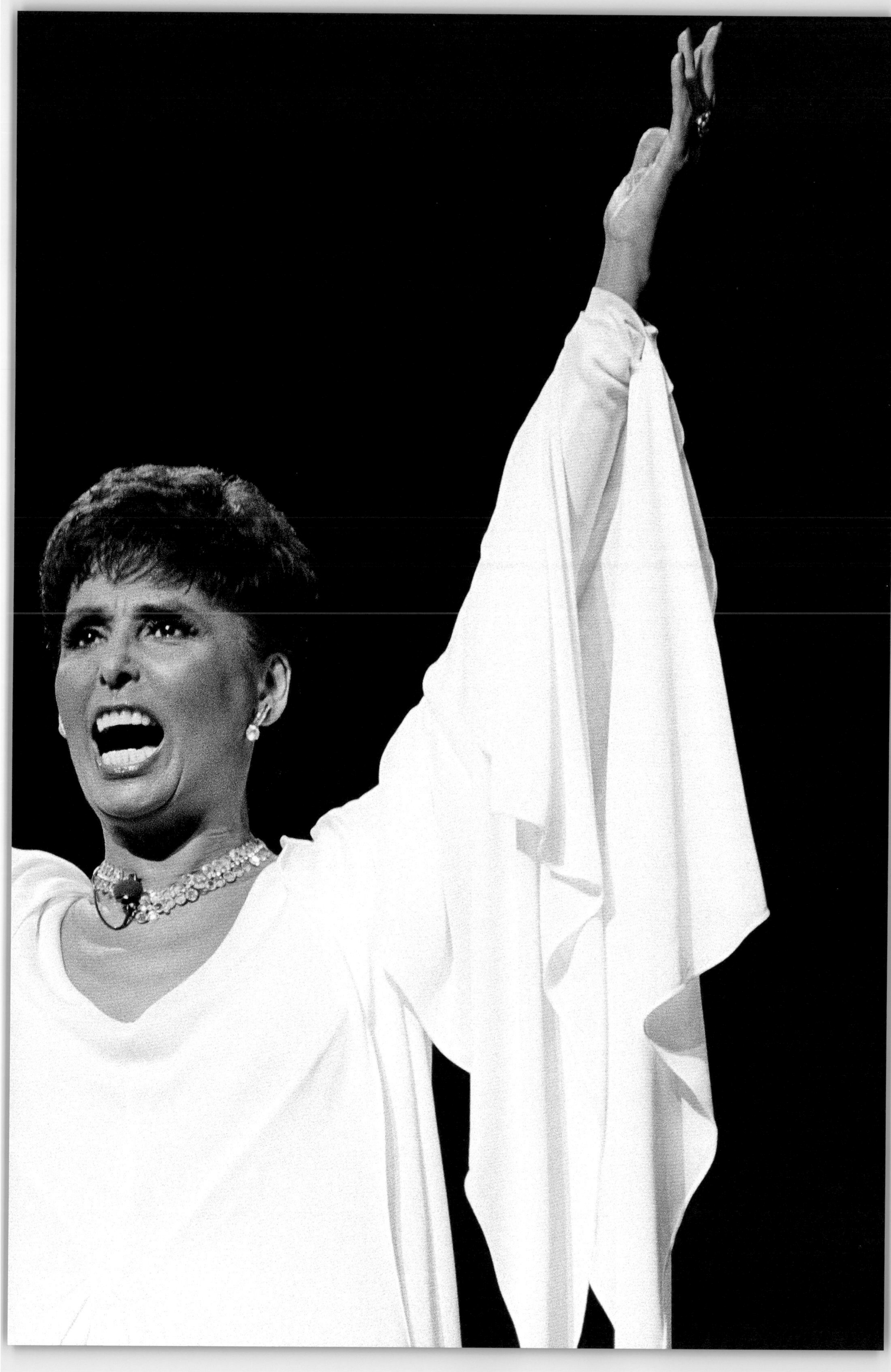

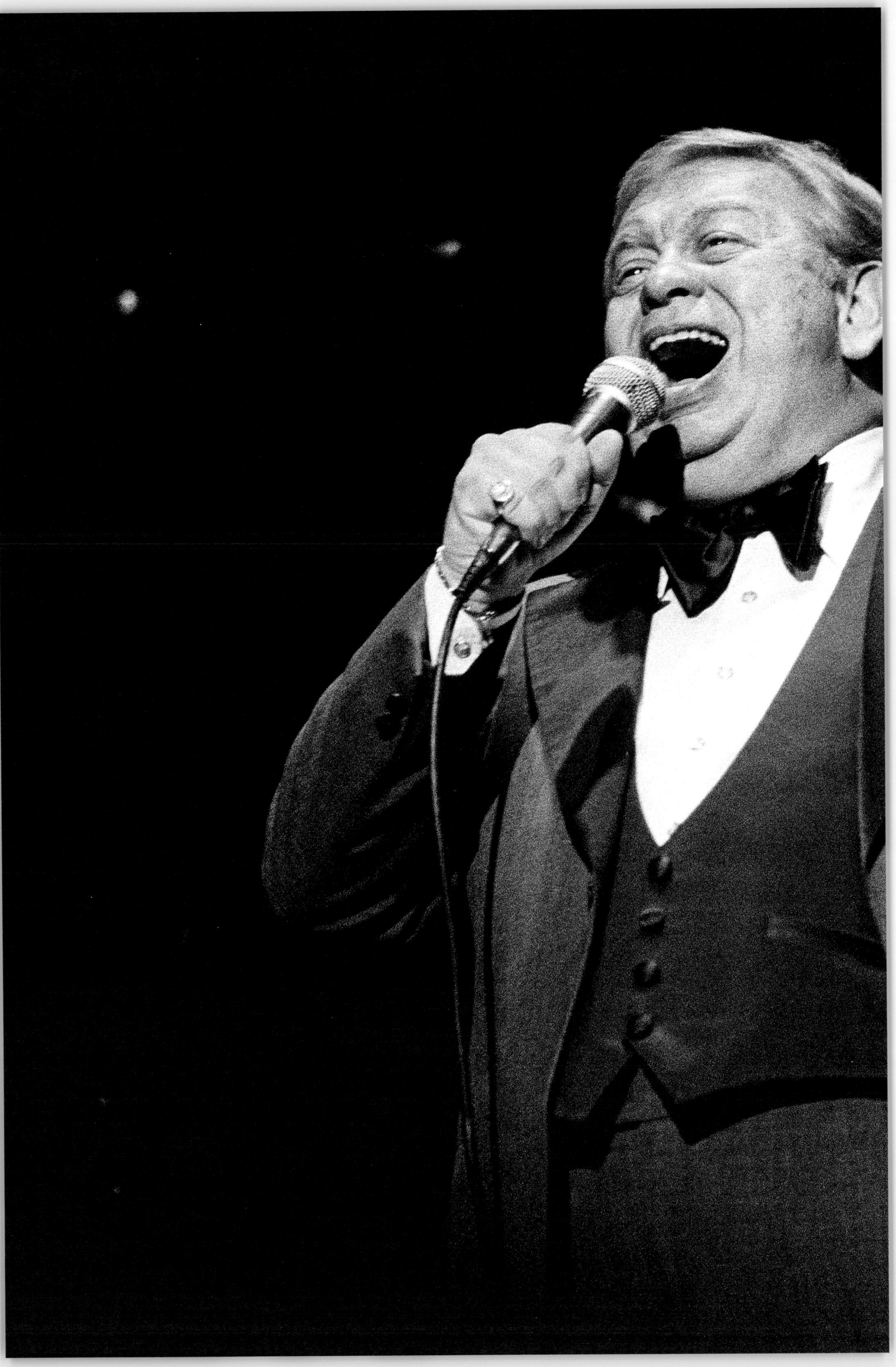

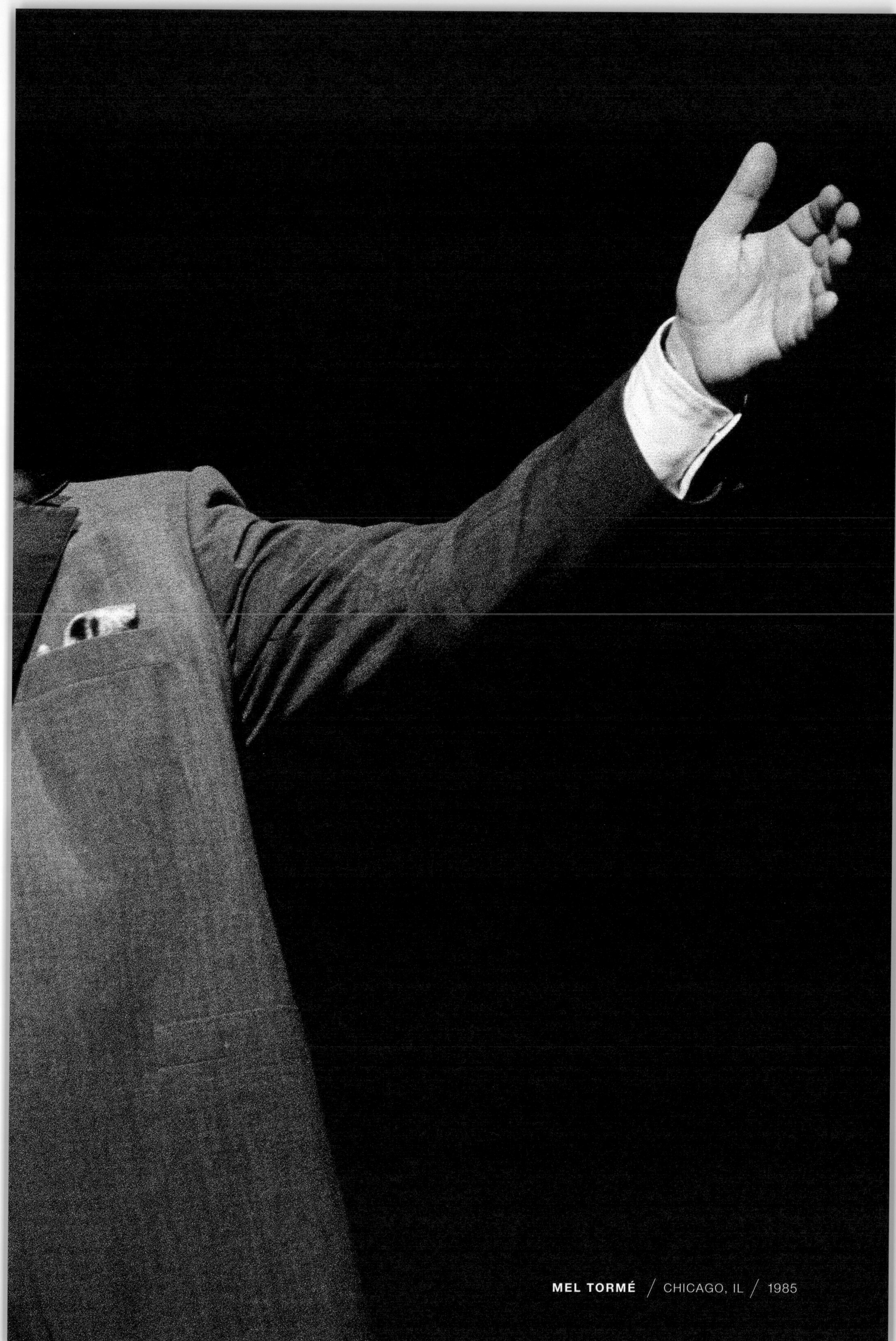

MEL TORMÉ / CHICAGO, IL / 1985

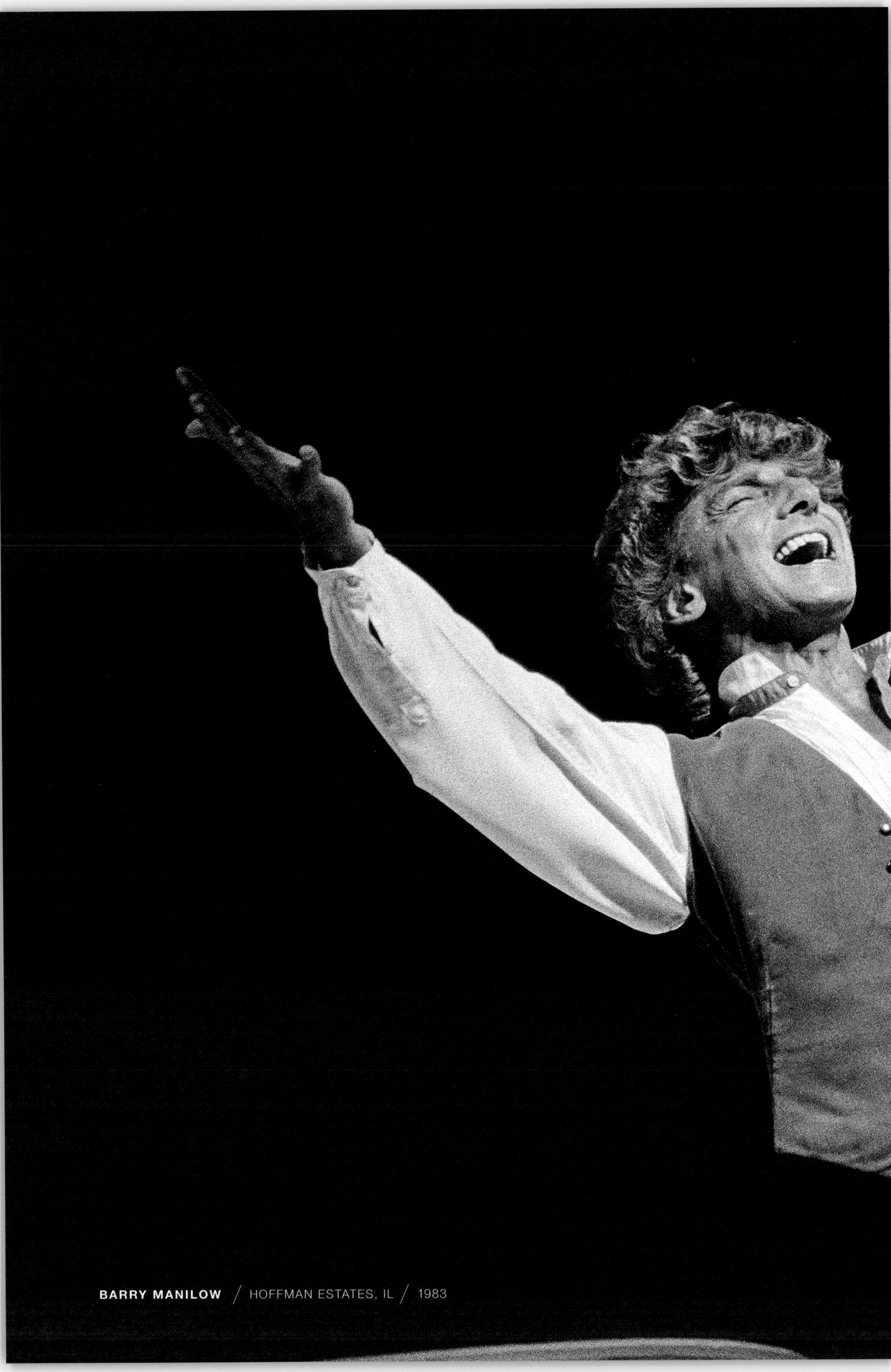

BARRY MANILOW / HOFFMAN ESTATES, IL / 1983

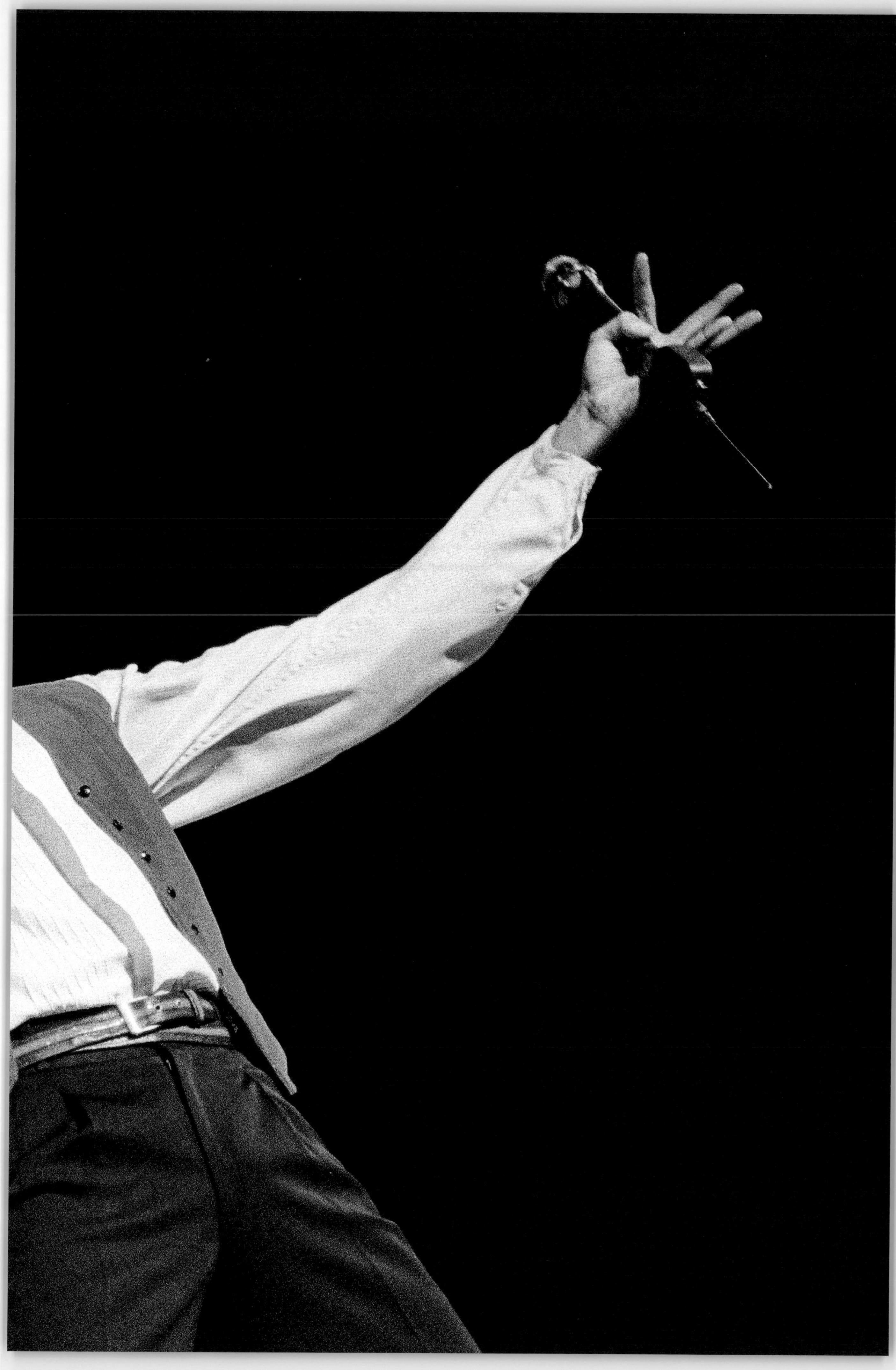

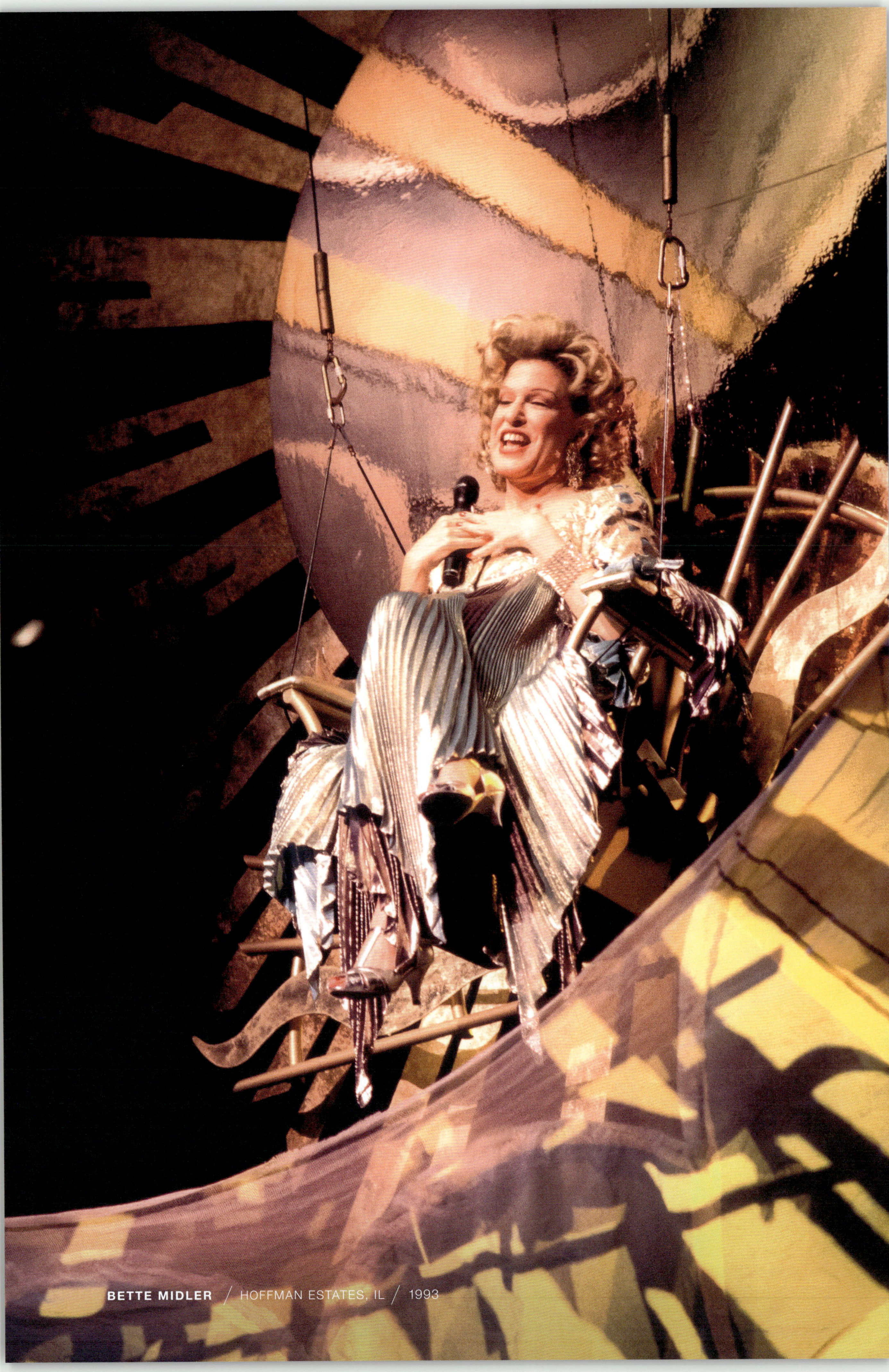

BETTE MIDLER / HOFFMAN ESTATES, IL / 1993

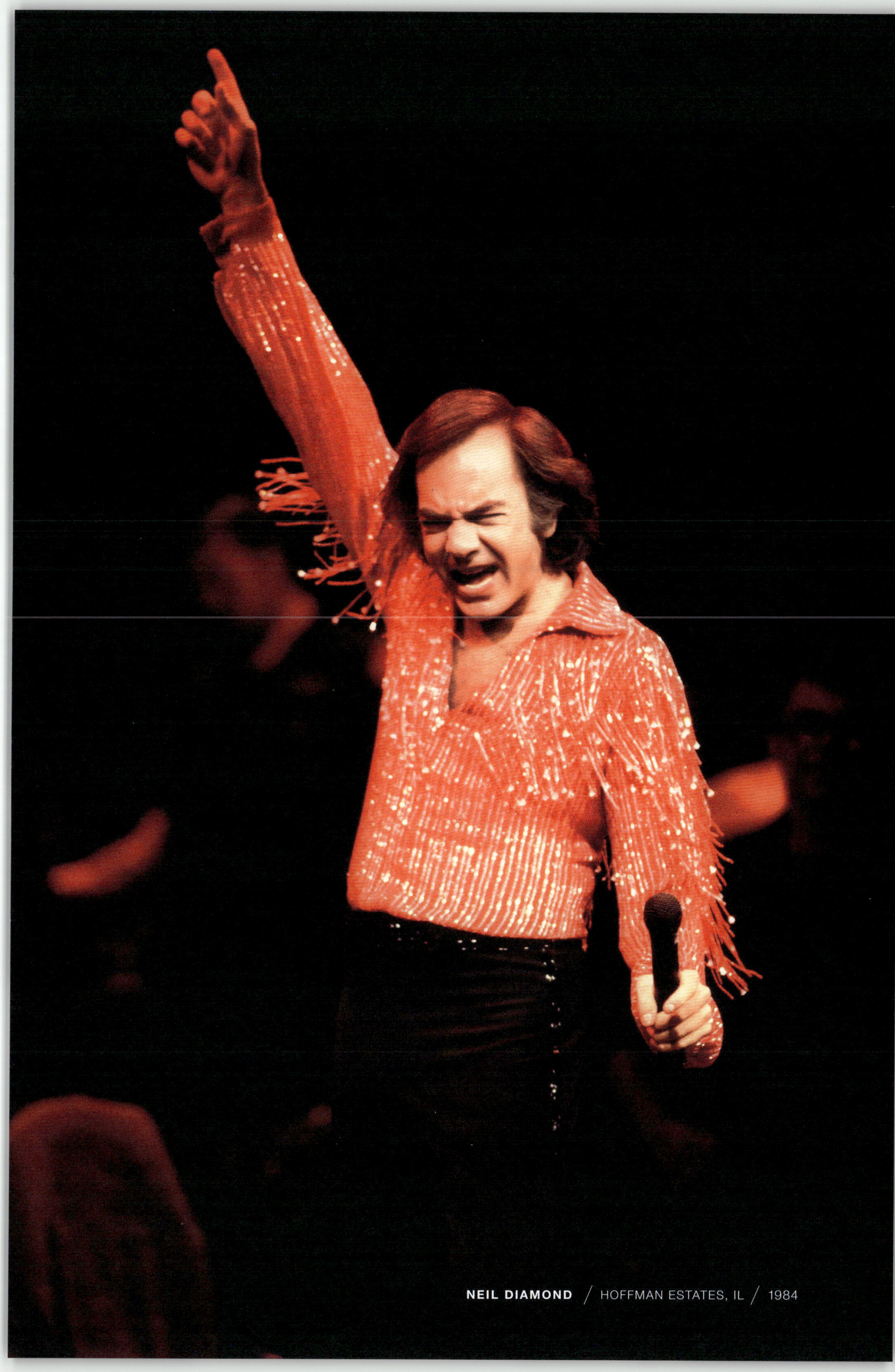

NEIL DIAMOND / HOFFMAN ESTATES, IL / 1984

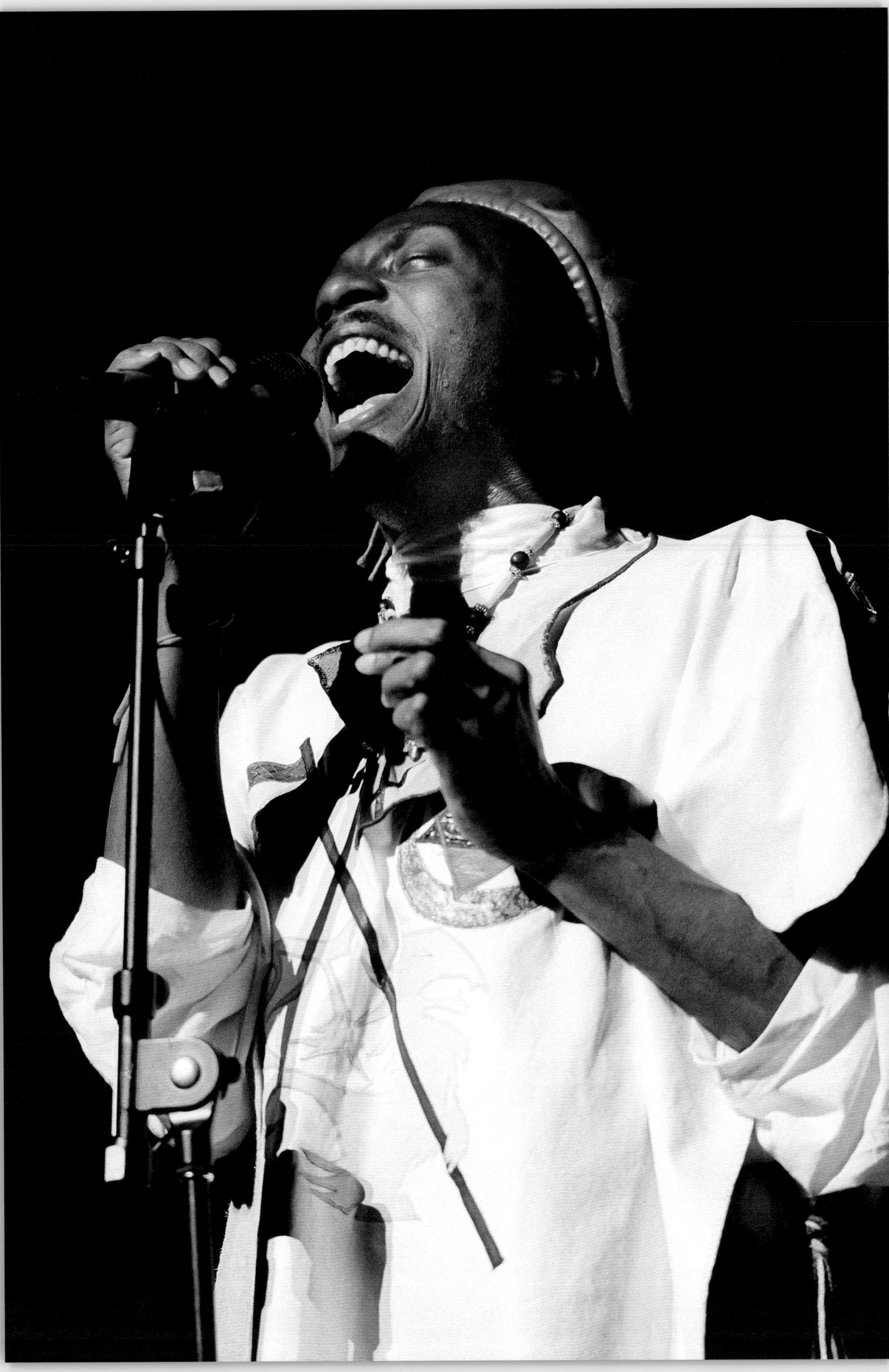

12

WORLD
REGGAE & INTERNATIONAL

It is disorienting to hear 20,000 people cheering wildly, and not understand the language of the lyrics they are cheering about. The music is fabulous to listen to while photographing, though. And the artists are some of the nicest people I have ever met in the business–maybe because they haven't been as exposed to the world of the American music business. They are a joy to work with.

JIMMY CLIFF / CHICAGO, IL / 1980

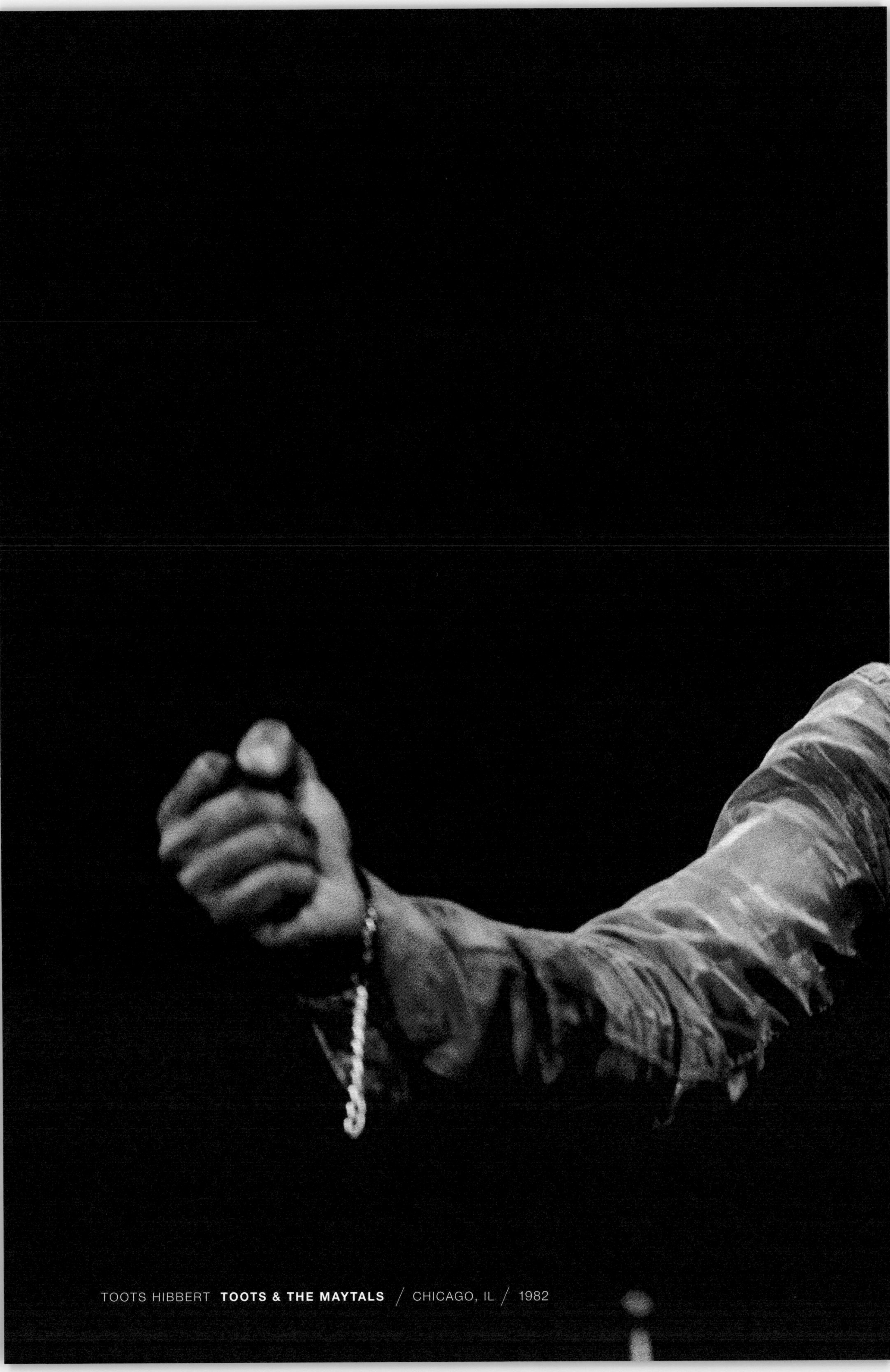

TOOTS HIBBERT **TOOTS & THE MAYTALS** / CHICAGO, IL / 1982

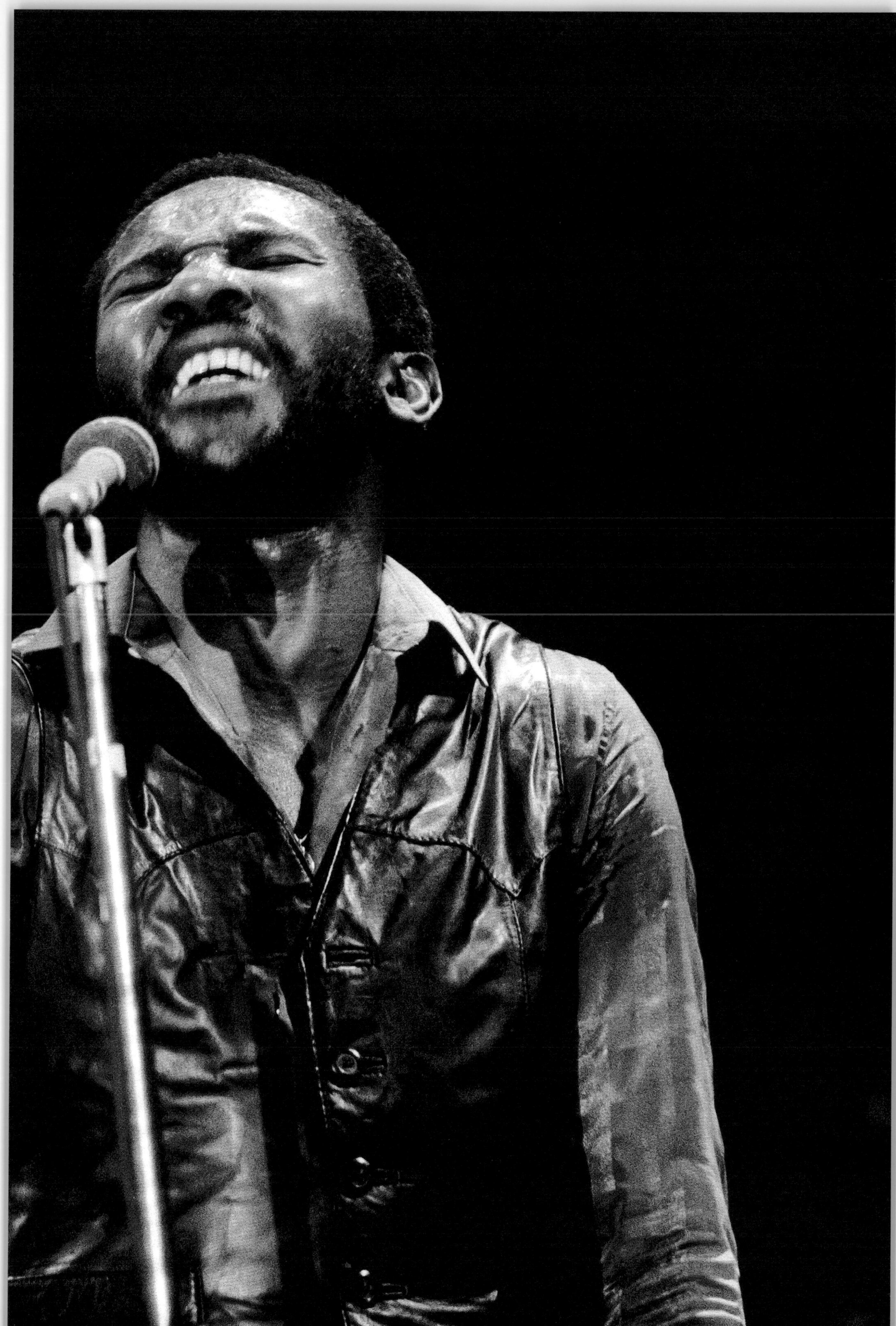

BOB MARLEY / CHICAGO, IL / 1979

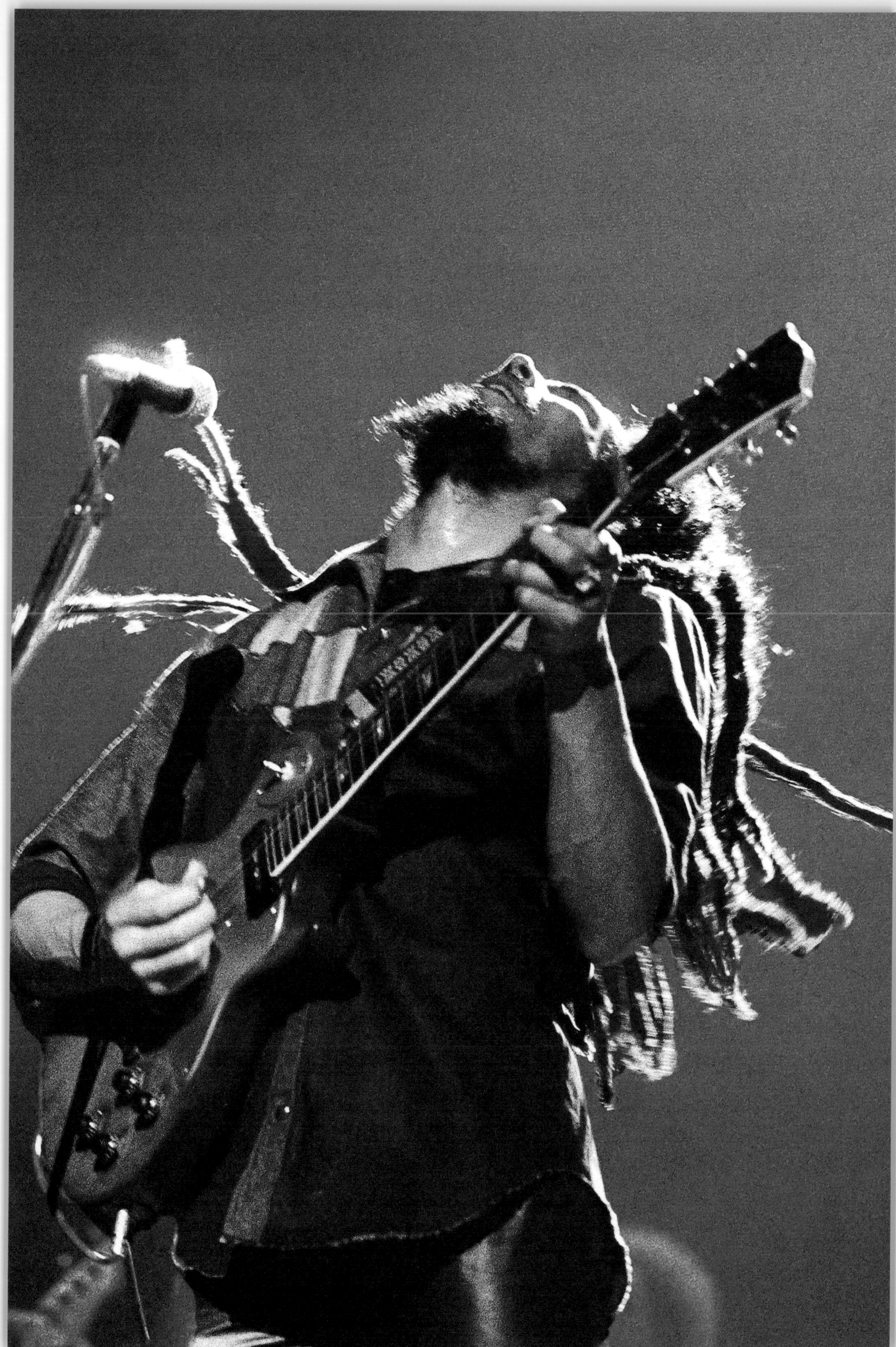

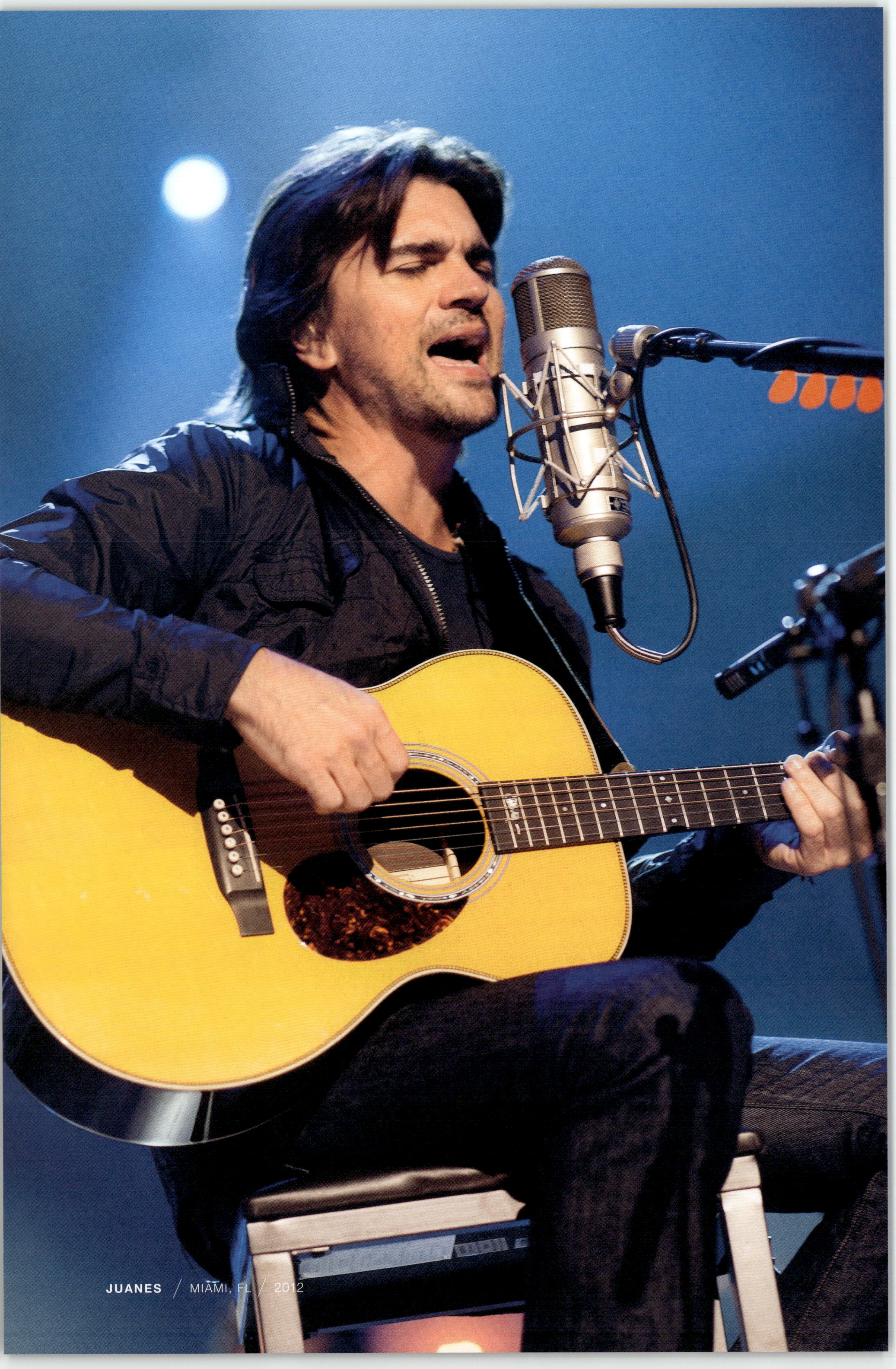

JUANES / MIAMI, FL / 2012

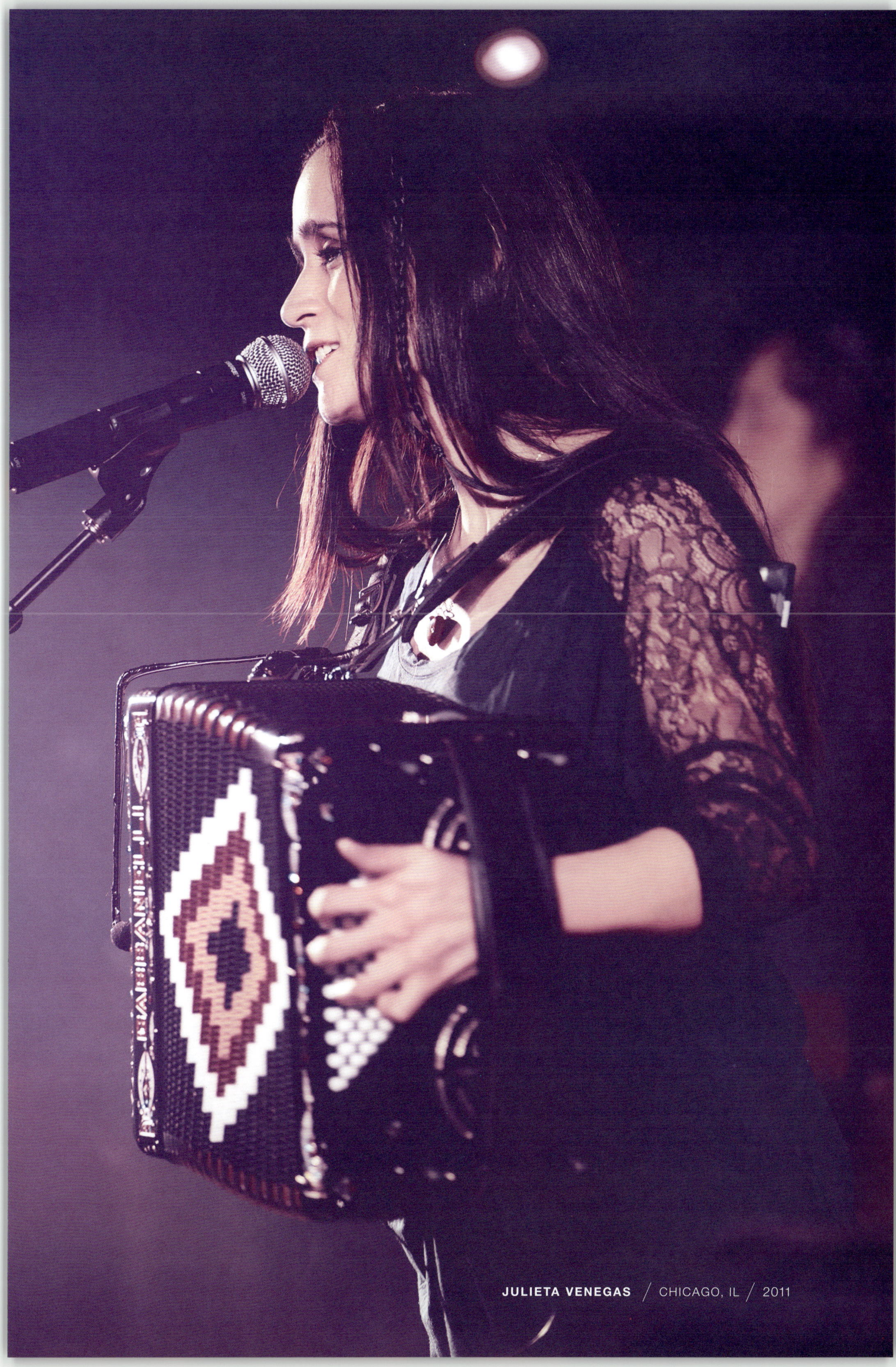

JULIETA VENEGAS / CHICAGO, IL / 2011

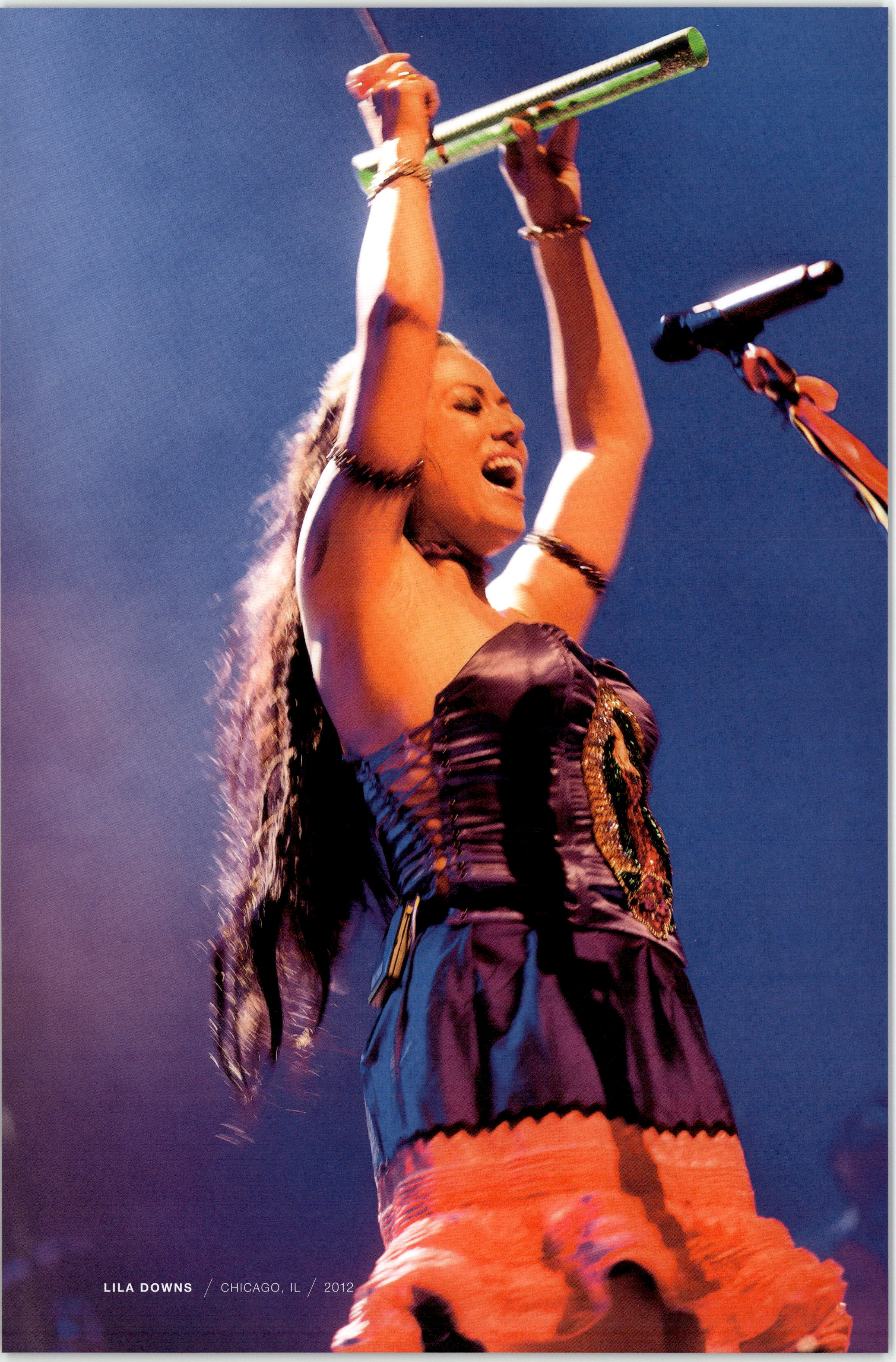

LILA DOWNS / CHICAGO, IL / 2012

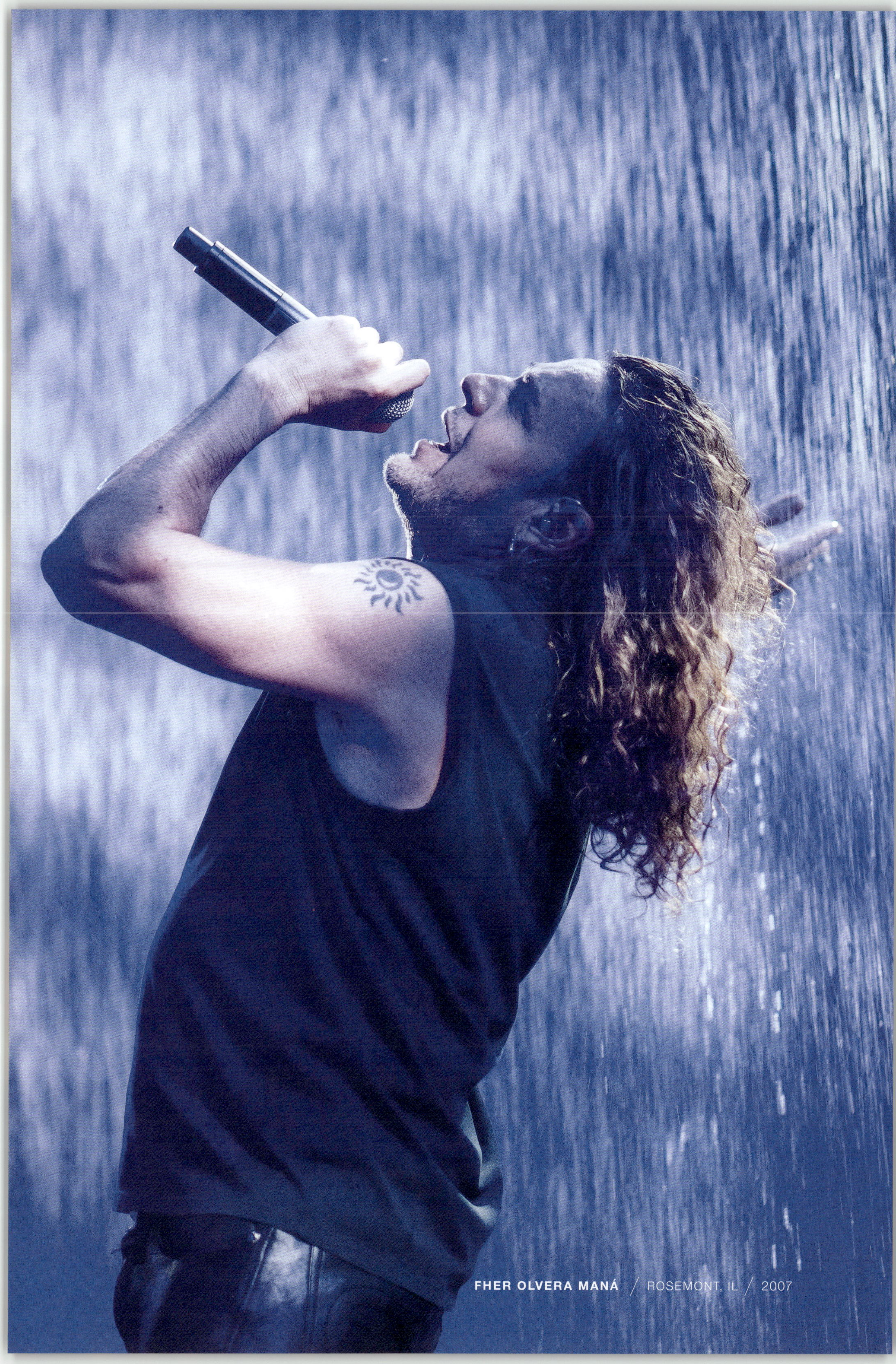

FHER OLVERA MANÁ / ROSEMONT, IL / 2007

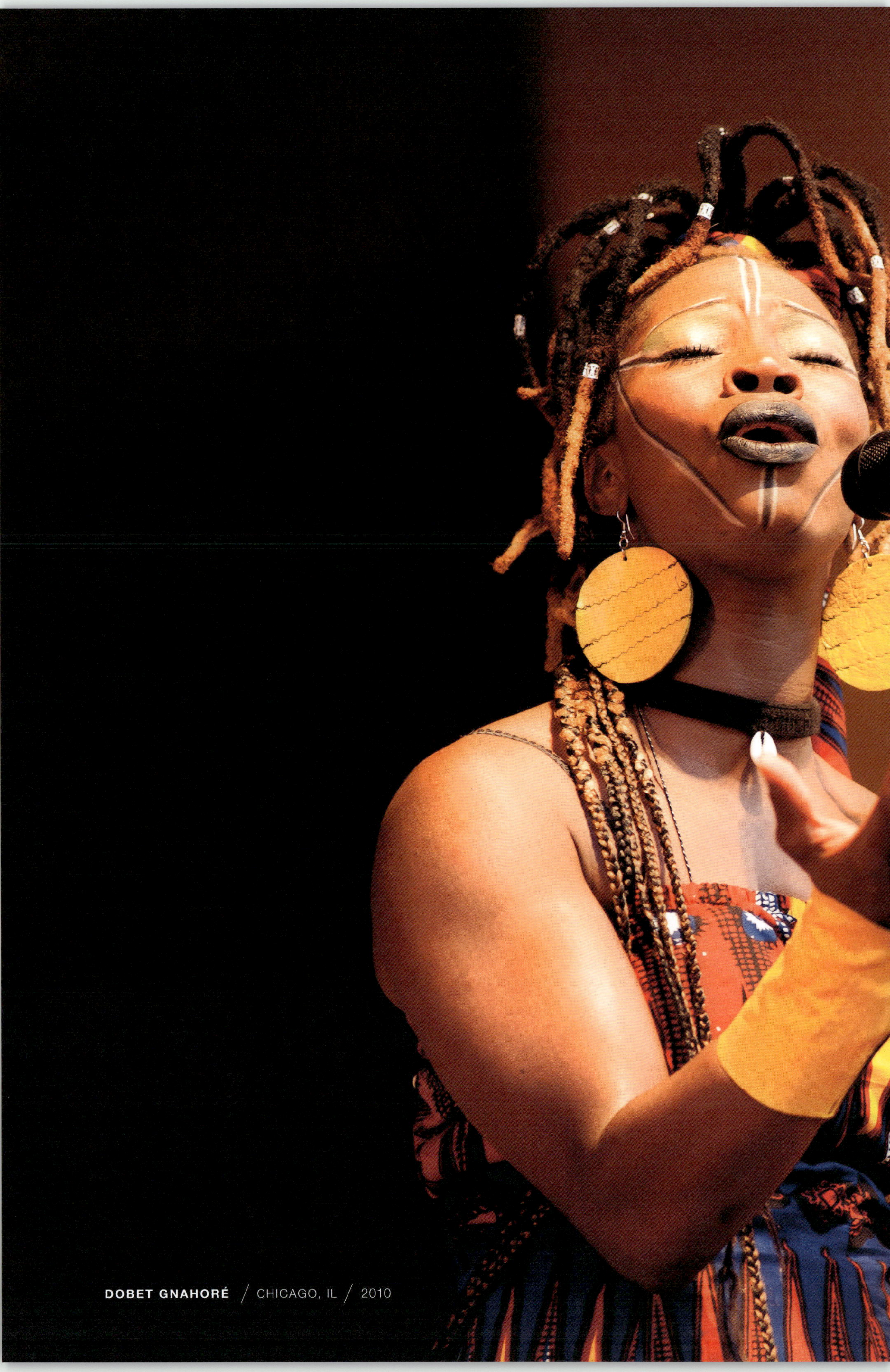

DOBET GNAHORÉ / CHICAGO, IL / 2010

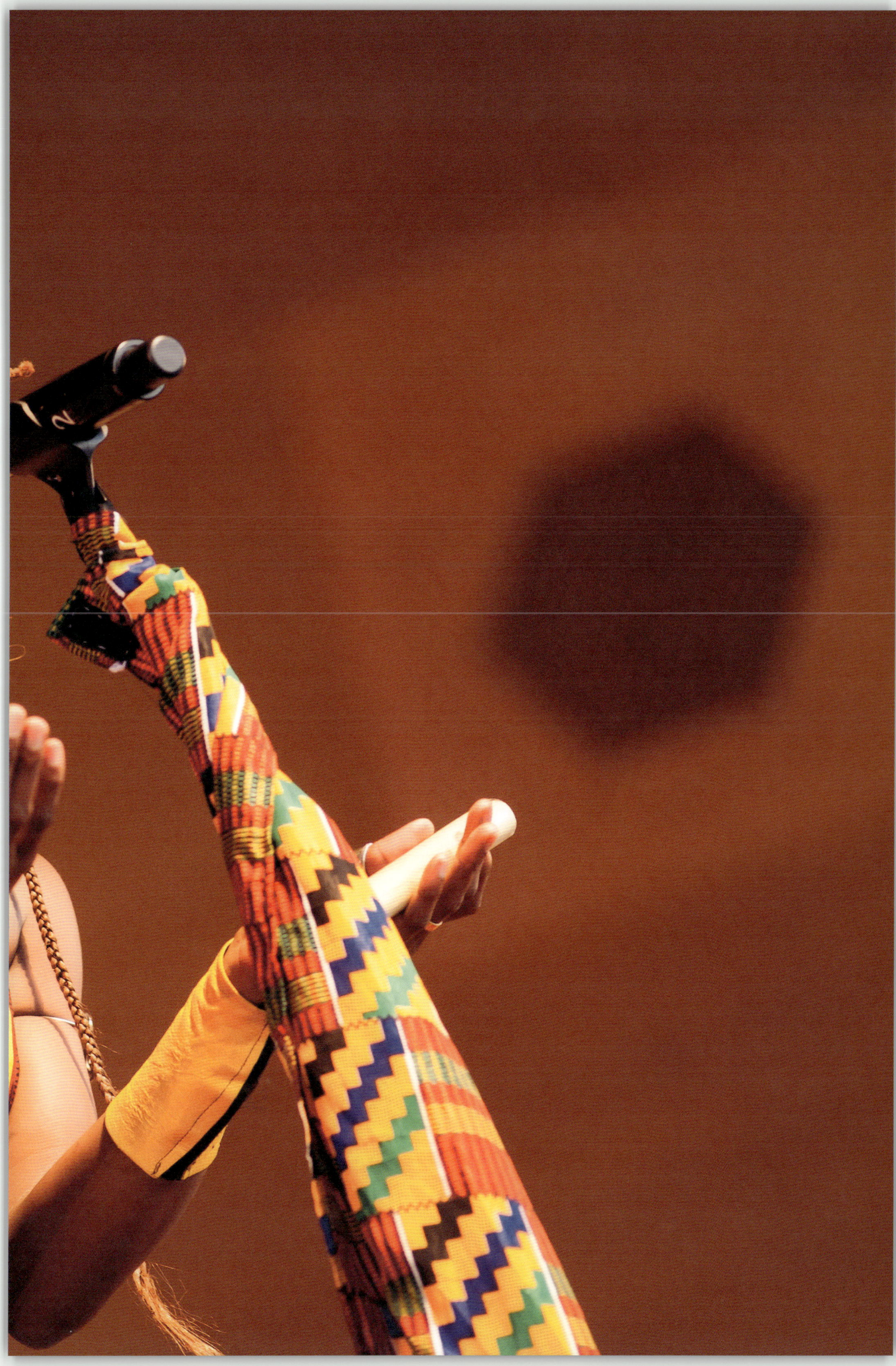

NATKIN
THE MOMENT OF TRUTH

For a band that was never too thrilled to be doing photos to begin with, if Paul walked in with a camera, everyone relaxed instead of tensed up. He was immediately trusted, and that's the main thing when you are working with people. In the course of those few decades there were plenty of photographers who showed up and they were just the photographer and you wanted to get them out of the room, but with Paul it was always our friend who just happened to have a camera.

Of all the shots of us he took, obviously the live shots from gigs speak for themselves, but the stuff in the dressing rooms and solo portrait shots and band shots–I do know that we never felt rushed, never wanted to rush. I think he did capture some really great, personal and human images of the band. We weren't taking pictures, we were hanging out with a buddy who had a camera in his hands.

When you're talking about Paul and you're talking about photo shoots and he's showing you some old stuff and then you see a photo of Sinatra in between images of Guns N' Roses and Slaughter, you're like "Who is this guy?" We recognized he's not entering our world, we're entering his. And that's just the thing, as time went on and we understood what Paul had already done and how great he is at what he does, it was always a pleasure to know he was still hanging around.

There are a few photos Paul took of the band that are in the book I wrote about The Black Crowes, *Hard to Handle: The Life and Death of the Black Crowes*. He's the first guy that I emailed to say, "I'm writing a book and do you want to dig through your files and send me some pics that might work?"

Steve Gorman

The Black Crowes

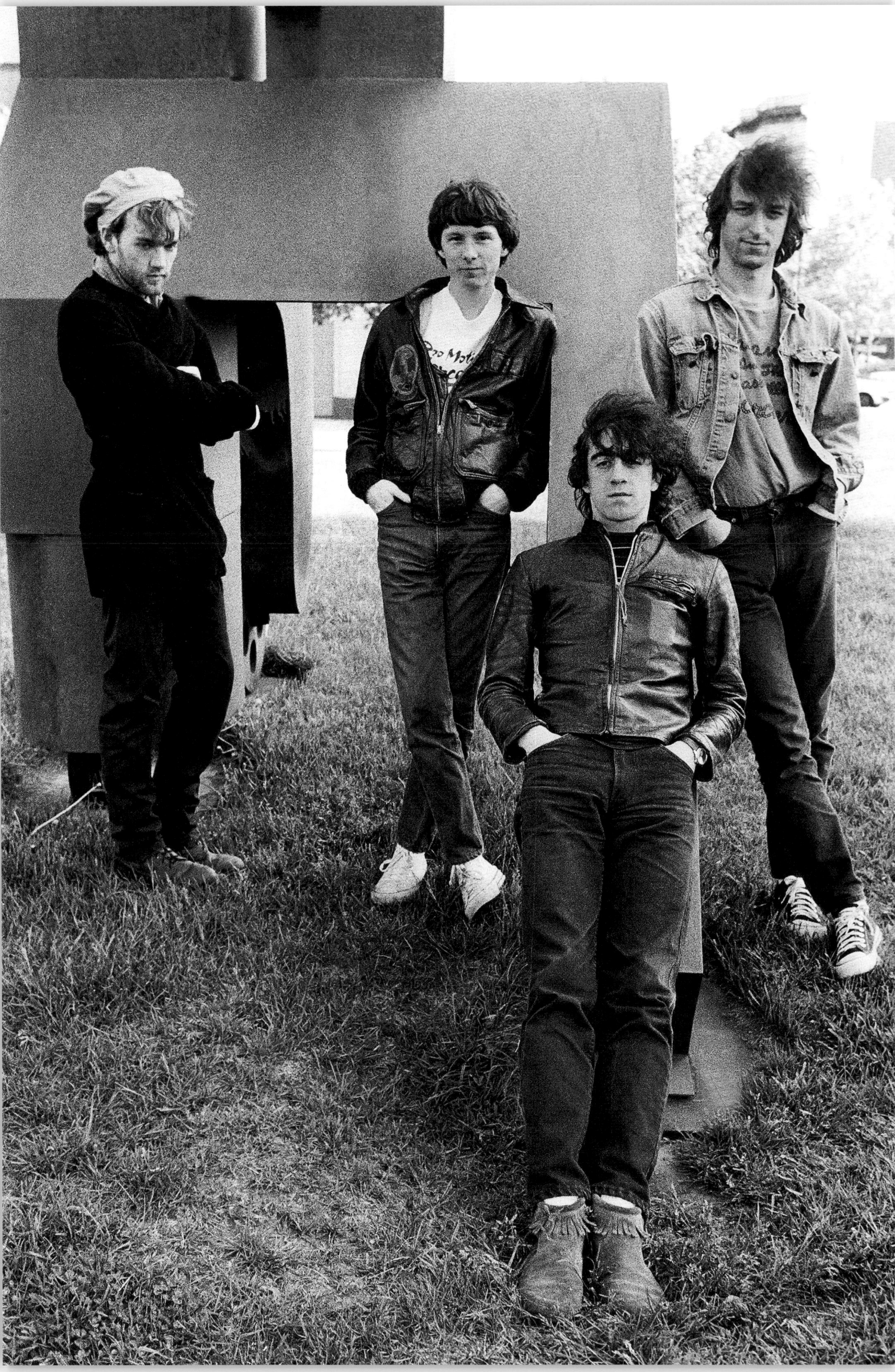

TROPE PUBLISHING Co.

LCCN: 2021932476
ISBN: 978-1-9519630-3-3

Manufactured in China
First printing, 2022

Trope Publishing Co.
www.trope.com

Images from *Natkin: The Moment of Truth* are available for purchase. For inquiries, go to trope.com or email the gallery at info@trope.com.

Contributors:

Dave Hoekstra is a Chicago writer and documentarian. He collaborated with Paul Natkin on the books *The People's Place: Soul Food Restaurants*; *Reminiscences From the Civil Rights Era to Today;* and *Disco Demolition: The Night Disco Died* with Steve Dahl. Dave was a staff writer for 29 years at the *Chicago Sun-Times* and was a 2013 Studs Terkel Community Media Award winner. Dave has known Paul for 40 years.

Selena Fragassi is a freelance music journalist and publicist. Her work has appeared regularly in the *Chicago Sun-Times* as well as *Nylon*, *Paste*, *Blurt*, *Under the Radar*, *PopMatters* and the former *Venus Zine* where she was music editor.

Tom Maday is a portrait and location photographer whose assignments take him around the world. His images appear in the books *Trope Chicago*, *Trope London*, and *In the Arena*. Tom's work is also included in the titles *Great Chicago Stories* and *After the Fall: Srebrenica Survivors in St. Louis*.

A special thanks to **Cathy Domanico** for making this book possible.

R.E.M.

A publicist from IRS Records asked me to do a photo shoot with one of their new bands. I knew the club's dressing room was pretty drab, and as I was walking in, I noticed a weird modern art sculpture across the street. I introduced myself to this new band, R.E.M., and asked them to follow me. I'm not sure if they had ever done a shoot on the road, but they went along with it and across the street we went. We shot for about three minutes before they got cold; they are from the South, after all. That meeting started a relationship that lasted for about 20 years.

ZZ Top

In 1979, a new hard rock magazine called *RIP* started up. One of its editors knew my work and asked me to spend a few days on the road with ZZ Top for an upcoming cover story. Everything that happened on that trip was a photographable moment, and I tried to capture it all. Those guys know how to make every moment count–besides being great musicians, they really understand how to put on a show.

The Go–Go's

Chicago used to have a festival called ChicagoFest, where for almost two weeks bands would play on four stages (for blues, jazz, country and rock) laid out on a long pier with a roadway behind. As the festival's official photographer, I would just walk back and forth along the pier, taking pictures as I walked. One day, I decided to start at the pier's far end–the rock stage. The day's opening act had just arrived, and I asked if I could take their picture in their trailer dressing room. It was 11 a.m., and they weren't really awake yet, but they said, "Sure, come on in." The dressing room wasn't much to look at; I was about to ask them to step outside to shoot when one of them said, "Hey, we can all hang on this clothes rack." That photo shoot took all of two minutes and sparked a lifelong friendship.

John Mellencamp

A local rock magazine asked me to photograph a new singer staying at a hotel downtown. Knowing nothing about him, I figured I would just ask him to walk outside and get a few pictures. He shrugged–very much not into being photographed–and when we went outside, he immediately dove head-first into a garbage can. I only took two pictures before he got up and said "OK, you've got your shot," and walked back into the hotel. He was right.

Tom Petty / Back cover

The *Chicago Sun-Times* asked me to cover Tom Petty's first big homecoming concert in Gainesville, Florida. I flew down to St. Petersburg the day before and did a quick photo shoot with Tom on the roof of our hotel. We headed to the airport for the half-hour flight to Gainesville, filling all the seats on the small commuter plane. We then proceeded to fly into one of the worst storms I have ever flown through–when we got off the plane in Gainesville, Tom dropped down and kissed the ground. He must have been energized by the near-death experience, though, because that night he put on one of the greatest shows I have ever seen him do.

NATKIN

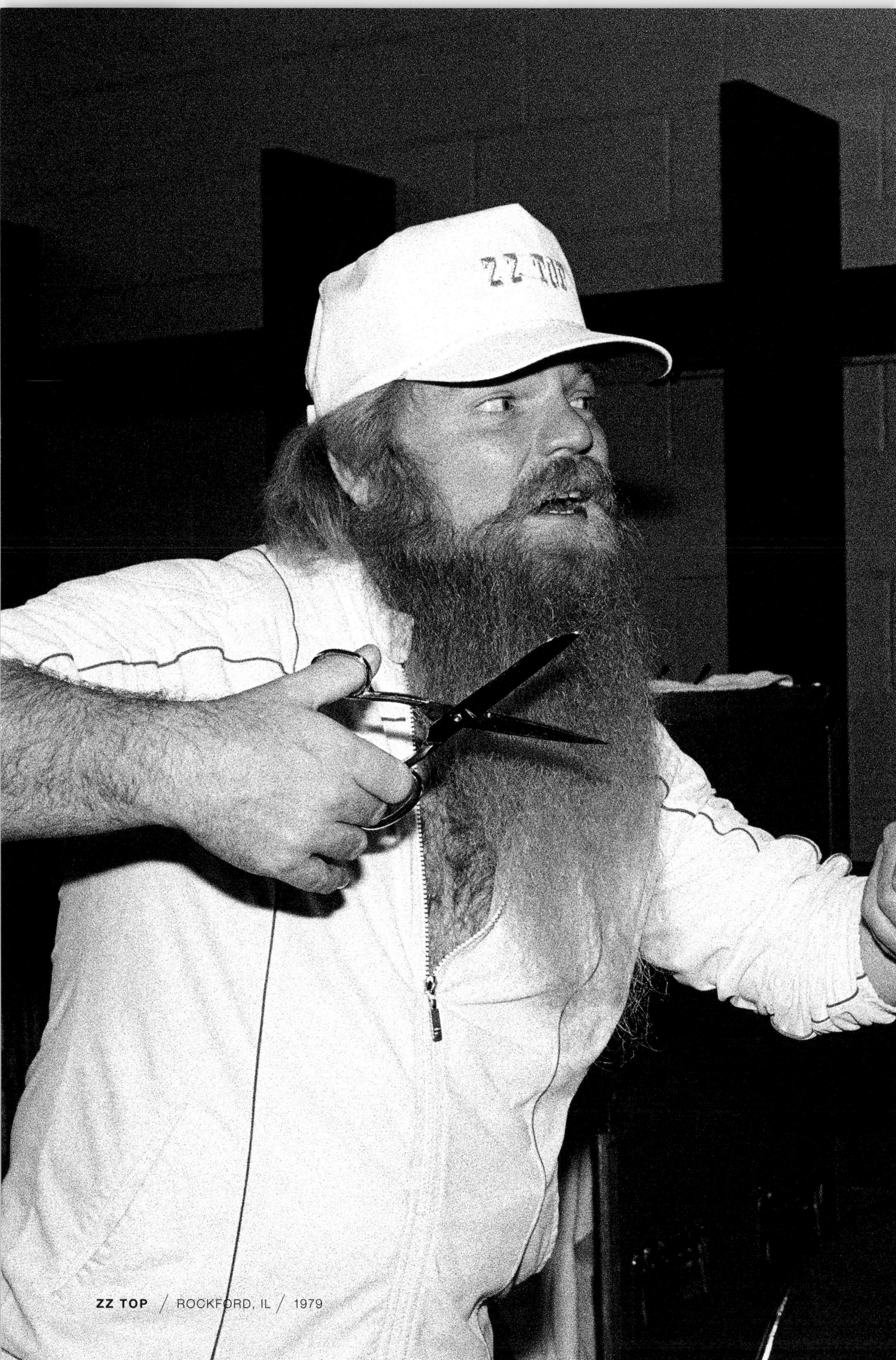

ZZ TOP / ROCKFORD, IL / 1979

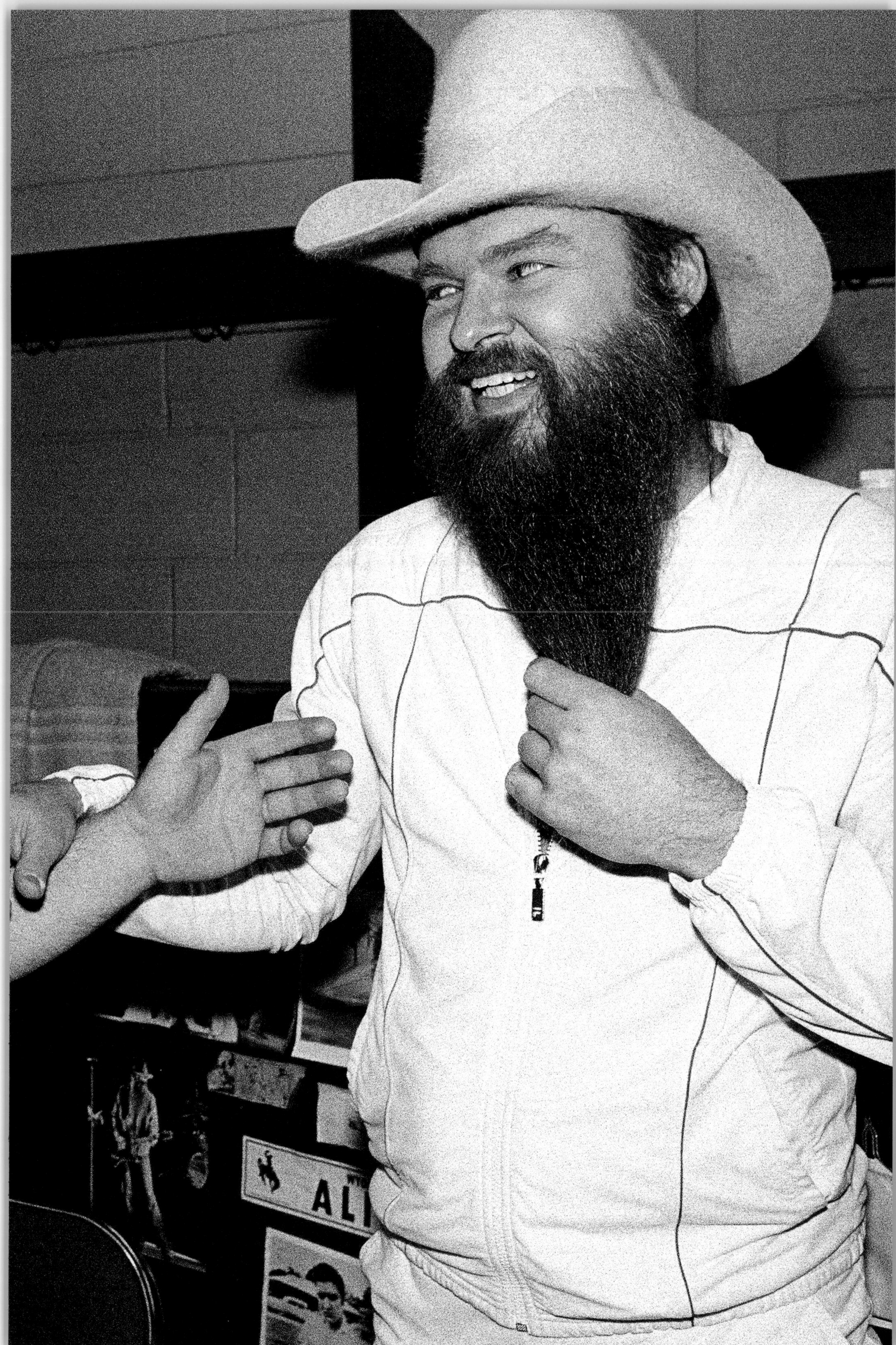

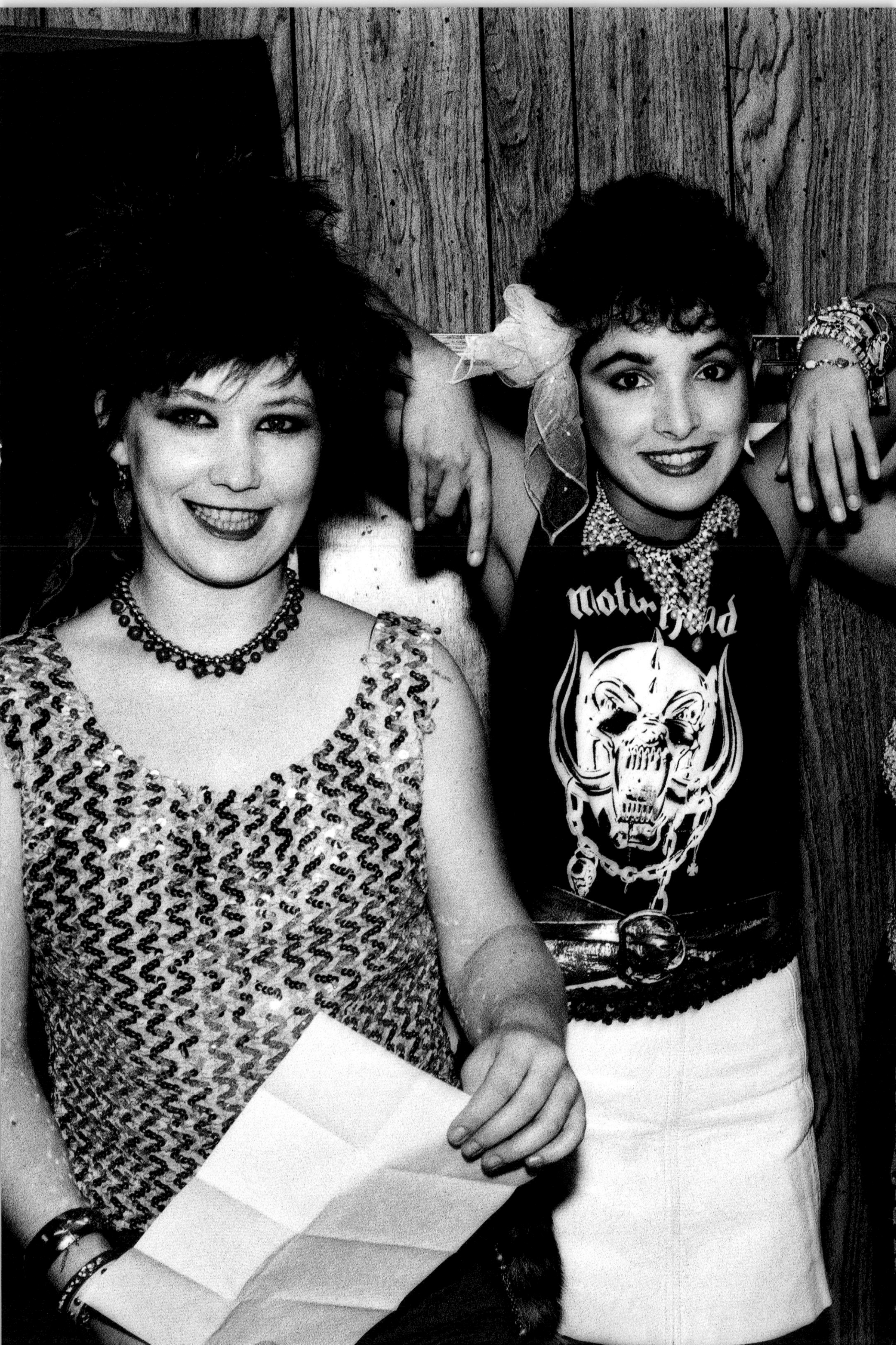

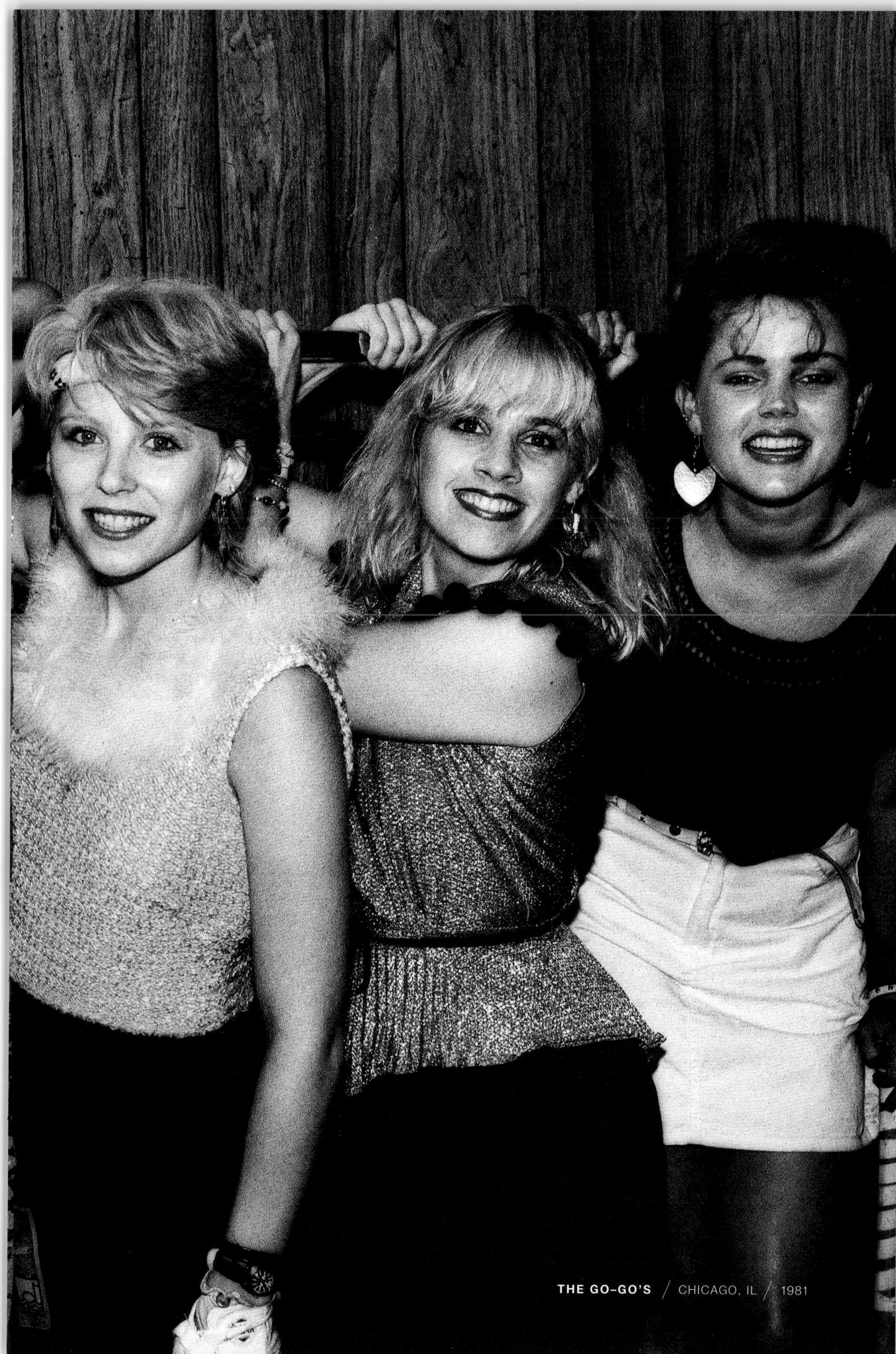

THE GO-GO'S / CHICAGO, IL / 1981

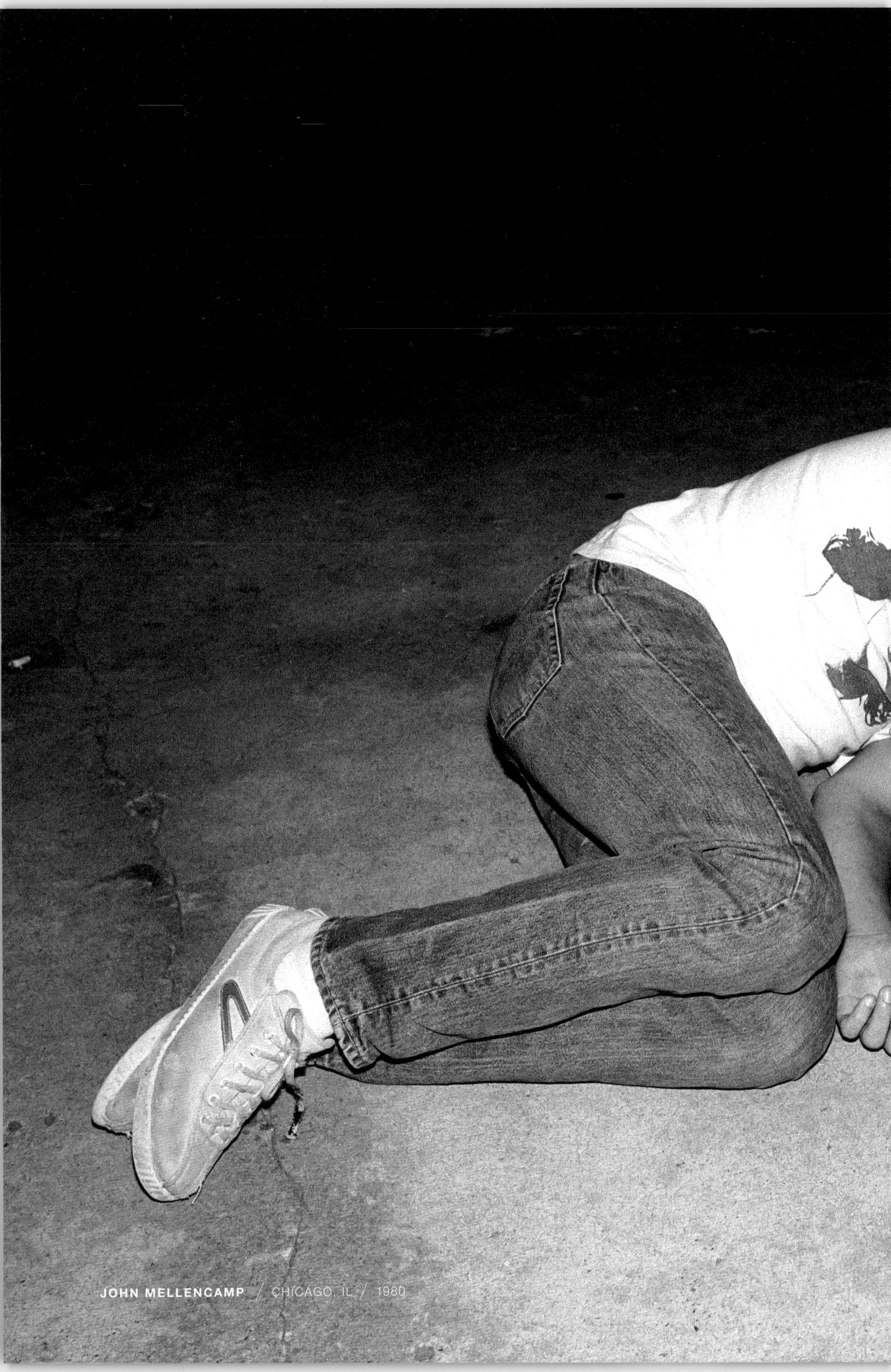

JOHN MELLENCAMP / CHICAGO, IL / 1980